Fodor's

BEST ROAD TRIPS
IN THE USA

Welcome to the Road

Americans didn't invent the road trip—that honor goes to Germany's adventurous Bertha Benz, whose husband patented the first gas-powered carriage in 1886—but they did perfect it. They opened the first gas station (in Pittsburgh in 1905), paved the first modern highway (in New York in 1911), and pioneered a new kind of lodging called the "motor hotel" (in California's San Luis Obispo in 1925). Although today you might be searching for different amenities, such as a place to plug in your car, the lure of the open road still draws tens of millions of travelers every year.

TOP REASONS TO GO

★ **Iconic Drives:** From the Blue Ridge Parkway to the Pacific Coast Highway.

★ **Roadside Attractions:** The perfect places to stretch your legs along the way.

★ **Favorites Eats:** Eat at foodie destinations and diners only the locals know about.

★ **Getting There:** Take the fastest route or meander along the road less traveled.

★ **Where to Sleep:** Discover the best national park lodges or beachfront getaways.

★ **Shop Therapy:** Sample local delicacies and uncover one-of-a-kind artsworks.

Contents

MAPS

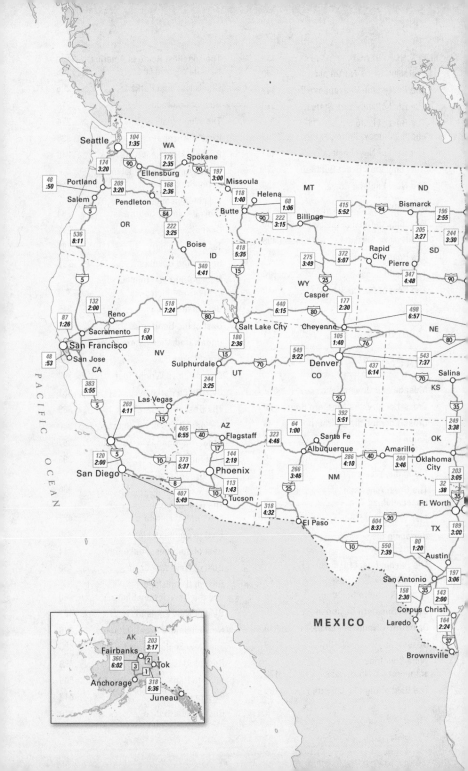

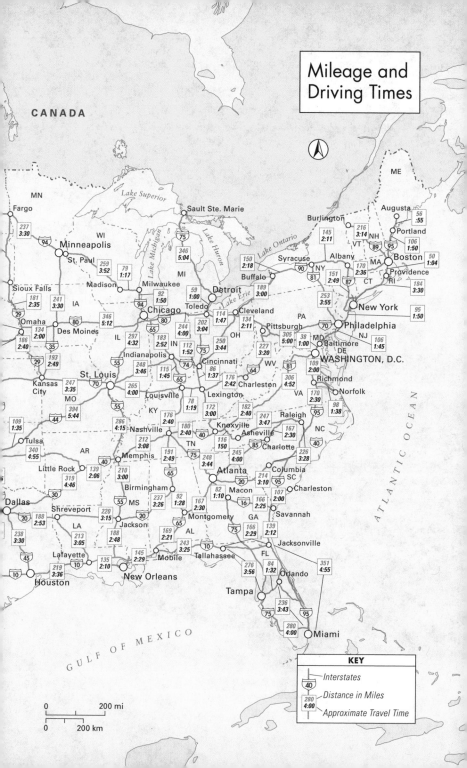

Mileage and Driving Times

CANADA

MN

Fargo — 237 / 3:30 — 94

WI

Minneapolis
St. Paul — 259 / 3:52 — 79 / 1:17

Lake Superior

Sault Ste. Marie — 75 — 346 / 5:04

ME

Burlington — 216 / 3:14 — NH — Augusta 56 / :55

Portland — 106 / 1:50 — 89 — 95

Lake Huron

145 / 2:11 — VT

Boston 50 / 1:04

Madison — 92 / 1:50 — Milwaukee

MI

Lake Michigan

Syracuse — 150 / 2:18 — 90 — Albany — 170 / 2:36 — MA — Providence

Sioux Falls — 181 / 2:35 — 241 / 3:30 — IA — 29

59 / 1:00 — Detroit — Buffalo — NY — 81 — 151 / 2:49 — 87 — CT — RI

New York — 184 / 3:30

Chicago — 80 — Toledo — 114 / 1:47 — Cleveland — Lake Erie

189 / 3:00

95 / 1:50

Omaha — 134 / 2:00 — Des Moines — 346 / 5:12 — 80 — IL — 65 — 244 / 4:00 — 202 / 3:04 — 134 / 2:11 — Pittsburgh — PA — 70 — Philadelphia

186 / 2:40 — 35 — 29

297 / 4:32 — 183 / 2:52 — IN — 112 / 1:52 — 250 / 3:44 — OH — 227 / 3:20 — 305 / 5:00 — 38 / 1:00 — MD — Baltimore — NJ — 106 / 1:45 — DE

Indianapolis — 74 — Cincinnati — 86 / 1:37 — WV — 81 — 109 / 2:00 — WASHINGTON, D.C.

193 / 2:49

St. Louis — 248 / 3:46 — 115 / 1:45 — 65 — 64 — 176 / 2:42 — Charleston — VA — 306 / 4:52 — Richmond

Kansas City — 247 / 3:35 — 70 — MO — 265 / 4:00 — Louisville — KY — 78 / 1:19 — Lexington — 170 / 2:30 — Norfolk — 98 / 1:38

109 / 1:35 — 44 — 394 / 5:44 — 55 — 286 / 4:15 — 176 / 2:40 — 172 / 3:00 — 182 / 2:40 — 247 / 3:47 — Raleigh — 167 / 2:30 — NC — 95

Tulsa — 340 / 4:55 — AR — 212 / 3:08 — Nashville — Knoxville — Asheville — 116 / 150 — 85 — Charlotte — 40 — 226 / 3:28

Little Rock — 139 / 2:06 — 40 — Memphis — 191 / 2:49 — TN — 75 — 248 / 3:44 — 245 / 4:00 — Columbia — 214 / 3:10 — SC — 95 — Charleston

319 / 4:46 — 210 / 3:00 — 65 — Atlanta — 82 / 1:10 — Macon — 166 / 2:25 — 107 / 2:00 — Savannah

30

Dallas — 188 / 2:53 — Shreveport — 220 / 3:15 — Birmingham — 237 / 3:26 — 92 / 1:28 — 167 / 2:30 — 16 — 166 / 2:29 — 139 / 2:12 — GA

LA — 55 — MS — Jackson — 188 / 2:48 — Montgomery — AL — 75 — Jacksonville — 351 / 4:55

238 / 3:30 — 213 / 3:05 — 169 / 2:21 — 65 — 243 / 3:25 — 10 — Tallahassee — FL

20 — 45 — Lafayette — 135 / 2:10 — Mobile — 145 / 2:29 — 276 / 3:56 — 84 / 1:32 — Orlando

10 — 219 / 3:36 — New Orleans — Tampa — 236 / 3:43 — 95

Houston — 280 / 4:00 — Miami

75

GULF OF MEXICO

ATLANTIC OCEAN

0 — 200 mi

0 — 200 km

KEY

40 — Interstates

280 / 4:00 — Distance in Miles / Approximate Travel Time

Chapter 1

EXPERIENCE THE BEST ROAD TRIPS IN THE USA

10 ULTIMATE EXPERIENCES

Road trips across the United States offer terrific experiences that should be on every traveler's list. Here are Fodor's top picks for a memorable trip.

1 The Blue Ridge Parkway

Running 469 miles through North Carolina and Virginia, this scenic mountain drive links Great Smoky Mountains and Shenandoah national parks, taking you through stunning Appalachian vistas and charming small towns. *(Ch. 7)*

2 The Going-to-the-Sun Road

One of the West's most magnificent drives, this 50-mile-long road spans the width of Glacier National Park. *(Ch. 2, 4)*

3 Florida Keys Scenic Highway

Florida's "Overseas Highway" is a destination unto itself, one that crosses 42 bridges over water, including the Seven Mile Bridge. *(Ch. 7)*

4 The Road to Hāna

One of the world's most famous drives, this precarious Maui road has more than 600 curves and crosses some 50 gulch-straddling bridges in just 52 coastline miles. *(Ch. 9)*

5 The Million Dollar Highway

Whether named for the cost of building it or the incredible views, this 25-mile highway in southwestern Colorado is a breathtaking journey through the San Juan Skyway. *(Ch. 4)*

6 Monument Valley

This remarkably remote region of Arizona and Utah is impossible to view in a single frame. A scenic 17-mile strip of Valley Drive will have you channeling Ansel Adams. *(Ch. 5)*

7 The High Road to Taos

For a scenic adventure, drive the 56 miles between Taos and Santa Fe via this breathtaking alpine route through quaint Spanish-colonial villages and past sweeping vistas. *(Ch. 5)*

8 Lake Champlain Byway

For classic New England vistas, travel along the 185-mile route that borders Vermont's Lake Champlain; it's especially scenic during peak fall foliage season. *(Ch. 8)*

9 Historic Route 66

The Mother Road, spanning from Chicago to Los Angeles, was one of America's first national highways and still provides travelers with a classic Americana experience. *(Ch. 2)*

10 The Pacific Coast Highway

One of the world's most spectacular coastal drives, Highway 1 winds around the Pacific Ocean and through jagged mountains and redwood trees. *(Ch. 3)*

Best Iconic Landmarks

HOLLYWOOD SIGN

Fun fact: these 50-foot letters didn't originally spell "Hollywood." They advertised "Hollywoodland," an upscale real estate development. When they fell into disrepair, the city of Los Angeles came to its rescue with a new coat of paint, removing the last four letters in the process.

GOLDEN GATE BRIDGE

Named for the mile-long strait at the mouth of San Francisco Bay that it crosses, this suspension bridge is known around the world for its graceful towers and rusty orange color. (It was originally intended to be blue and yellow, but the color of the primer stuck.)

MOUNT RUSHMORE

South Dakota's Black Hills would be famous without it, but this colossal sculpture of four presidents—Washington, Jefferson, Lincoln, and, slightly behind the other three, Theodore Roosevelt—makes them iconic. By artist Gutzon Borglum, Mount Rushmore's design changed several times before debuting in 1941.

STATUE OF LIBERTY

People throw the word *iconic* around a lot these days, but New York's Statue of Liberty is perhaps the one landmark that truly represents the United States in the eyes of the world. You can visit the island, but the best way to enjoy the statue is standing on the deck of the (free) Staten Island Ferry.

SPACE NEEDLE
Built for the World's Fair in 1962, Seattle's 604-foot Space Needle is an unforgettable part of the Seattle skyline. The futuristic design was a compromise between two powerful men, one who wanted it to look like a balloon, the other like a flying saucer.

EDMUND PETTUS BRIDGE
The most potent symbol of America's Civil Rights struggle is this bridge outside Selma, Alabama. In 1965, state troopers brutally attacked 400 mostly African American demonstrators peacefully marching to Montgomery.

TAOS PUEBLO
One of the oldest continuously inhabited communities in the United States, Taos Pueblo is both a UNESCO World Heritage site and a National Historic Landmark. The adobe structures were originally home to the Ancestral Puebloan people.

Washington Monument

GATEWAY ARCH
The nation's tallest monument, the 630-foot St. Louis Gateway Arch treats you to sweeping views of the Mississippi River. (A futuristic tram whisks you to the top.) Don't miss the museum, which strives to weave in the stories of Native American people who lived in the region.

WASHINGTON MONUMENT
The world is full of similarly shaped obelisks, but there's something about the 1884 Washington Monument—maybe its location on top of a small hill, or the ring of flags surrounding its base—that inspires us. It's Washington, D.C.'s compass: east is the Capital, north is the White House, and west is the Lincoln Memorial.

INDEPENDENCE HALL
A UNESCO World Heritage site, this 18th-century landmark is where the Declaration of Independence and the Constitution were adopted. It's the centerpiece of Philadelphia's Independence National Historical Park, home to the Liberty Bell, Congress Hall, and more.

Best National Parks

GRAND CANYON
You'll never forget your first visit to Arizona's Grand Canyon, gazing down at the seemingly endless expanse from the South Rim. Repeat visitors come for hiking, horseback riding, or white water rafting.

ARCHES
It took millions of years for erosion to form the sandstone arches that give this Utah park its name. Delicate Arch is the most famous and Landscape Arch is the longest, but there are more than 2,000 others to grab your attention, making this the largest collection of natural arches in the world.

ACADIA
It includes 17 other islands, but most visitors to this coastal paradise in Maine stick to easily accessible Mount Desert Island. Bike the carriage roads, hike lofty Cadillac Mountain, or trek to Bass Harbor Head Lighthouse.

OLYMPIC
Covering 1 million acres, Washington State's jewel in the crown offers what is essentially three parks in one, with glacier-topped mountains, misty primeval forests filled with evergreens, and pristine beaches where you can set up camp and watch the waves roll in past sea stacks.

GREAT SMOKY MOUNTAINS
The country's most popular national park—partly because it sits close to large cities in Tennessee (Gatlinburg and Pigeon Forge) and North Carolina (Bryson City and Cherokee)—the Great Smoky Mountains are especially beautiful for hiking and camping in spring and fall.

YELLOWSTONE
Occupying the northwest corner of Wyoming and parts of Montana and Idaho, the country's first national park is known for the Old Faithful geyser, but it's dotted with steaming pools and bubbling mud pots, too.

DEATH VALLEY
Straddling the border of California and Nevada, Death Valley is the hottest place in the United States. It sets other records, being the driest (barely two inches of rain a year) and the lowest (282 feet below sea level) national park.

Rocky Mountain NP

YOSEMITE
The record-breaking granite peak of El Capitan gets star billing, but this 1,200-square-mile park in California's Sierra Nevada mountains has plenty of superlatives, including Bridalveil Fall, the country's tallest waterfall.

ROCKY MOUNTAIN
Since it's split in two by the Continental Divide, the eastern half of this Colorado park is craggy mountains, while the western half is lush, green forests.

ZION
Other parks offer wide-open spaces, but Utah's Zion offers breathtaking spots like The Narrows, a slot canyon that often narrows to less than 20 feet wide. Its soaring red cliffs attract casual hikers and serious rock climbers.

DENALI
With North America's highest mountain at its center, Denali showcases an untamed Alaskan landscape teeming with wildlife and stunning vistas.

Best Roadside Attractions

CADILLAC RANCH

Outside the Texas town of Amarillo—mentioned prominently in the song "Route 66"—is this way-out art project. The brainchild of several San Francisco hippies, it's a series of 10 spray-painted Cadillacs buried grill-first in a pasture.

THE ENCHANTED HIGHWAY

If you're near Regent, North Dakota, locals will steer you to this 32-mile stretch of road north of town lined with metal sculptures. Massive pheasants dash across the plain, huge grasshoppers nibble on leaves, and trout leap from imaginary streams. The gift shop in Regent sells miniature versions of the larger-than-life sculptures.

HOLE N' THE ROCK

Within Utah's Canyonlands, Hole N' the Rock is a 5,000-square-foot home that was carved out of a huge sandstone rock in the early 1970s. You can take a guided tour of the home or visit its gift shop and trading post.

LUCY THE ELEPHANT

Built in 1881 just outside Atlantic City, New Jersey to promote real estate sales and tourism, this six-story structure is now America's oldest-surviving roadside attraction; Lucy is now even a popular overnight rental on Airbnb.

PRADA MARFA
Way out in the Texan desert, 26 miles northwest of the funky art town of Marfa, you'll find this art installation that captures a Prada storefront stuck in time in 2005.

CABAZON DINOSAURS
A frequent stop for anyone heading to Palm Springs and Joshua Tree from Los Angeles, the Cabazon Dinosaurs consist of two huge, steel-and-concrete dinos; you can even go inside the brontosaurus to visit the small gift shop.

BLUE WHALE OF CATOOSA
Rising out of its own little lake near Catoosa, Oklahoma, the Blue Whale is one of the region's most whimsical sights. Built in the 1970s as an anniversary present, it's taken on a life of its own as a tourist attraction.

Extraterrestrial Highway

MYSTERY HOLE
This spot in Fayetteville, West Virginia is the perfect example of the kitschy, side-show-esque roadside attractions of yore. The underground series of rooms are built at different angles to give the illusion of not following the laws of gravity.

EXTRATERRESTRIAL HIGHWAY
As Nevada Route 375 makes its way around mysterious Area 51 in the Nevada desert, it becomes the tourism-inspired Extraterrestrial Highway, where alien-inspired landmarks, restaurants, and shops abound.

Road-Tripping 101

USING THIS GUIDE

These trips are jam-packed with suggestions for making the most of your road trip and seeing the best of the regions they cover. They are designed for the road-tripper who actually enjoys being on the road and who believes the journey is really the biggest part of the adventure. Most of these trips suggest staying only one night at each destination, and while a two- or three-hour drive per day is typical, some days you'll see five or even more hours of driving. Feel free to mix and match the destinations of our itineraries so they work for you and your optimal driving schedule.

Our trips were designed with the typical vacation schedule in mind, so if you have time to extend your trip and spend more time at certain destinations, feel free. Ultimately these trips are meant to act as inspiration for your road-trip travels, providing a framework for the best way to see these regions and the unmissable stops along the way.

WHEN TO GO

In a country as vast and diverse as the United States, there's no bad time to do a road trip, and you'll find trips in this book that work with any season. But it's still important to be smart as certain regions of the country can have worse winters than others. It's a good idea to avoid a winter road trip in any place that regularly sees snow; indeed, many destinations might have sights and hotels that close during this time. National parks can be particularly fraught to drive through during the winter, and some roads might be impassable. Depending on your destination, summer can also be a tricky time to hit the open road. Hurricanes and wildfires are big issues in the South and the West, and while you can't predict when they might hit, you can be prepared in case they happen while you're there. Beach and lake destinations tend to get booked up far in advance, so it's best to plan ahead if your summertime trip involves water. Generally, spring and fall are the best times to enjoy a road trip in the United States, no matter where you might be headed.

CAR RENTALS

All these trips begin and end at cities with major airports, with plenty of rental car companies for you to choose from. Not all the trips are round-trips, so be sure that your rental company also exists in your final destination and be prepared for potential extra fees to drop off at a different location.

It's always best to reserve your rental car before arriving. To rent a car, you need a valid driver's license and to be at least 25 years old. Many companies will still rent to those younger than 25 for an additional fee. Note that there are also often fees for adding additional drivers. Always be sure to purchase insurance with your rental car; if you already have your own, confirm with your insurance company that your personal insurance will carry over to any rental.

BEFORE YOU GO

Be sure that your driver's license is up-to-date as is your vehicle registration and car insurance information if you're bringing your own car. It's smart to take your car into a shop for a tune-up and oil change before you leave. Also be sure to pack an emergency kit to keep in your car at all times; this should include a first aid kit, extra water, a blanket, a flashlight, and extra batteries; make sure your car also has a spare tire, flares, and jumper cables. If you're able, it's not a bad idea to splurge for a AAA membership for your trip just in case. If you're planning on relying on your phone for directions, make sure you have a workable setup to mount your phone on your car's dashboard (or a reliable copilot). Be sure to plan your route out in advance, including on a road atlas in case you lose Wi-Fi or your phone dies. And, of course, don't forget a phone charger you can use in the car.

PACKING LIST

Aside from the essentials mentioned above, your packing list should reflect the destination you're traveling to. It's always good to bring layers for a car ride as well as a reusable water bottle. Make sure you also bring cash and change for tolls or any place along the way that is cash-only. And of course, don't forget about your favorite road trip snacks.

RULES OF THE ROAD

Always be sure to obey traffic laws and speed limits while driving and never text and drive. Some recommended stops include wineries or pubs, so be sure to drive responsibly. Also be aware of when you're crossing state lines, as laws (especially speed limits) can change. If you're entering California, be prepared to stop at an agricultural inspection station, designed to prevent nonnative species of plants and animals from interfering with the state's careful ecosystem. You're not allowed to bring certain foods and plants into the state, so be sure to check in advance if you're planning on picking up any snacks on a trip that ends in California.

TRAFFIC

All travel times in this book don't factor in traffic, which we admit is going to be inevitable on any major road trip. Be sure to check travel times before you leave for the day, and if you have reservations at any destination you need to make, be ready to leave early in order to avoid traffic. It can be helpful to be flexible in terms of your stops, too. Make a list of the places you want to visit en route in order of importance to you; that way you know what to cut in case traffic hits. Coastal destinations in the summertime are notorious for traffic, so if you're on a summer road trip, be sure to factor traffic times into your planning.

TIME ZONES

Depending on your trip, it's quite possible you'll end up passing into one or more of the continental United States's four time zones. Be prepared for this in your travel plans and update your car's clock as needed.

SAFETY

Aside from having a good emergency kit in your car, the most important thing to keep in mind while setting off on a road trip is to know your limits. Long hours on the road can take their toll, so be sure to listen to your body if you're getting tired. Switch off with your travel companions regularly or don't hesitate to take a break if you need it. Also be sure to book all your accommodations in advance so you aren't left without a place to stay. It's a good idea to fill your gas tank at the start of every travel day; if you know your day's route will be particularly remote, look up the nearest gas stations in advance so you can plan on them if you need it. And be sure to look at the weather forecast for all your destinations, especially if you're going to be traveling through different regions. The American landscape can vary drastically, even in the same season, so be prepared for what you might encounter weather-wise at each destination.

What to Read and Watch

NOMADLAND

Moviegoers are fascinated with tales of people who leave everything behind and follow their dreams. This 2021 film features Oscar-winner Francis McDormand as Fern, a down-on-her-luck woman who buys a van and joins a community of nomadic people who gather in temporary communities. It just happens to be filmed in some gorgeous spots: Nevada's Black Rock Desert, California's San Bernardino National Forest, and the austerely beautiful Badlands of South Dakota.

TASTE THE NATION

Longtime *Top Chef* host Padma Lakshmi sets out on her own to discover the culinary traditions of various parts of the country, especially those whose roots here go back a generation at the most. The series is part cooking show, part travelogue, and part exploration of the immigrant experience. Most memorable is her conversation with a Thai woman whose high-end food was initially rejected by Las Vegas diners used to cheap and greasy fare. She triumphs, and so does the series.

CARS

This Pixar classic doesn't involve a road trip, but its cast of anthropomorphic cars will definitely give you a deeper appreciation for the many vehicles you'll pass on your journey. Most of the movie takes place in the fictional town of Radiator Springs, once a stop on Historic Route 66.

LITTLE MISS SUNSHINE

In this 2006 film, a dysfunctional family takes a cross-country trip in a yellow VW bus in order to help their daughter win the Little Miss Sunshine beauty pagent.

THELMA AND LOUISE

The ultimate road trip buddy movie, 1991's *Thelma and Louise* features two best friends who set off on a road trip where chaos (and crime) ensues.

ON THE ROAD BY JACK KEROUAC

A seminal work of the Beat Generation, this 1957 novel tells the adventures of a group of friends (based on Keroauc and his own counterculture friends) as they set off on a cross-country adventure, enjoying drugs, poetry, and jazz along the way.

THE PRICE OF SALT BY PATRICIA HIGHSMITH

The basis for the movie *Carol*, this 1952 novel focuses on two women in the 1950s who drive across the country to escape their lives and defy society's expectations.

LOVECRAFT COUNTRY BY MATT RUFF

Now an HBO miniseries, this horror-esque book set in the Jim Crow era follows a young Black man traveling from Chicago to New England, investigating his father's disappearance with his uncle, a writer for a guidebook focusing on traveling while Black.

Chapter 2

TRIPS OF A LIFETIME

WELCOME TO TRIPS OF A LIFETIME

TOP REASONS TO GO

★ **Yellowstone National Park:** The crowning jewel of the national park system is also an ultimate highlight of any northern cross-country trip.

★ **The Gulf Shores:** A southern cross-country trip takes you past some stunning landscapes, but also through the supremely underrated shores of the Gulf of Mexico.

★ **Route 66 Kitsch:** There's plenty to see along Route 66, but it might just be the many old-fashioned rest stops, diners, and motels that take you back to road trips past and keep the travelers coming.

★ **The Outer Banks:** As you hightail it up the East Coast, the Outer Banks of North Carolina give you some of the country's most stunning beach scenery.

★ **Gettysburg National Battlefield:** One of the country's most hallowed grounds, a visit to Gettysburg is a reminder of the history and horrors of the Civil War.

1 The Ultimate Cross-Country Road Trip: The Northern Route. From Seattle to Washington D.C., travel through Yellowstone, the Badlands, and the Midwest.

2 The Ultimate Cross-Country Road Trip: The Southern Route. The drive from Jacksonville to San Diego takes you past the Gulf Shores, Texas, and the Southwest.

3 Route 66. The quintessential American road trip.

4 The East Coast's Best Beaches. A journey up the East Coast that gives you the best the Atlantic Ocean has to offer.

5 Along the Mississippi. Follow America's mightiest river from New Orleans to Minneapolis.

6 The Great American Baseball Road Trip. From famous stadiums to the Baseball Hall of Fame, this trip is the perfect way to embrace America's favorite pastime.

7 Civil War Battlefields and History. Delve deep into the history of America's bloodiest conflict by visiting its battlefields and historic sites.

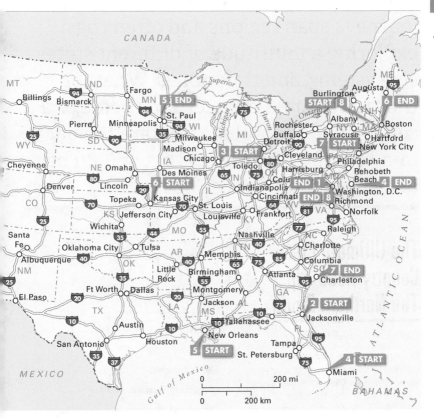

8 Retracing the American Revolution. See the essential sites associated with America's Founding Fathers.

While any road trip can be considered epic, there are certain itineraries that truly define the word. These multiday journeys span regions and often coasts, exploring a multitude of different states, ecosystems, and time zones. Whether they're centered on a certain theme or a certain body of water, these are the once-in-a-lifetime adventures that should be on every road-tripper's bucket list.

The Ultimate Cross-Country Road Trip: The Northern Route

Written by Andrew Collins

Driving across the country's northern tier offers a bit of something for everyone: some of the world's most magnificent national parks, long stretches of sparsely populated open country, enormous and gorgeous lakes, youthful and artsy college towns, and a few bigger cities with grand architecture and superb museums. And although there's a span from western Wyoming to eastern South Dakota that's a bit of a food desert (unless you don't get tired of beer and burgers), this drive passes through some impressive culinary destinations, from Washington's wine country to vibrant farm-to-table scenes in Minneapolis and Madison to the diverse international fare of Cleveland, Pittsburgh, and Washington, D.C. From some of the country's most remote scenery to some of its most accessible, this coastal trip will leave you with a true sense of America's diversity and beauty.

At a Glance

Start: Seattle, WA

End: Washington, DC

Miles Traveled: 3,600 miles

Suggested Duration: 16 days

States Visited: Idaho, Illinois, Indiana, Maryland, Michigan, Minnesota, Montana, Ohio, Pennsylvania, South Dakota, Washington, Wyoming

Key Sights: Glacier National Park; Mount Rushmore; National Museum of African American History and Culture; Taliesin; Yellowstone National Park

Best Time to Go: It's best not to even consider this route between mid-November and April, as you're going to hit road closures in parts of Glacier and Yellowstone national parks and pretty brutal, cold, windy, and potentially snowy weather across much of the route. The absolute best time weather-wise is July and August, but places can get crowded and expensive, so try to plan and reserve rooms well in advance if planning a summer adventure. Spring and fall are ideal for nice weather and fewer crowds.

Day 1: Seattle, WA, to Wenatchee, WA

140 miles (2 hours, 30 minutes without traffic and stops)

It's quickest to take I–90 east to U.S. 97, but you'll add only a little extra time to your adventure if you take the more scenic Highway 522 to U.S. 2, over gorgeous Stevens Pass in the Cascade Range, and by way of Leavenworth.

ALONG THE WAY

Shop: Just 20 miles northwest of Seattle, the town of Woodinville is entirely about selling one very specific product: wine. And we're talking about some of the greatest wine in North America, as nearly all of the town's 130 tasting rooms source grapes from the vaunted wine regions of eastern Washington, including Walla Walla, Yakima Valley, and the Columbia Valley. With limited time, make a visit to the granddaddy of all Washington wineries, **Chateau Ste. Michelle** (✉ *14111 N.E. 145th St.* ☎ *425/488–1133* ⊕ *www.ste-michelle.com*).

Town: A favorite weekend getaway, Leavenworth is a charming (if a touch kitschy) Bavarian-style village that thrives with both old-fashioned and urbane restaurants and inns. It's also a hub for outdoor fun, including easily accessible hikes in the surrounding Okanogan-Wenatchee National Forest; the Icicle Ridge Trail is a favorite. The **Nutcracker Museum and Shop** (✉ *735 Front St.* ☎ *509/548–4573* ⊕ *www.nutcrackermuseum.com*)

contains nearly 7,000 modern and antique nutcrackers—some of them centuries old, along with interesting exhibits on the region's Native American heritage.

Eat & Drink: Go full-on old-school Bavarian with a meal at **Andreas Keller Restaurant** (✉ *829 Front St.* ☎ *509/548–6000* ⊕ *www.andreaskellerrestaurant.com*) in Leavenworth. Merry "oompah" music bubbles out from marching accordion players at this festive restaurant, where the theme is "Germany without the Passport." You can feast on a selection of wursts—bratwurst, knackwurst, and weisswurst—beef goulash, and schnitzel cordon bleu.

WENATCHEE

Do: Gaining popularity with an outdoorsy crowd and sophisticated wine lovers, Wenatchee is an attractive, fast-growing city located in a shallow valley at the confluence of the Wenatchee and Columbia Rivers. Stretch your legs with a stroll on the paved Apple Valley Recreation Loop Trail, which runs for 26 miles on both sides of the Columbia River, or by ambling through **Ohme Gardens** (✉ *3327 Ohme Rd.* ☎ *509/662–5785* ⊕ *www.ohmegardens.org*), where you can commune with an artful arrangement of native rocks, ferns, mosses, pools, waterfalls, rock gardens, and conifers.

Eat & Drink: Set in a renovated warehouse along the Columbia River, Pybus Public Market is modeled loosely on Seattle's Pike Place Market and features vendors selling all manner of local farm goods, including locally made wines, and several excellent restaurants, including **Pybus Bistro** (✉ *3 N. Worthen St.* ☎ *509/888–3900* ⊕ *www.pybuspublicmarket.org*). **McGlinn's** (✉ *111 Orondo Ave.* ☎ *509/663–9073* ⊕ *www.mcglinns.com*) is a beloved downtown gastropub with rustic brick walls, soaring wood-beam ceilings, and an extensive menu of elevated comfort fare.

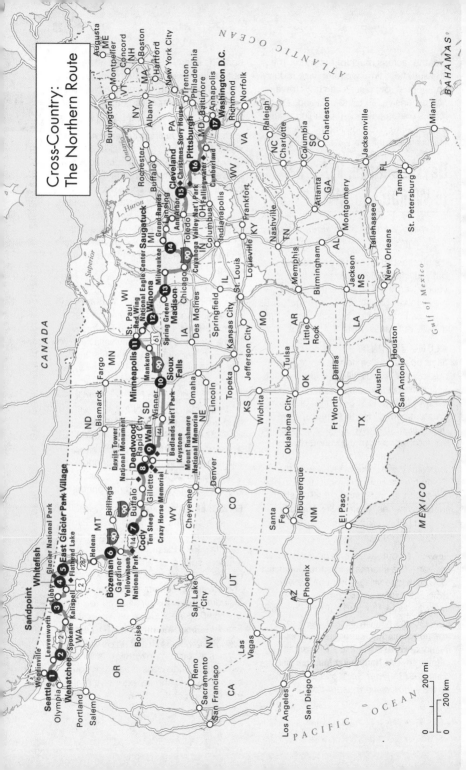

Cross-Country: The Northern Route

Stay: One of the most charming lodgings in the area, the 1917 **Warm Springs Inn & Winery** (✉ *1611 Love La.* ☎ *509/662–5683* ⊕ *www.warmspringsinn.com*) is set amid 10 acres of gardens and grape vines and offers elegant, well-appointed rooms filled with art and antiques.

Breakfast: Prodigious breakfast sandwiches with delicious fillings—such as the "monster biscuit"—are the specialty of **Sage Hills Bakery** (✉ *826 N. Wenatchee Ave.* ☎ *509/888–3912* ⊕ *www.facebook.com/sagehillsbakery*), a contemporary café that also serves decadent cookies and cinnamon rolls.

Day 2: Wenatchee, WA, to Sandpoint, ID

240 miles (4 hours, 30 minutes without traffic and stops)

Head north for a short but pretty drive along U.S. 97 bordering the Columbia River, then take U.S. 2 across the dramatic, windswept high desert of central and eastern Washington, passing through the attractive city of Spokane, and then cutting north up U.S. 2 to Newport and across the border to Sandpoint.

ALONG THE WAY

Town: Washington's second-largest city, Spokane is known for its beautiful public gardens and greenery as well as its wealth of well-preserved late-19th-century and early-20th-century buildings. The city's magnificent waterfalls form the heart of **Riverfront Park** (✉ *507 N. Howard St.* ☎ *509/625–6600* ⊕ *www.riverfront-spokane.org*), a 100-acre oasis that spans several islands and offers attractions like a 1909 hand-carved Looff carousel, a giant red slide shaped like a Radio Flyer wagon, and the Numerica SkyRide gondola, which whisks passengers directly over the dramatic falls.

Eat & Drink: Right off the Maple Street Bridge in Spokane, **Frank's Diner** (✉ *1516 W. 2nd Ave.* ☎ *509/747–8798* ⊕ *www.frankdiners.com*) is set in a 1906 railroad observation car with original stained glass windows. It's a colorful stop for generously portioned American fare, including salmon BLTs and turkey pot pie.

SANDPOINT

Do: A laid-back vacation community in rugged northern Idaho's panhandle, the pine-shaded town of Sandpoint sits along the northwest shore of the nation's fifth-deepest body of water, Lake Pend Oreille (pronounced pond-oh-ray). The area draws snow-sport enthusiasts to Schweitzer Mountain, the largest ski resort in the state, and in summer it's a hot spot for hiking (ride the chairlift up to the half-mile Summit View Loop). Other engaging pursuits include renting kayaks or taking a picturesque **Lake Pend Oreille Cruises** tour (☎ *208/255–5253* ⊕ *www.lakependoreillecruises.com*) of the lake along with browsing the galleries and specialty shops of **Cedar Street Bridge Public Market** (✉ *334 N. 1st Ave.* ☎ *208/304–7383* ⊕ *www.cedarstreetbridge.com*).

Eat & Drink: With breathtaking views of the lake, **Forty One South** (✉ *41 Lakeshore Dr., Sagle, ID* ☎ *208/265–2000* ⊕ *www.41southsandpoint.com*) lies just a bit out of town at the Lodge at Sand Point and has both a romantic environment and some of the region's most refined contemporary cuisine. Downtown's convivial **Idaho Pour Authority** (✉ *203 Cedar St.* ☎ *208/597–7096* ⊕ *www.idahopourauthority.com*) is a nice spot for craft sips and getting to know the locals.

Stay: You'll find cushy rooms with distinctive accents—colorful Talavera tiles in one, a 30-foot octagonal copper ceiling in another—at the **Talus Rock Retreat** (✉ *291 Syringa Heights Rd.* ☎ *208/255–8458* ⊕ *www.talusrockretreat.com*), a contemporary boutique lodge with a pool and hot tub that's close to downtown but set on 18 quiet woodland acres.

Breakfast: Get your morning caffeine fix—and a hearty organic breakfast burrito—at **Evans Brothers Coffee** (✉ *524 Church St.* ☎ *208/265–5553* ⊕ *www.evansbrotherscoffee.com*).

Day 3: Sandpoint, ID, to Whitefish, MT

200 miles (3 hours, 30 minutes without traffic and stops)

This scenic, sparsely populated route passes beneath the jagged peaks of the Cabinet and Purcells mountain ranges, from Idaho's panhandle into western Montana. From Sandpoint, follow U.S. 2 north through Bonners Ferry, and then east into Montana and through verdant evergreen forests to Kalispell, and then to picturesque Whitefish.

ALONG THE WAY

Eat & Drink: Roughly at the halfway point of today's drive, the **Cabinet Mountain Brewing Company** (✉ *206 Mineral Ave.* ☎ *406/293–2739* ⊕ *www.cabinetmountainbrewing.com*) bills itself as the "living room" of Libby, an easygoing Montana town on the Kootenay River. Stop in for a plate of street tacos or a panini, along with a pint of the signature Yaak Attack IPA.

Town: The main drag of Kalispell, northwestern Montana's largest town, is lined with galleries, boutiques, and restaurants. An Andrew Carnegie library is now home to the **Hockaday Museum of Art** (✉ *302 2nd Ave. E* ☎ *406/755–5268* ⊕ *www.hockadaymuseum.com*) and Kalispell's first school building has been turned into the **Northwest Montana History Museum** (✉ *124 2nd Ave. E* ☎ *406/756–5381* ⊕ *www.nwmhistory.org*), but the highlight is visiting the **Conrad Mansion National Historic Site Museum** (✉ *330 Woodland Ave.* ☎ *406/755–2166* ⊕ *www.conradmansion.com*), a Norman-style mansion from the 1890s that sits on a ridge with dramatic mountain views.

Nature: From Kalispell, it's just a 10-mile drive south to explore the north shore of 370-foot-deep Flathead Lake, the largest natural freshwater lake in the western United States. It's a wonderful—and popular—place for sailing, fishing, and swimming.

WHITEFISH

Do: A hub for golfing, boating, hiking, mountain biking, and skiing, Whitefish sits at the base of Big Mountain Ski and Summer Resort, which provides outstanding views into Glacier National Park and the Canadian Rockies. In addition to offering plenty of outdoorsy diversions, this attractive and increasingly affluent town has a cute, shop-filled downtown.

Eat & Drink: The Louisiana-raised chef-owner of convivial **Tupelo Grille** (✉ *17 Central Ave.* ☎ *406/862–6136* ⊕ *www.tupelogrille.com*) prepares excellent southern-inflected fare, such as Low Country shrimp and grits and fried green tomatoes remoulade. For a satisfying ending to any meal, be sure to check out **Sweet Peaks Ice Cream** (✉ *419 E. 3rd St.* ☎ *406/862–4668* ⊕ *www.sweetpeaksicecream.com*), a mini-chain of artisan parlors that offers a slew of interesting flavors, like huckleberry-lemon pie and honey-cinnamon.

Stay: With a private beach and marina, the luxurious **Lodge at Whitefish Lake** (✉ *1380 Wisconsin Ave.* ☎ *406/863–4000* ⊕ *www.lodgeatwhitefishlake.com*) has beautifully appointed rooms with rich wood tones, granite countertops, and slate bathrooms with large walk-in showers and deep soaking tubs—lovely for relaxing after a long day of driving or a strenuous hike.

Breakfast: In downtown Whitefish, **Loula's Cafe** (✉ *300 2nd St. E* ☎ *406/862–5614* ⊕ *www.loulaswhitefish.com*) has become a favorite morning gathering spot for both locals and visitors. Regulars swear by the lemon-stuffed French toast and spicy-sausage breakfast enchiladas,

Extend Your Trip

From Seattle: The Pacific Coast Highway and Highway 101; the Best of the Pacific Northwest; Wine Countries of the Pacific Northwest *(Ch. 3)*

From Yellowstone and Cody: Big Sky County; The Ultimate Wild West Road Trip *(Ch. 4)*

From Mount Rushmore: The Best of the Dakotas *(Ch. 5)*

From Minneapolis: Along the Mississippi *(Ch. 2)*

From Madison: The Best of the Heartland; Underrated Cities of the Midwest *(Ch. 6)*

From Cleveland: All the Great Lakes *(Ch. 6)*

From Pittsburgh: A Frank Lloyd Wright Tour *(Ch. 6)*

From Washington D.C.: Retracing the American Revolution *(Ch. 2)*

but Loula's is also famous for homemade fruit pies, which are available in about 20 different flavors.

Day 4: Whitefish, MT, to East Glacier Park Village, MT

105 miles (3 hours without traffic and stops)

One of the most spectacular drives of your cross-country adventure can happen on this day, assuming it's late June to mid-September, and the incredible Going-to-the-Sun Road through the heart of Glacier National Park is open. Take U.S. 2 east from Whitefish to West Glacier, and follow Going-to-the-Sun Road alongside the crystalline shore of Lake McDonald over Crystal Point and Logan Pass, along the north shore of St. Mary Lake, and south down U.S. 89 to East Glacier Park Village. If you're visiting when Going-to-the-Sun Road is closed, you can still explore the southern reaches of the park, and then take U.S. 2 around the southern end of the park to East Glacier (cutting about 20 miles off your trip).

ALONG THE WAY

Eat & Drink: In **Russell's Fireside Dining Room** at historic **Lake McDonald Lodge** (✉ *288 Lake McDonald Lodge Loop* ☎ *855/733–4522* ⊕ *www.glaciernationalparklodges.com*), take in a great view while choosing between standards such as pasta and wild game, or local favorites, like the huckleberry elk burger or the Montana rainbow trout.

Nature: Although you currently need to make a reservation in order to drive the legendary Going-to-the-Sun Road, this is the **Glacier National Park** (☎ *406/888–7800* ⊕ *www.nps.gov/glac*) experience that you absolutely shouldn't miss. Be sure to stop at Avalanche Creek Campground and make the 30-minute stroll along the fragrant Trail of the Cedars, and at the Jackson Glacier Overlook to view one of the park's largest glaciers.

EAST GLACIER VILLAGE

Do: A convenient, quiet base that's also home to the gorgeous Glacier Park Lodge, East Glacier also provides easy proximity to some notable attractions in the southeastern side of the park, such as Two Medicine Valley, a rugged, often windy, and always beautiful spot accessed via a stunning 9-mile drive from Highway 49, and Running Eagle Falls, a pair of cascades that originate from two different sources.

Eat & Drink: A unique natural log structure made from enormous trees, the **Great Northern Dining Room in Glacier Park Lodge** (✉ 499 MT-49 ☎ 844/868–7474 ⊕ www. glaicerparkcollection.com) provides a rustic environment for hearty comfort-food classics, from beef pot roast to butternut squash ravioli.

Stay: Just east of the park, the beautiful Glacier Park Lodge, dating to 1913, is supported by 500- to 800-year-old fir and 3-foot-thick cedar logs. Entertainers delight guests with storytelling and singing in the spectacular great hall. Rooms are sparsely decorated, but historic framed posters hang on the hallway walls.

Breakfast: Although Glacier Park Lodge is the most memorable place for breakfast, the friendly **Whistle Stop Restaurant** (✉ 1024 MT-49 ☎ 406/226–9292 ⊕ www. brownieshostel.com) is a reliable option for omelets, French toast, and the like.

Day 5: East Glacier Park Village, MT, to Bozeman, MT

280 miles (5 hours without traffic and stops)

Follow U.S. 2 east to Browning, and turn south on U.S. 89, following it through Choteau. Then pick up U.S. 287 south to Wolf Creek for a turn on I–15 to Helena, then U.S. 287 again south to Interstate 90 for a final jog east to Bozeman.

ALONG THE WAY

Town: Montana's state capital, Helena is known for its numerous city parks, several museums, and thriving arts community. The southern part of town is hilly and thick with lush greenery in summer, and you'll find a trove of ornate brick-and-granite historic buildings

along Last Chance Gulch. Be sure to at least view the exterior of the imposing **Cathedral of St. Helena** (✉ 530 N. Ewing St. ☎ 406/442–5825 ⊕ www.sthelenas. org)—modeled after a cathedral in Vienna, Austria, and known for its stained glass windows and 230-foot-tall twin spires.

Eat & Drink: If it's serious sustenance you're craving, order a heaping plate of smoked chicken or Texas-style brisket at folksy **Bad Betty's Barbecue** (✉ 812 Front St. ☎ 406/459–2303 ⊕ www.badbettysbarbecue.com)—saving room for the creamy banana pudding.

Nature: For a bird's-eye view of the city, scramble to the peak of Mount Helena, the crowning feature of 620-acre Mount Helena City Park. Several trails lead to the peak, with the 2.9-mile round-trip offering perhaps the best scenery. It's a moderately strenuous trek, but it only takes just 1½ to 2 hours.

BOZEMAN

Do: A mix of cowboys, professors, students, skiers, and celebrities makes Bozeman one of the more diverse communities in the northern Rockies as well as one of the fastest-growing towns in Montana. The boom has led to stylish new hotels and trendy eateries, but this recreation hub retains a decidedly easygoing, western vibe. The must-see is the impressive **Museum of the Rockies** (✉ 600 W. Kagy Blvd. ☎ 406/994–2251 ⊕ www.museumoftherockies.org), where you'll find a celebration of the history of the entire region, with exhibits ranging from prehistory to pioneers, plus a planetarium with laser shows.

Eat & Drink: Inside the cavernous former Northern Pacific Railroad depot, **Montana Ale Works** (✉ 611 E. Main St. ☎ 406/587–7700 ⊕ www.montanaaleworks.com) offers a huge selection of Montana microbrews, and a restaurant serving bison pot stickers, baked pasta dishes, and Caribbean and Spanish dishes. You'll find some fun bars downtown, including **Plonk Wine** (✉ *29 E. Main St.* ☏ *406/587–2170* ⊕ *www.plonkwine.com*), a long narrow space that's as much fun for people-watching as it is for sipping vino from the extensive and impressive list.

Stay: With a striking art deco design, the gorgeous **Kimpton Armory Hotel** (✉ *24 W. Mendenhall St.* ☏ *406/551–7700* ⊕ *www.armoryhotelbzn.com*), located in Bozeman's former armory building, provides urbane accommodations and amenities in an appealing downtown location. There's a fantastic restaurant and bar, too.

Breakfast: Colorful murals, high ceilings, and exposed air ducts create a mod-industrial environment at **Jam!** (✉ *25 W. Main St.* ☏ *406/585–1761* ⊕ *www.jamonmain.com*), a bustling downtown café that serves breakfast all day as well as a selection of tasty lunch items. Specialties include the crab cake Benedict and challah bread French toast stuffed with jam-infused mascarpone cheese.

Day 6: Bozeman, MT, to Cody, WY

250 miles (7 hours without traffic and stops)

Of course, you could simply zoom along I–90 and U.S. 310 from Bozeman to Cody, for a straightforward 3½-hour drive. But by far the most rewarding route takes you through the heart of **Yellowstone National Park** (☏ *307/344–7381* ⊕ *www.nps.gov/yell*). If you don't have time for an extra night, you can make this drive in a long day—passing through the Mammoth Springs, Old Faithful, Canyon Village, and Yellowstone Lake section of the park, albeit perhaps having to rush a bit in places (get a very early start!).

ALONG THE WAY

Eat & Drink: An enjoyable stop for lunch just before you enter Yellowstone, the **Iron Horse Bar & Grille** (✉ *606 Jackson St.* ☏ *814/889–8955*) in Gardiner is a rollicking roadhouse with a huge wooden deck overlooking the Yellowstone River and the mountains in the distance.

Nature: With limited time, concentrate on the two biggest attractions in Yellowstone: Old Faithful geyser and the Grand Canyon of the Yellowstone. After entering the park via the North Entrance, stop at Mammoth Hot Springs and walk the Lower Terrace Interpretive Trail past Liberty Cap and the other strange, brightly colored travertine formations. Then continue south to Old Faithful, where you should allow at least two hours to explore its eye-popping geothermal features. Eruptions occur approximately 90 minutes apart but can vary, so check with the visitor center for predicted times. As you backtrack north, it's well worth stopping to walk around Grand Prismatic Spring in Midway Geyser Basin. Next, make your way east through Madison and Norris to Canyon Village to see the Grand Canyon of the Yellowstone—the Artist Point overlook on the South Rim offers one of the best photo ops. Then continue south through sweeping Hayden Valley, keeping an eye out for buffalo roaming the prairies.

CODY

Do: Founded in 1896 and named for Pony Express rider, army scout, Freemason, and entertainer William F. "Buffalo Bill" Cody, this easygoing western town is best known as a base for visiting Yellowstone National Park, but it actually boasts its own impressive array of diversions. Part of the fun here is sauntering down Sheridan Avenue, stopping by the Irma Hotel for a refreshment, and attending the **Cody Nite Rodeo** (✉ *519 W. Yellowstone Ave.* ☏ *307/587–5155* ⊕ *www.codystampederodeo.com*), an intimate, family-friendly affair that takes place nightly all summer. Whatever you do, do not miss the **Buffalo Bill Center of the West** (✉ *720 Sheridan Ave.* ☎ *307/587–4771* ⊕ *www.centerofthewest.org*), an extraordinary complex—and an affiliate of the Smithsonian Institution—that contains the Buffalo Bill Museum, the Whitney Western Art Museum, the Plains Indian Museum, the Cody Firearms Museum, and the Draper Natural History Museum.

Eat & Drink: The handsome **Cody Steakhouse** (✉ *1367 Sheridan Ave.* ☎ *307/586–2550* ⊕ *www.cody-steak-house.business.site*) is a favorite of red-meat eaters, but there's also a surprising variety of internationally inspired seafood and poultry dishes, including prawns with a spicy mango-jalapeño salsa. A trip to Cody isn't complete without a scooting your boots to live music, usually provided by the local group West the Band, at **Cassie's** (✉ *214 Yellowstone Ave.* ☎ *307/527–5500* ⊕ *www.cassies.com*).

Stay: The quirkiest lodging in town is the **Irma Hotel** (✉ *1192 Sheridan Ave.* ☎ *307/587–4221* ⊕ *www.irmahotel.com*), built in 1902 by Buffalo Bill and named for his daughter. It's not fancy, but the Irma exudes character.

Breakfast: Set in an airy former Texaco garage, the **Station by Cody Coffee** (✉ *919 16th St.* ☎ *307/578–6661* ⊕ *www.cody-coffee.com*) can fuel you with well-made lattes, nitro cold brews, and chai teas, while the kitchen serves an assortment of sweet and savory crepes as well as fresh-fruit smoothies.

Day 7: Cody, WY, to Deadwood, SD

370 miles (6 hours without traffic and stops)

This is a big day of driving, so try to set out early. Head east through the rugged mountains and grassy plains of eastern Wyoming, taking U.S. 14, Highway 30, and Highway 31 to the tiny and scenic village of Ten Sleep, continuing on U.S. 16—known along this stretch as the Cloud Peak Skyway Scenic Byway—over the Bighorn Mountains and through charming Buffalo to I–90 and continuing east for Deadwood.

ALONG THE WAY

Eat & Drink: You won't encounter a ton of dining options on this journey, although the towns of Buffalo and Gillette offer some perfunctory options in a pinch. Nevertheless, in the incredibly scenic foothills of the Bighorn Mountains in the town of Ten Sleep, you will pass by one of the coolest little brewpubs in the state, **Ten Sleep Brewing Co.** (✉ *2549 U.S. 16* ☎ *307/366–2074* ⊕ *www.tensleepbrewingco.com*), which serves first-rate porters and golden ales to a friendly crowd. Most days, there's either a taco or pizza truck on hand by late in the afternoon.

Detour: As you drive east from Gillette, the highways begin to rise into the forested slopes of the Black Hills. A detour north will take to **Devils Tower National Monument** (☎ *307/467–5283* ⊕ *www.nps.gov/deto*), a grooved butte that juts upward 1,280 feet above the plain of the Belle Fourche River. The tower was a tourist magnet long before a spaceship landed here in *Close Encounters of the Third Kind*—Teddy Roosevelt designated it the nation's first national monument in 1906. A stroll along the 1.3-mile paved trail around the base takes less than an hour and affords impressive views.

DEADWOOD

Do: You'll discover brick streets fronted by Victorian buildings—which house shops, restaurants, and gaming halls—in this relentlessly kitschy town that has boomed especially since the 2004–2006 run of its eponymous TV show. Highlights among the historic attractions include the **Adams Museum** (✉ *54 Sherman St.* ☎ *605/578–1714* ⊕ *www.deadwoodhistory.com*)—which showcases the region's first locomotive, photographs of the town's early days, and an exhibit featuring the largest gold nugget ever discovered in the Black Hills—and **Mount Moriah Cemetery** (✉ *10 Mt. Moriah Dr. ☎ 605/722–0837 ⊕ www.cityofdeadwood.com*), also known as Boot Hill. It's the final resting place of Wild Bill Hickok, Calamity Jane, and other notable Deadwood residents. From the top of the cemetery, you'll have the best panoramic view of the town.

Eat & Drink: On the second floor of historic Saloon No. 10, **Deadwood Social Club** (✉ *657 Main St. ☎ 605/578–1533 ⊕ www.saloon10.com*) is filled with old-time photographs of Deadwood. And while the decor is western, the food is northern Italian, a juxtaposition that keeps patrons coming back.

Stay: One of the stateliest Victorian buildings in town, the **Martin Mason Hotel** (✉ *33 Deadwood St. ☎ 605/722–3456 ⊕ www.martinmasonhotel.com*) offers elegantly furnished rooms, a small casino with a pressed-tin ceiling, and a high-ceilinged café that serves reliably good comfort fare.

Breakfast: An active glass-blowing studio and gallery set in a former service station, **Pump House Coffee & Deli** (✉ *73 Sherman St. ☎ 605/571–1071 ⊕ www.mindblownstudio.com*) serves tasty egg sandwiches and espresso drinks.

Day 8: Deadwood, SD, to Wall, SD

150 miles (3 hours without traffic and stops)

Drive south along U.S. 385, stopping to view the Crazy Horse Memorial, then backtrack slightly and follow Highway 244 east via Mount Rushmore National Memorial, the U.S. 16A and U.S. 16 through Rapid City, and picking up I–90 east for the quickest route.

ALONG THE WAY

Attraction: Designed to be the world's largest work of art, **Crazy Horse Memorial** (☎ *605/673–4681 ⊕ www.crazyhorsememorial.org*) is a tribute to the spirit of the Lakota people. It depicts Crazy Horse, the legendary Lakota leader who helped defeat General Custer at Little Bighorn. A work in progress, thus far the warrior's head has been carved from the mountain, and the colossal head of his horse is beginning to emerge.

Attraction: One of the nation's most recognized public art works in the country, **Mount Rushmore** (✉ *13000 SD-244 ☎ 605/574–2523 ⊕ www.nps.gov/moru*) can be enjoyed in as little as 15 minutes, but you'll get more out of your visit if you stay a bit longer and walk through the excellent interpretive center and explore the network of easy trails.

Eat & Drink: Perfect for a bite to eat before or after visiting nearby Mount Rushmore, the **Powder House Restaurant** (✉ *24125 U.S. 16A ☎ 605/666–4646 ⊕ www.powerhouselodge.com*) in Keystone serves stick-to-your-ribs country fare, including local game dishes like elk burgers and buffalo stew.

WALL

Do: This tiny railroad hub—apart from being a gateway to Badlands National Park—is known for being home to one of the daffier roadside attractions in the country, **Wall Drug Store** (✉ *510 Main St. ☎ 605/279–2175 ⊕ www.walldrug.com*), which got its start in 1931 by offering free ice water to road-weary travelers. Today its four dining rooms can seat more than 520 customers at once, and a life-size mechanical Cowboy Orchestra and Chuckwagon Quartet greet curious customers as they enter. The attached Western Mall has more than a dozen shops selling all kinds of keepsakes, from cowboy hats, boots, and Black Hills gold jewelry to T-shirts and fudge.

Eat & Drink: With limited dining options in these parts, your best option is the **Badlands Saloon & Grille** (✉ *509 Main St.* ☎ *605/279–2210*), which offers a lot more of what you've probably experienced over the past couple of days: cold beer, buffalo burgers, and plenty of local color.

Stay: Wall's best option is the pleasant, if functional, **Best Western Plains Motel** (✉ *712 Glenn St.* ☎ *605/279–2145* ⊕ *www.bestwestern.com*), which has a pool and a central location.

Breakfast: Stop by venerable Wall Drug for traditional American fare (and the store's famous homemade doughnuts).

Day 9: Wall, SD, to Sioux Falls, SD

330 miles (6 hours without traffic and stops)

The most interesting route today is by way of Highway 240 south from Wall to Badlands National Park to the town of Interior, exiting the park and following Highway 44 east across the prairie, then north on U.S. 81 and east on Highway 42.

ALONG THE WAY

Nature: So stark and forbidding are the chiseled spires, ragged ridgelines, and deep ravines of **Badlands National Park** (☎ *605/433–5361* ⊕ *www.nps.gov/badl*) that Lieutenant Colonel George Custer once described them as "hell with the fires burned out." Ruthlessly ravaged over the ages by wind and rain, the 380 square miles of wild terrain continue to erode and evolve, sometimes visibly changing shape in a few days. Prairie creatures thrive on the untamed territory, and animal fossils are in abundance. Badlands Loop Road circles through the park and accesses several overlooks along the way, including Pinnacles and Yellow Mounds, which are outstanding places to examine the landscape's sandy pink- and brown-toned ridges and bizarre spires.

Eat & Drink: The pickings remain slim until you get to Sioux Falls, but laid-back **Shirley's Diner** (✉ *142 E. 2nd St.* ☎ *605/842–3903* ⊕ *shirleys-diner-winner. edan.io*) in Winner is handily situated about midway along your route and serves unfussy home cooking.

SIOUX FALLS

Do: South Dakota's largest city is also one of the fastest-growing communities in the upper Midwest, thanks to a high quality of life, a favorable business climate, and good balance of art, culture, and outdoor recreation. A highlight of any visit is strolling around the 128-acre **Falls Park** (✉ *131 E. Falls Park Dr.* ☎ *605/367–7430* ⊕ *www.siouxfalls.org*), where the Big Sioux River drops more than 100 feet over a series of rocky ledges. Throughout the city's downtown, you'll find dozens of appealing shops and eateries as well as the **Sioux Falls SculptureWalk** (✉ *300 S. Phillips Ave.* ☎ *605/838–8102* ⊕ *www. sculpturewalksiouxfalls.com*), an urban trail featuring more than 60 diverse works.

Eat & Drink: Close to Falls Park and just off the city's pleasing Sioux Falls Bike Trail, **Ode to Food and Drinks** (✉ *300 N. Cherapa Pl.* ☎ *605/275–6332* ⊕ *www. odetofoodanddrinks.com*) is smartly decorated—with curving stone walls and big windows overlooking the river—and serves an eclectic mix of American and international dishes. The classy tiki-inspired cocktail bar **Hello Hi** (✉ *120 S. Phillips Ave.* ☎ *605/275–4544* ⊕ *www. thehellohi.com*) is an inviting place to wind down your evening.

Stay: Occupying a stunningly restored 1918 bank tower, the **Hotel on Phillips** (✉ *100 N. Phillips Ave.* ☎ *605/274–7445* ⊕ *www.hotelonphillips.com*) has plush rooms that showcase the building's ornate design accents. Common spaces include a beautiful mezzanine overlooking the lobby, and the swish and clubby Treasury bar and restaurant.

Breakfast: Start the day with blackened-salmon omelet or corned beef hash and eggs at hipster-favorite **Josiah's Coffeehouse and Café** (✉ *104 W. 12th St.* ☎ *605/759–8255* ⊕ *www.josiahscoffee. com*), an inviting space with a bakery serving delectable caramel rolls and scones.

Day 10: Sioux Falls, SD, to Minneapolis, MN

240 miles (4 hours without traffic and stops)

Start your drive from Sioux Falls along I-90 east to Worthington, turning northeast on Highway 60 to Mankato, then turning north on U.S. 169 to reach Minneapolis. It's a relaxing and mostly flat journey through wide-open prairies, with little traffic.

ALONG THE WAY

Town: Another fast-growing community with a high quality of life, Mankato is also home to Minnesota State University, which imbues it with a youthful, progressive personality. Set at the confluence of the Minnesota and Blue Earth rivers, the city makes an especially pleasant stopover from late spring through early fall, when you can hike to a dramatic waterfall at **Minneopa State Park** (✉ *54497 Gadwall Rd.* ☎ *507/386–3910* ⊕ *www.dnr.state. mn.us*), or stroll along downtown's **Mankato Walking Sculpture Tour** (✉ *127 S. 2nd St.* ☎ *507/388–1062* ⊕ *www.cityartmankato.com*).

Eat & Drink: A short walk from Mankato's pleasant Minnesota River Trail, **Coffee Hag** (✉ *329 N. Riverfront Dr.* ☎ *507/387–5533* ⊕ *www.facebook.com/thecoffeehag*) is an artsy, offbeat café that serves tasty vegetarian fare, chai lattes, and smoothies.

MINNEAPOLIS

Do: Whether you're looking for highbrow sophistication or a quiet picnic on the Chain of Lakes, Minneapolis offers a great mix of outdoor adventures and cultural attractions, plus a justly acclaimed, independent-spirited dining and retail scene. The gorgeously designed **Walker Art Center** (✉ *725 Vineland Pl.* ☎ *612/375–7600* ⊕ *www.walkerart.org*) contains an outstanding collection of 20th- and 21st-century American and European sculpture, prints, and photography, as well as acclaimed traveling exhibits. Set aside an extra half hour to walk through the adjacent and also excellent Minneapolis **Sculpture Garden** (✉ *725 Vineland Pl.* ☎ *612/375–7600* ⊕ *www.walkerart.org*). Take a walk to the Mill District, a patch of historic and stately old flour mill buildings and one very new, enthralling modern structure—the Guthrie Theater, with its 178-foot cantilevered bridge. The neighborhood is home to the excellent **Mill City Museum** ✉ *(704 S. 2nd St.* ☎ *612/341–7555* ⊕ *www.millcitymuseum.org*), whose interactive exhibits document the city's industrial history, and that overlooks Saint Anthony Falls. You can get an especially nice look at this series of cascades, locks, and dams on the Mississippi River by walking across the Stone Arch Bridge, which was built in 1883 for trains but is now used exclusively by pedestrians and bicycles.

Eat & Drink: A visit to Minneapolis presents the opportunity to experience the robustly flavored, beautifully plated dishes of Yia Vang, who's perhaps the most celebrated Hmong chef in the United States (the Twin Cities' vibrant Hmong community is the largest outside Asia). As of this writing, his food was available at the **Union Hmong Kitchen** (✉ *693 Raymond Ave.* ☎ *612/431–5285* ⊕ *www. unionhmongkitchen.com*) pop-up, but a new permanent restaurant, **Vinai** (✉ *1717 N.E. 2nd St.* ⊕ *www.vinaimn.com*), is expected to open by late 2021. Housed in a 1920s Ford auto garage, the beloved

Bryant Lake Bowl (✉ *810 W. Lake St.* ☎ *612/825–3737* ⊕ *www.bryantlake-bowl.com*)is a lively bar, fun all-day restaurant, renowned cabaret theater, and very popular bowling alley.

Stay: In the city's lively Warehouse District, the **Hewing Hotel** (✉ *300 N. Washington Ave.* ☎ *651/468–0400* ⊕ *www.hewinghotel.com*) is an artfully executed boutique hotel. The stunner occupies a late 1890s former lumber warehouse that's also home to acclaimed Tullibee restaurant as well as a sixth-floor rooftop bar with grand views of the neighborhood.

Breakfast: Head to the **Hi-Lo** (✉ *4020 E. Lake St.* ☎ *612/353–6568* ⊕ *www.hi-lo-diner.com*), a landmark 1950s stainless-steel diner that offers a wide selection of breakfast greatest hits, from huevos rancheros with chorizo to lavender crème brûlée French toast.

Day 11: Minneapolis, MN, to Winona, MN

120 miles (2 hours, 30 minutes without traffic and stops)

This drive follows a picturesque stretch of the Mississippi River southeast, starting from St. Paul, then continuing on U.S. 10 along the east side of the river in Wisconsin, crossing back into Minnesota on U.S. 63 into Red Wing, and then following U.S. 61 along the west side of the river through Lake City and Wabasha to Winona.

ALONG THE WAY

Town: You might recognize the town of Red Wing because of its eponymous shoe manufacturer or for the beautiful glazed pottery that Red Wing Stoneware has been producing since 1877. But the town also stands out for its well-preserved 19th-century architecture and dramatic riverfront terrain, which you can fully appreciate from the top of Barn

Bluff—it's an easy half-mile scramble to the 340-foot summit of this rocky promontory that affords sweeping views of downtown and the countryside.

Eat & Drink: In Red Wing, the historic St. James Hotel's hip **Scarlet Kitchen & Bar** (✉ *406 Main St.* ☎ *651/385–5544* ⊕ *www.st-james-hotel.com*) is a wonderfully atmospheric venue for brunch or dinner.

Nature: A fantastic place to learn about bald eagles, of which hundreds inhabit the Upper Mississippi River Valley, the **National Eagle Center** (✉ *50 Pembroke Ave.* ☎ *651/565–4989* ⊕ *www.nationaleaglecenter.org*) sits on the banks of the river in downtown Wabasha, offering two floors of interactive exhibits, huge windows for glimpsing these birds in the wild, and the opportunity for up close interactions with the rescued golden and bald eagles who reside here.

WINONA

Do: A little bigger than Red Wing but also with a historic downtown and a pleasing riverside location, Winona is notable for its superb **Minnesota Marine Art Museum** (✉ *800 Riverview Dr.* ☎ *507/474–6626* ⊕ *www.mmam.org*), containing a remarkable permanent collection of nautical art and artifacts from around the world, including Emanuel Leutze's famous *Washington Crossing the Delaware* and works by J. M.W. Turner, Picasso, and several Hudson River School artists. If it's a nice day, climb to Winona's highest point, Sugar Loaf, a rocky butte reached via a 1.2-mile round-trip hike—be prepared for a pretty good workout.

Eat & Drink: The bright, fresh cuisine served at **Nosh Scratch Kitchen** (✉ *102 Walnut St.* ☎ *507/474–7040* ⊕ *www.noshrestaurant.com*) showcases the seasonal bounty of the Upper Mississippi River Valley and beyond. More casual fare and great ales are the specialty of **Island City Brewing** (✉ *65 E. Front St.*, ☎ *507/961–5015* ⊕ *islandcitybrew.com*), which occupies a handsome old building with views of the levee and river.

Stay: Downtown Winona has a pair of charming B&Bs within a few blocks of each other: the stately **Alexander Mansion** (✉ *274 E. Broadway St.* ☎ *507/474–4224* ⊕ *www.alexandermansionbb.com*), which was built for one of the town's early judges in 1886, and the white-clapboard **Carriage House** (✉ *420 Main St.* ☎ *507/452–8256 www.chbb.com*), a 1870 Victorian—both include sumptuous full breakfasts in the rates.

Breakfast: In a redbrick storefront near the riverfront, the **Acoustic Cafe** (✉ *77 Lafayette St.* ☎ *507/453–0394* ⊕ *www. acousticcafewinona.com*) serves house-roasted coffees and light sandwiches and pastries throughout the day.

Day 12: Winona, MN, to Madison, WI

160 miles (3 hours, 30 minutes without traffic and stops)

Drive a short way down U.S. 61 from Winona and cross the Mississippi River again on U.S. 14 into the city of La Crosse, and follow this hilly route through leafy southwestern Wisconsin through towns now famous for the architecture of Frank Lloyd Wright, before entering Madison from the west.

ALONG THE WAY

Town: The small town of Spring Green would make a charming stop even without its most famous attraction, **Taliesin** (✉ *5481 County Rd.* ☎ *608/588–7900* ⊕ *www.taliesinpreservation.org*), the 800-acre former estate, school, studio, and summer home of Frank Lloyd Wright; tours of which are an absolute must if you have even a slight interest in design and architecture.

Eat & Drink: Close to Taliesin, designed by Frank Lloyd Wright, and offering lovely views of the Wisconsin River, the **Riverview Terrace Cafe** (✉ *5607 County Rd.* ☎ *877/588–7900* ⊕ *www.taliesinpreservation.org*) serves farm-to-table fare, including aged-cheddar grilled-cheese sandwiches and homemade cookies.

MADISON

Do: This picturesque and progressive city—the center of which lies along an eight-block-wide isthmus—is known as much for being home to the lakefront campus of University of Wisconsin–Madison as for being the state's political center. Start your explorations at the regal **Wisconsin State Capitol** (✉ *2 E. Main St.* ☎ *608/266–0382* ⊕ *www.wisconsin. gov*), and also set aside time to tour the gorgeous, glass-walled **Madison Museum of Contemporary Art** (✉ *227 State St.* ☎ *608/257–0158* ⊕ *www.mmoca.org*), which contains a fantastic permanent collection by mostly 20th-century luminaries and a stunning rooftop sculpture garden. On the pretty campus of the University of Wisconsin–Madison, go for a stroll at Memorial Union, overlooking Lake Monona and home to beloved **Babcock Ice Cream** (✉ *1605 Linden Dr.* ☎ *608/262–3045* ⊕ *www.babcockhall-dairystore.wisc.edu*).

Eat & Drink: One of the most renowned farm-to-table restaurants in the Upper Midwest, **L'Etoile** (✉ *1 S. Pinckney St.* ☎ *608/251–0500* ⊕ *www.letoile-restaurant.com*) has been an exemplar of the Slow Food movement since it opened in 1976—try to reserve in advance, and prepare to be blown away by the five-course tasting menu. Later in the evening, drop by **One Barrel Brewing** (✉ *2001 Atwood Ave.* ☎ *608/630–9286* ⊕ *www.onebarrelbrewing.com*) for a pint of BBL Aged Scotch Ale.

Stay: For eye-popping water views and a great location near the University of Wisconsin, consider the historic **Edgewater** (✉ *1001 Wisconsin Pl.* ☎ *608/535–8200* ⊕ *www.theedgewater.com*), which is home to a very nice full-service spa and the convivial Boathouse Bar & Grill.

Breakfast: Do as plenty of locals have been doing for years and grab a booth at retro-cool **Monty's Blue Plate Diner** (✉ *2089 Atwood Ave.* ☎ *608/244-8505* ⊕ *www. montysblueplatediner.com*), where you can start your day off with meat loaf hash or eggs Mornay with poached eggs and smoked ham.

Day 13: Madison, WI, to Saugatuck, MI

315 miles (5 hours without traffic and stops)

With a lot of ground to cover today, it's best to stick with interstates. Take I-94 east to Milwaukee, and follow it south to Chicago and around the south shore of Lake Michigan via I-90, continuing through the northern end of Indiana and then back up I-94 into Michigan, passing through Benton Harbor and picking up I-196 to Saugatuck.

ALONG THE WAY

Town: Wisconsin's largest city, Milwaukee is an international seaport with a handsome skyline of modern steel-and-glass high-rises and well-kept 19th-century buildings. If you have time for just one attraction, make it the singularly stunning **Milwaukee Art Museum** (✉ *700 N. Art Museum Dr.* ☎ *414/224-3200* ⊕ *www. mam.org*), with its pleasing Lake Michigan location and spectacular curvilinear addition, designed by Santiago Calavatra.

Eat & Drink: This very traditional metropolis with deep central European roots has long been famous for its old-world restaurants—casual **Von Trier** (✉ *2235 N. Farwell Ave.* ☎ *414/272-1775* ⊕ *www. vontriers.com*) is a good lunch stop. Wherever you dine, save time for a trip to **Leon's Frozen Custard** (✉ *3131 S. 27th St.* ☎ *414/383-1784* ⊕ *www.leonsfrozen-custard.us*), a neon-lit landmark on your

way south out of town that dispenses luscious cherry milk shakes and banana split sundaes.

SAUGATUCK

Do: This small, well-established art colony and LGBTQ+-friendly vacation town at the mouth of the Kalamazoo River and along the Lake Michigan shoreline makes for a relaxing pause as you transition from the more sparsely populated western half of the country to the bigger cities of the Midwest. Saugatuck and its sister village Douglas sit along a wide section of river that's actually classified as Kalamazoo Lake, which is great for kayaking or taking a boat cruise around Lake Michigan. There are also plenty of cool art galleries, chic cafés, and stylish boutiques to explore. And there's **Oval Beach** (✉ *690 Perryman St.* ☎ *269/857-2603* ⊕ *www.saugatuck.com*), one of the prettiest stretches of sand along Lake Michigan's shoreline, with its acres of protected sand dunes and blissful sunset views.

Eat & Drink: A 15-minute drive away in nearby Fennville, rustic yet sophisticated **Salt of the Earth** (✉ *114 E. Main St.* ☎ *269/561-7258* ⊕ *www.saltoftheearth-fennville.com*) sources as much of its menu as possible from within 50 miles and even offers some excellent Michigan wine, beer, and cider options.

Stay: Built in 1913 by a colleague of Frank Lloyd Wright in a loose interpretation of Prairie style, the grand **Belvedere Inn & Restaurant** (✉ *3656 63rd St.* ☎ *269/857-5777* ⊕ *www.thebelvedereinn.com*) is now a sumptuous boutique hotel on 5 tranquil acres of gardens and lawns. The dining room is perfect for a leisurely romantic dinner, too.

Breakfast: In the heart of bustling Saugatuck village, **Uncommon Coffee Roasters** (✉ *127 Hoffman St.* ☎ *269/857-3333* ⊕ *www.uncommoncoffeeroasters.com*) offers sunny sidewalk seating as well as a cozy indoor space for enjoying yogurt parfaits and pesto-egg bagels.

Day 14: Saugatuck, MI, to Cleveland, OH

320 miles (5 hours without traffic and stops)

Follow I–196 and I–96 through Grand Rapids and Lansing, then head down U.S. 23 through the lively college town of Ann Arbor to Toledo, Ohio, where you'll pick up on I–90 to Cleveland. As this route passes through some urban areas, be prepared for more traffic, especially during the morning and evening rush hours.

ALONG THE WAY

Eat & Drink: If you're starting to feel a little peckish or thirsty when you pass through Grand Rapids, and especially if you're a fan of craft ale, pause in this attractive river town with an acclaimed beer scene for a bite to eat at **Founders Brewing** (✉ *235 Grandville Ave. SW* ☎ *616/776–1195* ⊕ *www.foundersbrewing.com*), a high-ceilinged tap room with hefty sandwiches and pub fare and lots of interesting sips on tap.

Town: Most famous as the location of the University of Michigan, Ann Arbor is roughly at the midway point between Saugatuck and Cleveland, and can be easily explored in a few hours. Ann Arbor's attractive downtown blends almost imperceptibly with the U. of M. campus, many of whose stately buildings were designed by architectural icons Albert Kahn and Eero Saarinen. East Liberty Street is lined with fun eateries and shops, and leads to the heart of campus and its picturesque "Diag," a huge green where you're apt to find students sunbathing and studying on warm days.

Shop: Ann Arbor's distinctive **Kerrytown Market & Shops** (✉ *407 N. 5th Ave.* ☎ *734/662–5008* ⊕ *www.kerrytown.*

com) anchors an eclectic neighborhood of redbrick lanes and dynamic cultural spaces. The market spreads across three carefully preserved late-Victorian industrial buildings and features vendors proffering all kinds of specialty foods, vintage clothiers, antiques shops, art spaces, several excellent restaurants, and both the Ann Arbor Farmers Market and Ann Arbor Artisans Market.

CLEVELAND

Do: Occupying a sweeping stretch of shoreline along Lake Erie, Cleveland was America's fifth-largest city a century ago, and its impressive wealth of early-20th-century landmarks is a testament to this fact. Its greatest draw is the striking I. M. Pei–designed **Rock & Roll Hall of Fame** (✉ *1100 E. 9th St.* ☎ *216/781–7625* ⊕ *www.rockhall.com*), which is enormously fun to explore. The crown jewel of the city's cultural hub, the **Cleveland Museum of Art** (✉ *11150 East Blvd.* ☎ *216/421–7350* ⊕ *www.clevelandart.org*) is another must-see, with 70 galleries spanning Mediterranean antiquity to the present.

Eat & Drink: Don't miss the legendary **West Side Market** (✉ *1979 W. 25th St.* ☎ *216/664–3387* ⊕ *www.westsidemarket.org*), which occupies a grand 1912 building with 44-foot-high vaulted ceilings and carries more than 75 vendors specializing in pierogi, Cambodian food, Middle Eastern specialties, and every other amazing cuisine under the sun.

Stay: The **Kimpton Schofield Hotel** (✉ *2000 E. 9th St.* ☎ *216/357–3250* ⊕ *www.theschofieldhotel.com*) occupies a dapper 14-story tower from the early 1900s in the heart of the city's theater district. Rooms have top-of-the-line bedding and bath amenities, and the restaurant, Betts, turns out artfully plated modern American fare.

Breakfast: Amid the striking bridges, viaducts, and beautifully restored warehouses and factory buildings in the city's formerly industrial and increasingly hip Flats district, **Lucky's Cafe** (✉ *777 Stark-weather Ave.* ☎ *216/622–7773* ⊕ *www.luckyscafe.com*) works closely with Ohio farmers to source the ingredients for its gingerbread waffles topped with warm maple-roasted apples, and brûléed steel-cut oatmeal with dried-fruit compote.

Day 15: Cleveland, OH, to Pittsburgh, PA

135 miles (2 hours, 30 minutes without traffic and stops)

Follow I–77 south from Cleveland, allowing at least two hours to wander around Cuyahoga Valley National Park, then pick up I–80 east toward Youngstown, where you'll catch I–76 (the Pennsylvania Turnpike) southeast to Pittsburgh.

ALONG THE WAY

Photo Op: On your way out of Cleveland, we "triple-dog-dare ya" to stop in front of the **Christmas Story House** (✉ *3159 W. 11th St.* ☎ *216/298–4919* ⊕ *www.achristmas-toryhouse.com*), which will forever be associated with the eponymous 1983 holiday movie.

Nature: One of the country's newer national parks, **Cuyahoga Valley National Park** (✉ *330/657–2752* ⊕ *www.nps.gov/cuva*) is a 33,000-acre patch of greenery that extends for 22 meandering miles along the Cuyahoga River between Cleveland and Akron. There's fishing, biking, snowshoeing, and hiking throughout the park, which includes a 19.5-mile stretch of the historic Ohio and Erie Canal Towpath, and you can take a ride (especially nice in autumn) on the Cuyahoga Valley Scenic Railroad. Most of the park's top attractions are easily accessed from major roads, including Brandywine Falls, which is the most photogenic of about 100 cascades throughout the park.

Eat & Drink: The best dining venue located within Cuyahoga Valley National Park, enchanting **Sarah's Vineyard** (✉ *1204 W. Steels Corners Rd.* ☎ *330/929–8057* ⊕ *www.sarahsvineyardwinery.com*) is set amid several acres of grapevines and includes a winery and tasting room. You can walk through a butterfly garden, sip wine on a breezy deck, and order cheese plates, hummus, sandwiches, and pizzas to enjoy with your tasting.

PITTSBURGH

Do: Hilly and colorful Pittsburgh is one of the country's most distinctive urban environments. Once a center of steel manufacturing, today it's better known as a center of health care, finance, education, and technology. It's also home to some exceptional museums and lots of neighborhoods that, despite having gentrified to varying degrees, still maintain close-knit communities of various European, Asian, and Latin-American immigrants. One of the country's best museums devoted to a single artist, the **Andy Warhol Museum** (✉ *117 Sandusky St.* ☎ *412/237–8300* ⊕ *www.warhol.org*) devotes seven floors to the work of the native Pittsburgher and pop-art icon. From there, it's a short walk to the **Mattress Factory** (✉ *500 Sampsonia Way* ☎ *412/231–3169* ⊕ *www.mattress.org*), whose contemporary installations and experimental art exhibits often carry environmental themes; the rock garden outside is breathtaking.

Eat & Drink: Among the North Side's continuously evolving supply of restaurants, you'll find both old-school treasures—like **Max's Allegheny Tavern** (✉ *537 Suismon St.* ☎ *412/231–1899* ⊕ *www.maxsalleghenytavern.com*), with its Tiffany lamps, wooden booths, and hearty traditional German fare—and modern hot spots. Just over the river and back downtown, **Bridges & Bourbon** (✉ *930 Penn Ave.* ☎ *412/586–4287* ⊕ *www.bridgesandbourbonpgh.com*) is a chic cocktail lounge with tasty bar snacks.

Stay: A classic downtown hotel in a historic 1906 building just a stone's throw from PNC Park, the Andy Warhol Museum, and Pittsburgh's Cultural District, the **Renaissance Pittsburgh Hotel** (✉ *107 6th St.* ☎ *412/562–1200* ⊕ *www.marriott. com*) is an elegant place to spend the night—many rooms have giant windows with river views.

Breakfast: Kick off your morning a couple of blocks from the Mattress Factory with an expertly prepared latte or lapsang souchong tea at **Commonplace Coffee** (✉ *100 S. Commons* ☎ *724/541–6016* ⊕ *www. commonplacecoffee.com*), which has several other inviting locations around the city.

Day 16: Pittsburgh, PA, to Washington, DC

240 miles (4 hours, 30 minutes without traffic and stops)

The most direct route to the nation's capital is entirely via interstates, but it's well worth taking a slightly more circuitous and quite scenic route, following I-76 east to Somerset, following Route 160 southeast to Cumberland, Maryland, and then heading east via I-68, I-70, I-270, I-495, and George Washington Memorial Parkway to Washington, DC.

ALONG THE WAY

Detour: Just slightly off the main route an hour and a half southeast of Pittsburgh, you can tour **Fallingwater** (✉ *1491 Mill Run Rd., Mill Run, PA* ☎ *724/329–8501* ⊕ *www.fallingwater.org*), Frank Lloyd Wright's residential masterwork—a stone, concrete, and glass house dramatically cantilevered over a waterfall. The only way to see this amazing house is on a guided tour, and it's best to book at least a couple of weeks ahead, especially in summer and on spring and fall weekends.

Town: Surrounded by the deep blue Allegheny Mountains, Cumberland, Maryland, developed as a major transportation hub where the Chesapeake & Ohio Canal, the Baltimore & Ohio Railroad, and the National Pike met. You can get a feel for the city's rich history at the **C&O Canal National Historical Park** (✉ *205 W. Potomac St.* ☎ *301/582–0813* ⊕ *www. nps.gov/choh*), which is the starting point for walking and biking the towpath, and taking tours on replica canal boats.

Eat & Drink: Set near a fountain on the brick pedestrian walkway, **City Lights** (✉ *59 Baltimore St.* ☎ *301/722–9800* ⊕ *www.citylightsamericangrill.com*) brings urbane charm to downtown Cumberland. The menu of upscale American classics features seafood with a distinctively Chesapeake touch, hand-cut steaks, freshly made pies, and espresso drinks.

WASHINGTON, DC

Do: Having wrapped up your cross-country journey in the nation's capital, one of North America's truly remarkable museum cities, you could easily spend a week here without running out of memorable things to see and do. It can be tough to prioritize, as the 19 Smithsonian Museums—all of them offering free admission—focus on a wide range of subjects. But in keeping with this itinerary's themes of Americana and natural scenery, put these four at the top of your list: the **Smithsonian National Museum of Natural History** (✉ *10th St. and Constitution Ave. NW* ☎ *202/633–1000* ⊕ *www.naturalhistory.si.edu*), the **Smithsonian National Museum of American History** (✉ *1300 Constitution Ave. NW* ☎ *202/633–1000* ⊕ *www.americanhistory.si.edu*), the **National Museum of the American Indian** (✉ *4th St. SW* ☎ *202/633–1000* ⊕ *www.americanindian.si.edu*), and the newest in the group, the **National Museum of African American History and Culture** (✉ *1400 Constitution Ave. NW* ☎ *844/750–3012* ⊕ *www.*

nmaahc.si.edu). As these fantastic cultural draws put you squarely on the Capitol Mall, you'll also want to set aside time to explore the leafy rectangle's other sites, such as the Washington Monument and Lincoln Memorial.

Eat & Drink: In a city with no shortage of exceptional restaurants, the Logan Circle neighborhood—in particular 14th Street between Rhode Island Avenue and U Street—stands out for its variety of hip, inviting options. Drop by **The Pig** (✉ 1320 14th St. NW ☎ 202/290–2821 ⊕ www.thepigdc.com) for seriously smokin'-good porchetta, pulled-pork sandwiches, and baby back ribs.

Stay: The snazzy **Kimpton Banneker** (✉ 1315 16th St. NW ☎ 202/234–6399 ⊕ www.thebanneker.com) has a cool rooftop bar for fair-weather socializing and roomy accommodations with colorful contemporary artwork and soft Frette linens.

Breakfast: Beloved breakfast restaurant **Ted's Bulletin** (✉ 1818 14th St. NW ☎ 202/265–8337 ⊕ www.tedsbulletin.com) has a few locations in the metro area, including one close to 14th and U streets, and serves both traditional (breakfast burritos, French toast) and more creative (crab Benedicts, Pop-Tarts-inspired blueberry-cheesecake pastries) breakfast dishes all day long.

The Ultimate Cross-Country Road Trip: The Southern Route

Written by Andrew Collins

Arguably the warmest route across the United States, this far-southern route that skirts the Gulf of Mexico and the Mexico–U.S. border provides a compelling glimpse into the remarkably diverse heritage, folkways, and personality of the South and the Southwest. Starting in northern Florida, the route passes through the Gulf South, connecting enchanting jewels of Spanish colonial, French, and Creole architecture with small, easygoing coastal communities. At the route's midpoint, in San Antonio, the verdant, humid landscape of the South gives way to the dry, sun-bleached, big-sky aspect of the American Southwest, with its vibrant though complicated mix of Indigenous, Hispanic, and Anglo culture.

This most southerly trans-U.S. route is relatively direct, especially if you stick to efficient if less interesting Interstate 10 (switching to Interstate 8 for the final stretch from Tucson to San Diego). For much of this adventure, however, it's best to drive along the more engaging surface roads, U.S. 90 in particular, that pass directly along the shore of the Gulf of Mexico and through the vast prairies and high deserts of Texas, New Mexico, Arizona, and Southern California.

At a Glance

Start: Jacksonville, FL

End: San Diego, CA

Miles Traveled: 2,800 miles

Suggested Duration: 14 days

States Visited: Alabama, Arizona, California, Florida, Louisiana, Mississippi, New Mexico, Texas

Key Sights: The Alamo; Anza-Borrego State Park; Big Bend National Park; the French Quarter; Saguaro National Park

Best Time to Go: Although summer is quite popular for exploring this part of the country, it's also the one season that has some significant drawbacks: it's hot (humid on the Gulf Coast and arid but scorching in the Southwest), the beaches can get crowded, and traffic can get heavy in areas. Spring and fall offer the ideal balance, although beware the hordes of college students and families during spring break from the Florida Panhandle to Galveston. Winter is arguably the most rewarding time for this drive, with cool but sunny weather.

Day 1: Jacksonville, FL, to Pensacola, FL

360 miles (5 hours, 30 minutes without traffic and stops)

The most direct route is simply to follow I–10 west right across the top of Florida and across the Panhandle. But if you're up for seeing more of the scenery, U.S. 90 parallels the interstate and takes you right through a number of pleasant small towns. It's almost exactly the same number of miles, but it'll add two hours to your trip.

ALONG THE WAY

Town: Whichever route you take, you'll pass right through the heart of Tallahassee, a pleasant and relatively nontouristy city that looks and feels distinctly southern, with its looming live oak trees, fragrant flower gardens, and Greek Revival and Craftsman-style houses. Florida's capital is worth exploring for an hour or two, including downtown's historic 1845 Old Capitol building (now a museum) and, behind it, the "new" working capital. If you're the kind of road-tripper who's also an automobile buff, stop briefly to explore the **Tallahassee Antique Car Museum** (✉ 6800 Mahan Dr. ☎ 850/942–0137 ⊕ www.tacm. com), which contains about 130 vintage autos as well as actual Batmobiles used in several Hollywood films. Another easy stop north of town is **Alfred B. Maclay Gardens State Park** (✉ 3540 Thomasville Rd. ☎ 850/487–4556 ⊕ www.floridastateparks.org), whose 1,200-acres of gorgeous dogwoods, azaleas, and magnolias are laced with gracious pathways.

Eat & Drink: Go for a stroll around Tallahassee's lively All Saints District, which is close to Florida State University's campus and abounds with cool bars, food trucks, and beer gardens—be sure to check out the galleries around Railroad Square, too. **Voodoo Dog** (✉ 805 S. Macomb St. ☎ 850/224–0005 ⊕ www. eatvoodoodog.com) serves creative burgers and hot dogs.

PENSACOLA

Do: Take a stroll among the brick streets of the city's oldest neighborhood, Seville Square, which is centered on an attractive park shaded by live oak trees—it's also the site of one of the country's oldest European settlements, dating back to 1559. It includes **Historic Pensacola Village** (✉ 24 Zaragoza St. ☎ 850/595–5993 ⊕ www.historicpensacola.org), with its several history museums and restored homes. Then drive 10 miles southwest to see Pensacola's most renowned attraction, the mammoth **National Museum of Naval Aviation** (✉ 1750 Radford Blvd. ☎ 850/452–3604 ⊕ www.navalaviationmuseum.org), with its more than 140 aircraft, including the first plane to fly across the Atlantic (in 1919), the NC-4. The museum is next to Fort Barrancas, part of Gulf Islands National Seashore and a pleasant spot for a picnic or short hike along a nature trail.

Eat & Drink: For stellar, contemporary southern fare, book a table at **Restaurant Iron** (✉ 22 N. Palafox St. ☎ 850/476–7776 ⊕ www.restaurantiron.com). Whatever you order as a main dish, be sure to try a side of the jalapeño cornbread with sorghum butter. For a nightcap, stop nearby at **Old Hickory Whiskey Bar** (✉ 123 S. Palafox St. ☎ 850/332–5916 ⊕ www. oldhickorywhiskeybar.com), known for its encyclopedic menu of whiskies from around the world.

Stay: Steps from historic Seville Square, the smartly furnished **Oyster Bay Boutique Hotel** (✉ 400 Bayfront Pkwy. ☎ 850/912–8770 ⊕ www.stayoysterbay.com) has

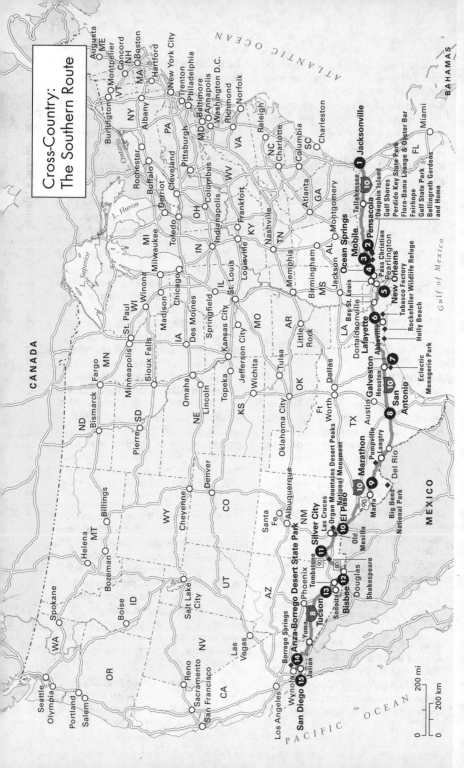

Alabama's Gulf State Park is filled with white sand beaches.

roomy suites, some of them with verandas overlooking Pensacola Bay.

Breakfast: A few blocks from Seville Square, **Cafe Single Fin** (✉ *380 N. 9th Ave.* ☎ *850/433–2929* ⊕ *www.cafesinglefin. com*) turns out delicious açaí bowls, smoothies, strawberry muffins, and scrambled-egg wraps.

Day 2: Pensacola, FL, to Mobile, AL

85 miles (2 hours without traffic and stops)

Forgo the interstate and stick to the scenic coastal route for this relatively easy day on the road. Follow Route 292 and 182 along the barrier islands overlooking the Gulf, then zigzag north and west via Route 59 and U.S. 98—through Foley and Fairhope—to Mobile.

ALONG THE WAY

Nature: Here's hoping for sunny weather, as today's drive on Alabama's Gulf Coast is perfect for beachcombers. Southwest of Pensacola, while still in Florida, the first notable stop you'll come to is **Perdido Key State Park** (✉ *15301 Perdido Key Dr.* ☎ *850/492–1595* ⊕ *www.floridastateparks.org*), a beautiful, sweeping stretch of sand that's a perfect place to lounge on the beach for a bit. After crossing the state border, continue west to **Gulf State Park** (✉ *20115 State Park Rd.* ☎ *251/948–7275* ⊕ *www.alapark.com*), where you can saunter out along the longest pier on the Gulf Coast—keep an eye out for nurse sharks and dolphins.

Roadside Attraction: It's kitschy, often overrun with spring breakers, and slightly goofy, but the **Flora-Bama Lounge & Oyster Bar** (✉ *17401 Perdido Key Dr., Perdido Key* ☎ *850/492–0611* ⊕ *www.florabama. com*) has been party central in these parts since it opened in 1964. It contains an astounding 22 different bars and hosts top country bands throughout the year.

If you pass through around lunch time, it's a surprisingly good spot for burgers, baked oysters, and bay shrimp tacos.

Eat & Drink: Treat yourself to a sweet snack at the **Yard Milkshake Bar** (✉ 3800 Gulf Shores Pkwy. ☎ 251/948–0121 ⊕ www.theyardmilkshakebar.com) in Gulf Shores—the enormous, elaborate, and very Instagrammable shakes with names like the Peanut Butter Finger Waffle are served in monogrammed Mason jars and festooned with garishly colored toppings. The charming town of Fairhope is a good place to be for dinner (and to watch the sunset from the town pier); the stylish **Dragonfly Foodbar** (✉ 7 S. Church St. ☎ 251/990–5722) offers a great selection of creative fusion tacos.

MOBILE

Do: With tree-lined boulevards and grassy squares, French and Spanish colonial architecture, and a picturesque location on Mobile Bay, Mobile bears some resemblance to New Orleans—in fact, the celebration of Mardi Gras began here, and you can learn all about the festival's history at the entertaining **Mobile Carnival Museum** (✉ 355 Government St. ☎ 251/432–3324 ⊕ www.mobilecarnivalmuseum.com). Walk a few blocks northeast, past the stunning 1927 Saenger Theater, to bustling Dauphin Street and over to Bienville Square, the historic heart of the city, where you can relax on a park bench and take in the scene.

Eat & Drink: Mobile's **Meat Boss** (✉ 5401 Cottage Hill Rd. ☎ 251/591–4842 ⊕ www.meatboss.com) is a perfect opportunity to try Alabama-style white (mayo-based) barbecue sauce, which is great with chicken or pulled pork. Steps from Bienville Square, dimly lighted **Haberdasher** (✉ 113 Dauphin St. ☎ 251/436–0989 ⊕ www.facebook.com/thehabmobile) earns kudos for its superbly crafted cocktails.

Stay: Downtown Mobile's opulent **Battle House Renaissance Hotel** (✉ 26 N. Royal St. ☎ 251/338–2000 ⊕ www.marriott.com) has been popular with dignitaries and road-trippers alike since the mid-19th century—the on-site spa is exceptional as well.

Breakfast: A favorite breakfast and brunch venue along bustling Dauphin Street, cheerful **Spot of Tea** (✉ 310 Dauphin St. ☎ 251/433–9009 ⊕ www.spotoftea.com) serves decadent Belgian pecan waffles and Monte Christo sandwiches.

Day 3: Mobile, AL, to Ocean Springs, MS

100 miles (2 hours, 30 minutes without traffic and stops)

Follow I–10 west from Mobile for about 10 miles, then sidetrack south along Route 193 to spend some time on Dauphin Island. From there, backtrack north, then take Route 188 west to U.S. 90, and continue across the border into Mississippi to Ocean Springs.

ALONG THE WAY

Nature: Although this outdoor romp through fabulous gardens is a decidedly curated form of nature, gracious **Bellingrath Gardens and Home** (✉ 12401 Bellingrath Gardens Rd. ☎ 251/973–2217 ⊕ www.bellingrath.org) in Theodore is a wonderful place to stroll amid the flowers and greenery.

Detour: A narrow barrier island with several notable attractions, Dauphin Island is a 165-square-mile swatch of picturesque beaches and pine groves that's worth the detour. The highlight is the Estuarium at **Dauphin Island Sea Lab** (✉ 102 Bienville Blvd. ☎ 251/861–7500 ⊕ www.disl.edu), a public aquarium and research institute where you can view more than 30 aquariums inhabited by myriad Gulf marine life and flora, including red snappers, octopus, sea turtles, and alligators (kids love the stingray touch pool). If you have an extra hour or so, consider stopping by the island's **Audubon Bird Sanctuary** (✉ *211 Bienville Blvd.* ☎ *251/861–3607* ⊕ *www.dauphinisland.org*), which has a 1,000-foot-long boardwalk and nature trail, and is a great place to view plovers, sandpipers, terns, and cormorants.

Eat & Drink: On Dauphin Island, laid-back **Lighthouse Bakery** (✉ *919 Chaumont Ave.* ☎ *251/861–2253* ⊕ *www.facebook.com/ LighthouseBakery*) is a good bet for sandwiches, pastries, and coffee, tea, and lemonade.

OCEAN SPRINGS

Do: Quiet, historic, and without the intense casino and resort development of nearby Biloxi and Gulfport, this artsy community makes an appealing overnight stop. The walkable downtown buzzes with cute eateries and galleries, and the beachfront is pretty but mellow, lined by homes rather than high-rises (although the intense damage from Hurricane Katrina is still evident in places). On a charming live-oak-lined lane on the edge of downtown, the **Walter Anderson Museum of Art** (✉ *510 Washington Ave.* ☎ *228/872–3164* ⊕ *www.walterander-sonmuseum.org*) contains more than 1,000 works by the eponymous local artist (1903–65) who became famous for his fanciful paintings and murals of coastal scenery, plants, and animals. The town is also home to the Mississippi District Headquarters of **Gulf Islands National Seashore** (✉ *3500 Park Rd.* ☎ *228/230–4100* ⊕ *www.nps.gov/guis*). You can learn about the region's natural history at the William M. Colmer Visitor Center, picnic, hike, and hang out on the fishing pier.

Eat & Drink: A romantic downtown bistro whose walls are lined with local artwork, Vestige (✉ *715 Washington Ave.* ☎ *228/818–9699* ⊕ *www.vestigerestau-rant.com*) serves superb contemporary Asian-inspired southern fare. Whether you stay at the snazzy Roost hotel, do check out its stunning **Wilbur** speakeasy (✉ *604 Porter Ave.* ☎ *228/217–7160* ⊕ *www.wilburcraftbar.com*), designed

with ancient reclaimed wood and decorated with Walter Anderson block prints.

Stay: With chic yet unfussy rooms, a cool grab-and-go market with tasty bites, and the aforementioned Wilbur speakeasy, **The Roost** (✉ *604 Porter Ave.* ☎ *228/285–7989* ⊕ *www.roostoceansprings.com*) is one of the most distinctive and inviting little hotels on the Gulf Coast.

Breakfast: Start the day with a pour-over or cold brew at the verdant **Greenhouse on Porter** (✉ *404 Porter Ave.* ☎ *228/238–5680* ⊕ *www.biscuitsprings.com*)—dine on fluffy biscuits with honey butter or homemade jam in the actual solari-um-style greenhouse or at a table on the quiet lawn.

Day 4: Ocean Springs, MS, to New Orleans, LA

100 miles (2 hours without traffic and stops)

Although faster I–10 is an option, stick with U.S. 90 for the most enjoyable route, passing through the Mississippi coastal cities of Biloxi and Gulfport, and stopping in the more engaging smaller towns of Pass Christian and Bay St. Louis. From here, continue along U.S. 90 through the wetlands of southeastern Louisiana and Bayou Sauvage National Wildlife Refuge to New Orleans.

ALONG THE WAY

Towns: Two small towns across the mouth of Bay St. Louis, Pass Christian and Bay St. Louis don't have much in the way of formal attractions, but have cute downtowns with a smattering of intriguing boutiques and eateries. In Pass Christian, walk the two or three blocks north on Davis Avenue from U.S. 90. After crossing the Bay St. Louis Bridge, turn left on North Beach Boulevard and a few blocks later you'll be in the heart of little downtown Bay St. Louis, with its fishing pier, pretty beachfront, and easygoing bars and shops.

Eat & Drink: Shortly before you cross the Pearl River into Louisiana, you'll come to **Turtle Landing Bar & Grill** (⊠ *16463 U.S. 90* ☎ *228/533–7000* ⊕ *www.turtlelanding. com*) in Pearlington, famous for its views of alligators hanging around behind the restaurant in Cowan Bayou (note the "Beware, dock is weak, but the gators are hungry." sign out back). The burgers, po'boys, and fried seafood are all fine, but it's more about the location.

NEW ORLEANS

Do: The inimitable jewel of the Gulf Coast, New Orleans is the highlight of many a southern cross-country adventure. With limited time in this incredible city, try this strategy: spend half your time in the famous, or infamous, tourist heart, the French Quarter, and set aside the rest simply to amble around one of the city's many charming neighborhoods, like the historic Garden District or the increasing hip Faubourg Marigny and Bywater. No need to feel guilty if all you do is eat, drink, shop, and people-watch during your stay, but if you're up for getting a genuine sense of the city's rich history, check out the museums at **Jackson Square** (⊠ *701 Decatur St.*) that make up part of the Louisiana State Museum (☎ *800/568–6968* ⊕ *www. louisianastatemuseum.org*), including the **Presbytère** (⊠ *751 Chartres St.*), with its excellent exhibits on Mardi Gras and Hurricane Katrina; the **Cabildo** (⊠ *701 Chartres St.*), where the Louisiana Purchase was finalized in 1803; and the **1850 House** (⊠ *523 St. Ann St.*), a beautifully maintained townhouse and courtyard that's part of the fashionable Pontalba Buildings.

Eat & Drink: It's not so much that you can't go wrong in New Orleans (as the city does have its overpriced tourist traps), but you can eat incredibly well, every day, for weeks, without dining at the same place twice. For an all-out, special-occasion, old-school experience, head to **Commander's Palace** (⊠ *1403 Washington Ave.* ☎ *504/899–8221* ⊕ *www.commanderspalace.com*), setting aside time to stroll amid the gracious old homes of the surrounding Garden District. For a memorable meal in the less-touristy downriver neighborhoods, try **The Joint** (⊠ *701 Mazant St.* ☎ *504/949–3232* ⊕ *www.alwayssmokin. com*) in Bywater for fantastic barbecue. For nightlife, drop by the Spotted Cat (⊠ *623 Frenchmen St.* ⊕ *www.spotted-catmusicclub.com*) in Faubourg Marigny for old-time jazz and swing, and **Bacchanal Fine Wine & Spirits** (⊠ *600 Poland Ave.* ☎ *504/948–9111* ⊕ *www.bacchanalwine. com*) in Bywater for stellar drinks and bar food, plus great music every night.

Stay: Due to potential traffic and parking issues in the French Quarter, consider staying in quieter but cool Bywater or Faubourg Marigny. The intimate and historic **Macarty House** (⊠ *3820 Burgundy St.* ☎ *504/267–1564* ⊕ *www.macarty-house.com*) has six lovely rooms and a cloistered pool.

Breakfast: In Bywater, funky **Elizabeth's Restaurant** (⊠ *601 Gallier St.* ☎ *504/944–9272* ⊕ *www.elizabethsrestaurantnola. com*) lives up to its "real food, done real good" motto with its heavenly praline bacon and "redneck eggs" (fried green tomatoes with poached eggs and hollandaise).

Day 5: New Orleans, LA, to Lafayette, LA

190 miles (4 hours without traffic and stops)

Start out on I–10 and then I–310 to Luling, then follow the south bank of the Mississippi River along Highway 18 for a scenic riverside drive. At Donaldsonville, turn south onto Highway 308, then southwest on Highway 70 to U.S. 90,

The French Quarter in New Orleans comes alive at night.

and from there continue west through Morgan City to the heart of Louisiana's Cajun Country, centered around New Iberia and Lafayette.

ALONG THE WAY

Eat & Drink: Set in a handsome 1920s storefront building in downtown Donald-sonville, the dapper **Grapevine Cafe** (✉ 211 Railroad Ave. ☎ 225/473–8463 ⊕ www.grapevine.cafe) serves superb crab cakes with roasted-garlic aioli and an extensive drinks menu.

Roadside Attraction: Sure, it's a bit silly, but for a spicy side trip, make the 10-mile drive southwest of New Iberia to Avery Island (not an island in the conventional sense but a salt dome) to visit the **Tabasco Factory** (✉ 32 Wisteria Rd. ☎ 337/373–6129 ⊕ www.tabasco.com), where one of the world's favorite hot sauces has been distilled and bottled since the mid-19th-century.

LAFAYETTE

Do: Here you'll find exceptionally interesting opportunities to learn about Cajun Louisiana's rich history, starting with the **Acadian Cultural Center** (✉ 501 Fisher Rd. ☎ 337/232–0789 ⊕ www.nps.gov/jela), which is one of six units of the outstanding Jean Lafitte National Park and Preserve, of which three relate to Cajun heritage. At Acadian Village, you can watch a poignant film that dramatizes the Expulsion of the Acadians by the British from Canada's Maritime provinces and explore exhibits on Cajun folklore, food, and music. In spring and fall, ranger-guided boat tours along Bayou Vermilion are also offered. Right behind the center, you can tour the excellent Cajun living history museum, **Vermilionville** (✉ 300 Fisher Rd. ☎ 337/233–4077 ⊕ www.bayouvermiliondistrict.org), which comprises about 20 historic structures, many with docents demonstrating various elements of early life in this part of the state.

Eat & Drink: The giant stuffed alligator that greets you at the door to **Prejean's** (✉ *3480 N.E. Evangeline Throughway* ☎ *337/896–3247* ⊕ *www.prejeans.com*) is a good indication of the Cajun aesthetic—and great food—inside this festive roadhouse that's been serving smoked duck–and–tasso ham gumbo, sautéed crab fingers, and shrimp and grits for decades. It's also a great spot to listen to live Cajun music, as is downtown's **Blue Moon Saloon** (✉ *215 E. Convent St.* ☎ *337/234–2422* ⊕ *www.bluemoonpresents.com*), an infectiously festive place to listen to great zydeco, Cajun, country, rockabilly, and other local and regional bands.

Stay: Most of the lodging options in town are major chains, with downtown's **Doubletree by Hilton Lafayette** (✉ *1521 W. Pinhook Rd.* ☎ *337/235–6111* ⊕ *www.hilton.com*) being one of the best.

Breakfast: Downtown's **Rêve Coffee Roasters** (✉ *200-A Jefferson St.* ☎ *337/534–8336* ⊕ *www.revecoffeeroasters.com*) is the best spot in this small city for expertly crafted coffee drinks, from nitro cold brews to single-origin pour overs.

Day 6: Lafayette, LA, to Galveston, TX

240 miles (5 hours without traffic and stops)

By far the fastest route is I–10 to I–45, but this is a pretty dull drive, too. Better to take a leisurely drive along the Gulf, which takes about 90 minutes longer but offers rewarding scenery. When you reach the scenic Bolivar Peninsula, you'll have to catch the short ferry ride across the mouth of Galveston Bay to Galveston Island. The 20-minute ride is free, but there can be a long wait on busy weekends, so check the website for live updates. Your other option from Port Arthur, which is less scenic but often

Essential Listening

There's something about the traditional music of Louisiana—zydeco, swamp pop, Afro-Caribbean, and other Cajun and Creole subgenres—that sounds inherently more enjoyable when you're actually here. You'll find great playlists on Spotify, and you can buy many of the top compilations from Louisiana Music Factory.

faster, is to follow Highway 73 to I–10, and take that Highway 146 to I–45, which leads right onto the island.

ALONG THE WAY

Photo Op: As you head south toward the coast, take your time passing through the small town of Abbeville, a cute Cajun hamlet with two alluring and utterly photogenic squares surrounded by historic buildings, including the gorgeous 1915 St. Mary Magdalen Catholic Church.

Eat & Drink: In Abbeville, the famous **Dupuy's Oyster Shop** (✉ *108 S. Main St.* ☎ *337/893–2336* ⊕ *www.dupuys.com*) has been serving heaping platters of bivalves on the half shell or fried, along with other Cajun specialties, since 1869.

Nature: Pick up Highway 82 in Abbeville, which is a designated scenic byway known as the Creole Nature Trail. The road meanders through lush wetlands on its way toward Pecan Island and then through the 71,000-acre **Rockefeller Wildlife Refuge** (✉ *5476 Grand Chenier Hwy.* ☎ *337/491–2593* ⊕ *www.wlf.louisiana.gov/page/rockefeller-wildlife-refuge*), a pristine marshland flanking the Gulf of Mexico that's home to more than 400 species of birds as well as alligators, otters, nutria, and other critters. Just past the small hamlet of Cameron, you'll take a short ferry (it crosses west every half hour) across the Calcasieu River/Ship Channel, and then you'll pass through Holly Beach, aka the "Cajun Riviera," which is a good spot to relax on the sand and take in views of the Gulf of Mexico. The Creole Nature Trail officially ends when you cross the Sabine River and enter Texas, but the scenery remains quite pretty as you drive through the small border city of Port Arthur and onto the Bolivar Peninsula.

GALVESTON

Do: Situated on a narrow barrier at the mouth of Galveston Bay, this picturesque city delights visitors with its long and broad beaches, ornate Victorian architecture, and friendly, free-spirited personality. Part of the fun here is simply milling around the beautiful **Historic Downtown Strand Seaport District** (⊠ 502 20th St. ☎ 409/795–7777 ⊕ www.downtowngalveston.org), ducking into galleries and boutiques, and marveling at the plaques on many older buildings that reveal the high-water lines during the several hurricanes that have inundated the island over the years (the most catastrophic was the Great Storm of 1900, during which at least 8,000 residents perished). You can learn about the storm and Galveston's storied naval and shipping history at the excellent **Texas Seaport Museum** (⊠ Pier 22 ☎ 409/763–1877 ⊕ www.galvestonhistory.org). A 20-minute drive west, be sure to visit the island's most impressive modern attraction, Moody Gardens (⊠ 1 Hope Blvd. ☎ 409/683–4200 ⊕ www.moodygardens.org), a complex of three glass pyramids that contain a science museum, aquarium, and—the highlight of the bunch—a tropical rain forest.

Eat & Drink: Steps from the beguiling Grand 1894 Opera House in the Strand district, **Rudy and Paco** (⊠ 2028 Postoffice St. ☎ 409/762–3696 ⊕ www.rudyandpaco.com) is a romantic venue for steaks and seafood prepared with Latin American recipes and ingredients. At sunset, the loveliest place in town to

sip a margarita or glass of champagne is the Rooftop Bar, atop the **Tremont House Hotel** (⊠ 2300 Ship Mechanic Row St. ☎ 409/763–0300 ⊕ www.thetremonthouse.com), which offers dazzling panoramic views of downtown and the bay.

Stay: The most memorable of Galveston's many lodging options are its two sumptuous grand dames (they're sister properties), each of which has a different vibe. The turreted **Hotel Galvez & Spa** (⊠ 2024 Seawall Blvd. ☎ 409/765–7721 ⊕ www.hotelgalvez.com) dates to 1911 and is the best choice if you want one last beachside experience before cutting inland. If you would rather be close to the Strand's shops and restaurants, the stately Tremont House is a four-story Victorian-era gem whose rooms have soaring ceilings and windows.

Breakfast: Jumpstart your morning with a dirty chai latte or a fresh-fruit smoothie at funky **MOD Coffeehouse** (⊠ 2126 Postoffice St. ☎ 409/765–5659 ⊕ www.modcoffeehouse.com) in the Strand.

Day 7: Galveston, TX, to San Antonio, TX

250 miles (4 hours without traffic and stops)

Although it's possible to zigzag along back roads through Victoria and Karnes City, this scenery isn't especially memorable. The better option is sticking with I–45 and I–10, as the time you save driving you can spend with a stop in the underrated and thoroughly engaging city of Houston.

ALONG THE WAY

Town: It's understandable if trying to make a short visit to the nation's fourth-most populous city sounds a little daunting—greater Houston is more than 10,000 square miles (it's nearly the size of Massachusetts). If you have just a few hours at the most, your best strategy is to focus on one area or key attraction, like **Space Center Houston** (✉ 1601 E. NASA Pkwy. ☎ 281/244–2100 ⊕ www. spacecenter.org) or **Bayou Bend Collection and Gardens** (✉ 6003 Memorial Dr. ☎ 713/639–7750 ⊕ www.mfah.org). In the city's Museum District around Rice University, the must-see is the **Menil Collection** (✉ 1533 Sul Ross St. ☎ 713/525–9400 ⊕ www.menil.org), a peaceful campus of spectacular galleries and museum spaces. Although not officially part of the Menil, the neighborhood also includes the impressive **Rothko Chapel** (✉ 3900 Yupon St. ☎ 713/524–9839 ⊕ www.rothkochapel.org), which Philip Johnson designed, and whose walls house 14 large paintings by Mark Rothko.

Eat & Drink: Just a few blocks north of the Menil Collection, you'll find dozens of hip eateries and bars in the lively Montrose District, long a center of Houston's LGBTQ community, and an all-around hot spot for shopping and dining. **Blacksmith Houston** (✉ 1018 Westheimer Rd. ☎ 832/360–7470 ⊕ www.blacksmithhouston.com) is an airy, modern coffeehouse with tasty breakfast and lunch fare.

Roadside Attraction: On your way through Houston, stop to see the larger-than-life steel sculptures of animals—from a rust-colored armadillo to colorfully painted cows on a saucerlike pedestal—and small planes at the **Eclectic Menagerie Park** (☎ 715/598–9577 ⊕ www. texaspipe.com), a free, private collection of figures located on the grounds of a 108-acre pipe and supply company.

SAN ANTONIO

Do: San Antonio is the point in your cross-country journey when you truly transition from the lush, humid, and somewhat densely populated Gulf South to the sweeping, dry, and more sparsely inhabited Southwest. No visit to San Antonio is complete without at least a brief stroll along its famed **River Walk** (✉ 849 E. Commerce St.

☎ 210/227–4262 ⊕ www.thesanantonioriverwalk.com), a picturesque 15-mile pathway set below street level, the heart of which curves through downtown and is lined with bars and hotels. Many of San Antonio's top attractions, including the iconic **Alamo** (✉ 300 Alamo Plaza ☎ 210/225–1391 ⊕ www.thealamo.org), are within a block of this walkway, which in recent years has been extended several miles south to Mission Reach (where you can visit the excellent San Antonio Missions National Historical Park), north past the superb **San Antonio Art Museum** (✉ 200 W. Jones Ave. ☎ 210/978–8100 ⊕ www.samuseum.org), and up to the trendy Pearl Brewery District, a mixed-used development set around a historic brewery campus with cool boutiques, bars, and restaurants.

Eat & Drink: As you stroll up the River Walk from downtown, have a seat at the lushly landscaped **Elsewhere Garden Bar & Kitchen** (✉ 103 E. Jones Ave. ☎ 210/446–9303 ⊕ www.elsewheregarden.com), which offers a great selection of craft beer and other beverages along with addictively good deep-fried chicken with pickled jalapeños on a stick, double-cheese burgers, and Baja-style shrimp tacos. For drinks, **The Modernist** (✉ 516 E. Grayson St. ☎ 210/901–8646) is a swanky midcentury-modern haunt with a festive patio and well-crafted cocktails.

Stay: The architectural centerpiece of the Pearl neighborhood, the elegant **Hotel Emma** (✉ 136 E. Grayson St. ☎ 210/448–8300 ⊕ www.thehotelemma. com) showcases the historic opulence of its building while also reflecting a chic 21st-century design.

Breakfast: For old-school traditional Mexican breakfast fare, you can't beat **Pete's Tako House** (✉ 502 Brooklyn Ave. ☎ 210/224–2911 ⊕ www.petestakohouse.com), where a plate of chorizo-egg tacos or chilaquiles will fill you up for the day.

Day 8: San Antonio, TX, to Marathon, TX

330 miles (5 hours without traffic and stops)

It's a straight shot through the rocky and wide-open plains of southwestern Texas, along U.S. 90 to the small town of Marathon.

ALONG THE WAY

Eat & Drink: In Del Rio, **830 Kitchen** (⊠ *301 Ave. B* ☎ *830/308–3806* ⊕ *www.830kitchen.com*) is one of the best lunch stops along this route and a good spot to break up your journey. Expect big portions of chorizo burgers, avocado fries, carne asada fries, and other flavorful, filling, if not-exactly healthy comfort fare.

Town: Barely a blip along the otherwise largely uninhabited 185-mile stretch of U.S. 90 between Del Rio and Marathon, the hamlet of Langtry makes for a quirky pause, as does the dramatic 275-foot-high Pecos River Bridge, which you cross 17 miles before you get to Langtry. The town is closely associated with colorful, if notorious, saloon keeper, justice of the peace, and self-proclaimed "only law west of the Pecos," Judge Roy Bean (portrayed famously by Paul Newman in *The Life and Times of Judge Roy Bean*). You can visit the **Judge Roy Bean Visitor Center** (⊠ *526 State Loop 25* ☎ *432/291–3340* ⊕ *www.txdot.gov*), which contains some colorful exhibits and artifacts related to this legendary figure. You can also follow Torres Avenue a short way to a bluff overlooking the Rio Grande and a remote patch of Mexico across it—a historical marker notes that this was once a popular border crossing that traces back centuries.

Roadside Attraction: About 18 miles west of Langtry, a short detour from U.S. 90 on Highway 1865 leads to the ghost town of Pumpville, whose only building

still in use is a tiny, well-maintained stone Baptist church that bills itself the "gospel west of the Pecos" and still draws a handful of ranchers, from as far as 50 miles away, each Sunday.

MARATHON

Do: This tiny, historic railroad town is most famous for being one of the key bases for a foray into the breathtaking wilderness of **Big Bend National Park** (☎ *432/477–2251* ⊕ *www.nps.gov/bibe*), with the northern Persimmon Gap entrance just 40 miles south. Stop at the main Panther Junction Visitor Center, and then spend half your day hiking any of the well-marked trails amid the spectacular mountain peaks of Chisos Basin. Then make your way to the park's southwestern corner, where you can explore (on a 1.6-mile round-trip trail) Santa Elena Canyon, whose sheer 1,500-foot walls were carved by the Rio Grande. Get there via the stunning Ross Maxwell Scenic Drive, which curls for some 30 miles past silent deserted homesteads, grand overlooks, and the Castolon Historic District's ancient old adobe buildings.

Eat & Drink: When the sun sets, the intimate 12 Gage Restaurant at the **Gage Hotel** (1 ⊠ *02 N.W. 1st St.* ☎ *432/386–4205* ⊕ *www.gagehotel.*

Extend Your Trip

From New Orleans: Along the Mississippi *(Ch. 2)*; The Great American Music Road Trip *(Ch. 7)*

From San Antonio: The Best of Texas; Texas Hill Country *(Ch. 5)*

From Tuscon: The Best of Arizona *(Ch. 5)*

From San Diego: Pacific Coast Highway; The Best of Southern California *(Ch. 3)* com) is Marathon's most memorable and romantic place for dinner (consider the hefty rib-eye steak with Hatch green chili cream corn). Also run by the Gage and set in an 1880s mercantile, the nearby Brick Vault Brewery and Barbecue (⊠ 102 N.W. 1st St. ☎ 432/386–7538 ⊕ www.brickvaultbreweryandbbq.com) is a more casual microbrewery serving reliably good Texas-style barbecue.

Stay: Cowboy, Native American, and Hispanic cultures are reflected in the furnishings and artwork of the gorgeously restored and historic Gage Hotel, built in the 1920s by renowned architect Henry Trost.

Breakfast: Yet another excellent dining option adjacent to and run by the Gage Hotel, **V6 Coffee Bar** (⊠ 109 N.E. 1st St. ☎ 432/308–6877) is a good bet for hearty breakfast fare like biscuits with jalapeño gravy or avocado toast.

Day 9: Marathon, TX, to El Paso, TX

250 miles (4 hours without traffic and stops)

Follow U.S. 90 through the colorful towns of Alpine and Marfa, and then up to the tiny railroad town of Van Horn, where you'll pick up I–10 to El Paso.

ALONG THE WAY

Town: The cultural oasis of Marfa enjoys a devoted following among artists, hipsters, LGBTQ+ folks, and free spirits, thanks to its clutch of avant-garde galleries, ranch-chic restaurants and indie hotels, and endless opportunities for people-watching—from poetry readings to gallery openings to bar-hopping. Its relative proximity to Big Bend as well as the Davis and Guadalupe mountain ranges has made this offbeat design mecca a favorite destination with hikers and other outdoors enthusiasts, too. You can tour one of the world's largest permanent installations of contemporary

art at the **Chinati Foundation** (⊠ 1 Cavalry Row ☎ 432/729–4362 ⊕ www.chinati. org), which displays works by American minimalist Donald Judd and others in buildings spread over 340 acres.

Eat & Drink: The hearty fare, potent coffee, and fresh-squeezed juices at **Aster Marfa** (⊠ 215 Highland St. ☎ 432/729–4500 ⊕ www.astermarfa.com), a small patio café across from the Presidio County Courthouse, will help you fuel up for a day of hiking or art touring.

Shop: Marfa's arty vibe shines through in its clutch of distinctive shops. **Cobra Rock Boot Company** (⊠ 211 S. Dean St. ⊕ www.cobrarock.com) is beloved for its bespoke leather boots while the **Wrong Marfa** (⊠ 110 Highland St. ☎ 432/729–1976 ⊕ www.wrongmarfa.com) carries distinctive pottery, drawings, and housewares. Check out the extensive selection of books, jewelry, and well-curated sundries at **Hey I Like It Here** (⊠ 105 S. Highland Ave. ☎ 817/262–3261 ⊕ www.marfasaintgeorge.com) in the Hotel Saint George, and vintage wear, skin and body products, and whimsical cards at Raba Marfa (⊠ 212 E. San Antonio St. ☎ 432/295–0064 ⊕ www.rabamarfa.com).

EL PASO

Do: With an attractive desert location fringed by mountains, this friendly city forms a culturally vibrant borderland region that encompasses neighboring Ciudad Juárez, Mexico, and Las Cruces, New Mexico. With distinctive hotels and restaurants (many of them set in artfully restored Victorian and early-20th-century buildings), excellent museums, and a gorgeous minor league baseball stadium, downtown El Paso is in the midst of an exciting revitalization. Make a point of visiting the superb (and free) **El Paso Museum of Art** (⊠ 1 Arts Festival Plaza ☎ 915/212–0300 ⊕ www.elpasoartmuseum.org), which features a striking array of contemporary and historic Latin American, Spanish, and native artworks. Within Franklin Mountains State Park's 37 square miles of majestic scenery, you'll discover more than 100 miles of hiking trails—the southern section offers amazing views of the city below.

Eat & Drink: A culinary jewel of downtown's cultural district, elegant **Anson 11** (✉ *303 N. Oregon St.* ☎ *915/504–6400* ⊕ *www.anson11.com*) offers both a refined dining room that turns out creatively prepared American dishes and a lively, more casual bistro where you might tuck into a flat-bread pizza or the kitchen's signature meat loaf with smoked-tomato gravy. Downtown has some cool spots for drinks and bar snacks, including **Craft and Social** (✉ *305 E. Franklin Ave.* ☎ *915/401–1909* ⊕ *www.craftandsocial.com*), a stylish but unpretentious lounge that stands out for its well-curated beer and wine list.

Stay: Following a five-year closure and a tremendously ambitious renovation, the city's 1912 grande dame, **Hotel Paso Del Norte** (✉ *10 Sheldon Ct.* ☎ *915/534–3000* ⊕ *www.marriott.com*), has reopened as part of Marriott's posh Autograph Collection. With a stunning historic design, it has superb restaurants, a hip bar, and a luxurious spa.

Breakfast: Bright and cheerful **Salt + Honey Bakery Café** (✉ *801 N. Piedras St.* ☎ *915/313–4907* ⊕ *www.saltandhoneyep.com*) anchors the city's up-and-coming Five Points West district and is a great place to kick off your day with a well-crafted espresso drink and the Mediterranean-inspired all-day brunch and sandwich menu.

Day 10: El Paso, TX, to Silver City, NM

180 miles (3 hours, 30 minutes without traffic and stops)

Southern New Mexico is one section of this drive where there's a great payoff in venturing a little off-the-beaten path. Your day starts straightforwardly with a drive up I–10 to Las Cruces, then picks up I–25 north, passing through the self-proclaimed world capital of green chilis, Hatch, before turning onto Highway 152—the Geronimo Scenic Byway—through the tiny, picturesque mountain towns of Hillsboro and Kingston, before catching U.S. 180 the final stretch to Silver City.

ALONG THE WAY

Town: The largest city in the Mesilla Valley, fast-growing Las Cruces is home to New Mexico State University and adjacent to the historic village of Old Mesilla, which was established by a group of Mexican residents when the territory of New Mexico was acquired by the United States in 1848. The town's Old Mesilla Plaza and Historic District has seen celebrations, weddings, bloody political battles, and the milestone trial of Billy the Kid. Walk through to admire the many mid-19th-century adobe buildings, many of them now housing distinctive shops, restaurants, and bars.

Eat & Drink: Southern New Mexico has a surprisingly good winemaking scene, with **Mesilla's Luna Rossa Winery & Pizzeria** (✉ *1321 Avenida de Mesilla* ☎ *575/526–2484* ⊕ *www.lunarossawinery.com*) among the best. At the winery's casual restaurant, you can sample great vino alongside terrific pizzas, pastas, panini sandwiches, and homemade gelato.

Detour: Reached via U.S. 70 east, the western section of Organ Mountains–Desert Peak National Monument is just 15 miles east of Las Cruces and offers dozens of great hikes through stunning, jagged mountains.

SILVER CITY

Do: This artsy little mountain town began as a mining hub, was the boyhood home of Billy the Kid, and today supports a sizable population of artists, academics, and free spirits. You can spend the afternoon walking around the community's historic downtown and dropping by the funky galleries of the Yankee–Texas Arts & Cultural

District. Or get behind the wheel and take in the stunning alpine scenery of the surrounding Gila National Forest.

Eat & Drink: Little Toad Creek Brewery & Distillery (⊠ 119 N. Main St. ☎ 575/556–9934 ⊕ www.littletoadcreek.com) is in the center of downtown in a handsome historic building and serves tasty pub fare, like green-chili cheese fries and smoked pulled pork tacos, not to mention well-crafted drinks. The most historic and arguably the most colorful spot in the area, though, is the **Buckhorn Saloon & Opera House** (⊠ 32 Main St. ☎ 575/538–9911 ⊕ www.buckhornsaloonandoperahouse.com), which is 10 miles north of town in the pretty mountain hamlet of Pinos Altos. It offers live music and old-fashioned melodramas in an atmospheric 1860s building with pressed-tin ceilings and a fireplace.

Stay: Within walking distance of downtown galleries and restaurants, the **Murray Hotel** (⊠ 200 W. Broadway St. ☎ 575/956–9400 ⊕ www.murray-hotel.com) is a neatly restored 1930s art deco gem with compact, tastefully appointed rooms.

Breakfast: For first-rate espresso drinks on a relaxing patio in the colorful Yankee–Texas Arts District, check out **Tranquilbuzz Coffee House** (⊠ 300 N. Arizona St. ☎ 575/956–6476 ⊕ tranquil-buzz-coffee.business.site).

Day 11: Silver City, NM, to Bisbee, AZ

170 miles (3 hours without traffic and stops)

Drive southwest on Highway 90 through Lordsburg, then Highway 80 south and west through the very southeastern corner of Arizona to Bisbee.

ALONG THE WAY

Town: There aren't a whole lot of formal attractions, or even towns, on the drive from Silver City to Bisbee, and that's part of the charm—the great views of the Big Burro Mountains in New Mexico, the Chiricahua Mountains in Arizona, and miles of sweeping expanses of cactus-studded desert make for a lovely drive. But just outside the otherwise very sleepy town of Lordsburg, the once thriving mining town of **Shakespeare** (☎ 575/543–9034 ⊕ www.shakespeareghosttown.com) attracted some of the West's fiercest outlaws—Billy the Kid and Black Jack Ketchum among them. By 1900, most of the mines had disappeared, and these days you can take a guided tour of this well-preserved ghost town said to have its share of haunted buildings.

Eat & Drink: By far the most intriguing spot for dinner and drinks along this route is **Saddle & Spur Saloon** (⊠ 1046 G Ave.) ☎ 520/364–4481, inside the gorgeous early 1900s Gadsden Hotel in the border town of Douglas, Arizona. The filling steak-centric southwestern fare is quite good, and the smartly decorated tavern is a stunner.

BISBEE

Do: Another quirky community that thrived during its copper-mining boom years in the early 20th century, Bisbee was for a time one of the biggest cities between the Mississippi River and the Pacific. In the 1970s and 1980s, artists, hippies, and free spirits began settling here, buying and fixing up its colorful Victorian buildings and homes, which cling to the often steep hills that rise up around downtown. It's a great place for strolling around, admiring the colorful architecture, and stopping by the several acclaimed art galleries. You can learn about the town's colorful history at the excellent **Bisbee Mining and Historical Museum** (⊠ 5 Copper Queen Plaza ☎ 520/432–7071 ⊕ www.

bisbeemuseum.org) or on an underground tour of the Copper Queen Mine—these 75-minute excursions are led by knowledgeable and entertaining retired Phelps Dodge miners and go some 1,500 feet into the mine.

Eat & Drink: Informal burgers joints, Mexican restaurants, and coffeehouses are the norm in Bisbee, but upscale **Cafe Roka** (✉ 35 Main St. ☎ 520/432–5153 ⊕ www.caferoka.com) stands out from the pack for its creative, locally sourced contemporary Mediterranean—mostly Italian—fare. Among several colorful saloons, the subterranean **Bisbee Social Club** (✉ 67 Main St. ☎ 520/366–3898 ⊕ www.bisbeesocialclub.com) impresses with its well-crafted cocktails.

Stay: A great option if you're seeking some extra space to kick around in and appreciate having a fully equipped kitchen, **Canyon Rose Suites** (✉ 27 Subway St. ☎ 520/432–5098 ⊕ www.canyonrose. com) is set inside a former boarding house in the stately Allen Block Building.

Breakfast: The considerable lore of the **Bisbee Breakfast Club** (✉ 75 Erie St. ☎ 520/432–5885 ⊕ www.bisbee-breakfastclub.com), which you'll find set along a row of old buildings in the town's historic Lowell district, has spawned a small empire of restaurants around the state. But the original location has the most colorful personality, and the home-style cooking—chicken-fried steak with eggs and spicy sausage gravy, cinnamon French toast, chorizo rancheros—will provide plenty of sustenance for the day ahead.

Day 12: Bisbee, AZ, to Tucson, AZ

110 miles (2 hours without traffic and stops)

Head northwest on Highway 80 to Tombstone, then cut across Highway 82 to Sonoita, a scenic drive through the Santa Rita Mountains and Coronado National Forest, and follow Highway 83 north to I–10, which leads west to Tucson.

ALONG THE WAY

Town: Immortalized in western lore and Hollywood movies (*Gunfight at the O.K. Corral*, *Tombstone*, *Wyatt Earp*), the bustling little hamlet of Tombstone prospered almost unimaginably in the 1880s thanks to a highly profitable silver mining boom and today makes for a fun, if slightly cheesy, stop to soak up the colorful history of the Earp brothers, Clanton gang, and Doc Holliday. Hop out for a stroll along historic Allen Street, where you can stop by the Gunfighter Hall of Fame and watch entertaining gunfight reenactments three times a day at the **O.K. Corral** (✉ 326 E. Allen St. ☎ 520/457–3456 ⊕ www.okcorral.com).

Eat & Drink: As you continue west through the Santa Cruz Mountains, you'll enter one of the state's best-known (if underrated outside of Arizona) wine regions, Sonoita, which has about a dozen vintners. Some of these are outstanding and well-worth a stop for a taste, including the self-described "off-grid" producer **Rune Wines** (✉ 3969 AZ-82 ☎ 520/338–8823 ⊕ www.runewines. com), where you can sip on a backyard terrace overlooking the mountains.

TUCSON

Do: Arizona's second-largest city offers immediate proximity to gorgeous natural scenery—it's a favorite destination of hikers, golfers, and spa goers. But it's also a youthful, laid-back college town (home to the University of Arizona) with plenty of cool cafés and bars, as well as myriad offbeat shops, especially along Historic Fourth Avenue. The must-see in this sunny city is **Saguaro National Park** (☏ 520/733–5153 ⊕ www.nps.gov/sagu), whose eastern and western units bracket Tucson. Arriving from the east, pick up a trail map at the Rincon Mountain Visitor Center. Drive south along the paved Cactus Forest Drive to the Javelina picnic area, where you'll see signs for the Free-man Homestead Trail, an easy 1-mile loop that winds through a stand of mesquite as interpretive signs describe early inhabitants in the Tucson basin.

Eat & Drink: Tucson offers one of the more diverse dining scenes along this itinerary, but don't overlook the city's stellar Mexican food, which South Tucson's **Mi Nidito** (⊠ 1813 S. 4th Ave. ☏ 520/622–5081 ⊕ www.miniditorestaurant.com) has been serving since 1952. Cap off the evening with classic cocktails at the dark and alluring Owls Club (⊠ 236 S. Scott Ave. ☏ 520/207–5678 ⊕ www.owlsclubwest.com).

Stay: Offering wallet-friendly rates and a handy location just off I-15, the vintage-cool **Hotel McCoy** (⊠ 720 W. Silverlake Rd. ☏ 844/782–9622 ⊕ www.hotelmccoy.com) has its own modern art gallery, bookstore, and plenty of engaging common spaces.

Breakfast: Downtown's scene-y **5 Points Market & Restaurant** (⊠ 756 S. Stone Ave. ☏ 520/623–3888 ⊕ www.5pointstucson.com) is an attractive spot (with a great patio) to fuel up on smoked-salmon Benedicts and chilled rice pudding with ponzu sauce, coconut, and cashews.

Day 13: Tucson, AZ, to Anza-Borrego Desert State Park, CA

365 miles (5 hours, 30 minutes without traffic and stops)

The best approach for this drive is mostly along I–10 and I–8, across southern Arizona via Yuma. Just before you reach the small city of El Centro, drive north on Highway 111, then turn west in Brawley on Highway 78 to **Anza-Borrego Desert State Park Visitor Center** (⊠ 200 Palm Canyon Dr. ☏ 760/767–4205 ⊕ www.parks.ca.gov).

ALONG THE WAY

Town: Once a thriving port on the Colorado River back when it was navigable (before the advent of numerous dams), the town of Yuma borders California as well as the adjoining Mexican states of Baja California and Sonora. Give yourself about an hour to explore the **Yuma Territorial Prison State Historic Park** (⊠ (220 Prison Hill Rd. ☏ 928/783–4771 ⊕ www.azstateparks.com), the hilltop site of the late-19th-century prison where as many as six inmates inhabited a tiny cell. Nearby, **Colorado River State Historic Park** (⊠ 201 N. 4th Ave. ☏ 928/329–0471 ⊕ www.azstateparks.com) preserves the grounds and some buildings from an 1860s U.S. Army depot and interprets the natural history of the 1,450-mile river.

Eat & Drink: Close to the Colorado River and Yuma's historic parks, **Prison Hill Brewing** (⊠ 278 S. Main St. ☏ 928/276–4001 ⊕ www.prisonhillbrewing.com) occupies a handsome vintage downtown building with ample sidewalk seating and a large indoor dining room. Share an appetizer sampler of pretzels, sausage, fried chicken, and homemade beer cheese, and save room for the stout-chocolate brownies à la mode.

ANZA-BORREGO DESERT STATE PARK

Do: At about 586,000 acres, this stunning desert landscape, part of the UNESCO-designated Mojave and Colorado Deserts Biosphere Reserve, is larger than most of the country's national parks. Anza-Borrego itself has plenty to keep you busy, including some 500 miles of unpaved roads, some suitable for standard cars, others—including the famed road to Fonts Point—better suited to four-wheel drive. Start by picking up maps at the excellent park visitor center (be sure to check out its colorful desert garden), then drive a short way to Borrego Palm Canyon Campground, where you can embark on the Panoramic Overlook Trail, a short, moderately hilly 1.5-mile out-and-back trek with a payoff of spectacular 360-degree views. Another favorite scramble is the Slot, a steep but rewarding 0.8-mile hike through a narrow ravine of massive rock formations. As you explore the park, keep your eyes peeled for bighorn sheep, coyotes, and rattlesnakes. Later in the day, drive just north of the area's main town, Borrego Springs, to view the more than 130 massive bronze Sky Art sculptures—which include a sabertooth cat, a velociraptor, and a giant serpent—created by Mexican-American artist Ricardo Breceda that dot the sweeping 1,500-acre grounds of **Galleta Meadows** (✉ *1700–1844 Borrego Springs Rd.* ☎ *760/767–5555* ⊕ *www. underthesunfoundation.org*).

Eat & Drink: In tiny Borrego Springs, you'll find a few mostly simple options, including long-running **Carlee's Place** (✉ *660 Palm Canyon Dr.* ☎ *760/767–3262* ⊕ *www.carleesplace.com*), a lively roadhouse known for its massive menu of down-home American comfort fare, including hefty charbroiled steaks.

Stay: With a clothing-optional pool and close proximity to the park, adults-only **Borrego Valley Inn** (✉ *405 Palm Canyon Dr.* ☎ *760/767–0311* ⊕ *www.*

borregovalleyinn.com) is an inviting place to unwind after a day of driving or hiking through the desert. Camping enthusiasts take note: you're welcome to pitch a tent anywhere in the state park, and with so little light pollution, the stargazing is pretty incredible.

Breakfast: Centrally located **Red Ocotillo** (✉ *721 Ave. Sureste* ☎ *760/767–7400* ⊕ *www.redocotillo.com*) is a good place in the morning for eggs Benedict or blueberry-buttermilk pancakes.

Day 14: Anza-Borrego Desert State Park to San Diego, CA

90 miles (2 hours without traffic and stops)

The last day of your adventure entails a relatively short drive through the desert mountains east of San Diego, but it's a memorable drive. Head south on Highway S3, then southwest on Highway 78 to Julian. From there, follow Highway 79 south as it cuts directly through the desert peaks, oak woodlands, and giant lake in the heart of Cuyamaca Rancho State Park. Then pick up I-8 east, for the final leg to San Diego.

ALONG THE WAY

Town: A quirky Victorian gold rush town, Julian lies just over the mountains from Anza-Borrego and bursts with antiques shops, galleries, old timey stores, and cafés specializing in fruit—especially apple—pies.

Eat & Drink: By far the area's most acclaimed stop for lunch, **Jeremy's on the Hill** (✉ *4354 CA-78* ☎ *760/765–1587* ⊕ *www.jeremysonthehill.com*) in quaint Wynola specializes in farm- and ranch-to-table burgers, meat loaf, and salads.

SAN DIEGO

Do: Congratulations! You've made it all the way from coast to coast, and what better way to celebrate the completion of this journey than by taking in a grand view of the Pacific Ocean. For a vista perched high on a sea cliff that also takes in Point Loma Peninsula, San Diego Bay, and the downtown skyline, head to **Cabrillo National Monument** (✉ 1800 Cabrillo Memorial Dr. ☎ 619/557–5450 ⊕ www.nps.gov/cabr). Or to see a gorgeous inlet with a white-sand beach, tidal pools, and often a view of barking sea lions lazing on the rocks, drive to La Jolla Cove, the centerpiece of the affluent seaside community of La Jolla.

Eat & Drink: Close to Cabrillo National Monument and anchoring a mixed-use development on the site of a former navy training campus on San Diego Bay, **Liberty Market** (✉ 2820 Historic Decatur Rd. ☎ 619/487–9346 ⊕ www.bluebridgehospitality.com) is a fabulous food hall brimming with gourmet vendors and several hip sit-down bars and eateries. When in San Diego, do make a point of eating fish tacos, which you can grab on-the-go at inexpensive takeout places like the local chain **Oscars Mexican Seafood** (✉ 646 University Ave. ☎ 619/230–5560 ⊕ www.oscarsmexicanseafood.com).

Stay: To be close to the festive energy of downtown's historic Gaslamp Quarter and hip East Village districts, book a room at the swanky **Pendry** (✉ 550 J St. ☎ 619/738–7000 ⊕ www.pendry.com), with its rooftop pool, artfully decorated rooms, and outstanding on-site restaurants and bars. On the coast, the California Craftsman–style **Lodge at Torrey Pines** (✉ 11480 N. Torrey Pines Rd. ☎ 858/453–4420 ⊕ www.lodgetorreypines.com) has an absolutely stunning cliff-top location with ocean views, a celebrated golf course, and access to the wonderful trails of Torrey Pines State Natural Reserve.

Breakfast: A beloved tradition for breakfast for several decades, **Big Kitchen Cafe** (✉ 3003 Grape St. ☎ 619/234–5789 ⊕ www.judysbigkitchen.com) in Golden Hill is a delight for its colorful art-filled dining room and hefty omelets (the one with avocado, cream cheese, and chives is a favorite).

Route 66

Written by Aimee Heckel

Historic Route 66 is the most famous highway in the United States, making it a must-drive for road-trippers and history buffs alike. The so-called "Mother Road" dates back to 1926, connecting Chicago and Los Angeles. The original road covered nearly 2,500 miles, winding through small towns in various states and quickly becoming synonymous with a particular vision of Americana. The road and the communities it crosses have changed a lot over the years, with improvements, new sections, and growth, but you can still plan an adventurous trip from Illinois to California, hitting many of the historical highlights along the way.

At a Glance

Start: Chicago, IL

End: Los Angeles, CA

Miles Traveled: 2,300 miles

Suggested Duration: 9 days

States Visited: Arizona, California, Illinois, Missouri, New Mexico, Oklahoma, Texas

Key Sights: Cadillac Ranch; Gateway Arch National Park; Grand Canyon National Park; London Bridge; Petrified Forest National Park

Best Time to Go: Midwestern roads can be treacherous in the wintertime, so make this a warm-weather trip.

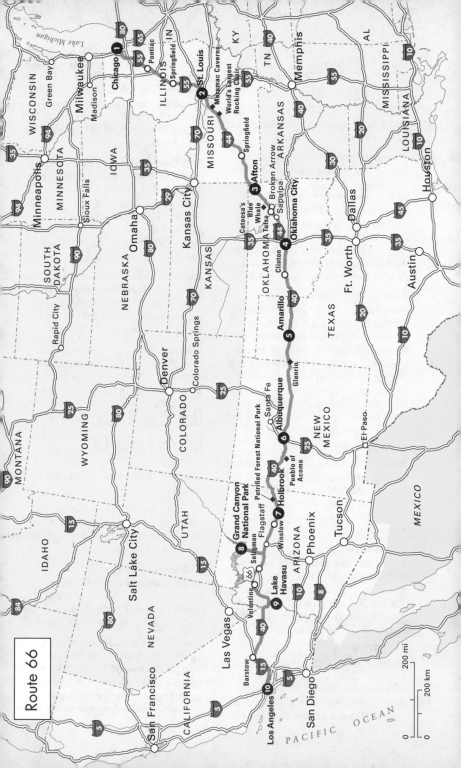

Route 66

Day 1: Chicago, IL, to St. Louis, MO

300 miles (4 hours, 40 minutes without traffic and stops)

Start your trip in the Midwest's biggest city, Chicago, where major airports like O'Hare offer plenty of rental car options. As you leave the city, Interstate 55 is dotted with Route 66 attractions, and you can follow them all the way into St. Louis. This is the official starting point of Route 66; while much of the country was still dirt roads, Illinois was the first to pave its part of the famous route.

ALONG THE WAY

Photo Op: Just over an hour-and-half outside Chicago, the small town of Pontiac is home to the **Illinois Route 66 Hall of Fame and Museum** (✉ 110 W. Howard St. ☎ 815/844–4566 ⊕ www.il66assoc.org), a fitting introduction to the adventure you've just embarked on. Even if you don't have time to explore the museum itself, be sure to stop for a photo of the world's largest Route 66 road sign outside the museum.

Town: Check out the self-guided **Living Legends Tour** in Springfield, Illinois, (⊕ visitspringfieldillinois.com/Landing/LivingLegends.aspx) where you can learn about Route 66 via Springfield's local entrepreneurs.

Eat & Drink: Have a hot dog on a stick for lunch at **Springfield's Cozy Dog Drive Inn** (✉ 2925 S. 6th St. ☎ 217/525–1992 ⊕ www.cozydogdrivein.com) opened in 1949 on Route 66. The casual eatery of today is located next door to the original site, now a historic landmark.

ST. LOUIS

Do: Route 66 runs right through St. Louis, Missouri, where you can visit the historic landmark, the Chain of Rocks Bridge. While in the area, see a true natural wonder, the **Meramec Caverns** (✉ 1125 MO-W

☎ 573/468–2283 ⊕ www.americascave.com), "Missouri's buried treasure." And, of course, no visit to St. Louis is complete without a visit to **Gateway Arch National Park** (✉ 11 N. 4th St. ☎ 314/655–1600 ⊕ www.nps.gov/jeff), home to the city's famous arch.

Eat & Drink: While St. Louis has a vast dining scene, from elegant to budget-friendly, a one-of-a-kind, relaxed option is Crown Candy Kitchen (✉ 1401 St. Louis Ave. ☎ 314/621–9650 ⊕ crowncandykitchen.net) located downtown. Decorated in 1930s style, the eatery makes its own (very delicious) candy.

Stay: Treat yourself to an elegant night at the four-star **Fleur-de-Lys Mansion** (✉ 3500 Russell Blvd. ☎ 314/773–3500 ⊕ www.thefleurdelys.com), a B&B in a 1913 home with a garden.

Breakfast: If you stay at Fleur-de-Lys, breakfast is included in your stay, all made from scratch. Even the bread is baked daily from a sourdough starter.

Day 2: St. Louis, MO, to Afton, OK

325 miles (5 hours without traffic and stops)

Interstate 44 is the main highway to transport you from Missouri to Oklahoma, through small towns and big cities, valleys and hills.

ALONG THE WAY

Roadside Attraction: As you approach Fanning, Missouri, be sure to check out the World's Largest Rocking Chair on Route 66. Yes, it's exactly what it sounds like.

Town: You've visited Springfield, Illinois, so why not Springfield, Missouri? This Springfield has the **Route 66 Springfield Visitor Center** (✉ 815 E. St. Louis St. ☎ 800/678–8767 ⊕ www.springfieldmo.org) and the well-preserved **Rock Fountain Court Historic**

District, a group of stone cabins facing Route 66 that used to be public lodging.

Eat & Drink: Springfield has more than 1,000 restaurants to pick from, but one that stands out (for its quirkiness, not local significance) is the **London Calling Pasty Company** (⊠ 2825 Glenstone Ave. ☏ 415/705–6000 ⊕ www.londoncalling-pastycompany.com), where you can eat British food in a converted double-decker red bus converted. There are two locations and a food truck in Springfield.

Nature: The Springfield area has more than 100 parks and is known for its trails—a good excuse to get out and stretch your legs. A good intro trail to the area is **Wilson's Creek Greenway** (⊠ 3825 W. Farm Rd. 146 ☏ 417/864–2015 ⊕ ozarkgreenways.org).

AFTON

Do: While it might be easy to drive right past this tiny town in Oklahoma, it really is a Route 66 mecca, with a ton of different related museums, classic Route 66 architecture, and nostalgic attractions, including the **Darryl Starbird's National Rod & Custom Hall of Fame Museum** (⊠ 55251 E. OK-85A ☏ 918/257–4234 ⊕ www.darrylstarbird. com), dedicated to custom car builders. You can even multiple stretches of the original Route 66 that are only 9 feet wide.

Eat & Drink: The best place to eat in Afton: **Nowhere** (⊠ 300 S. 1st St. ☏ 918/919–4111 ⊕ www.facebook.com/ nowhereonroute66). That's not cheekiness; it's the actual name of a tasty local barbecue joint. Nowhere on Route 66 (the full name, for its location right on the historical road) offers hand-rubbed, wood-smoked meats and an impressive collection of specialty sandwiches. Add some fried green beans and spicy pickles for a true American meal.

Shop: Shop a pecan grove at Afton's **Miller Pecan Company** (⊠ 21853 U.S. 69 ☏ 918/257–6887 ⊕ www.millerpecancom-pany.com). Bet you've never had blackstrap molasses or scuppernong jelly before.

Stay: Stay in the Elvis Room with its shiny purple comforters at the **Route 66 Motel** (⊠ 21751 S. U.S. 69 ☏ 918/257–8313 ⊕ www.route66motels.com); it's far from fancy, but each room has a different, fun theme.

Breakfast: Green Country Cafe (⊠ 21601 U.S. 69 ☏ 918/257–5140 ⊕ www.route-66motels.com) is a sweet, small-town restaurant with excellent pie, but the classic breakfast dishes won't disappoint either. If you're there too early for dessert, grab a slice of pie to go for a midday snack.

Day 3: Afton, OK, to Oklahoma City, OK

180 miles (2 hours, 45 minutes without traffic and stops)

Take I-44 down past Tulsa and Broken Arrow, Oklahoma, to Oklahoma City. The longest driveable length of Route 66 runs through Oklahoma. Keep your eyes open for landmarks, such as the Bridge No. 18 at Rock Creek, part of the Historic Route 66 in Sapulpa.

ALONG THE WAY

Roadside Attraction: Another Route 66 roadside attraction that can't be missed is Catoosa's Blue Whale, an 80-foot-long sperm whale made out of concrete and pipe.

Town: Tulsa, the second-largest city in Oklahoma, may be best known for its art deco architecture, but it's also home to several Route 66 markers, such as the 11th Street Arkansas River Bridge and the charming, cottage-style Vickery Phillips 66 Station. If you have time, a visit to the city's **Greenwood Cultural Center** (⊠ 322 N. Greenwood Ave. ☏ 918/596–1020 ⊕ www.greenwoodculturalcenter. com) is an essential stop to learn more about the 1921 Tulsa Massacre and the history of Greenwood, once America's Black Wall Street.

Eat & Drink: Get a fresh seafood lunch at Tulsa's **White River Fish Market and Restaurant** (✉ *1708 N. Sheridan Rd.* ☎ *918/835–1910* ⊕ *www.whiteriverfish-market.com*). Yes, some of the best food in this land-locked state is surprisingly from the sea.

OKLAHOMA CITY

Do: Do your best cowboy impression at the **National Cowboy and Western Heritage Museum** (✉ *1700 N.E. 63rd St.* ☎ *405/478–2250* ⊕ *www.nationalcow-boymusuem.org*), which boasts more than 28,000 western and Native American art and artifacts.

Eat & Drink: Pop's Soda Ranch (✉ *660 U.S. Rte. 66* ☎ *405/928–7677* ⊕ *www.pops66.com*) in nearby Arcadia is exactly the kind of mom-and-pop stop you want to eat at on a road trip like this. Just look for the massive, neon, glowing soda bottle as you cruise down 66.

Stay: The Route 66 road trip is all about time travel, and you can continue that at the **Colcord Hotel** (✉ *15 N. Robinson Ave.* ☎ *405/601–4300* ⊕ *www.colcordhotel.com*), built in 1909 originally as a sky-scraper office tower. Today, it's a swanky luxury hotel.

Breakfast: The Colcord has several different restaurants on-site. Breakfast at Flint, one such restaurant, is a winner, thanks to its fluffy vanilla pancakes and breakfast tacos.

Day 4: Oklahoma City, OK, to Amarillo, TX

260 miles (4 hours without traffic and stops)

Continue along I–40 East. You'll find scattered small towns along the way with frequent Route 66 sites, such as old service stations, as you make your way into Texas.

Extend Your Trip

From St. Louis: Along the Mississippi *(Ch. 2)*; The Best of the Ozarks *(Ch. 6)*

From Albuquerque: The Best of New Mexico *(Ch. 5)*

From Grand Canyon: The Best of Arizona *(Ch. 5)*

From Los Angeles: The Pacific Coast Highway; The Best of Southern California *(Ch. 3)*

ALONG THE WAY

Town: Clinton, Oklahoma, is located on Route 66. Stop here to tour (and take some great selfies at) the **Oklahoma Route 66 Museum** (✉ *2229 W. Gary Blvd.* ☎ *580/323–7866*) and to learn more about Oklahoma's part in the historic road.

Eat & Drink: The **Route 66 Cafe at the Market** (✉ *301 W. Gary Blvd.* ☎ *580/445–7008*) in Clinton not only pays homage to the Mother Road, but it also has drool-worthy, old-fashioned comfort food. Take your pick from the meat loaf, catfish fry, chicken-fried steak, and homemade Frito pie, all just like Grandma used to make (okay, maybe not the Frito pie).

AMARILLO

Do: When in Amarillo, you have to take photos at one of the country's most famous roadside attraction, the **Cadillac Ranch** (✉ *13651 I–40 Frontage Rd.* ☎ *806/848–0764*), where a row of Caddys curiously balance upright, noses down in the ground and tail fins up in the air.

Eat & Drink: Everything is bigger in Texas, right? Then order a 72-ounce steak at the **Big Texan Steak Ranch** (✉ *7701 I–40 East* ☎ *806/372–6000* ⊕ *www.bigtexan.com*).

Stay: If you attempt the 72-ounce-steak challenge, you will be waddling back to your bed. Luckily, there's a motel and "horse motel" (yes, for your horses) on-site. The **Big Texan Motel** (✉ *7701 I–40 Access Rd.* ☎ *806/372–6000* ⊕ *www.bigtexanmotel.com*) was built to look like an old Wild West town, complete with a Texas-shaped swimming pool.

Breakfast: Ye Olde Pancake Station
(✉ *2800 Virginia Circle* ☎ *806/355–0211* ⊕ *www.pancakestation.com*) is where the locals start their day. There's more than pancakes; you can actually order green eggs and ham (the green here is green chili).

Day 5: Amarillo, TX, to Albuquerque, NM

290 miles (4 hours without traffic and stops)

I–40 will shoot you straight west to New Mexico, passing a handful of Route 66 landmarks as you go.

ALONG THE WAY

Town: Glenrio is unincorporated and considered to be both in Texas and New Mexico at the same time. Here you can see the Historic Route 66 roadbed in a well-preserved, midcentury ghost town of the American West.

Eat & Drink: Russell's Truck and Travel Center (✉ *1–25, Springer, NM* ☎ *575/483–5004* ⊕ *www.russellsttc.com*) is a convenience store as well as an authentic Route 66 diner. It's not fancy, but it's the real deal.

ALBUQUERQUE

Do: There's so much to do in Albuquerque, but the **ABQ BioPark** (✉ *901 10th St. SW* ☎ *505/764–6200* ⊕ *www.cabq.gov*) is a true wonderland for animal lovers. Round out the day with a sunset ride on the **Sandia Peak Tramway** (✉ *30 Tramway Rd. NE* ☎ *505/856–1532* ⊕ *www.sandiapeak.com*).

Eat & Drink: Campo at Los Poblanos (✉ *4803 Rio Grande Blvd. NW, Los Ranchos de Albuquerque, NM* ☎ *505/338–1615* ⊕ *www.lospoblanos.com*) is the definition of farm-to-table; it's located on an organic farm in the Rio Grande River Valley.

Stay: Stay in the **Hyatt Regency Tamaya Resort and Spa** (✉ *1300 Tuyuna Trail, Santa Ana Pueblo, NM* ☎ *505/867–1234* ⊕ *www.hyatt.com*) if you want a luxurious stay with a focus on Native American culture (it's actually built on the Santa Ana Pueblo), or at the **Hotel Parq Central** (✉ *806 Central Ave. SE* ☎ *505/242–0040* ⊕ *www.hotelparqcentral.com*) for a unique and historical experience; the latter is a former infirmary transformed into an elegant hotel with a sultry rooftop bar.

Breakfast: Swing by the healthy and hip **Grove Cafe and Market** (✉ *600 Central Ave. SE* ☎ *505/248–9800* ⊕ *www.thegrovecafemarket.com*) for a fresh breakfast in a bright, enclosed patio.

Day 6: Albuquerque, NM, to Holbrook, AZ

230 miles (30 hours, 30 minutes without traffic and stops)

I–40 West will take you to Arizona, past pink cliffs, wide-open spaces, tiny towns, and the Continental Divide, which is also the highest point on Route 66.

ALONG THE WAY

Detour: If you want to immerse yourself in Native American culture and the Pueblo of Acoma, take a small detour (about 20 minutes) to Sky City, New Mexico. Start at the **Sky City Cultural Center and Haak'u Museum** (✉ *Haaku Rd.* ☎ *505/552–7861* ⊕ *www.acomaskycity.org*) and learn about the oldest continuously inhabited settlement in North America.

Eat & Drink: Taste authentic Acoma food at the **Yaak'a Cafe** inside the Sky City cultural center. In addition to traditional fare, you can also find modern American food, all made by a member of the tribe.

Photo Op: The **Rio Puerco Bridge** (✉ *14311 Central Ave NW* ⊕ *www.nps.gov*) in Rio Puerco, New Mexico, is located west of Albuquerque on Route 66, after a scenic drive into the valley. You can walk across the bridge, which is on the National Register of Historic Places, and take photos of the old Highway 66 fading into the desert beyond.

HOLBROOK

Do: In the Holbrook area, take some time to enjoy the fairy tale–esque **Petrified Forest National Park** (☎ *928/524–6228* ⊕ *www. nps.gov/pefo*) and glimpse some fossils.

Eat & Drink: Locals love **Sombreritos Mexican Food** (✉ *2101 Navajo Blvd.* ☎ *928/524–1538* ⊕ *www.sombreritos-food.com*) for its unpretentious, authentic Mexican dishes.

Stay: Spend the night in the **Wigwam Motel** (✉ *811 W. Hopi Dr.* ☎ *928/524–3048* ⊕ *www.sleepinawigwam.com*), which is on the National Register of Historic Places. Instead of a typical room, guests stay in a concrete teepee.

Breakfast: **Joe and Aggie's Cafe** (✉ *120 W. Hopi Dr.* ☎ *928/524–6540*) is a local gem in Holbrook. This family-style restaurant even has a mini-museum inside with old photos, news clippings, and other Route 66 mementos.

Day 7: Holbrook, AZ, to Grand Canyon National Park

175 miles (2 hours, 30 minutes without traffic and stops)

Follow I-40 to the Grand Canyon, past the city of Flagstaff, Arizona's famous red rocks, and the Coconino National Forest's thick pine trees. Although the route to

the Grand Canyon veers away from the traditional Route 66, it's still a must-see for a true vision of America.

ALONG THE WAY

Town: Although this stretch of the drive is short and straightforward, a bonus site along the way is the 11-acre architectural treasure, the **La Posada Historic District** (✉ *303 E. 2nd St.* ☎ *928/289–4366* ⊕ *www.laposada.org*) in Winslow, Arizona. Stroll through the grounds and pick up a souvenir.

Shop: La Posada's Trading Post and Book Store is a great place to find Mimbres design replica pottery, southwestern jewelry, and Native American crafts.

Eat & Drink: The La Posada Hotel houses a restaurant called **The Turquoise Room** (✉ *303 E. 2nd St.* ☎ *928/289–2888* ⊕ *www.theturquoiseroom.net*), considered the finest restaurant in the region. It specializes in southwestern cuisine.

GRAND CANYON NATIONAL PARK

Do: Witnessing the 10-mile-wide **Grand Canyon** (✉ *Grand Canyon National Park Visitor Center, S. Entrance Rd.* ☎ *928/638–7888* ⊕ *www.nps.gov/grca*) is awe-inspiring, even life-changing. Explore it via hiking, a mule ride, biking, or even rafting down the Colorado River.

Eat & Drink: The best restaurant by the Grand Canyon is hands down **El Tovar** on the South Rim (✉ *1 El Tovar Rd.* ☎ *928/638–2631* ⊕ *www.grandcanyonlodges.com*), which serves both international and southwestern cuisine. It's also a bit expensive. If you're on a budget, you can also find food trucks on the South Rim. If you are on the North Rim and want another solid option that's less pricey, check out the **Grand Canyon Lodge Dining Room** (✉ *AZ-67, North Rim* ☎ *928/638–8598* ⊕ *www.grandcanyonforever.com/dining*).

Stay: Stay at the beautiful El Tovar Hotel on the South Rim. Let's be honest: you're going to want to stay here for a few days,

Did You Know?

Sure-footed mules take riders along the rim for half-day trips and down into the Grand Canyon for longer excursions. Two-day trips include an overnight stay at Phantom Ranch on the canyon floor.

thanks to the Euro-style hunting lodge feel and canyon-view rooms.

Breakfast: Grab quick coffee and a light breakfast at the **Canyon Coffee House at The Fountain** (✉ *9 Village Loop Dr.* ☎ *928/638–2631* ⊕ *www.grandcanyon-lodges.com*) (inside the Bright Angel Lodge).

Day 8: Grand Canyon National Park, AZ, to Lake Havasu, AZ

240 miles (3 hours, 45 minutes without traffic and stops)

Head from one natural delight to another via the simple I–40 route, which takes you from the Grand Canyon to Lake Havasu City.

ALONG THE WAY

Town: The small town of Seligman, Arizona, calls itself a "birthplace" of Route 66. It feels like you've stepped back in time with the retro signs and classic cars.

Eat & Drink: When in Seligman, you must dine at **Delgadillo's Snow Cap** founded in the 1950s (✉ *301 AZ-66* ☎ *928/422–3291*), with quirky menu items like Oink Burgers, "male" or "female" sundaes, and a "cheeseburger with cheese."

LAKE HAVASU

Do: In Lake Havasu, visit the world-famous **London Bridge** (✉ *1340 McCulloch Blvd.* ⊕ *www.londonbridgetour.com*). Yes, the London Bridge from the timeless nursery rhyme now resides in Arizona. It was built in the 1830s in London and moved to Arizona in the 1960s. In addition to a wealth of Route 66 attractions, this surprising beachfront resort in the middle of the desert state boasts ample hiking, boating, biking, fishing, golfing, and special events—so much, in fact, that you may want to extend your trip and stay here for a few days.

Eat & Drink: Lake Havasu has a good selection of food, mostly casual. A brewery can provide a great glimpse into a community, so refuel at award-winning **Barley Brothers Restaurant and Brewery** (✉ *1425 McCulloch Blvd. N* ☎ *928/505–7837* ⊕ *www.barleybrothers.com*). With wood-fired-oven pizza, local brews, and a view of London Bridge, you can't go wrong.

Stay: It's an Arizona rite of passage to go camping on the lake, although there are other lodging options if you don't feel like roughing it, like the hip boutique **Heat Hotel** (✉ *1420 McCulloch Blvd. N* ☎ *928/854–2833* ⊕ *www.heathotel.com*) overlooking Bridgewater Channel.

Breakfast: Fill up on breakfast at the Lake Havasu City **Black Bear Diner** (✉ *1900 McCulloch Blvd. N* ☎ *928/855–2013* ⊕ *www.blackbeardiner.com*). This restaurant claims the "biggest portions for the hungriest bears," such as a 10-ounce "Bigfoot Chicken Fried Steak and Eggs" that's a whopping 2,580 calories.

Day 9: Lake Havasu, AZ, to Los Angeles, CA

300 miles (5 hours without traffic and stops)

There are two different routes from Havasu to L.A., both similar in time and distance. Choose I–40 so you can make one final, historical stop in Barstow, California.

ALONG THE WAY

Town: Barstow, California, is home of the former Harvey House Railroad Depot, originally built in 1885. Today it's the **Route 66 Mother Road Museum** (✉ *681 N. 1st Ave.* ☎ *760/255–1890* ⊕ *www.route66museum.org*), featuring a spread of old photos and artifacts.

Eat & Drink: While in Barstow, you can snag some great Mexican food. **Lola's**

Kitchen (✉ *1244 E. Main St.* ☎ *760/255–1007*), a hidden gem in a strip mall, has tasty green chilis that are worth the stop.

LOS ANGELES

Do: Wrap up your Route 66 road trip by spending a day exploring the many historic sites in Los Angeles, including the Broadway Theater District and the **Million Dollar Theater** (✉ *301 S. Broadway* ☎ *213/687–4247* ⊕ *www.milliondollar.la*). Head to the Hollywood area for more Route 66–era landmarks, such as the Griffith Observatory, the giant Chicken Boy statue, the TCL Chinese Theatre, and, of course, the Hollywood sign. But the best way to end your adventure is with a photo op at Santa Monica Pier, where the famous "End of the Trail" sign marks the official end to your journey; you can even add your name to the list of fellow Route 66 travelers at the nearby information booth.

Eat & Drink: Finalize this history buff's journey where the French dip sandwich is said to have been invented, at **Philippe the Original** (✉ *1001 N. Alameda St.* ☎ *213/628–3781* ⊕ *www.philippes.com*).

Stay: On Santa Monica's busy Main Street, the **Sea Shore** (family-owned for almost 50 years) is a charming throwback to Route 66 and to 1960s-style roadside motels in an trendy neighborhood (✉ *2637 Main St.* ☎ *310/392–2787* ⊕ *www.seashoremotel.com*).

Breakfast: Founded by Santa Monica natives, **Huckleberry Bakery and Café** (✉ *1014 Wilshire Blvd.* ☎ *310/451–2311* ⊕ *www.huckleberrycafe.com*) brings together the best ingredients from local farmers and growers to craft diner-style comfort food with a chic twist. Everything is made on-site, even the hot sauce and almond milk.

The East Coast's Best Beaches

Written by Brandon Schultz

California may be known for its surfing and laid-back coastal attitude, but many of the country's best beaches are actually found on the East Coast, where more than 2,000 miles of coastline are dotted with scores of popular seaside destinations. For a highlights tour of the East Coast's best beaches south of New Jersey, follow this trail from Miami to Delaware, stopping in each state along the way at least once. It'll take at least eight days to hit them all, but don't be afraid to stay longer in any given spot or hit a few extra shores along the way. There's plenty to see in each town, and so many more gorgeous beaches along the route. ■TIP→ **This route ends in Delaware so to truly experience the best of the East Coast, extend your trip even longer by linking it with two other road trips: The Best of Long Island and the Jersey Shore (Ch. 8) and Coastal New England (Ch. 8).**

At a Glance

Start: Miami Beach, FL

End: Rehoboth Beach, DE

Miles Traveled: 1,450 miles

Suggested Duration: 8 days

States Visited: Delaware, Florida, Georgia, Maryland, North Carolina, South Carolina, Virginia

Key Sights: Myrtle Beach; Palm Beach; the Outer Banks; Tybee Island; Virginia Beach

Best Time to Go: If you want to hit all the beaches at the height of activity with all local businesses open, you'll need to visit in summer. The earlier you go, the less soaring and scorching the temperatures will be, and some crowds may be marginally smaller. Keep in mind that the summer will also mean accommodations book up quickly, so plan accordingly.

Day 1: Miami, FL, to Cocoa Beach, FL

210 miles (3 hours, 45 minutes without traffic and stops)

Miami International Airport (MIA), with more than a dozen on-site car rental agencies, should be your point of entry for this adventure; Fort Lauderdale (FLL) may seem close, but traffic from here could easily add an additional hour to your day. When leaving Miami, it's a simple drive up I–95 N to FL-404, which will take you island-hopping through Thousand Islands to Cocoa Beach.

ALONG THE WAY

Town: About 2 hours from Miami, stop in West Palm Beach for a culture break. There's plenty of dining and shopping around the Palm Beaches, but the **Norton Museum of Art** (✉ 1450 S. Dixie Hwy. ☎ 561/832–5196 ⊕ www.norton.org) in West Palm is worth the stop alone. Here you'll find more than 8,000 pieces between the collection's five primary focuses: American, Chinese, European, contemporary, and photography.

Eat & Drink: While in West Palm Beach, grab a bite at **Batch New Southern Kitchen & Tap** (✉ 223 Clematis St. ☎ 561/708-0000 ⊕ www.batchsouthernkitchen. com), where local ingredients supply from-scratch recipes of modern southern dishes like shrimp and grits, chicken and waffles, and an entire mac-and-cheese menu. Garden fresh cocktails mixed with craft American spirits are a hit here.

Shop: West Palm's Antique Row is brimming with hidden treasures, but the bargains are found at **Palm Beach Outlets** (✉ 1751 Palm Beach Lakes Blvd. ☎ 561/515–4400 ⊕ www.palmbeachoutlets.com), also in West Palm.

COCOA BEACH

Do: Cocoa Beach is best known for two things: surfing and space. The **Florida Surf Museum** (✉ 4275 N. Atlantic Ave. ☎ 321/720–8033 ⊕ www.floridasurfmuseum.org) provides a good look into the state's surfing history for serious devotees, but the casually curious may have more fun simply watching the surfers at Westgate Cocoa Beach Pier. Transitioning from the sea to the sky, Cocoa Beach is equally famed as the gateway to the **Kennedy Space Center** (✉ Space Commerce Way, Merritt Island, FL ☎ 855/433–4210 ⊕ www.kennedyspacecenter.com) at Cape Canaveral. There are plenty of tours and exhibits available year-round, but you'll create a lifelong memory if you time your visit to catch a rocket launch.

Eat & Drink: Drop by **Q's Crackin' Crab & Seafood Kitchen** (✉ 5240 N. Atlantic Ave. ☎ 321/613–4044 www.qscrackincrab.com) for a signature seafood boil drenched in garlic butter or one of a vast array of mixed seafood platters with lobster, crab, and shrimp dominating the menu. For the classic local cocktail experience, head back to Cocoa Beach Pier and visit the **Rikki Tiki Tavern** (✉ 401 Meade Ave. ☎ 321/783–7549 ⊕ www.resort.to) at the very tip, 800 feet from the shore, for cocktails over the ocean and under the thatched roof.

Stay: If a hotel can be both retro and contemporary, **Beachside Hotel & Suites** (✉ 3901 N. Atlantic Ave. ☎ 321/783–2221 ⊕ www.beachsidehotelcocoabeach.com) is it. Grab a complimentary surfboard and head to the beach 300 feet away or snag a cruiser for some more land-focused exercise. If exertion is out of the question, just float on the lazy-river-style pool.

Breakfast: Follow your nose to **Sunrise Bread Company** (✉ 315 S. Hopkins Ave, Titusville, FL 321/268—1009 ⊕ www.sunrisebread.com) for baked goods and breakfast sandwiches on your way out of Cocoa Beach. You'll also find plenty of specialty coffees and smoothies to power you for your drive today.

Day 2: Cocoa Beach, FL, to Jekyll Island, GA

240 miles (3 hours, 30 minutes without traffic and stops)

Head back to I–95 N and continue up the coast until you reach GA-520 E. From here, it's a quick jaunt to the ocean to reach Jekyll Island across the East River. Don't forget that there's a small toll to access the island, so have cash ready.

ALONG THE WAY

Town: About an hour before Jekyll Island, make a stop in Jacksonville, Florida, the country's largest city by surface area. Jacksonville is home to a handful of notable art and history museums, a couple of historic forts, plenty of parks, and its top attraction, the **Jacksonville Zoo and Gardens** (✉ *370 Zoo Pkwy.* ☎ *904/757–4463* ⊕ *www.jacksonvillezoo.org*).

Eat & Drink: Chow down on tacos and margaritas at **TacoLu** (✉ *1712 Beach Blvd.* ☎ *904/249–8226* ⊕ *www.tacolu.com*) in Jacksonville Beach. This local favorite offers classics like Baja fish tacos and carnitas alongside a serious tequila list in a festive atmosphere of colorful art and murals.

JEKYLL ISLAND

Do: The former playground of America's wealthiest families, you'll still find plenty of lovely "cottages" (mansions, to any sane person) on Millionaire's Row, but the island today is better known for its impressive natural gifts. From the eerie beauty of epic **Driftwood Beach** (☎ *800/933–2627* ⊕ *www.goldenisles. com*), where the still-standing remains of 200-year-old oaks and pines line the coast, to the **Georgia Sea Turtle Center** (✉ *214 Stable Rd.* ☎ *912/635–4444* ⊕ *www.gstc.jekyllisland.com*), where you can get up close with the rehabbing

patients, Jekyll Island is ideal for a quiet escape.

Eat & Drink: To enjoy live music at a waterfront location, have dinner at the **Wharf** (✉ *370 Riverview Dr.* ☎ *912/635–3612* ⊕ *www.jekyllwharf.com*). Located on the Historic District pier, the view is idyllic any time of day, but can be particularly dramatic at sundown. Directly across the island (a whopping 4-minute drive or 20-minute walk), **Tortuga Jacks** (✉ *201 Beachview Dr. N* ☎ *912/342–2600* ⊕ *tortuga-jacks.business.site*) also offers waterfront bites and sips and is a top choice if you're road-tripping with a pet.

Stay: Settle into the **Beachview Club Hotel** (✉ *721 Beachview Dr. N* ☎ *912/635–2256* ⊕ *www.beachviewclubjekyll.com*) to experience quiet coastal living on Jekyll Island. The outdoor pool is shaded by live oaks and the shoreline is just steps beyond.

Breakfast: Snag coffee or an indulgent frappe to-go from **The Pantry at Jekyll Island Club Resort** (✉ *371 Riverview Dr.* ☎ *888/445–3179* ⊕ *www.jekyllclub.com*). It's a short drive for Day 3, so consider a simple breakfast order like the Jekyll cinnamon roll or a danish.

Day 3: Jekyll Island, GA, to Tybee Island, GA

110 miles (2 hours without traffic and stops)

Continue up I–95 N to I–16 E and cross the Wilmington River and Bull River on your way to Tybee Island.

ALONG THE WAY

Photo Op: Just off I–95 in Townsend, the self-proclaimed "Smallest Church in America" offers a quaint photo op with its tiny chapel and miniature bell tower among the (much taller) trees.

Town: Savannah is one of the most alluring cities in the South and it's directly

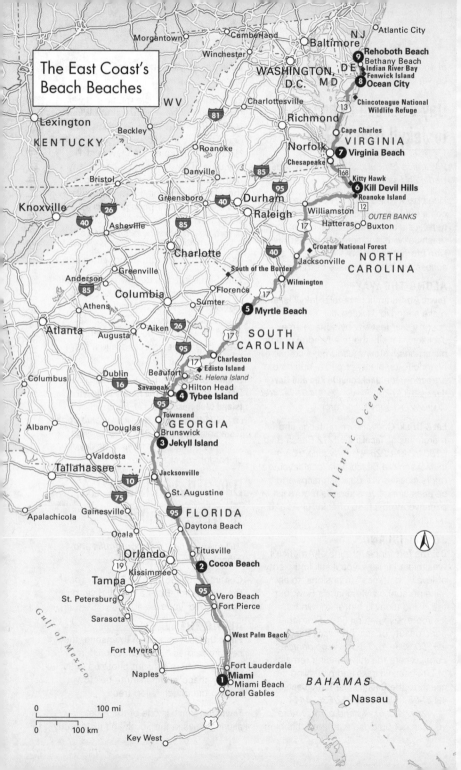

The East Coast's
Beach Beaches

Morgantown
Cumberland
Baltimore
NJ
Atlantic City

Winchester
WASHINGTON,
D.C.
MD
DE
9 **Rehoboth Beach**
Bethany Beach
Indian River Bay
Fenwick Island
8 **Ocean City**

WV
Charlottesville
13
Chincoteague National
Wildlife Refuge

Lexington
81
Richmond
Cape Charles

KENTUCKY
Beckley
Roanoke
VIRGINIA
Norfolk
7 **Virginia Beach**

Bristol
Danville
85
Chesapeake
168
Kitty Hawk

Knoxville
40
Greensboro
Durham
95
6 **Kill Devil Hills**
Roanoke Island

26
Raleigh
Williamston
12
Hatteras
Buxton
OUTER BANKS

40
Asheville
85
17

Anderson
Greenville
40
Croatan National Forest
NORTH
CAROLINA
Jacksonville

Charlotte
South of the Border

Columbia
Florence
Wilmington

Atlanta
Athens
Aiken
26
Sumter
17
5 **Myrtle Beach**

Augusta
95
SOUTH
CAROLINA

Columbus
Dublin
17
Charleston
Edisto Island
St. Helena Island

16
Beaufort
Hilton Head

Savannah
95
4 **Tybee Island**

Albany
Douglas
Townsend
GEORGIA

Brunswick
3 **Jekyll Island**

Tallahassee
Valdosta
10
Jacksonville

75
St. Augustine

Apalachicola
Gainesville
95
FLORIDA

Ocala
Daytona Beach

Orlando
Titusville

19
Kissimmee
2 **Cocoa Beach**

Tampa
95
Vero Beach
Fort Pierce

St. Petersburg
Sarasota

Fort Myers
West Palm Beach

Naples
Fort Lauderdale
1 **Miami**
Miami Beach
Coral Gables

Atlantic Ocean

Gulf of Mexico

BAHAMAS
Nassau

0   100 mi
0   100 km

1
Key West

Georgia's Jekyll Island is a peaceful place filled with nature excursions.

on your route to Tybee, so don't miss the chance to stop. Stroll River Street, gawk at the unnamed fountain in **Forsyth Park** (✉ *2 W. Gaston St.* ☎ *912/351–3841* ⊕ *www.savannahga.gov*), and ogle the majestic mansions surrounding many of the 22 square parks found within a single square mile of downtown Savannah.

Eat & Drink: Mrs. Wilkes Dining Room (✉ *107 W. Jones St.* ⊕ *www.mrswilkes. com*) remains the top table in Savannah, but the no-reservations system makes it difficult for day-trippers to score a seat. Feel free to stop by and check—miracles can happen—but you're guaranteed a great meal at **Sisters of the New South** (✉ *2605 Skidaway Rd.* ☎ *912/335–2761* ⊕ *www.thesistersofthenewsouth.com*), a "meat and three" eatery with traditional sides like collard greens, red rice, and green beans. The peach cobbler is famous here, and sweet tea is a must.

Detour: Make a pit stop at **Bonaventure Cemetery** (✉ *330 Bonaventure Rd., Thunderbolt, GA* ☎ *912/651–6843* ⊕ *www. savannahga.gov*) on your way out of Savannah. This waterfront cemetery isn't just the titular "garden" of *Midnight in the Garden of Good and Evil* and the location of one of the book's most important scenes, it's also a gorgeous collection of stunning monuments and swaying Spanish moss hanging from towering oaks.

TYBEE ISLAND

Do: Just beyond Savannah, Tybee is a barrier island with both ocean and river beaches, the most popular of which is South Beach with its soft-sand shoreline. Beach bums will prefer the ocean beaches while fishing fans should head to the river beaches, while the historic 18th-century lighthouse and **Tybee Island Marine Science Center** (✉ *37 Meddin Dr.* ☎ *912/786–5917* ⊕ *www.tybeemarinescience.org*) should appeal to all.

Eat & Drink: Embrace the island vibe with a meal at the **Crab Shack** (✉ *40 Estill Hammock Rd.* ☎ *912/786–9857* ⊕ *www. thecrabshack.com*). What started as a charter boat company and marina slowly expanded as the owners began cooking up the day's catch; it's now a waterfront restaurant serving fresh seafood daily.

Stay: If you loved the Crab Shack, consider staying at the owners' Airbnb, Purple Haze, within walking distance of the restaurant and also overlooking the water (the restaurant's website has a direct link to the listing). If you prefer a more traditional stay, try the **Admiral's Inn** (✉ *1501 Butler Ave.* ☎ *912/786–0700* ⊕ *www. admiralsinntybee.com*) for a three-star night with an outdoor pool.

Breakfast: There's a bit of a longer drive coming up, so treat yourself to a full meal at **Sunrise Breakfast** (✉ *1511 Butler Ave.* ☎ *912/786–7473* ⊕ *www.sunrisesavannah.com*), where the Hash Brown Deluxe is the star of the signature menu. Potatoes are piled with broccoli, mushrooms, onions, and tomatoes, and you can add all manner of meats or eggs for protein.

Day 4: Tybee Island, GA, to Myrtle Beach, SC

220 miles (4 hours, 30 minutes without traffic and stops)

Instead of staying on I–95 N for most of the trip north into South Carolina, stick to U.S. 17, which will take you through Charleston and its nearby collection of popular islands and beaches.

ALONG THE WAY

Town: Charleston itself would make an excellent stop, and if you're in a rush to make it to Myrtle Beach, by all means just take a half hour or so to wander around the city's cobblestone streets that ooze with southern charm. But if you have some time to spare, any of the city's outlaying islands make a fine detour, from golf-famous Kiawah Island to historic Sullivan's Island. But don't miss rural Edisto Island, where you'll find magnificent stands of age-old oaks festooned with Spanish moss, and side roads that lead to Gullah hamlets and

Extend Your Trip

From Miami: The Best of Southern Florida *(Ch. 7)*

From Cocoa Beach: The Best of Northern and Central Florida *(Ch. 7)*

From Myrtle Beach or the Outer Banks: The Best of the Carolinas *(Ch. 7)*

From Rehoboth Beach: The Best of Long Island and the Jersey Shore *(Ch. 8)*

aging wooden churches. A driving tour around **Botany Bay Heritage Preserve** (✉ *1066 Botany Bay Rd.* ☎ *843/869–2713* ⊕ *www.dnr.sc.gov*) passes through impoundments and maritime forest and past saltwater marsh, making it one of the most diverse and car-accessible coastal habitats in the Southeast.

Eat & Drink: Once a 1940s-era filling station (the pumps are still outside), **Whaley's** (✉ *2801 Myrtle St.* ☎ *843/869–2161* ⊕ *www.whaleyseb.com*) on Edisto Island has been converted into a fun and eclectic bar and restaurant. The menu ranges from bar food like Buffalo wings and burgers to local shrimp, crab cakes, and pan-seared mahimahi.

MYRTLE BEACH

Do: Myrtle Beach is the crown jewel of the 60 miles of beach that make up South Carolina's Grand Strand. Light brown sands, gentle waves, and mild water temps make the beach itself enjoyable for all ages, but there's plenty of off-sand fun to be had, too. The main action is found at **Broadway at the Beach** (✉ *1325 Celebrity Cir.* ☎ *843/444–3200* ⊕ *www. broadwayatthebeach.com*), which is actually on Lake Broadway, where you could spend anywhere from an hour to a day touring attractions, catching shows, and riding amusements like the SkyWheel, one of the tallest Ferris wheels in the nation.

Eat & Drink: If you packed a dressy outfit and are in the mood for steak and lobster, **The Library** (✉ *6613 N. Kings Hwy.* ☎ *843/448–4527* ⊕ *www.thelibraryrestaurantsc.com*) should be your dinner reservation of choice in Myrtle Beach. For a more casual place, choose **Hook & Barrel** (✉ *8014 N. Kings Hwy. B* ☎ *843/839–5888* ⊕ *www.hookandbarrelrestaurant.com*) for honey-glazed salmon, crab cakes, or filet mignon. Continue the tiki trend of this trip with after-dinner drinks at **8th Avenue Tiki Bar** (✉ *708 N. Ocean Blvd.* ☎ *843/712–2340* ⊕ *www.8thavetikibar.net*) on the boardwalk.

Stay: Aside from the view, there's a very practical reason to spring for a beachfront property in Myrtle Beach: there aren't a lot of public restrooms along the water, so you'll want easy access to your hotel if you'll be spending all day on the sand (especially if you're enjoying cocktails or beer). **Island Vista Resort** (✉ *6000 N. Ocean Blvd.* ☎ *843/449–6406* ⊕ *www.islandvista.com*) is an affordable option that also comes with its own indoor and outdoor pools and plenty of other creature comforts.

Breakfast: It's a long day ahead, so you may want to grab breakfast to go and make an early start. Start with an espresso from **Boardwalk Coffeehouse** (✉ *104 9th Ave. N* ☎ *843/839–1230* ⊕ *www.boardwalkcoffeehouse.com*) and have a breakfast sandwich on a croissant along with a frappé for the road.

Day 5: Myrtle Beach, SC, to Kill Devil Hills, NC

310 miles (5 hours, 30 minutes without traffic and stops)

If you've fallen in love with I–95 N and want to continue on the same path, you could take this to U.S.-64 E, but there's a slightly shorter route today. You'll save about 15 minutes if you take SC-31 N instead, hugging the coast a bit tighter.

ALONG THE WAY

Roadside Attraction: Perhaps the weirdest and wildest pit stop on the East Coast, South of the Border (⊕ *www.sobpedro.com*) is a wonderland of towering, colorful figures (animal and human), neon lights, souvenir shopping, and roadside dining. You'll need to take the I–95 N route (or an alternative path up U.S.-501 N from Myrtle Beach) to hit this one, found immediately before the North Carolina border, but you won't regret it.

Town: Roughly 80 miles into your drive, take a break in Wilmington, North Carolina. The 230-block Historic District is packed with charming architecture that oozes southern grace as you say goodbye to the true South with today's drive. Don't miss the sprawling **Airlie Gardens** (✉ *300 Airlie Rd.* ☎ *910/798–7700* ⊕ *www.airliegardens.org*) for a romantic location that has attracted a slew of film and television crews.

Eat & Drink: Grab some pub fare at **Fork 'N' Cork** (✉ *122 Market St.* ☎ *910/228–5247* ⊕ *www.theforkncork.com*) in Wilmington. Start with fried pickles or crispy Brussels sprouts before choosing from a dozen burgers or sandwiches. If you're aiming to have seafood with every meal on this beach itinerary, give the Rattlesnake Bites a try; they're shrimp-and-corn-stuffed, deep fried jalapeños served with habanero jelly.

Nature: Croatan National Forest

(☎ 252/638–5628 ⊕ www.fs.usda.gov) is the only coastal forest in the East, and you'll find it around the halfway point between Myrtle Beach and the Outer Banks, ideally situated for a brief stretch break.

KILL DEVIL HILLS

Do: The Outer Banks refers to 175 miles of barrier islands off the coast of North Carolina, and the numerous beaches have varying appeals. Kitty Hawk is one of the best for general interest, from surfing or lying on the beach to nature walks on nearby trails; there's something for everyone here. But Kill Devil Hills is a solid choice with great surfing, restaurants, and hotels. And don't miss nearby Roanoke Island, site of the first English settlement in 1585, all of whose inhabitants mysteriously vanished without a trace.

Eat & Drink: If you're ready for oysters, it's off to **Awful Arthur's** (⊠ 2106 N. Virginia Dare Trail ☎ 252/441–5955 ⊕ www. awfularthursobx.com) you go. This Kill Devil Hills institution was the first oyster bar in Outer Banks and is still riding high in popularity. The ocean-view lounge, a surprisingly rare occurrence in the Outer Banks, certainly adds to the appeal.

Stay: The **Sea Ranch Resort** (⊠ 1731 N. Virginia Dare Trail ☎ 252/441–7126 ⊕ www.searanchresort.com) is a no-fuss stay in Kill Devil Hills with clean, spacious rooms, many of which include ocean views and private balconies. The Beachside Bistro with its oceanfront deck is great for evening drinks, too.

Breakfast: Miller's Seafood & Steakhouse (⊠ 1520 S. Virginia Dare Trail ☎ 252/441–7674 ⊕ www.millersseafood.com) may not sound like a breakfast bonanza, but it's the top choice in Kill Devil Hills for a filling breakfast, with plenty of lighter options, too.

Day 6: Kill Devil Hills, NC, to Virginia Beach, VA

90 miles (1 hour, 40 minutes without traffic and stops)

Breaking from tradition, there's no I–95 N option today. Take NC-168 N to I–264 E and stop when you reach the coast.

ALONG THE WAY

Town: Between canals, rivers, and lakes, Chesapeake, Virginia, has more waterways than you can see in a day, but that shouldn't stop you from dropping by to check a few out. You'll also find the lush **Chesapeake Arboretum** (⊠ 624 Oak Grove Rd. ☎ 757/382–6411 ⊕ www. cityofchesapeake.net), a planetarium, a couple of farms, and the **Great Dismal Swamp** (⊠ 3120 Desert Rd., Suffolk, VA ☎ 757/986–3705 ⊕ www.fws.gov).

Eat & Drink: Have lunch at **Baker's Crust Artisan Kitchen** (⊠ 1244 Greenbrier Pkwy. ☎ 757/547–2787 ⊕ www.bakerscrust. com) in Chesapeake. Start with tuna and avocado poke or mozzarella arancini then dive into the sandwich menu, Neapolitan pizzas, farm fresh salads, street tacos, or burgers. If that's not enough, there's a specialty entrée selection, too. More than a dozen signature drinks round out the craft cocktail menu (try the Bourbon Brûlée).

VIRGINIA BEACH

Do: Wide beaches along the boardwalk are the top feature of Virginia Beach, but there's a thriving locavore scene fed by numerous area farms, plenty of public art, an 18th-century lighthouse, and the fascinating Edgar Cayce's Association for Research and Enlightenment. **First Landing State Park** (⊠ 2500 Shore Dr. ☎ 757/412–2300 ⊕ www.dcr.virginia. gov), Virginia's most visited, is the site of the first landing by English colonists in 1607, before they moved on to Jamestown.

Eat & Drink: Dine at **Heirloom** (✉ *2484 N. Landing Rd.* ☎ *757/689–3339* ⊕ *www. heirloomvb.com*) for an upscale taste of the city's fresh bounty. Start with a Virginia apple and baby kale salad with she crab soup, then move on to the steamer pot of crab, shrimp, clams, and sausage or southern fried chicken with pimento mac-and-cheese and local collards.

Stay: If you're treating yourself, check in to **The Cavalier** (✉ *4200 Atlantic Ave.* ☎ *757/425–8555* ⊕ *www.marriott.com*) and surround yourself with artful luxury at this Autograph Collection property. If you'd rather save a bit, **The Founders Inn and Spa** (✉ *5641 Indian River Rd.* ☎ *757/424–5511* ⊕ *www.hilton.com*) offers fuss-free accommodations within a brick manor accented by formal English gardens.

Breakfast: Stop by **The Bee & The Biscuit** (✉ *1785 Princess Anne Rd.* ☎ *757/800–5959* ⊕ *www.beebiscuit.com*) for a memorable breakfast. Whether you opt for the breakfast tostada on blue corn tortilla, crumbled-bacon pancakes, or Bay crab Benedict, be sure to add an order of biscuits with honey butter and jam to your selection.

Day 7: Virginia Beach, VA, to Ocean City, MD

245 miles (1 hour, 40 minutes without traffic and stops)

Cross the Chesapeake Bay via U.S. 13 N to Old Ocean City Boulevard for a straightforward path directly into Ocean City, Maryland.

ALONG THE WAY

Town: Make a quick stop in Cape Charles just beyond the Chesapeake Bay Bridge-Tunnel. Cape Charles Beach offers the opportunity to satisfy yesteryear seaside nostalgia with ice cream on the boardwalk, a quiet pier, and spotting fish along the coast.

Eat & Drink: While in Cape Charles, peek into **Coastal Baking Co.** (✉ *555 Mason Ave., Cape Charles, VA* ☎ *757/331–2482* ⊕ *www.coastalbakingco.com*) for flaky turnovers, mini Bundt cakes, and seasonal cupcakes. If you're still hungry despite your big breakfast, there are more serious menu items here, but it's more fun to indulge in a few baked goods.

Nature: The **Chincoteague National Wildlife Refuge** (✉ *8231 Beach Rd.* ☎ *757/336–6122* ⊕ *www.fws.gov*), located on the Virginia part of Assateague Island, features more than 14,000 acres of beach, dunes, marsh, and maritime forest, all home to an incredible amount of wildlife. The refuge is most famous for its resident wild ponies, which have lived on the island for hundreds of years. You can see the ponies by hiking the 7½-mile Service Road or taking a tour bus or scenic boat tour.

OCEAN CITY

Do: Ocean City, Maryland, sits on a strip of land between the Atlantic Ocean and Isle of Wight Bay, offering tons of beach and water sport opportunities. Most visitors enjoy the lively boardwalk, and Trimper's Rides of Ocean City has been a rite of passage for area vacationers for decades. If you're an avid fisherperson, you might want to take the chance to land a white marlin while you're here.

Eat & Drink: Ocean City's atmosphere is on the casual/party side, so embrace the grab-and-go culture with dinner at **OC Street Food** (✉ *11505 Coastal Hwy.* ☎ *443/664–6322* ⊕ *www.ocstreetfood-md.com*), offering an array of New York City street foods at the beach. Choose from kebabs, gyros, and pita platters, and don't forget the ice cream.

Stay: If you're looking for quieter nights, head toward **Condo Row** above 85th Street and rent a condo away from the hotels located in the much busier, party-forward southern end of Ocean City. If you do prefer a proper hotel, **Castle**

in the Sand Hotel (✉ *3701 Atlantic Ave.* ☎ *410/289–6846* ⊕ *www.castleinthe-sand.com*) offers reasonable beachfront rooms with standard amenities.

Breakfast: Soriano's Coffee Shop (✉ *306 S. Baltimore Ave.* ☎ *410/289–6656* ⊕ *www.sorianoscoffeeshop.com*) is your go-to morning stop before heading out of Ocean City. Cream chipped beef is the house specialty, but there are plenty of breakfast sandwiches and all the staples you'd expect from pancakes to omelets.

Day 8: Ocean City, MD, to Rehoboth Beach, DE

28 miles (50 minutes without traffic and stops)

Take MD-528 N, which becomes DE-1 N, as you travel up the scenic Delmarva Peninsula and through Delaware Seashore State Park. When you're ready to head home, the closest major airport is in Philadelphia, about two hours away.

ALONG THE WAY

Town: Make a stop in Fenwick Island to check out the **DiscoverSea Shipwreck Museum** (✉ *708 Coastal Hwy.* ☎ *302/448–0933* ⊕ *www.discoversea.com*). There you'll be able to explore a collection of artifacts (such as coins, weapons, and a "mermaid") that were recovered from shipwrecks that occurred in the mid-Atlantic region and from around the world.

Eat & Drink: At **Bluecoast Seafood Grill** (✉ *30904 Coastal Hwy.* ☎ *302/539–7111* ⊕ *www.bluecoastseafoodgrill.com*) in Bethany Beach, the seafood is fresh, the dishes are beautifully yet simply prepared, and the wine list has been expertly curated.

Nature: This stretch of Delaware coast is also home to canals, ponds, and creeks, as well as the Indian River Bay. Rent a kayak or a stand-up paddleboard and explore the bay on your own or with

an outfitter like **EcoBay Kayak & SUP** (✉ *30048 Cedar Neck Rd., Ocean View, DE* ☎ *302/841–2722* ⊕ *www.ecobaykayak.com*). You can also opt for a leisurely hike on the Prickly Pear Trail, an easy 3½-mile loop that offers views of pine trees, meadows, and the bay.

REHOBOTH BEACH

Do: Delaware's beach towns are perhaps some of the country's most underrated, offering no-frills and low-key fun among sparkling water, inviting beaches, and indisputably good vibes. Rehoboth Beach is one of the most popular, so be sure to spend some time on its relaxing sandy shores. Stroll the Rehoboth Beach Boardwalk, an old-fashioned boardwalk with shops, restaurants, and saltwater taffy shops. If you're lucky, you might be able to catch some live music at the **Rehoboth Beach Bandstand** (✉ *Rehoboth Ave.* ☎ *302/644–2288* ⊕ *www.rehoboth-bandstand.com*).

Eat & Drink: Check out **La Fable** (✉ *26 Baltimore Ave.* ☎ *302/227–8510* ⊕ *www.bonjourfable.com*), a traditional French-style bistro in the heart of downtown Rehoboth. The menu features classic French dishes such as escargot, duck confit, and boeuf bourguignon, all served in an intimate, romantic environment. Afterward, shift back into beach-town mode with a couple of after-dinner drinks at **Rehoboth Ale House** (✉ *15 Wilmington Ave.* ☎ *302/278–7433* ⊕ *www.rehobothalehouse.com*), where you'll find an impressive collection of rotating craft beers as well as a menu of delicious craft cocktails.

Stay: The **Bellmoor Inn and Spa** (✉ *6 Christian St.* ☎ *302/227–5800* ⊕ *www.thebellmoor.com*) creates a luxurious experience for its guests. Amenities include a spa, pool, a shuttle that takes guests directly to the beach, and beach chair and umbrella rentals. For classic beach-town charm outfitted with contemporary tastes in mind, try the **Ocean Glass Inn** (✉ *37299 Rehoboth Ave.* ☎ *302/227–2844* ⊕ *www.oceanglassinn.com*).

Breakfast: Start your last morning on a healthy note with breakfast at **Greenman Juice Bar & Bistro** (✉ *12 Wilmington Ave.* ☎ *302/227–4909* ⊕ *www.green-manjuicebar.com*), where you can enjoy the homemade quiche or coconut rice porridge with a fresh juice or smoothie on the cozy patio.

Along the Mississippi River

Written by Stratton Lawrence

On the west side of Yellowstone National Park, a small spring emerges in Montana. Across the country, the Allegheny River descends from the Pennsylvania mountains. And in Minnesota, at Lake Itasca, a river forms and heads south. Fed by a watershed spanning 31 states, the Mississippi River is the circulatory system of our nation, and exploring its route reveals a clear view of America. It is 2,320 miles from the Gulf of Mexico to Lake Itasca, where the Upper Mississippi River forms, laying claim as the river's official headwaters. This artery helps to define the borders of 10 states, and even of our nation, through historic moments like the Louisiana Purchase.

Today's Mississippi River is not the one that pioneers encountered. Levees line the majority of its banks, preventing Big Muddy from overflowing into the floodplain that once formed wetlands along much of the route. The river's transformation into a controlled canal for barges has changed its character, but it still shows glimpses of its might when it overflows—and in the river's northern reaches where natural floodplain forests still exist.

What's most impressive about a drive up the Big River is the culture that emerged along its banks, from Cajun cuisine in Louisiana to soul music in Memphis to Mark Twain's literary portraits of Americana in

Missouri. This road trip traces the mighty Mississippi from New Orleans (75 miles before the river spills into the Gulf of Mexico) to Minneapolis, where the river forms the heart of the city.

At a Glance

Start: New Orleans, LA

End: Minneapolis, MN

Miles Traveled: 1,400 miles

Suggested Duration: 7 days

States Visited: Illinois, Iowa, Louisiana, Minnesota, Missouri, Mississippi, Tennessee, Wisconsin

Key Sights: Delta Blues Museum; Gateway Arch; Graceland; Mark Twain's Boyhood Home; Mississippi National River and Recreation Area

Best Time to Go: In summer, you'll swelter through the early days of the trip, but a good sweat feels appropriate in the Mississippi Delta. As you head north, you'll reach weather divinity, and find that more restaurants and attractions are open and accessible than during the cold winter months.

Day 1: New Orleans, LA, to Natchez, MS

170 miles (3 hours without traffic and stops)

Take I–10 west to Baton Rouge, where you'll pick up U.S. 61 north to Natchez. U.S. 61 runs the length of the river and will be a constant companion on this trip.

ALONG THE WAY

Town: Before your trip starts, spend two or three days in the Big Easy. Eat Chicken Creole Captain at **Palm & Pine** (✉ *308 N. Rampart St.* ☎ *504/814–6200* ⊕ *www. palmandpinenola.com*). Discover the origins of the cocktail at **Sazerac House**

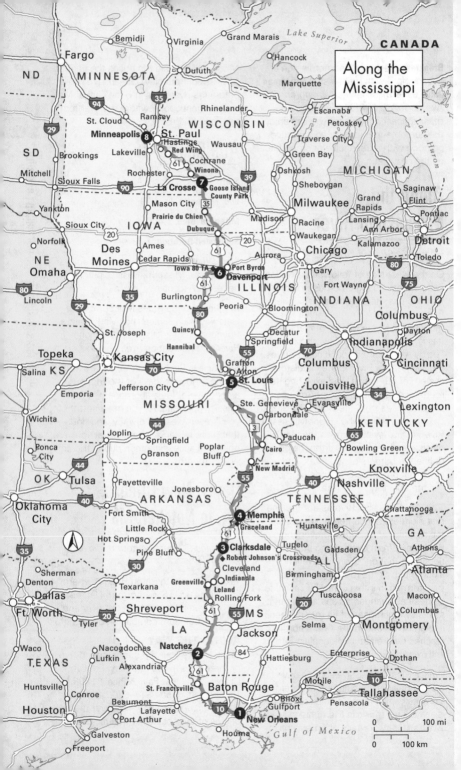

(✉ 101 Magazine St. ☎ 504/910–0100 ⊕ www.sazerachouse.com), and prep yourself for the trip by getting rowdy at the Rivershack Tavern (✉ 3449 River Rd. ☎ 504/834–4938 ⊕ www.rivershack-tavern.com). Then load up on coffee and beignets at **Café Du Monde** (✉ 800 Decatur St. ☎ 504/525–4544 ⊕ www.cafedumonde.com), and hit the road.

Eat & Drink: Halfway between Baton Rouge and the Mississippi state line, the **St. Francisville Inn** (✉ 5720 Commerce St. ☎ 225/635–6502 ⊕ www.stfrancisvilleinn.com) in St. Francisville drapes the southern hospitality on as heavy as the Spanish moss on the trees outside. The French Creole cuisine here is a memorable treat.

NATCHEZ

Do: The **Natchez National Historical Park** (✉ Melrose Montebello Pkwy. ☎ 601/446–5790 ⊕ www.nps.gov/natc) encompasses the city's waterfront district, including exhibits at Fort Rosalie, a strategic site for the French, British, and Spanish explorers who controlled the region through different eras. There are also well-maintained mansions and former plantations along the river, including the Melrose estate, a brick mansion whose surviving structures include a cabin where the plantation's enslaved people lived.

Eat & Drink: Watch boats ply the river while noshing on oysters Bienville at the **Magnolia Grill** (✉ 49 Silver St. ☎ 601/446–7670 ⊕ www.magnoliagrill.com), where the catfish is served chargrilled and spicy.

Stay: With views of the river from many of the rooms, **Hotel Vue** (✉ 130 John R Junkin Dr. ☎ 601/653–8888 ⊕ www.choicehotels.com) is a comfortable place to lay your head. Its star attraction is the Pilot House, a top-floor restaurant and cocktail bar with a glass wall overlooking the Mississippi; it hosts live music most evenings.

Essential Listening

Start your trip with Satchmo setting the mood. Let Louis Armstrong sing and play you to Baton Rouge, before pivoting to a modern-day horn man, Trombone Shorty. Once you head into the Mississippi Delta, aka blues country, add Robert Johnson's "Me and the Devil Blues" and B. B. King's "Everyday I Have the Blues" to the playlist. As you approach Memphis, put Elvis, Sam and Dave, Otis Redding, and Isaac Hayes in the rotation.

Breakfast: Get up early to hit the **Donut Shop** (✉ 501 John R. Junkin Dr. ☎ 601/442–2317) before they run out of the day's batch of hot glazed goodness, and grab a beef tamale to take with you on the road.

Day 2: Natchez, MS, to Clarksdale, MS

220 miles (4 hours without traffic and stops)

Take U.S. 61/U.S. 278 north all the way to Clarksdale, through the heart of the Mississippi Delta. In Rolling Fork, you have the option of shifting to MS-1 to more closely follow the river, visiting Greenville and Rosedale along the way.

ALONG THE WAY

Detour: Indianola, B. B. King's birthplace, is a 10-minute detour that's worth the stop to tour the **B. B. King Museum** (✉ 400 2nd St. ☎ 662/887–9539 ⊕ www.bbkingmuseum.org) and pay homage at his grave. Across the street, you can load up on catfish, shrimp, and the Earlberta burger at **The Blue Biscuit** (✉ 501–503 2nd St. ☎ 662/645–0258) if you're hungry.

Photo Op: Stop in Leland, Jim Henson's boyhood home, to tour the **Birthplace of Kermit the Frog Museum** (✉ *415 S. Deer Creek Dr. E* ☎ *662/686–7383* ⊕ *www.birthplaceofthefrog.com*) and pose with everyone's favorite friendly green amphibian.

Eat & Drink: Just north of Cleveland, **Airport Grocery** (✉ *3608 U.S. 61* ☎ *662/843–4817* ⊕ *www.airportgrocerycleveland.com*) is a laid-back blues joint known for pork barbecue, chili cheese tamales, and catfish hoagies. Or if you find yourself in Greenville after 5 pm, the original **Doe's Eat Place** (✉ *502 Nelson St.* ☎ *662/334–3315* ⊕ *www.doeseatplace.com*) is the finest place in the Delta for a hearty steak. Then stick around to catch a show at the **Walnut Street Blues Bar** (✉ *128 S. Walnut St.* ☎ *662/378–2254* ⊕ *www.highway61blues.com*), a staple along the Mississippi Blues Trail.

CLARKSDALE

Do: Start by taking the Clarksdale Walk of Fame self-guided tour, where the many stars that called this small town home are memorialized, including Sam Cooke, Son House, and Tennessee Williams. After immersing yourself in Robert Johnson and Muddy Waters at the **Delta Blues Museum** (✉ *1 Blues Alley* ☎ *662/627–6820* ⊕ *www.deltabluesmuseum.org*), head next door to the **Ground Zero Blues Club** (✉ *387 Delta Ave.* ☎ *662/621–9009* ⊕ *www.groundzerobluesclub.com*), a happening blues joint that's co-owned by Morgan Freeman.

Eat & Drink: The menu at **Hooker Grocer & Eatery** (✉ *316 John Lee Hooker La.* ☎ *662/624–7038* ⊕ *www.hookergrocer.com*) is sophisticated southern, with international flair (think gumbo meets chicken karaage), but the blues vibe is pure Delta, with live music on indoor and outdoor stages.

Stay: Travelers Hotel (✉ *212 3rd St.* ☎ *662/483–0693* ⊕ *www.stayattravelers.com*) has come a long way since it housed itinerant railroad workers a century ago—today, it's a boutique space with modern, Instagram-worthy furnishings and a lobby bar that serves as a community hub.

Breakfast: Meraki Roasting Company (✉ *282 Sunflower Ave.* ☎ *662/351–2233* ⊕ *www.merakiroasting.com*) is more than a coffee shop—it's an in-house mentorship program for young locals to build entrepreneurial experience through a 16-week employment program. It's also home to Big River Bagels (order a smear of the honey vanilla cream cheese).

Day 3: Clarksdale, MS, to Memphis, TN

75 miles (1 hour, 30 minutes without traffic and stops)

It's a short drive up U.S. 61 today, leaving plenty of time to explore Memphis.

ALONG THE WAY

Photo Op: Before leaving Clarksdale, stop by the old intersection of Highways 61 and 49, where a three-guitar sculpture marks the place where blues legend Robert Johnson allegedly sold his soul to the devil to gain his guitar-playing abilities.

Detour: Before cruising into downtown Memphis, spend a few hours south of town at **Graceland** (✉ *Elvis Presley Blvd.* ☎ *901/332–3322* ⊕ *www.graceland.com*). If you're not an Elvis fan, you will be after touring the hip-shaking legend's mansion, airplane, and gardens while tracing his remarkable career.

Eat & Drink: After your quick drive, head straight for **Sunrise Memphis** (✉ *670 Jefferson Ave.* ☎ *901/552–3168* ⊕ *www.sunrise901.com*) for hearty sandwiches like the Hen House, or the Crunchy Tiger Hidden Salad.

MEMPHIS

Do: Tour the **Stax Museum of American Soul Music** (⊠ *926 E. McLemore Ave.* ☎ *901/261–6338* ⊕ *www.staxmuseum. com*), where you'll be floored by how many soul music hits emerged from the studio known as Stax Records, from Booker T. & the MGs to Otis Redding to the Staples Singers. The piece de resistance is Isaac Hayes's Cadillac Eldorado with fur carpeting and 24-carat-gold trim. Leave time to tour **Mud Island River Park** (☎ *901/312–9190* ⊕ *www.memphisriverparks.org*), where a scale model of the lower Mississippi stretches over 2,000 feet.

Eat & Drink: The barbecue scene in Memphis is legendary, and **Charlie Vergos' Rendezvous** (⊠ *52 S. 2nd St.* ☎ *901/523–2746* ⊕ *www.hogsfly.com*) is a multilevel temple to smoked pork. Order a rack of ribs and ask for a table in the subterranean basement for an experience that feels like slipping 70 years back in time. Or for a taste of Memphis' farm-to-table scene, visit **Sweet Grass** (⊠ *937 Cooper St.* ☎ *901/278–0278* ⊕ *www.sweetgrassmemphis.com*), where the loaded Dirty Pig Fries aren't the healthiest option but are always worth the order.

Stay: Prepare for the most memorable hotel of your trip—**The Peabody Memphis** (⊠ *118 S. 2nd St.* ☎ *901/529–4000* ⊕ *www.peabodymemphis.com*) sparkles from top (where the resident ducks live in their rooftop Royal Duck Palace) to the bottom (where the magnificent lobby features a fountain that said ducks swim in each day). Arrive in time to sip a cocktail as the ducks march to the elevator at 5 pm. Rooms are spacious, with stately furniture and details.

Breakfast: Inside the Peabody, the **Capriccio Grill's** (⊠ *149 Union Ave.* ☎ *901/529–4199* ⊕ *www.peabodymemphis.com*) Italianate art and decor feel like stepping into Old Europe, and thoughtful breakfast entrées like almond toast and an Elvis Smoothie (peanut butter yogurt and bananas served with banana nut bread) will fuel the drive ahead.

Day 4: Memphis, TN, to St. Louis, MO

290 miles (4 hours, 30 minutes without traffic and stops)

Today's drive leaves the Delta behind as you head into the Mississippi River Valley. I–55 N runs directly to St. Louis, although you have plenty of options for detours and stops to experience the river along the way.

ALONG THE WAY

Town: Just minutes off I–55, New Madrid is a charming Missouri town situated along a horseshoe bend in the river. It's best known as the site of a major fault that led to massive earthquakes in 1811. Take the five-minute walk from Riverside Park to an observation deck with terrific views of the river. Enjoy local art and photography at the **River Walk Gallery** (⊠ *711 Water St.* ☎ *573/748–4060* ⊕ *www. new-madrid.mo.us*), set in the town's oldest home, and tour the 19th-century mansion at the **Hunter-Dawson State Historic Site** (⊠ *312 Dawson Rd.* ☎ *573/748–5340* ⊕ *www.mostateparks.com*).

Detour: The southernmost point in Illinois, Cairo is a town that's well past its prime, but it's a fascinating place to visit, both historically and geographically. The flood-prone city sits on a peninsula at the confluence of the Ohio and Mississippi rivers. At **Fort Defiance Park** (☎ *618/734–4127* ⊕ *www.stateparks.com*), you can see where the rivers and the state lines of Illinois, Missouri, and Kentucky all come together. If time allows, continue south to **Columbus Belmont State Park** (⊠ *350 Park Rd.* ☎ *270/677–2327* ⊕ *www.parks.ky.gov*), an important Civil War site along a tranquil stretch of the river.

The Gateway Arch in St. Louis stands proud over the Mississippi River.

Eat & Drink: Crown Valley (✉ 23589 State Rte. WW ☎ 573/756–9463 ⊕ www.crownvalleywinery.com) in Ste. Genevieve, MO, pulls triple duty as a winery, brewery, and distillery. Whatever your libation of choice, its views of the Ozarks' rolling hills and a regular live-music schedule make it an attractive pit stop.

ST. LOUIS

Do: After taking in the view from 630 feet at **Gateway Arch National Park** (✉ 11 N. 4th St. ☎ 314/655–1600 ⊕ www.nps.gov/jeff), spend the afternoon at **City Museum** (✉ 750 N. 16th St. ☎ 314/231–2489 ⊕ www.citymuseum.org), an all-ages playground that includes an endless array of fun things to climb over and through, from a 10-story spiral staircase slide to a series of caves to the MonstroCity, an outdoor complex of cages and stairs that's capped by an airplane.

Eat & Drink: St. Louis has several foods unique to the city: slingers (eggs, a beef patty, and hash browns, covered with chili), toasted ravioli, and St. Louis–style pizza (thin crust with gooey cheese).

Grab a classic pie from **Pizza-A-Go-Go** (✉ 6703 Scanlan Ave. ☎ 314/781–1234 ⊕ pizzaagogostl.wixsite.com/pizza-gogostl), breaded and fried ravioli from **Mama Toscano's** (✉ 2201 Macklind Ave. ☎ 314/776–2926 ⊕ www.mamatoscano.com), and a late-night slinger from **City Diner** (✉ 3139 S. Grand Blvd. ☎ 314/772–6100 ⊕ www.citydinerstl.com).

Stay: Union Station is an architectural landmark that's now home to the St. Louis Aquarium, several restaurants, and the modern, well-appointed **Union Station Hotel** (✉ 1820 Market St. ☎ 314/231–1234 ⊕ www.hilton.com). Check in by 5 pm to see the 3-D light show on the vaulted ceiling in the Grand Hall.

Breakfast: Egg (✉ 3100 Locust St. ☎ 314/899–0036 ⊕ www.eggstl.com) has two locations where you can score their delicious hashes (meat, veggies, and eggs over potatoes), chakchouka, and breakfast tacos. On weekends, be sure to make a reservation.

Day 5: St. Louis, MO, to Davenport, IA

280 miles (4 hours, 30 minutes without traffic and stops)

Leave St. Louis on I-64 W before taking U.S. 61 to Hannibal. After taking some time to explore, cross the river to reach I-172, passing through Carthage and a brief stretch on U.S. 136 before taking U.S. 67 north to Davenport.

ALONG THE WAY

Eat & Drink: If you're up for the scenic route, take IL-100 from St. Louis along the east bank of the river, and stop for lunch at **Grafton Oyster Bar** (✉ *215 Water St.* ☎ *618/786–3000* ⊕ *www. graftonoysterbar.com*) in Grafton, Illinois, a floating restaurant that takes cues from New Orleans. The signature appetizer is a savory shrimp and alligator sausage cheesecake.

Town: Hannibal is as quaint and purely American as one can imagine. Visit **Mark Twain's boyhood home** (✉ *120 N. Main St.* ☎ *573/221–9010* ⊕ *www.marktwainmuseum.org*), cruise the river on a paddleboat, and see the statue of Huck Finn and Tom Sawyer. Finally, climb the **Mark Twain Memorial Lighthouse** (✉ *E. Rock St.* ☎ *573/221–0154* ⊕ *www.hannibalparks. org*) for a sweeping view of the river and town.

Roadside Attraction: Along the river in Quincy, IL, sits **Villa Kathrine** (✉ *532 Gardner Expy.* ☎ *217/224–3688* ⊕ *www. quincyparkdistrict.com*), an impressive but odd late-19th-century mansion built by an eccentric millionaire who drew inspiration from his travels to Morocco. The home now serves as the tourist information center for Quincy.

DAVENPORT

Do: Take a walk through the **Vander Veer Botanical Park** (✉ *215 W. Central Park Ave.* ☎ *563/326–7818* ⊕ *www.*

cityofdavenportiowa.com), which includes a grand walkway lined with trees and a conservatory with seasonal blooms. In the evening, catch a concert or theatrical performance at the historic **Adler Theatre** (✉ *136 E. 3rd St.* ☎ *563/326–8500* ⊕ *www.adlertheatre. com*) before walking the Davenport Skybridge after dark, when it lights up with multicolored LEDs.

Eat & Drink: Front Street Brewery (✉ *421 W. River Dr.* ☎ *563/324–4014* ⊕ *www. frontstreetbrew.com*) has midwestern craft beer clout, brewing an array of porters, pales, and light ales since opening in 1992. Their kitchen serves upscale pub grub, and the taproom lets you sip a pint in view of the river.

Stay: Hotel Blackhawk (✉ *200 E. 3rd St.* ☎ *563/322–5000* ⊕ *www.marriott.com*) is a classy, modern hotel in a renovated historic building, with many rooms offering views of the river. There's an on-site old-timey barber shop, and a bowling alley on the bottom floor that's known for its martinis.

Breakfast: You can expect a little more creativity from the menu than its name might suggest at **The Diner** (✉ *421 W. River Dr.* ☎ *563/323–0895* ⊕ *www.thedinerqc.com*), where extensive breakfast options include Bonnie's Huggabunch, a deconstructed bacon cheeseburger with eggs, sandwiched between pancakes.

Day 6: Davenport, IA, to La Crosse, WI

190 miles (3 hours, 30 minutes without traffic and stops)

Your route today is due north on U.S. 61 to Dubuque, where you'll hop across the water to WI-35 to more closely follow the river. After passing Prairie du Chien, you'll enjoy a largely undeveloped 50 miles with constant river views.

ALONG THE WAY

Roadside Attraction: Just west of Davenport is the world's largest truck stop, **Iowa 80 TA** (✉ *755 W. Iowa 80 Rd.* ☎ *563/284–6961* ⊕ *www.iowa80truckstop.com*), with room for 900 trucks to park. In addition to everything you could ever need for a truck, there are plenty of T-shirts and gimmicky souvenirs.

Roadside Attraction: In Port Byron, Illinois, a 30-foot-tall statue of a man riding a vintage penny-farthing bicycle (dubbed *Will B. Rolling*) highlights a stroll or ride along the Great River Bike Trail.

Town: Set along scenic hills and bluffs overlooking the river, Dubuque is an excellent way station. Tour the **National Mississippi River Museum & Aquarium** (✉ *350 E. 3rd St.* ☎ *563/557–9545* ⊕ *www.rivermusem.com*), where the exhibits include fish native to the river and the National Rivers Hall of Fame. Then take the short ride on the **Fenelon Place Elevator** (✉ *491 W. 4th St.* ☎ *563/582–6496* ⊕ *www.felelonplaceelevator.com*), which takes you up a steep hill to the former mansion of a businessman who built the small railway to avoid the walk up and down.

Eat & Drink: Valley Fish & Cheese (✉ *304 S. Prairie St.* ☎ *608/326–4719* ⊕ *www.valleyfishpdc.com*) in Prairie du Chein prides itself on "good, quality oddball stuff." That might mean snapping turtle jerky or a delicious filet of hickory-smoked perch. Owner "Mississippi Mike" Valley fishes on the Mississippi to harvest the smoked fish for sale in the rustic building that's adorned floor to ceiling with river effects and memorabilia.

Nature: The Upper Mississippi River National Wildlife and Fish Refuge stretches for much of the river on today's drive, allowing you to see more of the Mississippi as it looked before levees. Near the end of the drive, walk or bike the Shady Maple Interpretive Trail in Goose Island County Park to explore a healthy floodplain forest.

LA CROSSE

Do: Get your bearings in La Crosse by heading to the top of Grandad Bluff, a cliff that overlooks the city and the Mississippi nearly 600 feet below. Then cruise by the 54-foot-tall **World's Largest Six Pack** (✉ *3rd St. S*), adorned with La Crosse Lager labels. Finally, head to **Riverside Park** (✉ *100 State St.* ☎ *608/789–7533* ⊕ *www.explorelacrosse.com*) and the adjacent **Riverside International Friendship Gardens** (✉ *405 E. Veterans Memorial Dr.* ☎ *608/789–7533* ⊕ *www.riversidegardens.org*). Stroll through the gardens before a walk or jog along the river.

Eat & Drink: Treat yourself to fine dining with a view at **The Waterfront** (✉ *328 Front St. S* ☎ *608/782–5400* ⊕ *www.thewaterfrontlacrosse.com*), a seafood-oriented white-tablecloth spot known for steaks, impeccable service, and views of the Mississippi from the pleasant patio.

Stay: The most impressive residence in town—built for a lumber baron in the late-19th-century—is now the **Castle La Crosse Bed and Breakfast** (✉ *1419 Cass St.* ☎ *844/726–5808* ⊕ *www.castlecrossebnb.com*). This towering home with a stone façade feels legitimately regal, from the grand staircase to the spacious, luxuriously appointed rooms.

Breakfast: Grounded Patio Café (✉ *308 Main St.* ☎ *608/784–5282* ⊕ *www.groundedlax.com*) is a local favorite for coffee, smoothies, and egg sandwiches, including sandwich specialties like the Tuscan Sunrise with turkey, tomato, Swiss, and pesto on an English muffin.

Day 7: La Crosse, WI, to Minneapolis, MN

160 miles (3 hours without traffic and stops)

You've got options today, but skip the interstate on your last day of driving. Flank the river along U.S. 61 unless you're stopping for pizza at Suncrest Gardens. In Red Wing, cross the river to Hager City, before picking up U.S. 10 north of Hastings.

ALONG THE WAY

Town: Winona, Minnesota, is a pleasant riverfront college town where you can stretch your legs with a hike around the city's lake, go birding in the floodplain forest of Aghaming Park, or cool off with a swim in the river at Latsch Island Beach.

Eat & Drink: If you're traveling on a Friday or Saturday, plan on a late lunch at **Suncrest Gardens** (✉ S2257 Yaeger Valley Rd. ☎ 608/626–2122 ⊕ www. suncrestgardensfarm.com) in Cochrane, Wisconsin, where the "Pizza Farm" bakes pies in a wood-fired oven, made from ingredients grown right on the farm. Stick around for live music, or rent a room in the farmhouse on Airbnb and stay the night.

Nature: The National Park Service maintains and protects 72 miles of riverfront between Ramsey and Hastings, Minnesota. As you approach St. Paul, floodplain valleys curve into bluffs, offering one of the best opportunities for exploration via kayaking and canoeing on the river.

Roadside Attraction: If you head through Red Wing, the town's eponymous shoe company created **the world's largest boot** (✉ 315 Main St.), a 20-foot-tall size 638½ that required 80 cowhides to source its leather.

MINNEAPOLIS

Do: Brace yourself for city life by escaping into the green heart of Minneapolis at the 200-acre **Minnehaha Regional Park** (✉ 4801 S. Minnehaha Dr. ☎ 612/230–6400 ⊕ www.minneapolisparks.org), where a picture-perfect waterfall crashes 53 feet on its way downstream to the Mississippi. Then visit the **Minneapolis Sculpture Garden** (✉ 725 Vineland Pl. ☎ 612/375–7600 ⊕ www.walkerart.org) to pose with the city's famous *Spoonbridge and Cherry* sculpture. See one more example of oversized art by driving into the heart

of the city to see the **Bob Dylan mural** (✉ 1 S. 5th St.), depicting the musician at three stages in his career.

Eat & Drink: The dining scene in Minneapolis could fill weeks of exploration, but experience a taste from one of its most inventive kitchens at **Spoon and Stable** (✉ 211 N. 1st St. ☎ 612/224–9850 ⊕ www.spoonandstable.com), where the gorgeous presentations of entrées like trout and dry-aged duck breast insist that you photograph your food. In St. Paul, **The Lexington** (✉ 1096 Grand Ave. ☎ 651/289–4990 ⊕ www.thelexmn.com) is an upscale dining stalwart that's reinvented itself to remain relevant with dishes like walleye cakes and hot brussels sprouts (but they still serve their smoked chicken pot pie).

Stay: You don't have to stay at the Foshay Tower—home to the posh **W Minneapolis** (✉ 821 S. Marquette Ave. ☎ 612/215–3700 ⊕ www.marriott.com)—to take in the views of the city from the rooftop observation deck, but crash here and you may take frequent trips to the 30th floor. On weekends, the "living room" transforms into a hip club with live DJs.

Breakfast: Breakfast options in the Twin Cities are as wide and inviting as dinner, but **Nolo's** (✉ 515 N. Washington Ave. ☎ 612/800–6033 ⊕ www.noloskitchen. com) stands out by offering a signature breakfast fried rice, doused in yum yum sauce, and breakfast tacos that opt for crunch over soft tortillas.

The Great American Baseball Road Trip

Written by Mark Sullivan

For hardcore baseball fans, nothing beats a trip to some of the country's best ballparks, right? We've upped the ante a bit with this tour, throwing in some cool side trips, a couple of must-see museums, and a few bits of history about the game that you should know. You'll check out restaurants and pubs where you can discuss the big game with other sports fans, and stay at hotels that are walking distance to the stadiums (and sometimes look down onto the fields).

Just keep in mind that this itinerary doesn't factor in extra time if you really want to get to know the big cities like Chicago, Pittsburgh, and Boston. So feel free to add days in any of the baseball-loving cities along the way.

At a Glance

Start: Kansas City, MO

End: Boston, MA

Miles Traveled: 1,776 miles

Suggested Duration: 8 days

States Visited: Iowa, Illinois, Massachusetts, Michigan, Missouri, New York, Pennsylvania

Key Sights: Fenway Park; National Baseball Hall of Fame; Negro Leagues Baseball Museum; PNC Park; Wrigley Field

Best Time to Go: If you're actually planning to see a baseball game while on this trip (and you should), you'll need to make the trek during baseball season, from April through September.

Day 1: Kansas City, MO

Fly into Kansas City and spend your first day of the trip exploring the city's unique, baseball-loving history. In the morning, pick up your rental car to hit the road.

Do: In Kansas City's historic 18th and Vine District, once the heart of the city's African American community, you'll find the fantastic **Negro Leagues Baseball Museum** (✉ 1616 E. 18th St. ☎ 816/221–1920 ⊕ www.nlbm.com). The well-regarded museum chronicles the 100-year history of the historic league, formed in 1920

because players were banned from all-white teams. It has plenty about the hometown team, the Kansas City Monarchs, as well as Negro League greats like John Henry Lloyd, Satchel Paige, and Jackie Robinson (who played for the Monarchs).

In the same complex is the **American Jazz Museum** (✉ 1616 E. 18th St. ☎ 816/474–8463 ⊕ www.americanjazzmuseum.org), which has its own baseball connection; 18th and Vine was one of the only neighborhoods where Black players could find lodging, and they frequented the jazz clubs in the neighborhood. Of course, you'll also want to head to **Kauffman Stadium** (✉ 1 Royal Way ☎ 816/921–8000 ⊕ www.kansascity.royals.mlb.com) to catch a game with the Kansas City Royals. The crown-shaped scoreboard and a gushing outfield fountain make this park memorable. Don't miss the on-site Hall of Fame Museum.

Eat & Drink: There's absolutely no doubt about where you should eat here: **Arthur Bryant's BBQ** (✉ 1727 Brooklyn Ave. ☎ 816/231–1123 ⊕ www.arthurbryantsbbq.com), the place that perfected Kansas City-style barbecue. It's in the 18th and Vine District, so it's perfect timing after a trip to the Negro Leagues Baseball Museum. Just north of downtown, **Chappell's Restaurant and Sports Museum** (✉ 323 Armour Rd. ☎ 816/421–0002 ⊕ www.chappellskc.com) is jam-packed with baseball memorabilia.

Stay: Located with a handsome downtown landmark, the grand **Hotel Phillips** (✉ 106 W. 12th St. ☎ 816/221–7000 ⊕ www.hilton.com) is on the National Register of Historic Places. The art deco styling is impressive, especially in the ornate lobby. There's a tucked-away speakeasy for late-night imbibing.

Breakfast: Fortify yourself for the day's long drive with a stop at the upscale **Blue Bird Bistro** (✉ 1700 Summit St. ☎ 816/221–7559 ⊕ www.bluebirdbistro.

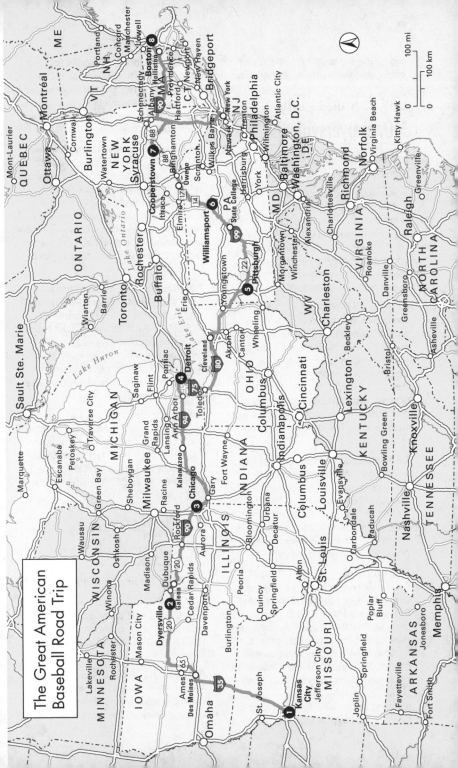

The Great American Baseball Road Trip

com), where everything is made with locally grown and organic ingredients.

Day 2: Kansas City, MO, to Dyersville, IA

367 miles (5 hours, 40 minutes without stops or traffic)

I–35 speeds you north from Kansas City to Des Moines. From there, continue north on I–35 or head diagonally through the farm towns on U.S. 65. Either way you'll connect to U.S. 20, which takes you to Dyersville, Iowa, which has a small-town vibe and a charming cluster of handsome brick buildings.

ALONG THE WAY

Town: Des Moines, Iowa, may not have a major league team, but locals couldn't care less. They cheer on the Iowa Cubs, a minor league team affiliated with the Chicago Cubs, at downtown's **Principal Park** (✉ *1 Line Dr.* ☎ *515/243–6111* ⊕ *www.iowacubs.com*). It has a great riverfront location and it's a perfect place to experience the local joy of a minor league stadium.

Eat & Drink: Not far from Principal Park, downtown's **Waterfront Seafood Market** (✉ *ClockTower Square, 2900 University Ave., West Des Moines, IA* ☎ *515/233–5106* ⊕ *www.waterfrontseafoodmarket. com*) expertly straddles the line between classic and contemporary with fresh fish prepared in a variety of ways.

DYERSVILLE

Do: The real reason the rural town of Dyersville is on the map is the **Field of Dreams Movie Site** (✉ *28995 Lansing Rd.* ☎ *563/875–8404* ⊕ *www.fieldofdreams-moviesite.com*), a baseball diamond built for one of the most famous baseball movies of all times, *Field of Dreams*. In the Kevin Costner film, an Iowa farmer plows up a cornfield to make a baseball diamond because he hears a mysterious voice whispering, "If you build it, he will

come," and indeed, long-dead baseball players appear to play a game in the movie. And in real life, the building of the field has also brought hordes of tourists: the site is now one of the most popular attractions in Iowa.

Eat & Drink: At **Textile Brewing Company** (✉ *146 2nd St. NE* ☎ *563/207–0357* ⊕ *www.textilebrews.com*), the name refers to the sewing factory that operated on the premises more than a century ago. Order a craft beer—the American-style lager named for the town is a favorite—and then pub grub like flatbreads topped with barbecued chicken or chorizo.

Stay: Baseball fans will want to book a night at the **Field of Dreams Farm House** (✉ *28995 Lansing Rd., Dyersville, IA* ☎ *563/875–8404* ⊕ *www.fieldofdreams-moviesite.com/home-rental*), the three-bedroom home that had a starring role in *Field of Dreams*. It sits near the famous field, so you can stroll over after the crowds have left.

Breakfast: A plaque on the wall here reads "Welcome Friends and Family," and you'll certainly feel right at home when you settle in for breakfast at the **Dyersville Family Restaurant** (✉ *226 1st Ave. E, Dyersville, IA* ☎ *563/875–0033*). It sits in Dyersville's historic downtown.

Day 3: Dyersville, IA, to Chicago, IL

204 miles (3 hours, 30 minutes without traffic and stops)

Take U.S. 20 east past Dubuque, Iowa, eventually reaching Rockford, Illinois. From there, I–90 takes you directly to Chicago.

ALONG THE WAY

Town: Galena, Illinois, is one of the most charming small towns between Dyersville and Chicago. The well-preserved

19th-century buildings hold more than 100 boutiques where you can shop to your heart's content. Pick up some baseball memorabilia at **Country Crafts and Sports** (✉ *113 S. Main St.* ☎ *815/776–0067* ⊕ *www.countycraftandsports. com*).

Eat & Drink: On Main Street in Galena is the intriguingly named **Fritz and Frites** (✉ *317 N. Main St.* ☎ *815/777–2004* ⊕ *www.fritzandfrites.com*), a storefront eatery that's a little bit German and a little bit French. It's basically Alsatian food, and it's all delicious. Look for the black-and-white awning.

CHICAGO

Do: There's plenty to do in the Windy City, but for this trip, head straight to **Wrigley Field** (✉ *1060 W. Addison St.* ☎ *773/404–2827* ⊕ *www.mlb.com/cubs/ ballpark*), one of baseball's best and most historic stadiums. It's easy to see why Chicago Cubs fans are so, well, fanatic about this beauty from 1914: the classic bright-red marquee over the entrance, the scoreboard that's still turned by hand, and the outfield wall covered with ivy. Tours of the park and dugouts are given from April to October.

And don't miss the **Chicago Sports Museum** (✉ *835 N. Michigan Ave.* ☎ *312/202–0500* ⊕ *www.chicagosportsmuseum. com*), where an interactive exhibit lets you learn to throw a curve ball with Cy Young Award–winner Steve Stone. There's also a massive trove of memorabilia related to the Cubs' historic 2016 World Series win, including manager Joe Maddon's famous "We Did Not Suck" T-shirt (for non–baseball fans: they hadn't won the World Series in a record 108 years).

Eat & Drink: A surprisingly sophisticated sports bar, **Harry Caray's 7th Inning Stretch** (✉ *Water Tower Place, 835 N. Michigan Ave.* ☎ *312/202–0500* ⊕ *www.harry-carays.com*) is named for the beloved announcer for the Chicago Cubs. Yes,

that's a photo of President Barack Obama on the wall; he was one of hundreds of celebrities who've come to pay tribute to Caray. For decades, the family-owned-and-operated **Slugger's World Class Sports Bar** (✉ *3540 N. Clark St.* ☎ *773/248–0055* ⊕ *www.sluggersbar. com*) has long been a favorite on game day. The location, around the corner from Wrigley Field, can't be beat.

Stay: Once a private men's club, the **Chicago Athletic Club** (✉ *12 S. Michigan Ave.* ☎ *312/940–3552* ⊕ *www.chicagoathletichotel.com*) has been transformed into one of the city's most opulent places to stay. It hasn't totally rid itself of the masculine vibe—for example, the Game Room bar is filled with billiard tables, a shuffleboard court, and a bocce bay. If that's not your scene, head to the solidly soundproofed Cherry Circle Room.

Breakfast: In Lincoln Park, the **Stray Hen Café** (✉ *2423 N. Clark St.* ☎ *773/697–8168* ⊕ *www.strayhencafe.com*) is a great choice for a bite as you head out of town. Don't miss one of the omelets, either the meat-filled Hunter or the veggie-stuffed Gatherer.

Day 4: Chicago, IL, to Detroit, MI

283 miles (4 hours without traffic and stops)

Believe it or not, I–94 takes you almost the entire way to Detroit. Along the way, you can catch glimpses of Lake Michigan for much of the trip.

ALONG THE WAY

Town: Kalamazoo, Michigan, is within easy driving distance for both Cubs and Tigers fans, but locals prefer to cheer on the Kalamazoo Growlers, who play in a summer collegiate baseball league. Their home is **Homer Stryker Field** (✉ *251 Mills St.* ☎ *269/337–8191* ⊕ *www. homer-stryker-field.lany.io*), where you'll be so close to the actions, you can hear the chatter in the dugout.

Eat & Drink: The name might make you think they'd give baseball fans the cold shoulder, but Kalamazoo's **Niskers Char-Grill & Slap Shot Hockey Bar** (✉ *5051 W. Main St.* ☎ *269/903–2427* ⊕ *www.niskerschargrill.com*) is for sports lovers of all stripes. No matter what the big game is that day, it's on the big-screen TVs at this friendly pub.

DETROIT

Do: Detroit might just be the most sports-loving city in America. It's the only downtown that's home to teams from all four major sports: baseball (the Tigers), football (the Lions), basketball (the Pistons), and hockey (the Red Wings). But the Tigers—which formed in 1901 and were charter members of the American League—hold a special place in the hearts of Detroiters. With a Ferris wheel with cars shaped like baseballs and a carousel with 30 hand-painted tigers, **Comerica Park** (✉ *2100 Woodward Ave.* ☎ *313/962–4000* ⊕ *www.detroit. tigers.mlb.com*) has a personality few other fields can match. The left-field concourse is dominated by statues of many of the greats—Al Kaline, Ty Cobb, and Hank Greenburg—who led the Tigers to winning seasons. The Beer Hall, with a 70-foot-long bar serving many microbrews, is the place to celebrate a victory or commiserate about a defeat.

Eat & Drink: After a Tigers home game, a free shuttle bus transports fans to **Tommy's Detroit Bar & Grill** (✉ *624 3rd Ave.* ☎ *313/965–2269* ⊕ *www.tommysdetroit.com*), where locals rave over the corned beef that's made right on the premises. Order it as a sandwich with Thousand Island dressing or as part of the belly-busting "Monstah" burger. In the evening, **Thomas Magee's Sporting House and Whiskey Bar** (✉ *1408 E. Fisher Service Dr.* ☎ *313/263–4342* ⊕ *www.thomasmagees.com*) is a lively tavern serving a long list of beers and a whiskey of the month.

Extend Your Trip

From Chicago: All the Great Lakes *(Ch. 6)*

From Detroit: Underrated Cities of the Midwest *(Ch. 6)*

From Pittsburgh: A Frank Lloyd Wright Tour *(Ch. 6)*

From Boston: Retracing the American Revolution *(Ch. 2)*; The Best of New England *(Ch. 8)*

Stay: Within walking distance of Comerica Park is the sultry **Siren** (✉ *1509 Broadway St.* ☎ *313/277–4736* ⊕ *www.thesirenhotel.com*), a boutique hotel located in the 1926 Wurlitzer Building. Splurge for the Penthouse, a lofty retreat with double-height windows looking out onto the ballpark.

Breakfast: Inside Downtown's Chrysler House, **Dime Store** (✉ *719 Griswold St.* ☎ *313/962–9106* ⊕ *www.eatdimestore. com*) is reputed to have the city's best brunch. Don't worry if you're not there during a weekend—the peach cobbler French toast and all the other favorites are also on the regular breakfast menu.

Day 5: Detroit, MI, to Pittsburgh, PA

286 miles (4 hours, 15 minutes without traffic and stops)

I–75 and I–80 take you around the southern shores of Lake Erie and past Cleveland. How can you be so close to a baseball-loving city like that and not stop by? It's just a quick detour on I–90. Then take I–77 south to return to I–80, which brings you to Pittsburgh.

Wrigley Field has been home to the Chicago Cubs since 1916.

ALONG THE WAY

Town: Cleveland's crowning glory is **Progressive Field** (✉ *2401 Ontario St.* ☎ *216/420–4487* ⊕ *www.cleveland.indians.mlb.com*), a neoclassical ballpark that is consistently ranked among the best in the country by baseball fans. The stadium has got its flaws, like way too many skyboxes, but the handsome facade and views of the skyline make it memorable.

Eat & Drink: One thing you should know about Cleveland is that there are two famous mustards in town: Authentic Stadium Mustard, favored at FirstEnergy Stadium (home to the NFL's Cleveland Browns), and Bertman's Original Ballpark Mustard, the winner at Progressive Field. Since this is a baseball trip, head to **Mabel's BBQ** (✉ *2050 E. 4th St.* ☎ *216/417–8823* ⊕ *www.mabelsbbq.com*), not far from Progressive Field, to sample Bertman's in any variety of burgers or sandwiches, either on its own or incorporated into a delectable barbecue sauce.

PITTSBURGH

Do: Known mostly for its Gilded Age history thanks to its role as an early-20th-century industrial city, Pittsburgh is also home to **PNC Park** (✉ *115 Federal St.* ☎ *412/321–2827* ⊕ *www.mlb.com/pirates/ballpark*), one of MLB's most intimate ballparks, with only two decks so you're never too far from the action. Unlike the beer-soaked scene at some stadiums, the home field of the Pittsburgh Pirates is somewhere to bring the whole family. Kids are even encouraged to run the bases after games on Sundays.

The Pirates used to play at Forbes Field, where second baseman Bill Mazeroski famously hit a home run over the left-center outfield wall in game seven of the 1960 World Series, defeating the Yankees. The stadium is long gone, but the **Forbes Field Wall** (✉ *Roberto Clemente Dr.*) still stands on the campus of the University of Pittsburgh. Have your photo taken in front of the wall, still marked with the number 406 to show how far Mazeroski sent the ball.

The **Western Pennsylvania Sports Museum** (✉ *1212 Smallman St.* ☎ *412/454–6000* ⊕ *www.heinzhistorycenter.org*) has lots of interesting exhibits, but nothing tops the one focusing on the history of the Negro Leagues. Pittsburgh was once home to both the Homestead Grays and the Pittsburgh Crawfords, making it the center of the circuit. Check out a glove belonging to pitcher Satchel Paige, whose legendary career with the Cleveland Indians came after decades of playing in the Negro Leagues for teams like the Chattanooga Black Lookouts.

Eat & Drink: A stone's throw from PNC Park, **Proper** (✉ *139 7th St.* ☎ *412/281–5700* ⊕ *www.properpittsburgh.com*) is a brick-oven pizzeria with some creative combinations like the Black & Gold, topped with cracked black pepper and slices of Yukon Gold potatoes. Across the river, **Redbeard's on Sixth** (✉ *144 6th St.* ☎ *412/261–2324* ⊕ *www.redbeardspgh. com*) is known for its mural of legendary ballplayers. The names of the burgers are all clever baseball references, too.

Stay: Talk about a room with a view: the sumptuous **Renaissance Pittsburgh Hotel** (✉ *107 6th St.* ☎ *412/562–1200* ⊕ *www. marriott.com*) gazes down on the mighty Allegheny River and the infield at PNC Park. This place is packed when there's a home game, so book well ahead.

Breakfast: Pamela's Diner (✉ *60 21st St.* ☎ *412/281–6366* ⊕ *www.pamelasdiner. com*) brags about serving the "breakfast of champions." Try the hearty "Pittsburgh Hash," fried with Lyonnaise potatoes, kielbasa, and sauerkraut and topped with Swiss cheese.

Day 6: Pittsburgh, PA, to Williamsport, PA

199 miles (3 hours, 15 minutes without traffic and stops)

Heading east from Pittsburgh, U.S. 22 takes you to I–99. Take this to State College, home of Penn State, then hop on I–80 for the rest of the trip to Williamsport.

ALONG THE WAY

Town: In the town of State College, a favorite activity every summer is catching a State College Spikes game, a collegiate summer baseball team that are part of the MLB Draft League. The team plays at **Medlar Field at Lubrano Park** (✉ *701 Porter Rd.* ☎ *814/272-1711* ⊕ *www.statecollege.spikes.milb.com*) on the campus of Pennsylvania State University.

Eat & Drink: Not far from Medlar Field is the **Sowers Harvest Café** (✉ *421 E. Beaver Ave.* ☎ *814/867–1007* ⊕ *www.sowersharvest.cafe*), a favorite with students. The emphasis at this bustling eatery is food that is good and good for you, so there are a lot of healthy sandwiches and salads.

WILLIAMSPORT

Do: If it's August, stop at **Howard J. Lamade Stadium** (✉ *100 Borderline Rd.* ☎ *570/326–1921* ⊕ *www.llbwsorg. com*) in Williamsport, home to the Little League World Series, where thousands of fresh-faced baseball players return year after year for their shot at the championship. The stadium, built in 1959, holds 40,000 fans, and even more stake out a spot on the hill rising up beyond the outfield. The rest of the year, check out the **World of Little League Museum** (✉ *525 U.S. 15, South Williamsport* ☎ *570/326–3607* ⊕ *www.littleleague. org/world-of-little-league*).

Eat & Drink: Grab a table on the umbrella-shaded patio beside **Barrel 135**

(✉ *Residence Inn by Marriot Williamsport, 135 W. 3rd St.* ☎ *570/322–7131* ⊕ *www.barrel135.com*), a chic eatery with a globetrotting menu (think Jamaican jerk chicken and Korean barbecue) and interesting beers on tap.

Stay: One of the region's most eye-catching lodgings is Williamsport's 19th-century **City Hall Grand** (✉ *454 Pine St.* ☎ *570/447–1010* ⊕ *www.cityhallgrandhotel.com*). Outside it's a little like a castle, but inside the loftlike spaces have a cool, contemporary vibe. The Little League Room, with some historic photos of the ballfield, is stunning.

Breakfast: On Southern Avenue, **The Buttery Biscuit** (✉ *715 W. Southern Ave.* ☎ *570/601–4558* ⊕ *www.facebook.com/thebutterybiscuit570*) is the kind of place that locals don't like to share with out-of-towners. This diner knows how to make a stick-to-your-ribs meal.

Day 7: Williamsport, PA, to Cooperstown, NY

199 miles (3 hours, 30 minutes without traffic and stops)

You're headed into the mountains today, so be prepared for lots of twists and turns on this route. Basically, you take U.S. 15 north of Williamsport, changing to PA-14 when you reach Trout Run. This road takes you through hamlets like Roaring Branch and Cedar Ledge on your way to Waverly, where you change to NY-17 on your way to the college town of Binghamton, New York. From here, It's I-88 and NY-28 to Cooperstown.

ALONG THE WAY

Eat & Drink: Facing the Susquehanna River, the waterfront community of Owego, New York, is a pleasant place to stop for lunch. Try the **Owego Kitchen** (✉ *13 Lake St.* ☎ *607/223–4209* ⊕ *www.theowegokitchen.com*), a funky little spot that attracts students from the local

university. The "Not Your Mom's Tuna Salad Sandwich" spices things up with Albacore Tuna and Jamaican relish.

COOPERSTOWN

Do: Considered a mecca for baseball lovers, Cooperstown is home to the **National Baseball Hall of Fame** (✉ *25 Main St.* ☎ *888/425–5633* ⊕ *www.baseballhall.org*). This don't-miss destination is jam-packed with memorabilia from the earliest days of baseball. One of the most interesting exhibits documents the challenges Black players faced before and after Jackie Robinson was recognized as the first Black player in the major leagues when he joined the Brooklyn Dodgers in 1947. (It also documents how a formerly enslaved man named Moses Fleetwood Walker actually broke the color line in 1884.) If you're in town in May, catch the annual Hall of Fame Classic at **Doubleday Field** (✉ *1 Doubleday Ct.* ☎ *607/547–2270* ⊕ *www.doubledayfield.com*), a handsome ballfield dating back to 1920.

Eat & Drink: Named for the man who supposedly invented baseball, **Doubleday Café** (✉ *93 Main St.* ☎ *607/547–5468* ⊕ *www.doubledaycafe.com*) occupies one of several beautiful brick buildings on Cooperstown's main street. If you're thinking it serves pub grub, you'd be right. But it also has seriously delicious dinner specials that make it seem like fine dining.

Stay: A seven-minute walk from Main Street, **The Otesaga Resort Hotel** (✉ *60 Lake St.* ☎ *607/547–9931* ⊕ *www.otesaga.com*) feels a world away. The back of this Colonial-style showplace faces Blackbird Bay, which you'll enjoy from one of the rockers on the wraparound porch. Many of the traditionally decorated rooms and suites share the same stellar views.

Breakfast: With its own coffee bean roaster in the corner, **Stagecoach Coffee** (✉ *31 Pioneer St.* ☎ *607/547–6229* ⊕ *www.stagecoachcoffee.com*) is an eye-opening experience. Bagels range from the "Usual" (cream cheese and tomato slices) to the "Unusual" (add avocado) to the "Ultimate" (add bacon).

Day 8: Cooperstown, NY, to Boston, MA

238 miles (3 hours, 45 minutes without traffic and stops)

From Cooperstown, NY-166 takes you east to Warnerville, where you'll switch to I–88. Around the town of Rotterdam, you'll hop on I–90, detour onto I–87 to stick to the outskirts of New York's capital city of Albany, then return to I–90 for the entire way to Boston. It's a surprisingly pretty drive, especially if you happen to be here in early October, the height of leaf-peeping season.

ALONG THE WAY

Detour: It doesn't seem right to have a baseball-focused trip and not mention the New York Yankees, one of the MLB's most historic teams that has seen some of the sport's most famous players as well as the team with the most World Series wins (27 since being established in 1901). The original House That Ruth Built was torn down and rebuilt in 2009, but the new **Yankee Stadium** (✉ *1 E. 161st St., The Bronx, NY* ☎ *718/293–4300* ⊕ *www.mlb.com/yankees/ballpark*) incorporated some of the designs of its predecessor and offers plenty of insight into Yankee history. The Bronx stadium is a two-hour-plus, often traffic-filled drive south of Albany, so it's best added as a full extra day side trip, but it's a can't-be-missed experience for any baseball fan.

Town: Several towns claim to be the inspiration for Ernest L. Thayer's 1888 ode to baseball, "Casey at the Bat," but Holliston, Massachusetts, has perhaps the most compelling case. Thayer grew up in nearby Worcester, and his family owned a wool mill less than a mile from the baseball

diamond in the Holliston neighborhood called Mudville, Take a selfie with the statue of "Mighty Casey" while you're here.

Eat & Drink: On Railroad Street in Mudville, **Casey's Publichouse** (✉ *81 Railroad St., Holliston, MA* ☎ *508/429–4888* ⊕ *www.caseyspublichouse.com*) memorializes the fictional ballplayer and his team, the Mudville Nine. The atmosphere is relaxed, and the menu is a step or two above your typical pub grub.

BOSTON

Do: Even if you're not a baseball fan, you haven't really visited Boston until you've visited **Fenway Park** (✉ *4 Jersey St.* ☎ *877/733–7699* ⊕ *www.mlb.com/redsox/ballpark*). The home of the Red Sox since 1912, baseball's best-loved ballpark has a stately entrance at street level that makes it feel like part of the neighborhood. Seats atop the "Green Monster," the 37-foot left field wall that's a goal for many batters, come at a premium, but it's hard to find a seat here that doesn't give you a great vantage point. Tours are a great way to get to know the place. They're usually given every hour on the hour, but they end four hours before the opening pitch on game day.

Eat & Drink: The founder of **Bennett's Sandwich Shop** (✉ *84 Peterborough St.* ☎ *857/239–9736* ⊕ *www.bennettssandwichshop.com*) had an unsuccessful tryout with the Red Sox when he was in high school, but that didn't stop him from offering the luscious lobster rolls to fans leaving Fenway Park. If you didn't score tickets to the game, head to **Bleacher Bar** (✉ *82A Landsdowne St.* ☎ *617/262–2424* ⊕ *www.bleacherbarboston.com*), with an unbeatable view of Fenway Park's third base. It's always packed, but that's part of the appeal.

Stay: A short stroll from Fenway Park, the upscale Hotel Commonwealth (✉ *500 Commonwealth Ave.* ☎ *617/933–5000* ⊕ *www.hotelcommonwealth.com*) has views of the scoreboard from some rooms. The accommodations are luxurious, and the service is top-notch. If you're looking for something a bit more reasonably priced, the rock-and-roll-theme **Verb Hotel** (✉ *1271 Boylston St.* ☎ *617/566–4500* ⊕ *www.theverbhotel.com*) is just as close to the ballpark. There's a pretty pool in the courtyard where a cool crowd gathers.

Breakfast: On fashion-forward Boylston Street, hip **Pavement Coffeehouse** (✉ *1334 Boylston St.* ☎ *857/263–7355* ⊕ *www.pavementcoffeehouse.com*) roasts its own beans, so you're guaranteed a primo cup of joe. The pastries are delectable, too.

Civil War Battlefields and History

Written by Barbara Noe Kennedy

As the bloodiest war in American history, the Civil War ravaged the United States from 1861 to 1865, pitting brother against brother, father against son, and neighbor against neighbor, all while fighting to end the chattel slavery that the country was built on from its inception. Today the bloody battlefields have been preserved in a mantle of peaceful escape, where one can—and must—learn from the past. From Gettysburg in the North all the way to Vicksburg in the South and back again, this epic drive explores the history and realities of the periods before, during, and after the Civil War. Along the way, an array of fascinating stops includes unsung towns, beloved dining establishments, and lesser-known sites that tell the fuller story of the war that will appeal to hardcore history buffs and high school students alike.

At a Glance

Start: Harrisburg, PA

End: Charleston, SC

Miles Traveled: 2,263 miles

Suggested Duration: 10 days

States Visited: Georgia, Maryland, Mississippi, North Carolina, Pennsylvania, South Carolina, Tennessee, Virginia, West Virginia

Key Sights: Appomattox Court House National Historical Park; Gettysburg National Battlefield; Harpers Ferry; McLeo̓d Plantation Historic Site; Vicksburg National Battlefield

Best Time to Go: This trip is possible year-round, though spring is always lovely, with blossoms adding ephemeral color to the now-peaceful battlefields. Travel can be tough in the north during winter months.

Day 1: Harrisburg, PA, to Gettysburg, PA

38 miles (45 minutes without traffic and stops)

With the closest major airport to Gettysburg, state capital Harrisburg is a good place to pick up a rental car and begin your journey. Be sure to start your Civil War adventure with a visit to the city's **National Civil War Museum** (✉ *1 Lincoln Cir.* ☎ *717/260–1861* ⊕ *www.nationalcivilwarmuseum.org*). Follow U.S. 15 south through green countryside and rolling hills as you make your way to one of America's most hallowed grounds.

ALONG THE WAY

Town: About 15 miles southwest of Harrisburg, U.S. 15 cuts through the historic agricultural town of Dillsburg, packed with old-time charm. Stroll the historic streets and pick up apples, berries, and nectarines at family-owned **Paulus Mount Airy Orchards** (✉ *522 E. Mt. Airy Rd.* ☎ *717/432–2544* ⊕ *www.paulusmtairyorchards.com*).

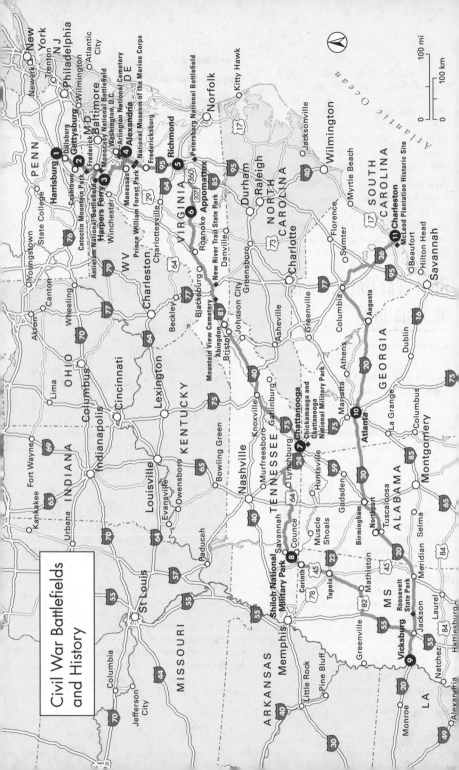

Eat & Drink: In Dillsburg, grab a bite at the landmark **Baker's Diner** (✉ *515 N. U.S. 15* ☎ *717/432–8800* ⊕ *www.bakersdinerpa. com*), which has served home-style meals in its cozy eatery since 1958.

Detour: Veer off at Straban Township for 12 miles on PA-394 to Cashtown, where Confederate officers used the **Cashtown Inn** (✉ *1325 Old Rte. 30* ☎ *717/334–9722* ⊕ *www.cashtowninn.com*) as their headquarters before Gettysburg broke out in July 1863; the basement served as a field hospital during the battle. The brick building has been preserved as a four-room inn and tavern, with New American dishes served in the 1797 Tavern Room.

GETTYSBURG

Do: Gettysburg is a picturesque town that's all about the famous battle that occurred here on July 1 to 3, 1863, turning the tide of the Civil War in favor of the Union. Get a solid introduction at the **Gettysburg National Military Park Museum and Visitor Center** (✉ *1195 Baltimore Pike* ☎ *717/334–1124* ⊕ *www.nps.gov/gett*); visit museums and historic houses in downtown Gettysburg (including the Jennie Wade House, which tells the story of the only civilian killed during the battle); tour the battlefield by bus, Segway, horseback, bike, or self-guided auto tour; and visit the cemetery where Lincoln gave his famous Gettysburg Address.

Eat & Drink: Built in 1776, the **Dobbin House Tavern** (✉ *89 Steinwehr Ave.* ☎ *717/334–2100* ⊕ *www.dobbinhouse. com*) served as a Confederate sniper roost due to its prime view over Cemetery Hill. Today it's a popular tavern and restaurant featuring Colonial-style cuisine in a historic location (try the baked king's onion soup or primal rib of beef).

Stay: The region has tons of adorable inns and B&Bs in historic buildings, including the peaceful **Baladerry Inn** (✉ *40 Hospital Rd.* ☎ *717/337–1342* ⊕ *www.baladerryinn.com*) and the **Lightner Farmhouse** (✉ *2350 Baltimore Pike* ☎ *717/321–3771*

⊕ *www.lightnerfarmhouse.com*); both served as field hospitals during the battle. The upscale, award-winning **Gettysburg Hotel** (✉ *1 Lincoln Sq.* ☎ *717/337–2000* ⊕ *www.hotelgettysburg.com*), established in 1797, has beautifully appointed historic rooms with modern trimmings.

Breakfast: The **Lincoln Diner** (✉ *32 Carlisle St.* ☎ *717/334–3900* ⊕ *www.thelincolndiner.com*) is a popular spot among locals and visitors alike for its home-style comfort food and desserts.

Day 2: Gettysburg, PA, to Harpers Ferry, WV

71 miles (1 hour, 30 minutes without traffic and stops)

Follow U.S. 15 and U.S. 340 south through hilly green countryside speckled with farms and small towns as you make your way to Harpers Ferry, known as the site of an 1859 raid by famed abolitionist John Brown.

ALONG THE WAY

Nature: Right off U.S. 15 near Thurmont, MD, leafy trails wind through **Catoctin Mountain Park** (✉ *14707 Park Central Rd., Thurmont, MD* ☎ *301/663–9388* ⊕ *www. nps.gov/cato*), filled with waterfalls, thick woods, and scenic vistas. Camp David hides somewhere nearby (search the skies for tell-tale helicopters).

Town: Frederick, MD's 18th-century historic district is filled with museums like the **Museum of Civil War Medicine** (✉ *48 E. Patrick St.* ☎ *301/695–1864* ⊕ *www. civilwarmed.org*), public artwork, galleries, innovative restaurants, and upscale boutiques.

Eat & Drink: In Frederick, **Family Meal** (✉ *882 N. East St.*) is a modern take on a classic diner, occupying an old car dealership.

Gettysburg was the site of the most famous battle of the Civil War as well as Lincoln's Gettysburg Address.

Attraction: A relatively unknown but significant battle unfolded in July 1864 on the fields at **Monocacy National Battlefield** (✉ *5201 Urbana Pike* ☎ *301/662–3515* ⊕ *www.nps.gov/mono*), south of Frederick. Though the Confederates won, the time they spent fighting delayed them from possibly capturing the nation's capital.

Detour: On September 17, 1862, the bloodiest single day of battle unfolded at Antietam, located southwest of Frederick via U.S. 40 and MD-34. Learn all about it at the **Antietam National Battlefield** (✉ *302 E. Main St., Sharpsburg, MD* ☎ *301/432–5124* ⊕ *www.nps.gov.anti*), take a self-guided driving tour around the battlefield, and walk several bucolic trails (including Snavely's Ford Creek). You can also see the sites via kayaking Antietam Creek.

HARPERS FERRY

Do: Located at the confluence of the Shenandoah and Potomac rivers, this charming mountain town was where John Brown attempted to initiate a revolt of enslaved people by taking over the town's federal arsenal in 1859; the mission failed and Brown was captured and eventually executed, but the event is considered an important precursor to the Civil War. His "fort" (the old firehouse), along with other related sites, have been preserved as part of **Harpers Ferry National Historical Park** (✉ *171 Shoreline Dr.* ☎ *304/535–6029* ⊕ *www.nps.gov/hafe*). There's also great hiking (including the soaring Marye's Heights Trail, with a fabulous bird's-eye view over Harpers Ferry), the John Brown Museum, and Jefferson Rock, where the third president stated in 1785: "The scene is worth the voyage across the Atlantic."

Eat & Drink: Kelley Farm Kitchen (✉ *1112 Washington St., Bolivar, WV* ☎ *304/535–9976* ⊕ *www.facebook.com/KelleyFarmKitchen*) offers hearty vegan cuisine, including all-day breakfasts, amazing impossible burgers, and addictive garlic knots. **Hamilton's Tavern 1840** (✉ *914 Washington St.* ☎ *304/535–8728* ⊕ *www.hamiltonstavern1840.com*) is popular for its globally inspired cuisine like salmon tartare, fish tacos, and butternut squash risotto.

Stay: Ledge House Bed & Breakfast (✉ *280 Henry Clay St.* ☎ *877/468–4236* ⊕ *www. theledgehouse.com*) provides a nature escape in the heart of town with balconies and decks overlooking the Potomac and Shenandoah rivers. Another good choice is **Light Horse Inn** (✉ *1084 Washington St., Bolivar, WV* ☎ *877/468–4236* ⊕ *www.lighthorseinn.com*), just up the road, occupying a historic house with early American flair.

Breakfast: Battle Grounds Bakery & Coffee (✉ *180 High St.* ☎ *304/535–8583* ⊕ *www. facebook.com/battlegroundsbakery*) has delicious breakfast sandwiches, fresh pastries, and what many say is the best coffee around.

Day 3: Harpers Ferry, WV, to Alexandria, VA

250 miles (4 hours, 25 minutes without traffic and stops)

Drive through pastoral Loudoun County via several local routes as you head to Manassas, and then on to Alexandria.

ALONG THE WAY

Attraction: Washingtonians flocked to Manassas, VA, in 1861 with picnic baskets and wine to watch the first major Civil War battle in Virginia. As the battle became unruly they fled, with any thought of a quick war swiftly extinguished. The visitor center at **Manassas National Battlefield** (✉ *6511 Sudley Rd.* ☎ *703/361–1339* ⊕ *www.nps.gov/mana*) has a good overview of both Manassas I and II, which unfolded in 1862; there are also walking trails and a self-guided auto route.

Detour: After Robert E. Lee left his Virginia home and plantation, Arlington House, to command the Confederate army, the Union confiscated the property and converted it into a burial site. Today the

Extend Your Trip

From Richmond: The Blue Ridge Parkway *(Ch. 7)*

From Atlanta or Charleston: The Civil Rights Trail *(Ch. 7)*

From Charleston: The Best of the Carolinas *(Ch. 7)*

renovated house stands in the center of **Arlington National Cemetery** (☎ *877/907–8585* ⊕ *www.arlingtoncemetery.mil*), where nearly 400,000 Americans who died during wartime, as well as many notable Americans (including William Howard Taft and John F. Kennedy), are interred in its 624 acres. It's about 20 minutes north of Alexandria via the George Washington Memorial Parkway.

ALEXANDRIA

Do: Alexandria was the first Southern city to be taken by the Union in May 1861, and there are plenty of historic sights to explore. The Carlyle House served as a field hospital (and the basis for the PBS series *Mercy Street*); the Stabler-Leadbeater apothecary shop sold residents everything from liquid opium to dental equipment to window panes; the site of Union Fort Ward harbors well-preserved earthen walls and a small museum; and over 1,800 African Americans who escaped from bondage during the Civil War are buried at the Contrabands and Freedmen Cemetery Memorial on Washington Street. Don't miss the **Freedom House Museum** (✉ *1315 Duke St.* ☎ *703/746–4554* ⊕ *www.alexandriava. gov*), which was the headquarters of the nation's largest domestic slave-trading firm until Union forces took the city; today it gives an important look into the realities of chattel slavery before the Civil War.

If you have time, cross the river into Washington, D.C., where President Abraham Lincoln was assassinated on April 15, 1865, at Ford's Theatre. He died at Petersen House across the street, now part of a fascinating museum that examines the Civil War in light of his murder.

Eat & Drink: King Street has a plethora of acclaimed restaurants offering a range of prices and styles. The **Fish Market** (✉ 105 King St. ☎ 703/836–5676 ⊕ www.fishmarketva.com) is the place to go for Chesapeake crab cakes and Virginia oysters while **Brabo Tasting Room** (✉ 1602 King St. ☎ 703/894–5252 ⊕ www.braborestaurant.com) is a Belgian favorite that serves Penn Cove mussels and crisp-skinned snapper with rock shrimp and shellfish butter.

Stay: The first officer killed in the war, Elmer Ellsworth, died at the Marshall House on King Street, which today is boutique hotel the **Alexandrian** (✉ 480 King St. ☎ 703/549–6080 ⊕ www.marriott.com). The **Morrison House** (✉ 116 S. Alfred St. ☎ 703/838–8000 ⊕ www.marriott.com), in a Federalist building with a literary theme, is another cozy historic choice.

Breakfast: Royal Restaurant (✉ 730 N. St. Asaph St. ☎ 703/548–1616 ⊕ www.royalrestaurantva.com) has been serving hearty traditional breakfasts for more than 100 years.

Day 4: Alexandria, VA, to Richmond, VA

105 miles (1 hour, 50 minutes without traffic and stops)

Today's drive is a straight shot down truck-hoarding, traffic-filled I–95.

ALONG THE WAY

Nature: Miles of tranquil trails lace **Prince William Forest Park** (✉ 18170 Park Entrance Rd. ☎ 703/221–7181 ⊕ www.nps.gov/prwi), a 15,000-acre oasis of oaks, maples, and poplars near Triangle, VA.

Attraction: The state-of-the-art **National Museum of the Marine Corps** (✉ 18900 Jefferson Davis Hwy. ☎ 703/432–1775 ⊕ www.usmcmuseum.com) relates American history through the eyes of the U.S. Marines. You'll know it by the dramatic, tilted, steel mass—inspired by the flag raisings at Iwo Jima—rising just off I–95 in Triangle.

Town: The historic town of Fredericksburg on the Rappahannock River has both Revolutionary and Civil War history (George Washington's mother lived here). Four major battles unfolded in the vicinity of Fredericksburg over the course of two years, providing an interesting look at changing war tactics. Highlights include the Sunken Wall in Fredericksburg, Spotsylvania's Bloody Angle, and the house where Stonewall Jackson died.

Eat & Drink: Mason Dixon Café (✉ 2100 Princess Anne St. ☎ 540/371–1950 ⊕ www.masondixoncafe.com) in Fredericksburg is a favorite local spot, offering sandwiches, burgers, and full-fledged entrées.

RICHMOND

Do: The long-time capital of Virginia is experiencing a cultural revival in its architecturally rich streets. The city was also the capital of the Confederacy during the Civil War, a history it attempts to reckon with via several historic sites. The **Richmond National Battlefield Park** (✉ 470 Tredegar St. ☎ 804/226–1981 ⊕ www.nps.gov/rich) comprises 13 Civil War sites, including battlefields and miles of defensive fortifications; its expansive visitor center is housed in an old wool mill overlooking the James River.

Eat & Drink: Try the seasonal, southern delights at **Shagbark** (✉ 4901 Libbie Mill E. Blvd. ☎ 804/358–7424 ⊕ www.shagbarkva.com) or slurp down fresh Chesapeake bivalves at **Rappahannock Oyster Company** (✉ 320 E. Grace St.

☏ 804/545–0565 ⊕ www.rroysters.com).
If you have time, see what appeals in
Carytown or Scott's Addition, just two of
the city's many up-and-coming neighborhoods filled with restaurants, shops, and
cafés.

Stay: The **Jefferson Hotel** (✉ 101 W.
Franklin St. ☏ 804/788–8000 ⊕ www.
jeffersonhotel.com) exudes historic
elegance with chandeliers, gilded trim,
and Tiffany stained glass windows. **Quirk
Hotel** (✉ 201 W. Broad St. ☏ 804/340–
6040 ⊕ www.destinationhotels.com) has
turned a 1916 luxury department store
into a hip retreat.

Breakfast: Dot's Back Inn (✉ 4030 MacAr-
thur Ave. ☏ 804/266–3167 ⊕ www.
dotsbackrichmond.com) is a retro diner
with all the classics (and an amazing crab
cake Benedict).

Day 5: Richmond, VA, to Appomattox, VA

*92 miles (1 hour, 40 minutes without
traffic and stops)*

Today head west across central Virginia
on U.S. 360, VA-307, and U.S. 460.

ALONG THE WAY
Detour: The 10-month siege at Petersburg, VA, from June 1864 to April 1864,
resulted in Richmond's fall and set the
path to surrender at Appomattox. Preserved as **Petersburg National Battlefield**
(✉ 5001 Siege Rd., Prince George, VA
804/732–3531 ⊕ www.nps.gov/pete), the
site offers a visitor center discussing the
siege (including the infamous Battle of
the Crater), self-guided auto routes, and
living history demonstrations.

APPOMATTOX
Do: General Robert E. Lee surrendered
to General Ulysses S. Grant on April 9,
1865, at the McLean House in the village
of Appomattox Court House, signaling
the end of the Civil War. **Appomattox**

Court House National Historical Park (✉ 111
National Park Dr. ☏ 434/352–8987
⊕ www.nps.gov/apco) has 27 structures
restored to their 1865 look, including the
parlor where the war-ending documents
were signed.

Eat & Drink: The **Babcock House** (✉ 250
Oakleigh Ave. ☏ 434/352–7532 ⊕ www.
babcockhouse.com) is a popular stop
for burgers, sandwiches, meat loaf, and
other hearty entrées as well as Sunday
brunch (it's also a B&B). Mamma Terez-
inha's (✉ 1952 Church St. ☏ 434/352–
4444) serves New York–style pizza by the
pie or by the slice.

Stay: The five-room **Longacre of Appomattox** (✉ 1670 Church St. ☏ 434/352–9251
⊕ www.longacreofappomattox.com)
offers English-style charm in the Virginia
countryside.

Breakfast: Granny Bee's (✉ 179 Main St.
☏ 434/352–2259 ⊕ www.facebook.com/
GrannyBeesRestaurant) serves good
old-fashioned heartiness. For something
lighter, check out **Baine's Books and
Coffee** (✉ 205 Main St. ☏ 434/229–8157
⊕ www.bainesbooks.com).

Day 6: Appomattox, VA, to Chattanooga, TN

*440 miles (6 hours, 40 minutes without
traffic and stops)*

After enjoying Appalachian scenery on
U.S. 460, bite the bullet today for the
long-haul drive on interstate highways,
via I–81, I–40, and I–75.

ALONG THE WAY
Nature: Stretch your legs on the peaceful
trails along the New River in Virginia's
New River Trail State Park (✉ 116 Orphan-
age Dr., Max Meadows, VA ☏ 276/699–
6778 ⊕ www.dcr.virginia.gov); it's about
10 miles south of I–81 at Max Meadows
off I–77. The fishing there is superb, too.

Roadside Attraction: Although Dr. Charles T. Pepper didn't invent the spicy, cherry-root-beer-esque soda, he did give his name to it—he had offered the real inventor, Charles Alderton, his first job, who then named his liquid invention in his former boss's honor. You'll find his pilgrimage gravesite at Mountain View Cemetery in Rural Retreat, Virginia, just west of the I–77 interchange.

Town: In the outdoorsy town of Abingdon, Virginia, jump on the 34.3-mile Virginia Creeper rail-to-recreation trail or attend a performance at the **Barter Theatre** (✉ 127 W. Main St. ☎ 276/628–3991 ⊕ www.bartertheatre.com), the nation's longest-running professional theater, performing since 1933.

Eat & Drink: Dead End BBQ (✉ 3621 Sutherland Ave. ☎ 865/212–5655 ⊕ www.deadendbbq.com) in Knoxville, Tennessee, stands out for its award-winning, nationally recognized fare that takes you back to the dead-end street where the owners originally served barbecue to neighbors.

CHATTANOOGA

Do: Some of the Civil War's hardest fought battles unfolded in and around Chattanooga, with the Union repelling the Confederacy back to Georgia in 1863, in effect paving the way for Sherman's March to the Sea. Civil War veterans established the **Chickamauga and Chattanooga National Military Park** (✉ 3370 Lafayette Rd., Fort Oglethorpe, GA ☎ 706/866–9241 ⊕ www.nps.gov/chch) in 1889, making it the nation's oldest (and at nearly 10,000 acres, the largest) military park. Tour the park on your own or with a park ranger, visit two different visitor centers, hike trails, and more.

Eat & Drink: The burgers at Tremont Tavern (✉ 1203 Hixson Pike ☎ 423/266–1996 www.tremonttavern.com) have a cult following, though if you're hungry for fried chicken, **Champy's World Famous Fried Chicken** (✉ 526 E. Martin Luther King Blvd. ☎ 423/752–9198 ⊕ www.champyschicken.com) is the place to go.

Stay: Sleep in a Victorian-era luxury sleeper car at the **Chattanooga Choo Choo Hotel** (✉ 1400 Market St. ☎ 423/266–5000 ⊕ www.choochoo.com); standard suites are available as well. The hotel is a hub of activity, with several on-site restaurants and a distillery.

Breakfast: Family-owned **Bluegrass Grill** (✉ 55 E. Main St. ☎ 423/752–4020 ⊕ www.bluegrassgrillchattanooga.com) on Main Street is beloved for its homemade diner favorites; try the alderwood-smoked salmon frittata or corned beef—or tofu—hash.

Day 7: Chattanooga, TN, to Shiloh, TN

220 miles (3 hours, 50 minutes without traffic and stops)

Follow I–24 north and U.S. 64 west on a rustic drive to Shiloh National Military Park.

ALONG THE WAY

Eat & Drink: You're in whiskey country, so, of course, you need to visit the **Jack Daniels Distillery** (✉ 280 Lynchburg Hwy. ☎ 931/759–6357 ⊕ www.jackdaniels.com) in Lynchburg, Tennessee, 25 miles north of Winchester via TN-50. A variety of sampling tours are offered. The distillery's Miss Mary Bobo's Restaurant serves standard southern fare for lunch.

SHILOH NATIONAL MILITARY PARK

Do: Shiloh may mean "place of peace," but in 1862, these pristine lands saw a pivotal battle that resulted in a Union victory and killed more soldiers than in all previous Civil War battles combined (23,746 casualties over two days). Today the 5,000-acre **Shiloh National Military Park** (✉ 1055 Pittsburg Landing Rd. ☎ 731/689–5696 ⊕ www.nps.gov/shil)

offers interpretive centers, a self-guided auto tour, ranger programs, living history exhibits, and special events. Don't miss Fraley Field, where the battle began; the Hornet's Nest, where Union troops held back waves of Confederates; and Pittsburg Landing, where Grant received reinforcements that turned the tide for the North.

Eat & Drink: You won't find a more authentic place for fried catfish than **Hagy's Catfish Hotel** (⊠ 1140 Hagy La. ☎ 731/689–3327 ⊕ www.catfishhotel. com) in Savannah, Tennessee, where the southern delicacy is served on the banks of the Tennessee River alongside hush puppies, coleslaw, and fries. The original shack, built in 1825 by ancestor-settler Henry Hagy, was occupied by Union forces during the Battle of Shiloh before opening as a restaurant in 1938.

Stay: There aren't tons of choices in the area surrounding Shiloh, but the **Lodge at Pickwick Landing** (⊠ 120 Playground Loop ☎ 731/689–3135 ⊕ www.tnstateparks. com) in Counce offers basic rooms with river views.

Breakfast: Dae Break (⊠ 990 Pickwick Rd. S ☎ 731/438–3461) in Savannah has everything you want in a home-style breakfast joint.

Day 8: Shiloh, TN, to Vicksburg, MS

300 miles (4 hours, 45 minutes without traffic and stops)

Hop onto U.S. 45 south to the fabled Natchez Trace Parkway, one of the nation's most scenic byways. You'll enjoy 60 miles of historic sites, hiking enclaves, and bountiful springtime azaleas before veering off at Mathiston, following U.S. 82 to I–55 to I–20 southwest, finally bringing you into Vicksburg.

ALONG THE WAY

Town: The **Civil War Interpretive Center** (⊠ 501 W. Linden St. ☎ 662/287–9273 ⊕ www.nps.gov/shil) in Corinth, Mississippi, about 23 miles southwest of Shiloh, stands on the site where the Battle of Corinth took place just a few months after Shiloh, offering videos, interactive exhibits, and multimedia presentations. In addition, the **Corinth Contraband Camp** (⊠ 800 N. Parkway St. ☎ 662/287–9273 ⊕ www.nps.gov/shil) commemorates the settlement where formerly enslaved African Americans fled to safety behind Union lines; a quarter-mile path leads past six life-size bronzes depicting denizens of the camp. Historic buildings filled with boutiques and art galleries line Fillmore Street.

Town: Honor the king of rock 'n' roll at the **Elvis Presley Birthplace** (⊠ 306 Elvis Presley Dr. ☎ 662/841–1456 ⊕ www. elvispresleybirthplace.com) in Tupelo, Mississippi, on the Natchez Trace Parkway, where he was born in 1935 and learned to play the guitar. **Tupelo National Battlefield** (⊠ 2005 Main St. ☎ 662/680–4025 ⊕ www.nps/gov/tupe) recalls the Battle of Tupelo on July 13–15, 1864, in which the Union successfully kept the Confederates from interfering with Sherman's March to the Sea.

Eat & Drink: Hal and Mal's (⊠ 200 Commerce St. ☎ 601/948–0888 ⊕ www. halandmals.com) in Mississippi's capital city of Jackson is a honky-tonk serving music and drinks alongside soul food.

VICKSBURG

Do: In May 1863, Vicksburg was the last major Confederate stronghold on the Mississippi River, and the Union's decisive victory in the Siege of Vicksburg in July 1863 (along with the recent win at Gettysburg) is considered a turning point in the war. **Vicksburg National Military Park** (⊠ 3201 Clay St. ☎ 601/636–0583 ⊕ www.nps.gov/vick) has more than 1,400 monuments and markers, restored and original trenches, and a cemetery.

Eat & Drink: Authentic tastes of the South include **10 South Rooftop Bar & Grill** (✉ *1301 Washington St.* ☎ *601/501–4600* ⊕ *www.10southrooftop.com*), a casual rooftop bar with views over the Mississippi; Beechwood Restaurant (✉ *4451 Clay St.* ☎ *601/636–3761* ⊕ *www. beechwoodrestaurantandlounge.com*), an old-timey favorite serving steaks and seafood; and **Bovina Café** (✉ *191 Tiffentown Rd.* ☎ *601/636–6802*), beloved for its soul food.

Stay: Many of the town's historic abodes have been converted to inns and B&Bs, including **Anchuca** (✉ *1010 First East St.* ☎ *601/661–0111* ⊕ *www.anchuca.com*), a Greek Revival mansion outfitted with period antiques, and **Cedar Grove Mansion Inn** (✉ *2200 Oak St.* ☎ *601/636–1000* ⊕ *www.cedargroveinn.com*), overlooking the Mississippi River.

Breakfast: The Tomato Place (✉ *3229 U.S. 61* ☎ *601/661–0040* ⊕ *www.thetomatoplace.com*) is known for its fried green tomatoes, bread pudding, and welcoming atmosphere.

Day 9: Vicksburg, MS, to Atlanta, GA

420 miles (6 hours, 20 minutes without traffic and stops)

It's freeway-driving all the way today via I-20, with some serious mileage to get under your belt before reaching Atlanta.

ALONG THE WAY

Nature: Encircling Shadow Lake an hour east of Vicksburg, **Roosevelt State Park** (✉ *2149 MS-13, Morton, MS* ☎ *601/732–6316* ⊕ *www.mdwfp.com*) offers hiking, fishing, and camping in a peaceful forest that ignites with autumn foliage.

Town: Boutiques and restaurants in the artsy, 20-block Northport Historic District in Northport, Alabama, occupy 19th- and early-20th-century buildings; walking tours are offered.

Town: Though it's Alabama's largest city, Birmingham has a small-town feel. Stop here for the Birmingham Civil Rights District, where you can delve into African American history, and **Sloss Furnaces National Historic Landmark** (✉ *20 32nd St. N* ☎ *205/254–2025* ⊕ *www.slossfurnaces.com*), where two blast furnaces long fired the city's steel industry.

Eat & Drink: Some of the South's best fried chicken can be found at **Café Dupont** (✉ *113 20th St. N* ☎ *205/322–1282* ⊕ *www.cafedupont.net*) in Birmingham.

ATLANTA

Do: This humming metropolis has museums, luxury shopping, and great food and art scenes. As the site of the 1864 Battle of Atlanta and the starting point for Sherman's March to the Sea, it has plenty of Civil War sights, too, including the **Atlanta History Center's Cyclorama** (✉ *130 West Paces Ferry Rd. NW* ☎ *404/814–4000* ⊕ *www.atlantahistorycenter.com*), which depicts the battle, and **Kennesaw Mountain National Battlefield Park** (✉ *900 Kennesaw Mountain Dr.* ☎ *770/427–4686* ⊕ *www.nps.gov/kemo*), where Sherman's Atlanta campaign started.

Eat & Drink: If you're looking for something upscale in this culinary haven, **Miller Union** (✉ *999 Brady Ave. NW* ☎ *678/733–8550* ⊕ *www.millerunion.com*) is an ode to modern southern cuisine while Bacchanalia focuses on creatively prepared local produce. Or go the picnic route and swing by **Ponce City Market** (✉ *675 Ponce De Leon Ave. NE* ☎ *404/900–7900* ⊕ *www.poncecitymarket.com*), a vibrant food hall. Dine-in restaurants include W. H. Stiles Fish Camp and H&F Burger.

Stay: The late neo-futuristic architect John Portman designed downtown's **Hyatt Regency** (✉ *265 Peachtree Rd. NE* ☎ *404/577–1234* ⊕ *www.hyatt.com*) in 1967 and updated it before his death in

2017 with personal touches including pieces from his own art collection. The **Hotel Clermont** (✉ *789 Ponce De Leon Ave. NE* ☎ *470/485–0485* ⊕ *www.hotelclermont.com*) is a funky stay in a century-old building near Ponce City Market.

Breakfast: R. Thomas' Deluxe Grill (✉ *1812 Peachtree St. NW* ☎ *404/881–0246* ⊕ *www.rthomasdeluxegrill.net*) on Peachtree Street has been serving healthy breakfasts for more than 30 years. The **Silver Skillet** (✉ *200 14th St. NW* ☎ *404/874–1388* ⊕ *www.silverskillet.com*) has been around even longer (since 1956), and is always packed with patrons enjoying skillet country ham, fried seasoned catfish strips, and other southern classics.

Day 10: Atlanta, GA, to Charleston, SC

300 miles (4 hours, 45 minutes without traffic and stops)

Today has more freeway driving in store, heading southeast on I-20 and I-26 as you end your trip where the Civil War first started.

ALONG THE WAY

Town: Augusta, GA, is known as the host of The Masters golf tournament, but it's also the birthplace of James Brown and offers a revitalized Broad Street and a bucolic Riverwalk explore. You can also take a cruise on the Augusta Canal.

Eat & Drink: Just one of the many exciting food options in Columbia, the **Motor City Supply Company Bistro** (✉ *920 Gervais St.* ☎ *803/256–6687* ⊕ *www.motorsupplyco-bistro.com*) offers casually upscale meals like steamed mussels and Dijon-fried eggplant.

Attraction: Located just outside Charleston, **McLeod Plantation Historic Site** (✉ *325 Country Club Dr.* ☎ *843/762–9514*

⊕ *www.ccprc.com*) is the only former plantation in the area where the visitor experience is focused on the lives of the enslaved people who toiled here. Guided and self-led tours are organized around a "Transition to Freedom" program that imagines what life was like for the people working on the cotton plantation and the ramifications these injustices still have on society today. The site is an essential reminder of what the Civil War was really fought over: the desire of Southern plantation-owners to keep enslaving people.

CHARLESTON

Do: Charleston is a bevy of historic houses, thriving restaurants, and booming art galleries all found along charming cobblestone streets. The Civil War officially kicked off at Fort Sumter, in Charleston Harbor, on April 12, 1861, when a shot fired from Fort Johnson across the way initiated a 34-hour battle. The fort has been preserved as the **Fort Sumter and Fort Moultrie National Historical Park** (☎ *843/883–3123* ⊕ *www.nps.gov/fosu*), accessible by ferry from downtown Charleston.

Eat & Drink: Charleston has a legendary food scene, and you'd have to actively try to have a bad meal while here. **Graze** (✉ *863 Houston Northcutt Blvd., Mt. Pleasant, SC* ☎ *843/606–2493* ⊕ *www.grazecharleston.com*), **Husk** (✉ *76 Queen St.* ☎ *843/577–2500* ⊕ *www.huskrestaurant.com*), and **Xiao Bao Biscuit** (✉ *224 Rutledge Ave.* ⊕ *www.xiaobiscuit.com*) are just a few of the city's best, while **Edmund's Oast** (✉ *1081 Morrison Dr.* ☎ *843/727–1145* ⊕ *www.edmundsoast.com*) is a cutting-edge brewery/dining dynamo.

Stay: Charleston reigns in the world of refined inns and B&Bs. **Charleston Place** (✉ *205 Meeting St.* ☎ *843/722–4900* ⊕ *www.belmond.com*) is all marble, antiques, and chandeliers while the **French Quarter Inn** (✉ *166 Church St.* ☎ *843/722–1900* ⊕ *www.fqicharleston.com*) is a little more cozy but still luxurious.

Breakfast: Hannibal's Soul Kitchen (✉ *16 Blake St.* ☎ *843/722–2256* ⊕ *www. hannibalkitchen.com*) is the go-to for a seafood breakfast, while Three Little Birds Café (✉ *65 Windermere Blvd.* ☎ *843/225–3065* ⊕ *www.threelittlebird-cafe.com*) believes in "Peace, Love, and Pancakes"—and has a lovely porch to dine on during nice weather.

Retracing the American Revolution

Written by Brandon Schultz

At its most basic, the birth of the United States can be defined by the years of the American Revolutionary War, but it's important to understand the foundation built in the more than 150 years leading up to the rebellion and the country's rapid development in the years following. Whether you're a historian or a history newbie, this road trip will explore the origins of the United States, from its first British settlement to the first and last major engagements of the Revolution. You'll end among the awe-inspiring museums and monuments of Washington, D.C., where you'll uncover the modern evolution of the capital, originally ordered by Congress with the Residence Act in 1790.

At a Glance

Start: Boston, MA

End: Washington, D.C.

Miles Traveled: 906 miles

Suggested Duration: 8 days

States Visited: Maryland, Massachusetts, New Jersey, New York, Pennsylvania, Virginia, Washington, D.C.

Key Sights: Colonial Williamsburg; The Freedom Trail; Independence Hall; James-town; Washington Crossing Historic Park

Best Time to Go: Various stops along this route have stronger connections to different seasons (Washington's Crossing is best reimagined in snowy winter, while Philadelphia will be in its full Revolutionary glory in July), but autumn would be the most agreeable average for the destinations as a whole. The only month that you should completely avoid is December, as Colonial Williamsburg is typically closed for the whole month.

Day 1: Boston, MA

If you're flying to the trip's starting point, you'll arrive at Boston Logan International Airport. It's just a 10-minute drive from there to Downtown Boston, and you should plan to spend a full day in the city before hitting the road.

Do: From the Boston Tea Party to the ride of Paul Revere (whose house still stands in the city's North End), Boston's connec-tions to the American Revolutionary War are legendary. At the very least, you'll want to visit the **Bunker Hill Monument & Museum** (✉ *43 Monument Sq., Charles-town, MA* ☎ *617/242–7275* ⊕ *www.nps. gov/bost*), the **Boston Tea Party Ships & Museum** (✉ *306 Congress St.* ☎ *617/338–1773* ⊕ *www.bostonteapartyship.com*), **Granary Burial Ground** (✉ *Tremont St.* ⊕ *www.boston.gov*) where Sam Adams and Paul Revere are buried, **Old North Church** and the **Paul Revere House** (✉ *193 Salem St.* ☎ *617/858–8231* ⊕ *www. oldnorth.com*), the **Boston Massacre site** (✉ *Corner of State and Congress Streets* ☎ *617/357–8300* ⊕ *www.bostonmas-sacre.net*), and the **USS *Constitution*** (✉ *Bldg. 22, Charlestown Navy Yard* ☎ *617/426–1812* ⊕ *www.ussconstitu-tionmuseum.org*), which is the world's oldest ship still afloat. If you're up for a 2½-mile walk, you could follow the **Freedom Trail** (www.thefreedomtrail.org) for 16 significant sites, including most of the ones mentioned above.

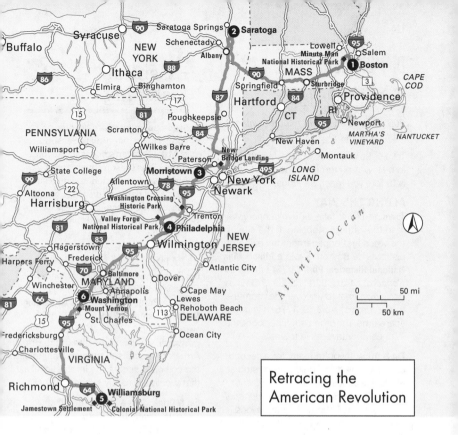

Retracing the
American Revolution

Eat & Drink: Abigail's Tea Room (✉ *306 Congress St.* ☎ *866/955–0667* ⊕ *www. bostonteapartyship.com*) at the Boston Tea Party Ships & Museum offers a fun period experience for a cup of tea and a light lunch. For dinner with a historic twist, try the **Green Dragon Tavern** (✉ *11 Marshall St.* ☎ *617/367–0055* ⊕ *www. greendragonboston.com*). The original Union Street location, where Paul Revere, John Hancock, and other Sons of Liberty met, is gone, but the tradition lives on in the current location on Marshall Street.

Shop: Faneuil Hall (⊕ *faneuilhallmarketplace.com*) has been a beloved Boston marketplace since the 1740s, and certainly played its part in Revolutionary history with the likes of Samuel Adams and George Washington addressing crowds here. Today you'll find four large markets, including the foodie favorite known as Quincy Market.

Stay: Most of Boston's historic hotels date to the late 19th century, so leave the Revolution behind for some R&R at a charming B&B like the **Samuel Sewall Inn** (✉ *143 St. Paul St.* ☎ *617/713–1230* ⊕ *www.samuelsewallinn.com*) in Brookline. Enjoy a leap back to the future with a night at this Queen Anne–style Victorian before returning to the Colonial period in the morning.

Breakfast: Stop by **Render Coffee** (✉ *563 Columbus Ave.* ☎ *617/262–4142* ⊕ *www.rendercoffeebar.com*) in the South End before heading out of town. Build your own breakfast sandwich (try the rosemary, potato, egg) and grab a cup of premium coffee from local roaster Gracenote.

Day 2: Boston, MA, to Saratoga, NY

200 miles (3 hours, 15 minutes without traffic and stops)

Take I–90 W across Massachusetts and into New York, turning on to I–87 N shortly before you reach Saratoga.

ALONG THE WAY

Town: You can't take a Revolutionary War road trip without stopping at the site of the war's first engagement in Lexington, just outside Boston. Explore **Minute Man National Historical Park** (✉ *174 Liberty St., Concord, MA* ☎ *978/369–6993* ⊕ *www. nps.gov/mima*) to uncover the momentous events of April 19, 1775. If you have spare time after the park, check out the 17th-century taverns in town.

Eat & Drink: If you're ready for a second cup of coffee and a quick lunch, stop at **Sturbridge Coffee House** (✉ *407 Main St.* ☎ *508/347–2288* ⊕ *www.sturbridgecoffeehouse.com*) about an hour beyond Lexington. Largely considered the best local coffee in town, this amiable shop also happens to be two minutes from **Old Sturbridge Village** (✉ *1 Old Sturbridge Village Rd.* ☎ *800/733–1830* ⊕ *www. osv.org*), a living history museum recreating late 18th-century life (a great spot to stroll with your brew and to-go sandwich).

Roadside Attraction: You'll find the largest cuckoo clock in New England in Sturbridge, just 5 miles off I–90. The functional clock stands over 20 feet tall and is "hidden" in the Secret Garden of **The Bird Store and More** (✉ *4 Cedar St.* ☎ *508/347–2473* ⊕ *www.thebirdstoreandmore.com*). The quirky clock itself is also a shop, and the cuckoo appears hourly from 9 am to 6 pm.

Essential Listening

Study up on all that's to come on your trip by listening to Season 2 of Mike Duncan's podcast, "Revolutions." This season covers the American Revolution, so you'll gain increased perspective throughout your journey as you progress with both the itinerary and the series.

SARATOGA

Do: Fast-forward from the beginning of the war to its decisive turning point with the Battles of Saratoga. At **Saratoga National Historical Park** (✉ *648 NY-32, Stillwater, NY* ☎ *518/670–2985* ⊕ *www.nps. gov/sara*), you'll find the site of the British Army's first-ever surrender, which helped the colonists secure the international aid that would ultimately support victory.

Eat & Drink: Just a 10-minute drive from the park, **Sweet Lou's Bistro** (✉ *161 Broad St.* ☎ *518/507–6013* ⊕ *www.sweetlousdeli23.com*) is a Schuylerville favorite for quality plates with no pretension. Choose from the signature corned beef and pastrami menu, or try something a little less classic, like a grilled macaroni-and-cheese sandwich with Bourbon bacon.

Stay: Reserve one of the lakeview rooms at **The Nest** on Saratoga Lake (✉ *511 NY-9P* ☎ *518/306–5531* ⊕ *www.brownsbeachresort.com*) for a special sunset experience. This quaint inn is the coziest stay you'll find within 10 minutes of Saratoga National Historical Park.

Breakfast: Farmer's Hardware (✉ *35 Maple Ave.* ☎ *518/934–3444* ⊕ *www.farmershardwaresaratoga.com*) will take you about 15 minutes out of your way, but the creative brunch fare and custom hot chocolates and Bloody Marys are worth it. You don't need to wait for brunch to hit

From Fanueil Hall to Bunker Hill, Boston is filled with Revolution-era sights.

this Saratoga favorite, though; it's open during traditional breakfast hours, too.

Day 3: Saratoga, NY, to Morristown, NJ

180 miles (3 hours without traffic and stops)

Head back down I–87 S into New Jersey and follow I–287 most of the way to your next destination.

ALONG THE WAY

Town: Make a stop in Albany, the capital of New York. The oldest house in the city is the Quackenbush House, dating to around 1730, but the most famous house around is quickly becoming the **Schuyler Mansion** (✉ *32 Catherine St.* ☎ *518/434–0835* ⊕ *www.parks.ny.gov*), a name brought back to national fame with Broadway's *Hamilton*. At **First Church** (✉ *110 N. Pearl St.* ☎ *518/463–4449*) in Albany, you'll also be able to glimpse the oldest pulpit in America, brought to the United States in 1656.

Eat & Drink: The Hollow Bar + Kitchen (✉ *79 N. Pearl St.* ☎ *518/426–8550* ⊕ *www. thehollowalbany.com*) in downtown Albany offers classic pub fare like chicken tenders, chili, and nachos alongside fresh takes like Buddha bowl salad, vegan meat loaf, and a risotto of the day.

Detour: New Bridge Landing (✉ *1205 Main St., River Edge, NJ* ☎ *201/343–9492* ⊕ *www.bergencountyhistory.org*) is a little-known North Jersey spot about 15 minutes off today's route, but the tiny town had tremendous hypothetical impact on the Revolution and stands as a reminder of one of life's most important lessons. Here, a tactical retreat by Washington is widely believed to have saved the Continental Army from a rebellion-crushing defeat in 1776. The original bridge is gone, but the current edition (circa 1889) still has a spot on the National Register of Historic Places. Three Colonial houses also remain nearby.

MORRISTOWN

Do: America's first national historical park (established in 1933), **Morristown National Historical Park** (✉ *30 Washington Pl.* ☎ *973/543–1949* ⊕ *www.nps.gov/morr*) is a bit unusual in that it's home to four separate sites, not all connected, which each played a part in the war. The most interestingly (and mysteriously) named is Fort Nonsense, but the most significant are the Ford Mansion and adjacent Washington's Headquarters Museum. The surviving mansion was home to Washington during the infamous "hard winter" and the museum tells the story of his remarkable leadership in keeping an army together and motivated through harsh conditions. Don't miss the replica soldier huts at Jockey Hollow.

Eat & Drink: Despite the name, **Jockey Hollow Bar & Kitchen** (✉ *110 South St.* ☎ *973/644–3180* ⊕ *www.jockeyhollow-barandkitchen.com*) has nothing to do with the historical park, but the four dining spaces inside the former Vail Mansion demand a visit for the seafood, famous house-made pastas, or both. The wine list is equally significant.

Stay: If you're feeling a bit presidential after today's itinerary, finish the day with a dignified stay at **The Madison Hotel** (✉ *1 Convent Rd.* ☎ *800/526–0729* ⊕ *www.themadisonhotel.com*). The reasonably priced four-star hotel is stately inside and out, and offers both an indoor pool and an elegant steak house worth peeking into even if you're not dining.

Breakfast: The breakfast menu at **The Artistic Baker** (✉ *16 Cattano Ave.* ☎ *973/267–5540* ⊕ *www.theartistbaker.com*) changes daily, but you can always count on a hot cup of specialty coffee and irresistible pastries from this top local bakery.

Day 4: Morristown, NJ, to Philadelphia, PA

85 miles (1 hour, 30 minutes without traffic and stops)

It's a quick drive through the rest of New Jersey today, heading south toward I–95 S, taking you directly into Philadelphia.

ALONG THE WAY

Town: Just before crossing the Delaware River into Pennsylvania, stop at **Washington Crossing Historic Park** (✉ *355 Washington Crossing Pennington Rd., Titusville, NJ* ☎ *609/737–0623* ⊕ *www.state.nj.us*) in New Jersey. Then called Johnson's Ferry, this is the spot where Washington famously crossed the river on the icy Christmas night of 1776 in a surprise attack that tipped the scales back in the Continental Army's favor.

Eat & Drink: Cross the bridge for lunch at **Washington Crossing Inn** (✉ *1295 General Washington Memorial Blvd.* ☎ *215/493–3634* ⊕ *www.washingtoncrossinginn.com*) in Pennsylvania. (Both states have a Washington Crossing on either side of the river.) Affordable meals are served inside the refined home preserved from the early-19th-century; weekend brunch is especially adored here.

Detour: A half-hour detour on your way to Philly, **Valley Forge National Historical Park** (✉ *1400 N. Outer Line Dr., King of Prussia, PA* ☎ *610/783–1077* ⊕ *www.nps.gov/vafo*) was the site of the Continental Army's winter encampment after the British took Philadelphia. The site became the equivalent of America's fourth-largest city as 12,000 soldiers (and several hundred women and children) built 1,500 cabins. This is where Washington resupplied, retrained, and reinspired the entire army during a brutal winter that temporarily halted fighting.

PHILADELPHIA

Do: Tomorrow you'll catch the museums and historical sites that only offer daytime hours, but this evening you can stroll the historic streets of Old City, including the impossibly picturesque Elfreth's Alley, the oldest continuously inhabited residential street in the country. You can also stroll by Benjamin Franklin's grave at **Christ Church Burial Ground** (✉ 340 N. 5th St. ☎ 215/922–1695 ⊕ www.christchurch-phila.org) and toss a penny on it for luck (he's the one who coined the adage "A penny saved is a penny earned.").

Eat & Drink: While in Old City, dine at **The Olde Bar** (✉ 125 Walnut St. ☎ 215/253–3777 ⊕ www.theoldebar.com) on Walnut Street if you like seafood. This oyster bar and retro cocktail lounge is always a stylish choice. Otherwise, head to **Amada** (✉ 217–219 Chestnut St. ☎ 215/625–2450 ⊕ www.amadarestaurant.com) on Chestnut Street for modern Spanish tapas from the same chef.

Stay: If you're looking for a period stay, book a room at **Morris House Hotel** (✉ 225 S. 8th St. ☎ 215/922–2446 ⊕ www.morrishousehotel.com). This boutique hotel was originally built in 1787 and is a National Historic Landmark with easy access to many of the city's historic sites.

Breakfast: Pop over to the **Reading Terminal Market** (✉ 51 N. 12th St. ☎ 215/922–2317 ⊕ www.readingterminalmarket.org) for breakfast. This huge facility is one of the oldest public markets in the country and frequented by locals and tourists daily. At breakfast, the must-try bites are the homestyle cooking of several Pennsylvania Dutch vendors, including Dutch Eating Place.

Day 5: Philadelphia

Stay put today. You'll need to spend a full day in Philadelphia to catch even a sampling of its impact on early America.

Do: You won't find a city with deeper ties to the Revolution than Philadelphia, so even a full day here will still require a highlights tour. Don't miss: **Independence Hall** (✉ 520 Chestnut St. ☎ 215/965–2305 ⊕ www.nps.gov/inde); the **Liberty Bell** (✉ 526 Market St. ☎ 215/965–2305 ⊕ www.nps.gov/inde); the **National Constitution Center** (✉ 525 Arch St. ☎ 215/409–6700 ⊕ www.constitutioncenter.org); the **Museum of the American Revolution** (✉ 101 S. 3rd St. ☎ 215/253–6731 ⊕ www.amrevmuseum.org); **Carpenter's Hall** (✉ 320 Chestnut St. ☎ 215/925–0167 ⊕ www.carpentershall.org), site of the First Continental Congress; and **Graff House** (✉ 700 Market St. ☎ 215/965–2305 ⊕ www.nps.gov/inde), where the Declaration of Independence was written. For a bit of fun that's more a space of legend than fact, you can also tour the **Betsy Ross House** (✉ 239 Arch St. ☎ 215/629–4026 ⊕ www.historicphiladelphia.org).

Eat & Drink: Have a sandwich at **High Street Philly** (✉ 101 S. 9th St. ☎ 215/625–0988 ⊕ www.highstreetphilly.com). The breads are baked in-house and the fillings range from roast pork with broccoli rabe (a Philly staple) to poached salmon with roasted red pepper and olive tapenade. Or you can take a detour to nab a classic Philly cheesesteak at **Jim's Steaks** (✉ 400 South St. ☎ 215/928–1911 ⊕ jimssouthstreet.com) on South Street. You've probably heard that the real battle of the best Philly cheesesteak is between Geno's and Pat's, but Jim's is a sleeper favorite and is a bit closer to the city center.

Breakfast: Luna's Café (✉ 317 Market St. ☎ 215/309–3140 ⊕ www.lunaphilly.com) has plenty of breakfast sandwiches, jazzed-up pancakes, and, of course, avocado toast, but the breakfast specialties may provide more of the sustenance you need for the long drive ahead. Consider the loaded breakfast bowl with tofu scramble or some biscuits and sausage gravy with eggs and fried chicken.

Day 6: Philadelphia, PA, to Williamsburg, VA

290 miles (4 hours, 45 minutes without traffic and stops)

Hop on I-95 S and settle in for the nearly 5-hour drive down to Williamsburg. It's a long one, but you just had a day off from driving so you should be ready for it.

ALONG THE WAY

Town: The capital of the United States is simply the location of the U.S. Congress and, for a brief period of about two months ending in February 1777, that was Baltimore. There's plenty to see in this harbor city, but no actual battle action was seen here during the Revolution, despite the construction of **Fort McHenry** (✉ *2400 E. Fort Ave.* ☎ *410/962–4290* ⊕ *www.nps.gov/fomc*) in anticipation of a British approach. The fort did see action during the War of 1812, though, and is where Francis Scott Key penned "The Star-Spangled Banner," which would become the young country's national anthem.

Eat & Drink: Five minutes from Fort McHenry, have lunch at **Hull Street Blues Café** (✉ *1222 Hull St.* ☎ *410/727–7476* ⊕ *www.hullstreetblues.com*). This small, local favorite takes full advantage of its river/harbor location with a seafood focus, and any meal should begin with the cream of crab soup.

Attraction: Sprawling **Mount Vernon** (✉ *3200 Mount Vernon Memorial Hwy.* ☎ *703/780–2000* ⊕ *www.mountvernon. org*), the plantation and home of George and Martha Washington, serves as a reminder of the power and complex legacy of our first president and many of the Founding Fathers: leaders in the American Revolution and, simultaneously, enslavers of hundreds of people. Of course, Mount Vernon is a stunning historic home with gorgeous grounds; Washington was a student of landscape design and agriculture who transformed his estate into gardens and fields for observation and production. Even if you don't go inside the revered house, exploring the waterfront grounds is a worthwhile peek into Washington's masterful manipulation of nature. You should also make time to explore the various outbuildings in which enslaved people ran Mount Vernon's many operations. You can learn more about these enslaved people—who represented 90% of Mount Vernon's residents at the time of Washington's death—by visiting one of their living quarters on the property, such as Pioneer Farm.

WILLIAMSBURG

Do: By the time you arrive, many of Williamsburg's Colonial attractions will be closed, but you'll spend a full day here tomorrow so don't fret. In the meantime, enjoy a low-key evening and consider getting to know the area casually with something fun like a candlelight ghost tour.

Eat & Drink: Colonial Williamsburg is the place to embrace full immersion, so kick it off right with dinner at **Josiah Chowning's Tavern** (✉ *109 E. Duke of Gloucester St.* ☎ *800/447–8679* ⊕ *www.colonial-williamsburghotels.com*). The menu is inspired by Colonial pub grub and the restaurant itself is designed as an authentic 18th-century alehouse, complete with period-appropriate entertainment like balladeers and old-timey games nightly.

Stay: Keep the theme going strong with a stay at **Colonial Houses Historic Lodging** (✉ *136 Francis St. E* ☎ *757/565–8440* ⊕ *www.colonialwilliamsburghotels.com*). These Colonial reproductions will blast you to the past with furniture and decor, but you won't have to leave modern luxuries and conveniences behind. Best of all, guests receive discounts and special incentives for Colonial Williamsburg.

Breakfast: Williamsburg is also a college town, and that means there's a proper breakfast scene. Among the most popular is the no-fuss **Colonial Pancake House** (✉ *301 Page St.* ☎ *757/253–5852* ⊕ *www.colonialpancake.com*), which specializes in piles of pancakes and waffles, with plenty of other traditional breakfast-nook fare available.

Day 7: Williamsburg, VA

Today's the day to catch all that Colonial Williamsburg has to offer while the sun's up, so skip the highway and traverse the cobblestone streets on foot. You'll continue onward tomorrow.

Do: Colonial Williamsburg is an enormous living history museum of original and re-created buildings that represent the era when the town was the capital of the 18th-century Virginia colony. More than 300 acres are populated not just with architecture, but period actors strolling the streets and working in shops that were relevant to the once-thriving town. Strolling through town is free, but most historic houses, shops, and performances are ticketed. Start with a visit to the **Colonial Williamsburg Visitor Center** (✉ *101 Visitor Center Dr.* ☎ *855/771–3290* ⊕ *www.colonialwillamsburg.org*) to map your afternoon based on your personal interests, like blacksmithing, letterpress printing, or, if you're a Loyalist, ogling the personal effects of British nobility at Governor's Palace (just kidding … Thomas Jefferson also lived here when he was governor after the war).

Eat & Drink: Have one last dose of Williamsburg-style immersion with a final dinner at **King's Arms Tavern** (✉ *416 E. Duke of Gloucester St.* ☎ *855/578–0080* ⊕ *www.colonialwilliamsburghotels.com*), where servers in period-dress present updated plates inspired by 18th-century recipes that would have been served when the original tavern opened in 1772.

Breakfast: Now with three locations, **AromasWorld** (✉ *431 Prince George St.* ☎ *757/221–6676* ⊕ *www.aromasworld.com*) originated in Williamsburg and serves an extensive menu of house-roasted specialty coffees and teas with delicious freshly baked bites. Breakfast is served until noon and, if you're making a later start today, you could also pick up some sandwiches for lunch any time after 10:30 am.

Day 8: Williamsburg, VA, to Washington, D.C.

150 miles (2 hours, 30 minutes without traffic and stops)

Backtrack today by taking I–95 N up to the nation's capital, Washington, D.C., where you'll find flights to just about anywhere in the country from Ronald Reagan Washington National Airport, Dulles International Airport, or even Baltimore/Washington International Airport.

ALONG THE WAY

Town: There are two worthwhile spots to stop today and, if you still have the energy, it's recommended to hit both. Though they're in opposite directions from Williamsburg, they're only about 30 minutes apart from each other; it's certainly possible to see it all, but feel free to choose just one for a more relaxed day. To the west, your first option is **Jamestown** (✉ *1368 Colonial Pkwy.* ☎ *757/856–1250* ⊕ *www.historicjamestowne.org*), where you can explore the ruins of the first European settlement in the colonies (this area is called Historic Jamestowne) as well as re-creations of the fort with a Powhatan village at a living history museum (this area is called Jamestown Settlement). To the east, you'll find the site of the last major battle of the Revolution, a fitting final day stop. The Siege of Yorktown resulted in a captured British Army and prompted negotiations to end the war. You can visit the battlefield at **Colonial National**

Historical Park (☎ 757/898–3400 ⊕ www.
nps.gov/colo).

Depending where you head today, you
could grab a bite at **Dale House Café**
(✉ 1368 Colonial National Historic Pkwy.
☎ 757/229–1170 ⊕ www.historic-
jamestowne.org) on the James River in
Historic Jamestowne or at **Water Street
Grille** (✉ 323 Water St. ☎ 757/369–5644
⊕ www.waterstreetgrille.net) on
Yorktown Beach. If you're starting early
because you plan to hit both stops, visit
Yorktown second and snag a snack and
a microbrew with a view at Water Street
Grille before journeying onward.

WASHINGTON, D.C.

Do: Since it didn't quite exist until after
the Revolution, the U.S. capital has
admittedly little to do with the early
days of the nation, but it still provides a
fascinating perspective on where these
revolutionary efforts led. Consider Daughters of the **American Revolution Memorial
Hall** (✉ 1776 D St. NW ☎ 202/628–1776
⊕ www.dar.org); the **National Museum
of American History** (✉ 1300 Constitution
Ave. NW ☎ 202/633–1000 ⊕ www.
americanhistory.si.edu), where you'll find
Washington's uniform and Jefferson's
desk; **Anderson House** (✉ 2118 Massachusetts Ave. NW ☎ 202/785–2040
⊕ www.societyofthecincinnati.org); and,
of course, the Washington and Jefferson
Memorials. One essential stop is the
phenomenal **National Museum of African
American History and Culture** (✉ 1400
Constitution Ave. NW ☎ 844/750–3012
⊕ www.nmaahc.si.edu), which seeks to
view American history through the African American experience, giving insight
into how chattel slavery was deeply
entwined with our country's founding
and the contributions African Americans
made to the Revolutionary War.

Eat & Drink: Have an elegant final
dinner at **Plume** (✉ 1200 16th St. NW
☎ 202/448–2300 ⊕ www.plumedc.com)
in The Jefferson hotel. Here you'll find
dishes inspired by the harvests of Monticello in a location fit for a president.

Stay: Rest up at the **Dupont Circle Hotel**
(✉ 1500 New Hampshire Ave. NW
☎ 202/483–6000 ⊕ www.doylecollection.
com) for a chic reentry to the present
day. In this neighborhood, you'll also find
the gorgeous embassies of many United
States' allies—a testament to the international powerhouse that rose from the
struggles and successes of the American
Revolutionary War.

Breakfast: Depending on your departure
time, you may be able to squeeze in an
egg sandwich or huevos revueltos at
Emissary (✉ 2032 P St. NW ☎ 202/748–
5655 ⊕ www.emissarydc.com), but if
time is tight you can at least score your
caffeine of choice from the neighborhood
coffeehouse and wake up on the way to
the airport.

Chapter 3

THE WEST COAST

WELCOME TO THE WEST COAST

TOP REASONS TO GO

★ **Big Sur:** The Pacific Coast Highway is scenic the whole way through, but nothing matches the rugged beauty and winding coastal roads of Big Sur.

★ **Santa Monica Pier:** More than just an old-school amusement park, Santa Monica's famed pier along the Pacific Ocean offers family fun and gorgeous coastal views.

★ **Yosemite National Park:** By merely standing in Yosemite Valley and turning in a circle, you can see more natural wonders in a minute than you could in a full day pretty much anywhere else.

★ **Olympic National Park:** Edged on all sides by water, the forested landscape of Olympic National Park is remote and pristine, capturing the particular beauty of the Pacific Northwest.

★ **The Willamette Valley:** Oregon's famed wine country delivers some of the country's best wine alongside stunning scenery and charming small towns.

1 The Pacific Coast Highway and Highway 101. A drive up the entire West Coast of the United States is completely unforgettable.

2 The Best of Northern California. San Francisco, Lake Tahoe, Yosemite, and more.

3 The Best of Southern California. Los Angeles, Joshua Tree, Orange County, and more.

4 California's National Parks. Hit up every single one of California's nine national parks in one epic trip.

5 The Best of the Pacific Northwest. See the hip cities and stunning landscapes of Washington and Oregon.

6 Wine Countries of the Pacific Northwest. Several of the country's best wine regions are found in its Northwest corner.

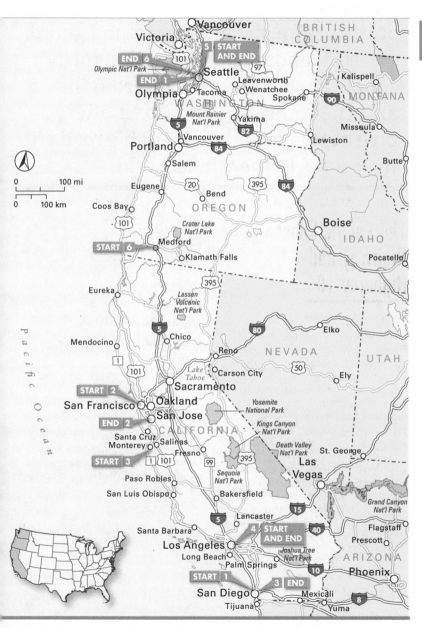

Whether you're looking for curving coastlines overlooking an endless expanse of ocean, treks through misty forests where ancient trees stand guard, or desert landscapes containing rocky monoliths that seem to rise from the sand, the country's West Coast offers some of the most unforgettable road trip adventures in the whole world.

The Pacific Coast Highway and Highway 101

Written by Shoshi Parks

In the pages of Great American Road Trips, the drive from San Diego to Seattle should be at the very top. The route, which glides along the world-famous Pacific Coast Highway from the sunny beaches in Southern California to the redwoods and windswept vistas in the north, then on to rocky Oregon shores and the rain forests of Olympic National Park, is beyond beautiful. Along the way, the West Coast's most dynamic cities, each one a worthy destination in and of itself, line up like the pearls in a 2,878-mile-long necklace. From its epic views and its incredible food to its hiking trails and its city streets, San Diego to Seattle along the 101 is the trip of a lifetime.

At a Glance

Start: San Diego, CA

End: Seattle, WA

Miles Traveled: 1,622 miles

Suggested Duration: 12 days

States Visited: California, Oregon, Washington

Key Sights: Golden Gate Bridge; Hearst Castle; Lewis & Clark National Historic Park; Los Angeles County Museum of Art; Redwood National Park

Best Time to Go: This trip is gorgeous all year long (especially along the Pacific Coast Highway), but you'll get the best weather in the Pacific Northwest in summer and early fall.

Day 1: San Diego, CA, to Los Angeles, CA

125 miles (2 hours without traffic and stops)

California-dream your way out of San Diego and along the southernmost part of the Pacific Coast Highway (PCH). Pass through Orange County's classic beach communities before heading slightly inland to the heart of Los Angeles.

ALONG THE WAY

Town: Take a walk along the wooden Oceanside Pier, one of the state's longest, in Oceanside and catch a wave at South Carlsbad State Beach. Swing by the **California Surf Museum** (✉ 312 Pier View Way ☎ 760/721–6876 ⊕ www.surfmuseum.org) for a look at the popular Southern California sport and the legendary athletes who have made their mark.

Eat & Drink: Drink in ocean views and a craft cocktail or two from the outdoor patio at **Pierside Kitchen & Bar** (✉ 610 Avenida Victoria ☎ 949/218–0980 ⊕ www.piersidesc.com) in San Clemente. On the menu, you'll find delights from the sea including spicy ceviche, octopus al fuego, and a raw bar.

Nature: Get out on the water, post up at **Doheny State Beach** (✉ 25300 Dana Point Harbor Dr. ☎ 949/496–6171 ⊕ www.dohenystatebeach.org), or walk the trails at **Dana Point Headlands Conservation Area** (✉ 34558 Scenic Dr.) to get a glimpse of the majestic mammals that frequent these waters. Whale-watching tours depart from Dana Point Harbor.

LOS ANGELES

Do: The options for things to do in Los Angeles are virtually endless. Wander through massive **Griffith Park** (✉ 4730 Crystal Springs Dr. ☎ 323/913–4688 ⊕ www.laparks.org) or stop by the **La Brea Tar Pits** (✉ 5801 Wilshire Blvd. ☎ 213/763–3499 ⊕ www.tarpits.org) for a glimpse

of prehistoric Los Angeles. Some of the country's best modern art is housed at the **Los Angeles County Museum of Art** (✉ 5905 Wilshire Blvd. ☎ 323/857–6000 ⊕ www.lacma.org), and you can get a glimpse of Hollywood history and movie magic at the **Academy Museum of Motion Pictures** (✉ 6067 Wilshire Blvd. ☎ 323/930–3000 ⊕ www.academymuseum.org).

Eat & Drink: Dig into Korean fried chicken and banchan at Grand Central Market hot spot **Shiku** (✉ 317 S. Broadway ☎ 213/359–6007 ⊕ www.grandcentralmarket.com/vendors/shiku) or Middle Eastern specialties from beloved chef Ori Menashe at **Bavel** (✉ 500 Mateo St. ☎ 213/232–4966 ⊕ www.baveldtla.com). After dinner, **The Slipper Clutch** (✉ 351 S. Broadway), a Downtown Los Angeles bar inspired by New York punk rock, offers highballs and craft beer with a side of pinball.

Stay: Los Angeles is huge and getting from one neighborhood to another can be a major time-suck, so choose your hotel's location carefully. In Koreatown, between Hollywood and Downtown, the boutique **LINE LA** (✉ 3515 Wilshire Blvd. ☎ 213/381–7411 ⊕ www.thelinehotel.com) boasts local art and hosts regular events. Or find art deco nostalgia with a contemporary edge in the casually sophisticated **Mayfair Hotel** (✉ 717 Hartford Ave. ☎ 213/632–1200 ⊕ www.members.love) in Downtown L.A.

Breakfast: Get a classic L.A. diner breakfast at the **House of Breakfast** (✉ 3728 W. Olympic Blvd. ☎ 323/731–5405).

Day 2: Los Angeles, CA, to San Luis Obispo, CA

189 miles (3 hours without traffic and stops)

Navigate north up the PCH toward celebrity hangout Santa Barbara. Outside the city, you enter the state's lesser-known wine country and pass through Solvang, one of

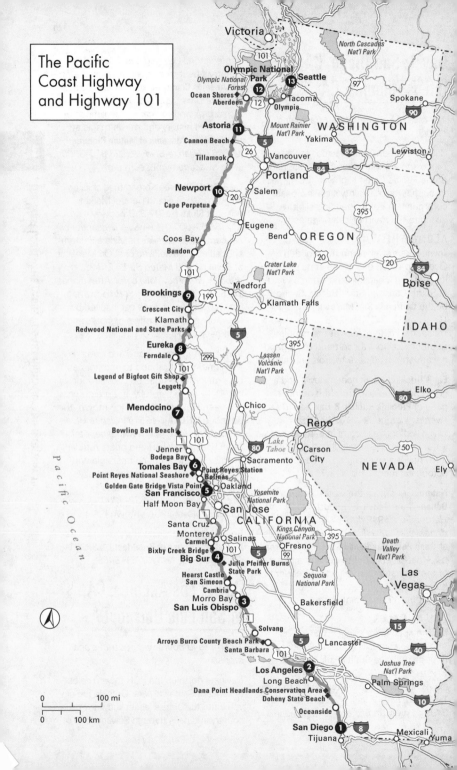

California's quirkiest towns, before returning to the coast and San Luis Obispo.

ALONG THE WAY

Town: In Santa Barbara, see what's blooming at the **Santa Barbara Botanic Garden** (⊠ 1212 Mission Canyon Rd. ☎ 805/682–4726 ⊕ www.sbbg.org) or visit the Old Mission (⊠ 2201 Laguna St. ☎ 805/682–4713 ⊕ www.santabarbara-mission.org), one of California's original 18th-century Spanish missions. There's plenty of shopping to be done downtown where luxury retailers and boutique stores rub elbows with larger chains.

Eat & Drink: The longtime local favorite **La Super-Rica Taqueria** (⊠ 622 N. Milpas St. ☎ 805/963–4940 ⊕ www.facebook.com/lasuperricataqueria) in Santa Barbara packs authentic flavor and is the perfect introduction to Southern California tacos.

Nature: Sprawl out on the sand or take a swim at **Arroyo Burro County Beach Park** (⊠ 2981 Cliff Dr. ☎ 805/687–3714 ⊕ www.countyofsb.org), called Hendry's Beach by locals.

Roadside Attraction: The bizarre wine country town of Solvang is equal parts Danish village and Disney movie.

SAN LUIS OBISPO

Do: There are vineyards galore just outside San Luis Obispo in the Edna Valley. Join an organized wine tour or plan your own with a wine-touring map available at the Old Edna Townsite. A historic Mission, the **Mission San Luis Obispo de Tolosa** (⊠ 751 Palm St. ☎ 805/781–8220 ⊕ www.missionsanluisobispo.org), still stands in the Old Town Historic District.

Eat & Drink: The craft eatery **Taste!** (⊠ 2900 Broad St. ☎ 805/200–2978 ⊕ www.taste2900.com), which serves everything from classic burgers to pork banh mi, has been winning awards in SLO since it opened in 2014. At the **Sidecar Cocktail Co.** (⊠ 1040 Broad St. ☎ 805/439–3563 ⊕ www.sidecarslo.com), sip on margaritas and tiki drinks

Essential Listening

Make your way through Southern California with the classic surf rock tunes of *The Beach Boys Greatest Hits.*

or go for dinner, when the brick-walled bar/restaurant serves some of the best comfort food in town.

Stay: The popular themed rooms at the world-famous **Madonna Inn** (⊠ 100 Madonna Rd. ☎ 805/543–3000 ⊕ www.madonnainn.com) include everything from "Yosemite Rock" to "Love Nest." The kitschy on-site Silver Bar Cocktail Lounge is worth a visit whether you are staying here or not.

Breakfast: Over 100 different delectable doughnut flavors are available every day (including vegan and gluten-free options) at **SloDoCo Donuts** (⊠ 793F Foothill Blvd. ☎ 805/782–9766 ⊕ www.slodoco.com).

Day 3: San Luis Obispo, CA, to Big Sur, CA

107 miles (2 hours, 15 minutes without traffic and stops)

Head north past Cambria and toward the rocky bluffs, towering redwoods, and rushing waterfalls of Big Sur, where the California coast puts on one of its most spectacular shows.

ALONG THE WAY

Eat & Drink: Get fresh seafood plucked straight from Morro Bay at **The Galley** (⊠ 899 Embarcadero ☎ 805/772–7777 ⊕ www.galleymorrobay.com), a waterfront restaurant on the Morro Bay Embarcadero.

Town: The laid-back beach town of Cambria extends from beautiful Moonstone Beach to a quaint downtown peppered with antiques shops and boutiques. Swing by **Nitt Witt Ridge** (✉ *881 Hillcrest Dr., Cambria, CA* ☎ *805/927–2690* ⊕ *nitwit-ridge.business.site*), a house made completely of garbage and a bastion of folk art, for a tour or a photo.

Roadside Attraction: The lavish **Hearst Castle** (✉ *750 Hearst Castle Rd., San Simeon, CA* ☎ *800/444–4445* ⊕ *www.hearstcastle.org*), built for publishing magnate William Randolph Hearst by early 19th-century architect extraordinaire Julia Morgan, has more than 40 bedrooms, 61 bathrooms, indoor and outdoor swimming pools, a movie theater, and 127 acres of gardens. Tours are offered regularly.

Photo Op: The descendants of the zebras (yes, zebras) once kept at Hearst Castle are often visible from the side of Highway 1 in San Simeon.

BIG SUR

Do: Get a look at Big Sur's McWay Falls from Highway 1, then hit the trail at **Julia Pfeiffer Burns State Park** (✉ *52801 CA-1* ☎ *831/667–1112* ⊕ *www.parks.ca.gov*) or the water at **Sand Dollar Beach** (✉ *CA-1* ☎ *805/434–1996* ⊕ *www.parks.ca.gov*) or **Andrew Molera State Park** (✉ *45500 CA-1* ☎ *831/667–2315* ⊕ *www.parks.ca.gov*).

Eat & Drink: **Nepenthe** (✉ *48510 CA-1* ☎ *831/667–2345* ⊕ *www.nepenthe.com*) isn't the cheapest spot in town, but its location alone, crowning the top of a ridge overlooking the Pacific, is worth the splurge. Get a cocktail or enjoy a full dinner of steak and seafood out on the patio.

Stay: If you have the gear for a night under the stars, snag a campsite at Julia Pfeiffer Burns State Park. To get a reservation, plan to book as far in advance as possible. Otherwise, the **Big Sur Lodge** (✉ *47225 CA-1* ☎ *831/667–3100* ⊕ *www.bigsurlodge.com*) is a clean, comfortable option.

But if you've got cash to burn, you won't regret a night at the epic **Post Ranch Inn** (✉ *47900 CA-1* ☎ *831/667–2200* ⊕ *www.postranchinn.com*).

Breakfast: The rustic-modern **Big Sur Bakery** (✉ *47540 CA-1* ☎ *831/667–0520* ⊕ *www.bigsurbakery.com*) has coffee, fresh-baked bread and pastries, and a selection of heartier breakfast options.

Day 4: Big Sur, CA, to San Francisco, CA

149 miles (3 hours without traffic and stops)

Travel on toward San Francisco. As you pass the artist colony of Carmel and the town of Monterey (the setting for John Steinbeck's 1945 novel *Cannery Row* and the more modern HBO series *Big Little Lies*), stick to Highway 1 and the beach towns that line the coast of the Bay Area. This route adds 30 minutes to the trip but is a much more interesting drive than going up Highway 101.

ALONG THE WAY

Photo Op: Cross the world-famous Bixby Creek Bridge on the northern end of Big Sur then pull over to get the perfect shot.

Town: Tiny Carmel has long drawn artists with its charm. Explore the town's galleries and boutiques and, if you have the time, take a quick detour down the aptly named 17-Mile Drive for lovely views and a look at how the other half lives.

Eat & Drink: Stop at the roadside favorite **Sam's Chowder House** (✉ *4210 CA-1* ☎ *650/712–0245* ⊕ *www.samschowderhouse.com*) in Half Moon Bay for a bowl of clam chowder and a beer on the patio.

SAN FRANCISCO

Do: From the "Painted Ladies" (Victorian homes) of the Haight to the back alleys of the largest Chinatown outside Asia, San Francisco is one of the country's most enchanting cities. The murals in the

One of the most photographed spots along the coast, Bixby Bridge has amazing views of Big Sur.

Mission neighborhood, North Beach's **Coit Tower** (✉ *1 Telegraph Hill Blvd.* ☎ *415/249–0995* ⊕ *www.sfrecpark.org*), and downtown museums like the **SFMoMa** (✉ *151 3rd St.* ☎ *415/357–4000* ⊕ *www.sfmoma. org*) are among the many must-sees.

Eat & Drink: Get an authentic modern take on Chinese food at **Mister Jiu's** (✉ *28 Waverly Pl.* ☎ *415/857–9688* ⊕ *www. misterjius.com*) or a San Francisco–style burrito from a city favorite, **La Taqueria** (✉ *2889 Mission St.* ☎ *415/285–7117* ⊕ *www.facebook.com/LaTaqSF*). After dinner, head to Haight Street for a drink at the classic dive **Aub Zam Zam** (✉ *1633 Haight St.* ☎ *415/861–2545*) or craft-cocktail favorite the **Alembic** (✉ *1725 Haight St.* ☎ *415/666–0822* ⊕ *www.alembicsf.com*).

Stay: The stylish **Proper Hotel** (✉ *45 McAllister St.* ☎ *415/735–7777* ⊕ *www.properhotel.com*) near the Civic Center is a carefully orchestrated gallery of art and design with a popular rooftop bar, while the boutique **Hotel Kabuki** (✉ *1625 Post St.* ☎ *415/922–3200* ⊕ *www.jdvhotels.com*) in Japantown will swath you in its Zen aesthetic.

Breakfast: Before heading over the Golden Gate Bridge to Marin, grab a satisfying southern breakfast at **Brenda's French Soul Food** (✉ *652 Polk St.* ☎ *415/345–8100* ⊕ *www.frenchsoulfood.com*) in the Tenderloin.

Day 5: San Francisco, CA, to Tomales Bay, CA

50 miles (1 hour, 40 minutes without traffic and stops)

It's a short drive today over the iconic Golden Gate Bridge and up Highway 1 to the Point Reyes National Seashore and the oyster-rich waters of Tomales Bay.

ALONG THE WAY
Photo Op: Cross the Golden Gate then pull over at the **Golden Gate Bridge Vista Point** (⊕ *www.goldengatebridge.org*) for a view of the architectural marvel in all its glory.

Detour: The "hidden" town of **Bolinas**, a small surfing community in a cove of Bolinas Bay, is about a 10-minute drive from Highway 1. The community abuts Mount Tamalpais and you can hike straight from town into the redwoods that sprout from Marin's tallest mountain.

Town: The tiny, historic town of **Point Reyes Station** has a handful of pleasant shops and restaurants. It's a lovely stop before hitting the wild lands of the national seashore a few miles down the road.

Eat & Drink: One of Northern California's best cheese purveyors, **Cowgirl Creamery** (✉ 80 4th St. ☎ 415/663–9335 ⊕ cowgirl-creamery.square.site) in Point Reyes Station is the perfect stop. Pick up a round of Mt. Tam, the creamery's flagship triple cream, along with bread, charcuterie, and wine for lunch alfresco.

TOMALES BAY

Do: Head to **Point Reyes National Seashore** (☎ 415/464–5137 ⊕ www.nps.gov/pore) is an unusual mix of historical ranching and dairy lands and protected wilderness. See the wild Tule Elk at Tomales Point, whale-watch from the 150-year-old Point Reyes Lighthouse, and get a look at the elephant seal colony at Chimney Rock.

Eat & Drink: When you've had your fill of Point Reyes, hit the road to drive up the inland side of Tomales Bay. **The Marshall Store** (✉ 19225 CA-1 ☎ 415/663–1339 ⊕ www.themarshallstore.com), a roadside joint with barbecued oysters, Dungeness crab sandwiches, and other delights from the bay, is always worth a stop.

Stay: About four miles up the road from the Marshall Store, **Nick's Cove** (✉ 23240 CA-1 ☎ 415/663–1033 ⊕ www.nickscove.com) has well-appointed cabins that hang out over the calm Tomales waters. Nick's also has a fantastic farm-to-table restaurant (and their own hillside farm, The Croft, a historic boathouse for sipping cocktails, and a small beach with a fire pit for roasting marshmallows after dark.

Breakfast: It's a 10-mile drive to Valley Ford and the **Estero Cafe** (✉ 14450 CA-1 ☎ 707/876–3333 ⊕ www.estero.cafe), a local café with a knack for breakfast.

Day 6: Tomales Bay, CA, to Mendocino, CA

129 miles (3 hours without stops)

It's a day of spectacular views and quaint coastal towns as you continue up the PCH toward Mendocino.

ALONG THE WAY

Town: In Bodega Bay, tool around town on a bike or rent a kayak for a few hours on the water. Four miles from the coast is the village of Bodega, the filming location for Alfred Hitchcock's 1963 film *The Birds*.

Eat & Drink: In Jenner, the Russian River meets the sea. Find stunning views of both at the intimate **River's End Restaurant** (✉ 11048 CA-1 ☎ 707/865–2484 ⊕ www.ilovesunsets.com), which specializes in local seafood and seasonal produce.

Nature: In Point Arena, Bowling Ball Beach is littered with perfectly round boulders carefully carved by the waves.

MENDOCINO

Do: This laid-back town is a mecca for artists and gallery owners. Check out the **Mendocino Art Center** (✉ 45200 Little Lake St. ☎ 707/937–5818 ⊕ www.mendocinoartcenter.org), then browse some of the many galleries in town. If you prefer your art in liquid form, there are a number of wineries in nearby Anderson Valley.

Eat & Drink: Farm-to-table California cuisine is on the menu at the cozy **Trillium Cafe** (✉ 10390 Kasten St. ☎ 707/937–3200 ⊕ www.trilliummendocino.com). End the night with a shot and a beer at **Dick's Place** (✉ 45070 Main St. ☎ 707/937–6010), a dive on Main Street over a century old.

Stay: The **Blue Door Inn** (✉ 10481 Howard St. ☎ 707/937–4892 ⊕ www.

bluedoorgroup.com) is an elegant Victorian bed-and-breakfast with a modern aesthetic. Many of the rooms have fireplaces, soaking tubs, and views of the Pacific.

Breakfast: Grab a coffee and breakfast (or just a pastry for the road) at the **Goodlife Cafe & Bakery** (✉ *10483 Lansing St.* ☎ *707/937–0836* ⊕ *www.goodlifecafe-mendo.com*).

Day 7: Mendocino, CA, to Eureka, CA

143 miles (3 hours without traffic and stops)

Today's route takes you away from the coast and into the weird and wonderful world of rural Northern California on the Redwood Highway (also known as Highway 101). At the day's end, you're back at the coast in Eureka, a city that rose to prominence during the gold rush era.

ALONG THE WAY

Town: Leggett is crawling with unusual attractions just kitschy enough to be fun. Drive through a massive Sequoia at the **Chandelier Drive-Through Tree** (✉ *67402 Drive Thru Tree Rd.* ☎ *707/925–6464* ⊕ *www.drivethruthree.com*), visit the **One Log House** (✉ *705 N. Hwy. 1* ☎ *707/247–3417* ⊕ *www.oneloghouse.com*), and take home a Sasquatch effigy at the **Legend of Bigfoot Gift Shop** (✉ *2500 U.S. 101, Garberville, CA* ☎ *707/247–3332*).

Eat & Drink: The roadside café **The Peg House** (✉ *69501 U.S. 101* ☎ *707/925–6444* ⊕ *www.thepeghouse.com*) in Leggett has a large patio, live music, and burgers and oysters hot off the grill.

Roadside Attraction: All of Leggett's roadside attractions are amusing, but **Confusion Hill** (✉ *75001 U.S. 101* ☎ *707/925–6456* ⊕ *www.confusionhill.com*) takes

the cake. Built for midcentury road-trippers, this mysterious spot is home to the "gravity house," the "chipalope," and the world's tallest freestanding redwood chainsaw carving.

Detour: The well-maintained Victorian town of Ferndale is so charming that it has shown up in a number of movies and TV shows, including 1995's *Outbreak* and 2001's *The Majestic*. It's also got a spectacular hillside cemetery as creepy as it is lovely. You'll find Ferndale a 10-mile drive toward the coast from Highway 101.

EUREKA

Do: The entire town of Eureka has been named a historic landmark, but the best-preserved blocks are located in Old Town. Explore the neighborhood on foot and don't forget to check out the **Carson Mansion** (✉ *143 M St.* ☎ *707/443–5665* ⊕ *www.ingomar.org*), considered the grandest Victorian home in the United States.

Eat & Drink: The sophisticated yet unstuffy **Humboldt Bay Provisions** (✉ *205 G St.* ☎ *707/672–3850* ⊕ *www.humboldtbayprovisions.com*) deals in fresh local oysters and handcrafted cheeses, meats, breads, and desserts. For a more laid-back meal, hit the **Lost Coast Brewery Taproom** (✉ *1600 Sunset* ☎ *707/267–9651* ⊕ *www.lostcoast.com*), where they've got a menu full of sandwiches, salads, and appetizers along with some of the best beer in town.

Stay: Get your own slice of Victorian heaven with a night's stay at the historic **Carter House Inn** (✉ *301 L St.* ☎ *800/404–1390* ⊕ *www.carterhouse.com*).

Breakfast: Fill up on breakfast favorites like French toast, biscuits and gravy, and eggs Benedict at the **Greene Lily Cafe** (✉ *307 2nd St.* ☎ *707/798–6083* ⊕ *www.thegreenlilycafe.com*).

Day 8: Eureka, CA, to Brookings, OR

106 miles (2 hours, 10 minutes without stops)

Bouncing back and forth from coast to forest, today's drive takes you north through Redwood National and State Parks and over the Oregon state border.

ALONG THE WAY

Nature: Redwood National and State Parks (✉ 707/464–6101 ⊕ *www.nps.gov/redw*) are a collection of protected spaces stretching almost 50 miles from Crescent City to Orick, California. Walk among the giant redwood trees in Jedediah Smith Redwoods, visit lush Fern Canyon in Prairie Creek Redwoods, and watch the Roosevelt elk graze near Gold Bluffs Beach.

Eat & Drink: Fill up on sandwiches, soups, and salads at the **Log Cabin Diner** (✉ 301 CA-169 ☎ 707/482–0400 ⊕ *www.logcabindiner.net*) in Klamath, California. After lunch, say hello to the emus that live next door.

Town: Stop in at Crescent City, California, to check out the beautiful **Battery Point Lighthouse** (✉ 235 Lighthouse Way ☎ 707/464–3089 ⊕ *www.delnortehistory.org*), one of the oldest on the West Coast. In town, you'll find plenty of shops and galleries to peruse as well as cafés and restaurants.

BROOKINGS

Do: The redwoods and coastal views don't stop at the Oregon border. In Brookings, take a hike along the **Oregon Redwoods Trail** (☎ 541/247–3600 ⊕ *www.fs.usda.gov*) and admire the rock formations rising out of Lone Ranch Beach.

Eat & Drink: Indulge in superfresh sushi and seafood at local favorite, the **Pacific Sushi & Grill** (✉ 613 Chetco Ave. ☎ 541/251–7707 ⊕ *www.pacifisushi.com*). At the **Oxenfre Public House** (✉ 631

Extend Your Trip

From Los Angeles: The Best of Southern California; California's National Parks *(Ch. 3)*

From Big Sur: The Best of Southern California *(Ch. 3)*

From San Francisco: The Best of Northern California *(Ch. 3)*

From Seattle: The Best of the Pacific Northwest; Wine Countries of the Pacific Northwest *(Ch. 3)*; Ultimate Cross Country Road Trip North *(Ch. 2)*

Chetco Ave. ☎ 541/813–1985 ⊕ *www.oxenpub.com*), a gastropub serving local organic food late into the night, you can down a stiff drink and check out live music.

Stay: Wake up with a view of the Pacific at the comfortable and modern **Beachfront Inn** (✉ 16008 Boat Basin Rd. ☎ 541/469–7779 ⊕ *www.beachfrontinn.com*).

Breakfast: Get pancakes and other classic breakfast dishes at the rustic diner **Mattie's Pancake House** (✉ 15975 U.S. 101 ☎ 541/469–7211).

Day 9: Brookings, CA, to Newport, OR

205 miles (4 hours, 15 minutes without traffic or stops)

The Oregon Coast pulls out all the stops today as you head north from Brookings, through the fishing town of Bandon, past the Oregon Dunes National Recreation Area, and on to Newport.

ALONG THE WAY

Town: Once a major fishing hub on the Oregon Coast, Bandon now caters more to tourists with fun shops, harborside eats, and a cheese-producing creamery, **Face Rock** (✉ 680 2nd St. S.E. ☎ 541/347–3223 ⊕ www.facerockcreamery.com).

Eat & Drink: Nosh on award-winning fish tacos, Dungeness crab rolls, and local oysters at the no-frills **Tony's Crab Shack** (✉ 155 1st St. SE ☎ 541/347–2875 ⊕ www.tonyscrabshack.com) by the water in Bandon.

Photo Op: The rocky coastline in Cape Perpetua forms delightful natural fountains and churns at the Spouting Horn and Thor's Well.

NEWPORT

Do: See otters and fish endemic to this region of the Pacific at the **Oregon Coast Aquarium** (✉ 2820 S.E. Ferry Slip Rd. ☎ 541/867–3474 ⊕ www.aquarium.org) or walk along the town's historic bayfront where seafood processing has been ongoing for over 100 years. At the northern end of town, the **Yaquina Head Lighthouse** (✉ 750 N.W. Lighthouse Dr. ☎ 541/574–3100 ⊕ www.blm.gov) stands tall above Nye Beach's long stretch of sand.

Eat & Drink: Splurge on a dinner of seafood prepared with unique international flavors at Local Ocean (✉ 213 S.E. Bay Blvd. ☎ 541/574–7959 ⊕ www. localocean.net), then head to the historic local dive, the **Bay Haven Inn** (✉ 608 S.W. Bay Blvd. ☎ 541/265–7271 ⊕ www. bay-haven-inn.poi.place). Before going in, stop across the street to visit the colony of sea lions that post up at the harbor.

Stay: Let the sounds of the sea lull you to sleep at the **Ocean House Bed & Breakfast** (✉ 4920 N.W. Woody Way ☎ 541/265–3888 ⊕ www.oceanhouse.com) at Nye Beach or enjoy a stay at the **Whaler** (✉ 155 S.W. Elizabeth St. ☎ 541/272–3630 ⊕ www.whalernewport.com), a cozy motel with ocean views and a private balcony in every room.

Breakfast: The hole-in-the-wall **Cafe Stephanie** (✉ 411 N.W. Coast St. ☎ 541/265–8082 ⊕ www.facebook.com/nyebeach-cafestephanie) serves an excellent daily breakfast menu with options like quiche, crepes, and breakfast burritos.

Day 10: Newport, OR, to Astoria, OR

133 miles (3 hours without stops)

Highway 101 sweeps inland today, passing through the outer edge of Tillamook State Forest before heading back to the coast and the site where Lewis and Clark first saw the Pacific. The day's drive ends in Astoria, a port town and one of the stars of 1985's *The Goonies*.

ALONG THE WAY

Eat & Drink: Brake for some cheese (and a tour) at the **Tillamook Creamery** (✉ 4165 N. Hwy. 101 ☎ 503/815–1300 ⊕ www. tillamook.com) in Tillamook. The on-site café sells multiple iterations of mac and cheese along with pizza, sandwiches, and ice cream.

Town: Go for a stroll along Cannon Beach, a wide swath of golden sand punctuated by massive monoliths, including the 235-foot-tall Haystack Rock.

ASTORIA

Do: Learn about Lewis and Clark's epic adventure to discover the West in the early 19th century and peek inside their winter shelter, Fort Clatsop, at the **Lewis & Clark National Historic Park** (✉ 92343 Fort Clatsop Rd. ☎ 503/661–2471 ⊕ www.nps.gov/lewi). In town, *Goonies* fans will get a kick out of the **Oregon Film Museum** (✉ 732 Duane St. ☎ 503/325–2203 ⊕ www.oregonfilmmuseum.org), while aficionados of architecture and design will enjoy the **Flavel House Museum** (✉ 714 Exchange St. ☎ 503/325–2203 ⊕ www.astoriamuseums.org).

Eat & Drink: Astoria's food-and-drink scene is best known for its seafood and beer, both of which you can find tasty versions of at the **Buoy Beer Company** (✉ 1 8th St. ☎ 503/325–4540 ⊕ www.buoybeer. com). For something different, check out the traditional eastern European dishes served at **Drina Daisy Bosnian Restaurant** (✉ 915 Commercial St. ☎ 503/338–2912 www.drinadaisy.com).

Stay: Find modern elegance for a song at the boutique **Hotel Elliot** (✉ 357 12th St. ☎ 503/325–2222 www.hotelelliott.com) or check in at the stylish **Selina Commodore Hotel** (✉ 258 14th St. ☎ 786/485–0498 ⊕ www.selina.com), a historic property downtown.

Breakfast: Delicious breads and seasonal, organic breakfast dishes are made fresh daily at the worker's collective, the **Blue Scorcher Bakery & Cafe** (✉ 1493 Duane St. ☎ 503/338–7473 ⊕ www. bluescorcher.coop).

Day 11: Astoria, OR, to Olympic National Park

132 miles (2 hours, 45 minutes without stops)

Take in the last of the ocean views on your last day driving the coast. Then cross over the Washington border and head north to Lake Quinault in Olympic National Park.

ALONG THE WAY

Town: In the industrial harbor town of Aberdeen, Washington, you'll find several homages to Kurt Cobain, who grew up here in the 1970s and 1980s. See memorials to the musician above and below the bridge in Kurt Cobain Memorial Park and get a look at his childhood home at 1210 E. 1st Street.

Eat & Drink: Have a pint alongside high-quality gastropub fare at the more-than-a-century-old **8th Street Ale House** (✉ 207 8th St. ☎ 360/612–3455 ⊕ www.8thstreetalehouse.com) in Aberdeen.

Detour: It's about a 15-minute drive from the fork in the road north of Gray's Harbor City to Ocean Shores, a well-loved summer vacation spot with an endless beach.

OLYMPIC NATIONAL PARK

Do: Although you won't be able to see the entirety of **Olympic National Park** (☎ 360/565–3130 ⊕ www.nps.gov/olym), a place that covers more than a million acres of diverse landscape, you can explore its lower reaches. Head for Lake Quinault where you can swim, fish, or boat in the lake or hike the Quinault Rain Forest Trail.

Eat & Drink: Dine on the delights of the Pacific Northwest at the **Salmon House** (✉ 516 S. Shore Rd. ☎ 360/288–2535 ⊕ www.rfrv.com) at the Rainforest Resort. Their menu includes house-smoked salmon, steak, pasta, and selections from their full bar.

Stay: A perfect remnant of midcentury Americana, the waterfront **Lake Quinault Lodge** (✉ 345 S. Shore Rd. ☎ 888/896–3818 ⊕ www.olympicnationalparks.com) has a wide lawn set with Adirondack chairs, outdoor games and a swimming dock. Or find camping nearby at the **Falls Creek Campground** (✉ S. Shore Rd. ☎ 360/288–0203 ⊕ www.recreation.gov).

Breakfast: Grab breakfast with a view of the lake in the Lake Quinault Lodge's Roosevelt Room.

Day 12: Olympic National Park to Seattle, WA

154 miles (2 hours, 45 minutes without traffic and stops)

On the last day of your road trip, backtrack to Aberdeen, then head east through the state capital of Olympia and then north on I–5 to the bustling city of Seattle,

ALONG THE WAY

Town: Make a stop in the Washington state capital, Olympia, for a tour of the legislature and supreme court or check out the **Monarch Sculpture Park** (✉ 8431 Waldrick Rd. SE ☎ 360/264–2408 ⊕ www.monarchsculpturepark.org) and its many outdoor works of art. If you're traveling with kids, they'll get a kick out of the **Hands On Children's Museum** (✉ 414 Jefferson St. NE ☎ 360/956–0818 www.hocm.org).

Eat & Drink: Order an oh-so-satisfying sandwich or salad at the popular **Lucky Lunchbox** (✉ 2826 Capitol Blvd. SE ☎ 360/259–8164 ⊕ www.theluckylunchbox.com) in Olympia.

SEATTLE

Do: Whether it's your first time in Seattle or your 100th, the city's greatest hits—including the delicate sculptures at the **Chihuly Garden & Glass Museum** (✉ 305 Harrison St. ☎ 206/753–4940 ⊕ www.chihulygardenandglass.com), the bustling seafood market **Pike Place** (✉ 85 Pike St. ☎ 206/682–7453 ⊕ www.pikeplacemarket.org), and the iconic **Space Needle** (✉ 400 Broad St. ☎ 206/905–2100 ⊕ www.spaceneedle.com)—never get old. Options a little farther off the beaten track include a visit to the Fremont Troll, the **Museum of Pop Culture** (✉ 325 5th Ave. N ☎ 206/770–2700 ⊕ www.mopop.org), and the interconnecting tunnels of the **Seattle Underground** (✉ 102 Cherry St. ⊕ www.undergroundtour.com).

Eat & Drink: Seattle's food scene is nothing short of fantastic. Find excellent Latin American and Cuban food at **Mojito** (✉ 7545 Lake City Way N.E. ☎ 206/525–3162 ⊕ www.mojitoseattle.com), masterful Indian at Pioneer Square's **Nirmal's** (✉ 106 Occidental Ave. S. ☎ 206/683–9701 ⊕ www.nirmalseattle.com), and fresh seafood at **Matt's in the Market** (✉ 94 Pike St. ☎ 206/467–7909 ⊕ www.mattsinthemarket.com). Sip martinis and more at **Bathtub Gin & Co.** (✉ 2205 2nd Ave. ☎ 206/728–6069 ⊕ www.

Essential Listening

Grunge may not be king in Seattle anymore, but Washington state still has a special place in its heart for Nirvana and their magnum opus, *Nevermind*.

bathtubginseattle.com), an unpretentious basement speakeasy in Belltown.

Stay: Get an affordable night's stay at the colorful, art-accented **Maxwell Hotel** (✉ 300 Roy St. ☎ 206/286–0629 ⊕ www.staypineapple.com) at the base of Queen Anne Hill. The **Alexis Royal Sonesta Hotel** (✉ 1007 1st Ave. ☎ 206/624–4844 ⊕ www.sonesta.com) epitomizes the aesthetic of the Pacific Northwest, with contemporary style and a palette of marine blues and forest greens.

Breakfast: Start the day off with a comforting spread from **Fat's Fried Chicken and Waffles** (✉ 2726 E. Cherry St. ☎ 206/602–6863 ⊕ www.fatschickenandwaffles.com).

The Best of Northern California

Written by Shoshi Parks

Northern California is indisputably one of the country's most spectacular regions and on this road trip it puts on its most spectacular show. The 10-day drive will take you from San Francisco and Napa Valley to Lake Tahoe and Yosemite National Park, and then on to the Monterey Bay. In between the dramatic Pacific coastline in the west and the rugged Sierra Nevada Mountains in the east, you'll find three major cities, incredible ecological diversity, and some of the best wine regions in the world.

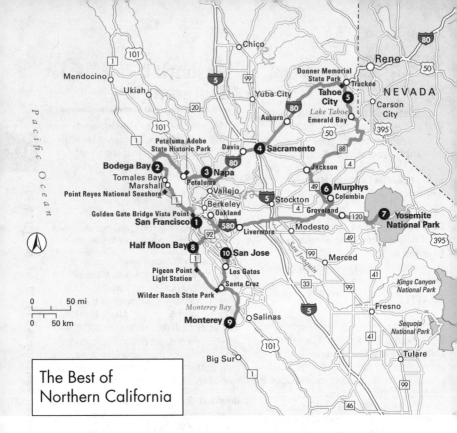

The Best of
Northern California

At a Glance

Start: San Francisco, CA

End: San Jose, CA

Miles Traveled: 880 miles

Suggested Duration: 9 days

States Visited: California

Key Sights: Golden Gate Bridge; Lake
Tahoe; Napa Valley; Winchester Mystery
House; Yosemite National Park

Best Time to Go: Thanks to Northern
California's mild Mediterranean climate,
this trip is just as enjoyable in the dead of
winter as it is in the heat of summer.

Day 1: San Francisco to Bodega Bay

*53 miles (1 hour, 30 minutes without
traffic and stops)*

Your first day takes you from the San
Francisco Airport north on Highway
101 and into the city of San Francisco.
After seeing the sights, drive down Park
Presidio and cross the majestic Golden
Gate Bridge. Continue north through
Marin, then head west to Tomales Bay
and Bodega Bay just beyond.

ALONG THE WAY

Town: San Francisco is worth a full day of
exploration (or more), but if you're just
passing through on the way to Bodega
Bay, you can still do a quick circuit of
some of the city's greatest hits. Check

out the old-school Italian neighborhood North Beach, Coit Tower, and the cable cars on Russian Hill or visit Mission Dolores, the painted ladies of NoPa and Haight Street, and scenic **Golden Gate Park** (☎ 415/831–2700 ⊕ www. sfrecpark.org).

Eat & Drink: San Francisco is hands down one of the best food cities in the country. In the North Beach area, try pizza from a 13-time world champion at **Tony's Pizza Napoletana** (✉ 1570 Stockton St. ☎ 415/835–9888 ⊕ www.tonspizzanapo-letana.com). In the Mission, choose from a variety of small women-owned eateries at the **LaCocina Municipal Marketplace** (✉ 101 Hyde St. ☎ 415 570–2595 ⊕ laco-cinamarketplace.com). Over in NoPa, check out **Che Fico Alimentari** (✉ 834 Divisadero St. ☎ 415/416–6980 ⊕ www. cheficoalimentari.com), a nationally renowned Italian salumeria.

Photo Op: There's no better photo op than the Golden Gate Bridge, especially when the fog rolls through in the afternoon. Pull over at the **Golden Gate Bridge Vista Point** (⊕ www.goldengatebridge.org) on its northern side for the best view.

Detour: Cross to the western side of Tomales Bay near the adorable town of Point Reyes Station for a visit to **Point Reyes National Seashore** (☎ 415/464–5137 ⊕ www.nps.gov/pore), where there are miles of beach, hiking trails that weave among herds of endangered Tule elk, and a historic lighthouse.

BODEGA BAY

Do: Rent a kayak and hit the water or take a tour with **Blue Waters Kayaking** (✉ 11401 CA-1 ☎ 415/669–2600 ⊕ www.bluewa-terskayaking.com) after dark for a chance at seeing glowing bioluminescence in Tomales Bay. If you prefer to stay on dry land, try your hand at shucking the area's famous oysters at the rustic-hip **Hog Island Oyster Company** (✉ 20215 Shore-line Hwy. ☎ 415/663–9218 ⊕ www.

hogislandoysters.com) in Marshall (reser-vations recommended).

Eat & Drink: The no-frills **Marshall Store** (✉ 19225 CA-1 ☎ 415/663–1339 ⊕ www.themarshallstore.com) has fantastic raw and barbecued oysters, not to mention rolls piled high with Dunge-ness crab. For a more extensive meal of fresh local seafood and farm-fresh produce, continue up the road to **Nick's Cove** (✉ 23240 CA-1 ☎ 415/663–1033 ⊕ www.nickscove.com), a historic road-house that's a destination in itself.

Stay: Spend the night in the beautifully renovated bayside cottages at Nick's Cove or head up the road to the **Bodega Bay Lodge** (✉ 103 CA-1 ☎ 707/875–3525 ⊕ www.bodegalodge.com), a comfort-able hotel with sweeping views of the shoreline.

Breakfast: Feast on crab cakes and a view at **Spud Point Crab Co.** (✉ 1910 Westshore Rd. ☎ 707/875–9472 ⊕ www.spudpoint-crabco.com) or grab coffee and a bagel at **Roadhouse Coffee** (✉ 1580 Eastshore Rd.), both in Bodega Bay.

Day 2: Bodega Bay to Napa

42 miles (1 hour without traffic and stops)

Drive east on Adobe Road over the hills and into Sonoma County. Spend some time in historic downtown Petaluma then continue east through the famed vineyards of Napa Valley on Highways 116 and 121.

ALONG THE WAY

Town: In Petaluma, you'll find a fetching historic downtown rife with Victorian-era homes, boutiques, and antiques stores. For a self-guided walking tour, stop in at the **Petaluma Visitors Center** (✉ 210 Lakeville St. ☎ 707/769–0429 ⊕ www. visitpetaluma.com).

Eat & Drink: While in town, stop for lunch at Petaluma's cozy riverside **Wild Goat Bistro** (✉ 6 Petaluma Blvd. N.

☎ 707/658–1156 ⊕ www.wildgoatbistro.com) or the **Tea Room Cafe** (✉ 316 Western Ave. ☎ 707/765–0199 ⊕ www.tearoomcafe.com), a sweet bakery where breakfast and sandwiches are served all day.

Roadside Attraction: Tour one of the best-preserved early-19th-century adobes left in California at the **Petaluma Adobe State Historic Park** (✉ 3325 Adobe Rd. ☎ 707/762–4871 ⊕ www.parks.ca.gov), which was once the seat of an agricultural empire owned by General Mariano Guadalupe Vallejo.

NAPA

Do: Wine taste the day away in the vineyards of Napa Valley. It would take you weeks to get through even just the best of the best, but you can't go wrong with the midcentury modern vibes of **Ashes & Diamonds** (✉ 4130 Howard La. ☎ 707/666–4777 ⊕ www.ashesdiamonds.com), the French chateau–inspired sparkling purveyor **Domaine Carneros** (✉ 1240 Duhig Rd. ☎ 707/257–0101 ⊕ www.domainecarneros.com), picturesque **Bouchaine Vineyards** (✉ 1075 Buchli Station Rd. ☎ 707/252–9065 ⊕ www.bouchaine.com), and style-drenched **Clos du Val** (✉ 5330 Silverado Trail ☎ 707/261–5212 ⊕ www.closduval.com).

Eat & Drink: Nibble on Spanish tortillas, smoky garlic shrimp, and paella at downtown Napa's tapas restaurant **Zuzu** (✉ 829 Main St. ☎ 707/224–8555 ⊕ www.zuzunapa.com), or head a few miles north to Santa Helena for pork chops, cioppino, and burrata at **Longmeadow Ranch's Farmstead Restaurant** (✉ 738 Main St. ☎ 707/963–4555 ⊕ www.longmeadowranch.com).

Stay: Stay the night in Napa's glamorous boutique **Archer Hotel** (✉ 1230 1st St. ☎ 707/690–9800 ⊕ www.archerhotel.com) or check in at the somewhat more affordable but equally lovely **Blackbird Inn** (✉ 1755 1st St. ☎ 707/226–2450 ⊕ www.blackbirdinnnapa.com) or **Cedar Gables Inn B&B** (✉ 486 Coombs

St. ☎ 707/224–7969 ⊕ www.cedargablesinn.com).

Breakfast: Find a mouthwatering breakfast of Benedicts, griddle cakes, and flatbreads at the farm-style **Boon Fly Cafe** (✉ 4048 Sonoma Hwy. ☎ 707/299–4870 ⊕ www.boonflycafe.com).

Day 3: Napa to Sacramento

113 miles (1 hour, 15 minutes without traffic and stops)

Today's drive heads east through the rich agricultural lands of the northern Central Valley and into the state capital, Sacramento.

ALONG THE WAY

Town: Davis, home to one of the University of California campuses, is a weird and wonderful haven rooted within the rural farmlands of the Central Valley. Perhaps not surprisingly, some of the best things to do here are plant-and-animal-based. Take a peaceful walk through the **UC Davis Arboretum and Public Garden** (✉ 448 La Rue Rd. ☎ 530/752–4880 ⊕ www.arboretum.ucdavis.edu), visit hawks and owls at the **California Raptor Center** (✉ 1340 Equine La. ☎ 530/752–6091 ⊕ www.crc.cetmed.ucdavis.edu), or learn about pollinators at the **Häagen-Dazs Honey Bee Haven** (✉ Bee Biology Rd. ☎ 530/867–9429 ⊕ www.beegarden.ucdavis.edu).

Eat & Drink: There are plenty of affordable eats in Davis, including poke and sushi-burritos at **Good Friends** (✉ *400 G St.* ☎ *530/231–5537*), tacos at **Taqueria Davis** (✉ *505 L St.* ☎ *530/758–8453* ⊕ *www.taqueriadavis.com*), and vegan fast-food favorites at **Burger Patch** (✉ *500 1st St.* ☎ *530/231–5023* ⊕ *www.theburgerpatch.com*).

SACRAMENTO

Do: In recent years, California's state capital has finally come into its own as a city worth spending some time in. While here, get a look at the city's past at the **Old Sacramento State Historic Park** (✉ *111 I St.* ☎ *916/445–7387* ⊕ *www.parks.ca.gov*) on the banks of the Sacramento River. The **Crocker Art Museum** (✉ *216 O St.* ☎ *916/808–7000* ⊕ *www.crockerart.org*) near the waterfront has an impressive collection of work from artists throughout California and beyond.

Eat & Drink: Sacramento has some excellent Asian eateries, including the Vietnamese/Thai **Lemon Grass Restaurant** (✉ *601 Munroe St.* ☎ *916/486–4891* ⊕ *www.lemongrassrestaurant.com*), the contemporary Japanese spot **Kru Sushi** (✉ *3135 Folsom Blvd.* ☎ *916/551–1559* ⊕ *www.krurestaurant.com*), and the Taiwanese/Sichuan **Yang's Noodles** (✉ *5860 Stockton Blvd.* ☎ *916/392–9988* ⊕ *www.yangs-noodles.com*). After dinner, you'll find creative cocktails at the midcentury-evoking **Ten Ten Room** (✉ *1010 10th St.* ☎ *916/272–2888* ⊕ *www.tentenroom.com*) or the vintage dive **b-side** (✉ *1430 S St.* ☎ *916/706–1830* ⊕ *www.b-sidesacramento.com*).

Stay: The sophisticated **Kimpton Sawyer Hotel** (✉ *500 J St.* ☎ *916/545–7100* ⊕ *www.sawyerhotel.com*) comes with a third-floor pool deck and cocktail lounge while the modern **The Exchange** (✉ *1006 4th St.* ☎ *916/931–3300* ⊕ *www.hilton.com*) downtown has a rooftop restaurant-bar.

Extend Your Trip

From San Francisco: Pacific Coast Highway and Highway 101 *(Ch. 3)*

From Yosemite: California's National Parks *(Ch. 3)*

From Monterey: The Best of Southern California *(Ch. 3)*

Breakfast: Breakfast with the locals at the bizarrely wonderful diner **Pancake Circus** (✉ *2101 Broadway* ☎ *916/452–3322* ⊕ *www.pancakecircus.net*).

Day 4: Sacramento to Tahoe City

113 miles (2 hours without traffic and stops)

Head into the foothills of the Sierra Nevada Mountains and through some of the earliest gold mining camps in the state. At Truckee, where the Donner Party infamously overwintered in 1846, turn south onto Highway 89. It will take you all the way to the shores of Lake Tahoe.

ALONG THE WAY

Town: A mining camp during California's mid-19th-century gold rush, Auburn's carefully restored Old Town is a charming blast from the past outfitted with restaurants, boutiques, and a fantastic old firehouse. In the **Placer County Historical Museum** (✉ *101 Maple St.* ☎ *530/889–6500* ⊕ *www.placer.ca.gov*) inside the monumental Placer County Courthouse, get a look at the raw gold that made Northern California known around the world.

Eat & Drink: In Auburn, fill up on grown-up pub fare and beer at the craft brewery **Auburn Alehouse** (✉ *289 Washington St.* ☎ *530/885–2537* ⊕ *www.*

auburnalehouse.com) or enjoy Texas-style barbecue at the **Smokey Pit** (✉ 160 Harrison Ave. ☎ 530/889–9080 ⊕ www.smokeypitbarbeque.com).

Nature: Stop for a hike at legendary Donner Lake in Truckee, where the Donner Party resorted to cannibalism to survive a brutal winter stuck in the Sierra Nevada Mountains. In **Donner Memorial State Park** (✉ 12593 Donner Pass Rd. ☎ 530/582–7892 ⊕ www.parks.ca.gov), you'll find a monument to those early settlers and the mellow 2½-mile round-trip Lakeshore Interpretive Trail.

TAHOE CITY

Do: For those who love the outdoors, Tahoe is a world-class playground in both summer and winter. In the winter months, rent yourself some skis or a snowboard and head to **Northstar** (✉ 5001 Northstar Dr. ☎ 530/562–2267 ⊕ www.northstarcalifornia.com) or **Alpine Meadows** (✉ 2600 Alpine Meadows Rd. ☎ 800/403–0206 ⊕ www.squawalpine.com). In summer, hike, kayak, or get some sun at Kings Beach. Floating down the Truckee River in an innertube is an unbeatable way to spend a hot afternoon.

Eat & Drink: Dig into wood-fired pizzas and craft cocktails at **The Pioneer Cocktail Club** (✉ 521 N. Lake Blvd. ☎ 530/523–0402 ⊕ www.pioneertahoe.com) or go highbrow at **Wolfdale's Cuisine Unique** (✉ 640 N. Lake Blvd. ☎ 530/583–5700 ⊕ www.wolfdales.com), a lake-view restaurant with surf-and-turf delights like seared bay scallops and ling cod.

Stay: Stay the night amid the modern mountain stylings of **Basecamp Tahoe City** (✉ 955 N. Lake Blvd. ☎ 530/580–8430 ⊕ www.basecamptahoecity.com), or find panoramic views of the lake at **Sunnyside Lodge** (✉ 1850 W. Lake Blvd. ☎ 530/583–7200 ⊕ www.sunnysideresort.com).

Breakfast: Wake up to breakfast burritos and Benedicts at the adorable **Fire Sign Cafe** (✉ 1785 W. Lake Blvd. ☎ 530/583–0871 ⊕ www.firesigncafe.com).

Day 5: Tahoe City to Murphys

148 miles (3 hours, 15 minutes without traffic and stops)

Skirt along the western side of Lake Tahoe on Highway 89 then head west on Highway 88 to Highway 49, the scenic Golden Chain Highway. From there you'll head south through historic gold rush towns, stopping for the night in Murphys, a charismatic village populated with wineries, boutiques, and restaurants.

ALONG THE WAY

Nature: Before leaving Tahoe, stop at Emerald Bay, one of the most beautiful areas of the lake. Hike to the bottom of the hill to see **Vikingsholm** (☎ 530/525–9530 ⊕ www.vikingsholm.com), a castle built on the lake's shore in the 1920s. For a fun adventure, rent a kayak and paddle out to the lake's only island, Fanette, where the ruins of a teahouse used by the castle's mistress still remain.

Town: In Jackson, one of the deepest gold mines in the world is also one of the last where the original mill still remains. See the inner workings of the **Kennedy Gold Mine** (✉ 12594 Kennedy Mine Rd. ☎ 209/223–9542 ⊕ www.kennedygoldmine.com) on a guided tour or walk the self-guided trail on your own.

Eat & Drink: Fill up on blackened salmon, chicken sandwiches, and portobello burgers at **Bistro 49** (✉ 250 French Bar Rd. ☎ 209/223–2564 ⊕ www.bistro49jackson.com) in Jackson.

MURPHYS

Do: Many of the historic towns in Gold Country are cute, but Murphys takes the cake. Before strolling around town, hit one of the many local wineries, starting with **Ironstone Vineyards** (✉ 1894 6 Mile Rd. ☎ 209/728–1251 ⊕ www.ironstonevineyards.com) just a few minutes down Highway 4. On a tour through the nearby

The Golden Gate Bridge is perhaps California's most recognizable landmark.

Mercer Caverns (✉ *1665 Sheep Ranch Rd.* ☎ *209/728–2101* ⊕ *www.mercercaverns.net*), you can get a glimpse of what Calaveras County looks like from under the earth.

Eat & Drink: For such a small town, Murphys has a surprising number of fantastic eateries. Find an unexpected pairing of authentic Mexican and classic Italian dishes at **Gabby's Cuisine** (✉ *260 Jones St.* ☎ *209/813–7043* ⊕ *www.gabbscuisine-murphys.com*), carefully crafted seared mahimahi and lamb shank at **Alchemy** (✉ *191 Main St.* ☎ *209/728–0700* ⊕ *www.alchemymurphys.com*), and Vietnamese favorites at the **Asian Cafe** (✉ *64 Mitchler St.* ☎ *209/728–8898*).

Stay: Spend the night at the romantic **Victoria Inn** (✉ *402 Main St.* ☎ *209/728–8933* ⊕ *www.victoriainn-murphys.com*) or at the clean and comfortable **Murphys Inn Motel** (✉ *76 Main St.* ☎ *209/728–1818* ⊕ *www.murphysinnmotel.com*).

Breakfast: Grab breakfast at **Grounds Restaurant** (✉ *402 Main St.* ☎ *209/728–8663* ⊕ *www.groundrestaurant.com*), where the coffee is fresh and the waffles are fluffy.

Day 6: Murphys to Yosemite National Park

67 miles (1 hour, 30 minutes without traffic and stops)

From Murphys continue down the Gold Chain Highway to its terminus at Yosemite Junction. From there, you'll travel east on Highway 120 all the way to one of the country's most stunning national parks.

ALONG THE WAY

Town: Columbia Living History (✉ *22708 Broadway St.* ☎ *209/588–9128* ⊕ *www.parks.ca.gov*), a re-created gold mining village about 20 miles south of Murphys, is kitschy fun, and the old-timey candy shop is not to be missed.

Eat & Drink: Stop by Columbia's historic **St. Charles Saloon** (✉ *22801 Main St.* ☎ *209/288–2258*) for a pint and the best pizza in town.

Photo Op: In Groveland, don't miss the oldest continuously operating saloon in the state, the **Iron Door** (✉ *18761 Main St.* ☎ *209/962–8904* ⊕ *www.irondoorsaloon.com*).

YOSEMITE NATIONAL PARK

Do: Take in the sights by car or lace up your boots and hit the trails and head to **Yosemite National Park** (☎ *209/372–0200* ⊕ *www.nps.gov.yose*). Yosemite Valley is where you'll find the park's most famous landmarks, including Bridalveil Falls, Half Dome, and El Capitan, but if you're traveling in the summer, the sights along Tioga Road are just as spectacular (and less crowded).

Eat & Drink: Casual eats can be found at several spots around Yosemite Valley, including the **Curry Village Pizza Patio & Bar** (✉ *9010 Curry Village Dr.* ⊕ *www.travelyosemite.com*) and the **Village Grill** (✉ *Yosemite National Park Rd.* ☎ *209/372–0200* ⊕ *www.travelyosemite.com*). For more upscale dining, check out **The Mountain Room** in the Yosemite Valley Lodge (✉ *9006 Yosemite Lodge Dr.* ☎ *888/413–8869* ⊕ *www.travelyosemite.com*) or **The Ahwahnee Dining Room** (✉ *1 Ahwahnee Dr.* ☎ *209/372–1489* ⊕ *www.travelyosemite.com*).

Stay: If you have the gear, car camping or even backpacking in Yosemite is well worth the effort. You'll have to make a reservation if you want to stay in a campground, but wilderness permits to camp in the backcountry are readily available. If you'd prefer a comfortable bed, try the elegant Ahwahnee or the more affordable **Yosemite Valley Lodge** (✉ *9006 Yosemite Lodge Dr.* ☎ *888/413–8869*.

Breakfast: Coffee and light bites are available at **Degnan's Kitchen** (✉ *9015 Village Dr.* ☎ *888/413–8869* ⊕ *www.travelyosemite.com*) in Yosemite Village and **Base Camp Eatery** (✉ *9006 Yosemite Lodge Dr.* ☎ *888/413–8869* ⊕ *www.travelyosemite.com*) in the Yosemite Valley Lodge.

Day 7: Yosemite National Park to Half Moon Bay

174 miles (3 hours, 15 minutes without traffic and stops)

On your longest drive of the road trip, today you'll shoot straight west out of the Sierras, through the Central Valley and back into the Bay Area. Cross the San Mateo-Hayward Bridge over the San Francisco Bay and continue to the Pacific coast and the town of Half Moon Bay.

ALONG THE WAY

Town: Around Livermore, you'll find an under-the-radar wine region known for its Chardonnay, Sauvignon Blanc, and Petite Sirah. Among the best local wineries are **Page Mill** (✉ *1960 S. Livermore Ave.* ☎ *925/456–7676* ⊕ *www.pagemillwinery.com*), **McGrail Vineyards** (✉ *5600 Greenville Rd.* ☎ *925/215–0717* ⊕ *www.mcgrailvineyards.com*), and **BoaVentura de Caires** (✉ *9309 Tesla Rd.* ☎ *925/606–9672* ⊕ *www.boaventuravineyard.com*).

Eat & Drink: Soak up the wine with a big bowl of ramen or udon at **Kiseki** (✉ *1510 N. Vasco Rd.* ☎ *925/292–9664* ⊕ *www.eatkiseki.com*) in Livermore, or stop in San Mateo across the bay for Filipino pork knuckles and beef salpicao at **Avenida Restaurant** (✉ *201 E. 3rd Ave.* ☎ *650/781–3637* ⊕ *www.avenidarestaurant.net*).

Detour: Before crossing the bay, take a detour to the vibrant city of Oakland. Picnic at Lake Merritt, visit the shops along Temescal Alley or Piedmont Avenue, and visit the always innovative **Oakland Museum of California** (✉ *1000 Oak St.* ☎ *510/318–8400* ⊕ *www.museumca.org*).

HALF MOON BAY

Do: Separated from the core of the Silicon Valley by rolling hills, the beach enclave of Half Moon Bay remains quiet and surprisingly idyllic. Here you can ride horses on the beach with **Sea Horse Ranch** (✉ *1828 Cabrillo Hwy. N*

☎ *650/726–9903* ⊕ *www.seahorseranch. org*), surf the waves at world-famous Mavericks, and relax on the sand at **Gray Whale Cove State Beach** (☎ *650/726–8819* ⊕ *www.parks.ca.gov*).

Eat & Drink: Almost anywhere you go in Half Moon Bay, seafood is on the menu. Try the famous chowder beachside at **Sam's Chowder House** (✉ *4210 CA-1* ☎ *650/712–0245* ⊕ *www.samschowderhouse.com*), or gorge on cioppino and fried scallops at the **Flying Fish Grill** (✉ *4100 Cabrillo Hwy. N* ☎ *650/712–0220* ⊕ *www.beach-house.com*).

Stay: Let the sound of the ocean lull you to sleep at the **Beach House** at Half Moon Bay (✉ *4100 Cabrillo Hwy. N* ☎ *650/712–0220* ⊕ *www.beach-house.com*) or the **Cypress Inn** on Miramar Beach (✉ *407 Mirada Rd.* ☎ *650/726–6002* ⊕ *www.cypressinn.com*). Or if you don't mind a splurge, you can hobnob with celebrities at the glamorous **Ritz-Carlton** (✉ *1 Miramontes Point Rd.* ☎ *650/712–7000* ⊕ *www.ritzcarlton.com*).

Breakfast: Start your morning with crepes from **Mavericks Creperie** (✉ *146 San Mateo Rd.* ☎ *650/713–5298* ⊕ *www.maverickscreperie.com*).

Day 8: Half Moon Bay to Monterey

90 miles (2 hours without traffic and stops)

Travel south along the Pacific Coast Highway. The ocean will be your quiet companion most of the way to Monterey.

ALONG THE WAY

Photo Op: The **Pigeon Point Light Station** (✉ *210 Pigeon Point Rd.* ☎ *650/879–2120* ⊕ *www.parks.ca.gov*) in Pescadero has kept its lonely watch over this section of the Pacific coast since 1872.

Town: Ride one of the country's oldest wooden roller coasters, the Giant

Dipper, at Northern California's last remaining beachside amusement park, the **Boardwalk** (✉ *400 Beach St.* ☎ *831/423–5590* ⊕ *www.beachboardwalk.com*) in Santa Cruz.

Eat & Drink: While in Santa Cruz, fuel up on food-truck fare and beer from local favorite **Humble Sea Brewing Co.** (✉ *820 Swift St.* ☎ *831/621–2890* ⊕ *www.humblesea.com*); you can watch the surfers hang ten as you eat.

Nature: Hike to a magical sea cave on Fern Grotto Beach (or along any number of other trails) at **Wilder Ranch State Park** (✉ *1401 Coast Rd.* ☎ *831/423–9703* ⊕ *www.parks.ca.gov*) on Highway 1.

MONTEREY

Do: Rent a bike and ride the waterfront Monterey Bay Coastal Trail, hunt for starfish and sea urchin in the tide pools at **Asilomar State Beach** (✉ *Sunset Dr.* ☎ *831/646–6440* ⊕ *www.parks.ca.gov*), tour the boardwalk-like Cannery Row, or go whale-watching. Though the tickets are costly, the **Monterey Bay Aquarium** (✉ *886 Cannery Row* ☎ *831/648–4800* ⊕ *www.montereybaysquarium.org*) is not to be missed.

Eat & Drink: Dig into a heaping plate of Italian-style seafood at **Monterey's Fish House** (✉ *2114 Del Monte Ave.* ☎ *831/373–4647* ⊕ *www.montereyfishhouse.com*) or old-school surf and turf at the eccentric **Sardine Factory** (✉ *701 Wave St.* ☎ *831/373–3775* ⊕ *www.sardinefactory.com*) near Cannery Row. Late night, sip cocktails over the fire pit at the **Pearl Hour** (✉ *214 Lighthouse Ave.* ☎ *831/657–9447* ⊕ *www.pearlhour.com*) or craft beer at downtown's **Alvarado Street Brewery** (✉ *426 Alvarado St.* ☎ *831/655–2337* ⊕ *www.asb.beer*).

Stay: Just a few steps from Cannery Row, the renovated **Wave Street Inn** (✉ *571 Wave St.* ☎ *831/375–2299* ⊕ *www.wavestreetinnmonterey.com*) has a comfortable coastal vibe. Down the bluff in Pacific Grove, you can spend the night overlooking the bay in the gorgeous **Victorian Seven Gables Inn** (✉ *555 Ocean View Blvd.* ☎ *831/372–4341* ⊕ *www. thesevengablesinn.com*).

Breakfast: Housed in an historic adobe downtown, the buzzy **Alta Bakery** (✉ *502 Munras Ave.* ☎ *831/920–1018* ⊕ *www. altamonterey.com*) makes incredible coffee, breakfast pastries, and breads.

Day 9: Monterey to San Jose

72 miles (1 hour, 20 minutes without traffic and stops)

On the last day of your road trip, you'll retrace your steps up the coast to Santa Cruz then cut through redwoods that tower over the Santa Cruz Mountains on windy Highway 17. Over the hill, stop in bougie Los Gatos before traveling on to San Jose. The airport and its rental car agencies are conveniently located right near the city's downtown core.

ALONG THE WAY

Town: Located at the base of the Santa Cruz Mountains, Los Gatos is as cute as they come. Stroll along the shops and eateries of North Santa Cruz Avenue, stopping anywhere that catches your fancy.

Eat & Drink: While in Los Gatos, lunch on mango red curry and spicy eggplant basil at the Asian fusion restaurant, **Golden Triangle** (✉ *217 N. Santa Cruz Ave.* ☎ *408/402–5092* ⊕ *goldentrian-glecuisine.weebly.com*). If you need a caffeinated or sugary pick-me-up, stop by **Manresa Bread** (✉ *276 N. Santa Cruz Ave.* ☎ *408/402–5372* ⊕ *www.manresabread. com*), the accessible bakery offshoot of a Michelin-starred restaurant in town.

SAN JOSE

Do: In massive, sprawling San Jose, there are a wide variety of museums, parks, and oddities to keep you occupied. Take

Essential Listening

Listen to *Cannery Row*, John Steinbeck's novel about workers in the sardine factories that once formed the economic backbone of Monterey. Or if you're a *Big Little Lies* fan, make sure you listen to the television show's haunting theme song "Cold Little Heart" by Michael Kiwanuka as you approach the coastal town.

a tour of the bizarre **Winchester Mystery House** (✉ *525 S. Winchester Blvd.* ☎ *408/247–2000* ⊕ *www.winchester-mysteryhouse.com*), explore modern art at the **San Jose Museum of Art** (✉ *110 S. Market St.* ☎ *408/271–6840* ⊕ *www. sjmusart.org*) or the smaller but more cutting-edge **Institute of Contemporary Art** (✉ *560 S. 1st St.* ☎ *408/283–8155* ⊕ *www.icasanjose.org*), or hike through the ghost town of a mercury mining settlement at **Almaden Quicksilver County Park** (✉ *21785 Almaden Rd.* ☎ *408/268–3883* ⊕ *www.sccgov.org*).

Eat & Drink: Find a wide range of tasty, affordable eats at the downtown **San Pedro Square Market** (✉ *87 N. San Pedro St.* www.sanpedrosquaremarket.com), gourmet Mexican fusion at Willow Glen's **Zona Rosa** (✉ *1411 The Alameda* ☎ *408/275–1411* ⊕ *www.zonarosadin-ing.com*), or flavorful Ethiopian at **Walia** (✉ *2208 Business Cir.* ☎ *408/645–5001* ⊕ *www.waliaethiopian.com*). Celebrate your last night on the road with cocktails from the **Haberdasher** (✉ *43 W. San Salvador St.* ☎ *408/792–7356* ⊕ *www. haberdashertogo.com*).

Stay: Spend your final night at the storied **Hotel De Anza** (✉ *233 W. Santa Clara St.* ☎ *408/286–1000* ⊕ *www.destinationho-tels.com*) downtown or the sophisticated hacienda-style **Hotel Valencia** (✉ 355 Santana Row ☎ 408/551–0010 ⊕ www. hotelvalencia-santanarow.com) at Santana Row.

Breakfast: Have a farewell breakfast of tri tip and hash or French toast at the **Park Station Hashery** (✉ 1701 Park Ave. ☎ 408/320–1711 ⊕ www.parkstationhashery.com).

The Best of Southern California

Written by Amber Gibson

This eight-day road trip from Big Sur to San Diego spans some of California's most breathtaking landscapes, navigating from forests to beaches to deserts, all while driving down the Pacific Coast Highway with unobstructed views of the dramatic coastline below. Along the way, taste luscious wines in Paso Robles and Santa Barbara and experience big city living in Los Angeles and San Diego. This region of the country marks the ideal balance between urban and rural, adventure and relaxation, simplicity and luxury.

At a Glance

Start: Monterey, CA

End: San Diego, CA

Miles Traveled: 900 miles

Suggested Duration: 8 days

States Visited: California

Key Sights: Big Sur; Joshua Tree National Park; Pebble Beach; San Diego Zoo; Santa Monica Pier

Best Time to Go: The weather in Southern California is great year-round, but Joshua Tree and Palm Springs can get mighty hot in summer.

Day 1: Monterey to Big Sur

40 miles (1 hour, 20 minutes without traffic and stops)

Rent a car from one of the half-dozen car-rental providers located at Monterey Regional Airport (if you'd rather fly direct, San Jose International Airport is about an hour and 20 minutes from Monterey). Enjoy a leisurely hourlong drive along the coast through Andrew Molera State Park and Julia Pfeiffer Burns State Park.

ALONG THE WAY

Detour: Relish the scenic 17-mile drive through Pebble Beach, best known for its championship golf courses, raw white beaches, and rugged coastal cliffs. Admission is $10.50 per vehicle, but the fee is reimbursed with a $35 purchase at Pebble Beach Resorts restaurants. The gates are open to the public from sunrise to sunset.

Town: Clint Eastwood was once mayor of Carmel-by-the-Sea, where he legalized ice-cream cones, although high heels are still verboten without a permit from city hall. The quirky seaside town is home to art galleries aplenty and storybook cottages.

BIG SUR

Do: Between **Julia Pfeiffer Burns State Park** (✉ 52801 CA-1 ☎ 831/667–1112 ⊕ www. parks.ca.gov) and **Andrew Molera State Park** (✉ 45500 CA-1 ☎ 831/667–2315 ⊕ www.parks.ca.gov), there are dozens of hikes through redwood groves you can take to discover secluded coves, rushing waterfalls, and blossoming meadows. You may even spot migrating gray whales from December to May. **Limekiln State Park** (✉ 63025 CA-1 ☎ 805/434–1996 ⊕ www.parks.ca.gov) is much smaller, but the abandoned limestone kilns and easy beach access make it worth a visit.

Eat & Drink: Big Sur Bakery & Restaurant (✉ 47540 CA-1 ☎ 831/667–0520 ⊕ www. bigsurbakery.com) serves humble and hearty plates in a small ranch-style home; the wood-fired pizza is always a sure bet.

The Best of
Southern California

Stay: Deetjen's Big Sur Inn (✉ 48865 CA-1 ☎ 831/667–2377 ⊕ www.deetjens. com) was built in the 1930s and the cozy rooms and cabins are listed on the National Register of Historic Places. Guests are forced to unplug and focus on the surrounding nature—there are no TVs, Wi-Fi, or cell phone coverage on the property. If Internet and cell service are a must, **Glen Oaks Big Sur** (✉ 47080 CA-1 ☎ 831/667–2105 ⊕ www.glenoaks-bigsur.com) has more modern amenities and an equally immersive woodland atmosphere.

Breakfast: Enjoy a substantial meal of pancakes and huevos rancheros at the **Ripplewood Cafe** (✉ 47047 CA-1 ☎ 831/667–2242 ⊕ www.ripplewoodresort.com).

Day 2: Big Sur to Paso Robles

140 miles (2 hours, 30 minutes without traffic and stops)

Cruise along the legendary Pacific Coast Highway in the lane closest to the ocean, passing through Cambria and Cayucos before cutting inland at Morro Bay to Paso Robles.

ALONG THE WAY

Photo Op: Snap a pic of the opulent hilltop **Hearst Castle** (✉ 750 Hearst Castle Rd., San Simeon, CA ☎ 800/444–4445 ⊕ www.hearstcastle.org) built by media magnate William Randolph Hearst, which is now a National Historic Landmark.

Eat & Drink: Stop by **Cambria Coffee Roasting Company** (✉ 761 Main St.

☎ 805/927–0670 ⊕ www.cambriacof-feesales.com) in Cambria to try meticulously brewed single-origin coffee from Central America. Farther south, get lunch at **Ruddell's Smokehouse** (✉ 101 D St. ☎ 805/995–5028 ⊕ www.smokerjim.com) in Cayucos, where they smoke their own oysters, salmon, and albacore tuna for tasty tacos with a beach view.

Town: Morro Bay is a sleepy, foggy beach town located on a natural harbor. It's popular with fishermen and surfers, although you'll want to rent a wet suit to catch waves in these cold waters. Visit Morro Rock Beach to see the famous volcanic stone that helped early sailors navigate the coast. Peregrine falcons, harbor seals, sea otters, and sea lions can often be spotted at this nature reserve.

PASO ROBLES

Do: There are more than 200 wineries in Paso Robles and the up-and-coming wine region is famous for Zinfandel, Cabernet Sauvignon, and Rhône-style reds. Visit a few family-owned wineries while you're here, including **Opolo Vineyards** (✉ 7110 Vineyard Dr. ☎ 805/238–9593 ⊕ www.opolo.com), which has an adjacent distillery, and the chic open-air tasting room at **Booker Winery** (✉ 2644 Anderson Rd. ☎ 805/237–7367 ⊕ www.bookerwines.com), where you can play bocce ball and escape the heat in underground wine caves.

Eat & Drink: Niner Wine Estates (✉ 2400 CA-46 ☎ 805/239–2233 ⊕ www.niner-wine.com) offers a full-service restaurant overlooking their Malbec and Cabernet Sauvignon vineyards. They make their own olive oil, sourdough focaccia, farmer's cheese, and ice cream in-house, and plates like grilled trout with leeks and lemons and pan-roasted strip loin pair beautifully with their wide variety of estate-grown wines.

Stay: Allegretto Vineyard Resort (✉ 2700 Buena Vista Dr. ☎ 805/369–2500 ⊕ www.allegrettovineyardresort.com)

resembles an opulent Tuscan villa decorated with an amalgamation of globally inspired art and sculptures. Across 20 acres, manicured Mediterranean gardens, grapevines, lavender plants, and olive trees thrive.

Breakfast: Spearhead Coffee (✉ 619 12th St. ☎ 805/296–3328 ⊕ www.spread-headcoffee.com) roasts their own beans, including a local whiskey-infused variety, and uses homemade syrups in their inventive lattes, like the Cortijo, sweetened with condensed milk and clove.

Day 3: Paso Robles to Santa Barbara

130 miles (2 hours, 30 minutes without traffic and stops)

After a brief glimpse of the Pacific at Pismo Beach, take the 101 and cut across inland before ending back with ocean views in Santa Barbara.

ALONG THE WAY

Town: San Luis Obispo is an energetic college town that's the cultural and commercial hub of the Central Coast. Its dynamic downtown is easily walkable, with numerous local boutiques and public art installations along Higuera Street. The city's ambitious climate action plan includes becoming carbon neutral by 2035 and they've protected a 54,000 acre greenbelt around the city from development.

Eat & Drink: Load up on carbs at **Bob's Well Bread** (✉ 550 Bell St. ☎ 805/344–3000 ⊕ www.bobswellbread.com) in Los Alamos. The breads here, including baguettes and pain au levain for sandwiches, are all made with natural starters in old-world European traditions resulting in a satisfying crust and springy crumb.

Photo Op: The small village of Solvang is famous for its Danish-style architecture, including thatched-roof cottages and four wooden windmills.

SANTA BARBARA

Do: Known as the American Riviera, Santa Barbara invented the concept of an urban wine trail, with nearly 30 tasting rooms to choose from, concentrated in the Presidio and eclectic Funk Zone neighborhoods. **Au Bon Climat** (✉ 813 Anacapa St. ☎ 805/963–7999 ⊕ www. aubonclimat.com) makes world-class Pinot Noir and Chardonnay while **Margerum** (✉ 19 E. Mason St. ☎ 805/845–8435 ⊕ www.margerumwines.com) has elegant Rhône blends and a standout food menu, too. For nondrinkers, **Los Padres Outfitters** (✉ Asegra and Greenwell Ave. ☎ 805/755–8687 ⊕ www.lospadresoutfitters.com) offers private guided horseback rides on the beach for all experience levels, allowing you to splash into the ocean along the cragged bluffs.

Eat & Drink: Secret Bao (✉ 1201 Anacapa St. ☎ 805/259–3226 ⊕ www. secretbaosb.com) is a fun stop for fast, casual contemporary Korean food, while vegetarian restaurant **Satellite** (✉ 1117 State St. ☎ 805/364–3043 ⊕ satelittesb. com) has bountiful salads and toasts topped with balsamic smoked shiitake mushrooms, accompanied by an intriguing selection of natural wines. For dinner, share authentic Spanish tapas and heaping bowls of paella among friends at **Loquita** (✉ 202 State St. ☎ 805/880–3380 ⊕ www.loquitasb.com). Don't skip the Basque cheesecake for dessert.

Stay: Belmond **El Encanto** (✉ 800 Alvarado Pl. ☎ 805/845–5800 ⊕ www.belmond. com) is the grand dame of Santa Barbara's luxury resorts, originally opened in 1918 and restored to its Spanish Colonial Revival glory, with bungalows tucked away amid 7 acres of lush gardens and bougainvillea-draped walls. **Palihouse** (✉ 915 Garden St. ☎ 805/564–4700 ⊕ www.palihousesantabarbara.com) has a preppy vintage vibe and quaint courtyard, centrally located downtown. All 24 rooms at this boutique property have gas fireplaces, balconies or terraces, and a minibar well-stocked with local snacks.

Breakfast: Cajé Coffee Roasters (✉ 1316 State St. ⊕ www.caje.coffee) has the best blended coffee drinks, smoothies, and açai bowls in town. For a taste of Paris, visit **Bree'osh** (✉ 2700 De La Vina St. ☎ 805/770–2238 ⊕ www.breeosh. com) in Montecito, run by a soigné French couple and serving exquisitely laminated croissants and kouign-amann.

Day 4: Santa Barbara to Los Angeles

100 miles (2 hours without traffic and stops)

Meander along the coastline for a leisurely drive before heading east on I–10 to Downtown Los Angeles.

ALONG THE WAY

Eat & Drink: Little Dom's Seafood (✉ 686 Linden Ave. ☎ 805/749–7400 ⊕ www. ldseafood.com) in Carpinteria is the premier place for local seafood fresh from the docks, including live Santa Barbara uni, local halibut, and yellowfin tuna, freshly prepared with Ojai olive oil and vibrant Calabrese pepper sauce. Plus, pastry chef Ann Kirk makes the best biscotti this side of the Atlantic and incredible small-batch gelato. If you're in a hurry, the market next door has sandwiches, prepared salads, and Italian cookies to take away.

Photo Op: El Matador's powerful rock formations are a popular spot for engagement photos and coastline drone shots.

Town: Scores of A-list celebrities, from Julia Roberts to Lady Gaga, call Malibu home. Stretch your legs at one of the famous beaches, like **Zuma Beach**, where the original *Baywatch* was filmed.

LOS ANGELES

Do: The Broad (✉ 221 S. Grand Ave.
☎ 213/232–6250 ⊕ www.thebroad.org)
is one of L.A.'s finest museums, offering
free general admission and rotating exhibitions of contemporary art. Golden hour
at **Griffith Observatory** (✉ 2800 E. Observatory Rd. ☎ 213/473–0800 ⊕ www.grif-
fithobservatory.org) is the best vantage
point for 360-degree views of the city,
including the iconic Hollywood Sign.

Eat & Drink: The patio at **Piccalilli** (✉ 3850
Main St. ☎ 424/298–8450 ⊕ www.
piccalillila.com) is a pleasant place for
people-watching in Culver City, where you
can enjoy miso pork jowl, smashed Szechuan cucumbers, and tomato curry with
garlic naan. Los Angeles also has the best
vegan food scene in the country, and **Little
Pine** (✉ 2870 Rowena Ave. ☎ 323/741–
8148 ⊕ www.littlepinerestaurant.com)
in Silver Lake serves vegan comfort food
that even carnivores love. The impossible
meatballs, creamy macaroni and cheese,
and fennel flatbread with savory vegan
"sausage" crumbles are undeniably good,
and better for the planet.

Stay: Hotel Figueroa (✉ 939 S. Figueroa
St. ☎ 213/627–8971 ⊕ www.hotelf-
igueroa.com) first opened in 1926 as a
safe haven for solo female travelers who
couldn't check into most hotels without a
male chaperone. Today the hotel continues to champion local women in the arts,
and the notorious coffin-shaped pool is a
cheeky nod to burying the patriarchy. **JW
Marriott Los Angeles L.A. LIVE** (✉ 900 W.
Olympic Blvd. ☎ 213/765–8600 ⊕ www.
marriott.com) is a great hotel for families,
located next to the Staples Center, with
spacious rooms and a lively rooftop pool.
Downtown L.A. Proper (✉ 1100 S. Broadway ☎ 213/806–1010 ⊕ www.proper-
hotel.com) is the coolest new property
in Downtown, with a Mexican modern-
ism–inspired design by Kelly Wearstler
and restaurants by L.A. dining doyennes
Suzanne Goin and Caroline Styne.

Extend Your Trip

From Monterey: The Best of
Northern California (Ch. 3)

From Los Angeles: California's
National Parks (Ch. 3)

From San Diego: The Pacific Coast
Highway (Ch. 3); Ultimate Cross
Country Trip South (Ch. 2)

Breakfast: Aussie all-day café **Strings of Life**
(✉ 609 N.W. Knoll Dr. ☎ 424/313–8136
⊕ www.sol-losangeles.com) in West Hollywood combines the best of both worlds:
specialty coffee and chef-driven food.
Crispy potato cake with smoked salmon,
mango coconut chia pudding, and fluffy
omelets are a few breakfast favorites.

Day 5: Los Angeles to Palm Springs

Hit the road early to maximize your time
in Joshua Tree National Park, then trace
your route back to Palm Springs, where
you'll spend the night.

ALONG THE WAY

Roadside Attraction: Life-size dinosaurs
Dinny the Brontosaurus and Mr. Rex are
visible from the freeway as you pass
through **Cabazon** (✉ 50770 Seminole Dr.
☎ 909/272–8164 ⊕ www.cabazondino-
saurs.com). The surrounding open-air
museum includes robotic dinosaurs,
gemstone and fossil panning, and a gift
shop inside Dinny's belly.

Eat & Drink: Coachella Valley produces
more than 90% of the dates grown in the
United States, and **Shields Date Garden**
(✉ 80–225 CA-111 ☎ 760/347–0996
⊕ www.shieldsdategarden.com) is a
great place to sample them all: gold-
en Zahidi dates, amber-color Halawi
dates, firm Deglet Noor dates, and

Did You Know?

Found only in Arizona, California, Nevada, and Utah, the Joshua tree (Yucca brevifolia) is actually a member of the agave family. Native Americans used the Joshua tree's hearty foliage like leather, forming it into everyday items like baskets and shoes. Later, early settlers used its core and limbs for building fences to contain their livestock.

soft caramel-like Medjool dates. Try the supersweet date milkshake and pick up an assortment to go—they're the perfect road trip and hiking snack.

Nature: Enter **Joshua Tree National Park** (☎ 760/367–5500 ⊕ www.nps.gov/jotr) through the less crowded south entrance off Interstate Highway 10 east of Indio. You can see a lot just driving through, including Joshua trees galore, molten magma monoliths, and the cholla cactus garden. If you have the time and stamina, there are hundreds of granite rock formations for rock climbing and bouldering, too. Cell phone service is weak, so consider picking up a physical map at the Cottonwood Visitor Center before wandering off to explore the desert scenery.

PALM SPRINGS

Do: The **Palm Springs Aerial Tramway** (☒ 1 Tram Way ☎ 760/325–1391 ⊕ www. pstramway.com) offers spectacular views of the entire valley along Chino Canyon to Mt. San Jacinto State Park from the world's largest rotating tram car. The 10-minute ride brings you up to 8,516 feet with restaurants, a natural history museum, and more than 50 miles of hiking trails.

Eat & Drink: Visit **Copley's** on Palm Canyon (☒ 621 N. Palm Canyon Dr. ☎ 760/327–9555 ⊕ www.copleypalmsprings.com) for a romantic dinner alfresco on Cary Grant's former estate. **Wildest Restaurant & Bar** (☒ 72990 El Paseo ☎ 760/636–0441 ⊕ www.wildestrestaurant.com) has creative vegan options like sautéed king oyster mushroom "scallops" along with excellent seafood and grass-fed steaks.

Stay: The intimate bungalows at adults-only **L'Horizon Palm Springs** (☒ 1050 E. Palm Canyon Dr. ☎ 760/323–1858 ⊕ www.lhorizonpalmsprings.com) are a quintessential example of the midcentury modern architecture that Palm Springs is famous for. Geometric tiled courtyards at **Villa Royale** (☒ 1620 S. Indian Trail ☎ 760/327–2314 ⊕ www.villaroyale. com), beloved by movie stars during Hollywood's golden age, burst with color and raw desert beauty. The **Ritz-Carlton Rancho Mirage** (☒ 68900 Frank Sinatra Dr. ☎ 760/321–8282 ⊕ www.ritzcarlton. com) is a family-friendly option with the most luxurious spa in Palm Springs and fantastic hiking right on the property.

Breakfast: Breakfasts at **Cheeky's** (☒ 622 N. Palm Canyon Dr. ☎ 760/327–7595 ⊕ www.cheekysps.com) are practically a rite of passage in Palm Springs, thanks to its bacon bar and hangover-halting mimosas.

Day 6: Palm Springs to Santa Monica

130 miles (2 hours, 30 minutes without traffic and stops)

The drive today isn't too long if you make sure to avoid peak traffic times. Just be sure to arrive in Santa Monica in time for sunset on the pier.

ALONG THE WAY

Town: Claremont is the most endearing small town between the desert and Los Angeles. You can play hundreds of unique instruments from around the globe at **Ben Harper's Folk Music Center** (☒ 220 Yale Ave. ☎ 909/624–2928 ⊕ www. folkmusiccenter.com) and wander across 86 acres of native California plants at the **California Botanic Garden** (☒ 1500 N. College Ave. ☎ 909/625–8767 ⊕ www. calbg.org).

Eat & Drink: Destroyer (☒ 3578 Hayden Ave. ☎ 310/360–3860 ⊕ www.destroyer. la) in Culver City is the more casual sister restaurant to avant-garde fine-dining Vespertine, with elevated breakfast fare like buttery smoked cod on Icelandic seeded rye bread and sunchoke sourdough waffles with creamed kale and country ham. Sip a sweet potato latte and grab a pastry from the case to go.

SANTA MONICA

Do: An afternoon at the **Santa Monica Pier** (✉ *200 Santa Monica Pier* ☎ *310/458–8900* ⊕ *www.santamonicapier.org*) will bring you back to the 1920s, when the Pleasure Pier and its amusement park attractions thrived. Take a ride on the historic merry-go-round and the world's only solar-powered Ferris wheel, or sign up for trapeze school if you're feeling daring. Download the Secret Story Tour app and solve digital puzzles while unlocking secrets from the pier's past.

Eat & Drink: Pasjoli (✉ *2732 Main St.* ☎ *424/330–0020* ⊕ *www.pasjoli.com*) is a sophisticated bistro that transports you to Paris, imbuing the freshest local California produce with precise French technique. Dishes range from delicate blue crab and poached rhubarb to signature pressed duck straight from Escoffier's culinary bible, an indulgence for two that must be ordered in advance.

Stay: Many of the guest rooms at **Viceroy Santa Monica** (✉ *1819 Ocean Ave.* ☎ *310/260–7500* ⊕ *www.viceroyhotelsandresorts.com*) offer panoramic Pacific Ocean views and marble bathrooms featuring luxury toiletries from ROIL and Natura Bissé. Reserve one of six open-air cabanas in advance for poolside rest and relaxation. Just down the road, reduce your energy consumption at eco-friendly **Shore Hotel** (✉ *1515 Ocean Ave.* ☎ *310/458–1515* ⊕ *www.shorehotel.com*), a LEED-Gold-certified hotel with a solar-reflecting roof and heated swimming pool powered by solar energy. Finally, the historic **Fairmont Miramar Hotel & Bungalows** (✉ *101 Wilshire Blvd.* ☎ *310/576–7777* ⊕ *www.fairmont.com*) has been a pied-à-terre for Hollywood royalty for a century—Greta Garbo even lived here for four years.

Breakfast: Breadblok (✉ *1511 Montana Ave.* ☎ *310/310–8576* ⊕ *www.breadblok.com*) specializes in gluten-free, soy-free, and refined sugar–free breads and pastries, including an ethereal honey lavender cake and delectable doughnuts. They even make their own plant-based almond, coconut, and oat milks to pair with coffee.

Day 7: Santa Monica to Laguna Beach

70 miles (2 hours without traffic and stops)

Be sure to check the traffic before departing today. Highway 1 is usually significantly slower, but with prettier ocean views than if you cut inland on I–405. Both routes are a straight shot to Laguna Beach.

ALONG THE WAY

Eat & Drink: Puesto Mexican Artisan Kitchen & Bar (✉ *7821 Edinger Ave.* ☎ *714/316–0151* ⊕ *www.eatpuesto.com*) has three Orange County locations, including one in Huntington Beach, all serving modern Mexico City cuisine in a colorful and casual location. Order their tacos, served on handmade, organic stone-ground blue-corn tortillas with line-caught seafood and from-scratch salsas.

Town: Newport Beach has plenty to offer to nature lovers, shopaholics, and the young at heart. **Crystal Cove State Beach** (✉ *8471 N. Coast Hwy.* ☎ *949/494–3539* ⊕ *www.crystalcovestatepark.org*) is one of the more pristine and rustic beaches in Orange County, with an underwater park for scuba divers and snorkelers. **Fashion Island** (✉ *401 Newport Center Dr.* ☎ *949/721–2000* ⊕ *www.fashionisland.com*) is Orange County's premier luxury shopping center and **Balboa Fun Zone** (✉ *600 E. Bay Ave.* ☎ *949/675–8915* ⊕ *www.ocfunzone.com*) has been a family favorite since the 1930s, with a nautical museum, arcade games, whale-watching, and chocolate-dipped ice-cream Balboa Bars.

LAGUNA BEACH

Do: Explore the tide pools at Crescent Bay Beach, Rockpile Beach, and Thousand Steps to discover colorful marine life including anemones, hermit crabs, and sea stars. Main Beach and Treasure Island are some of the most easily accessible tide pools in the area. You'll want to visit at low tide and keep an eye on the swell. Sea kayaking is another way to get up close with ocean critters in the protected Laguna Beach State Marine Preserve.

Eat & Drink: Chef and owner Miki Izumisawa has been delighting diners in Laguna for more than 20 years at **242 Cafe Fusion Sushi** (✉ 242 N. Coast Hwy. ☎ 949/494–2444 ⊕ www.242cafefusionsushi.net) with her iconoclastic nigiri and sashimi, using untraditional ingredients like mango and pine nuts (she even tops one plate of sashimi with chili lemon ice cream).

Stay: Nestled in the Aliso and Wood Canyons, **The Ranch at Laguna Beach** (✉ 31106 Coast Hwy. ☎ 949/499–2271 ⊕ www.theranchlb.com) is all about laid-back luxury, with a nine-hole golf course and access to Aliso Beach via a pedestrian walkway, where you can relax under turquoise umbrellas and roast s'mores by beach bonfires at night. Sustainability is core to their mission; in order to lower their carbon footprint, they compost, crush glass bottles to fill bunkers, use reclaimed water for irrigation, and more.

Breakfast: Blk Dot Coffee (✉ 656 N. Coast Hwy. ☎ 949/371–0288 ⊕ www.blkdotcoffee.com) is a fun stop for breakfast and Vietnamese coffee, including unique specialty drinks like iced sea salt foam–topped coffee and the Vietnamese Tiger, gussied up with brown sugar syrup and black jelly.

Day 8: Laguna Beach to San Diego

70 miles (1 hour, 40 minutes without traffic and stops)

This gorgeous drive down the coastline on Historic Highway 101 is short and scenic, past Camp Pendleton and on to San Diego.

ALONG THE WAY

Town: Sea walls divide the series of small sandy beaches that line Carlsbad, a charming town with fun for the whole family, including prestigious golf courses, hidden lagoons, delicious eats at the **Windmill Food Hall** (✉ 890 Palomar Airport Rd. ☎ 760/214–9127 ⊕ www.windmillfoodhall.com), and **LEGOLAND** (✉ 1 Legoland Dr. ☎ 888/690–5346 ⊕ www.legoland.com) for the kids.

Shop: Enjoy health-conscious shopping at **One Paseo** (✉ 3725 Paseo Pl. ☎ 858/523–2298 ⊕ www.onepaseo.com) in Del Mar, an outdoor development featuring chic homegrown brands like Shop Good for clean beauty, Roark for outdoorsy menswear, and Pigment for home décor and flora.

SAN DIEGO

Do: Torrey Pines Gliderport (✉ 2800 Torrey Pines Scenic Dr. ☎ 858/452–9858 ⊕ www.flytorrey.com) is the largest tandem flight center in the country, and all ages and physical abilities can soar like a bird above the seaside cliffs in a peaceful tandem flight. If you prefer to see the mighty Pacific by sea, book a leisurely sunset cruise with **San Diego Sailing Tours** (✉ 1450 Harbor Island Dr. ☎ 619/786–0173 ⊕ www.sandiegosailingtours.com) and see the historic vessels at the Maritime Museum up close. And, of course, be sure to pay a visit to Balboa Park and the famous **San Diego Zoo** (✉ 2920 Zoo Dr. ☎ 619/231–1515 ⊕ www.zoo.sandiegozoo.org).

Eat & Drink: Addison (✉ *5200 Grand Del Mar Way* ☎ *858/314–1900* ⊕ *www.addisondelmar.com*) is the most glamorous fine-dining experience in town, and the tasting menu will surprise you with novel dishes like white asparagus ice cream drizzled with extra virgin olive oil. **Ironside Fish & Oyster** (✉ *1654 India St.* ☎ *619/269–3033* ⊕ *www.ironsidefishandoyster.com*) is another delicious pick for fresh local seafood including peel 'n' eat Baja shrimp, rockfish ceviche, roasted yellowtail collar, and ruby-red bigeye tuna fillets. Save room for dessert at **Stella Jean's Ice Cream** (✉ *4404 Park Blvd.* ☎ *619/501–8252* ⊕ *www.stellajeans.com*), where scoops of colorful mango sticky rice, ube pandesal toffee, and matcha pistachio await.

Stay: Fairmont Grand Del Mar (✉ *5300 Grand Del Mar Ct.* ☎ *858/314–2000* ⊕ *www.fairmont.com*) is a sprawling Mediterranean estate with opulent Spanish, Venetian, and Moroccan architecture, a glamorous courtyard pool, golf, tennis, pickleball, and beds so comfortable you'll never want to get up. The gardens at hacienda-style **Estancia La Jolla** (✉ *9700 N. Torrey Pines Rd.* ☎ *855/430–7503* ⊕ *www.meritagecollection.com*) are filled with stylish succulents and host live musical performances.

Breakfast: The cacao waffle topped with coconut yogurt at **Parakeet Cafe** (✉ *1680 India St.* ☎ *619/255–1442* ⊕ *www.parakeetcafe.com*) is a decadently sweet way to start your day; there's also shakshuka with labneh or chilaquiles if you're looking for something savory.

California's National Parks

Written by Andrew Collins

From otherworldly desertscapes and soaring sequoias to eye-popping canyons and rocky islands, California contains some of the country's most celebrated national parks. You probably already know about the "bucket list" destinations like Yosemite and Death Valley, but on this journey north through inland California's Sierra Nevada mountain range and then back down along the state's breathtaking coastline, you'll also discover some of the park system's hidden treasures—underrated yet dazzling landscapes like Lassen Volcanic, Point Reyes, Pinnacles, and Channel Islands.

This itinerary covers a lot of ground, and you'll need at least 10 days to spend even a day at every park highlighted. If you're able to set aside two to three weeks, you'll be able to explore and appreciate the landscape more thoroughly.

At a Glance

Start: Los Angeles, CA

End: Los Angeles, CA

Miles Traveled: 2,300 miles

Suggested Duration: 10 days

States Visited: California

Key Sights: Keys View, Joshua Tree National Park; Generals Highway, Sequoia National Park; Yosemite Valley, Yosemite National Park; Bumpass Hell, Lassen Volcanic National Park; Newton B. Drury Scenic Highway Redwood National and State Park

Best Time to Go: You can access parts of every California national park year-round, but the desert parks are better avoided during the sizzling hot June to August months, and access on some key park roads is limited in winter in Lassen Volcanic, Yosemite, and Sequoia and Kings Canyon.

Day 1: Los Angeles to Joshua Tree

145 miles (3 hours without traffic and stops)

Grab your rental car at LAX, and then follow I-10 east to Exit 117. Continue north on Highway 62, which leads to the park's West Entrance, off Park Boulevard in the small town of Joshua Tree. This is a mostly prosaic freeway drive through suburbia, but Highway 62 is a scenic and sometimes twisty route through Morongo Valley.

ALONG THE WAY

Town: The Coachella Valley's classic desert resort community—long famous with Hollywood folks and one of the country's top LGBTQ+ destinations—Palm Springs is a popular gateway to Joshua Tree National Park, worth at least a short stop to stroll among its distinctive design shops, galleries, and eateries and maybe even to ride the thrilling **Palm Springs Aerial Tramway** (✉ *1 Tram Way* ☎ *760/325–1391* ⊕ *www.pstramway. com*), which carries passengers through Chino Canyon to an elevation of 8,516 feet, near the summit of Mt. San Jacinto.

Eat & Drink: Downtown Palm Springs pulses with inviting restaurants, many with sprawling patios cooled off on hot days by misting machines. One favorite is **Cheeky's** (✉ *622 N. Palm Canyon Dr.* ☎ *760/327–7595* ⊕ *www.cheekysps.com*) for daily brunch and lunch, where you can order chilaquiles, buttermilk corn pancakes, and a "flight" of five types of bacon.

Shop: The Uptown Design District along North Palm Canyon Drive is a stretch of cool shops—including colorful **Trina Turk** (✉ *891 N. Palm Canyon Dr.* ☎ *760/416–2856* ⊕ *www.trinaturk.com*) for swimwear and fashion, and 1950s-chic **Shag** (✉ *745 N. Palm Canyon Dr.* ☎ *760/322–3400* ⊕ *www.shagstore.com*) for art and housewares—specializing in the

midcentury modern aesthetic for which Palm Springs is internationally famous

JOSHUA TREE NATIONAL PARK

Do: An 800,000-acre expanse of the Mojave and Sonoran deserts, **Joshua Tree National Park** (☎ *760/367–5500* ⊕ *www. nps.gov/jotr*) contains hundreds of the distinctive Joshua trees for which it is named. Joshua Tree's Park Boulevard extends for more than 50 miles through the park, and it's worth either starting or ending on this drive via the park's southeastern entrance off I-10. Must-sees that are easy to access from the main park road include the boulder-strewn paths around Skull Rock and the Jumbo Rocks Campground, and Hidden Valley and Cap Rock, which you can tour via easy loop trails dotted in places with Joshua trees. Be sure to make the 6-mile side drive to Keys View overlook, from which you can see the San Andreas Fault and the Salton Sea, and on clear days, the craggy mountain peaks of northern Mexico.

Eat & Drink: Near Yucca Valley, **Pappy & Harriet's Pioneertown Palace** (✉ *53688 Pioneertown Rd., Pioneertown, CA* ☎ *760/228–2222* ⊕ *www.pappyandharriets.com*) is located on an old Hollywood set that figured in dozens of movies in the 1940s and 1950s and is now an offbeat venue for watching live bands while eating stick-to-your-ribs burgers, steaks, and Tex-Mex fare. After dinner, stop to people-watch at the retro-cool **Virginian** (✉ *73643 Twentynine Palms Hwy.* ☎ *760/361–3050* ⊕ *www. virginiancocktails.com*) cocktail bar.

Stay: If you stay in Palm Springs, consider one of the lodgings near the north end of town—which puts you a little closer to the park—such as stylish **Arrive Palm Springs** (*1551 N. Palm Canyon Dr.* ☎ *760/507–1650* ⊕ *www.arrivehotels. com*), with its chic vibe and an on-site ice-cream shop. Closer to the park, the funky, moderately priced **29 Palms** Inn (✉ *73950 Inn Ave.* ☎ *760/367–3505* ⊕ *www.29palmsinn.com*) is set amid 70

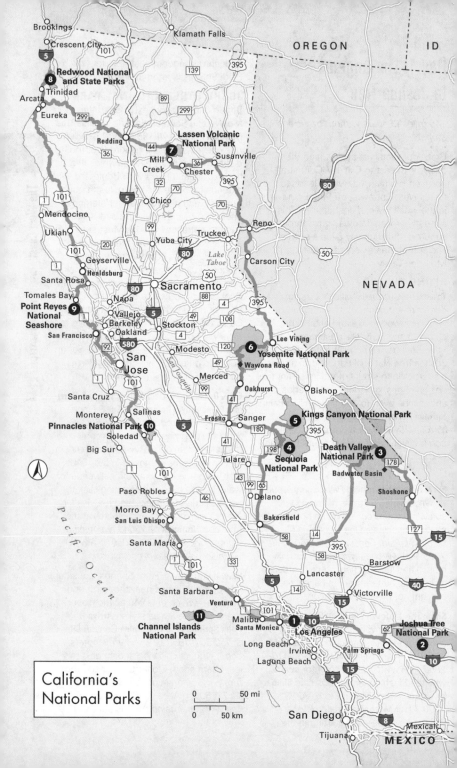

California's National Parks

acres of palm trees, with desert gardens, an art gallery, and a colorful restaurant.

Breakfast: Fuel for your day at **JT Country Kitchen** (✉ 61768 Twentynine Palms Hwy. ☎ 760/366–8988 ⊕ www.jtcountrykitchen.com) in the town of Joshua Tree, a down-home diner where biscuits and gravy, breakfast burritos, French toast, and other breakfast treats are served all day.

Day 2: Joshua Tree to Death Valley

240 miles (4 hours without traffic and stops)

The journey northward runs along both state highways and some unnumbered side roads, but all are paved and well-signed. Start in Twentynine Palms, turn north toward Baker via Amboy and Kelso, pick up Highway 127 north to Death Valley Junction, and then take Highway 190 west to the Furnace Creek area, in the heart of the park.

ALONG THE WAY

Town: In tiny Shoshone, the **Crowbar Cafe & Saloon** (✉ Old State Hwy. 127 ☎ 760/852–4123 ⊕ www.shoshonevillage.com) is filled with old mining paraphernalia and photos of the region, and is a colorful stop for enjoying flame-grilled rainbow trout, fish tacos, and other hearty western dishes.

Detour: There's not a lot to see or do—beyond soaking up the sweeping Mojave Desert vistas—along this remote route, but once you reach the town of Shoshone, about three hours into your drive, you have the option of accessing Death Valley via the southeastern route along Highway 178 through stark yet desolately beautiful Badwater Basin. At 282 feet below sea level, this is the lowest point in the Western Hemisphere. As you continue north toward Furnace Creek, check out the dramatic rock formations at Natural Bridge and Devil's Golf Course.

Traveling this route adds about an hour to the drive without stops.

DEATH VALLEY NATIONAL PARK

Do: At 5,270 square miles, **Death Valley** (☎ 760/786–3200 ⊕ www.nps.gov.deva) is the largest U.S. national park outside Alaska, and although its name hints at some of the hottest temperatures and most unforgiving terrain in the world, it's also a land of considerable diversity, with multicolored canyons, 11,000-foot peaks, undulating sand dunes, and fragrant wildflower meadows. Start with a drive along 9-mile Artist's Drive, admiring the brilliantly hued landscape, then continuing on to the rewarding 2-mile Golden Canyon Interpretive Trail. Next, check out Zabriskie Point, which takes in the park's dramatic, multihued hills, and Dante's View, a mile-high lookout in the Black Mountains from which you can see many of Death Valley's most remarkable features.

Eat & Drink: With its astounding valley views, the **Inn at Death Valley Dining Room** (✉ CA- 190 ☎ 760/786–2345 ⊕ www.oasisatdeathvalley.com) is the park's signature restaurant, serving innovatively prepared seasonal cuisine and refreshing prickly-pear margaritas.

Stay: Given how far Death Valley is from other cities, it's advisable to stay inside the park, which has a handful of options. It tends to book up early during busy periods, but the beautifully restored 1927 Inn at Death Valley is the most treasured of these. Offering simpler motel-style accommodations, **Stovepipe Wells Village Hotel** (✉ 51880 CA-190 ☎ 760/786–7090 ⊕ www.deathvalleyhotels.com) is a more economical option with a peaceful location near striking Mesquite Flat Sand Dunes.

Breakfast: Located in Stovepipe Wells Village, **Panamint Springs Resort Restaurant** (✉ 40440 CA-190, Darwin, CA ☎ 775/482–7680 ⊕ www.panamintsprings.com) turns out a popular breakfast buffet and has an attractive patio with grand vistas of Panamint Valley.

Day 3: Death Valley to Sequoia and Kings Canyon

325 miles (6 hours, 30 minutes without traffic and stops)

Because getting here entails a long drive, and Sequoia and Kings Canyon are actually two distinct but contiguous parks, it's worth developing a strategy before deciding on your exact route. Plan to spend one night in Kings Canyon's Grant Corner Village, arriving via Highway 180 and limiting your time in Sequoia to the park's northern reaches.

ALONG THE WAY

Town: Bakersfield in California's Central Valley is a good place to break up today's journey. Highlights include an emerging Downtown Arts District and the California Living Museum (✉ *10500 Alfred Harrell Hwy.* ☎ *661/872-2256* ⊕ *www.calmzoo. org*), which includes an exceptional zoo, botanical garden, and natural history museum.

Eat & Drink: An Italian grocery and restaurant that's been a fixture in Bakersfield since 1910, **Luigi's** (✉ *725 E. 19th St.* ☎ *661/322–0926* ⊕ *www.shopluigis. com*) remains a favorite place for big portions of hot-pastrami sandwiches, pasta Bolognese, and homemade cheesecake.

SEQUOIA AND KINGS CANYON NATIONAL PARKS

Do: These spectacular alpine parks each offer a different kind of landscape, with Sequoia all about the towering, ancient conifers—the world's largest trees—for which it's named, and Kings Canyon renowned for its sweeping alpine peaks and valleys. You can gain a real sense of Sequoia's awe-inspiring landscape by arriving on Highway 198 through the Ash Mountain Entrance, and then climbing some 3,500 feet along Generals Highway where you can visit the engaging Giant Forest Museum, and stroll amid the sequoia trees in Round Meadow and

Extend Your Trip

From Yosemite: The Best of Northern California *(Ch. 3)*

From Los Angeles: The Best of Southern California; The Pacific Coast Highway *(Ch. 3)*

along the Big Trees Trail. Other highlights include the famed 274.9-foot General Sherman Tree, which ranks among the world's oldest and highest trees, and climbing the stone steps to the scenic overlook from Moro Rock. To explore Kings Canyon, base yourself around Grant Grove Village with a short trek to Panoramic Point, a look at Grizzly Falls, and a stroll through magnificent Zumwalt Meadow, with its grand views of the Kings River and the Grand Sentinel and North Dome rock formations.

Eat & Drink: In Sequoia, **The Peaks Restaurant** inside Wuksachi Lodge (✉ *64740 Wuksachi Way* ⊕ *www.visitsequoia. com*) is famous for its giant fireplace and locavore-minded seasonal cuisine—reservations are essential. The top dining option in Kings Canyon, **Grant Grove Restaurant** (✉ *86728 CA-180* ☎ *866/807-3598* ⊕ *www.visitsequoia.com*) has a large dining room overlooking expanses of sequoia trees; the kitchen turns out creative American cuisine with a focus on sustainable ingredients.

Stay: The lodging options in these parks are amazing thanks to their jaw-dropping designs, especially the grand, cedar-and-stone Wuksachi Lodge in Sequoia. The timber-frame **John Muir Lodge** (✉ *86728 CA-180* ☎ *866/807–3598* ⊕ *www. visitsequoia.com*) in Kings Canyon has relatively simple rooms, but offers a bit of quiet away from the crowds of nearby Grant Grove village.

Breakfast: Convenient options in the park include the aforementioned Grant Grove Restaurant in Kings Canyon, and the casual **Lodgepole Market, Deli, and Cafe** (✉ *63204 Lodgepole Rd.* ☎ *559/565–3301* ⊕ *www.visitsequoia.com*) in Sequoia.

Day 4: Sequoia and Kings Canyon to Yosemite

150 miles (3 hours, 30 minutes without traffic and stops)

Take Highway 180 west from Kings Canyon to Fresno, then follow Highway 41 north, which leads directly to the Yosemite's South Entrance and Wawona section.

ALONG THE WAY

Eat & Drink: The stylish **School House Restaurant & Tavern** (✉ *1018 S. Frankwood Ave.* ☎ *559/787–3271* ⊕ *www.schoolhousesanger.com*) in Sanger occupies a 1920s redbrick schoolhouse and turns out locally sourced fare, such as steak Cobb salads, spiced-lamb-and-beef burgers, and a house favorite: pear bread pudding with vanilla ice cream, candied walnuts, and fresh basil.

Town: In the heart of California's San Joaquin Valley, Fresno offers some standout attractions that make it worth a stop. Highlights include the fanciful grottoes and tunnels of **Forestiere Underground Gardens** (✉ *5021 W. Shaw Ave.* ☎ *559/271– 0734* ⊕ *www.undergroundgardens.com*) and the considerable pre-Columbian Mesoamerican and Andean holdings of the **Fresno Art Museum** (✉ *2233 N. 1st St.* ☎ *559/441–4221* ⊕ *www.fresnoartmuseum.org*).

Photo Op: Inside the park, Wawona Road (Hwy. 41) continues north from the South Entrance up into Yosemite Valley. As you approach the valley, you'll pass through a tunnel, and the view as you emerge is mesmerizing.

Essential Listening

Driving through the sierras provides the perfect backdrop for listening to any of the several audiobooks by the preeminent 19th-century naturalist and oft-described "father of the national parks" system, John Muir, whose writings and conservation advocacy helped secure the designation of Sequoia and Yosemite national parks. Great choices include *Our National Parks* and *Wilderness Essays*.

YOSEMITE NATIONAL PARK

Do: One of the most celebrated landscapes in America, **Yosemite** (☎ *209/372– 0200* ⊕ *www.nps.gov/yose*) ranges across nearly 1,200 square miles and could really be described as several parks in one. During a short stay, you can view the stands of imposing sequoia trees in Mariposa Grove in Wawona, which is the easiest area to access if coming from Fresno. And you can focus the rest of your time on the best-known sites of Yosemite Valley: admiring legendary El Capitan (the largest exposed-granite monolith on the planet), checking out the roaring triple cascades of 2,425-foot-tall Yosemite Falls, driving to the overlook atop Glacier Point for an astounding view of the valley, and embarking on one or two shorter hikes, such as the 3-mile Mist Trail to Vernal Fall or the 8.5-mile Panorama Trail from Glacier Point, which provides you terrific views of Half Dome. In summer, as you exit the park through the Eastern Entrance, you can drive the breathtaking 59-mile Tioga Road to Tuolumne Meadows and on to Lee Vining.

Eat & Drink: Dinner at the vaunted **Ahwahnee Dining Room** (✉ *1 Ahwahnee Dr.* ☎ *888/413–8869* ⊕ *www.travelyosemite.*

com) is an unforgettable experience, where rarefied modern American cuisine is served beneath ornate chandeliers and a 34-foot ceiling.

Stay: Designed by Gilbert Stanley Underwood in the late 1920s, the grand stone-and-timber Ahwahnee is one of the country's singular national parks lodges. It's expensive and always booked well in advance, but it's absolutely worth the splurge. Outside the park, the town of Oakhurst has plenty of options, and you'll find some nifty lodgings in Groveland, Fish Camp, Mariposa, and other towns to the west as well.

Breakfast: Especially convenient if you're headed toward Tuolumne Meadows, the **White Wolf Lodge** (✉ *White Wolf Rd.* ☎ *888/413–8869* ⊕ *www.travelyosemite. com*) is a pleasingly rustic spot 30 miles northwest of Yosemite Valley, offering all-you-can-eat home-style breakfasts.

Day 5: Yosemite to Lassen Volcanic

281 miles (5 hours, 10 minutes without traffic and stops)

Although open only from around early June through late October, Yosemite's Eastern Entrance leads to the most scenic route to Lassen and allows you to explore Tuolumne Meadows. This route follows Highway 120 east out of the park to the small town of Lee Vining, where you turn north on U.S. 395 and pass gorgeous Mono Lake, cutting up through Carson City and Reno, Nevada. U.S. 395 leads back into California, where you turn west in Susanville onto Highway 36, which leads to Lassen's southern sections. The rest of the year, you'll have to leave Yosemite from the west, driving by way of Stockton via Highways 120 and 4. Then turn north on Highway 99, continuing through Sacramento to Chico, and then following Highway 32 to Highway

36/89 west to the park's southerly Kohm Yah-mah-nee Visitor Center. These routes take roughly the same amount of time.

ALONG THE WAY

Nature: Not far from Yosemite's eastern entrance, Lee Vining is a cute, friendly village that's home to remote, enormous Mono Lake, with its eerie calcium-carbonate tufas (hoodoo-like rock formations), which you can get a better look at on free nature walks offered in summer through the **Mono Basin Scenic Area Visitor Center** (✉ *Lee Vining Creek Trail* ☎ *760/647–3044* ⊕ *www.fs.usda.gov*).

Eat & Drink: Many who pass through Reno give it no more than a quick look, perhaps taking in its glitzy skyline of neon-streaked casino towers, but "the biggest little city in the world" has a revitalized downtown with attractive promenades along the Truckee River and a number of excellent restaurants. **Old World Coffee Lab** (✉ *104 California Ave.* ☎ *775/391–0189* ⊕ *www.oldworldcoffee. co*) is a hip stop for well-crafted espresso drinks and fresh bagels. Beside the river, **Sierra Street Kitchen and Cocktails** (✉ *50 N. Sierra St.* ☎ *775/686–6669* ⊕ *www. sierrastkitchen.com*) offers tasty internationally inspired tapas, creative sips, and live music some evenings.

LASSEN VOLCANIC NATIONAL PARK

Do: Although named for the now dormant plug volcano at its heart, which erupted dramatically in 1915, the 165-square-mile **Lassen Volcanic National Park** (☎ *530/595–4480* ⊕ *www.nps.gov/lavo*) is more diverse than its name suggests, offering miles of trails through dense alpine forests and wildflower meadows. The drive north along Lassen Park Highway is a gem, passing by the Devastated Area, which still shows evidence of the 1915 eruption, and leading to the gorgeous scenery around Manzanita Lake, where you can visit the excellent Loomis Museum and enjoy a stroll along the 1-mile Lily Pond Nature Trail. Other draws include

Did You Know?

Found within Sequoia National Park, sequoias once grew throughout the northern hemisphere, until they were almost wiped out by glaciers. Some of the fossils in Arizona's Petrified Forest National Park are extinct sequoia species.

the 3-mile round-trip Bumpass Hell Trail, which reveals some of the park's most exciting geothermal features, including steam vents, mud pots, and boiling lakes, and assuming you're fit for a 2,000-foot climb, undertaking the 2.5-mile hike to the 10,457-foot summit of Lassen Peak.

Eat & Drink: Dining options in the park are limited, but the **Restaurant at Highlands Ranch Resort** (✉ *41515 CA-36 E, Mill Creek, CA* ☎ *530/595–3388* ⊕ *www.highlandranchresort.com*), just outside the park's southern entrance, doles out sophisticated fare overlooking a pastoral meadow. You'll find a smattering of cafés and bars a bit east in the small town of Chester and larger community of Susanville, which is home to **Lassen Ale Works** (✉ *702-000 Johnstonville Rd.* ☎ *530/257–4443* ⊕ *www.lassenale-works.com*), a lively spot for gourmet pizza and distinctive craft beers.

Stay: About 10 miles from the park's southern entrance, the upscale Highlands Ranch Resort is a standout for its plush bungalows, many with outdoor hot tubs. Inside the park, near the northern entrance, **Manzanita Lake Camping Cabins** (✉ *39489 CA-44, Shingletown, CA* ☎ *530/779–0307* ⊕ *www.lassenlodging.com*) is a great, reasonably priced option comprising 20 rustic but handsome modern cabins.

Breakfast: In Chester, bright and cheerful **Cravings Cafe** (✉ *278 Main St.* ☎ *530/258–2229* ⊕ *www.facebook.com/chestercravings*) serves flavorful breakfast burritos and Belgian waffles.

Day 6: Lassen Volcanic to Redwood

215 miles (4 hours without traffic and stops)

Redwood National Park comprises several different units spanning a 60-mile corridor from just above Trinidad north to Crescent City, almost to the Oregon border, with several key sites and visitor centers in between. From the Manzanita Lake section of Lassen, it's about 200 miles west via Highways 44 and 299. Then head north on U.S. 101 to reach the Thomas H. Kuchel Visitor Center, the southernmost in the park, before continuing north to explore the park.

ALONG THE WAY

Town: Redding is far Northern California's main hub, and it's worth a stop to visit its **Turtle Bay Exploration Park** (✉ *844 Sundial Bridge Dr.* ☎ *530/243–8850* ⊕ *www.turtlebay.org*), a highlight of which is the stunning Santiago Calatrava–designed Sundial Bridge, a metal-and-translucent-glass pedestrian walkway, suspended by cables from a single tower and spanning a broad bend in the Sacramento River.

Eat & Drink: The panorama from the patio and glass-walled dining room at **View 202** (✉ *202 Hemsted Dr.* ☎ *530/226–8439* ⊕ *www.view202redding.com*), which sits on a hilltop above the Sacramento River in Redding, takes in the snowcapped mountains in the distance. The modern American menu emphasizes grilled meats and fish from noted California purveyors but also includes bouillabaisse and homemade ravioli.

REDWOOD NATIONAL AND STATE PARKS

Do: Made up of both federal lands administered by the national park service and several state parks, the officially named **Redwood National Park and State Parks** (☎ *707/464–6101* ⊕ *www.nps.gov/redw*) is the definitive place to walk amid redwood trees, which can rise to more than 350 feet (they differ from sequoias in that they grow near the coast, and are taller but generally don't attain the same girth as their inland counterparts). The best place to spend the bulk of your time is the Prairie Creek Redwoods State Park section, which is just off U.S. 101. Here you can drive 10-mile Newton B. Drury Scenic Parkway, admiring trees along the way and stopping at several points—notably the Big Tree Wayside—for short hikes. Another highlight is driving to Gold Bluffs Beach and making the short fourth-of-a-mile hike into Fern Canyon, a magical 50-foot-canyon carpeted with deer, sword, and five-finger ferns—the dizzyingly lush landscape appeared famously in Jurassic Park 2. As you continue north, make the beautiful Coastal Drive Loop, a narrow and partially unpaved 9-mile journey through stands of redwoods with expansive vistas of the Pacific. Both a retro-kitschy must for photo ops and fun souvenirs, and an opportunity to explore the area's redwoods via a six-passenger gondola, Trees of Mystery sits right along U.S. 101. Upon pulling into this goofy place, you'll be greeted by a talking 49-foot-tall Paul Bunyan statue—and yes, Babe the Blue Ox stands dutifully beside him.

Eat & Drink: At the southern end of the park, the best dining is in the funky college town of Arcata and the North Coast's largest city, Eureka. **Cafe Brio** (⊠ 791 G St. ☎ 707/822–5922 ⊕ www. cafebrioarcata.com) overlooks Arcata's town plaza, bakes its own breads, and serves superb focaccia sandwiches, leafy salads, and creative dinner fare. In Eureka's Old Town, **Cafe Waterfront** (⊠ 102 F St. ☎ 707/443–9190 ⊕ www.cafewaterfronteureka.com) occupies an old former brothel and is well-regarded for its oyster burgers, chowders, steamed clams, and other locally caught seafood.

Stay: Eureka and Arcata have a wealth of accommodations, from chain properties to "PaintedLadies" Victorian B&Bs, including the **Carter House Inns** (⊠ 301 L St. ☎ 800/404–1390 ⊕ www.carterhouse.com), which stands out for its central Old Town Eureka location. You'll also find some distinctive options near the park's core attractions, such as **Elk Meadow Cabins** (⊠ 7 Valley Green Camp Rd. ☎ 800/544–0300 ⊕ www.elkmeadowcabins.com), a cluster of spacious,

restored former millworkers' cabins with kitchens and a communal fire pit.

Breakfast: In Trinidad, **Beachcomber Cafe** (⊠ 363 Trinity St. ☎ 707/677–0106 ⊕ www.beachcombertrinidad.com) is a great place to pick up bagels topped with chevre, poached eggs, lox, and other delicious toppings, along with organic espresso drinks.

Day 7: Redwood National Park to Point Reyes National Seashore

340 miles (6 hours without traffic and stops)

Today's drive is from coastal Humboldt County to coastal Marin County near San Francisco, most of it inland through magnificent old-growth forest on Highway 101. When you get to Petaluma, cut toward the coast via D Street and then Point Reyes–Petaluma Road, which takes you to Highway 1 and then the park's entrance.

ALONG THE WAY

Eat & Drink: You won't lack for notable dining options along this route, especially once you get to Sonoma County. **Catelli's** (⊠ 21047 Geyserville Ave. ☎ 707/857–3471 ⊕ www.mycatellis.com) Italian restaurant in Geyserville beckons hungry diners with exceptional homemade pastas.

Town: One of several picturesque communities in the heart of Sonoma's Wine Country, Healdsburg has an attractive downtown anchored by a tree-shaded square. Here you'll find dozens of winery tasting rooms, fashionable boutiques, and fine restaurants. If you have a little extra time, venture west from town via Westside Road, where you can enjoy tastings at some of California's most esteemed wineries, such as **Gary Farrell** (⊠ 10701 Westside Rd. ☎ 707/473–2909 ⊕ www.garyfarrellwinery.com).

POINT REYES NATIONAL SEASHORE

Do: The 71,000-acre **Point Reyes National Seashore** (☎ 415/464–5137 ⊕ www. nps.gov/pore), set on a lush, windswept peninsula in the Pacific, lies just 30 miles north of San Francisco but feels as though it could be galaxies away. It's a pristine patchwork of drives and hikes atop 100-foot sea cliffs, along pristine beaches, and past wildlife-rich estuaries. It's worth driving to the farthest point in the park, Lighthouse Visitor Center, for a trek over a dramatic headland where you can often spy gray whales just off the coast during the winter and spring migratory periods. Among the seashore's most scenic beaches, Limantour Spit is a gorgeous spot to watch the waves crash dramatically against the shore. Keep an eye out for harbor seals and all kinds of migratory birds, too.

Eat & Drink: Just north of the park with a magnificent location overlooking Tomales Bay, Hog Island Oyster Co.'s Marshall Oyster Farm and **The Boat Oyster Bar** (✉ 20215 Shoreline Hwy. ☎ 415/663–9218 ⊕ www.hogislandoysters.com) is a delightful spot for locally harvested raw and barbecued oysters—you can even shuck and barbecue them yourself if you're feeling adventurous. Not far from the park entrance, the village of Point Reyes Station has several inviting restaurants, including **Tomales Bay Foods** (✉ 80 4th St. ☎ 415/663–9335 ⊕ www.cow-girlcreamery.com), a smartly retrofitted old barn that's now a gourmet market. It houses the famed **Cowgirl Creamery** dairy as well as shops and counters selling creative sandwiches, luscious gelato, and other treats and picnic goods.

Stay: Just south of Point Reyes Station, the **Olema House** (✉ 10021 Coastal Hwy. 1 ☎ 415/663–9000 ⊕ www.olemahouse. com) is a smartly restored 1860s stage-coach stopover that's close to the park. Another good option that's a little easier on the wallet, the **Cottages at Point Reyes Station** (✉ 13275 Sir Francis Drake Blvd., Inverness, CA ☎ 415/669–7250 ⊕ www. cottagepointreyes.com) offer cabins with fireplaces encompassing a gorgeous private 8-acre wildlife preserve.

Breakfast: In Point Reyes Station, don't miss the delectable blueberry-buttermilk scones, blackberry-lemon-pear muffins, and ham-and-cheese croissants at **Bovine Bakery** (✉ 11315 CA-1 ☎ 415/663–9420 ⊕ www.bovinebakeryptreyes.com), where you can also fuel up on espresso and chai lattes.

Day 8: Point Reyes National Seashore to Pinnacles

170 miles (3 hours without traffic and stops)

Although it covers one relatively small (by national park standards) tract of about 26,600 acres, Pinnacles National Park feels like two separate places, as it's accessed from either the east or west, and there's no road connecting the two entrances. From Point Reyes National Seashore, take Highway 1 through the gorgeous Marin Headlands to U.S. 101, continue south over the Golden Gate Bridge through San Francisco, connect with I–280 south through Silicon Valley, pick up U.S. 101 southeast of San Jose, and then, if you're heading to the western side of the park, follow U.S. 101 to Soledad, and then turn east on Highway 146. Or if you're entering the east side of the park, branch off the U.S. 101 south of Gilroy at Exit 353 and take Highway 25 south to Highway 146. Note that the road to the western entrance is windy and meanders through some hilly terrain while the road to the eastern entrance is much more direct.

ALONG THE WAY

Town: One of the world's most beautiful cities needs no introduction, and sure enough, it's right on the way between these two parks. Once you cross the

Golden Gate Bridge, hop onto Highway 1 and head south through the Richmond District. Pause for anywhere from an hour to a few hours in **Golden Gate Park** (☎ 415/831–2700 ⊕ www.sfrecpark.org), which is home to exceptional cultural treasures like the **de Young Museum** (✉ 50 Hagiwara Tea Garden Dr. ☎ 415/750–3600 ⊕ www.deyoung.famsf.org) and **California Academy of Sciences** (✉ 55 Music Concourse Dr. ☎ 415/379–8000 ⊕ www.calacademy.org).

Eat & Drink: Near San Francisco's Golden Gate Park, you'll find a wealth of great restaurants, especially in the Richmond District (just north) and the Sunset District (just south). Asian eateries are particularly good in these parts, and a couple of standouts are trendy **Burma Superstar** (✉ 309 Clement St. ☎ 415/387–2147 ⊕ www.burmasuperstar.com) in the Richmond, and bare-bones **San Tung** (✉ 1031 Irving St. ☎ 415/242–0828 ⊕ www.santung.net) in the Sunset, which is revered for its dry-fried chicken wings and steamed dumplings.

PINNACLES NATIONAL PARK

Do: Upgraded in 2013 from a national monument to a national park, **Pinnacles** (☎ 831/389–4485 ⊕ www.nps.gov/pinn) is nonetheless somewhat underrated, despite being barely more than two hours away from San Francisco. This remarkable volcanic landscape is bisected by a ridge of jagged mountains. In the eastern section of the park, you can view the excellent exhibits at Bear Gulch Nature Center, before embarking on the Bear Gulch Trail to the famed Bear Gulch Caves. On the western side, drive to the Chaparral Trailhead area for a grand view of the park's High Peak, and take the 2½-mile Balconies Cliffs-Cave Loop. For any of these hikes to the park's caves, make sure you pack a flashlight before setting out.

Eat & Drink: Dining options are quite limited near the park, but you'll find a handful of inexpensive, informal options in Soledad, including some excellent Mexican restaurants, like **Taqueria Pacheco** (✉ 325 Front St. ☎ 831/678–1808), a no-frills spot with mouthwatering *al pastor*, *carne asada*, and other tacos. A little farther south in Kings City, **The Cork & Plough** (✉ 200 Broadway St. ☎ 831/386–9491 ⊕ www.thecorkandplough.com) serves updated comfort fare using locally sourced ingredients—from lamb burgers to braised-oxtail gnocchi—and features a great selection of Monterey County wines.

Stay: The top lodging option near the park, the **Inn at Pinnacles** (✉ 32025 Stonewall Canyon Rd. ☎ 831/678–2400 ⊕ www.innatthepinnacles.com) is just outside Soledad; it's a stunning Mediterranean-inspired home set on 160 acres of vineyards.

Breakfast: There's not much near the park, but up in Salinas, you can count on the friendly folks at **First Awakenings** (✉ 171 Main St. ☎ 831/784–1125 ⊕ www.firstawakenings.net) to fill you up with delicious ways to start the day, including green chili and carnitas scrambles and several varieties of eggs Benedict.

Day 9: Pinnacles to Channel Islands

240 miles (4 hours without traffic and stops)

It's a direct shot down the U.S. 101 to reach the park's visitor center in the small seaside city of Ventura.

ALONG THE WAY

Eat & Drink: Famous in the 19th century for its hot springs resorts, Paso Robles is today a font of superb wine country restaurants and tasting rooms. Among the best eateries in town, upscale **Thomas Hill Organics** (✉ 1313 Park St. ☎ 805/226–5888 ⊕ www.thomashillorganics.com) is one of the Central Coast's most vaunted destinations for fine locavore-driven cuisine. For a simpler and less expensive meal, duck into the **Hatch Rotisserie & Bar** (✉ 835 13th St. ☎ 805/221–5727

⊕ *www.hatchpasorobles.com*), a casual spot with elevated comfort fare and a first-rate drinks program.

Town: San Luis Obispo is home to prestigious California Polytechnic State University and has an attractive downtown anchored by the 18th-century **Mission San Luis Obispo de Tolosa** (✉ *751 Palm St.* ☎ *805/781–8220* ⊕ *www.missionsanluisobispo.org*). It also anchors an ever-growing wine region, and you'll find numerous wineries and tasting rooms nearby.

CHANNEL ISLANDS NATIONAL PARK

Do: Visiting the **Channel Islands National Park**, a nautical park (☎ *805/658–5730* ⊕ *www.nps.gov/chis*) that comprises five islands off the coast of Santa Barbara, Ventura, and Oxnard, takes a little extra effort, as the only way to visit any of them is via a boat excursion (or your own private boat). A few different companies offer a variety of cruises to the archipelago, some specializing in scuba diving, kayaking, and other activities. If you have just a day, the best plan is to stop by the park **visitor center** (✉ *1901 Spinnaker Dr.*) in Ventura, which features exhibits and shows a film about the islands, which range in size from 1-square-mile Santa Barbara to the quite extensive 96-square-mile Santa Cruz Island. You could then take an hour-long excursion on one of the **Island Packers** (✉ *1691 Spinnaker Dr.* ☎ *805/642–1393* ⊕ *www.islandpackers. com*) high-speed catamarans to Santa Cruz Island. Once on the island, you can hike amid the unspoiled landscape of 2,500-foot mountains and dramatic canyons, viewing the many kinds of flora and fauna that thrive here and learning about the indigenous Chumash communities that once lived here.

Eat & Drink: There are no facilities on the islands, but **Andria's Seafood** (✉ *1449 Spinnaker Dr.* ☎ *805/654–0546* ⊕ *www. andriasseafood.com*), in Ventura near the visitor center, overlooks the harbor and

marina, and offers delicious clam chowder and fish-and-chips.

Stay: For convenience to the park visitor center and cruises to the islands, the **Ventura Beach Marriott** (✉ *2055 E. Harbor Blvd.* ☎ *805/643–6000* ⊕ *www.marriott. com*) in Ventura is an excellent choice.

Breakfast: Ventura's **Harbor Cove Cafe** (✉ *1867 Spinnaker Dr.* ☎ *805/658–1639* ⊕ *www.harborcovecafe.net*) is next to the park visitor center and is a great option for picking up a breakfast burrito and coffee, as well as box lunches for the rest of your day, before setting sail for Santa Cruz Island.

Day 10: Channel Islands to Los Angeles

70 miles (1 hour, 30 minutes without traffic and stops)

From Ventura, the U.S. 101 is the fastest and most direct way into Los Angeles, but branching off onto coastal Highway 1 in Oxnard and continuing along it through Malibu and Santa Monica offers much prettier scenery, and depending on traffic, it doesn't necessarily take much longer.

ALONG THE WAY

Eat & Drink: A funky, old-school spot in Malibu that's perfect for a casual seafood feast, the **Reel Inn** (✉ *18661 Pacific Coast Hwy.* ☎ *310/456–8221* ⊕ *www. reelinnmalibu.com*) is perhaps most famous for its mahimahi sandwiches and pepper-seared ahi salads.

Town: Santa Monica provides a scenic entry into metro L.A. and is notable for its pedestrian-friendly downtown (especially jacaranda-shaded Third Street Promenade and Santa Monica Place), old-school Santa Monica Pier, and gorgeous Santa Monica State Beach.

The Best of the Pacific Northwest

Written by Margot Bigg

With its beautiful scenery, bohemian cities, celebrated regional fare, and world-famous beer and wine, the Pacific Northwest is like nowhere else in the country, or—frankly—on earth. This weeklong road trip will give you a solid sampling of what the region has to offer, taking you through temperate rain forests, along windswept beaches, up ancient mountains, and past crystalline lakes, hitting four national parks along the way. And while the great outdoors is what beckons many to this little corner of America, this itinerary will also give you plenty of time to hang out in cities such as Portland and Seattle, both of which have thriving culinary scenes and plenty of unique experiences.

At a Glance

Start: Seattle, WA

End: Seattle, WA

Miles Traveled: 1,806 miles

Suggested Duration: 8 days

States Visited: Oregon, Washington

Key Sights: Crater Lake National Park; Mount Rainier National Park; North Cascades National Park; Olympia National Park; the Space Needle

Best Time to Go: It's no secret that the Pacific Northwest gets a lot of rain, and it's a good idea to pack a waterproof jacket whatever time of year you visit. The driest weather tends to be in summer and early fall, and heavy winter snowfall in the mountainous parts of the region makes visiting national parks and other outdoor attractions challenging, even with four-wheel drive.

Day 1: Seattle, WA, to Port Angeles, WA

258 miles (6 hours without traffic and stops)

Pick up your rental car on the early side and make your way to the Hoh River Rain Forest, one of the most photographed stretches of Olympic National Park. Then trace your route back part of the way to Port Angeles, where you'll spend your first night.

ALONG THE WAY

Town: At the base of the Olympic Mountains, Sequim is an old mill town overlooking the Strait of Juan de Fuca. Stop for a stroll or a bite to eat in the compact city center. If you come on a Saturday, don't miss the chance to browse for local produce and crafts at the **Sequim Farmers and Artisans Market** (✉ *152 W. Cedar St.* ⊕ *www.sequimmarket.com*).

Eat & Drink: Stick around Sequim for lunch at **Dockside Grill** (✉ *2577 W. Sequim Bay Rd.* ☎ *360/638–7510* ⊕ *www. docksidegrill-sequim.com*), which serves everything from fish-and-chips to oyster po' boys, all with fantastic views over the Sequim Bay.

Nature: Within the Hoh River Rain Forest, take in towering spruce and hemlock trees in this rainy stretch of **Olympic National Park** (☎ *360/565–3130* ⊕ *www. nps.gov/olym*). For the best views without much effort, consider a hike through the 0.8-mile-long Hall of Mosses loop trail.

PORT ANGELES

Do: Popular with weekending Seattleites, this cute coastal town offers lots of shops and dining, along with the **Clallam Historical Society** (✉ *933 W. 9th St.* ☎ *360/452–2662* ⊕ *www.clallamhistoricalsociety.com*) and the Feiro Marine Life Center (✉ *315 N. Lincoln St.* ☎ *360/417–6254* ⊕ *www.feiromarinelifecenter.org*).

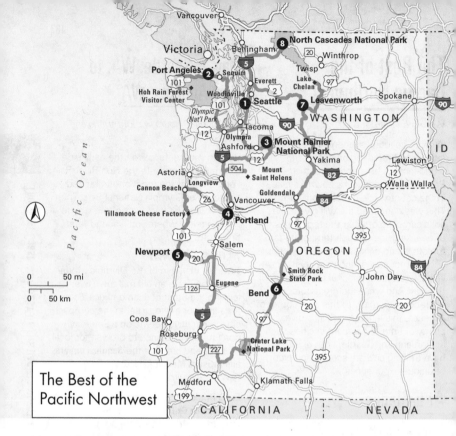

The Best of the
Pacific Northwest

Eat & Drink: Treat yourself to a fancy dinner at the swanky **C'est Si Bon** (⊠ *23 Cedar Park Dr.* ☎ *360/452-8888* ⊕ *www.cestsibon-frenchcuisine.com*), with its changing menu of Franco-Northwest fusion fare and its fantastic global wine list.

Stay: Spread across two manicured acres overlooking the sea, the Victorian **Sea Cliff Gardens Bed & Breakfast** (⊠ *397 Monterra Dr.* ☎ *360/452-2322* ⊕ *www. seacliffgardens.com*) features elegant, antiques-filled rooms and suites, some with whirlpool tubs. If you'd rather stay inside Olympic National Park, the **Sol Duc Hot Springs Resort** (⊠ *12076 Sol Duc-Hot Springs Rd.* ☎ *888/896-3818* ⊕ *www. olympicnationalparks.com*) offers cabins and campsites plus a few sprawling hot springs-fed pools.

Breakfast: At the **Oak Table Café** (⊠ *292 W. Bell St.* ☎ *360/683-2179* ⊕ *www. oaktablecafe.com*) in nearby Sequim, carefully crafted breakfasts and lunches are the focus. Try the huge soufflé-style apple-cinnamon pancakes.

Day 2: Port Angeles, WA, to Mount Rainier National Park

183 miles (4 hours without traffic and stops)

Head south along Highway 101 to Olympia, and then continue southeast all the way to Mount Rainier National Park via the town of Ashford.

ALONG THE WAY

Town: Although it's the capital of Washington State, Olympia is best known for its bohemian atmosphere and easy access to the great outdoors. Learn about wildlife at the **Wolf Haven International** (✉ *3111 Offut Lake Rd. SE, Tenino, WA* ☎ *360/264–4695* ⊕ *www.wolfhaven.org*) wolf sanctuary or take a three-mile hike along the Ellis Cove Trail, which runs through the wetlands of Priest Point Park (✉ *2600 E. Bay Dr. NE* ☎ *360/753–8380* ⊕ *www.olympiawa.gov*).

Eat & Drink: Olympia is a great spot to stick around for lunch. For fresh, from-scratch Italian fare, consider **Mercato Ristorante** (✉ *111 Market St. NE* ☎ *360/528–3663* ⊕ *www.mercatoristorante.com*). This popular spot offers a solid menu of salads, antipasto, pasta, and pizza plus an always-solid wine list with plenty of regional and imported options.

MOUNT RAINIER NATIONAL PARK

Do: Mount Rainier National Park (☎ *360/569–2211* ⊕ *www.nps.gov/mora*) is one of the most popular places for mountain climbing and backpacking in the Pacific Northwest, and for good reason. Its namesake perpetually snowcapped volcano is the fifth-highest mountain in the Lower 48 and has some 26 glaciers. It's divided into five sections, four with their own visitors' centers. Most visitors stop at the main Henry M. Jackson Memorial Visitor Center, which offers educational exhibits, guided hikes, and a cafeteria. Also worth visiting is the Grove of the Patriarchs in the Ohanapecosh section of the park, with its old-growth trees believed to be over 1,000 years old.

Eat & Drink: At the top of Crystal Mountain, some 6,872 feet above sea level, **Crystal Mountain Resort's Summit House** (✉ *33914 Crystal Mountain Blvd., Enumclaw, WA* ☎ *360/663–3085* ⊕ *www.crystalmountainresort.com*) is worth visiting for the views alone. The menu here is simple but far from plain, with

Essential Listening

The Hoh Rainforest is the quietest place in the contiguous United States. Prepare yourself with *One Square Inch of Silence*, an audio preview of the pristine forest, courtesy of acoustic ecologist Gordon Hempton.

Wagyu beef burgers, wild game chili, and veggie curry wraps, plus chocolate mousse s'mores for dessert.

Stay: If you want to stay inside the park, the **National Park Inn** (✉ *47009 Paradise Rd. E* ☎ *360/569–2411* ⊕ *www.mtrainierguestservices.com*) is your best noncamping bet, with year-round accommodations and an inviting lobby with a big fireplace. For a romantic alternative, consider booking a cabin at nearby **Wellspring Spa** (✉ *54922 Kernahan Rd. E* ⊕ *www.wellspringspa.com*), which offers quiet cabins, spa services, cedar saunas, and two outdoor hot tubs.

Breakfast: Fuel up with a hearty breakfast at Ashford's **Copper Creek Restaurant** (✉ *35707 WA-706* ☎ *360/569–2799* ⊕ *www.coppercreekinn.com*), which dates to 1946, making it the oldest continuously operating restaurant in the state. The interiors are rustic and lodge-like down to the antler chandeliers and wood-paneled everything, and the food is hearty, with scrambles, French toast, pancakes, and biscuits and gravy on the menu.

Day 3 : Mount Rainier National Park to Portland, OR

222 miles (4 hours, 30 minutes without traffic and stops)

Head back to I–5 and drive south until you reach Exit 22, for a detour to Mount Saint Helens. After visiting the site, head back to I–5 and continue south until you reach Portland.

ALONG THE WAY

Town: If you need a place to stretch your legs, Longview is a great option. At the heart of the city, Lake Sacajawea is a sprawling man-made lake surrounded by parkland; there's even a small Japanese garden. The city is also home to a number of squirrel bridges, which allow squirrels to avoid traffic by crossing high above roads, from tree to tree—don't forget to look up!

Eat & Drink: One of the newer additions to Longview's restaurant scene, **NADO** (✉ *902 14th Ave.* ☎ *360/232–8483* ⊕ *www.nadointown.com*) offers Korean treats such as bibimbap and hot pot, along with a smattering of unusual specials, from vegan "chicken" to Korean-style hot dogs.

Detour: Famous for its 1980 eruption, Mt. St. Helens is a must-see for anyone interested in national history. You can learn about the eruption at the **Johnston Ridge Observatory** (✉ *24000 Spirit Lake Hwy., Toutle, WA* ☎ *360/274–2140* ⊕ *www.fs.usda.gov*), or explore the subterranean Ape Cave, the longest continuous lava tube in the continental U.S.

PORTLAND

Do: Just south of the Oregon-Washington border, Portland is known for its free-spirited atmosphere, great dining, and ample opportunities to get out in nature. You don't even need to leave the city limits to experience the area's natural beauty, with highlights such as **Forest Park** (☎ *503/823–4492* ⊕ *www.portlandoregon.gov*), the **International Rose Test Garden** (☎ *503/238–7433* ⊕ *www.trimet.org*), and the **Lan Su Chinese Garden** (✉ *239 N.W. Everett St.* ☎ *228–8131* ⊕ *lansugarden.org*) all within a few minutes' drive from downtown. Book lovers won't want to miss **Powell's City of Books** (✉ *1005 W. Burnside St.* ☎ *800/878–7323* ⊕ *www.powells.com*), the world's largest new-and-used bookstore on the planet, occupying an entire city block. If you'd rather spend more time in nature, make your way out to the nearby **Columbia River Gorge** (✉ *714 Cascade Ave, Hood River, OR* ⊕ *www.columbiagorgetomthood.com*) to check out Multnomah Falls, the second-highest year-round waterfall in the United States.

Eat & Drink: For a romantic evening, make a reservation at **Departure Restaurant + Lounge** (✉ *525 S.W. Morrison St.* ☎ *503/802–5370* ⊕ *www.departureportland.com*), which is as known for its great city views as it is for its fantastic cocktails and delicious Pan-Asian fare, served tapas-style.

Stay: Portland has tons of hotel options to choose from, ranging from the quirky to the swanky. If you're looking for an unusual stay, consider **McMenamins Kennedy School** (✉ *5736 N.E. 33rd Ave.* ☎ *503/249–3983* ⊕ *www.mcmenamins.com*), an old schoolhouse turned hotel where you can sleep in refurbished classrooms. If you'd rather be downtown, the **Heathman Hotel** (✉ *1001 S.W. Broadway* ☎ *503/241–4100* ⊕ *www.heathmanhotel.com*) is a Portland classic, with elegant rooms and a popular afternoon tea service. For a more contemporary vibe in the heart of the city, artsy **Woodlark** (✉ *813 S.W. Alder St.* ☎ *877/239–0882* ⊕ *www.provenancehotels.com/woodlark*) features fresh rooms with sleek, modern decor spread across two historic buildings.

Breakfast: Over the past couple of decades, Portland has gained a reputation for its doughnuts owing largely to the tourist-fave **Voodoo Doughnut** (✉ *22 S.W. 3rd Ave.* ☎ *503/241–4704* ⊕ *www. voodoodoughnut.com*) with its curiously shaped (and arguably gimmicky) pastries. But locals in the know are more likely to send you to **Blue Star Donuts** (✉ *672 S. Gaines St.* ☎ *503/954–3672* ⊕ *www. bluestardonuts.com*), with its cakey, gourmet donuts, including some standout vegan options.

Day 4: Portland, OR, to Newport, OR

188 miles (4 hours without traffic and stops)

Head out to the Oregon Coast via Highway 26, which will take you through the forested Coastal Mountain Range before eventually joining up with Highway 101. Stop in Cannon Beach before continuing south along the coast to Newport.

ALONG THE WAY

Town: One of the most popular and easily accessed towns on the Oregon coast, Cannon Beach is known for its art galleries, boutiques, and—unsurprisingly—seafood restaurants. It's also home to Haystack Rock, one of Oregon's oft-photographed natural features.

Eat & Drink: One of a handful of Pelican Brewing outlets along the coast, the **Pelican Brewing Company** (✉ *1371 S. Hemlock St.* ☎ *503/908–3377* ⊕ *www. pelicanbrewing.com*) offers a wide variety of microbrews on tap and a menu of seafood-heavy pub fare, including a popular clam chowder.

Roadside Attraction: Oregon's cheesiest attraction, the **Tillamook Cheese Factory** (✉ *4165 N. Hwy. 101* ☎ *503/815–1300* ⊕ *www.tillamook.com*) is open to visitors for free self-guided tours. After your tour, you'll get the chance to try all sorts of

Extend Your Trip

From Portland, Newport, or Seattle: Highway 101 *(Ch. 3)*

From Seattle: Wine Countries of the Pacific Northwest *(Ch. 3)*; The Ultimate Cross Country Trip North *(Ch. 2)*

free cheese samples; just save room for ice cream, served at the Tillamook ice-cream parlor.

NEWPORT

Do: Famous for its Dungeness crab, Newport is one of the busier cities on the 101, with plenty more to do than just stroll the sand. Star attractions include the **Yaquina Head Lighthouse** (✉ *750 N.W. Lighthouse Dr.* ☎ *541/574–3100* ⊕ *www.blm.gov*) and the **Oregon Coast Aquarium** (✉ *2820 S.E. Ferry Slip Rd.* ☎ *541/867–3474* ⊕ *www.aquarium.org*), with its underwater tunnel and seabird aviary.

Eat & Drink: Offering some of the best views in Newport, the ocean-facing **Georgie's Beachside Grill** (✉ *744 S.W. Elizabeth St.* ☎ *541/265–9800* ⊕ *www.georgies-beachsidegrill.com*) serves a reasonably priced seafood-dominant menu in a casual setup.

Stay: One of the sleeker options on this stretch of the Oregon coast, the **Inn at Nye Beach** (✉ *729 N.W. Coast St.* ☎ *541/265–2477* ⊕ *www.innatenye-beach.com*) offers contemporary rooms, many with views out over the sea. For something a bit more secluded, the **Moolack Shores Inn** (✉ *8835 N. Coast Hwy.* ☎ *541/265–2326* ⊕ *www.mool-ackshores.com*) offers reasonably priced hotel rooms just north of town.

Breakfast: Start your day at the snug **Panini Bakery** (✉ *232 N.W. Coast St.* ☎ *541/272–5322*) for delicious espresso

Even on the hottest days, Mount Rainier still glistens with snow.

drinks, fresh-baked pastries, and freshly squeezed orange juice.

Day 5: Newport, OR, to Crater Lake National Park to Bend, OR

332 miles (6 hours, 30 minutes without traffic and stops)

Drive inland on Highway 20 before continuing southeast to Crater Lake. From here, make your way north to Bend for the night.

ALONG THE WAY

Town: Home of the University of Oregon, Eugene is the state's second-largest city, and offers lots of great dining and green spaces without the crowds of Portland.

Eat & Drink: Eugene has had a strong hippie influence since the 1960s, and nowhere can this aesthetic be felt more than at the vegetarian **Morning Glory Café** (✉ *450 Willamette St.* ☎ *541/687–0709*

⊕ *www.morninggloryeugene.com*). The lunch menu focuses on soups, salads, and sandwiches while the café's sweet-and-savory breakfast offerings are served well into the afternoon.

Detour: Rather than heading straight for Bend, head south to the only national park in Oregon: **Crater Lake National Park** (☎ *541/594–3000* ⊕ *www.nps.gov/crla*). Spanning over 5 miles in length, and with a depth of 1,943 feet, this ancient caldera lake is the deepest in the country. To get the best views of the park, take time to drive the 33-mile-long Rim Drive, which loops along the lake, with plenty of spots to pull off for photos along the way. If you decide to linger for a day or two, you can take a boat out to Wizard Island, a cinder cone island that sits in the heart of the lake.

BEND

Do: Central Oregon's main economic hub, Bend is a small but quickly growing city celebrated for its sunny climate and easy access to year-round outdoor recreation. Along with a cute downtown area full of shops and restaurants, you'll find ample parks, hiking areas, and even a couple of museums—don't miss the **High Desert Museum** (✉ 59800 U.S. 97 ☎ 541/382–4754 ⊕ www.highdesertmuseum.org), a family-friendly cross between a living history museum and a zoo.

Eat & Drink: Housed in a Craftsman-style bungalow, **Ariana Restaurant** (✉ 1304 N.W. Galveston Ave. ☎ 541/330–5539 ⊕ www.arianarestaurantbend.com) is a chef-owned fine-dining spot that offers European fare with a Northwest twist, along with an extensive wine and cocktail menu.

Stay: Rather than stay right in downtown Bend, head a few miles out into the surrounding countryside for a night (or a few nights) at **Brasada Ranch** (✉ 16976 S.W. Brasada Ranch Rd., Powell Butte, OR ☎ 888/487–3563 ⊕ www.brasada.com), an 1,800-acre resort with spacious cabins and suites plus golf, horseback riding, multiple pools, a fantastic gourmet restaurant, and a luxury spa, all set against a backdrop of the snowcapped Cascade Range. If you're on a budget, the cozy **Pine Ridge Inn** (✉ 1200 S.W. Mount Bachelor Dr. ☎ 800/600–4095 ⊕ www.pineridgeinn.com) features homey rooms with gas fireplaces, mini-refrigerators, and microwaves.

Breakfast: Before you hit the road, make a pit stop at **Lone Pine Coffee Roasters** (✉ 910 N.W. Harriman St. ☎ 541/306–1010 ⊕ www.lonepinecoffeeroasters.com) for a fresh pastry and a cup of joe made from beans roasted on-site.

Day 6: Bend, OR, to Leavenworth, WA

311 miles (5 hours, 30 minutes without traffic and stops)

Head north back into Washington State on Highway 97, and continue driving until you reach the Bavarian-inspired town of Leavenworth.

ALONG THE WAY

Photo Op: If you want an image that sums up the natural beauty of Central Oregon, **Smith Rock State Park** (☎ 800/551–6949 ⊕ www.oregonstateparks.org) won't disappoint. This tuff and basalt monolith, located just off Highway 97 is one of the most popular spots in the Pacific Northwest for rock climbing. You can easily get a great shot of the rock from the parking area; keep your eyes peeled for bald eagles and raptors.

Town: Just north of the border with Washington, the little town of Goldendale serves local rural communities and travelers passing through on their way to or from local attractions such as the **Goldendale Observatory State Park** (✉ 1602 Observatory Dr. ☎ 509/773–3141 ⊕ www.goldendaleobservatory.com) and the **Maryhill Winery** (✉ 9774 WA-14 ☎ 509/773–1976 ⊕ www.maryhillwinery.com).

Eat & Drink: Situated at the entrance of Goldendale's St. John the Forerunner Greek Orthodox Monastery, **St. John's Bakery** (✉ 2378 U.S. 97 ☎ 509/773–6650 ⊕ www.stjohnmonastery.org) provides an unusual alternative to the diner fare that dominates along Highway 97, with everything from sweet baklava to savory lunch treats such as spanakopita and gyros. They also serve outstanding coffee.

Roadside Attraction: If you want to see England's most famous Neolithic site but don't want to fly across the Atlantic to do it, fear not: you can still get your Stonehenge fix in Goldendale at the **Stonehenge Memorial** (✉ 41–97 Stonehenge Dr. ⊕ www.maryhillmuseum.org). This full-scale replica was built in 1918 as a WWI veterans' memorial and offers views out over the Columbia River.

LEAVENWORTH

Do: Revamped in the 1960s to look like a Bavarian village (even the gas stations and chain restaurants use hand-painted signage), Leavenworth is most popular for its shopping, dining, and general atmosphere. It's especially popular around Christmastime, but the Kris Kringle vibes are year-round here, particularly at the **Nutcracker Museum** (✉ 735 Front St. ☎ 509/548-4573 ⊕ www. nutcrackermuseum.com), which boasts around 3,000 nutcrackers, some dating back centuries. The town's location due east of Seattle also makes it a popular jumping-off point for regional outdoor activities, from winter snowshoeing to summer rock climbing.

Eat & Drink: It's always Oktoberfest at **München Haus Bavarian Grill and Beer Garden** (✉ 709 Front St. ☎ 509/548-1158 ⊕ www.munchenhaus.com), a popular sausage-and-beer joint on the northern end of town. The menu is dominated by sausages, including a few veggie options, all served with a huge range of mustards and other condiments, from apple cider vinegar sauerkraut to German curry ketchup.

Stay: A short drive from downtown Leavenworth, the lodge-style **Sleeping Lady Mountain Resort** (✉ 7375 Icicle Rd. ☎ 509/548-6344 ⊕ www.sleepinglady. com) offers rooms and cabins (some with bunk beds), plus an on-site spa with treatments and a dry sauna. If you're on a budget or visit during the holiday season, when accommodations can be hard to come by, there are also plenty of options in the nearby city of Wenatchee, about a 25-minute drive south of town.

Breakfast: In the heart of Leavenworth, the **Gingerbread Factory** (✉ 829 Front St. ☎ 509/548-6592 ⊕ www.gingerbreadfactory.com) serves espresso drinks and a variety of gingerbread cookies and houses as well as classic breakfast pastries such as marionberry scones and cinnamon rolls. There's also a small indoor seating area designed to resemble a forecourt (complete with an artificial tree adorned with heart-shaped cookie ornaments) for those who want to dine in.

Day 7: Leavenworth, WA, to North Cascades National Park

195 miles (4 hours without traffic and stops)

There are multiple ways to access North Cascades National Park. If you want to bring your car with you, take U.S. 2 to Everett and then take the I–5 N to the North Cascades Highway. However, make sure to check road conditions ahead of time, as parts of both U.S. 2 and the North Cascades Highway frequently experience snow-related closures well into the spring months. You can also access the park by heading to Lake Chelan, about an hour's drive northeast of Leavenworth, and taking a passenger ferry four hours into the remote town of Stehekin, which is accessible only by boat, floatplane, or by hiking 23 miles from the Cascade Pass Trailhead.

ALONG THE WAY

Town: Part of the larger Seattle metro area, the port city of Everett is best known as the home to one of Boeing's major factories. Aviation fans can visit the factory alongside the adjacent **Boeing Future of Flight** (✉ 8415 Paine Field Blvd., Mukilteo, WA ☎ 800/464-1476 ⊕ www.boeingfutureofflight.com), an airplane museum that houses a range of airplane-related displays, including a flight simulator and a real 727. Not far from the factory, the **Flying Heritage & Combat Armor Museum** (✉ 3407 109th St. SW ☎ 877/342-3404 ⊕ www.flyingheritage.com) focuses on military vehicles, and showcases a number of rare WWII aircraft.

Eat & Drink: One of a handful of the popular Seattle-area seafood restaurant empire, **Anthony's HomePort Everett** (✉ 1726 W. Marine View Dr. ☎ 425/252-3333 ⊕ www.anthonys.com) offers fresh, locally sourced seafood with indoor and outdoor seating and views out over Port Gardner Bay.

NORTH CASCADES NATIONAL PARK

Do: Among the most remote natural areas in Washington State, the glacier-filled **North Cascades National Park** (☎ 360/854–7200 ⊕ www.nps.gov/noca) features over half a million acres of alpine scenery and an extensive network of hiking trails. You can learn about the park and get hiking tips from Parks Service staff at the North Cascades Visitor Center, though it's only open in the summer. Another great place to get oriented is at the **North Cascades Environmental Learning Center** (✉ 1940 Diablo Dam Rd., Rockport, WA ☎ 360/854–2599 ⊕ www.ncascades. org) at Diablo Lake, where you can learn all about the local ecosystem or book a guided tour or canoe trip. If you end up visiting the Stehekin part of the park, you can get your bearings at the National Parks Service Golden West Visitor Center, a few minutes' walk from the passenger ferry port.

Eat & Drink: If you're staying in the Winthrop/Twisp area, **Arrowleaf Bistro** (✉ 207 White Ave. ☎ 509/996–3919 ⊕ www.arrowleafbistro.com) is a great place to grab dinner, with a changing menu of classic European dishes and solid dessert and cocktail offerings. The options in Stehekin are limited, and most visitors end up eating at either the Lodge at Stehekin's on-site restaurant or at the **Stehekin Valley Ranch** (☎ 509/682–4677 ⊕ www.stehekinvalleyranch.com).

Stay: There aren't a ton of overnight options in and around the park, and many visitors end up renting independently owned cabins or camping in the Ross Lake area. A bit farther east, the towns of Winthrop and Twisp have a larger number of hotel options. **Winthrop's Sun Mountain Lodge** (✉ 604 Patterson Lake Rd. ☎ 509/996–2211 ⊕ www.sunmountainlodge.com) is an excellent choice,

and offers beautiful views and lots of outdoor activities. For something cheaper, **Idle-A-While Motel** (✉ 505 Methow Valley Hwy. ☎ 509/997–3222 ⊕ www.idle-a-while-motel.com) in Twisp offers cabin-like rooms with mini-refrigerators and microwaves. If you're visiting the Stehekin portion of the park, the **North Cascades Lodge at Stehekin** (✉ 1 Stehekin Valley Rd. ☎ 855/685–4167 ⊕ www.lodgeatstehekin.com) offers a wide range of accommodations ranging from hotel rooms to large cabins, and even a lake house.

Breakfast: If you're in Stehekin, the **Stehekin Pastry Company** (✉ 200' S.W. Of Bakery ☎ 509/682–7742 ⊕ www.stehekinpastry.com) is one of the most popular spots in town, with a wide range of baked goods served fresh every morning. If you're staying in Twisp or Winthrop, head to the **Cinnamon Twisp Bakery** (✉ 116 Glover St. N ☎ 509/997–5030 ⊕ www.facebook.com/CinnamonTwispBakery) for a fresh bagel sandwich.

Day 8: North Cascades National Park to Seattle, WA

117 miles (2 hours, 15 minutes without traffic and stops)

If you're returning from the North Cascades Highway, head back the way you came until you reach I–5. Drive south to the I–405 S, stopping in Woodinville before continuing south to the Evergreen Point Floating Bridge, from where you can cross Lake Washington into Seattle. If you've opted to visit Stehekin via Lake Chelan, you can take Highway 2 east all the way to Woodinville and then continue on to Seattle.

ALONG THE WAY

Town: Home to more than 100 wineries, distilleries, and cideries, Woodinville is a must-visit for anyone itching to try some Pacific Northwest wine.

Eat & Drink: The Bistro at Hollywood Schoolhouse (✉ 14810 N.E. 145th St. ☎ 425/892–2575 ⊕ www.hollywood-schoolhousebistro.com) in Woodinville features a French-inspired menu created with local ingredients and, of course, a huge wine list. In the true Pacific North-west style, there's even dog-friendly seating on the outdoor patio.

SEATTLE

Do: Seattle offers a ton to see and do, from visiting the first branch of Star-bucks at **Pike Place Market** (✉ 85 Pike St. ☎ 206/682–7453 ⊕ www.pikeplacemar-ket.org) to strolling through some of its many area parks. And while Seattle is a relatively big city by Pacific Northwest standards, many of its star attractions are grouped together at the Seattle Center area, including the **Museum of Pop Culture** (✉ 325 5th Ave. N ☎ 206/770–2700 ⊕ www.mopop.org), **Chihuly Garden and Glass** (✉ 305 Harrison St. ☎ 206/753–4940 ⊕ www.chihulygardenandglass.com), and—of course—the iconic **Space Needle** (✉ 400 Broad St. ☎ 206/905–2100 ⊕ www.spaceneedle.com).

Eat & Drink: Situated in the Queen Anne neighborhood, the romantic **Eden Hill Restaurant** (✉ 2209 Queen Anne Ave. N ☎ 206/708–6836 ⊕ www.edenhillrestau-rant.com) offers whimsical tasting menus that change frequently, but always draw from the produce of the region.

Stay: Smack-dab in the heart of Pike Place Market, the boutique **Inn at the Market** (✉ 86 Pine St. ☎ 206/443–3600 ⊕ www.innatthemarket.com) offers spacious, contemporary rooms, many with views out over Puget Sound. If you'd prefer something more intimate, the **Shafer Baillie Mansion Bed & Breakfast** (✉ 907 14th Ave. E ☎ 206/322–4654 ⊕ www.

sbmansion.com) in the Capitol Hill area offers old-fashioned rooms done up with lavish antique furnishings, including four-poster beds.

Breakfast: In Seattle's Phinney Ridge area, north of downtown, **Coyle's Bakeshop** (✉ 8300 Greenwood Ave. N ☎ 206/257–4736 ⊕ www.coylesbakeshop.com) is the place to go if you've got a hankering for a croissant worthy of a French boulan-gerie or a big slice of cake. If you'd prefer a more savory start to the day, consider a rosemary cretzel, a hybrid between a croissant and pretzels.

Wine Countries of the Pacific Northwest

Written by Margot Bigg

It should come as little surprise that some of the best wines in the country are produced in the Pacific Northwest; after all, much of this lush region is on the same latitude as France's most celebrated wine regions. Oregon and Washington, while notoriously rainy, are also blessed with the ideal balance of sunshine and rainfall to produce some fantastic varietals, particularly Pinot, Syrah, and Chardonnay.

This itinerary will introduce you to the Pacific Northwest's most important wine regions, while highlighting not-to-miss wineries, dining options, and attractions along the way. You'll start in Southern Oregon before making your way north to the largest AVA (American Viticultural Area) in the state: the Willamette Valley, known for its relatively mild climate and world-famous Pinot Noirs. From there, you'll head north up to the Columbia Gorge AVA, which spans both Oregon and Washington on the north and south banks of the Columbia River, continuing on to Walla Walla and the Yakima Valley. Then it's on to Woodinville, a Seattle-area city that's centered on the wine industry, before wrapping your trip up with a visit to Seattle proper.

Finally, remember that the most important thing to keep in mind on this trip is to always drive responsibly. Alternate designated drivers each day, use car services to get to wineries from your hotels, or stick to the sip and spit method.

At a Glance

Start: Medford, OR

End: Seattle, WA

Miles Traveled: 859 miles

Suggested Duration: 6 days

States Visited: Oregon, Washington

Key Sights: Chateau Ste. Michelle; Hiyu Wine Farm; Maryhill Stonehenge; Prosser Vineyard & Winery; Seven Hills Winery

Best Time to Go: The best time to visit the Pacific Northwest is late spring through early autumn, when temperatures are pleasant and there's less chance of heavy rain. Late summer is particularly pretty for winery visits, when grapevines are at their most bountiful (though if you visit this time of year, you may find that the wine harvest has already begun). Note that while many wineries in the Pacific Northwest are open year-round, some do shutter for the winter holidays and a few even remain closed until early spring.

Day 1: Medford, OR, to Ashland, OR

51 miles (1 hour, 15 minutes without traffic and stops)

Start your trip in Southern Oregon—the main airport for the region is in the city of Medford, but the pretty university town of Ashland makes for a better base. Although Ashland is only a 20-minute drive from Medford, a more scenic

option is to take Highway 238 down to the town of Jacksonville and the surrounding Applegate Valley before looping back up to Ashland for the evening.

ALONG THE WAY

Town: You can't take more than a few steps in the tiny town of Jacksonville without ending up in front of a winery. **Anchor Valley Wine Bar and Tasting Room** (✉ *150 S. Oregon St.* ☎ *541/702–2355* ⊕ *www.anchorvalleywine.com*) and **South Stage Cellars** (✉ *125 S. 3rd St.* ☎ *541/899–9120* ⊕ *www.southstagecellars.com*) are great options, while rosé lovers won't want to miss out on **Quady North** (✉ *255 E. California St.* ☎ *541/702–2123* ⊕ *www.quadynorth.com*). Not far from town in the surrounding Applegate Valley, **Cowhorn** (✉ *1665 Eastside Rd.* ☎ *541/899–6876* ⊕ *www.cowhornwine.com*) is one of only a few certified biodynamic vineyards in the United States and offers beautiful Rhône-style wines served out on a patio or in their sustainably built tasting room.

Eat & Drink: Stick around Jacksonville for lunch at **C St. Bistro** (✉ *230 E. C St.* ☎ *541/261–7638* ⊕ *www.cstbistro.com*), which serves salads, soups, sandwiches, and pizzas made largely from locally sourced ingredients.

ASHLAND

Do: There's no shortage of wineries in and around Ashland, many clustered just to the east of town. Popular options include the expansive **Irvine & Roberts Vineyards** (✉ *1614 Emigrant Creek Rd.* ☎ *541/482–9383* ⊕ *www.irvinerobertsvineyards.com*), which specializes in wines normally associated with the Willamette Valley (think Pinots) and the long-established **Weisinger Family Winery** (✉ *3150 Siskiyou Blvd.* ☎ *541/488–5989* ⊕ *www.weisingers.com*), which has been producing wine in the region since 1988. If you're a performing arts fan, the **Oregon Shakespeare Festival** (✉ *15 S. Pioneer St.* ☎ *541/482–2111* ⊕ *www.osfashland.org*) is an Ashland-must, showing multiple

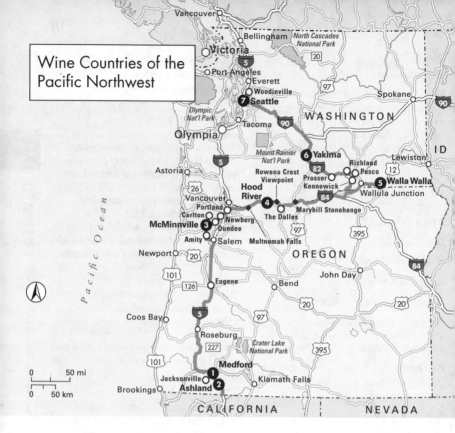

Wine Countries of the Pacific Northwest

plays (not all Shakespeare) across three theaters from February through October of every year.

Eat & Drink: Sit down for a snazzy dinner at **Alchemy Bistro** (✉ *35 S. 2nd St.* ☎ *541/488–1115* ⊕ *www.alchemyashland.com*), where you'll find everything from steak tartare to vegan burgers on the menu.

Stay: Ashland has its own thermal hot springs source and you can bathe in the waters from the comfort of your own hotel room's soaking tub at **Lithia Springs Resort** (✉ *2165 W. Jackson Rd.* ☎ *800/482–7128* ⊕ *www.lithiaspringsresort.com*) on the northern end of town. For something more traditionally elegant, the historic **Ashland Springs Hotel** (✉ *212 E. Main St.* ☎ *888/795–4545* ⊕ *www.ashlandspringshotel.com*) offers classically furnished rooms, a gorgeous lobby with stately chandeliers, and a fantastic on-site restaurant.

Breakfast: Start your day with a hearty breakfast at **Morning Glory** (✉ *1149 Siskiyou Blvd.* ☎ *541/482–2017* ⊕ *www.morninggloryashland.com*), where the options range from lemon ricotta stuffed French toast to Alaskan red crab omelets; they even do a breakfast risotto.

Day 2: Ashland, OR, to McMinnville, OR

267 miles (4 hours, 30 minutes without traffic and stops)

From Ashland, drive straight up I–5 until you reach the state capital, Salem. From here, head northwest to McMinnville, stopping at a few Willamette Valley wineries along the way.

ALONG THE WAY

Town: Oregon's second-largest city, Eugene, makes for a good midway stop, with good dining and shopping options and plenty of parks to stretch your legs. It's also home to a few excellent wineries, including the cozy **Civic Winery** (✉ 50 E. 11th Ave. ☎ 541/636–2990 ⊕ www. civicwinery.com) downtown and the massive **King Estate Winery** (✉ 80854 Territorial Hwy. ☎ 541/685–5189 ⊕ www. kingestate.com) just outside town.

Eat & Drink: Your best bet for lunch is at the **5th Street Public Market** (✉ 296 E. 5th Ave. ☎ 541/484–0383 ⊕ www.5stmarket.com), a multilevel complex with a solid mix of shops and tasting rooms, plus restaurants offering everything from seafood to burritos. If it's a nice day, you may want to grab some cheese and charcuterie at the **Provisions Market Hall** (✉ 296 E. 5th Ave. ☎ 541/606–4563 ⊕ www.provisionsmarkethall.com), a large specialty market with extensive deli offerings, a bakery, and a solid selection of wine from the Willamette Valley and beyond.

MCMINNVILLE

Do: There are countless possible ways to explore the Willamette Valley, with many of the wineries situated in and around the towns of Amity, Carlton, Dundee, Newberg, and McMinnville. One possible approach is to start at the Salem area's **Bryn Mawr Vineyards** (✉ 5935 Bethel Heights Rd. NW ☎ 503/581–4286 ⊕ www.brynmawrvineyards.com), notable for their hilltop views, continuing to **Maysara Winery** (✉ 15765 S.W. Muddy Valley Rd. ☎ 503/843–1234 ⊕ www. maysara.com), a biodynamic winery with a strong focus on sustainability. From here, make your way northeast to Dundee's beloved **Argyle Winery** (✉ 691 OR-99W ☎ 503/538–8520 ⊕ www. argylewinery.com), known for its sparkling options, and then onto Utopia Vineyards (don't leave without grabbing a bottle of Estate Pinot). Continue to the

Carlton Winemakers Studio (✉ 801 N. Scott St. ☎ 503/852–6100 ⊕ www.winemakersstudio.com), a cooperative winery with 16 vintners, before dipping south to McMinnville for the evening.

Eat & Drink: One of the oldest spots in McMinnville, **Nick's Italian Café** (✉ 521 N.E. 3rd St. ☎ 503/434–4471 ⊕ www. nicksitaliancafe.com) focuses on northern Italian fine dining, with homemade pastas, a standout wine list, and excellent desserts. They also offer wood-fired pizzas, topped with mozzarella made in house.

Stay: Although there are plenty of excellent spots to stay throughout the Willamette Valley, from cozy winery B&Bs to reliable chain hotels, you'll find some of the most interesting options in and around McMinnville, the largest city in this winery dense region. Its compact downtown alone is home to a number of stellar choices, from the sleek **Atticus Hotel** (✉ 375 N.E. Ford St. ☎ 503/472–1975 ⊕ www.atticushotel.com) to the quirky **McMenamins Hotel Oregon** (✉ 310 N.E. Evans St. ☎ 503/472–8427 ⊕ www.mcmenamins.com), with budget-friendly rooms and a multilevel rooftop bar. For a retro glamping experience, the **Vintages Trailer Resort** (✉ 16205 S.E. Kreder Rd., Dayton, OR ☎ 971/267–2130 ⊕ www.the-vintages.com) offers sleekly refurbished trailers complete with a pool and a small gym on-site.

Breakfast: Situated a short drive north of McMinnville in Dundee, **Red Hills Market** (✉ 155 S.W. 7th St. ☎ 971/832–8414 ⊕ www.redhillsmarket.com) offers everything from avocado toast dressed in locally produced olive oil to hearty plates of chilaquiles.

Vineyards in Oregon's Willamette Valley are best known for producing Pinot Noirs.

Day 3: McMinnville, OR, to Hood River, OR

100 miles (2 hours without traffic and stops)

Take Highway 99 to I–5, stopping in Portland for lunch along the way. Then make your way out to Hood River via I–84, which runs parallel to the Columbia River in the Columbia Gorge.

ALONG THE WAY

Town: Oregon's biggest city of Portland definitely merits a stop along the way, even if just to pop into one of its best-known attractions, the gargantuan **Powell's City of Books** (✉ *1005 W. Burnside St.* ☎ *800/878–7323* ⊕ *www.powells. com*). The so-called City of Roses is also home to one of the coolest wine shops out there, the quirky and unpretentious **Pairings** (✉ *455 N.E. 24th Ave.* ☎ *541/531–7653* ⊕ *www.pairingsport-land.com*), which offers an ever-changing selection of wines from around the world, with heavy emphasis on organic and biodynamic options.

Eat & Drink: Portland offers an exceptionally large number of dining options for a city of its relatively modest size, but hitting up a food cart "pod" (a cluster of independent food carts, usually on a former parking lot) is arguably the most quintessential Portland dining experience. Among the more famous pods is **Cartopia** (✉ *1207 S.E. Hawthorne Blvd.* ⊕ *www. instagram.com/cartopiafoodcarts*), in Southeast Portland, where you can get everything from Egyptian fare to meals based entirely on French fries, not to mention plenty of beer and wine. The heated, covered seating is a huge bonus on rainy Portland days.

Shop: Oregon doesn't have sales tax, which makes it a popular shopping stop for road-trippers from nearby states. For some of the best bargains, head to the **Columbia Gorge Outlets** (✉ *450 N.W. 257th Way, Troutdale, OR* ☎ *503/669–8060* ⊕ *www.shopcolumbiagorgeoutlets.com*) on the edge of town, where you'll find tax-free factory outlets of brands such as Columbia Sportswear, Tommy Hilfiger, and even Coach.

Nature: The best-known attraction in the Columbia Gorge is also one of the most photogenic. At 620 feet tall, Multnomah Falls is the second-highest year-round waterfall in the United States, and while you can hike up to the top of the falls via a mile-long trail, the best photo ops are conveniently right by the parking lot.

HOOD RIVER

Do: Hood River's compact city center is a great place to start your visit, with plenty of tasting rooms within walking distance of one another; popular options include **Stoltz Winery** (⊠ *514 State St.* ☎ *541/716–1330* ⊕ *www.stoltzwinery. com*) and **Evoke Winery** (⊠ *606 Oak St.* ☎ *541/386–3700* ⊕ *www.evokewinery. com*). It's also worth dipping into the tasting room of **Hood River Distillers** (⊠ *660 Riverside Dr.* ☎ *541/386–1588* ⊕ *www. hrdspirits.com*), the oldest distillery in the Northwest, to sample its range of whiskeys, gins, and vodkas. Then make your way down to **Marchesi Vineyards & Winery** (⊠ *3955 Belmont Dr.* ☎ *541/386–1800* ⊕ *www.marchesivineyards.com*), known for its Italian-style options, and then on to **Hiyu Wine Farm** (⊠ *3890 Acree Dr.* ☎ *541/436–4680* ⊕ *www.hiyuwinefarm. com*) to sample sustainably grown wines and ciders beautifully packaged in bottles with whimsical watercolor labels.

Detour: If you don't mind tacking a little driving on to the beginning or end of your Hood River stay, it's worth taking a drive along the Hood River "Fruit Loop," a popular driving loop that takes you past a variety of produce stands and wineries, plus a bakery and a lavender farm. U-pick options are available throughout the warmer months; if you visit in the late summer or autumn, be sure to stock up on some of the region's famous pears and apples.

Eat & Drink: The aptly named **Riverside** (⊠ *1108 E. Marina Dr.* ☎ *541/386–4410* ⊕ *www.riversidehoodriver.com*) offers indoor and outdoor dining with fabulous views of the Columbia River and beyond. While the views alone merit a visit, the menu is equally impressive, with a huge selection of salads and pastas plus meat-dominant and plant-based main courses, excellent desserts, and, unsurprisingly, a spectacular wine list.

Stay: Hood River offers plenty of spots to stay across a range of price points. Solid options include the centrally located **Hood River Hotel** (⊠ *102 Oak St.* ☎ *541/386–1900* ⊕ *www.hoodriverhotel.com*) and its hipster-chic rooms with local flair plus a 10-person bunkhouse for larger groups, and the budget-friendly **Adventure Lodge** (⊠ *1306 Oak St.* ☎ *541/239–2391* ⊕ *www.adventurelodge.co*); it has motel-style digs updated with sleek decorative touches.

Breakfast: Start your day Scandinavian-style at the Hood River branch of Portland's beloved **Broder** (⊠ *102 Oak St.* ☎ *541/436–3444* ⊕ *www.brodereast. com*). The huge breakfast menu features dishes such as chevre-stuffed Norwegian lefse and unnipurro, a Finnish-style "oven porridge."

Day 4: Hood River, OR, to Walla Walla, WA

191 miles (3 hours, 15 minutes without traffic and stops)

Continue east along the Columbia River until you reach Highway 12 in Wallula Junction, which will take you all the way to Walla Walla.

ALONG THE WAY

Photo Op: Situated at an elevation of around 700 feet and located between Hood River and The Dalles on the Historic Columbia River Highway, the **Rowena Crest Viewpoint** (⊠ *6500 Historic Columbia*

River Hwy. ☏ 800/551–6949 ⊕ www.oregonstateparks.org) is among the best places to snap an epic photo of the Columbia River Gorge. Better still, it's fully accessible by road, so while you could theoretically hike up to it, you certainly don't need to.

Town: Just east of Hood River, The Dalles is worth a stop for anyone interested in local history. Noteworthy attractions include the **Fort Dalles Museum** (✉ 500 W. 15th and Garrison St. ☏ 541/296–4547 ⊕ www.fortdallesmuseum.org), the **Columbia Gorge Discovery Center & Museum** (✉ 5000 Discovery Dr. ☏ 541/296–8600 ⊕ www.gorgediscovery.org), and Sunshine Mill, a former wheat mill that now houses the Quenett and Copa Di Vino wineries.

Eat & Drink: Stop for lunch and a wine tasting at **Maryhill Winery's Bistro** (✉ 9774 WA-14 ☏ 509/773–1976 ⊕ www.maryhillwinery.com), which offers classic options such as charcuterie, cheese, and dips along with crab cakes, steamer oysters, and substantial sandwiches.

Roadside Attraction: On the Washington side of the Columbia River, flanked on the west by a large cow field, sits an exact replica of Stonehenge, known as the **Maryhill Stonehenge** (✉ 41–97 Stonehenge Dr. ⊕ www.maryhillmuseum.org). It was built in the early 20th century as a World War I memorial. Like its namesake, the copy is oriented so that its altar stone matches up with the Summer Solstice sunrise.

WALLA WALLA

Do: Walla Walla has a huge number of wineries right within its city limits, and it's easy enough to go wine tasting without having to get behind the wheel, especially if you're staying downtown. Popular choices include **Seven Hills Winery** (✉ 212 N. 3rd Ave. ☏ 509/529–7198 ⊕ www.sevenhillswinery.com), **Kontos Cellars** (✉ 10 N. 2nd Ave. ☏ 509/204–2141 ⊕ www.kontoscellars.

com), and **Dama Wines** (✉ 123 E. Main St. ☏ 509/525–2299 ⊕ www.damawines.com). If you do want to get out and explore the region, L'Ecole No. 41 Winery, Caprio Cellars, and Valdemar Estates Winery are all worth the short drives, as is the Port of Walla Walla Incubators, a collection of start-up wineries situated in a collection of old WWII buildings, located right next to the regional airport.

Eat & Drink: In the heart of the city center, **T.Macs** (✉ 80 N. Colville St. ☏ 509/522–4776 ⊕ www.tmacsww.com) serves Italian-inspired meals that rely heavily on locally sourced produce, plus a changing selection of rich desserts.

Stay: Among Walla Walla's most historic buildings, the **Marcus Whitman Hotel** (✉ 6 W. Rose St. ☏ 509/525–2200 ⊕ www.marcuswhitmanhotel.com) has been hosting travelers since first opening back in 1928; today it features classic rooms plus an on-site restaurant and a wine lounge. For something more contemporary, The **Finch** (✉ 325 E. Main St. ☏ 509/956–4994 ⊕ www.finchwallawalla.com) has bright, modern rooms in an unfussy, boutique environment. If you'd rather stay somewhere a bit more bucolic, **Eritage Resort** (✉ 1319 Bergevin Springs Rd. ☏ 833/374–8243 ⊕ www.eritageresort.com) features beautiful, intimate suites with private patios and countryside views.

Breakfast: Grab a light breakfast at the **Colville Street Patisserie** (✉ 40 S. Colville St. ☏ 509/301–7289 ⊕ www.colvillestreetpatisserie.com) before continuing your trip through wine country. Along with Danishes, cakes, and cookies, they offer unusual options such as goat cheese and herb croissants and *kouign-amanns*, butter pastries originating in the French region of Brittany.

Day 5: Walla Walla, WA, to Yakima, WA

83 miles (1 hour, 30 minutes without traffic and stops)

Backtrack west along Highway 12 and continue until you reach the Tri-Cities of Kennewick, Pasco, and Richland. After stopping for a meal and maybe some wine, hop on I-82 and head northeast until you reach Yakima.

ALONG THE WAY

Town: Wine is a big deal in the Tri-Cities area; there are over 200 wineries in the region and it's home to Washington State University's Ste. **Michelle Wine Estates WSU Wine Science Center** (✉ *University Dr.* ☎ *509/372-7224* ⊕ *www.wine. wsu.edu*). If you have to choose just one winery, make it **Badger Mountain Vineyard** (✉ *1106 N. Jurupa St.* ☎ *509/627-4986* ⊕ *www.badgermtnvineyard.com*), Washington's first wine grape vineyard to earn USDA organic certification.

Eat & Drink: Stop for lunch at **Fiction Restaurant** (✉ *894 Tulip La.* ☎ *509/627-5000* ⊕ *www.bookwalterwines.com*), located at the J. Bookwalter Winery in Richland. The lunch menu here is dominated by salads, sandwiches, and pizzas, but there's also plenty of interesting appetizers for sharing, including panko-battered avocado fries.

YAKIMA

Do: After visiting the Tri-Cities, you'll head into the Yakima Valley, home to the oldest AVA in Washington. Start in the town of Prosser, dubbed the "birthplace of Washington wine," and home to 30-odd wineries; **14 Hands Winery** (✉ *660 Frontier Rd.* ☎ *509/786-5514* ⊕ *www.14hands. com*) and **Airfield Estates** (✉ *14450 Woodinville-Redmond Rd. NE* ☎ *425/877-1274* ⊕ *www.airfieldwines.com*) both merit visits. Continue northeast to the town of Yakima, stopping at **Treveri Cellars** (✉ *71 Gangl Rd.* ☎ *509/877-0925* ⊕ *www.*

treviericellars.com) in nearby Wapato before hitting Yakima's **Gilbert Cellars** (✉ *2620 Draper Rd.* ☎ *509/249-9049* ⊕ *www.gilbertcellars.com*) and **Tieton Cider Works** (✉ *619 W. J St.* ☎ *509/571-1430* ⊕ *www.tietonciderworks.com*). And if you need a break from wine tasting, drop into the **Yakima Valley Museum** (✉ *2105 Tieton Dr.* ☎ *509/248-0747* ⊕ *www.yvmuseum.org*), where you'll find a range of exhibits focused on local history, plus a few quirky highlights such as a collection of apple box labels and a "cabinet of curiosities" from around the world.

Eat & Drink: The Lab (✉ *910 Summitview Ave.* ☎ *509/367-6490* ⊕ *www. lunchatthelab.com*) touts a menu of what it calls "Asian New-American," featuring a variety of innovative dishes inspired by different Asian cuisines—think Thai-fried brussels sprout salads and katsu steak sandwiches.

Stay: Housed in an old Freemasons lodge dating to 1911, **The Hotel Maison** (✉ *321 E. Yakima Ave.* ☎ *509/571-1900* ⊕ *www. thehotelmaison.com*) is the swankiest option in town, with modernly furnished rooms and a well-equipped fitness center. For something more low-key (and pet-friendly), **The Hotel Y** (✉ *1700 N. 1st St.* ☎ *509/248-5650* ⊕ *www.thehotely. com*) offers modern rooms with exterior entrances, some with wet bars and microwaves.

Breakfast: Essencia Artisan Bakery and Chocolaterie (✉ *4 N. 3rd St.* ☎ *509/575-5570* ⊕ *www.facebook.com/EssenciaArtisanBakery*) is a good spot for breakfast, with à la carte pastries and breakfast sandwiches as well as set breakfasts that come with fresh fruit and tea, coffee, or juice.

Day 6: Yakima, WA, to Seattle, WA

167 miles (2 hours, 45 minutes without traffic and stops)

Continue north along I–82, which merges with I–90 and will take you northwest, all the way to Bellevue. From here, head north to the city of Woodinville to visit some of its celebrated wineries before making your way south to Seattle.

ALONG THE WAY

Town: A major hub for Washington wine, Woodinville is home to many of the state's top tasting rooms, including the oldest of the lot: **Chateau Ste. Michelle** (✉ 14111 N.E. 145th St. ☎ 425/488–1133 ⊕ www.ste-michelle.com). The city consists of four key districts, each with its own unique feel and plenty of wineries and bottle shops: the sleek Hollywood District, the more industrial Warehouse District, the sprawling West Valley, and the compact downtown.

Eat & Drink: Pair your lunch with some of Washington's finest wines at **Purple Café and Wine Bar** (✉ 14459 Woodinville–Redmond Rd. NE ☎ 425/483–7129 ⊕ www.purplecafe.com). The menu includes sandwiches, pastas, fresh seafood, and a smattering of vegan dishes. While the wine list features bottles from around the world, the majority of offerings are local favorites.

SEATTLE

Do: Wine lovers won't want to miss **SODO Urbanworks** (✉ 3931 1st Ave. S ☎ 206/973–1983 ⊕ www.sodo-urbanworks.com), an industrial complex that's been transformed into a one-stop shop for wine lovers, with many of the city's best tasting rooms under one roof. If you find yourself in the Capitol Hill area,

be sure to drop in for a drink at the sleek **Aluel Cellars** (✉ 801A E. Thomas St. ☎ 206/329–5994 ⊕ www.aluelcellars.com) or pick up a few bottles at **European Vine Selections** (✉ 522 15th Ave. E ☎ 206/323–3557 ⊕ www.evswines.com). If you want to get a feel for the city beyond its wine scene, head to the Seattle Center; there you'll find major attractions like the Space Needle, Chihuly Garden and Glass, and the Museum of Pop Culture.

Eat & Drink: Housed in the Melrose Market, a cluster of automotive buildings that have been revamped into a shopping and dining district, **Marseille** (✉ 1531 Melrose Ave. ☎ 206/659–1845 ⊕ www.marseillefoodandwine.com) offers seasonal fine dining and an extensive wine list. There's even an on-site bottle shop in case you want to pick up a bottle or two before leaving.

Stay: Wine takes center stage at downtown **Seattle's Hotel Kimpton** (✉ 1100 5th Ave. ☎ 206/624–8000 ⊕ www.hotelvintage-seattle.com), which offers nightly wine tastings and an on-site certified sommelier. If you'd rather be away from the city center, the **Ballard Inn** (✉ 5300 Ballard Ave. N.W. ☎ 206/789–5011 ⊕ www.ballardinnseattle.com) in the hip Ballard neighborhood, offers beautifully furnished rooms that mix 1920s vintage vibes with modern fixtures.

Breakfast: Wrap your trip up with a hearty breakfast at **The Fat Hen** (✉ 1418 N.W. 70th St. ☎ 206/782–5422 ⊕ www.thefathenseattle.com), which serves seasonal dishes such as homemade granola, salmon toast, and egg-based breakfast skillets.

Chapter 4

THE WEST AND THE ROCKIES

4

WELCOME TO
THE WEST AND THE ROCKIES

TOP REASONS TO GO

★ **Yellowstone National Park:** The nation's first national park is still one of its most popular. Wait for Old Faithful to erupt or glimpse the stupendous Grand Prismatic Spring, the largest hot spring in the United States.

★ **Great Basin National Park:** With one of the country's least-visited parks, pine trees make up Nevada's ancient forest. The Bristlecone pine is the world's longest-living tree and likely its oldest living organism.

★ **Arches National Park:** The sandstone arches here, famous symbols of the American West, have been carved by thousands of years of wind, water, and ice.

★ **The Million Dollar Highway:** These 25 miles in western Colorado take you on a spectacular journey through the San Juan Mountains.

★ **Deadwood:** The quintessential Wild West town still attracts visitors hoping to relive its rowdy and lawless past.

1 **Big Sky Country.** The wide open spaces of Montana, Idaho, and Wyoming are any road tripper's dream.

2 **The Loneliest Road in America: Nevada's Route 50.** Route 50 spans the entire middle of the country from coast to coast, but its most desolate stretch in Nevada is a perfect way to explore the state.

3 **Utah's National Parks.** These five parks highlight some of America's most stunning landscapes.

4 **The Best of Colorado.** The Centennial State is filed with Rocky Mountain adventures, Wild West lore, and glamorous ski towns.

5 **The Ultimate Wild West Road Trip.** Relive the legends and outlaws of the Old West on this epic trip that takes you to key spots in Arizona, Colorado, Wyoming, and South Dakota.

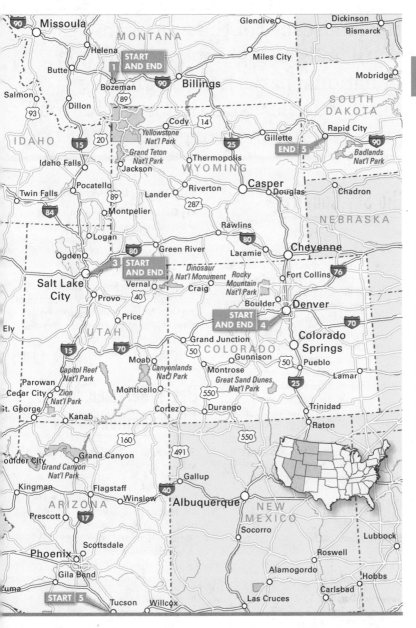

Defined by the Rocky Mountains, stunning expanses of open blue skies and unbelievable mountain ranges dot the landscapes of the American West. You'll find the highest concentration of national parks here, all offering unforgettable vistas that make for road trips nothing short of gorgeous.

Big Sky Country

Written by Shoshi Parks

Circling the northern reaches of the Rocky Mountains, this road trip through Montana, Idaho, and Wyoming is one of the most stunning exhibitions of nature to be found in this world. Out here, the landscape is dense with national forests and national monuments lauded for their stunning beauty and cultural histories, not to mention three separate national parks: Glacier, Yellowstone, and Grand Teton. Over 10 days, the itinerary careens over mountain passes, through emerald forests, and along the banks of sapphire lakes and rivers. Although this route will knock the socks off just about anyone, for those willing to get out in nature to hike, kayak, and horseback ride, the word *epic* doesn't even begin to describe it.

At a Glance

Start: Bozeman, MT

End: Bozeman, MT

Miles Traveled: 1,582 miles

Suggested Duration: 10 days

States Visited: Idaho, Montana, Wyoming

Key Sights: Craters of the Moon National Monument; Eaton's Ranch; Glacier National Park; Grand Teton National Park; Yellowstone National Park

Best Time to Go: The elevation and mountains make Big Sky Country cold and snowy more than six months out of the year. Although there is some great winter-weather adventuring along this route, you'll get the most out of the itinerary if you travel between May 1 and September 30.

Day 1: Bozeman, MT, to Glacier National Park

298 miles (5 hours without traffic and stops)

On your first day, head northwest out of Bozeman toward the Montana state capital, Helena, then north via I–15. By the time you hit Highway 89, the views of Flathead National Forest and the Rocky Mountains are in full bloom.

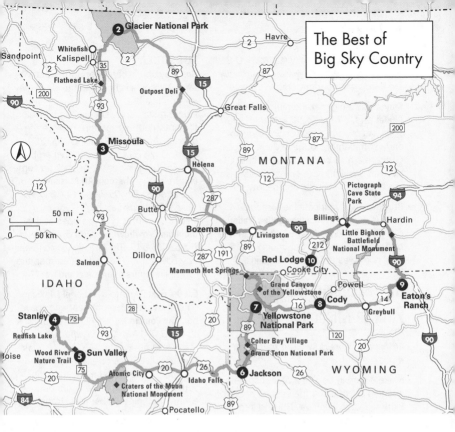

The Best of Big Sky Country

ALONG THE WAY

Town: Helena's Historic District, Last Chance Gulch, has a fascinating history rooted in the city's early pioneer and mining days. Take a self-guided walking tour through the neighborhood's 19th-century dry goods stores, hotels, and churches to get the backstory of what was once a remote outpost of the Wild West.

Eat & Drink: Fill up with a ham gobbler sandwich, French dip, or chef salad from Choteau's roadside **Outpost Deli** (⌂ 824 Main Ave. N ☎ 406/466–5330 ⊕ www. outpost-deli-edan.io).

GLACIER NATIONAL PARK

Do: The massive peaks of the Continental Divide in northwest Montana are the backbone of Glacier National Park and its sister park in Canada, Waterton Lakes, which together make up the International Peace Park. From their slopes, melting snow and alpine glaciers yield the headwaters of rivers that flow west to the Pacific Ocean, north to the Arctic Ocean, and southeast to the Atlantic Ocean via the Gulf of Mexico. Coniferous forests, thickly vegetated stream bottoms, and green-carpeted meadows provide homes and sustenance for all kinds of wildlife. **Glacier National Park** (☎ 406/888–7800 ⊕ www.nps.gov/glac) has more than 700 miles of hiking trails to do solo or with a guide. Fish at the park's many lakes and rivers (no permit required) and take a drive down the famed Going-to-the-Sun Road, one of the country's most spectacular National Historic Landmarks.

Eat & Drink: Get a Montana-style home-cooked meal and a sip (or a bottle) of handcrafted booze from **Josephine's Bar & Kitchen** (⌂ 10245 U.S. 2 ☎ 406/300–4755 ⊕ www.josephinesbar.com) and the

Glacier Distilling Company (✉ *10237 U.S. 2 E* ☎ *406/387–9887* ⊕ *www.glacierdistilling.com*) next door in Coram.

Stay: Book a night at the historic **Belton Chalet** (✉ *12575 U.S. 2* ☎ *406/888–5000* ⊕ *www.glacierparkcollection.com*), an early-20th-century lodge in West Glacier. Or there are 13 campgrounds within Glacier National Park; the one at Kintla Lake is a bastion of solitude and beauty.

Breakfast: Get your caffeine fix and a breakfast wrap at **Montana Coffee Traders** (✉ *30 9th St. W* ☎ *406/892–7696* ⊕ *www.coffeetraders.com*) in Columbia Falls, a local northwestern Montana chain.

Day 2: Glacier National Park to Missoula, MT

160 miles (3 hours without traffic and stops)

Make a stop in beautiful Whitefish before heading south along the eastern shore of Flathead Lake (Highway 35) and into the city of Missoula.

ALONG THE WAY

Town: Whitefish considers itself Montana's "outdoor recreation playground," and for good reason. In winter, skiers flock to **Whitefish Mountain Resort** (✉ *1015 Glades Dr.* ☎ *877/754–3474* ⊕ *www.skiwhitefish.com*) while during the warmer seasons, locals and visitors alike hit the hiking trails in the **Flathead National Forest** (☎ *406/758–5208* ⊕ *www.fs.usda.gov*) or the beachfront at Flathead Lake.

Eat & Drink: The Raven (✉ *15321 M-35* ☎ *406/837–2836* ⊕ *www.ravenbigfork.com*), a waterfront restaurant in Big Fork, has an eclectic menu, craft cocktails, live music and unparalleled views.

Nature: Get out on the water at Flathead Lake, the biggest freshwater lake west of the Mississippi. Rent a kayak or stand-up paddleboard in Woods Bay, go for a swim, or fish for trout and perch from shore.

MISSOULA

Do: The cultural center of northwest Montana, Missoula is home to the University of Montana, the Clark Fork River, and lots of restaurants, shops, and bars along the aptly named Hip Strip. Explore the ghostly remains of **Garnet** (☎ *406/329–3914* ⊕ *www.garnetghosttown.org*), an early gold-mining town, or soak up some culture at the **Missoula Art Museum** (✉ *335 N. Pattee St.* ☎ *406/728–0447* ⊕ *www.missoulaartmuseum.org*). If you're visiting in winter, hit the slopes at the **Montana Snowbowl** (✉ *1700 Snow Bowl Rd.* ☎ *406/549–9777* ⊕ *www.montanasnowbowl.com*). During the summer, they run zipline tours over the chairlifts.

Eat & Drink: Dig into traditional Mexican eats at the stylish restaurant and agave bar, **The Camino** (✉ *125 N. Pattee St.* ☎ *406/317–1260* ⊕ *www.thecaminomissoula.com*). At Gild (✉ *515 S. Higgins Ave.* ☎ *406/926–3258* ⊕ *www.gildbrewing.com*), a brewpub on the Hip Strip, you'll find three separate floors of fun, each with their own bar and atmosphere.

Stay: The Missoula lodging scene is a long list of chain hotels and motels. The regional outfit, the **C'mon Inn** (✉ *2775 Expo Pkwy.* ☎ *406/543–4600* ⊕ *www.cmoninn.com*), a lodge with an indoor courtyard and waterfall, is one of the more charming options.

Breakfast: Have a seat or take your coffee and breakfast to go at **Market on Front** (✉ *201 E. Front St.* ☎ *406/541–0246* ⊕ *www.marketonfront.com*), a bustling café and market downtown.

Day 3: Missoula, MT, to Stanley, ID

256 miles (5 hours without traffic and stops)

Today's route takes you through hundreds of miles of national forest and across the border into Idaho.

ALONG THE WAY

Town: In Salmon, Idaho, take a rigorous hike to the **Goldbug Hot Springs** (☎ 208/765–5100 ⊕ www.idahohotsprings.com) for a soak or stop in at the **Sacajawea Interpretive, Cultural, and Education Center** (✉ 2700 Main St. ☎ 208/756–1188 ⊕ www.sacajaweacenter.org), which delves into the history of the Lewis & Clark Expedition and the Agaidika Shoshone-Bannock Nation from which Sacajawea, their indigenous guide, hailed.

Eat & Drink: Tuck into a massive burger with all the fixins at **The Savage Grill** (✉ 907 Mulkey St. ☎ 208/756–2062 ⊕ www.facebook.com/SavageGrill) in Salmon.

STANLEY

Do: With access to the Sawhill Mountains and the Salmon River, Stanley is a good base for outdoor adventures on the Idaho frontier. Take an epic adventure on the Salmon River with one of Stanley's many whitewater-rafting outfitters or keep your feet planted firmly on the hiking trails around Redfish, Stanley, and Sawtooth lakes.

Eat & Drink: The log cabin **Sawtooth Luce's** (✉ 105 Niece Ave. ☎ 208/774–3361 ⊕ www.sawtoothluces.com) serves quality comfort food with solid vegetarian options. At the 90-year-old **Rod-N-Gun Saloon** (✉ 44 Ace of Diamonds St. ☎ 208/774–2922), you can get a stiff drink and a game of shuffleboard.

Stay: The suites and private cabins of **Stanley High Country Inn** (✉ 21 Ace of Diamonds St. ☎ 208/774–7000 ⊕ www.stanleyinn.com) have a rustic aesthetic adorned with modern touches.

Breakfast: Have a traditional breakfast straight from the griddle at **Limbert's** (✉ 401 Redfish Lodge Rd. ☎ 208/774–3536 ⊕ www.redfishlake.com) in the Redfish Lake Lodge.

Day 4: Stanley, ID, to Sun Valley, ID

62 miles (1 hour, 10 minutes without traffic and stops)

Take in the beauty of the Sawtooth National Forest on today's short drive from Stanley to Sun Valley and the neighboring town of Ketchum.

ALONG THE WAY

Eat & Drink: Stretch your legs and grab a cold drink or a bite at the **Galena Lodge** (✉ 15187 ID-75 ☎ 208/726–4010 ⊕ www.galenalodge.com), a community-owned home base for skiers and hikers in the town of Galena in the Boulder Mountains.

Nature: Hike one of the Sawtooth National Forest's two national recreation trails—the Fishhook Creek Boardwalk at Redfish Lake or the Wood River Nature Trail at Wood River Campground—or take a scenic drive along the Ponderosa Pine Scenic Byway (ID-21) or the City of Rocks Backcountry Byway.

SUN VALLEY

Do: Forget any assumption you might have about Idaho—Sun Valley is a posh, all-season outdoor getaway. At the **Sun Valley Resort** (✉ 1 Sun Valley Rd. ☎ 800/786–8259 ⊕ www.sunvalley.com), you can ski or snowboard in winter while in summer, you can golf, go for a horseback ride, or hike the trails of Bald Mountain.

Eat & Drink: Have an elegant dinner at Sun Valley's original dining room, **The Ram** (✉ 1 Sun Valley Rd. ☎ 208/622–2225 ⊕ www.sunvalley.com), or indulge in Tuscan favorites at nearby Ketchum's best Italian restaurant, **Cristina's** (✉ 520 2nd St. E ☎ 208/726–4499 ⊕ www.cristinasofsunvalley.com). At the historic **Pioneer Saloon** (✉ 320 N. Main St. ☎ 208/726–3139 ⊕ www.pioneersaloon.com), meat is on the menu, along with plenty of liquor to wet your whistle.

One of the most spectacular drives in the country is the Going-to-the-Sun Road in Glacier National Park.

Stay: One of Ketchum's newer properties, the **Limelight Hotel** (✉ *151 Main St. S* ☎ *208/726–0888* ⊕ *www.limelighthotels.com*) downtown has spacious guest rooms and large indoor and outdoor lounges. Art and design are woven into the fabric of **Hotel Ketchum** (✉ *600 N. Main St.* ☎ *208/471–4716* ⊕ *www.hotelketchum.com*), an affordably priced stay on Main Street.

Breakfast: Have breakfast at **The Kneadery** (✉ *260 N. Leadville Ave.* ☎ *208/726–9462* ⊕ *www.kneadery.com*) in Ketchum, a rustic eatery with Rocky Mountain-inspired takes on traditional dishes like Benedicts and omelets.

Day 5: Sun Valley, ID, to Jackson, WY

241 miles (4 hours, 30 minutes without traffic and stops)

Drive along the volcanic moonscape of Craters of the Moon National Monument and westward through southern Idaho until you hit Jackson, the southern gateway to Grand Teton National Park.

ALONG THE WAY

Nature: Explore the cinder cones and underground lava tubes of the spectacular **Craters of the Moon National Monument** (☎ *208/527–1335* ⊕ *www.nps.gov/crmo*), an alien landscape formed by fire.

Detour: A disaster at a nuclear power plant in 1961 left Atomic City a virtual ghost town. Get a look at what's left on this quick 6-mile detour (about ten minutes each way) on U.S. 26.

Town: In Idaho Falls, stroll along the River Walk to see the town's eponymous waterfall. If you don't intend to stop at Craters of the Moon, see similar lava formations at the bite-sized Hell's Half Acre just south of town.

Eat & Drink: Fuel up with "clean" comfort food at **Diablas Kitchen** (✉ *525 River Pkwy.* ☎ *208/522–1510* ⊕ *www.orderdiablaskitchen.com*) in Idaho Falls where everything from the quiche of the day to the mac and cheese is made fresh from scratch.

JACKSON

Do: A charming town at the base of the Tetons, Jackson is dense with art galleries and boutiques. The **National Museum of Wildlife Art** (✉ *2820 Rungius Rd.* ☎ *307/733–5771* ⊕ *www.wildlifeart.org*) has an impressive collection of artistic renderings of animals from around the world. Get your own look at those that frequent this region of Wyoming at the **National Elk Refuge** (✉ *675 E. Broadway Ave.* ☎ *307/733–9212* ⊕ *www.fws.gov*) on the edge of town.

Eat & Drink: Dig into plates piled high with mushroom pappardelle and chicken Parmesan at **Orsetto** (✉ *161 Center St.* ☎ *307/203–2664* ⊕ *www.orsettojh.com*) or order a wood-fired pizza from **Hand Fire Pizza** (✉ *120 N. Cache St.* ☎ *307/733–7199* ⊕ *www.handfirepizza.com*). After dinner, belly up to the bar at the **Million Dollar Cowboy** (✉ *25 N. Cache St.* ☎ *307/733–2207* ⊕ *www.milliondollarcowboybar.com*), a typical western dive.

Stay: Get a room in the western-styled **Hotel Jackson** (✉ *120 N. Glenwood St.* ☎ *307/733–2200* ⊕ *www.hoteljackson.com*), once named Wyoming's most beautiful hotel by *Architectural Digest*, or find a more affordable stay at the **Wyoming Inn** (✉ *930 W. Broadway* ☎ *307/734–0035* ⊕ *www.wyominginn.com*), a contemporary hotel styled in leather and wood.

Breakfast: Snag a table inside **Cafe Genevieve** (✉ *135 E. Broadway Ave.* ☎ *307/732–1910* ⊕ *www.genevievejh.com*) or on the outdoor patio for a breakfast made with fresh, seasonal ingredients.

Day 6: Jackson, WY, to Yellowstone National Park

57 miles (1 hour, 15 minutes without traffic and stops)

Today's drive is one of the most epic legs of all, cruising seamlessly through Grand Teton National Park into Yellowstone National Park.

ALONG THE WAY

Nature: Natural beauty surrounds you as you drive north through **Grand Teton National Park** (☎ *307/739–3300* ⊕ *www.nps.gov/grte*), which demands at least a few hours of exploration. Some of the most popular sites and trails in the park include Jenny Lake, the Taggart Lake Trail, the Mormon Row Historic District and, of course, Grand Teton itself.

Eat & Drink: There aren't a whole lot of options for lunch in Grand Teton National Park, but **Leek's Pizzeria** (Leeks Marina Rd. ☎ *307/543–2494* ⊕ *www.signalmtnlodge.com*) in nearby Colter Bay Village is worth a stop for tasty pies and a table with a view of Jackson Lake.

Photo Op: Grand Teton and Yellowstone are both teeming with wildlife. Keep your eyes peeled for bison, elk, moose, bears, and other incredible animals. If you plan to pull over for a photo, be sure to keep your distance (75 feet is recommended).

YELLOWSTONE NATIONAL PARK

Do: Considered one of the most spectacular national parks in the United States, **Yellowstone** (☎ *307/344–7381* ⊕ *www.nps.gov/yell*) is festooned with hot springs and geysers, including the granddaddy of them all, Old Faithful. Whether you plan to explore the backcountry on foot or to stick to the roads, you'll spend your day immersed in an epic natural world. Allow at least two hours to explore Old Faithful and the surrounding village. Eruptions occur approximately 90 minutes apart but can vary, so check with the visitor center for predicted times. Be sure to explore the surrounding geyser basin, including the 1½-mile Geyser Hill Loop, and Old Faithful Inn, from which you can watch the geyser erupt from the hotel's rear deck. A short drive north, make Grand Prismatic Spring in Midway Geyser Basin your can't-miss geothermal stop; farther north, near Madison, detour to the west along short Firehole Canyon Drive to see the Firehole River cut a small canyon and waterfall (Firehole Falls).

Eat & Drink: Have an upscale dinner of sustainable fresh fish and wild game at the **Lake Yellowstone Hotel Dining Room** (⊠ 236 Yellowstone Lake Rd. ☎ 307/344–7311 ⊕ www.yellowstonenationalparklodges.com). In the **Bear Pit Lounge** at the Old Faithful Inn (⊠ 3200 Old Faithful Inn Rd. ☎ 307/344–7311 ⊕ www.yellowstonenationalparklodges.com), sit back and relax with a cocktail and apps.

Stay: For the most authentic Yellowstone experience, spend the night under the stars. The quiet **Slough Creek Campground** (⊠ Slough Creek Campground Rd. ☎ 307/344–7381 ⊕ www.nps.gov/yell) in Lamar Valley is a stone's throw from some of the best wildlife-watching in the park. For more luxurious accommodations, try the historic **Lake Yellowstone Hotel** (⊠ 235 Yellowstone Lake Rd. ☎ 307/344–7311 ⊕ www.yellowstonenationalparklodges.com).

Breakfast: Get in on a breakfast buffet (individual specialties are also available) at the **Obsidian Room** in the Old Faithful Snow Lodge (⊠ 2 Old Faithful Rd. ☎ 307/344–7311 ⊕ www.yellowstonenationalparklodges.com).

Day 7: Yellowstone National Park to Cody, WY

52 miles (1 hour without traffic and stops)

Continue through Yellowstone and out its eastern entrance then on toward Cody, a historic town with a Wild West pedigree.

ALONG THE WAY
Nature: Start your adventure early today to explore even more of Yellowstone. You can make your way to the park's northern entrance to explore Mammoth Hot Springs, massive natural travertine terraces where mineral water flows continuously, building an ever-changing display. Or head to Lookout Point, which offers impressive views of the Grand Canyon of Yellowstone, through which the Yellowstone River has formed one of the most spectacular gorges in the world, with steep canyon walls and waterfalls.

Eat & Drink: Food options are limited within Yellowstone, so be sure to pack a picnic for your driving adventures today.

CODY
Do: Named for showman Buffalo Bill Cody, the town of Cody takes great pride in its Wild West history. Check out the authentic cabins and artifacts from Wyoming's pioneer days at **Old Trail Town** (⊠ 1831 Demaris Dr. ☎ 307/587–5302 ⊕ www.oldtrailtown.org) or stop in at the **Buffalo Bill Center of the West** (⊠ 720 Sheridan Ave. ☎ 307/587–4771 ⊕ www.centerofthewest.org), a complex of five museums that includes the Buffalo Bill Museum, the Plains Indians Museum, and the Cody Firearms Museum.

Eat & Drink: Get an unlimited chuckwagon dinner and a show at **The Cody Cattle Company** (⊠ 1910 Demaris Dr. ☎ 307/272–5770 ⊕ www.thecodycattlecompany.com). After dinner, grab a pint at the

WyOld West Brewing Company (⊠ 221 N. Bent St., Powell, WY ☎ 307/764–6200 ⊕ www.wyoldwest.com), which also has a wide-ranging menu of sandwiches, burgers, pasta, and more.

Stay: A former working cattle ranch, **K3 Guest Ranch Bed & Breakfast** (⊠ 30 Nielsen Trail ☎ 307/587–2080 ⊕ www.k3guestranch.com) offers western-themed accommodations and an all-inclusive breakfast cooked over a campfire.

Breakfast: Get your morning coffee and a light breakfast at friendly local favorite, **Rawhide Coffee** (⊠ 1155 Sheridan Ave. ☎ 307/578–8344 ⊕ www.rawhidecoffeecompany.com).

Day 8: Cody, WY, to Eaton's Ranch, WY

132 miles (2 hours, 30 minutes without traffic and stops)

Drift across northern Wyoming and into the pines of Bighorn National Forest. Eatons' Ranch has been flanking its eastern edge for over 140 years.

ALONG THE WAY

Town: Stop in the town of Greybull for a look at ancient dinosaur tracks in the painted badlands of Red Gulch and the bizarre rocks that form the geological anomaly, Devil's Kitchen.

Eat & Drink: Get quesadillas and burritos with a family touch at **Los Gabanes Mexican Restaurant** (⊠ 546 Greybull Ave. ☎ 307/765–2120 ⊕ los-gabanes-mexican. edan.io) in Greybull.

EATON'S RANCH

Do: This dude ranch in northeastern Wyoming is one of America's first. Located on the slopes of the Bighorn Mountains, **Eaton's** (⊠ 270 Eaton Ranch Rd., Wolf, WY ☎ 307/655–9285 ⊕ www.eatonsranch. com) is one of the few ranches where more experienced riders can still take horses out without a guide (guided trail

rides also happen twice a day). They also do overnight pack trips in the neighboring national forest.

Eat & Drink: All meals are communal at Eatons' Ranch and served in their large, cheery dining room (Saturday is outdoor barbecue night). If you're hankering for an adult beverage, stop in at The Apartment Bar or purchase wine or beer from the ranch store.

Stay: Almost all of Eatons' guests stay in individual cabins on the property, each rustic but comfortable with full bathrooms. Larger cabins have two to three bedrooms, fireplaces, and porches. There are also three suites in the Main Ranch House.

Breakfast: For breakfast, you're back at the communal dining room, but if you sleep in and miss the meal, stop by the on-site coffee shop.

Day 9: Eaton's Ranch, WY, to Red Lodge, MT

184 miles (3 hours without traffic and stops)

Today's drive takes you up through the Crow Nation, past the site of one of the most infamous battles of the 19th-century American Indian Wars, then west toward Billings, Montana. From there, travel southwest toward Red Lodge on the outskirts of the Custer Gallatin National Forest.

ALONG THE WAY

Attraction: Follow the **Battle of Little Bighorn** where Custer had his last stand on a self-guided driving tour of the battlefield (⊠ I–90 Frontage Rd., Crow Agency, MT ☎ 406/638–2621 ⊕ www.nps.gov/libi).

Town: In the city of Billings, see the carefully maintained treasures of **Moss Mansion** (⊠ 914 Division St. ☎ 406/256–5100 ⊕ www.mossmansion.com) or the contemporary **Yellowstone Art Museum** (⊠ 401

N. 27th St. ☎ 406/256–6804 ⊕ www.
artmuseum.org). Just outside town, step
into the ancient past at **Pictograph Cave
State Park** (✉ 3401 Coburn Rd. ☎ 406/254–
7342 ⊕ www.stateparks.mt.gov), which
boasts more than 100 rock paintings in
three easy-to-access caves.

Eat & Drink: At **The Fieldhouse** (✉ 2601
Minnesota Ave. ☎ 406/534–2556
⊕ www.thefieldhousemt.com) in Billings,
you'll find salads and sandwiches made
with produce and meat from local farms
and ranches.

RED LODGE

Do: In winter, the town of Red Lodge
draws thousands to its well-loved ski
resort, **Red Lodge Mountain** (✉ 305 Ski
Run Rd. ☎ 406/446–2610 ⊕ www.red-
lodgemountain.com). In warmer months,
there are plenty of outdoor activities to
be had, including hiking along the Lake
Fork Trail and visiting the rehabilitated
and rescued animals at the **Yellowstone
Wildlife Sanctuary** (✉ 615 2nd St. E
☎ 406/446–1133 ⊕ www.yellowstonewil-
dlifesanctuary.org).

Eat & Drink: Dig into the flavors and
aromas of Sicilian cuisine at the upscale
Piccola Cucina (✉ 7 Broadway Ave. N
☎ 406/446–1212 ⊕ www.piccolacucina-
group.com) at Ox Pasture or find a more
laid-back meal on the wide-ranging menu
at Prerogative Kitchen (✉ 104 Broadway
Ave. S ☎ 406/445–3232 ⊕ www.preroga-
tivekitchen.com).

Stay: Take in the mountain views from
the cozy **Inn on the Beartooth** (✉ 6648 U.S.
212 ☎ 406/446–1768 ⊕ www.innonthe-
beartooth.net). Or in town, you'll find a
great night's sleep within the wood-paneled rooms at the Alpine Lodge (1105
Broadway Ave. N 406/446–2213 www.
alpinelodge.com).

Breakfast: Wake up with traditional and
international breakfast favorites from
The Wild Table (✉ 113 Broadway Ave. N
☎ 406/446–0226 ⊕ www.thewildtable.
com).

Day 10: Red Lodge, MT, to Bozeman, MT

*149 miles (2 hours, 30 minutes without
traffic and stops)*

The last leg of your journey, Red Lodge to
Bozeman, is also one of the least event-
ful. Follow Highway 212 to Highway 421
and onto I–90 west through Livingston
and on to Bozeman.

ALONG THE WAY

Town: Take a break with a history
lesson in Livingston's railroad museum, the **Depot Center** (✉ 200 W. Park
St. ☎ 406/222–2300 ⊕ www.living-
stondepot.org), or the **Yellowstone
Gateway Museum** (✉ 118 W. Chinook
St. ☎ 406/222–4184 ⊕ www.yellow-
stonegatewaymuseum.org), which has
exhibitions on the region's natural and
cultural past.

Eat & Drink: Stop for a meal and a brew at
the charming, colorful **Neptune's** in Livingston (✉ 232 S. Main St. ☎ 406/333–2400
⊕ www.neptunestaphouse.com), which
specializes in coastal cuisine and sushi.

BOZEMAN

Do: There is much to do in the university
town of Bozeman. See an impressive
collection of dinosaur fossils at the **Museum of the Rockies** (✉ 600 W. Kagy Blvd.
☎ 406/994–2251 ⊕ www.museumoft-
herockies.org) or browse the shops and
galleries downtown. If you're traveling
in winter, hit the slopes at **Bridger Bowl
Ski Area** (✉ 15795 Bridger Canyon Rd.
☎ 406/587–2111 ⊕ www.bridgerbowl.
com).

Eat & Drink: Grab dinner at the **Blackbird
Kitchen** (✉ 140 E. Main St. ☎ 406/586–
0010 ⊕ www.blackbirdkitchen.com),
a cute Italian spot with a wood-fired
oven, or splurge on the last dinner of
your road trip at **Open Range** (✉ 241
E. Main St. ☎ 406/404–1940 ⊕ www.
openrangemt.com), a classic Montana

steak house. End your night on the town at the Bozeman institution, the **Haufbrau House** (✉ *22 S. 8th Ave.* ☎ *406/587–4931* ⊕ *www.haufbrauhouse.com*).

Stay: Book a room at the stylish **RSVP Hotel** (✉ *510 N. 7th Ave.* ☎ *406/404–7999* ⊕ *www.rsvphotel.co*) or **The Lark** (✉ *122 W. Main St.* ☎ *866/464–1000* ⊕ *www.larkbozeman.com*), a sunny downtown hotel with an outdoor wood-burning fireplace and a patio overlooking Main Street.

Breakfast: The Nova Cafe (✉ *312 E. Main St.* ☎ *406/587–3973* ⊕ *www.thenova-cafe.com*) in downtown Bozeman has a menu packed with both savory and sweet morning treats.

The Loneliest Road in America: Nevada's Route 50

Written by Stefanie Waldek

If you're looking for the cross-country road less traveled, you won't do better than U.S. Route 50, also called Highway 50, which spans more than 3,000 miles between West Sacramento, California, and Ocean City, Maryland, cutting right through the center of the United States. Its moniker is the "Loneliest Road in America," bestowed upon it by *Life* magazine in a 1986 feature. The most desolate, yet perhaps most interesting, stretch of the highway is its 300-mile span in Nevada, where the road crosses the expansive Great Basin Desert and passes through several quirky small towns. "We warn all motorists not to drive there unless they're confident of their survival skills," said an AAA representative in that story.

But Nevada's tourism board took that warning in stride, offering an official survival guide for drivers, complete with

a "passport" that you can stamp in the major towns along the highway. As it turns out, the drive is not at all dangerous—just make sure to top up your gas tank every chance you get—but it does offer beautiful mountain and desert views, a taste of the historic Wild West, and a chance to visit Nevada's only national park.

At a Glance

Start: Las Vegas, NV

End: Las Vegas, NV

Miles Traveled: 1,122 miles

Suggested Duration: 6 days

States Visited: Nevada

Key Sights: The Bellagio; Eureka Opera House; the Extraterrestrial Highway; Great Basin National Park; Pyramid Lake

Best Time to Go: Several stops on this route are only open from spring to fall—stick to May or September for milder weather.

Day 1: Las Vegas, NV, to Carson City, NV

433 miles (7 hours without traffic and stops)

While by no means close to Highway 50, Las Vegas is a good place to fly into and pick up a rental car. To start your road trip, take I–95 N all the way to Carson City, making a few fun pit stops throughout the drive.

ALONG THE WAY

Town: While most visitors to Beatty use the town as a base camp for nearby Death Valley National Park, it's also a great place to stretch your legs. Visit the retro **Atomic Inn** (✉ *350 S. 1st St.* ☎ *775/553–2250* ⊕ *www.atomicinnbeatty.com*) for a photo op, marvel at the Tom

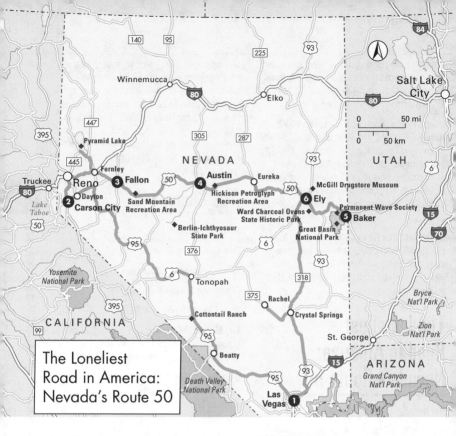

The Loneliest Road in America: Nevada's Route 50

Kelly Bottle House, or explore the ghost town of Rhyolite, known for outdoor art installations.

Roadside Attraction: Located near the intersection of I–95 and NV-266 is the infamous Cottontail Ranch, a now-abandoned legal brothel reportedly frequented by Howard Hughes. It closed in 2004 and has since been boarded up, but you can still make a quick stop to snap a photo or two.

Eat & Drink: Just shy of the halfway point of your drive today is the **Tonopah Brewing Company** (✉ 315 S. Main St. ☎ 775/482–2000 ⊕ www.tonopahbrewing.com), which has a tasting room that's perfect for lunch and a cold beer.

CARSON CITY

Do: Welcome to Nevada's state capital and the start (or end, depending on your direction) of Highway 50 in the state. Try to get to town before 5 pm so you can stop by the **Carson City Visitor Center** (✉ 1900 S. Carson St. ☎ 800/638–2321 ⊕ www.visitcarsoncity.com) to grab *The Official Hwy 50 Survival Guide*. If you arrive even earlier, try to visit one of the city's museums, like the **Nevada State Railroad Museum** (✉ 2180 S. Carson St. ☎ 775/687–6953 ⊕ www.carsonrailroad-museum.org), or simply stroll the walkable downtown and shop the boutiques.

Eat & Drink: Carson City is the largest town on this itinerary, and there's a wide variety of restaurants and bars to fill your evening. Try dinner at Thai restaurant **The Basil** (✉ 311 N. Carson St. ☎ 775/841–6100 ⊕ www.thebasilcarsoncity.com), followed by a round of beers at the **Tap @ Rice Street** (✉ *211 Rice St.* ☎ *775/434–7076*), where locals hang out.

Stay: In all honesty, Carson City isn't known for its hotels. There are plenty of national chains that are perfectly serviceable, like the **Hampton Inn & Suites Carson City** (✉ *10 Hospitality Way* ☎ *775/885–8800* ⊕ *www.hilton.com*). If you're looking for a more boutique stay, use Airbnb, where proprietors Jenny and Mark Lopicolo list rooms in the historic St. Charles Hotel.

Breakfast: Whether you've got time for a sit-down breakfast or you're itching to get out on the road, make your first stop of the day **L.A. Bakery Café and Eatery** (✉ *1280 N. Curry St.* ☎ *775/885–2253* ⊕ *www.labakerycafe.com*). There are café options for a leisurely meal, or you can simply grab a coffee and pastry to go.

Day 2: Carson City, NV, to Fallon, NV

62 miles (1 hour, 10 minutes without traffic and stops)

Today's your first day on historic Highway 50—but you should also take a little off-route detour to Pyramid Lake, just north of the town of Fernley, which is actually on Alternate U.S. 50 (a break-off that connects the main highway to the major cross-country interstate Route 80).

ALONG THE WAY

Town: You should stop in two towns along the route today: Dayton and Fernley, both of which are stamp stops in your survival guide (they're about 40 minutes apart). In the former, pop into the **Dayton Museum** (✉ *135 Shady La.* ☎ *775/246–6316* ⊕ *www.daytonsvhistory.org*) to learn about the town's gold rush days (in 1849, a prospector discovered gold here for the first time in what would eventually become the State of Nevada). In the

Essential Listening

As you officially start your Highway 50 journey, listen to the *Nevada Magazine Radio Show* hour-long podcast episode about the route to get jazzed for what's to come.

latter, stock up on food, supplies, and gas—the towns only get smaller from here on out.

Eat & Drink: Pop into **Black Bear Diner** (✉ *1190 E. Main St.* ☎ *775/835–8512* ⊕ *www.blackbeardiner.com*) for an old-fashioned road-trip lunch, and follow up with dessert at **Steve's Homemade Ice Cream** (✉ *1360 U.S. 95 N* ☎ *775/575–0500*), both in Fernley.

Detour: Head 25 miles north of Fernley to Pyramid Lake, one of the largest natural lakes in Nevada and all that's left of the former inland sea Lake Lahontan. The surreal scenery, including the unusual tufa rock formations, makes for a great photo op, but be sure to respect the landscape during your visit: this is sacred land to the Paiute tribe. Visit the **Pyramid Lake Paiute Tribe Museum and Visitors Center** (✉ *709 State St., Nixon, NV* ☎ *775/574–1088* ⊕ *www.pyramidlake. us*) to learn more about the history and significance of the lake.

FALLON

Do: There are two major reasons to come to Fallon, population roughly 9,000: to taste the region's famous Hearts of Gold cantaloupe and to drink at **Frey Ranch** (✉ *1045 Dodge La.* ☎ *775/423–4000* ⊕ *www.freyranch.com*), a distillery. You can also visit the **Churchill County Museum and Archives** (✉ *1050 S. Maine St.* ☎ *775/423–3677* ⊕ *www.ccmuseum.org*) to learn about the region's history.

Eat & Drink: If you think this trip is going to be all diners and fast food, think again. For dinner tonight, try **Vn Pho** (✉ 2183 W. Williams Ave. ☎ 775/428–5858 ⊕ www. vnphofallon.com).

Stay: You're pretty limited to chain hotels in Fallon, and of the handful in town, the **Best Western Fallon Inn & Suites** (✉ 1035 W. Williams Ave. ☎ 775/423–6005 ⊕ www.bestwestern.com) is one of the best options.

Breakfast: You can't go wrong with pastries or hot dishes at the **Courtyard Café and Bakery** (✉ 55 E. Williams Ave. ☎ 775/423–5505)—they're all delicious.

Day 3: Fallon, NV, to Austin, NV

111 miles (1 hour, 40 minutes without traffic and stops)

It's another day of traveling along Highway 50.

ALONG THE WAY
Photo Op: No, that 600-foot sand dune rising up from the rocky desert isn't a mirage: it's Sand Mountain, part of Sand Mountain Recreation Area.

Detour: Though it's about 60 miles off Highway 50, **Berlin-Ichthyosaur State Park** (☎ 775/964–2440 ⊕ www.parks.nv.gov) is a worthy detour—it has a ghost town and 225-million-year-old fossils of extinct marine reptiles (ichthyosaurs). The former mining town of Berlin was abandoned in 1911, and today its remnants can be explored by visitors to the park. As for the dinosaur bones? Those weren't discovered until 1928, but they're now on display in the Fossil House.

Eat & Drink: When you get back to Highway 50, stop for lunch at **Middlegate Station** (✉ 42500 Austin Hwy. ☎ 775/423–7134 ⊕ www.middlegatestation.com), known for its Monster Burger Challenge,

in which competitors must consume four pounds of food.

AUSTIN
Do: The former silver mining town of Austin only has a couple of hundred residents today, but it was once the second-largest city in Nevada, with a population of 5,000. Visit the town's three 150-year-old churches and the ruins of Stokes Castle, the summer home of 19th-century railroad magnate Anson Phelps Stokes.

Eat & Drink: Austin is home to the legendary **Lucky Spur Saloon** (✉ 306 Kingston Canyon Rd. ☎ 775/964–2000 ⊕ www. luckyspursaloon.com), frequently called the best bar in the middle of nowhere. Take in the views of Kingston Canyon from the worn leather barstools or play a game of pool as you sip a local brew.

Stay: In town your best bet is the quaint (read: clean, comfortable, and surprisingly modern) **Cozy Mountain Motel** (✉ 40 Main St. ☎ 775/346–1566 ⊕ www.cozymountainmotel.com). If you don't mind driving a little outside town, try the quirky **Paradise Ranch Castle Bed & Breakfast** (☎ 440/781–8768 ⊕ www.paradiseranchcastle.com).

Breakfast: The coffee and pastries at **Golden Club Coffee** (✉ 81 Main St. ⊕ goldenclub-coffee-coming-soon.business.site) are simple but do the trick.

Day 4: Austin, NV, to Baker, NV

210 miles (3 hours, 30 minutes without traffic and stops)

You're driving east along Highway 50 all day today, straight through to the state line.

ALONG THE WAY
Photo Op: Just east of Austin is the **Hickison Petroglyph Recreation Area** (☎ 775/635–4062 ⊕ www.blm.gov),

where you can see ancient petroglyphs along a half-mile walking trail.

Town: Prepare to spend a bit of time in Eureka, known as "the Friendliest Town on the Loneliest Road." The former mining town is incredibly well preserved so be sure to check out the restored historic sites like the **Eureka Opera House** (✉ *31 S. Main St.* ☎ *775/237–6006* ⊕ *www.co.eureka.nv.us*), the Eureka Courthouse, the Eureka Sentinel Museum (☎ *775/237–5010* ⊕ *www.co.eureka.nv.us*) in the former *Eureka Sentinel* newspaper building, the Victorian-style Carson Mansion, and the Jackson House Hotel, all of which date back to the late 19th century.

Eat & Drink: Stop for lunch at the **Owl Club Bar & Steakhouse** (✉ *61 N. Main St.* ☎ *775/237–5280* ⊕ *www.owlclubeureka.com*) or the Urban Cowboy Bar and Grill (✉ *121 N. Main St.* ☎ *775/237–5774*), both in Eureka.

Detour: Get a taste of the region's mining history with a quick visit to **Ward Charcoal Ovens State Historic Park** (☎ *775/289–1693* ⊕ *www.parks.nv.gov*), located just 6 miles off Highway 50 at Nevada Historical Marker No. 54, which denotes the Ward Mining District. Six massive beehive charcoal kilns from the 19th century still stand here, and you can take a peek inside them (legend has it they were used for shelter by stagecoach bandits).

BAKER

Do: This teensy town of fewer than 100 people is mostly known as the gateway to Great Basin National Park, so there's not a ton to do here beyond eat, drink, and gamble at the slot machines at the **Border Inn** (☎ *775) 234–7300* ⊕ *www.borderinncasino.com*). The inn is a quirky motel where the rooms are on the Utah side of the border, but the office, "casino," and restaurant are on the Nevada side. At night, remember to look up— Great Basin National Park is a designated International Dark Sky Park, meaning it's ideal for stargazing.

Eat & Drink: Try **Kerouac's Restaurant** at the Stargazer Inn (✉ *115 S. Baker Ave.* ☎ *775/234–7323* ⊕ *www.kerouacsnevada.com*), which is usually regarded as the best of the three eateries in town.

Stay: The aforementioned **Stargazer Inn** (✉ *115 S. Baker Ave.* ☎ *775/234–7323* ⊕ *www.stargazernevada.com*) is the place to stay in Baker, or you could head to the 375-acre **Hidden Canyon Retreat** (✉ *500 Hidden Canyon Rd.* ☎ *775/234–7172* ⊕ *www.hiddencanyonretreat.com*), a ranch just outside town. If you'd like to overnight in Great Basin National Park itself, there are campsites open year-round.

Breakfast: There's no better coffee and pastries in Baker than at **Sugar, Salt, & Malt Restaurant** (✉ *40 S. Baker Ave.* ☎ *719/237–5725* ⊕ *www.saltandsucre.com*).

Day 5: Baker, NV, to Ely, NV

62 miles (1 hour without traffic and stops)

The majority of your day should be spent at Great Basin National Park, after which you can make the short journey back west on Highway 50 to Ely.

ALONG THE WAY

Roadside Attraction: On the road between Baker and Great Basin is the Permanent Wave Society, a collection of punny folk art installations. Although a number of the sculptures were removed by the Nevada Department of Transportation in 2016, a few remain.

Nature: Great Basin National Park (☎ *775/234–7331* ⊕ *www.nps.gov/grba*) is one of the least visited national parks in the country, meaning you get to enjoy all of the nature and none of the crowds. Take a guided tour through the famous Lehman Caves, hike to the summit of Wheeler Peak during the summer, and go cross-country skiing or snowshoeing during the winter.

Great Basin National Park is Nevada's only national park.

Eat & Drink: The only restaurant in Great Basin is the **Great Basin Café** (✉ *100 NF-448* ☎ *775/234–7200* ⊕ *www.greatbasincafe.com*) in the Lehman Caves Visitors Center, and it's only open seasonally. If you're visiting during the off-season, bring a to-go lunch from Baker.

Detour: Just 15 minutes north of Ely is the **McGill Drugstore Museum** (✉ *11 S. 4th St.* ☎ *775/235–7276*), a former pharmacy that's been perfectly preserved with vintage goods on its shelves, therefore serving as somewhat of a time capsule.

ELY

Do: With a population of some 4,000 people, Ely is the biggest town around this neck of the woods. Its biggest year-round attraction is the **Nevada Northern Railway Museum** (✉ *1100 Ave. A* ☎ *775/289–2085* ⊕ *www.nnry.com*), while seasonal events like the White Pine County Fair and Horse Races in August and Race the Rails in September, in which cyclists race steam locomotives, are quite popular.

Eat & Drink: If you've had enough diner food on this trip, experience some fine dining with a side of gimmicks at **Jailhouse Cell Block Steak House** (✉ *211 5th St.* ☎ *775/289–3033* ⊕ *www.jailhousecasino.com*), part of the Jailhouse Motel & Casino complex, where you can also grab after-dinner drinks at the lounge or the sports bar, as well as gamble.

Stay: Hotels range from classic chains (the **La Quinta Inn & Suites by Wyndham Ely** ✉ *1591 Great Basin Blvd.* ☎ *775/289–8833* ⊕ *www.wyndhamhotels.com* is a good choice) to locally owned independent accommodations (try the **Bristlecone Motel** ✉ *700 Ave. I* ☎ *775/289–8838* ⊕ *www.bristleconemotelnv.com*).

Breakfast: Grab a coffee or a smoothie at **Flower Basket & Espresso Depot** (✉ *445 E. 11th St.* ☎ *775/289–2828* ⊕ *www.elyflowerbasket.com*), a flower shop and café.

Day 6: Ely, NV, to Las Vegas, NV

244 miles (3 hours, 50 minutes without traffic and stops)

It's time to make the long trek back to Vegas. Take NV-318 and U.S. 93 south through a stretch of Nevada almost as desolate as Highway 50; you might know it as Area 51. Gas stations are once again few and far between, so make sure you set out on a full tank of gas today.

ALONG THE WAY

Roadside Attraction: You can't actually visit the highly classified Area 51, of course (officially known as Homey Airport, the restricted Air Force installation was finally revealed to actually exist in 2013), but the areas surrounding it have embraced the extraterrestrial mythos. Nevada state Route 375 is actually called the Extra-terrestrial Highway. At Crystal Springs, take a quick hop on it until you reach the hamlet of Rachel and its collection of UFO-themed businesses.

Eat & Drink: The area's alien theme is most apparent at Rachel's **Little A'Le'Inn** (✉ *9631 Old Mill Rd.* ☎ *775/729–2515* ⊕ *www.littlealeinn.com*). Even if you aren't hungry for a tasty "alien burger," a pilgrimage to this restaurant/bar is practically a requirement to earn those Area 51 bragging rights. While the food is typical diner fare such as chili and sandwiches, it's very reasonably priced, and the owners put some tender-loving care into keeping their landmark shipshape.

LAS VEGAS

Do: Live it up on your last night of your trip by living large in Vegas. Take the traditional route and spend some time gambling in one of the major casinos (if you only have time for one, make it the Bellagio) or seeing a performance, like the Cirque de Soleil or whichever legendary musical artist currently has a residency. If nightlife isn't really your

style, enjoy the **Mob Museum** (✉ *300 Stewart Ave.* ☎ *702/229–2734* ⊕ *www. themobmusuem.org*) or the quirky **Neon Museum** (✉ *770 Las Vegas Blvd. N.* ☎ *702/387–6366* ⊕ *www.neonmuseum. org*)—basically a graveyard of old neon signs.

Eat & Drink: The first Hong Kong–style Chinese restaurant on the Las Vegas Strip, **Mott 32** (✉ *The Venetian, 3325 S. Las Vegas Blvd.* ☎ *702/607–3232* ⊕ *www.venetian.com*) offers its impeccable signature dish, Peking duck, in addition to myriad dumplings and street food. Afterward, get a cocktail at the **Chandelier Bar in the Cosmopolitan** (✉ *3708 Las Vegas Blvd. S* ☎ *702/698-7000* ⊕ *www. cosmopolitanlasvegas.com*), which offers innovative spins on an ever-changing menu of reinvented classics.

Stay: You can't go wrong spending the night at the **Bellagio** (✉ *3600 S. Las Vegas Blvd.* ☎ *888/987–6667* ⊕ *www.bellagio. mgmresorts.com*), but for something more affordable, **Harrah's** (✉ *3475 S. Las Vegas Blvd.* ☎ *800/214–9110* ⊕ *www. caesars.com*) on the Center Strip is old-school Vegas all the way.

Breakfast: Don't miss the indulgent pastries and artistic crepes at the **Bellagio Patisserie** (✉ *3600 S. Las Vegas Blvd.* ☎ *702/693–8865*).

Utah's National Parks

Written by Stefanie Waldek

Utah is an outdoor adventurer's dream, with spectacular landscapes comprising towering buttes, snowcapped mountains, winding slot canyons, lush forests, and mysterious hoodoos. The state is home to five national parks, not to mention a number of national forests and national monuments, each offering a range of experiences, from easily accessible scenic drives to multiday hikes through the backcountry. The best part is you can easily see them all in just over a week. This nine-day road trip itinerary covers the highlights of each national park—and much more—but if your schedule allows, it's highly recommended to spread your time out to add even more time in each park.

At a Glance

Start: Salt Lake City, UT

End: Salt Lake City, UT

Miles Traveled: 1,125 miles

Suggested Duration: 9 days

States Visited: Arizona, Utah

Key Sights: Arches National Park; Bryce Canyon National Park; Canyonlands National Park; Capitol Reef National Park; Zion National Park

Best Time to Go: Summer might be the most popular time to visit Utah's national parks, but visiting in the spring or in the fall is a great choice, as the weather is mild and the crowds are thinner. You'll see the fewest crowds in winter, but be mindful of road and trail closures due to snow.

Day 1: Salt Lake City, UT, to Arches National Park

230 miles (3 hours, 45 minutes without traffic and stops)

When your flight lands in Salt Lake City, don't dally—you'll want to get to Arches ASAP to maximize your time there. Pick up your rental car, and take I-15 S through the suburbs of Salt Lake City and Provo, veer east on U.S. 6 and I-70, and finally continue on U.S. 191 S.

ALONG THE WAY

Town: The approximate halfway point of today's drive is the town of Price. If you need a break to stretch your legs, consider visiting the **Utah State University**

Eastern Prehistoric Museum (✉ 155 E. Main St. ☎ 800/817–9949 ⊕ www.usueastern. edu) to see some dinosaur bones.

Eat & Drink: If you can hold out for lunch, drive another hour to historic **Ray's Tavern** (✉ 25 S. Broadway ☎ 435/564–3511 ⊕ www.facebook.com/RaysTavern) in Green River for burgers, beer, and homemade pie.

ARCHES NATIONAL PARK

Do: As one of Utah's most popular parks, **Arches** (☎ 435/179– 2299 ⊕ www.nps. gov/arch) has hikes for all levels, but favorites include Delicate Arch (the park's most famous arch), Double Arch (featured in *Indiana Jones and the Last Crusade*), and Landscape Arch (one of the longest arches on the planet).

Eat & Drink: There's no food to be found in the park, so you'll have to carry in any snacks or meals. If you're looking for a sit-down dinner, try **Desert Bistro** (✉ 36 S. 100 W ☎ 435/259–0756 ⊕ www.desert-bistro.com) in Moab, just 5 miles outside the park, for exquisite fine dining.

Stay: You can either camp in the park itself or you can stay in a hotel in Moab. If you go the latter route, consider the luxe resort **Sorrel River Ranch** (✉ Mile 17, HC 64 UT-128 ☎ 435/259–4642 ⊕ www. sorrelriver.com); the boutique **Hoodoo Moab, Curio Collection by Hilton** (✉ 111 N. 100 W ☎ 435/355–0595 ⊕ www.hilton. com); or the B&B **Sunflower Hill, a Luxury Inn** (✉ 147 N. 300 E ☎ 435/259–2974 ⊕ www.sunflowerhill.com).

Breakfast: Fuel up for your day with a quintessential diner breakfast at the old-school Moab Diner (✉ 189 S. Main St. ☎ 435/259–4006 ⊕ www.moabdiner. com).

Day 2: Arches National Park to Canyonlands National Park (Islands in the Sky)

26 miles (30 minutes without traffic or stops)

If you want to stay in a hotel, you'll keep Moab as your base tonight, so your route will be round-trip. Campers, however, can just take the one-way journey to Canyonlands. To get to Canyonlands's **Islands in the Sky Visitors Center** (⊠ *Grand View Point Rd.* ☎ *435/259–4712* ⊕ *www.nps.gov/cany*) from Moab, you can take UT-313 for a quick highway drive, or you can opt for the slower scenic route, which takes two hours on UT-279 that gives some great photo ops. Just be sure you have AWD and aren't afraid of a few narrow switchbacks.

ALONG THE WAY

Eat & Drink: You won't pass any restaurants between Moab and Canyonlands, so pack your lunch today.

Photo Op: On your way back to Moab, drive past the Potash Evaporation Ponds. They might not sound too interesting, but they're an incredible photo op—their brilliant turquoise waters pop against the orange-red rocks of the landscape. You can also catch sight of them from **Dead Horse State Park** (☎ *435/259–2614* ⊕ *www.stateparks.utah.gov*), the filming location of the epic finale of *Thelma & Louise*.

Nature: Along the scenic route, you'll pass the Corona Arch Trail, a 3-mile out-and-back hike that passes Bowtie Arch and Corona Arch. You can also tack on a 1.9-mile out-and-back diversion to Pinto Arch if you're feeling ambitious.

CANYONLANDS NATIONAL PARK (ISLANDS IN THE SKY)

Do: Canyonlands National Park (☎ *435/719–2313* ⊕ *www.nps.com/cany*) is split into four sections, and the area known as Islands in the Sky is the closest to Moab and the most popular overall. A few highlights include hiking Mesa Arch, hiking or simply taking in the vistas of Grand View Point, and the panoramic views from Buck Canyon Overlook.

Eat & Drink: There's no food in Canyonlands either, so bring some with you; otherwise you'll have to head back to Moab for a meal. For dinner, check out **Moab Brewery** (⊠ *686 S. Main St.* ☎ *435/259–6333* ⊕ *www.themoabbrewery.com*), one of the most popular spots in town. If beer's not your thing, don't worry—they've also opened an adjacent distillery.

Stay: Again, if you're not camping within the national park, you'll be staying in Moab. Make it easy on yourself and stay put at last night's accommodation.

Breakfast: Don't miss the eggs Benedict at the breakfast-only **Jailhouse Café** (⊠ *101 N. Main St.* ☎ *435/259–3900*), set in a late-19th-century home that was at one time the county courthouse.

Day 3: Canyonlands National Park: Islands in the Sky to the Needles

100 miles (2 hours without traffic and stops)

Today you're headed to the more off-the-beaten-path district of Canyonlands called the Needles. From the Islands in the Sky Visitors Center, head back toward Moab, south on U.S. 191, then west on UT-211 to get to the Needles Visitor Center (⊠ *UT-211* ☎ *435/259–4711* ⊕ *www.nps.gov/cany*).

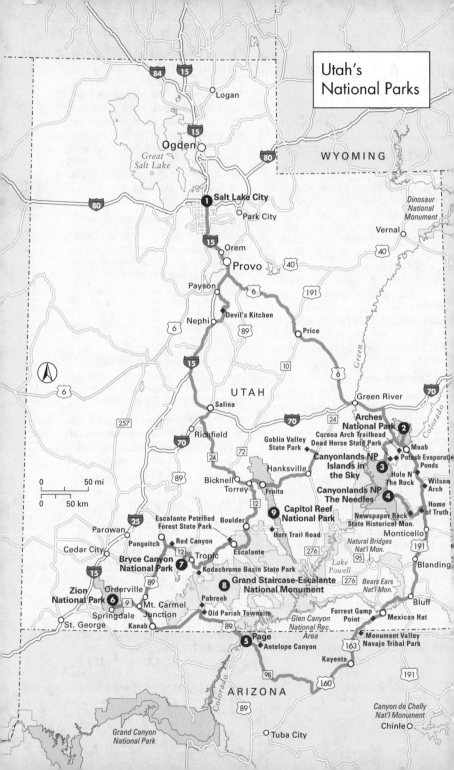

ALONG THE WAY

Eat & Drink: Once again, outside of Moab, there aren't any restaurants along the route. Eat a hearty breakfast and pack a to-go lunch.

Roadside Attraction: As its name implies, **Hole N' the Rock** (✉ 11037 U.S. 191 ☎ 435/686–2250 ⊕ www.theholeinth-erock.com) is a home carved right into a rock. Former owners Albert and Gladys Christensen began construction around 1940 and finished in 1952, opening a café and gift shop on-site. Today visitors can pay for a tour, shop for trinkets at the trading post, pick up an ice cream at the general store, or even pet some animals at the petting zoo.

Nature: If you're stopping for a picnic lunch, do so at Wilson Arch, just a five-minute hike off the highway. You can also see it from the road if you'd rather not stop.

Roadside Attraction: If you're fascinated by apocalyptic cults, don't miss the Home of Truth, a ghost town that was once a religious colony founded by Marie Ogden in the 1930s. The ruins are on private property, but you can see them from the road.

Photo Op: See more than 600 petroglyphs at **Newspaper Rock State Historic Monument** (✉ UT-211 ☎ 435/587–1500 ⊕ www.utahscanyoncountry.com), many of which are on a massive 200-foot rock face; yes, it's almost like it's a printed newspaper.

CANYONLANDS NATIONAL PARK (THE NEEDLES)

Do: The Needles region includes quite a bit of backcountry terrain, meaning you should be an experienced hiker and driver (with a 4x4 vehicle) if you decide to tackle some of the more advanced trails and drives. But there are plenty of options for beginner- and intermediate-level visitors, too. Options include the Roadside Ruin loop, which takes you past an 800-year-old structure; the half-mile Cave Spring loop, which includes a stop at a 19th-century cowboy camp; and the much more advanced Elephant Hill, which offers vistas of the park's famous sandstone needles.

Eat & Drink: As you might have guessed, there are no restaurants in the park, so carry your food in. The closest spot for a dine-in meal is the town of Monticello; go for Asian fusion at **Ja-Roen Thai Sushi** (✉ 380 S. Main St. ☎ 435/587–4000 ⊕ www.facebook.com/samjaroen).

Stay: If you're not camping in Canyonlands, book a stay at the quaint **Grist Mill Inn** (✉ 64 S. 300 E ☎ 435/587–2597 ⊕ www.thegristmillinn.com) in Monticello, a B&B housed in a former flour mill built in 1933.

Breakfast: The Grist Mill Inn also runs a restaurant, the **Granary Bar and Grill** (✉ 64 S. 300 E ☎ 435/587–2597 ⊕ www.granarybarandgrill.com), where breakfast is served to both guests and the public. It's also the spot for drinks at night.

Day 4: Canyonlands National Park to Page, AZ

215 miles (3 hours, 30 minutes without traffic and stops)

It's a bit of a haul between Canyonlands and Zion, the next national park on the itinerary, so take some time to explore the terrain: drive south on U.S. 191 and U.S. 163 through majestic Monument Valley, then continue on AZ-98 W to Page, Arizona, where you can spend the night.

ALONG THE WAY

Roadside Attraction: As you approach the village of Mexican Hat, you'll spot its namesake to the northeast: a sombrero-like rock that towers over the landscape.

Photo Op: You know the scene in Forrest Gump when Forrest stops running?

Well, you'll drive right past it on U.S. 163. Stop at the sign for Forrest Gump Point around mile 13, and make sure there are no cars coming before you run out into the middle of the road to snap a photo or record a video.

Nature: The big showstopper today is **Monument Valley Navajo Tribal Park** (☎ 435/727–5870 ⊕ www.navajonationparks.org), famous for its mitten-shaped buttes. The park is on Navajo land, and if you want to explore beyond the 17-mile Tribal Park Loop, also known as the Valley Drive, you'll have to secure a permit, hire a guide, or join a tour. The one exception is the self-guided Wildcat Trail, a 4-mile loop around the Mitten Buttes and Merrick Butte.

Town: About 40 minutes past Monument Valley, across the Arizona border, is the town of Kayenta, where you should pause to learn about the area's Navajo history and culture at the **Navajo Cultural Center of Kayenta** (⊠ U.S. 160 ☎ 928/697–3170). Then head to the local **Burger King** (yes, Burger King) to see an exhibit about the Navajo Code Talkers of World War II, organized by the fast-food joint's owner, the son of a Navajo Code Talker (⊕ www.facebook.com/BurgerKingHighway160).

Eat & Drink: If you're not up for dining at Burger King, **Kayenta's Amigo Cafe** (⊠ U.S. 163 ☎ 928/697–8448 ⊕ www.amigocafekayenta.com) serves Mexican, Navajo, and American cuisine for breakfast, lunch, and dinner.

PAGE

Do: Page is a base camp for a number of nearby outdoor activities, the most popular of which is touring **Antelope Canyon** (⊕ www.antelopecanyon.com). You're required to have a guide, and tours book up months in advance—don't expect to have the famous slot canyon all to yourself when you visit. Other Page attractions include Horseshoe Bend, Glen Canyon Dam, Lake Powell, and the **Navajo Village Heritage Center** (⊠ 1253 Coppermine Rd. ☎ 928/660–0304 ⊕ www.navajovillage.com).

Eat & Drink: For dinner, chow down at **Big John's Texas BBQ** (⊠ 153 S. Lake Powell Blvd. ☎ 928/645–3300 ⊕ www.bigjohnstexasbbq.com), then head to **State 48 Tavern** (⊠ 614 N. Navajo Dr. ☎ 928/645–1912 ⊕ www.state48tavern.com) for drinks.

Stay: Most hotels in Page are generic chains, but just outside town is the renowned luxury resort **Amangiri** (⊠ 1 Kayenta Rd., Canyon Point, UT ☎ 435/675–3999 www.aman.com). For something a little more wallet-friendly, book a stay at **Grandview Inn Bed and Breakfast** (⊠ 1601 Grandview St. ☎ 928/660–2614 ⊕ www.grandview-inn.com).

Breakfast: If your accommodations doesn't serve breakfast in the morning, head to **Hot N Sweet Coffee and Donut Shop** (⊠ 36 S. Lake Powell Blvd. ⊕ 928/612–2112) for a grab-and-go option.

Day 5: Page, AZ, to Zion National Park

115 miles (2 hours, 15 minutes without traffic and stops)

Today, simply take U.S. 89 to UT-9, and you'll be at the gates of Zion in no time.

ALONG THE WAY

Roadside Attraction: You'll want to hurry to Zion in order to maximize your time there, but take a brief stop at Pahreah and the Old Pariah Townsite. **Pahreah** is an old ghost town, though all that remains is a graveyard. The **Old Pariah Townsite** was a filming location for a number of Westerns, and while the set no longer exists, the striated landscape is a sight to behold.

Town: Kanab is just past today's halfway point, and while most people are here to get out into nature, there are some

More than 1.5 million visitors come to Arches annually, drawn to its wind- and water-carved rock formations

quirky stops in town that are worth a visit, namely the seasonal **Little Hollywood Museum** (✉ *297 W. Center St.* ☎ *435/644–5337* ⊕ *www.littlehollywoodmuseum.org*).

Eat & Drink: Pop by the **Kanab Creek Bakery** (✉ *238 W. Center St.* ☎ *435/644–5689* ⊕ *www.kanabcreekbakery.com*) for baked goods, soups, and sandwiches—and coffee, of course.

ZION NATIONAL PARK

Do: There's no way you could fit in all the highlights of **Zion** (☎ *435/772–3256* ⊕ *www.nps.gov/zion*) in a single-day visit, but definitely don't miss the Narrows, the Emerald Pools, and the Canyon Overlook. Remember that the park is one of the most visited in the country, meaning it's got the crowds—and the lines—to match.

Eat & Drink: Unlike the two other parks you've visited on this trip, there actually are food options inside Zion itself. There's the more upscale **Red Rocks Grill Dining Room** and the casual (and seasonal) **Castle**

Dome Café, both of which are located at Zion Lodge (✉ *1 Zion Lodge* ☎ *435/772–7700* ⊕ *www.zionlodge.com*).

Stay: Stay inside the park if you can—the historic Zion Lodge is the only accommodation within the park itself other than campgrounds. But if you can't score a reservation, there are dozens of hotels in the region (especially in the town of Springdale, right outside the park gates). There's everything from sprawling resorts like **Zion Mountain Ranch** (✉ *9065 West Hwy. 9* ☎ *866/648–2555* ⊕ *www.zmr.com*) to cozy, romantic B&Bs like **Under the Eaves Inn** (✉ *980 Zion Park Blvd.* ☎ *435/772–3457* ⊕ *www.undertheeaves.com*).

Breakfast: There's no shortage of breakfast cafés in Springdale, but for the best coffee, go to **Deep Creek Coffee Co.** (✉ *932 Zion Park Blvd.* ☎ *435/669–8849* ⊕ *www.deepcreekcoffee.com*).

Day 6: Zion National Park to Bryce Canyon National Park

85 miles (1 hour, 45 minutes without traffic and stops)

Bryce Canyon (☎ 435/834–5322 ⊕ www.nps.gov/brca) is less than two hours away from Zion via an extremely beautiful drive—just head east along UT-9, then north on U.S. 89, and finally east on UT-12, a scenic byway and All-American Road.

ALONG THE WAY

Eat & Drink: Grab a bite at **Thunderbird Restaurant** (✉ 4530 S. State St. ☎ 435/648–2262 ⊕ www.thunderbirdutah.com), a stalwart in Mt. Carmel Junction, serving classic American dishes and homemade pie.

Shops: Take a quick stop in Orderville to visit one of the several rock shops in town: you can buy rocks, jewelry, and refreshments before you hit the road again.

Detour: It's an ever-so-slight detour from the main route, but the town of Panguitch is a time capsule with a quintessential American main street lined with old buildings and vintage signs.

Nature: Stop in Red Canyon to hike the Pink Ledges Trail—it's just 0.7 miles long but has plenty of captivating scenery.

BRYCE CANYON NATIONAL PARK

Do: The easiest way to see some of Bryce Canyon's highlights is to traverse its 38-mile scenic drive, which stops at 13 viewpoints, including the popular Sunrise, Sunset, Inspiration, and Bryce

points. If you have time for a hike, try the Navajo Loop Trail, a 1.5-mile loop into a slot canyon called Wall Street. You can also tack on the Queen's Garden Trail, which is 1.8 miles out and back.

Eat & Drink: There are several in-park restaurants, including the dining room at the **Lodge at Bryce Canyon** (☎ 435/834–8700 ⊕ www.brycecanyonforever.com), though they're all seasonal. For year-round dining, head to **Idk BBQ** (✉ 161 N. Main St. ☎ 435/679–8353 ⊕ www.idkbarbecue.com) in Tropic, just outside the park.

Stay: Pitch a tent at one of the park's campsites or spend the night at the Lodge at Bryce Canyon. Otherwise, you can stay in one of the many hotels, B&Bs, or rentals in the villages of Bryce and Tropic; one of the best is **Stone Canyon Inn** (✉ 1380 W. Stone Canyon La. ☎ 866/489–4680 ⊕ www.stonecanyon-inn.com), a collection of guesthouses and bungalows.

Breakfast: Pick up a coffee and a pastry at **Bryce Canyon Coffee Co.** (✉ 21 N. Main St. ⊕ www.brycecanyoncoffee.com) for a to-go breakfast.

Day 7: Bryce Canyon National Park to Grand Staircase-Escalante National Monument

50 miles (1 hour without traffic and stops)

Continue along Scenic Byway 12 to **Grand Staircase-Escalante National Monument** (✉ 745 U.S. 89 ☎ 435/644–1300 ⊕ www. blm.gov).

ALONG THE WAY

Eat & Drink: There are no restaurants between Tropic and Escalante (the only major towns on today's route), so be sure to pack a lunch today.

Detour: If you have the time, drive south on Kodachrome Road at Cannonville to head to **Kodachrome Basin State Park** (☎ 435/679–8562 ⊕ www.stateparks. utah.gov), home to 67 monolithic spires. The park was named after the popular color film by the National Geographic Society during a 1948 survey.

Nature: Just to the northwest of Escalante is **Escalante Petrified Forest State Park** (✉ 710 Reservoir Rd. ☎ 435/826–4466 ⊕ www.stateparks.utah.gov), where you can hike through the petrified forest and see dinosaur bones and marine fossils.

GRAND STAIRCASE ESCALANTE NATIONAL MONUMENT

Do: Grand Staircase-Escalante National Monument covers more than 1,500 square miles—it's larger than the five Utah national parks combined—so there's no way you can see it all in one go. But in a short period of time, you can explore a number of slot canyons (Zebra Slot, Peek-a-Boo Slot, and Spooky Slot, to name three), plus hike a number of trails, like Devil's Garden and Lower Calf Creek Falls.

Eat & Drink: For dinner, visit the **Esca-Latte Internet Cafe & Pizza Parlor** inside Escalante Outfitters (✉ 310 W. Main St., Escalante, UT ☎ 435/826–4266 ⊕ www. escalanteoutfitters.com) for pizza and local beer.

Stay: It's primarily independent hotels in Escalante, each with its own personality. For a more unique stay, try **Escalante Yurts** (✉ 1605 Pine Creek Rd. ☎ 844/200–9878 www.escalanteyurts.com) or **Escalante Escapes** (✉ 500 W. 200 N ☎ 435/668–2108 ⊕ www.escalanteescapes.com), which has luxurious tiny homes.

Breakfast: **Kiva Koffeehouse** (✉ 7386 Hwy. 12, between mile marker 73 and 74, Escalante, UT ☎ 435/826–4550 ⊕ www. kivakoffeehouse.com) is a must-do when in Escalante—it has the best coffee for miles.

Day 8: Grand Staircase-Escalante National Monument to Capitol Reef National Park

70 miles (1 hour, 30 minutes without traffic and stops)

The last national park of your trip, Capitol Reef (☎ 435/425–3791 ⊕ www.nps.gov/ care) is an easy drive straight up Scenic Byway 12.

ALONG THE WAY

Town: Along the way, you'll drive through the town of Boulder. Make a stop at the **Anasazi State Park Museum** (✉ 460 UT-12 ☎ 435/335–7308 ⊕ www.stateparks. utah.gov) to visit an Ancestral Puebloan site and learn about the historic regional culture.

Eat & Drink: The seasonal **Hell's Backbone Grill & Farm** (✉ 20 UT-12 ☎ 435/335–7464 ⊕ www.hellsbackbonegrill.com) in Boulder has earned a number of James

Beard nominations for its farm-to-table cuisine—it's by far one of the most popular restaurants along Scenic Byway 12.

Detour: One of the most scenic drives off Scenic Byway 12 is Burr Trail Road, a backway that travels through the picturesque Long Canyon. Note that a portion of the road isn't paved, so you should only traverse it in dry conditions with a 4x4 vehicle.

CAPITOL REEF NATIONAL PARK

Do: Travel along the Capitol Reef Scenic Drive for incredible vistas in practically every direction, then stop in the town of Fruita to pick fruit from orchards planted by pioneers in the 1800s. Along the drive, you might also want to hike the Grand Wash Trail, a 4.5-mile out-and-back journey that passes Cassidy Arch, named for Butch Cassidy, who likely spent time hiding in the area.

Eat & Drink: There's no food inside Capitol Reef, so bring your own lunch or head to the **Capitol Burger** (✉ 12 W. Main St. ☎ 435/491-0742 ⊕ www.facebook.com/capitolburgertruck) food truck in nearby Torrey for very filling fare.

Stay: As with the other parks, you can camp in Capitol Reef or you can stay in a hotel in Torrey. At **Capitol Reef Resort** (✉ 2600 UT-24 ☎ 435/425-3761 ⊕ www.capitolreefresort.com), accommodations range from standard guest rooms to private cabins to Conestoga wagons.

Breakfast: The family-run **Wild Rabbit Cafe** (✉ 135 E. Main St. ☎ 435/425-3074 ⊕ www.thewildrabbitcafe.com) is a Torrey staple. While it's a great spot for breakfast, it also makes packed lunches for you to take into the park.

Day 9: Capitol Reef National Park to Salt Lake City, UT

235 miles (4 hours, 45 minutes without traffic and stops)

It's a long journey back to Salt Lake City today. Drive west on UT-24, then north on I-15. Once you hit the town of Nephi, get off the interstate to take the Nebo Loop Scenic Byway through the Uinta National Forest in the Wasatch Mountains. You'll meet back up with I-15 in Payson, and you can take that the rest of the way to Salt Lake City.

ALONG THE WAY

Detour: If you're feeling particularly ambitious, take a detour to **Goblin Valley State Park** (✉ Goblin Valley Rd., Green River, UT ☎ 435/275-4584 ⊕ www.stateparks.utah.gov), an hour in the opposite direction from Salt Lake City, to see a landscape full of hoodoos that looks like it's from another planet (which explains why the Mars Desert Research Station is located nearby). The park is an hour's drive east from Capitol Reef.

Eat & Drink: After your detour, backtrack toward Capitol Reef, then stop at the **Sunglow Restaurant and Motel** (✉ 91 E. Main St. ☎ 435/425-3821) in Bicknell, where you can get a slice of its legendary pickle pie, among other unusual flavors like oatmeal and pinto bean.

Town: Stop in the town of Salina for a little break. Grab a bite at the famous **Mom's Café** (✉ 10 E. Main St. ☎ 435/529-3921 ⊕ famousmomscafe.business.site), then stroll through the displays at **Miss Mary's Historical Museum** (✉ 204 S. 100 E ☎ 435/529-4108 ⊕ www.facebook.com/missmarysmuseum) or the Art Robinson Truck Museum (✉ 875 W. Main St.). For a more sobering history lesson, you can visit the **CCC & POW Camp** (✉ 598 E. Main St. ☎ 435/529-7304 ⊕ www.facebook.

com/CCCPOWCAMPUT), where a U.S. soldier infamously massacred German prisoners of war—the site now houses a museum remembering the event.

Nature: As you make your way along the Nebo Loop Scenic Byway, stop at the Devil's Kitchen for a quick hike to a scenic overlook.

SALT LAKE CITY

Do: Venture into Salt Lake's vibrant downtown, with its respected theater scene, farm-to-table restaurants, craft breweries and coffeehouses, and the impressive **City Creek Center** (⊠ 50 S. Main St. ☎ 801/521–2012 ⊕ www.shopcitycreek-center.com) retail plaza. Explore the city's namesake, the Great Salt Lake (⊕ www.utah.com/great-salt-lake-state-park), by car, on foot, or by bicycle. If you're here in summer, try floating off the beaches at Antelope Island—the water is so salty it's impossible to sink.

Eat & Drink: For dinner, enjoy the locally sourced ingredients and bold flavors at **Oquirrh** (⊠ 368 E. 100 S ☎ 801/359–0426 ⊕ www.oquirrhslc.com) or the authentic Mexican cuisine at **Red Iguana** (⊠ 736 W. North Temple ☎ 801/322–1489 ⊕ www.rediguana.com). Afterward, learn how SLC is trying to shed its teetotaler reputation with a drink at **Beehive Distilling** (⊠ 2245 S. West Temple ☎ 385/259–0252 ⊕ www.beehivedistilling.com) or **Fisher Brewing Company** (⊠ 320 W. 800 S ☎ 801/487–2337 ⊕ www.fisherbeer.com).

Stay: Splurge at the opulent **Grand America Hotel** (⊠ 555 S. Main St. ☎ 800/304–8696 ⊕ www.grandamerica.com) or enjoy a night at the hip **AC Hotel by Marriott Salt Lake City Downtown** (⊠ 225 W. 200 S ☎ 385/722–9600 ⊕ www.marriott.com).

Breakfast: Both the coffee and the breakfast menu will wow you at **Campos Coffee SLC** (⊠ 228 S. Edison St. ☎ 801/953–1512 ⊕ www.camposcoffee.com).

The Best of Colorado

Written by Aimee Heckel

A playground for nature lovers and outdoor enthusiasts, Colorado has majestic landscapes, raging rivers, and winding trails, all of which can be explored via the many scenic drives that make up the state's road system. In this 10-day road trip, you can truly explore the best of what Colorado offers: all four of the state's national parks, three major ski towns, and several different hot springs. You will visit Colorado's wine country and go on two of the most popular hikes (or more, if you're up for it). You will be awed by some of Colorado's natural wonders, such as the Cave of the Winds, the country's tallest sand dune, and the Garden of the Gods. And you'll also stop by tourist favorites, like Estes Park, Trail Ridge Road, and Grand Lake, all while keeping the driving time to four hours or less per day, so there's plenty of time to explore and enjoy all that Colorado has to offer.

At a Glance

Start: Denver, CO

End: Denver, CO

Miles Traveled: 1,100 miles

Suggested Duration: 10 days

States Visited: Colorado

Key Sights: Black Canyon of the Gunnison National Park; Garden of the Gods; Great Sand Dunes National Park; Mesa Verde National Park; Rocky Mountain National Park

Best Time to Go: This trip includes mountain driving, which can be challenging in winter even for the most seasoned mountain driver. And some of the roads may not even be open during winter, so this trip is best suited for warmer weather (or be prepared for potential closures and detours).

The Best of Colorado

0 — 40 mi
0 — 40 km

Day 1: Denver, CO, to Boulder, CO

35 miles (50 minutes without traffic and stops)

Start your Rocky Mountain road trip by heading west from Denver on U.S. 6 W to the classic mountain town of Golden, then head north on CO-93 to the hip college town of Boulder.

ALONG THE WAY

Town: Once the territorial capital of Colorado, Golden's growth was boosted by the high-tech industry as well as the **Molson Coors Brewery** (✉ 13th and Ford St. ☎ 866/812–2337 ⊕ www.coorsbrewerytour.com) and the Colorado School of Mines. Although that growth has slowed down in recent years, it remains a top draw for outdoors and history enthusiasts, not to mention beer enthusiasts. Beer snobs will probably send you to any of Colorado's hundreds of microbreweries, but it's hard for any beer lover to resist a pilgrimage to Coors Brewery; founded in 1873, today it's the largest single-site brewery in the world.

Eat & Drink: Woody's Wood Fired Pizza (✉ 1305 Washington Ave. ☎ 303/277–1443 ⊕ www.woodysgolden.com) in Golden has a full menu, with pastas, chicken, calzones, and burgers, but it's the pizza, with its smoky, wood fire–charred crust, that's the big draw.

BOULDER

Do: No place in Colorado better epitomizes the state's outdoor mania than Boulder, where sunny weather keeps locals busy through all seasons. For some of Boulder's prettiest views, head to

Chautauqua Park (✉ *Baseline Rd. and 9th St.* ☎ *303/442–3282* ⊕ *www.boulder-colorado.gov*), nestled at the base of the Flatirons; the park is a launching point for 40 miles of hiking trails. You should also make time to explore Pearl Street, the city's hub and an eclectic collection of boutiques, bookstores, art galleries, cafés, bars, and restaurants.

Eat & Drink: Feast your eyes on the intricately carved walls, pillars, and ceiling at the **Boulder Dushanbe Teahouse** (✉ *1770 13th St.* ☎ *303/442–4993* ⊕ *www. boulderteahouse.com*), a gift from Boulder's sister city Dushanbe, Tajikistan. Tajik artisans decorated the building in a traditional style, with ceramic Islamic art and a riot of colorful wood. The menu presents a culinary cross section of the world, with dishes including North African harissa chicken, spicy Indonesian peanut noodles, and Tajik shish kebab. Afterwards, spend some time trying out Boulder's many microbreweries, like **Avery Brewing Company** (✉ *4910 Nautilus Ct. N* ☎ *303/440–4324* ⊕ *www.avery-brewing.com*).

Stay: Located in what looks like a two-level motel, the **Basecamp Boulder Hotel** (✉ *2020 Arapahoe Ave.* ☎ *303/449–7550* ⊕ *www.basecampboulder.com*) is designed to be the base camp for your adventures—and it's as unique as Boulder, with a bouldering wall in the lounge, kombucha and local beer on tap in the lobby bar, bicycles guests can borrow, a canvas map of Boulder on guest room walls, and a dry sauna.

Breakfast: The Laughing Goat Coffeehouse (✉ *1709 Pearl St.* ⊕ *www.thelaughing-goat.com*) is bohemian-style café that serves bagels, muffins, pastries, and oatmeal for breakfast; try the locally roasted, organic espresso, too.

Day 2: Boulder, CO, to Grand Lake, CO

84 miles (2 hours, 30 minutes without traffic and stops)

Today's drive takes you up U.S. 36 W, past the charming mountain town of Lyons, and up the mountain to Estes Park, the gateway to Rocky Mountain National Park. After exploring one of the country's most popular (and beautiful) national parks, you'll end the day in Grand Lake, a mountain town that's usually less crowded than Estes Park.

ALONG THE WAY

Town: Estes Park boasts a postcard-worthy old town lined with charming shops and restaurants; wildlife, in particular elk, often wander the streets. Estes also has a solid craft beer and distillery scene and is home to the famous, dramatic **Stanley Hotel** (*333 E. Wonderview Ave.* ☎ *970/577–4000* ⊕ *www.stanleyhotel. com*), where it's said author Stephen King was inspired to write *The Shining*.

Eat & Drink: While Estes Park's old town area is fun for window-shopping, ice cream, and taffy, head a bit off the walking path to fill up at the alehouse **Latitude 105** (✉ *101 S. St. Vrain Ave.* ☎ *970/527–1500* ⊕ *ridgelinehotel.com/latitude-105*), where you can find gourmet burgers and Colorado-fresh menu items.

Nature: Rocky Mountain National Park (☎ *970/586–1206* ⊕ *www.nps.gov/romo*) is one of Colorado's four national parks, with 415 square miles of incredible trails, mountains, and wildlife. Take a scenic drive up Trail Ridge Road, the highest paved road in any national park, as well as North America's highest paved through-road.

GRAND LAKE

Do: Whereas Estes Park is the gateway to the Rocky Mountain National Park in the east, Grand Lake is considered the park's western gateway and it's a less crowded, but no less gorgeous, place to stop for the night. Located in the heart of this small mountain town is Colorado's largest natural lake.

Eat & Drink: Sagebrush BBQ and Grill (✉ *1101 Grand Ave.* ☎ *970/627–1404* ⊕ *www.sagebrushbbq.com*) is where to go for tasty local barbecue, as well as a relaxed western atmosphere: peanut shells on the floor, games on the TVs, and cowboy decor on the walls. You can even dare to try "Rocky Mountain oysters" here, which aren't oysters at all, but fried bull testicles.

Stay: Grand Lake must be experienced in a cabin. **Grand Mountain Rentals** (✉ *1028 Grand Ave.* ☎ *970/627–1131* ⊕ *www. grandmountainrentals.com*) is a locally owned company that can connect travelers with luxury lakeside properties.

Breakfast: The **Blue Water Bakery Cafe** (✉ *928 Grand Ave.* ☎ *970/627–5416* ⊕ *www.bluewaterbakery.com*) is a relaxed bakery and café with scrambles, burritos, and more—not to mention beautiful lake views and excellent coffee.

Day 3: Grand Lake, CO, to Vail, CO

110 miles (2 hours without traffic and stops)

Mountain driving can be challenging if you're new to it, but the scenery is absolutely worth the effort. Today you're heading south toward Colorado's stretch of famous ski towns, but you can stop for a dip in the natural springs to ease your muscles along the way.

ALONG THE WAY

Town: Relax in the natural mineral water at the **Hot Sulphur Springs Resort and Spa** (✉ *5609 Spring Rd.* ☎ *970/725–3306* ⊕ *www.hotsulphursprings.com*) in Hot Sulphur Springs. Here seven natural

springs emerge from a large fissure, filling more than 20 pools and baths at various temperatures.

Eat & Drink: Stop for lunch in the town of Dillon, home to Lake Dillon, one of the state's largest man-made reservoirs. At popular **Dillon Dam Brewery** (✉ *100 Little Dam St.* ☎ *970/262–7777* ⊕ *www. dambrewery.com*), one of the largest brewpubs in the Rockies, you can belly up to the horseshoe-shaped bar and sample ales and lagers while you munch on burgers, sandwiches, or pub grub.

VAIL

Do: Vail is one of the nation's biggest and most popular ski destinations with more than 5,300 acres and over 200 trails, but it's a five-star outdoor adventure year-round. You'll also find fine dining, a charming Swiss-inspired downtown, the **Walking Mountains Science Center** (✉ *318 Walking Mountains La., Avon, CO* ☎ *970/827–9725* ⊕ *www.walkingmountains.org*), and great hiking.

Eat & Drink: Vail has such a great food scene that it's tough to narrow it down, but **Mountain Standard** (✉ *193 Gore Creek Dr.* ☎ *970/476–0123* ⊕ *www.mtnstandard.com*) is at the top. Enjoy well-prepared New American food and local beer in the cozy restaurant on the banks of the river, right in the heart of downtown.

Stay: Although Vail is known for its ample luxury lodging options, a favorite way to stay is just outside town in nearby Wolcott, in luxury "glamping" tents by **Collective Retreats** (✉ *4098 CO-131, Wolcott, CO* ☎ *970/445–2033* ⊕ *www. collectivetreats.com*). Relax away from the crowds under unobstructed stars before retreating to your comfortable bed underneath an antler chandelier; toilets and running water are included in this not-so camping experience.

Breakfast: Made-to-order breakfast is part of your stay at Collective Retreats, or you can head back into Vail for champagne brunch at the French brasserie, **Vintage**

(✉ *12 Vail Rd.* ☎ *970/479–0175* ⊕ *www. vintage-vail.com*). Bacon-wrapped figs, crab Benedicts, croques madame and monsieur, and huckleberry bacon French toast are highlights, paired, of course, with breakfast cocktails.

Day 4: Vail, CO, to Aspen, CO

100 miles (2 hours without traffic and stops)

The mountainous drive from Vail to Aspen isn't far, but it passes right through Glenwood Springs. Take an extended break here for a relaxing soak in the hot springs, hiking, and a locally crafted cocktail.

ALONG THE WAY

Town: Glenwood Springs is home to the world's largest hot springs pool, as well as several other places to relax in the area's natural mineral water. **Iron Mountain Hot Springs** (✉ *281 Centennial St.* ☎ *970/945–4766* ⊕ *www.ironmountainhotsprings.com*) is on the banks of the Colorado River, and the **Yampah Vapor Caves** (✉ *709 E. 6th St.* ☎ *970/945–0667* ⊕ *www.yampahspa.com*) will take you underground to a dark and steamy hideaway.

Nature: One of Colorado's most beloved hikes is Hanging Lake Trail in Glenwood Canyon. This National Natural Landmark consists of a series of blue waterfalls spilling into a crystal lake; the lake even appears to be magically suspended off the edge of a cliff.

Eat & Drink: The **Colorado Ranch House** (✉ *704 Grand Ave.* ☎ *970/945–9059* ⊕ *www.coranchhouse.com*), a Western-inspired, modern-American restaurant serves cocktails made with alcohol from the local Woody Creek Distillers, as well as unique spins on classic dishes with locally sourced protein (think duck wings and an elk quesadilla); the Rocky Mountain ruby red trout is always a winner.

ASPEN

Do: Aspen Snowmass is one of the world's most famous skiing destinations, but skiing is not all Aspen offers. Have a picnic in the scenic **John Denver Sanctuary** (✉ *470 Rio Grande Pl.* ☎ *970/920–5120* ⊕ *www.aspenrecreation.com*), relax in a waterside garden on the Roaring Fork River, and stroll through Aspen's hoppin' downtown.

Eat & Drink: The Wild Fig (✉ *315 E. Hyman Ave.* ☎ *970/925–5160* ⊕ *www.thewild-fig.com*), right off the walking mall, feels like a European brasserie in Colorado. You can't leave Aspen without ordering the Fish in a Bag, the fish of the day expertly prepared and served in a brown paper bag.

Photo Op: One of the most photographed views in the nation is the famous Maroon Bells national landmark. Hike these popular mountains (there are several different trails of varying difficulty levels) or simply snap a selfie with them in the background.

Stay: Aspen is for luxury, so do it right and book a stay in one of the **Cuvée Aspen** (⊕ *www.cuvee.com*) properties. These luxe estates come with personalized details, like dinner prepared by a private chef, an in-room massage, or a champagne bubble bath.

Breakfast: Grab breakfast or brunch at **Village Smithy** (✉ *26 S. 3rd St.* ☎ *970/963–9990* ⊕ *www.villagesmithy.com*), a local favorite. In this historic building that used to be a blacksmith shop, you can enjoy deep-fried French toast made with a homemade baguette (or a tofu scramble if you're in the mood for something healthier).

Don't leave Colorado without snapping a photo of the peaks of the famous Maroon Bells.

Day 5: Aspen, CO, to Palisade, CO

115 miles (2 hours without traffic and stops)

Let the exploration of the mountains continue as you venture past more ski towns and into wine territory (yep, Colorado makes wine!). You'll be backtracking up CO-82 W for the first leg of the trip, but make a stop in quirky Carbondale for lunch to break it up.

ALONG THE WAY

Detour: If you don't mind adding another hour onto your drive, one of the most scenic drives in Colorado is on Independence Pass, on Colorado Highway 82 up and over the Continental Divide. Leaving from Aspen, it's in the opposite direction from Palisades, but in the fall, the yellow aspen leaves seem to transform the entire mountain into glittering gold, making the detour completely worth it.

Town: The artsy, outdoorsy town of Carbondale sits beneath Mount Sopris (12,965 feet), and its Main Street is lined with century-old brick buildings that house clothing boutiques, art galleries, and excellent restaurants.

Eat & Drink: The diner **Silo** (✉ *1909 Dolores Way* ☎ *970/963–1909* ⊕ *www.silocarbondale.com*) in Carbondale serves a small but well-prepared menu featuring a breakfast burrito stuffed with seasonal veggies and French toast with berry compote.

Shop: "Cocktails with a conscience" is the motto at **Carbondale's Marble Distilling Co.** (✉ *150 Main St.* ☎ *970/963–7008* ⊕ *www.marbledistilling.com*), a zero-waste craft distillery named for the famous pieces of marble, from the neighboring town of Marble, used in the filtering process. Creative cocktails featuring homemade vodka, rye, whiskey, and bourbon are served, but you can also purchase bottles to take home with you.

PALISADE

Do: Palisade is home to most of Colorado's vineyards and a quarter of the state's wineries. Do a winery tour, taste small-batch wine, and also pick up some fresh peaches, another one of Palisade's claims to fame. Just remember to drive responsibly.

Eat & Drink: Palisade might be famous for its wine, but it also has a local brewery, the **Palisade Brewing Company** (✉ 200 Peach Ave. ☎ 970/464–1462 ⊕ www. palisadebrewingcompany.com), with a full menu. If you're into spice, ask about the El Diablo Savory Cheesecake for dessert, made with ghost peppers, habanero peppers, jalapenos, sriracha, and pepper jack cheese, topped with an ancho/chipotle pesto.

Shop: Pick up a pie at **Palisade Pies** (✉ 3415 C ½ Rd. ☎ 970/549–0347), a family-owned shop that bakes pies packed with fresh fruit from their own orchard. On Sundays in mid-June through late September, don't miss the local farmers' market, where you can peruse produce, wine, and other local goods all in one spot.

Stay: Immerse yourself in Palisade's wine scene at **Wine Country Inn** (✉ 777 Grande River Dr. ☎ 970/464–5777 ⊕ www. coloradowinecountryinn.com), which features breakfast and afternoon wine receptions (with private label wines) and vineyard views.

Breakfast: Start the day with pastries (including sweet rolls and pie) made with local fruits at the **Slice O' Life Bakery** (✉ 105 W. 3rd St. ☎ 970/464–0577).

Day 6: Palisade, CO, to Telluride, CO

120 miles (2 hours, 30 minutes without traffic and stops)

All mountain drives through Colorado are scenic, so keep your camera on hand. This particular route takes you on CO-62 W to CO-134 S, which is part of the San Juan Skyway, one of the country's most stupendous drives.

ALONG THE WAY

Detour: A quick half-hour west of Palisade, traveling on I–70 W takes you to **Colorado National Monument** (✉ Rim Rock Dr., Fruita, CO ☎ 970/858–3617 ⊕ www. nps.gov/colm), where sheer red-rock cliffs open to 23 miles of steep canyons and thin monoliths that sprout as high as 450 feet from the floor. Created between 65 and 225 million years ago, the monument was designated in 1911 and has been popular with photographers, hikers, and those eager to drive its paved road, Rim Rock Drive, ever since. The 23-mile drive on the famed road will take you about an hour.

Nature: Another one of Colorado's famous parks, the **Black Canyon of the Gunnison National Park** (☎ 970/641–2337 ⊕ www. nps.gov/blca) is named for the black rocks lining its steep gorge, creating some of the steepest cliffs in the country.

Eat & Drink: Toast the canyon with a drink (and pizza, sausage, salad, and more) at the **High Alpine Brewing Company** (✉ 111 N. Main St. ☎ 970/642–4500 ⊕ www. highalpinebrewing.com) in Gunnison, a brewery located 7,700 feet above sea level.

TELLURIDE

Do: This European-influenced, historic town is considered one of the best ski destinations in North America thanks to its 300 inches of snow in the winter, and just as many days of sunshine per year. It's also home to one of Colorado's biggest annual music events, the Telluride Bluegrass Festival. To learn more about the city's mining history, make a visit to the **Telluride Historical Museum** (⊠ *201 W. Gregory Ave.* ☎ *970/728–3344* ⊕ *www. telluridemuseum.org*).

Eat & Drink: At dinnertime, take the Gondola up the mountain to **Allred's** (⊠ *San Sophia Station* ☎ *970/728–7474* ⊕ *www. tellurideskiresort.com*) for the town's best food and views. Locally inspired fare such as elk, bison, and lamb feature prominently on the menu.

Stay: A grand stone-and-wood structure, the luxury ski-in ski-out **Inn at Lost Creek** (⊠ *119 Lost Creek La., Mountain Village* ☎ *970/728–5678* ⊕ *www.innatlostcreek. com*) in the Mountain Village resembles an alpine lodge with contemporary furnishings.

Breakfast: Local institution **Baked** (⊠ *127 S. Fir St.* ☎ *970/728–4775* ⊕ *www.baked-intel.com*) serves fresh-baked goodies like sandwiches, pizza, and doughnuts.

Day 7: Telluride, CO, to Pagosa Springs, CO

170 miles (3 hours, 15 minutes without traffic and stops)

Today you can head out on CO-145, driving past scenic small towns that give you a taste of the old Wild West, as you make your way to Mesa Verde National Park, and then follow U.S. 160 on to Pagosa Springs. But if you don't mind an extra hour or so of driving time, loop back around the way you came from Telluride to take the Million Dollar Highway (aka U.S. 550) south from Ouray down to

Mesa Verde. This awesome stretch of road climbs over Red Mountain Pass (arguably the most spectacular part of the 236-mile San Juan Skyway). As it ascends steeply from Ouray, the road clings to the cliffs hanging over the Uncompahgre River. Guardrails are few, hairpin turns are many, and behemoth RVs seem to take more than their share of road.

ALONG THE WAY

Nature: Explore ancient history at **Mesa Verde National Park** (☎ *970/529–4465* ⊕ *www.nps.gov/meve*), home to about 5,000 archaeological sites. This national park has some of the best-preserved Ancestral Pueblo cliff dwellings in the country.

Eat & Drink: By far the best place to eat in the park is the **Metate Room** (⊠ *34879 U.S. 160, Mancos, CO* ☎ *970/529–4422* ⊕ *www.visitmesaverde.com*), a southwestern upscale restaurant attached to the Far View Lodge. Order a glass of wine and request a table outside on the rooftop (if you're there late enough, it's an excellent spot to watch the sunset).

Nature: As you leave Mesa Verde and head to Pagosa Springs, you can see **Chimney Rock** (⊠ *3179 CO-151* ☎ *970/883–5359* ⊕ *www.chimneyrock-co.org*) from the highway, a national monument and archaeological site that was considered sacred by the Ancestral Puebloans. Stop and hike to the top; a half mile will reward you with 360-degree panoramic views.

PAGOSA SPRINGS

Do: Pagosa Springs has the world's deepest geothermal hot spring, certified by the *Guinness World Records*. You can't swim here (it's more than 1,000 feet deep), but you can enjoy its waters in many pools nearby.

Eat & Drink: Riff Raff Brewing Company (⊠ *274 Pagosa St.* ☎ *970/264–4677* ⊕ *www.riffraffbrewing.com*) is a local brewery powered by the geothermal heat from the springs. How often can you say you had a beer that Mother Nature helped brew?

Stay: If you stay at the **Springs Resort and Spa** (✉ *323 Hot Springs Blvd.* ☎ *800/225–0934* ⊕ *www.pagosahotsprings.com*), you can wrap yourself in a big white spa robe and head directly for the 24 soaking pools that are terraced on several levels overlooking the San Juan River. As a hotel guest, you'll have 24-hour access.

Breakfast: The **Pagosa Baking Company** (✉ *238 Pagosa St.* ☎ *970/264–9348* ⊕ *www.pagosabakingcompany.com*) sells homemade goods and fresh, healthy breakfast offerings, from breakfast burritos to quiche.

Day 8: Pagosa, CO, to Great Sand Dunes National Park

110 miles (2 hours without traffic and stops)

It's time to hit up Colorado's fourth and final national park, in quirky San Luis Valley, a region full of roadside attractions.

ALONG THE WAY

Roadside Attraction: Not far from the sand dunes is a strange sight to behold: the **UFO Watchtower** (✉ *CO-17, Center, CO* ☎ *719/378–2296* ⊕ *www.ufowatchtower. com*), a supposed point of two energetic vortexes said to attract aliens. Come see for yourself if any aliens come to say hi and if not, leave a tribute for extraterrestrial guests in the sprawling yard of trinkets out front.

Nature: Another must-visit attraction nearby is the **Colorado Gators Reptile Park** (✉ *9162 CR 9 N, Mosca, CO* ☎ *719/378–2612* ⊕ *www.coloradogators.com)*; yes, hundreds of alligators live in southern Colorado.

GREAT SAND DUNES NATIONAL PARK

Do: The otherworldly **Great Sand Dunes National Park** (✉ *11999 CO-150* ☎ *719/378–6395* ⊕ *www.nps.gov/grsa*) seems out of place with mountains in the background and a creek running through them. You can even sled down the tallest sand dune in North America on a "sand-board."

Eat & Drink: Many people pack a picnic to enjoy in the dunes (you can even camp here), but another good bet in the valley is the **Crestone Brewing Company** (✉ *187 W. Silver Ave., Crestone, CO* ☎ *719/256–6400* ⊕ *www.facebook.com/Crestone-BrewingCo*). It's nothing fancy, but the burgers and wings do the job.

Stay: You can spend the night at stunning **Zapata Ranch** (✉ *5305 CO-150, Mosca, CO* ☎ *719/378–2356* ⊕ *www.zranch. org*), a working ranch owned by the Nature Conservancy and home to about 2,000 wild bison, as well as one domesticated bison that you can pet through the fence.

Breakfast: Food is included in your stay at Zapata Ranch. You will want to dine here; it's family-style dishes are all excellent.

Day 9: Great Sand Dunes National Park to Colorado Springs, CO

194 miles (3 hours, 30 minutes without traffic and stops)

There are two routes to Colorado Springs; the shorter one takes you on U.S. 160 and up 1–25 through historical towns like Pueblo, but the slightly longer route via Colorado 17 north to U.S. 285 and then U.S. 50 is much more scenic, taking you past several major mountains.

ALONG THE WAY

Town: The highlight of a stop in Cañon City is the Royal Gorge and its accompanying bridge, the highest bridge in the country and once the world's highest suspension bridge. Carved by the Arkansas River more than 3 million years ago, the Royal Gorge canyon walls tower up to 1,200 feet high. The 956-foot-high **Royal Gorge Bridge** (✉ *4218 County Rd. 3A* ☎ *719/275–7507* ⊕ *www. royalgorgebridge.com*) sways on gusty afternoons and the river can be seen clearly between gaps in the boards, adding to the thrill of a crossing. You can walk across the bridge nearly 1,000 feet above the river, and then book a wild white-water rafting trip in the Arkansas River to experience the bridge from below if there's time.

Eat & Drink: The **Whitewater Bar and Grill** (✉ *45045 W. U.S. 50* ☎ *719/269–1009* ⊕ *www.whitewaterbar.com*) is the ideal casual restaurant to break during an adventure-packed day. The vast backyard features sand volleyball, a playground for kids, horseshoes, fire pits, hammocks, and tons of tables with umbrellas—plus local beer, margaritas, and a full food menu.

COLORADO SPRINGS

Do: The contented residents of the Colorado Springs area believe they live in an ideal location, and it's hard to argue with them. The state's second-largest city has no shortness of outdoor and cultural adventures to enjoy. Immerse yourself in natural wonders at the **Cave of the Winds** (✉ *100 Cave of the Winds Rd.* ☎ *719/685–5444* ⊕ *www.caveofthewinds.com*), a 500-million-year-old underground cave system, and then see more mountain magic aboveground at the **Garden of the Gods** (✉ *Garden of the Gods Rd.* ⊕ *www.gardenofgods.com*), bizarre red-rock formations that tilt and balance in seemingly impossible ways. While you're here, be sure to take a train to the top of **Pikes Peak** (☎ *800/525–2250*

⊕ *www.pikes-peak.com*), the most visited mountain in North America.

Eat & Drink: While there are plenty of incredible restaurants in Colorado Springs, including perhaps Colorado's finest restaurant, the **Penrose Room** (✉ *1 Lake Ave.* ☎ *719/577–5773* ⊕ *www. broadmoor.com*), a fun road-trip experience is to dine at the **Airplane Restaurant** (✉ *1665 Newport Rd.* ☎ *719/570–7656* ⊕ *theairplanerestaurant.com*). A 1953 Boeing KC-97 tanker was converted into this quirky, casual restaurant, and you can sit in the cockpit and dine in the cabin.

Stay: It's expensive, but with its old-world style that emits pure luxury—including the signature pink building with the Mediterranean-style towers—**The Broadmoor** (✉ *1 Lake Ave.* ☎ *800/755-5011* ⊕ *www. broadmoor.com*) continues to redefine itself with settings where guests can unwind and be pampered.

Breakfast: At **Adam's Mountain Café** ✉ *(26 Manitou Ave.* ☎ *719/685–1430* ⊕ *www. adamsmountaincafe.com*), join the locals sitting at mismatched tables, viewing drawings by regional artists, and mingling at the community table. The food has an organic bent, with many vegetarian options.

Day 10: Colorado Springs, CO, to Denver, CO

70 miles (1 hour, 15 minutes without traffic and stops)

This relatively quick highway drive on 1–25 will shoot you back to Denver in no time flat. There's a lot to do in Colorado Springs, so it might be best to use this time to see anything you couldn't the previous day.

ALONG THE WAY

Town: Artsy, and very sleepy, Palmer Lake is a magnet for hikers who set out for the evergreen-clad peaks at several in-town trailheads. There are more good restaurants and working artists than one would expect from a population of about 2,800. The town developed around the railroad tracks that were laid here in 1871—the lake itself was used as a refueling point for steam engines.

Eat & Drink: Bella Panini (✉ *4 CO-105* ☎ *719/481–3244* ⊕ *www.bellapanini. com*) in Palmer Lake has a heavy Italian focus, but the chefs here aren't afraid to mix things up, whipping out such creative concoctions as crawfish-and-jalapeño pizza.

DENVER

Do: Wrap up your road trip with an art-filled day in Denver, the capital of Colorado. Visit the Golden Triangle Creative District, where you can see more than 16 different galleries and museums, including the **Denver Art Museum** (✉ *100 W. 14th Ave. Pkwy.* ☎ *720/865–5000* ⊕ *www.denverartmuseum.org*) and the **Clyfford Still Museum** (✉ *1250 Bannock St.* ☎ *720/354–4880* ⊕ *www.clyffordstillmuseum.org*). Hip Larimer Square is filled with boutiques, bars, and restaurants while taking a hike (and seeing a show, if you have the chance) at the **Red Rocks Park and Amphitheater** (✉ *18300 W. Alameda Pkwy., Morrison* ☎ *720/865–2494* ⊕ *www.redrocksonline.com*) is another must.

Eat & Drink: The most Colorado way to dine in Denver is at **Elway's** (✉ *2500 E. 1st Ave.* ☎ *303/399–5353* ⊕ *www. elways.com*), a steak house named after former Denver Broncos quarterback, John Elway. The wine list is solid, the food is filling and tasty, and, in true Colorado fashion, the atmosphere is sophisticated but far from stuffy.

Stay: Complete your artsy day by staying at the **Art Hotel** (✉ *1201 Broadway* ☎ *303/572–8000* ⊕ *www.hilton.com*), a modern hotel that also houses an impressive, curated art gallery. You may even find a famous piece of art in your room.

Breakfast: Locals line up for blocks to get a table at **Snooze** (✉ *1701 Wynkoop St.* ☎ *303/825–3536* ⊕ *www.snoozeeatery. com*), a breakfast eatery. The upbeat, retro vibe is only second to its popular pineapple upside-down pancakes.

The Ultimate Wild West Road Trip

Written by Aimee Heckel

If you've ever dreamed of being a cowgirl or cowboy, this trip back in time is for you. Luckily for history fans, the American Wild West is still alive in states like New Mexico, Colorado, Arizona, Wyoming, and South Dakota. While many things have changed since the 1800s, western hospitality remains, as do tons of historical sites, saloons, working ranches, and ghost towns that created the classic vision of the Wild West that so many people still have today (helped along with many a Hollywood Western and even more recent television shows like Westworld). Throughout this 10-day adventure, you'll explore ghost towns of former mining communities, watch re-enactments of shoot-outs, tip your hat at the same bars that once welcomed rebels and outlaws, and learn about America's history in the late 1800s as you journey through the country's most famous frontier towns. Each day is pretty driving-heavy with an average of four hours of driving per day, but it's the only way you'll be able to experience the best of the Wild West in just one trip.

At a Glance

Start: Tucson, AZ

End: Rapid City, SD

Miles Traveled: 2,160 miles

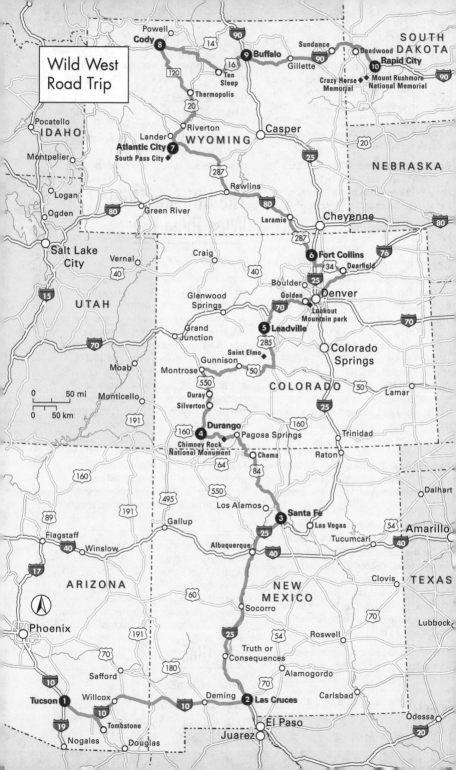

Suggested Duration: 9 days

States Visited: Arizona, Colorado, New Mexico, South Dakota, Wyoming

Key Sights: Buffalo Bill Center of the West; Deadwood, South Dakota; Dearfield Ghost Town; Mount Rushmore; Tombstone, Arizona

Best Time to Go: This is best as a warm-weather trip, because you won't love Wyoming's roads in a blizzard.

Day 1: Tucson, AZ, to Las Cruces, NM

325 miles (5 hours without traffic and stops)

Start your Wild West trip in southern Arizona, where many Hollywood Westerns have been filmed. Before you depart the city of Tucson, stop by Old Tucson just west of town for one of Hollywood's most popular filming locations (including *Three Amigos* and *Tombstone*). Today's drive to Las Cruces, New Mexico, is a straight shot east on Interstate 10, but any true Western fan needs to make the hourlong detour down to Tombstone before you leave Arizona.

ALONG THE WAY

Town: Tombstone, aka the Town Too Tough to Die, is one of the most popular Wild West attractions, thanks to famous past residents liké Doc Holliday and Wyatt Earp. Historic Allen Street is the site of the real 1881 gunfight at O.K. Corral, one of the Wild West's most famous shootouts that became the stuff of legend; you might even be able to catch a re-enactment. Afterwards, you can check out the replica gallows and other exhibits at the **Tombstone Courthouse State Historic Park** (✉ 223 E. Toughnut St. ☎ 520/457–3311 ⊕ www.azstateparks.com), visit the graves of outlaws at the **Boothill Cemetery** (✉ 408 AZ-80 ☎ 520/457–2540), and look for ghosts at the supposedly haunted **Bird Cage Theatre** (✉ 535 E. Allen St. ☎ 520/457–3421 ⊕ www.tombstonebirdcage.com). Tombstone is packed with tour options if you want to stay a while.

Eat & Drink: The first meal of your trip needs to be at a saloon. Tip a pint at **Doc Holliday's Saloon** (✉ 517 E. Allen St. ☎ 520/457–2247) or step back in time with a drink and a show at **Wyatt Earp's Oriental Saloon & Theater** (✉ 500 E. Allen St. ☎ 520/457–2407 ⊕ www.orientalsaloon.com).

LAS CRUCES

Do: The former stomping grounds of Billy the Kid, Las Cruces is the perfect place to feel like a cowboy for a day, thanks to the **New Mexico Farm & Ranch Heritage Museum** (✉ 4100 Dripping Springs Rd. ☎ 575/522–4100 ⊕ www.nmfarmandranchmuseum.org), which offers demos of cow milking, blacksmithing, and other ranching skills. You'll also enjoy wandering through Old Mesilla, a colorful village of historic adobe buildings and the former home of Billy the Kid.

Eat & Drink: Enjoy authentic, homemade Mexican food at **La Nueva Casita Cafe** (✉ 195 N. Mesquite St. ☎ 575/523–5434 ⊕ www.lanuevacasitacafe.com), a local favorite that dates back to the 1950s. After dinner, cruise around Main Street and the historic Mesquite District.

Stay: Immerse yourself in Spanish-colonial style at the posh **Hotel Encanto de Las Cruces** (✉ 705 S. Telshor Blvd. ☎ 575/522–4300 ⊕ www.hotelencanto.com). Relax by the outdoor pool as the sun goes down.

Breakfast: Breakfast is included in your stay at the Encanto, or pop over to the **Cafe de Mesilla** (✉ 2190 Hwy. 28, Avendia de Meilla ☎ 575/524–0000 ⊕ www.cafedemesilla.com), a charming adobe restaurant with classic New Mexican breakfast dishes you can enjoy on the patio. Try the Mesilla Morning Sandwich with green chilis.

Day 2: Las Cruces, NM, to Santa Fe, NM

280 miles (4 hours without traffic and stops)

Get a driving tour of the middle of New Mexico as you head north up Interstate 25.

ALONG THE WAY

Town: You'll drive through the big city of Albuquerque, so you may as well stop by the historic **San Felipe de Neri Church** (✉ *2005 N. Plaza St. NW* ☎ *505/243–4628* ⊕ *www.sanfelipedeneri.org*) in Old Town Plaza. The still-running adobe church was built in 1793, dating back to the Spanish colonial period, and is one of the oldest surviving buildings in the city. Albuquerque's early Wild West history was notorious for having minimal law enforcement—the wild Wild West.

Eat & Drink: Fill 'er up at the **High Noon Restaurant and Saloon** (✉ *425 San Felipe St. NW* ☎ *505/765–1455* ⊕ *www.high-noonrestaurant.com*) in Albuquerque's Old Town, housed in a historic 1785 building. The long-standing local restaurant serves ABQ's best hand-cut steaks and margaritas.

SANTA FE

Do: Santa Fe is the oldest capital city in the United States, and its history spanning Pueblo cultures and Spanish and Mexican rule is evident in its architecture and culture. But thanks to its role as the endpoint of the Santa Fe Trail, it's also a big draw for Wild West fans. While it'll be hard to pull yourself from the excitement of downtown, book a guided Jeep, bike, or walking tour with **Santa Fe Mountain Adventures** (☎ *505/988–4000* ⊕ *www.santafemountainadventures.com*), which will take you to see petroglyphs, historic ruins, and Ancestral Pueblo dwellings. The area surrounding Santa Fe is a popular filming location for Westerns, including the Netflix series *Godless*,

Extend Your Trip

From Santa Fe: The Best of New Mexico *(Ch. 5)*

From Cody: Big Sky Country *(Ch. 4)*

From Rapid City: The Best of the Dakotas *(Ch. 6)*

A Million Ways to Die in the West, *No Country for Old Men*, and the remakes of *3:10 to Yuma*, *The Magnificent Seven*, and *True Grit*. Alternatively, you can take a detour an hour east to visit Las Vegas, New Mexico, once considered the most violent town in the Wild West; many a Hollywood Western was filmed there, too.

Shop: Today Santa Fe is well-known for its art, with many artists showcasing a distinctly western style; you'll find examples at galleries like the **Sorrel Sky Gallery** (✉ *125 W. Palace Ave.* ☎ *505/501–6555* ⊕ *www.sorrelsky.com*).

Eat & Drink: The expert culinary team at the romantic **Anasazi Restaurant & Bar** (✉ *113 Washington Ave.* ☎ *505/988–3236* ⊕ *www.rosewoodhotels.com*) balances old-world techniques with southwestern spice in its approach to the menu. If you want a less formal vibe, dine in the more spacious, convivial bar or on the lively streetside patio.

Stay: The luxurious **Inn & Spa at Loretto** (✉ *211 Old Santa Fe Trail* ☎ *505/988–5531* ⊕ *www.hotelloretto.com*) features architecture inspired by Taos Pueblo. The southwestern, homey boutique hotel is just a few blocks from historic Santa Fe Plaza.

Breakfast: Start the day with a breakfast burrito smothered in spicy red chili at the casual diner, **Tia Sophia's** (✉ *210 W. San Francisco St.* ☎ *505/983–9880* www.tiasophias.com).

Day 3: Santa Fe, NM, to Durango, CO

215 miles (4 hours without traffic and stops)

It's time to giddy-up to Colorado, where today's drive will take you over a jaw-dropping mountain pass and past some photo-worthy attractions.

ALONG THE WAY

Town: Stop in Chama, New Mexico, where you can see (or ride, if time allows) the historic **Cumbres & Toltec Scenic Railroad** (✉ 888/286–2737 ⊕ www.cumbrestoltec.com). This coal-fueled steam train, built in 1880 for mining, is the country's most complete narrow-gauge railroad from that time. It chugs between Chama and Antonito, Colorado.

Eat & Drink: Pause in the hot springs town of Pagosa Springs at **Riff Raff Brewing Company** (✉ 274 Pagosa St. ☎ 970/264–4677 ⊕ www.riffraffbrewing.com), where you can get "earth-powered beer" (beer made via geothermal heat) and a goat burger smothered in onions and green chilis.

Nature: On U.S. 160, you'll pass the **Chimney Rock National Monument** (✉ 3179 CO-151, Chimney Rock ☎ 970/883–5359 ⊕ www.chimneyrockco.org), a sacred rock formation that sticks straight up. You can hike this Ancestral Puebloan site or simply appreciate it from the highway.

DURANGO

Do: The Wild West wouldn't have been the Wild West without the invention of the railroad, so dedicate this leg of the trip to trains and make a visit to Durango, the truest railroad town in the West. Visit the free **Durango and Silverton Narrow Gauge Railroad and Museum** (✉ 479 Main Ave. ☎ 888/872–4607 ⊕ www.durangotrain.com), with its railway dating back to the 1880s. If you don't have time for a full train ride, check out the inexpensive hourlong tour through the train yard.

Eat & Drink: For a raucous night, drink and dine at the **Diamond Belle Saloon,** an authentic Old West saloon with live ragtime piano located in the Strater Hotel (✉ 699 Main Ave. ☎ 970/247–4431 ⊕ www.strater.com).

Stay: The **Strater Hotel** (✉ 699 Main Ave. ☎ 970/247–4431 ⊕ www.strater.com), built in 1887, is a living history museum filled with Victorian antiques and an authentic Old West atmosphere. Or if you're looking for an off-the-beaten-path Old West escape, venture past Durango to **Dunton Hot Springs** (✉ 52068 Rd. 38, Dolores ☎ 877/288–9922 ⊕ www.duntondestinations.com), a former mining town (established in 1885) that's been renovated into luxurious cabins (yes, the whole town). Stay in a real miner's hand-hewn log cabin, dine in a 19th-century farmhouse, and relax in private hot springs.

Breakfast: El Moro Tavern (✉ 945 Main Ave. ☎ 970/259–5555 ⊕ www.elmorotavern.com), home of "Durango's strangest shoot-out" in 1906, serves weekend brunch. Otherwise, walk down to the 11th Street Station food truck court for various breakfast options.

Day 4: Durango, CO, to Leadville, CO

About 290 miles (6 hours without traffic and stops)

Prepare for the most beautiful part of your road trip, along Colorado's Million Dollar Highway with fittingly million-dollar mountain views.

ALONG THE WAY

Town: Stop in historic Silverton, an old mining community and National Historic Landmark perched at 9,318 feet above sea level. The town is heaven for history buffs and outdoor lovers alike.

Eat & Drink: Silverton's **Bent Elbow Restaurant** (✉ *1114 Blair St.* ☎ *970/387–5775* ⊕ *www.thebent.com*) is set inside an original Old West dining room and saloon, complete with a honky-tonk piano.

Nature: Pause as you enter Ouray, a fantasy-like mountain town built in a box canyon. You're surrounded by mountains on all sides, so take the time to explore by taking a jaunt to Box Canon Falls, where the turbulent waters of Clear Creek thunder 285 feet down a narrow gorge.

Detour: If you love a good ghost town, take a 45-minute detour to visit one of Colorado's finest: St. Elmo. This is one of Colorado's best-preserved ghost towns, with a dusty Main Street and saloon that looks straight out of a Western.

LEADVILLE

Do: Walk through the Victorian neighborhoods of the highest incorporated city in North America and a one-time silver-mining boomtown. Don't miss the **National Mining Hall of Fame and Museum** (✉ *120 W. 9th St.* ☎ *719/486–1229* ⊕ *www.mininghalloffame.org*), with fascinating replicas of mines.

Eat & Drink: The **Legendary Silver Dollar Saloon** (✉ *315 Harrison Ave.* ☎ *719/486–9914* ⊕ *www.legendarysilverdollarsaloon.com*), located in a historical building that feels plucked from the 1800s, used to be a favorite hangout of John Henry "Doc" Holliday. Many features at the saloon (and restaurant) are original.

Stay: The **Delaware Hotel** (✉ *700 Harrison Ave.* ☎ *800/748–2004* ⊕ *www.delaware-hotel.com*), in a Victorian brick building right in downtown, dates back to 1886. It's the last remaining grand hotel in town, and it's equal parts history museum and the crown architectural jewel of Leadville.

Breakfast: City on a Hill Coffee (✉ *508 Harrison Ave.* ☎ *719/486–0797* ⊕ *www.cityonahillcoffee.com*) claims to be North America's highest-elevation coffee business. So you can check that off your bucket list while you eat breakfast.

Day 5: Leadville, CO, to Fort Collins, CO

160 miles (2 hours, 30 minutes without traffic and stops)

Try to plan this drive outside of rush hour and weekends, so you can make it down busy Interstate 70 with less traffic.

ALONG THE WAY

Roadside Attraction: Visit the grave of William F. Cody (aka "Buffalo Bill") in **Lookout Mountain Park** (✉ *987 Lookout Mountain Rd.* ☎ *720/865–0900* ⊕ *www.denvergov.org*), on the way down Interstate 70. The on-site Buffalo Bill Museum (✉ *987½ Lookout Mountain Rd.* ☎ *303/526–0744* ⊕ *www.buffalobill.org*) tells all about the famous buffalo hunter's life and the Wild West history in the region.

Town: Golden, Colorado, is one of Colorado's oldest frontier towns. **Golden History Tours** (☎ *720/432–1162* ⊕ *www.goldenhistorytours.com*) offers guided tours through the streets and parks, relaying some pretty wild (and true) tales.

Eat & Drink: Located in the historic 1913 Armory building in Golden, **Café 13** (✉ *1301 Arapahoe St.* ☎ *303/278–2225* ⊕ *www.cafe13golden.com*) claims to be housed in one of the largest cobblestone buildings in the country. The menu is perfect for a healthy lunch of street tacos and sandwiches.

Detour: Swing east to Dearfield, a ghost town that used to be a Black majority settlement. It was formed in 1910 as a proposed colony for African Americans and ended up being one of Colorado's most successful African American communities until the population started dwindling in the 1920s. The spot is a fascinating look at the often-unexplored role of African Americans in the Wild West.

FORT COLLINS

Do: A relaxing way to spend the evening in Fort Collins is wandering through its historic Old Town, which was the real-life inspiration for Disneyland's Main Street USA. Look for live music, ample shopping, and quirky shops, like **Nuance Chocolate** (✉ *214 Pine St.* ☎ *970/484–2330* ⊕ *www.nuancechocolate.com*), a chocolatier that roasts and grinds chocolate beans nearby. It also claims to have the largest selection of single-origin chocolate in the world.

Eat & Drink: The Farmhouse at **Jessup Farm** (✉ *1957 Jessup Dr.* ☎ *970/631–8041* ⊕ *www.farmhousefc.com*) feels like home, if home were a 130-year-old farmhouse converted into a rustic restaurant. Although the stairs squeak with age and the brick is exposed, the food is modern, hip, and local.

Stay: In town, stay at the historic **Armstrong Hotel** (✉ *259 S. College Ave.* ☎ *970/484–3883* ⊕ *www.thearmstrong-hotel.com*), with a pressed-tin ceiling and guest rooms furnished with antiques. Or if you want to extend your stay, book time at the **Colorado Cattle Company and Guest Ranch** (✉ *70008 Weld, CR 132, Raymer* ☎ *970/437–5345* ⊕ *www.facebook.com/ColoradoCattleCompany*) about two hours east of Fort Collins. This is a real working ranch, where you can rope and drive cattle by day and sleep in a log cabin by night.

Breakfast: The **Silver Grill** (✉ *218 Walnut St.* ☎ *970/484–4656* ⊕ *www.silvergrill.com*) in downtown Fort Collins is the classic greasy spoon, in all the best ways.

Day 6: Fort Collins, CO, to Atlantic City, WY

300 miles (4 hours, 45 minutes without traffic and stops)

Say adios to Colorado; U.S. 287 will usher you into Wyoming for a quieter stretch of the drive. While Wyoming is packed with Wild West destinations, this route will take you into the realm of ghost towns.

ALONG THE WAY

Town: Laramie, Wyoming has historic buildings dating back to the 1800s, including a prison built on the river in 1872 where Old West outlaw Butch Cassidy was put behind bars.

Eat & Drink: The **Altitude Chophouse and Brewery** (✉ *320 S. 2nd St.* ☎ *307/721–4031* ⊕ *www.altitudechophouse.com*), with mountain-themed decor, is Laramie's finest restaurant, specializing in American favorites that highlight a true western heritage (think beef brisket and prime rib).

Detour: The ghost town of **South Pass City** (☎ *307/332–3684* ⊕ *www.wyoparks.wyo.gov*) used to be a stop near the Oregon Trail. More than 30 historic structures have since landed the community on the National Register of Historic Places. Be sure to tour the Carissa mine shaft.

ATLANTIC CITY

Do: No, not that Atlantic City. Wyoming's version has a population of only about 57, but this tiny former mining camp in Wind River Country is the real-deal West, with preserved buildings and an old-fashioned, small-town energy you won't find in busier tourist sites. This is the place to unplug and unwind.

Eat & Drink: If you want to experience the Wild West, follow the dirt roads to the **Miner's Grubsteak** (✉ *25 N. Granier Ave.*

While Mount Rushmore is impressive, so is the stunning landscape of the Black Hills that surround it.

☎ *307/332–0915*), which calls its menu "good ol' home cookin.'"

Stay: Spend the night in the humble **Miner's Delight Inn Bed & Breakfast** (✉ *290 S. Pass Rd.* ☎ *307/332–0248* ⊕ *www. minersdelightinn.com*), a two-story log cabin that started out as a hotel in 1904. You can also stay in one of five cabins on the property, complete with wood-burning stoves. Note that Miner's Delight is for adults only, but the Grubstake has a family-friendly cabin on-site.

Breakfast: The Miner's Delight serves breakfast, and so does the Miner's Grubsteak.

Day 7: Atlantic City, WY, to Cody, WY

200 miles (3 hours, 15 minutes without traffic and stops)

Wyoming roads can feel like ghost towns in and of themselves, so make sure you fill up on gas whenever you see a station.

This wide-open drive north gets you closer to Yellowstone National Park and just past the Shoshone National Forest.

ALONG THE WAY

Town: Stop at Thermopolis, with the world's largest mineral hot springs, to unwind in the 104-degree healing waters at the **Hot Springs State Park Bath House** (✉ *168 Tepee St.* ☎ *307/864–3765* ⊕ *www.wyoparks.state.wy.us*).

Eat & Drink: The **One Eyed Buffalo Brewing Company** (✉ *528 Broadway St.* ☎ *307/864–3555* ⊕ *www.oneeyedbuffalobrewingwyo.com*) in Thermopolis is a local brewery with a delicious menu (try the western-style charbroiled prime rib if it's on the menu).

CODY

Do: There's so much to do in this classic western town named after "Buffalo Bill" Cody. Start with a **Cody Trolley Tour** (✉ *1192 Sheridan Ave.* ☎ *307/527–7043* ⊕ *www.codytrolleytours.com*), an hour-long tour on a funky green trolley through Cody's historic Old West and "new

West" attractions. This provides an overview for what you might want to focus on in your short time here. In addition, cowboy culture lives on at the **Buffalo Bill Center of the West** (✉ *720 Sheridan Ave.* ☎ *307/587–4771* ⊕ *www.centerofthewest.org*); round out your day with a visit to the on-site Plains Indian Museum.

Eat & Drink: The Cody Cattle Company (✉ *1910 Demaris Dr.* ☎ *307/272–5770* ⊕ *www.thecodycattlecompany.com*) presents a family-style (read: bottomless) chuckwagon dinner and nightly western entertainment.

Stay: A Cody landmark, the **Irma Hotel** (✉ *1192 Sheridan Ave.* ☎ *307/587–4221* ⊕ *www.irmahotel.com*) was built by Buffalo Bill himself. In the summer, you can see shoot-out reenactments in front of the hotel. Grab a drink at the famous bar, a gift to Buffalo Bill from Queen Victoria.

Breakfast: Go to **Granny's Restaurant** (✉ *1550 Sheridan Ave.* ☎ *307/587–4829* ⊕ *www.grannysrestaurantwy.com*) for a homecooked, American breakfast.

Day 8: Cody, WY, to Buffalo, WY

170 miles (3 hours without stops and traffic)

This day has you crossing Wyoming east on the highway, through lush forests.

ALONG THE WAY

Town: Ten Sleep, Wyoming, is named for its Native American history (the "ten sleeps," or "ten nights," refers to the distance between the Sioux camps on the Platte River in the south and a Sioux campsite in the north). Pause at the **Ten Sleep Pioneer Museum** (✉ *436 2nd St.* ☎ *307/3662759*) to get an up-close look at pioneer life in the area.

Eat & Drink: The **Ten Sleep Saloon and Restaurant** (✉ *211 2nd St.* ☎ *307/366–2237* ⊕ *www.facebook.com/TenSleepSaloon*)

is a surprisingly delicious American restaurant in a tiny town with the population of about 200.

BUFFALO

Do: Buffalo is a trove of history and a hospitable little town in the foothills below Big Horn Pass. Here cattle barons who wanted free grazing and homesteaders who wanted to build fences fought it out in the Johnson County Cattle War of 1892. Visit the nearby **Fort Phil Kearny Historic Site** (✉ *528 Wagon Box Rd., Banner* ☎ *307/684–7629* ⊕ *www.wyoparks.wyo.gov*), home to two other major western battles: the Fetterman Fight of 1866 and Wagon Box Fight of 1867. You can also check out the famous **TA Ranch** (✉ *28623 Old Hwy. 87* ☎ *307/684–5833* ⊕ *www.taranch.com*), where you can see bullet holes in the barns where the Johnson County Cattle War ended. Another popular attraction is the **Jim Gatchell Museum** (✉ *100 Fort St.* ☎ *307/684–9331* ⊕ *www.jimgatchell.com*), which explores the frontier history of the region. And a detour an hour-and-a-half south will bring you to the Outlaw Caves, where Butch Cassidy and the Sundance Kid used to hide out.

Eat & Drink: Enjoy western hospitality at the **Occidental Saloon** (✉ *18 N. Main St.* ☎ *307/684–8989* ⊕ *www.occidentalwyoming.com*) and order from the same bar where cowboys, desperados, and western legends gathered, gambled, and drank. Look up for the original bullet holes in the ceiling.

Stay: The 140-year-old **Occidental Hotel** (✉ *10 N. Main St.* ☎ *307/684–0451* ⊕ *www.occidentalwyoming.com*), the oldest operating hotel in the state, has put up many a western legend, including Butch Cassidy and the Sundance Kid, Buffalo Bill, and Calamity Jane. A lot of this hotel remains in its original form, from the embossed ceilings to the antique chairs.

Breakfast: In the Occidental Hotel, the **Busy Bee Cafe** is a real spot that was a regular scene in the fictional western book and TV series, *Longmire*. Order author Craig Johnson's "the usual": eggs, hash browns, toast or biscuit, and a ham steak.

Day 9: Buffalo, WY, to Rapid City, SD

220 miles (3 hours, 20 minutes without traffic and stops)

Hop on Interstate 90 for a simple drive east to South Dakota, where you'll stop by one of the Wild West's most legendary towns and then head to Rapid City, the closest city with a major airport to return your rental car and head home.

ALONG THE WAY

Photo Op: Stop in Sundance, Wyoming, to take a photo next to the *Sundance Kid* statue; the Sundance Kid earned his name after he spent time in jail here for stealing a horse. It's also nice to take a small detour into nature and get a 360-degree panorama view from the old fire tower at Cement Ridge Lookout.

Town: Wind down your trip on a high note in Deadwood, South Dakota, the ultimate Wild West destination made even more famous thanks to the HBO television series of the same name. Walk through the historic downtown, visit the **Mount Moriah Cemetery** (✉ 10 Mt. Moriah Dr. ☎ 605/722–0837 ⊕ www.cityofdead-wood.com), see some of the area's greatest historical treasures in the **Adams Museum** (✉ 54 Sherman St. ☎ 605/578–1714 ⊕ www.deadwoodhistory.com), and take the trolley to the **Adams House** (✉ 22 Van Buren St. ☎ 605/578–3724 ⊕ www.deadwoodhistory.com).

Eat & Drink: Deadwood's spirit lives on at the city's oldest bar, the **Buffalo Bodega Saloon** (✉ 658 Main St. ☎ 605/578–1162 ⊕ www.buffalobodega.com).

RAPID CITY

Do: Rapid City is most famous for its proximity to **Mount Rushmore** (✉ 13000 SD-244, Keystone ☎ 605/574–2523 ⊕ www.nps.gov/moru), the iconic mountain carving with four presidential faces. But that's not the only mountain with a face in this region. See the world's largest in-progress mountain carving of **Crazy Horse** (☎ 605/673–4681 ⊕ www.crazyhorsememorial.com), an Oglala Sioux Indian chief who died in 1877.

Eat & Drink: Grab a hearty dish and beer at the state's first brewpub, **Firehouse Brewing Company** (✉ 610 Main St. ☎ 605/348–1915 ⊕ www.firehousebrewing.com), located in a 1915 firehouse.

Stay: Go glamping with **Under Canvas** (✉ 24342 Ranch Rd., Keystone ☎ 888/496–1148 ⊕ www.undercanvas.com) and their collection of luxury tents near the Black Hills National Forest just outside Rapid City. Sleep under the stars in an original gold-mining settlement, with unbelievable views of Mount Rushmore.

Breakfast: Under Canvas hooks you up with a locally sourced breakfast, or wrap up your trip with a classic American breakfast at the long-running **Colonial House Restaurant and Bar** (✉ 2315 Mt. Rushmore Rd. ☎ 605/342–4640 ⊕ www.colonialhousernb.com).

Chapter 5

THE SOUTHWEST AND TEXAS

WELCOME TO THE SOUTHWEST AND TEXAS

TOP REASONS TO GO

★ **Grand Canyon National Park:** Seeing the Grand Canyon for the first time is an astounding experience. Witness the sandstone canyon walls, pine and fir forests, mesas, plateaus, volcanic features, and the Colorado River far below.

★ **The High Road to Taos:** The scenic drive between Taos and Santa Fe is one of the country's most famous, and most beautiful, routes.

★ **Monument Valley:** This remote corner of Arizona and Utah features famous sandstone buttes that dot the stunning landscape.

★ **Houston:** The biggest city in Texas is home to an incredibly diverse food scene and a world-class art scene.

★ **Fredericksburg:** You'll find plenty of charming small towns in Texas Hill Country, but only one is the region's winemaking center.

1 The Best of Arizona. A true southwestern adventure includes visits to Phoenix, the Grand Canyon, Sedona, and more.

2 The Best of New Mexico. The Land of Enchantment will wow with its desert landscapes and hip cities.

3 Native American Homelands of the Southwest. Explore the parts of Arizona, New Mexico, Utah, and Colorado that were and continue to be most sacred to the Navajo, Paiute, Hope, Ancestral Puebloan, and Acoma Pueblo peoples.

4 Enlightenment and Wellness in the Southwest. A trip that takes you to some of the funkiest and spiritual places in the United States.

5 The Best of Texas. An epic trek that spans Austin, San Antonio, and Houston as well as the state's far-west corners.

6 Texas Hill Country. Between Austin and San Antonio, explore the small towns, wineries, and BBQ joints that beckon tourists.

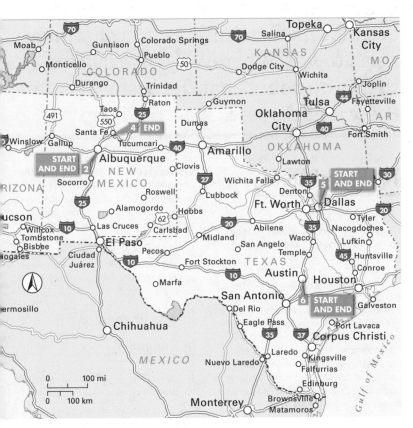

From the red rocks of Arizona to the Gulf Coast of Texas, the southwestern United States is a stunning mash-up of desertscapes, mountains, and charming small towns. Wherever you're headed, there's no doubt that the best way to see these landscapes is via a road trip.

The Best of Arizona

Written by Elise Riley

From the majestic saguaros of Arizona's southern deserts to the red rocks that make northern Arizona a bucket list destination for any photographer, this state is a road-tripper's paradise. While the urban areas of Phoenix and Tucson lure travelers with their luxurious resorts, golf courses, and near-constant sunshine, getting out onto the road will yield delightful discoveries. Grab some sunscreen, sensible footwear, and several bottles of water, and don't forget to download some podcasts—the nation's sixth-largest state awaits your adventurous eyes.

At a Glance

Start: Phoenix, AZ

End: Phoenix, AZ

Miles Traveled: 865 miles

Suggested Duration: 7 days

States Visited: Arizona

Key Sights: Heard Museum; Grand Canyon National Park; Kartchner Caverns State Park; Red Rock State Park; Saguaro National Park

Best Time to Go: This itinerary covers the whole state, which means that extreme temperatures can be an issue for some of your journey. Ideally, spring or fall are best for handling the desert heat of Phoenix and Tucson, while also seeing northern Arizona, without temperatures dipping too cold. Plan on bringing layers and preparing for temperature changes along the route.

Day 1: Phoenix, AZ, to Sedona, AZ

116 miles (2 hours, 30 minutes without traffic and stops)

Your first day is a relatively fast drive, but expect delays on Friday and Sunday, when desert dwellers leave the city en masse. Interstate 17 is easy to access from the Phoenix Sky Harbor International's rental car center, so hit the road and head north. You'll see a lot of cacti on your drive north and gradually—as the temperatures begin to drop—you'll also notice that they begin to disappear. The soil will also start getting redder as you make your way toward Sedona.

ALONG THE WAY

Eat & Drink: Pie is always a worthy diversion, right? The **Rock Springs Café** (✉ *35900 Old Black Canyon Hwy.* ☎ *623/374–5794* ⊕ *www.rocksprings. cafe*) in Black Canyon City is a must-stop for bikers and road-trippers alike.

Roadside Attraction: An experimental community of artists, **Arcosanti** (✉ *13555 S. Cross L Rd., Mayer, AZ* ☎ *928/632–7135* ⊕ *www.arcosanti.org*) remains a bit of a curiosity to visitors, and hasn't changed much in the 50 years since its founding. But this community of artisans crafts some of the most beautiful chimes and bells in the Southwest, which make for wonderful souvenirs.

Attraction: With such stiff competition from the Grand Canyon and Sedona, it's no surprise that **Montezuma Castle National Monument** (✉ *Montezuma Castle Rd., Camp Verde, AZ* ☎ *928/567–3322* ⊕ *www.nps.gov/moca*) rarely makes the must-do lists of Arizona attractions, but it's absolutely worth a visit. This 600-year-old structure was named by explorers who thought it had been erected by the Aztecs. Sinagua Native Americans actually built the five-story, 20-room cliff dwelling. Although you can't visit the cliff dwelling directly (the trail lets you view it from afar), you can still appreciate how impressive it is.

SEDONA

Do: Some people say Sedona simply needs to be breathed in for its mystical energy vortexes. Others visit it to hike its trails and red-rock formations at the spectacular **Red Rocks State Park** (✉ *4050 Red Rock Loop Rd.* ☎ *928/828–6907* ⊕ *www. azstateparks.com*) while still more see it as a marketplace for arts and crafts. No matter your choice, simply open your eyes and take in the town, whether it's from your vehicle, by foot, or in the back of a Jeep on a guided tour. Must-visit spots include Bell Rock, Cathedral Rock, and the Chapel of the Holy Cross.

Eat & Drink: Its artistic vibe allows Sedona to naturally blend with the culinary community. Bars and coffee shops are aplenty, although you'll quickly discover that this town is small. One not-to-be-missed dinner destination is **Elote** (✉ *350 Jordan Rd.* ☎ *928/203–0105* ⊕ *www. elotecafe.com*), which offers a modern twist on Mexican cuisine.

Stay: Sedona might be a tiny town, but the accommodations here run the gamut. Some of the finest resorts in the Southwest are here, like the superb **l'Auberge de Sedona** (✉ *301 Little La.* ☎ *800/905–5745* ⊕ *www.lauberge.com*), but a hotel like **El Portal** (✉ *95 Portal La.* ☎ *800/313–0017* ⊕ *www.elportalsedona. com*) checks just about every wish list. It's within walking distance of much of the area's shopping and nightlife, the staff is incredibly helpful, and the beautiful design includes authentic Tiffany and Roycroft pieces, French doors leading to balconies or a grassy central courtyard, stained-glass windows and ceiling panels, river-rock or tile fireplaces, and huge custom-designed beds.

Breakfast: Head to the **Coffee Pot** (✉ *2050 W. State Rte. 89A* ☎ *928/282–6626* ⊕ *www.coffeepotsedona.com*) to get your fuel for your journey north to the Grand Canyon.

Day 2: Sedona, AZ, to the Grand Canyon

109 miles (2 hours, 15 minutes without traffic and stops)

The best way to reach the Grand Canyon from Sedona is via Flagstaff, which is a relatively short morning drive. While the canyon's North Rim tends to be less crowded and has some underrated gems, the more popular South Rim of the Grand Canyon is the most accessible coming from Sedona.

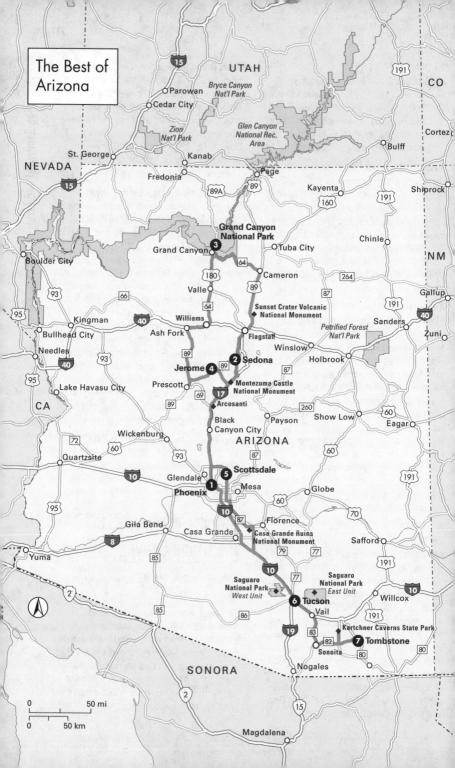

ALONG THE WAY

Town: College-town enthusiasm and high-country charm make Flagstaff one of Arizona's most outdoors-friendly towns. Hiking, skiing, and climbing are local passions, and there are state and national parks to explore.

Eat & Drink: At **Tourist Home All Day Café** (✉ 52 S. San Francisco St. ☎ 928/779–2811 ⊕ www.touristhomecafe.com) in Flagstaff, breakfast burritos, eggs Benedict, salads, and sandwiches all get a modern spin, and the quinoa falafel makes a great burger or vegan "hash-bowl." There's also an alluring selection of daytime cocktails.

Nature: A cinder cone that rises 1,000 feet, **Sunset Crater Volcanic National Monument** (✉ 6082 Sunset Crater Rd. ☎ 928/526–0502 ⊕ www.nps.gov/sucr) was an active volcano 900 years ago. Its final eruption contained iron and sulfur, which give the rim of the crater its glow and thus its name. You can walk around the base, but you can't descend into the huge, fragile cone. The Lava Flow Trail, a half-hour, mile-long, self-guided walk, provides a good view of the evidence of the volcano's fiery power: lava formations and holes in the rock where volcanic gases vented to the surface.

GRAND CANYON NATIONAL PARK

Do: The **Grand Canyon** (☎ 928/638–7888 ⊕ www.nps.gov/grca) is easily the most visited site in Arizona and one of the most popular vacation destinations in the whole country. It's estimated that nearly 6 million people a year make the trek, so anticipate crowds. If possible, that's the best advice about any Grand Canyon–centered vacation: anticipate. Reservations open a year ahead of time for guided hikes, rafting trips, stays at historic hotels, you name it. If an immersive experience is what you desire, plan on preparing at least a year in advance to secure your spot. Luckily, it's certainly possible to visit the park and enjoy it within a single day. While the canyon can be enjoyed via several hikes and bike rides around the rim, the best experience is actually getting into the canyon itself. Your comfort and mobility levels will determine how far you travel into it, but there are several trails to choose from of varying difficulty levels—among the most popular are the Bright Angel Trail (moderate) and the Rim Trail (easy). Most are wide enough to walk comfortably in well-soled shoes. Just remember that the journey back up takes significantly longer and is significantly more difficult.

Eat & Drink: The Grand Canyon isn't exactly a destination for fine dining. But securing a sought-after reservation for a meal at one of the park's historic hotels could make for some beautiful memories. The historic **El Tovar** (✉ 9 Village Loop Dr. ☎ 928/638–2631 ⊕ www.grandcanyonlodges.com) has a dining room that takes reservations 30 days in advance. It's the closest thing to a fine-dining experience you'll find for more than an hour's drive in any direction.

Stay: Historic South Rim hotels such as **Bright Angel Lodge** (✉ 9 Village Loop Dr. ☎ 928/638–2631 ⊕ www.grandcanyonlodges.com) and El Tovar are the most sought after, and with good reason. If rooms are unavailable, accommodations in nearby Tusayan will be spartan, but sufficient. Remember, this leg of the journey is about viewing nature's majesty. Creature comforts take a break for this part.

Breakfast: Since cafés and brunch spots are limited here, it's best to enjoy breakfast at your hotel.

Day 3: The Grand Canyon to Jerome, AZ

150 miles (3 hours without traffic and stops)

Head back south to the charming Verde Valley and its cluster of small towns via AZ-64 and AZ-89. This area of the state is certainly sleepy—it might make Sedona feel like a bustling metropolis—but the slowness of the Verde Valley is the point. Once a bustling area for copper mining, the valley is now known more for wine production, so plan on visiting some local wineries while you're here.

ALONG THE WAY

Town: The mountain town of Williams encompasses a nicely preserved half mile of historic Route 66. Sure, there are kitschy 1950s diners and souvenir shops, along with cowboys who enact staged gunfights on the streets, but you'll also find good restaurants, a few microbreweries, and outdoor activities like hiking, biking, and fishing.

Eat & Drink: For a nice taste of Route 66, enjoy a classic diner meal at **Cruisers Café 66** (⌧ *233 W. Rte. 66* ☎ *928/635–2445* ⊕ *www.cruisers66.com*) in Williams.

JEROME

Do: A good place to base yourself in the Verde Valley, Jerome was once known as the Billion Dollar Copper Camp, but after the last mines closed in 1953, the booming population of 15,000 dwindled to 50 determined souls. Although its population has risen back to almost 500, Jerome still holds on to its "ghost town" designation, and several bed-and-breakfasts and eateries regularly report spirit sightings. It's also home to a bourgeoning art community. Learn about its history at **Jerome State Historic Park** (⌧ *100 Douglas Rd.* ☎ *928/634–5381* www.azstateparks.com), visit its quirky

Extend Your Trip

From Sedona: Enlightenment and Wellness in the Southwest *(Ch. 5)*

From the Grand Canyon: Route 66 *(Ch. 2)*

From Tucson: The Ultimate Wild West Road Trip *(Ch. 4)*

galleries, and enjoy a visit to winery or two in nearby Cottonwood and Cornville, like **Page Springs Cellars** (⌧ *1500 N. Page Springs Rd., Cornville, AZ* ☎ *928/639–3004* ⊕ *www.pagespringcellars.com*).

Eat & Drink: Thankfully, the Verde Valley's emergence as a wine producer also has blossomed a newfound reputation for culinary excellence. You'll be charmed by a meal at **Asylum Restaurant** in Jerome (⌧ *200 Hill St.* ☎ *928/639–3197* ⊕ *www.asylumrestaurant.com*). Or for something a little more casual (and spooky), visit the **Haunted Hamburger** (⌧ *410 Clark St.* ☎ *928/634–0554* ⊕ *www.thehauntedhamburger.com*).

Stay: Jerome's hotels most certainly lean into the town's paranormal reputation. The **Ghost City Inn** (⌧ *541 Main St.* ☎ *928/634–4678* ⊕ *www.ghostcityinn.com*) and **Jerome Grand Hotel** (⌧ *200 Hill St.* ☎ *888/817–6788* ⊕ *www.jeromegrandhotel.net*) both offer comfortable accommodations.

Breakfast: Everyone heads to the **Flatiron** (⌧ *416 Main St.* ☎ *928/634–2733* ⊕ *www.theflatironjerome.com*) for coffee and breakfast in Jerome, and you should, too.

Day 4: Jerome, AZ, to Scottsdale, AZ

120 miles (2 hours without traffic and stops)

To reach southern Arizona, it's best to head back through Phoenix. But luckily, the Phoenix metro area also encompasses the whole of the East Valley, including upscale Scottsdale, which warrants a stop in its own right.

ALONG THE WAY

Eat & Drink: A classic Wild West town, Whiskey Row in Prescott still exudes turn-of-the-20th-century charm. For a lively frontier-style lunch, check out its historic **Palace Restaurant and Saloon** (✉ 120 S. Montezuma St. ☎ 928/541–1996 ⊕ www.whiskeyrowpalace.com). Legend has it that the patrons who saved the Palace's ornately carved 1880s Brunswick bar from a Whiskey Row fire in 1900 continued drinking at it while the row burned across the street. Whatever the case, the bar remains the centerpiece of the beautifully restored turn-of-the-20th-century structure, with a high, pressed-tin ceiling.

SCOTTSDALE

Do: Once an upscale Phoenix sibling, Scottsdale now flies solo as a top American destination. It's a bastion of high-end and specialty shopping, historic sites, elite resorts, restaurants, spas, and golf greens next to desert views. Don't miss the **Scottsdale Museum of Contemporary Art** (✉ 7374 E. 2nd St. ☎ 480/874–4666 ⊕ www.smoca.org) as well as Frank Lloyd Wright's masterpiece **Taliesin West** (✉ 12621 N. Frank Lloyd Wright Blvd. ☎ 480/860–2700 ⊕ www.franklloydwright.org), open for guided tours year-round. If you only have time to golf at one place, make it **Troon North** (✉ 10320 E. Dynamite Blvd. ☎ 480/585–5300 ⊕ www.troonnorthgolf.com) while your top spa destination should be the Wells & Being

Spa at the **Fairmont Scottsdale Princess** (✉ 7575 E. Princess Dr. ☎ 480/585–4848 ⊕ www.fairmont.com).

Eat & Drink: Dine at upscale steakhouse **Bourbon Steak** (✉ 7575 E. Princess Dr. ☎ 480/585–2694 ⊕ www.scottsdaleprincess.com), the hip **Citizen Public House** (✉ 7111 E. 5th Ave. ☎ 480/398–4208 ⊕ www.citizenpublichouse.com), or **The Mission** (✉ 3815 N. Brown Ave. ☎ 480/636–5005 ⊕ www.themissionaz.com) for modern Latin cuisine. Afterwards, head to Old Town Scottsdale, a walkable area filled with bars and restaurants that encourages revelry year-round.

Stay: For a true Scottsdale resort experience, splurge for a night at the **Four Seasons Resort Scottsdale** at Troon North (✉ 10600 E. Crescent Moon Dr. ☎ 480/513–5145 ⊕ www.fourseasons.com). For a slightly more affordable stay, check out the historic **Hotel Valley Ho** in Old Scottsdale (✉ 6850 E. Main St. ☎ 480/376–2600 ⊕ www.hotelvalleyho.com).

Breakfast: Enjoy authentic French crepes, quiches, and tartes at **Chez Vous** (✉ 8787 N. Scottsdale Rd. ☎ 480/443–2575), tucked into a Scottsdale shopping center.

Day 5: Scottsdale, AZ, to Tucson, AZ

113 miles (2 hours without traffic and stops)

The most direct route you'll have in your entire journey, the drive from Scottsdale to Tucson is an easy two-hour trip south.

ALONG THE WAY

Town: The midway point of your drive today is Casa Grande, which gets its name from the **Casa Grande Ruins National Monument** (✉ 1100 W. Ruins Dr. ☎ 520/723–3172 ⊕ www.nps.gov/cagr). The lone place to sight-see on the interstate, this national monument lets you see the ruins of a community dating

The Saguaro cacti that grow in Saguaro National Park are found only in the Sonoran Desert.

back to 1450. Although you can't tour the Great House up close, rangers are available to answer questions and help explain how ancient communities thrived in the desert.

Nature: Before you reach Tucson, be sure to make time to spend a few hours in **Saguaro National Park** (☎ 520/733–5153 ⊕ www.nps.gov/sagu). The park's two distinct sections flank the city of Tucson. Perhaps the most familiar emblem of the Southwest, the towering saguaros are found only in the Sonoran Desert. Saguaro National Park preserves some of the densest stands of these massive cacti. Known for their height (often 50 feet) and arms reaching out in weird configurations, these slow-growing giants can take 15 years to grow a foot high and up to 75 years to grow their first arm. Take a drive on either the Bajana Loop Drive or the Cactus Forest Drive.

TUCSON

Do: Don't think of Tucson as Phoenix's younger sibling. Several degrees cooler than the scorching heat of Phoenix,

Tucson also enjoys a slower pace and quite a different atmosphere. Thanks to its Western roots, university town vibe, and pop-culture connection to film, Tucson is an artist's haven. Don't miss the **Tucson Museum of Art and MOCA** (✉ 265 S. Church Ave. ☎ 520/624–5019 ⊕ www. moca-tucson.org). An hour southwest of the city, it's worth it to make the trek to **Kitt Peak National Observatory** (✉ AZ-386, Sierra Vista, AZ ☎ 520/318–8726 ⊕ www.noao.edu), famous for its ideal conditions for stargazing.

Eat & Drink: Thanks to its proximity to Mexico, Tucson is a town where Mexican food should be enjoyed and savored repeatedly. The oldest restaurant in town is **El Charro Café** (✉ 311 N. Court Ave. ☎ 520/622–1922 ⊕ www.elcharrocafe. com)—legend has it, the cheese crisp and chimichanga originated here. **Rollies Mexican Patio** (✉ 4573 S. 12th Ave. ☎ 520/300–6289 ⊕ www.facebook.com/ rolliestucson) offers a much newer and more modern take on Mexican cuisine. And finally, at some point in your Tucson leg you must visit **Eegee's** (✉ 3360 E. Ajo Way ☎ 520/294–3333 ⊕ www.eegees. com). Some might argue this is just a sandwich shop, but the real draw is the frozen-fruit drinks that have stained the lips of every Tucson child for generations. For decades, there have been promises of opening an Eegee's in Phoenix, but to no avail. Your only opportunity is in Tucson.

Stay: While golf resorts are plentiful in Tucson, this part of Arizona edges out its competition in two very distinct ways: ranching and spas. Visit **Tanque Verde Ranch** (✉ 14301 E. Speedway Blvd. ☎ 520/296–6275 ⊕ www.tanqueverderanch.com) to stay on a working, 640-acre guest ranch. For something a little more mind-body-spirit-oriented, **Canyon Ranch** (✉ 8600 E. Rockcliff Rd. ☎ 520/749–9655 ⊕ www.canyonranch.com) is regarded as one of the premier destination spas in the world. And if you're searching for something a little more middle-of-the-road, the **Arizona Inn** (✉ 2200 E. Elm St. ☎ 520/325–1541 ⊕ www.arizonainn.com) offers something a little more traditional.

Breakfast: Tucked inside the Stevens Home, part of the Tucson Museum of Art and Historic Block, **Café a la C'Art** (✉ 150 N. Main Ave. ☎ 520/628–8533 ⊕ www.cafealacarttucson.com) serves excellent breakfast frittatas, burritos, and pancakes.

Day 6: Tucson, AZ, to Tombstone, AZ

72 miles (1 hour, 15 minutes without traffic and stops)

It's a relatively quick drive out east to Arizona's ultimate Wild West town.

ALONG THE WAY
Nature: Get a workout and explore more than 2 miles of underground caves at **Kartchner Caverns State Park** (✉ 2980 AZ-90, Benson, AZ ☎ 520/586–4100

⊕ www.azstateparks.com), one of the only living cave systems in the world. Reservations are essential.

TOMBSTONE
Do: Channel your inner cowboy in this well-preserved western town with saloons, stagecoach rides, and a courthouse. Visit the actual **O.K. Corral** (✉ 326 E. Allen St. ☎ 520/457–3456 ⊕ www. okcorral.com), learn about Wyatt Earp and the town's history at **Tombstone Courthouse State Historic Park** (✉ 223 E. Toughnut St. ☎ 520/457–3311 ⊕ www. azstateparks.com), and go on a ghost tour of the **Bird Cage Theater** (✉ 535 E. Allen St. ☎ 520/457–3421 ⊕ www.tombstonebirdcage.com).

Eat & Drink: A meal at the historic **Crystal Palace Saloon** (✉ 420 E. Allen St. ☎ 520/457–3611 ⊕ www.crystalpalacesaloon.com) is a must, as is enjoying a drink at **Big Nose Kate's Saloon** (✉ 417 E. Allen St. ☎ 520/457–3107 ⊕ bignosekatestombestone.com).

Stay: Despite the town's touristy reputation, there aren't too many hotels in Tombstone. Your best bet is the **Tombstone Grand Hotel** (✉ 580 W. Randolph Way ☎ 520/457–9507 ⊕ tombstonegrand.com), nestled into a hill just outside town.

Breakfast: Get ready for hearty, generous helpings of classic breakfast dishes at **Longhorn Restaurant** (✉ 501 E. Allen St. ☎ 520/457–3405 ⊕ www.thelonghornrestaurant.com).

Day 7: Tombstone, AZ, to Phoenix, AZ

184 miles (2 hours, 55 miles without traffic and stops)

You'll have to backtrack a bit on your last day of driving as you head back north to finally spend some time in Arizona's bustling capital city.

ALONG THE WAY

Town: Vineyards, tasting rooms, and horse ranches dot the gently rolling hills and grasslands of Sonoita. Key wineries to visit if you have the time include **AZ Hops & Vines** (✉ 3450 AZ-82 ☎ 301/237–6556 ⊕ www.azhopsandvines.com) and **Callaghan Vineyards** (✉ 336 Elgin Rd., Elgin, AZ ☎ 520/455–5322 ⊕ www.callaghanvineyards.com).

Eat & Drink: While in Sonoita, take a lunch break from the wineries with a visit to **Copper Brothel Brewery** (✉ 3112 AZ-83 ☎ 520/405–6721 ⊕ www.copperbrotherbrewery.com); it serves bar fare and craft beer.

PHOENIX

Do: The ultimate playground for adults, Phoenix encourages yearlong activity (yes, even in summer). Golfers flock here and compete for tee times as early as sunrise. If you're anticipating something a little slower, some of the finest spas in the nation call the "Valley of the Sun" home and have menus full of treatments for body and soul. And of course, nothing beats an afternoon poolside under some shade. For a little more culture in your stay in the Valley, consider some of the area's museums. **The Heard** (✉ 2301 N. Central Ave. ☎ 602/252–8840 ⊕ www.heard.org) in Downtown Phoenix offers the finest collection of Native American art in the world.

Eat & Drink: Much more than a town for chips and salsa, Phoenix is earning a reputation as a culinary destination. Consider dining at **Richardson's** (✉ 6335 N. 16th St. ☎ 602/265–5886 ⊕ www.richardsonsnm.com) for New Mexican fare in Central Phoenix or **Kai** (✉ 5594 Wild Horse Pass Blvd. ☎ 602/225–0100 ⊕ www.wildhorsepassresort.com) for Native American-inspired fine dining.

Stay: Choose from hip and unabashedly quirky **Kimpton Hotel Palomar** (✉ 2 E. Jefferson St. ☎ 602/253–6633 ⊕ www.hotelpalomar-phoenix.com) in Downtown Phoenix or the luxurious **Sanctuary on Camelback Mountain Resort & Spa** (✉ 5700 E. McDonald Dr, Paradise Valley, AZ ☎ 855/421–3522 ⊕ www.santuaryoncamelback.com).

Breakfast: Fresh, filling, and simply fantastic, the food at **Matt's Big Breakfast** (✉ 825 N. 1st St. ☎ 602/254–1074), an itty-bitty, retro-cool diner, is a great way to start any day.

The Best of New Mexico

Written by Aimee Heckel

A road trip through New Mexico is a journey through one of the most fascinating regions of the country; this 9-day loop starting and ending in Albuquerque hits many of the state's top attractions. You'll be amazed by the diverse natural wonders here, from underground caves and mineral-rich, natural hot springs to glistening white sand dunes you can "surf" on.

History and culture are also rich here, which you can see as you visit important sites like the Gila Cliff Dwellings and Bandelier National Monument. This trip offers a variety of experiences, from fine dining to hidden gems, and it pays special attention to New Mexico's art offerings. Immerse yourself in Georgia O'Keeffe's artwork, gallery hop in Santa Fe, and find inspiration around every corner.

At a Glance

Start: Albuquerque, NM

End: Albuquerque, NM

Miles Traveled: 1,540 miles

Suggested Duration: 9 days

States Visited: New Mexico

Key Sights: Bandelier National Monument; Carlsbad Caverns National Park; Gila Cliff Dwellings National Monument; High

Road to Taos Scenic Byway; White Sands National Park

Best Time to Go: The weather in New Mexico is great in late spring, early summer, or fall, when temps are in the 70s and 80s. It can get pretty toasty during peak summertime, and it can snow in some regions in the wintertime, although any accumulation tends to melt pretty quickly.

Day 1: Albuquerque, NM, to Roswell, NM

252 miles (4 hours without traffic and stops)

This isn't the quickest route from Albuquerque to Roswell, but it permits a stop in Blue Hole, which is well worth the diversion. You'll take Interstate 40 east to Santa Rosa, then work your way to U.S. 285, which will shoot you to Roswell.

ALONG THE WAY

Town: The Blue Hole of Santa Rosa is a natural wonder that seems to appear like a mirage in the New Mexico desert. This crystal clear blue natural swimming pool is shockingly deep, boasting mysterious underground caves.

Eat & Drink: Get a taste of the historic Route 66 at the **Silver Moon Café** (✉ *2545 Rte. 66* ☎ *575/472–3162* ⊕ *www.facebook.com/silvermoonsantarosa*) in Santa Rosa, an old-school joint founded in the 1950s that feels like a step back in time.

Nature: If New Mexico's dry conditions have you craving more water , head to the **Santa Rosa Lake State Park** (✉ *NM-91* ☎ *575/472–3110* ⊕ *www.emnrd.state.nm.us*). Here you can go swimming, water skiing, and boating; you can even camp overnight if you want to extend your trip.

Essential Listening

The award-winning classic novel *Bless Me, Ultima* by Rudolfo Anaya, is based in the 1940s rural New Mexico (although due to some topics, it may be best for an adults-only road trip).

ROSWELL

Do: A truly underrated city, Roswell boasts its own zoo, a contemporary art museum, and another art museum that centers on southwestern work, but we all know what the city is really famous for: a supposed UFO crash in the 1940s. Learn more about it and tickle your supernatural curiosity at the **International UFO Museum and Research Center** (✉ *114 N. Main St.* ☎ *575/625–9495* ⊕ *www.roswellufomuseum.com*) and the **UFO Spacewalk** (✉ *116 E. 2nd St.* ☎ *575/910–2113* ⊕ *www.facebook.com/roswellufospacewalk*).

Eat & Drink: Part of the charm of Roswell is how hard it's leaned into the UFO kitsch. **Farley's Pub** (✉ *1315 N. Main St.* ☎ *575/627–1100* ⊕ *www.farleyspub.com*), a local chain, is adorned with sci-fi decor (such as posters and a wall of supernatural "heads") and serves casual wood-fired pizza, burgers, and ribs. The real draw here is the novelty décor more than the culinary expertise.

Stay: If you don't mind staying in a chain hotel, the **Holiday Inn Express & Suites Roswell** (✉ *3 Military Heights Dr.* ☎ *575/208–0736* ⊕ *www.ihg.com*) is your best bet for quality, but the inexpensive **Roswell Inn** (✉ *2101 N. Main St.* ☎ *575/623–6050* ⊕ *www.roswellinn.us*) is decorated with alien paraphernalia (it's about a mile from the UFO museum). Or for something even more memorable, look for a quirky vacation rental. Only in

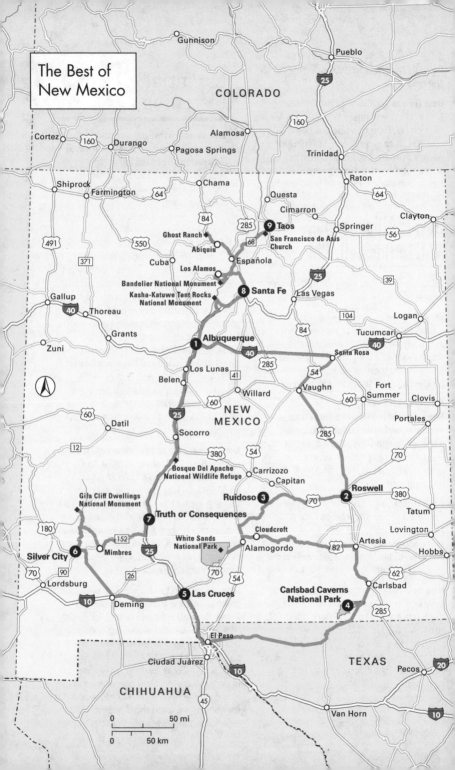

The Best of New Mexico

COLORADO

Gunnison

Pueblo

25

Cortez   160   Durango   Alamosa

Pagosa Springs   Trinidad

Shiprock   Farmington   64   Chama   Raton   64

491   550   Questa   Springer   56   Clayton

Ghost Ranch   285   Cimarron

Abiquiu   68   **9** Taos

371   Cuba   San Francisco de Asís
Church

Los Alamos   Española

Bandelier National Monument   25   39

Kasha-Katuwe Tent Rocks   **8** Santa Fe   Las Vegas
National Monument

Gallup   104   Logan

40   Thoreau   84

Zuni   Grants   **1** Albuquerque   Santa Rosa   Tucumcari   40

40   285   54

Los Lunas   285

Belen   41   Vaughn   Fort   Clovis
Summer

60   Willard   60   Portales

NEW
MEXICO   54

Datil   25   285   70

12   Socorro

380   Bosque Del Apache   54

National Wildlife Refuge   Carrizozo

Gila Cliff Dwellings   Capitan

National Monument   Ruidoso   **3**   70   **2** Roswell   380

7 Truth or Consequences   Tatum

180   152   Cloudcroft   Lovington

Silver City   **6**   Mimbres   25   White Sands   Alamogordo   82   Artesia   Hobbs

70   National Park

90   26   54   62   Carlsbad

Lordsburg   Deming   **5** Las Cruces   Carlsbad Caverns   285

10   National Park   **4**

70

El Paso

TEXAS   Pecos   20

Ciudad Juárez   10

CHIHUAHUA   Van Horn   10

45

0   50 mi

0   50 km

Roswell can you book an Airbnb that's actually a private 186-foot-deep, underground missile silo and a real-life Cold War relic.

Breakfast: The **Cowboy Cafe** (✉ *1120 E. 2nd St.* ☏ *575/622–6363* ⊕ *www.thecowboy. cafe*) plays into the town's extraterrestrial reputation with the Alien Omelet: ham, cheese and green chili, smothered in "Roswell Sauce" and topped with a sunny-side-up egg.

Day 2: Roswell, NM, to Ruidoso, NM

200 miles (3 hours, 45 minutes without traffic and stops)

Although you can get from Roswell to Ruidoso (a straight shot west) in just over an hour, add to your journey with a side trip to the White Sands National Park (a little farther west than Ruidoso).

ALONG THE WAY

Attraction: White Sands National Park
(☏ *575/479–6124* ⊕ *www.nps.gov/ whsa*) is named for its jaw-dropping (you guessed it) white sand dunes, comprised of shimmering, rare white gypsum—it's actually the world's biggest gypsum dunefield. Hike through the dunes, go sand sledding on special saucers, or simply take photos of this majestic site in an eight-mile scenic drive.

Eat & Drink: There are no restaurants in the national park, but nearby Alamogordo is home to authentic and filling Mexican food at **CJ's Si Senor Restaurant** (✉ *2300 N. White Sands Blvd.* ☏ *575/437–7879* ⊕ *www.facebook.com/AlamoSiSenor*). It doesn't get much better than a midday margarita after surfing the sand dunes.

RUIDOSO

Do: Ruidoso is an outdoor lover's paradise, with the nearby **Ski Apache!** resort (✉ *1286 Ski Run Rd., Alto, NM* ☏ *575/464–3600* ⊕ *www.skiapache.com*

Extend Your Trip

From La Cruces or Santa Fe: The Ultimate Wild West Road Trip (*Ch. 4*)

From Santa Fe or Taos: Enlightenment and Wellness in the Southwest (*Ch. 5*)

From Albuquerque: Route 66 (*Ch. 2*); Native American Homelands of the Southwest (*Ch. 5*)

and **Lincoln National Forest** (✉ *3463 Las Palomas Rd.* ☏ *575/434–7200* ⊕ *www. fs.usda.gov*), packed with trails and waterfalls. History comes to life here, too, with 19th-century buildings and an old church.

Eat & Drink: Casa Blanca Restaurant and Bar (✉ *501 Mechem Dr.* ☏ *575/257–2495* ⊕ *www.casablancaruidoso.com*) is known for its mouthwatering fried green chili strips and green chili chicken enchiladas. This local gem has roots in the 1950s, when it started out of a private residence.

Stay: Immerse yourself in mountain life by staying in a cabin; the area has many to choose from. The luxurious **Ruidoso Mountain View Cabins** (✉ *Kirkman Cir.* ☏ *832/305–7368* ⊕ *www.rentruidoso- cabins.com*) stand out for their views and location in the heart of the city, while still maintaining peace and privacy.

Breakfast: For giant portions in an intimate spot with a patio overlooking the river, locals love **Tina's Cafe** (✉ *2825 Sudderth Dr.* ☏ *575/257–8930* ⊕ *www.facebook.com/tinascaferuidoso*). Don't miss the cinnamon rolls with bacon crumbles and maple icing ("pig candy-style") or breakfast tacos stuffed with eggs

Day 3: Ruidoso, NM, to Carlsbad Caverns

170 miles (3 hours without traffic and stops)

The quickest route to Carlsbad Caverns will actually bring you back through Roswell, rather than winding through the Lincoln National Forest. But if you crave different scenery and have the time, head south and take U.S. 82 through the forest and connect back onto U.S. 285 for a slightly longer but scenic detour.

ALONG THE WAY

Town: Located within Lincoln National Forest, the town of Cloudcroft was established in 1898 when the El Paso–Northeastern Railroad crew laid out the route for the Cloud Climbing Railroad. Today, the mountain town has a kitschy, old-West atmosphere that's full of charm, along with countless trails and canyons on its outskirts; the Bridal View Falls and Grand View Trail is a popular one.

Eat & Drink: Superb wood-fired pizzas and craft beer are the draw at friendly, rustic **Cloudcraft Brewing Company** (✉ *1301 Burro Ave.* ☎ *575/682–2337* ⊕ *www.cloudcroft-brewing.com*).

CARLSBAD CAVERNS NATIONAL PARK

Do: Carlsbad Caverns National Park (☎ *575/785–2232* ⊕ *www.nps.gov/cave*) will awe you with its more than 119 caves lined with stalactites; when the sun goes down, you can see thousands of bats fly back into the caves. This is part of one of the best-preserved, exposed fossil reefs in the world, dating back to the Permian Period.

Eat & Drink: The **Yellow Brix Restaurant** (✉ *201 N. Canal St.* ☎ *575/941–2749* ⊕ *www.yellowbrixrestaurant.com*) in Carlsbad serves fresh food all day (from sandwiches and salmon to prime rib and margarita chicken as well as brunch on the weekends) in a historic yellow-brick house built in the 1920s.

Stay: You can't stay in the park, so most visitors make the town of Carlsbad (20 miles away) their home base. Stay in **Fiddler's Inn** (✉ *705 N. Canyon St.* ☎ *575/725–8665* ⊕ *www.fiddlersinnbb.com*), a country-style, family-run guesthouse in a century-old home, complete with a lovely garden and hot tub.

Breakfast: Breakfast is included in your stay at the Fiddler's Inn.

Day 4: Carlsbad Caverns to Las Cruces, NM

200 miles (3 hours without traffic and stops)

Get up early and take the straightforward route to Las Cruces, New Mexico, on U.S. 62 toward El Paso, close to the Mexican border.

ALONG THE WAY

Detour: El Paso, Texas, is a quick, 10-minute detour; this unique city is the intersection of two different countries (the United States and Mexico) and three states (Texas, New Mexico, and the Mexican state of Chihuahua). Visit the **Mission Ysleta** church (✉ *131 S. Zaragoza Rd.* ☎ *915/859–9848* ⊕ *ysletamission.org/about*), established in 1681 by Spanish refugees.

Eat & Drink: Just southwest of Las Cruces, stop by **Luna Rossa Winery & Pizzeria** (✉ *1321 Av. de Mesilla* ☎ *575/526–2484* ⊕ *www.lunarossawinery.com*) in Old Mesilla to check out New Mexico's wine scene. Skeptics are sometimes surprised by the high quality of southern New Mexico wines, with Mimbres Valley's Luna Rossa among the region's most impressive vintners, specializing in estate-grown, mostly Italian and Spanish varietals like Dolcetto and Tempranillo.

Within Carlsbad Caverns National Park, you'll find over 119 caves lined with stalactites.

LAS CRUCES

Do: Las Cruces has jaw-dropping scenery, a rich culture, fascinating history, and outdoor adventures galore. Don't miss the **Branigan Cultural Center** (✉ *501 N. Main St.* ☎ *575/541–2154* ⊕ *www.las-cruces. org*), with an interesting history display and rotating exhibits, housed in a 1935 Pueblo Revival building.

Eat & Drink: Enjoy craft beer with a view over the Mesilla Valley at the **Pecan Grill and Brewery** (✉ *500 S. Telshor Blvd.* ☎ *575/521–1099* ⊕ *www.pecangrill.com*). For dinner, try steak, chicken, or a burger grilled over pecan wood; in New Mexico style, always get your meats smothered in green chili.

Stay: The **Aguirre Spring Campground** (⊕ *www.blm.gov/visit/agu-irre-spring-campground*), perched high in the Organ Mountains, is the place to crash in Las Cruces. Campers get views of the Tularosa Basin and White Sands National Park.

Breakfast: Start the day with coconut French toast, green eggs and ham (that's eggs with basil-pesto sauce), or another unique dish on the patio at **The Shed** (✉ *810 S. Valley Dr.* ☎ *575/525–2636* ⊕ *www.ompctheshed.com*) in Las Cruces. This from-scratch menu always surprises.

Day 5: Las Cruces, NM, to Silver City, NM

155 miles (3 hours without traffic and stops)

This leg is mostly highway and takes you past several small towns as you head into the national forest that contains the famous Gila Cliff Dwellings, where you can explore before settling for the night in Silver City. There are several routes to Gila, but the quickest starts with Interstate 10.

ALONG THE WAY

Nature: The **Gila Cliff Dwellings National Monument** (☎ 575/536–9461 ⊕ www.nps.gov/gicl), located in the Gila National Forest, are mysterious, ancient Mogollon caves high above the canyon floor dating back to the late 1200s and early 1300s. See other artifacts, hike around the monument, and learn about the Mogollon, the wilderness and surrounding region in the museum.

Eat & Drink: Carmen's (✉ 113 Main St. ☎ 575/533–6999) in the tiny hamlet of Reserve is a great little place to stop on NM-12 in the northwestern reaches of the Gila National Forest, thanks to its spicy enchiladas and chicken-fried steak.

SILVER CITY

Do: Silver City began as a tough and lawless mining camp in 1870, and struggled for a long time to become a more respectable— and permanent—settlement. Henry McCarty spent part of his boyhood here, perhaps learning some of the ruthlessness that led to his later infamy under his nickname—Billy the Kid. Other mining towns in the area sparked briefly and then died, but Silver City eventually flourished and became the area's most populated city. Learn more about its history at the **Silver City Museum** (✉ 312 W. Broadway St. ☎ 575/538–5921 ⊕ www.silvercitymuseum.org).

Eat & Drink: Enjoy farm-to-table fare on the patio at **Revel** (✉ 304 N. Bullard St. ☎ 575/388–4920 ⊕ www.eatdrinkrevel.com). The casual restaurant is located downtown and serves from-scratch comfort food with locally sourced ingredients, like a fried green tomato–and–braised pork belly sandwich or the Gila River Ranch lamb Bolognese.

Stay: You can find a handful of lodging near the national forest, but a fun choice is to stay at the rustic **Gila Hot Springs and Campground** (☎ 575/536–9944 ⊕ www.gilahotspringscampground.com) in Silver City. Relax in the natural hot springs,

surrounded by the Gila Wilderness, just four miles from the national monument.

Breakfast: Diane's Restaurant and Parlor (✉ 510 N. Bullard St. ☎ 575/538–8722 ⊕ www.dianesrestaurant.com) is run by an award-winning chef. The bakery side features more than 20 different types of bread, European pastries, and more. Get upscale food in the restaurant and casual, lighter fare and drinks at the parlor.

Day 6: Silver City, NM, to Truth or Consequences, NM

88 miles (2 hours without traffic and stops)

It's just over a two-hour drive from Silver City to Truth or Consequences on NM-152.

ALONG THE WAY

Photo Op: Stop in Mimbres, New Mexico, near mile marker 4 on NM-35 N, to visit a world-famous archaeological site. Explore 1,000-year-old ruins of the Mimbres people at the **Mimbres Culture Heritage Site** (✉ 12 Sage Dr. ☎ 575/536–3333 ⊕ www.mimbrescultureheritagesite.org) and several 19th-century buildings.

TRUTH OR CONSEQUENCES

Do: Truth or Consequences is home to several naturally occurring, mineral-filled hot spring pools, filled from an ancient rift in the Rio Grande. These thermal springs are some of the most mineral-rich in the country and are touted for their health benefits (not to mention a soothing break on a long road trip).

Eat & Drink: A longstanding local staple is **Los Arcos Steak and Lobster** (✉ 1400 N. Date St. ☎ 575/894–6200 ⊕ www.losarcossteakhouse.com), which has been serving hand-cut steaks, seafood, and more since 1970. Enjoy dinner and a glass of wine on the patio, all while supporting a business run by a Truth or Consequences native.

Stay: The **Sierra Grande Lodge and Spa** (✉ *501 McAdoo St.* ☎ *877/288–7637* ⊕ *www.sierragrandelodge.com*) stands out for offering a full-service spa built above geothermal springs; private indoor and outdoor hot springs; locally crafted, organic skin care in each room; and optional adventurous experiences, like a hot air balloon ride.

Breakfast: The lodge's hot breakfast is included in your stay.

Day 7: Truth or Consequences, NM, to Santa Fe, NM

210 miles (3 hours without traffic and stops)

The route from Truth or Consequences to Santa Fe couldn't be simpler: just cruise up Interstate 25. It's also worth it to make a stop at the Bosque Del Apache National Wildlife Refuge. The refuge is about 45 minutes north of Truth or Consequences, and the bird-watching you'll find there is unmatched.

ALONG THE WAY

Attraction: Bosque Del Apache National Wildlife Refuge (✉ *1001 NM-1, San Antonio, NM* ☎ *575/835–1828* ⊕ *www.fws. gov*) is famous for the dramatic migration of sandhill cranes in the fall. These 30,000 acres between the Chupadera and San Pascual mountains are an important stop year-round for all kinds of other birds, too.

SANTA FE

Do: Santa Fe is an art and culture paradise. Stroll through the charming downtown and its historic Plaza, where several restaurants, creative shops, and famous markets line the crooked streets. Canyon Road is lined with many art galleries while there are several can't-miss museums like the **Georgia O'Keeffe Museum** (✉ *217 Johnson St.* ☎ *505/946–1000*

⊕ *www.okeeffemuseum.org*) and the **Museum of Indian Arts and Culture** (✉ *710 Camino Lejo* ☎ *505/476–1269* ⊕ *www. indianartsandculture.org*) located throughout the city. If you have time, don't miss **Meow Wolf** (✉ *1352 Rufina Cir.* ☎ *505/395–6369* ⊕ *www.meowwolf. com*), a madly imaginative and completely immersive 22,000-square-foot collaborative art installation.

Eat & Drink: Santa Fe's foodie scene is as great as its art offerings, but a classic is **The Shed** (✉ *113½ E. Palace Ave.* ☎ *505/982–9030* ⊕ *www.sfshed.com*), located in an ancient adobe building downtown; it's been a local favorite since the 1950s. You must try the locally grown red chile enchiladas with a (strong) margarita.

Stay: The **Rosewood Inn of the Anasazi** (✉ *113 Washington Ave.* ☎ *505/988–3030* ⊕ *www.rosewoodhotels.com*) is ideally located right on the Plaza (assuming you want to be in the heart of the action). This high-end, boutique hotel features incredible artwork throughout and top-notch service.

Breakfast: Start the day with breakfast rellenos on the patio at the **Tune-Up Café** (✉ *1115 Hickox St.* ☎ *505/983–7060* ⊕ *www.tuneupsantafe.com*); they also serve a mean brunch on the weekends.

Day 8: Santa Fe, NM, to Taos, NM

125 miles (2 hours, 45 minutes without traffic and stops)

After a stop at Bandelier National Monument, prepare for one of the most beautiful drives in the country. The 56-mile High Road to Taos Scenic Byway cuts through the Sangre de Cristo Mountains until you reach Taos. While the nonstop drive is just over 2½ hours, take your time to stop and explore the charming villages and farms along the way.

ALONG THE WAY

Detour: It takes less than an hour to drive the 40 or so miles from Santa Fe to **Bandelier National Monument** (✉ 15 Entrance Rd., Los Alamos, NM ☎ 505/672–3861 ⊕ www.nps.gov/band). Here you can see the preserved homes of Ancestral Puebloans. A hike along the main loop should take about an hour and a half, and you can add on additional trails for a deeper immersion in the history and scenery.

Eat & Drink: Fill up with a farm-to-table dish like a bacon-wrapped fillet or creative salad at a local favorite, the **Blue Window Bistro** (✉ 1789 Central Ave. ☎ 505/662–6305 ⊕ www.labluewindowbistro.com) in nearby Los Alamos. Don't let its unpretentious location in a shopping center fool you; Blue Window has been popular for more than 40 years for a reason. Los Alamos is also an interesting place that deserves further exploration; it was the headquarters for scientists in charge of·the Manhattan Project, which led to the development of the atomic bomb.

Photo Op: Don't miss the most photographed church in New Mexico, the **San Francisco de Asis Church** (✉ 60 St. Francis Plaza ☎ 575/758–2754 ⊕ www.sfranchos.org), located in Rancho de Taos just outside Taos itself.

TAOS

Do: Taos provides a slow and scenic escape bursting with art, outdoor activities, and nature galore (including skiing in the winter). While here, pay a visit to the **Taos Pueblo** (✉ 120 Veterans Hwy. ☎ 575/758–1028 ⊕ www.taospueblo.com), the biggest group of multistory Pueblo dwellings in the country, and take a walk on the Rio Grande Gorge Bridge, where you can see the mighty river flow 650 feet underfoot.

Eat & Drink: Enjoy a charming meal at the **Love Apple** (✉ 803 Paseo Del Pueblo Norte ☎ 575/751–0050 ⊕ www.theloveapple.net), a farm-to-table restaurant

housed in a former chapel. Tables are limited, but if you can land one, ask about the sweet-corn tamales with red-chili mole.

Stay: This B&B is a bit away from the action, but you'll appreciate the peaceful atmosphere at the **Adobe and Pines Inn** (✉ 4107 NM-68 ☎ 575/751–0947 ⊕ www.adobepines.com). The details here add up: Native American artifacts, mountain views, a historic adobe building, kiva fireplaces, and stunning gardens.

Breakfast: The **Farmhouse Cafe and Bakery** (✉ 1405 Paseo Del Pueblo Norte, El Prado ☎ 575/758–5683 ⊕ www.farmhousetaos.com) serves tasty huevos rancheros and freshly baked cinnamon rolls with spectacular views.

Day 9: Taos, NM, to Albuquerque, NM

130 miles (2 hours, 30 minutes without traffic and stops)

This fast highway drive will bring you back onto busy I–25 and past Santa Fe, back to Albuquerque, but not before passing a few more key sights in the Santa Fe/Taos area.

ALONG THE WAY

Town: The tiny, very traditional Hispanic village of Abiquiu was originally home to freed *genizaros*, indigenous and mixed-race enslaved people who were forced to work in Spanish, Mexican, and American households well into the 1880s. Today it's best known as the location of the **Georgia O'Keeffe Home and Studio** (✉ 21120 U.S. 84 ☎ 505/685–4016 ⊕ www.okeeffemuseum.org), where the famed artist spent the last 50 years of her life, inspired by the region's stunning vistas and landscapes. You can also visit nearby **Ghost Ranch** (✉ 280 Private Dr. 1708, U.S. 84 ☎ 505/685–1000 ⊕ www.ghostranch.org); O'Keeffe once lived on a

The Taos Pueblo are the largest group of multistory Pubelo dwellings in the country.

small parcel of the 22,000-acre dude and cattle ranch that today serves as a retreat center that offers O'Keeffe-focused tours to the public.

Eat & Drink: The inviting, art-filled restaurant at the **Abiquiú Inn** (✉ *21120 U.S. 84* ☎ *505/685–4378* ⊕ *www.abiquiuinn.com*) serves tasty New Mexican and American fare. Be sure to peek inside the adjoining art gallery featuring local work, and take a stroll through the graceful gardens.

Nature: Try to also pay a visit to **Kasha-Katuwe Tent Rocks National Monument** (✉ *NM-22, off I-25, Cochiti Pueblo* ☎ *505/331–6259* ⊕ *www.blm.gov/visit/kktr*), located just southwest of Santa Fe. The sandstone rock formations are a visual marvel, resembling stacked tents in a stark, water- and wind-eroded box canyon. The monument is managed in cooperation with Cochiti Pueblo, whose people call the area Kasha-Katuwe. It's an excellent choice for a day hike.

ALBUQUERQUE

Do: Albuquerque is adventure-packed, from water activities on the Rio Grande to vibrant art galleries. One surprise is the **Turquoise Museum** (✉ *400 2nd St. SW* ☎ *505/433–3684* ⊕ *www.turquoisemuseum.com*), where you can see some of the world's rarest pieces of turquoise and learn all about the stone; it's located in a mysterious Gothic castle that seems so out of place in this southwestern city. Another highlight is a visit to the **Petroglyph National Monumen**t (✉ *Western Trail NW* ☎ *505/899–0205* ⊕ *www.nps. gov*). Beneath the stumps of five extinct volcanoes, this park encompasses more than 25,000 ancient Native American rock drawings inscribed on the 17-mile-long West Mesa escarpment overlooking the Rio Grande Valley.

Eat & Drink: **Campo** at Los Poblanos (✉ *4803 Rio Grande Blvd. NW* ☎ *505/338–1615* ⊕ *www.lospoblanos. com*) is an ultralocal, field-to-fork restaurant located on an organic farm in the Rio Grande River Valley. The incredible menu is built around its own farm harvest and produce from other local purveyors. Say hello to the friendly barn cat who likes to walk guests to their car.

Stay: A newer gem in Albuquerque is the chic and luxurious **Hotel Chaco** (✉ *2000 Bellamah Ave. NW* ☎ *505/246–9989* ⊕ *www.hotelchaco.com*) right in Old Town, with a rooftop restaurant and bar, outdoor pool, and spacious rooms. It's located across from the hip Sawmill District, New Mexico's first food hall.

Breakfast: The **Grove Cafe and Market** (✉ *600 Central Ave. SE* ☎ *505/248–9800* ⊕ *www.thegrovecafemarket.com*) is all about supporting local farmers and products. Try sweet potato hash outside on the enclosed patio in this colorful, popular restaurant.

Native American Homelands of the Southwest

Written by Shoshi Parks

From New Mexico's 19 Pueblos to the land of Navajo, the American Southwest is a patchwork of Native Nations. For thousands of years, these Indigenous communities have called the high desert home, and remnants of early cities and ceremonial centers still exist at sites like New Mexico's Chaco Culture National Historical Park and Colorado's Mesa Verde National Park. Despite the hardships of desert life and the aftermath of conquest and colonization, the Native American people of the Southwest haven't disappeared—far from it. From Albuquerque to Tuba City, Native people continue to carry on the traditions of their ancestors and forge new paths of self-expression and self-determination. Winding through five states, this epic itinerary is a breathtaking trip through the natural splendor of the American Southwest and the cultural heritage of its resilient Native American communities.

At a Glance

Start: Las Vegas, NV

End: Las Vegas, NV

Miles Traveled: 1,643 miles

Suggested Duration: 9 days

States Visited: Arizona, Colorado, Nevada, New Mexico, Utah

Key Sights: Acoma Pueblo; Grand Canyon-Parashant National Monument; Mesa Verde National Park; Monument Valley; Navajo Nation

Best Time to Go: This trip can be done any time of year, but for the best weather for camping and hiking, visit in spring or fall.

Day 1: Las Vegas, NV, to Page, AZ

280 miles (4 hours, 40 minutes without traffic and stops)

The Las Vegas sprawl melts into an endless painted desert of towering cliffs and terraces on the first day's drive toward Lake Powell and Page, Arizona.

ALONG THE WAY

Town: The quirky town of Kanab, Utah, on the outskirts of Grand Staircase-Escalante National Monument was once a popular filming location for Westernss and television series featuring celebrities from Clint Eastwood to the Rat Pack. See leftover sets from Kanab's Hollywood heyday at the **Little Hollywood Movie Museum** (✉ *297 W. Center St.* ☎ *435/644–5337* ⊕ *www. littlehollywoodmuseum.org*).

Eat & Drink: While in Kanab, grab a bite at the eclectic restaurant and art gallery, the **Rocking V Cafe** (✉ *97 W. Center St.* ☎ *435/644–8001* ⊕ *www.rockingvcafe.com*). They've got a huge menu

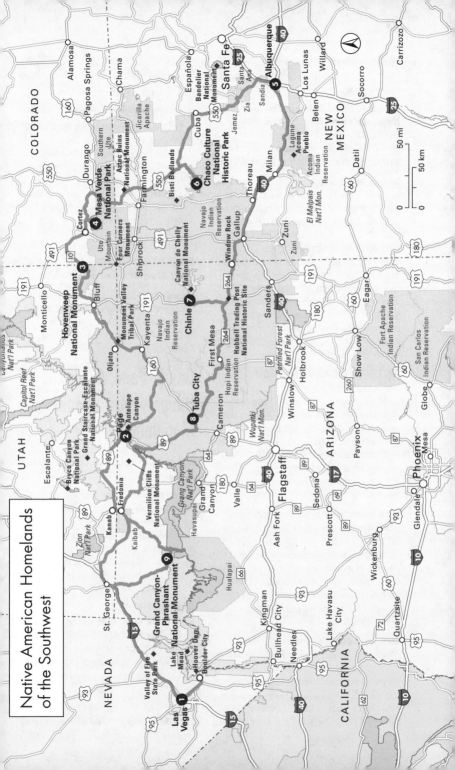

Native American Homelands of the Southwest

of sandwiches, salads, steaks, and more, all made with organic and natural ingredients.

Nature: At **Grand Staircase-Escalante National Monument** (✉ 745 U.S. 89 ☎ 435/644–1300 ⊕ www.blm.gov), a million acres of colorful cliffs and paper-thin slot canyons are waiting to be explored.

Detour: About an hour-and-a-half north of Kanab, the hoodoos grow in dense stands that fill the natural amphitheater at **Bryce Canyon National Park** (☎ 435/834–5322 ⊕ www.nps.gov/brca), part of the traditional tribal territory of the Paiute. The effect is otherworldly, a landscape not found anywhere else on the planet. During long winters, Bryce Canyon's views are at their most spectacular and some of its snow-covered trails can be traversed via snowshoe. Summertime hikes will get you up close to the massive stone formations.

ANTELOPE CANYON AND PAGE

Do: Possibly the world's most spectacular geological slots, the Navajo have long cherished **Antelope Canyon** (⊕ www.ante-lopecanyon.com). The tribe runs popular 90-minute tours through its rocky twists and turns several times a day. Advanced reservations are recommended. Low-key Page makes a good base for exploring the canyon.

Eat & Drink: Dig into brisket, ribs, and pulled pork at **Big John's Texas Barbeque** (✉ 153 S. Lake Powell Blvd. ☎ 928/645–3300 ⊕ www.bigjohnstexasbbq.com). Page isn't exactly known for its nightlife, but you'll find a good selection of beers on tap at the **State 48 Tavern** (✉ 614 N. Navajo Dr. ☎ 928/645–1912 ⊕ www.state48tavern.com).

Stay: The **Lake Powell Motel** (✉ 750 S. Navajo Dr. ☎ 480/452–9895 ⊕ www.lake-powellmotel.net) has both budget rooms and fully equipped apartments for a quiet night of rest. Get a few more amenities, including a pool, hotel bar, and views of beautiful Lake Powell at the **Lake Powell**

Resort (✉ 100 Lake Shore Dr. ☎ 888/896–3829 ⊕ www.lakepowell.com).

Breakfast: Order a hearty homestyle breakfast at local favorite, the **Ranch House Grille** (✉ 819 N. Navajo Dr. ☎ 928/645–1420 ⊕ www.ranch-house-grille.com).

Day 2: Page, AZ, to Hovenweep National Monument

204 miles (3 hours, 15 minutes without stops)

Green returns to the landscape as you travel over a rocky desert plateau and into the outskirts of southwestern Colorado's piñon forests where the skies are some of the darkest in the world. A detour will take you on one of the most incredible drives in the United States through Monument Valley.

ALONG THE WAY

Eat & Drink: A hip little adobe eatery, the **Amigo Cafe** (✉ U.S. 163 ☎ 928/697–8448 ⊕ www.amigocafekayenta.com) in Kayenta, Arizona, specializes in Native American and southwestern favorites like Navajo tacos and green chili cheeseburgers.

Detour: Just 20 minutes north of Kayenta, Monument Valley's towering rock formations at **Monument Valley Tribal Park** (☎ *435/727–5870* ⊕ *www.navajonationparks.org*) rise like spires from the hallowed ground on the Navajo Nation.

Photo Op: The only place in the United States where you can stand in four states at the same time, **Four Corners Monument** (✉ *597 NM-597, Teec Nos Pos, AZ* ☎ *928/206–2540* ⊕ *www.navajonationparks.org*) isn't thrilling, but you can't beat the photo op.

HOVENWEEP NATIONAL MONUMENT

Do: Archaeologists are still working to explain the exact use of the unusual 800-year-old stone towers and "castles" at **Hovenweep National Monument** (⊕ *www.nps.gov/hove*). Walk among them, then settle in for an evening of stargazing at this certified International Dark Sky Park.

Eat & Drink: There are no stores or restaurants for miles. Come prepared with your own food and drinks.

Stay: Hovenweep's 31-site year-round campground is first-come, first-served.

Breakfast: Break your fast at the campsite or make a beeline for **Silver Bean** (✉ *410 W. Main St.* ☎ *970/946–4404* ⊕ *www.facebook.com/thesilverbean*), an hour's drive toward your next destination in Cortez, Colorado. This adorable coffee shop in a retro airstream has hot and cold drinks, pastries, and breakfast burritos to eat on the artificial "lawn" or take away.

Day 3: Hovenweep National Monument to Mesa Verde

76 miles (1 hour, 45 minutes without traffic and stops)

It's about an hour through bucolic ranchlands and vineyards to Cortez, Colorado, before the climb to Mesa Verde begins. Even though the park's entrance is just ten miles from town, the drive up to the cliff dwellings is long, isolated, and quite beautiful.

ALONG THE WAY

Town: Colorado's gateway to the Southwest, the small town of Cortez has wineries, breweries, and the fascinating **Cortez Cultural Center** (✉ *25 N. Market St.* ☎ *970/565–1151* ⊕ *www.cortezculturalcenter.org*), with exhibits on Ancestral Puebloan history and art by local and Native artisans. In summer, Native American dance performances take place regularly.

Eat & Drink: Relax with apps and a pint of pale ale from local brewery collective, **WildEdge** (✉ *111 N. Market St.* ☎ *970/565–9445* ⊕ *www.wildedgebrewing.com*), in Cortez.

MESA VERDE NATIONAL PARK

Do: Take a self-guided tour of **Mesa Verde National Park** (☎ *970/529–4465* ⊕ *www.nps.gov/meve*) along the six-mile Mesa Top Loop Road which offers views of 12 of Mesa Verde's most famous cliff dwellings, including the Spruce Tree House. These cliff dwellings were once home to the Ancestral Puebloan people, who left behind over 4,000 archaeological sites. Go inside the precarious Balcony House, Cliff Palace, or Long House on regular guided tours. Advance recommendations are highly recommended.

Eat & Drink: Wild game, fresh fish, and organic produce are on the menu at the nationally recognized **Metate Room** (✉ *34879 U.S. 160* ☎ *970/529–4422* ⊕ *www.visitmesaverde.com*) within the park, open May through September.

Stay: Perched on a shoulder of the Mesa Verde, the **Far View Lodge** (✉ *Mile Marker 15, Mesa Verde National Park* ☎ *800/449–2288* ⊕ *www.visitmesaverde.com*) gives guests a magnificent panorama view of the Four Corners that stretches as far as the eye can see. There are no TVs in the rooms, just private balconies and unbeatable views; it's open May through October.

Breakfast: Take coffee to go or sit down for a full breakfast at the **Far View Terrace Café** on the lodge's first floor.

Day 4: Mesa Verde to Albuquerque, NM

266 miles (4 hours, 45 minutes without traffic and stops)

A southerly drive through the Pueblo lands of New Mexico takes you to the state capital, Albuquerque.

ALONG THE WAY

Town: The small town of Aztec is home to **Aztec Ruins National Monument** (✉ *725 Ruins Rd.* ☎ *505/334–6174* ⊕ *www.nps.gov/azru*), a massive Puebloan great house and UNESCO World Heritage site that's over 900 years old. Explore the three-story structure built by the ancestors of New Mexico's 19 living Pueblo communities then walk the Old Spanish Trail into town.

Eat & Drink: For lunch in Aztec, pair a wood-fired pie or calzone with a frosty pint at **550 Brewing & Pizza Parlor** (✉ *119 N. Main Ave.* ☎ *505/636–2261* ⊕ *www.550brew.com*).

Detour: For more of the Southwest's ancient splendor, take a 30-minute detour (25 miles each way) to **Bandelier National Monument** (✉ *15 Entrance Rd., Los Alamos, NM* ☎ *505/672–3861* ⊕ *www.nps.gov/band*) where an Ancestral Puebloan community lived, worked, and worshiped for around 350 years. Their descendants still remain, but were relocated to the banks of the Rio Grande in the 16th century following a long period of intense drought and social unrest.

ALBUQUERQUE

Do: Stroll through the streets of Albuquerque's charming Old Town or get a bird's-eye view of the city on the **Sandia Peak Tramway** (✉ *30 Tramway Rd. NE* ☎ *505/856–1532* ⊕ *www.sandiapeak.*

Extend Your Trip

From Mesa Verde: The Best of Colorado *(Ch. 4)*

From Albuquerque: Route 66 *(Ch. 2)*; The Best of New Mexico *(Ch. 5)*

From Las Vegas: The Loneliest Road in Nevada: Route 50 *(Ch. 4)*

com). In October, keep your eyes trained on the skies above, when more than 500 colorful hot-air balloons take flight during the city's weeklong **International Balloon Fiesta** (✉ *4401 Alameda Blvd. NE* ☎ *505/821–1000* ⊕ *www.balloonfiesta.com*). In Isleta Pueblo on the northern edge of town, you can see one of the country's oldest churches, a gorgeous adobe mission parish established in 1622.

Eat & Drink: Tucked inside the **Indian Pueblo Cultural Center** (✉ *2401 12th St. NW* ☎ *505/843–7270* ⊕ *www.indianpueblo.org*), **Indian Pueblo Kitchen** is a fine-dining restaurant helmed by Santa Clara Pueblo-Odawa chef Ray Naranjo and serves sophisticated pre- and post-contact Native dishes. Afterward, grab a southwestern-inspired pint at the rustic-modern **Bow & Arrow Brewing Company** (✉ *608 McKnight Ave. NW* ☎ *505/247–9800* ⊕ *www.bowandarrowbrewing.com*).

Stay: One of Route 66's first motels, the restored **El Vado Motel** (✉ *2500 Central Ave. SW* ☎ *505/361–1667* ⊕ *www.elvadoabq.com*) has a charming take on classic American road-trip culture complete with midcentury furnishings, local artwork, and a pool. On the northern edge of Albuquerque, the Sandia Pueblo operates the slick **Sandia Resort and Casino** (30 Rainbow Rd. 505/796–7500 www.sandiacasino.com) with a golf course, spa, and a gorgeous view of the mountains.

Breakfast: Pull up a chair at **The Farmacy** (✉ 3718 Central Ave. SE ☏ 505/227–0330 ⊕ www.facebook.com/farmacyabq), a chic modern café with high-octane coffee and breakfast favorites like waffles and biscuits and gravy.

Day 5: Albuquerque, NM, to Chaco Canyon National Historic Park

161 miles (3 hours without traffic and stops)

Head out of the city to Acoma, the oldest continuously occupied community in the United States, then back into the high desert for a visit to thousand-year-old Chaco, once the Southwest's largest city.

ALONG THE WAY

Town: The stunning mesa-top village of Acoma has survived drought, conquest, and colonization to earn the title of the oldest community in the United States. Members of the Acoma Pueblo still live here, thousands of feet in the sky, with no running water. The community's church and cemetery are its crown jewels, especially at Christmas when the paths are lit with candles for a midnight ceremony. The village can only be entered on guided tours, which leave from the **Sky City Cultural Center** (✉ Haaku Rd., Acoma Pueblo, NM ☏ 505/552–7861 ⊕ www.acomaskycity.org) multiple times daily.

Eat & Drink: Don't be fooled by its location across from a truck stop. The no-frills **Spicy Bite** (✉ 1203–1299 Motel Dr. ☏ 505/356–0044) in Milan serves fresh and authentic Indian food.

CHACO CANYON NATIONAL HISTORIC PARK

Do: Explore the ruins of the once-great city of **Chaco Canyon** (☏ 505/786–7014 ⊕ www.nps.gov/chcu), which dominated the Southwest between 850 and 1250

C.E. Walk or drive the canyon loop, take a guided tour of Pueblo Bonito, or lace up your boots for a backcountry hike to some of Chaco's more remote sites.

Eat & Drink: There is no food in the park, but you can snag a cold drink and firewood in the visitor's center.

Stay: The **Gallo Campground** (⊕ www. recreation.gov reservations necessary) is open year-round, and after dark, the night skies put on a spectacular display in this International Dark Sky Park.

Breakfast: This one's on you. Be sure to bring enough food and water for morning breakfast and coffee.

Day 6: Chaco Canyon National Historic Park to Chinle, AZ

170 miles (3 hours, 15 minutes without traffic and stops)

Travel through the Navajo Nation, stopping at the government seat at Window Rock, then on to the small town of Chinle, Arizona, which abuts the rugged, rocky Canyon de Chelly.

ALONG THE WAY

Detour: The bizarre rock formations of the Bisti Badlands form an otherworldly landscape of desolation and solitude. Find them northwest of Chaco Canyon, a 40-mile drive into the desert (about 1 hour and 12 minutes each way).

Eat & Drink: At the down-home roadside diner **Jerry's Cafe** (✉ 406 W. Coal Ave. ☏ 505/722–6775 ⊕ www.jerryscafenm. org) in Gallup, NM, dive into steaming plates of stuffed sopapillas and chiles rellenos.

Town: Named for the near-perfect circle shaped by snow and rain in the red cliff behind the Navajo Nation's tribal headquarters, Window Rock has both an interesting museum and a moving memorial to World War II's Navajo Code Talkers. At the **Ch'ihootso Indian Market Place** (⊠ *AZ-264* ☎ *928/871–4698* ⊕ *www.ch-ihootso-indian-edan.io*) vendors sell everything from utilitarian goods to rugs and jewelry.

Shop: In operation for over 140 years, the **Hubbell Trading Post National Historic Site** (⊠ *1/2 AZ-264, Ganado, AZ* ⊕ *www.nps.gov/hutr*) is a working trading post with exquisite handcrafted goods from local Navajo, Hopi, and Pueblo artisans. Stop by the visitor center to learn more about Hubbell's history, and take a walk around the grounds to visit its heritage Ganado sheep and Navajo hogans.

CHINLE

Do: With its painted rock formations and endless views, the **Canyon de Chelly National Monument** (☎ *928/674–5500* ⊕ *www.nps.gov/cach*) next door to Chinle is a geological wonder punctuated with ancient ruins. Take a self-guided or ranger-led hike or a scenic drive to the canyon's 10 overlooks.

Eat & Drink: The **Junction Restaurant** (⊠ *100 E. Indian Rte. 102* ☎ *928/674–8443* ⊕ *www.junctionrestaurantaz.com*), adjacent to Chinle's Best Western, serves some of this small town's best food with a menu that includes Navajo tacos and posole. Keep in mind that by Navajo law, alcohol cannot be bought, sold, or transported onto tribal lands.

Stay: The **Thunderbird Lodge** (⊠ *Canyon De Chelly* ☎ *928/674–5842* ⊕ *www.thunderbirdlodge.com*), owned and operated by the Navajo Nation, is a charming historic hotel with dependably clean and comfortable accommodations.

Breakfast: The Thunderbird Lodge Cafeteria next door to the lodge is inside a trading post more than a century old and has a wide selection of breakfast dishes, including supertasty blue-corn pancakes.

Day 7: Chinle, AZ, to Tuba City, AZ

132 miles (2 hours, 30 minutes without traffic and stops)

Cross the Navajo border and enter the heart of the Hopi Nation, where a drive along the Hopi Arts Trail offers a glimpse of the artistic heritage and craftsmanship of a legendary Native community.

ALONG THE WAY

Eat & Drink: Get a taste of tribal specialties like Hopi hot beef and lamb stew at the **Hopi Cultural Center Restaurant** (⊠ *AZ-264, Second Mesa, AZ* ☎ *928/734–2401* ⊕ *www.hopiculturalcenter.com*), located in the Hopi Cultural Center in Second Mesa.

Shop: Hopi artists are famed for their elaborately woven baskets, pottery, and silverwork, but these are just some of the gorgeous pieces you'll find for sale along the **Hopi Arts Trail** (⊕ *www.hopiartstrail.com*) stretching between First Mesa and Tuba City.

TUBA CITY

Do: Several museums in Tuba City illuminate the Navajo experience, from stories of creation at the **Navajo Interactive Museum** (⊠ *10 Main St.* ☎ *928/283–5441* ⊕ *www.discovernavajo.com*) to the role of the Navajo language in the Allied victory in World War II at the **Navajo Code Talkers Museum** (⊠ *10 Main St.* ☎ *928/283–5441* ⊕ *www.discovernavajo.com*). Take home a piece of Native artistry from the **Tuba City Trading Post** (⊠ *10 N. Main St.* ☎ *928/283-5441* ⊕ *www.discovernavajo.com*), which has been a working hub of commerce since 1870.

Eat & Drink: Tuba City doesn't have much in the way of food outside of fast food restaurants. **Pizza Edge** (⊠ *36 U.S. 160* ☎ *928/283–5938* ⊕ *www.pizzaedge.com*), a regional pizza chain with pizza, calzones, wings, and subs, is arguably the best of the bunch.

Stay: The **Moenkopi Legacy Inn & Suites** (⌧ *1 Legacy Lane* ☎ *928/283–4500* ⊕ *www.experiencehopi.com*), operated by the Hopi Nation, is a pleasant lodge accented with Native artwork and crafts-manship on the western edge of Hopi land. Amenities include a fitness center, pool, and a kiva garden.

Breakfast: At **Hogan Espresso** (⌧ *10 Main St.* ☎ *928/283–4545*), a cute little coffee shop with both indoor and outdoor seat-ing, the coffee, pastries, and other fare are well worth a morning stop.

Day 8: Tuba City, AZ, to Grand Canyon-Parashant

233 miles (4 hours without stops)

Today you'll take a northern route through the painted cliffs and high elevation deserts of northern Arizona to reach Grand Canyon-Parashant National Monument.

ALONG THE WAY

Nature: The route to Grand Canyon-Par-ashant passes right through **Vermilion Cliffs National Monument** (⊕ *www.blm. gov*), home of The Wave, a stunning geo-logical formation of crimson-and-gold that ripples across the Arizona desert. Enter the park's lottery online to score a permit to the site.

Town: The tiny town of Fredonia is worth a quick stop before heading into the rugged wilderness of Grand Canyon-Par-ashant. On North Main Street, check out the small but well curated **Red Pueblo Museum** (⌧ *U.S. 89* ☎ *928/643–7777* ⊕ *www.facebook.com/redpueblomu-seum*), which features everything from ancient Pueblo artifacts to an authentic pioneer-era log cabin.

GRAND CANYON-PARASHANT NATIONAL MONUMENT

Do: Less crowded than its national park counterpart, the views, hiking trails, and scenic drives at **Grand Canyon-Parashant National Monument** (☎ *435/688–3200* ⊕ *www.nps.gov*) in the traditional tribal lands of the Hualapai are no less spectacular.

Eat & Drink: Stock up on food and water in advance. There are no stores or potable water available within the monument.

Stay: Grand Canyon-Parashant has no developed campsites, but free backcoun-try camping is allowed throughout the park, including on the rim of the Grand Canyon. If you want to camp below the rim, you'll need a permit in advance.

Breakfast: At Grand Canyon-Parashant, the only breakfast for miles is the one you cook yourself.

Day 9: Grand Canyon-Parashant to Las Vegas, NV

131 miles (2 hours, 15 minutes without traffic or stops)

Get your last look at the desert as you roll into the mighty city of Las Vegas and the end of the road.

ALONG THE WAY

Town: Quaint Boulder City, Nevada, is dotted with a small downtown histor-ic district and neighborhoods, small businesses, and parks (and no casinos—this is the only town in Nevada where gambling is illegal). Over the hill from town, enormous Hoover Dam blocks the Colorado River as it enters Black Canyon. Backed up behind the dam is incongruous, deep-blue Lake Mead, the focal point of water-based recreation for southern Nevada and northwestern Arizo-na, and the major water supplier to seven southwestern states. The lake is ringed by miles of rugged desert country.

Nature: The breathtaking wonderland known as **Valley of Fire** (✉ 29450 Valley of Fire Hwy., Overton, NV ☎ 702/397–2088 ⊕ www.parks.nv.gov), with its red sandstone outcroppings, petrified logs, petroglyphs, and hiking trails, is along the northern reach of Lake Mead.

Eat & Drink: The **Coffee Cup** (✉ 512 Nevada Way ☎ 702/294–0517 ⊕ www.worldfamouscoffeecup.com) is a bustling breakfast-and-lunch diner that's been featured on Food Network's *Diners, Drive-Ins, and Dives.* Tourists line up on weekends for the quintessential small-town diner experience, complete with newspaper-strewn counter seating and the owners' family photos and water-sports memorabilia on the walls. It delivers on the food front, too, with giant portions of favorites such as huevos rancheros, biscuits and gravy, and barbecue sandwiches

LAS VEGAS

Do: You won't find much in the way of Indigenous culture in the City of Sin, but you will find a whole lot of debauchery. Head to big name casinos on the strip like the **Bellagio** (✉ 3600 S. Las Vegas Blvd. ☎ 888/987–6667 ⊕ www.bellagio.mgmresorts.com), **The Venetian** (✉ 3355 S. Las Vegas Blvd. ☎ 702/414–1000 ⊕ www.venetian.com), and **Mandalay Bay** (✉ 3950 Las Vegas Blvd. S ☎ 877/632–7800 ⊕ www.mandalaybay.mgmresorts.com) or make your way downtown for a more vintage experience at **The Neon Museum** (✉ 770 Las Vegas Blvd. N ☎ 702/387–6366 ⊕ www.neonmuseum.org), a graveyard for the city's retired neon signs.

Eat & Drink: Splurge on Cantonese delicacies at **Mott 32** (✉ 3325 S. Las Vegas Blvd. ☎ 702/607–3232 ⊕ www.venetian.com) in The Venetian or keep things casual at the **Park MGM's Crack Shack** (✉ 3770 S. Las Vegas Blvd. ☎ 702/820–5991 ⊕ www.crackshack.com), a fried-chicken and sandwich joint with a fine-dining pedigree. The truly hungry will find what they're looking for at the **Wynn Las Vegas** (✉ 3131 S. Las Vegas Blvd. ☎ 702/770–7000 ⊕ www.wynnlasvegas.com) and **The Mirage** (✉ 3400 S. Las Vegas Blvd. ☎ 800/374–9000 ⊕ www.mirage.mgmresorts.com), which have some of the best buffets in town. Off the strip, get a swanky drink at the **Downtown Cocktail Room** (✉ 111 S. Las Vegas Blvd. ☎ 702/880–3696 ⊕ www.downtowncocktailroom.com) or a cold one at famed Rat Pack hangout **Atomic Liquors** (✉ 917 E. Fremont St. ☎ 702/982–3000 ⊕ www.atomic.vegas).

Stay: Get the resort experience at the **ARIA** (✉ 3730 S. Las Vegas Blvd. ☎ 866/359–7757 ⊕ www.aria.mgmresorts.com), which has a soaring modernist aesthetic, three outdoor pools, a spa, and the Jewel nightclub. Downtown, the classic **Golden Nugget Hotel & Casino** (✉ 129 E. Fremont St. ☎ 702/385–7111 ⊕ www.goldennugget.com) has 2,400 well-appointed guest rooms and a three-story waterslide that twists and turns through a 200,000-gallon shark tank.

Breakfast: Recharge with one of the breakfast sandwiches at **Eggslut** (✉ The Boulevard Tower, 3708 Las Vegas Blvd. S ☎ 702/698–2344 ⊕ www.cosmopolitanlasvegas.com) or indulge in a French-inspired bistro-style brunch at **Bouchon** (✉ 3355 S. Las Vegas Blvd. ☎ 702/414–6203 ⊕ www.thomaskeller.com).

Enlightenment and Wellness in the Southwest

Written by Margot Bigg

The American Southwest has long been popular with spiritual seekers and those looking for healing and relaxation, and this itinerary will give you a whirlwind look at some of the best spiritual spots and wellness retreats the region has to offer. From New Age-y towns like Ojai and Sedona to mystical national parks that exude otherworldly vibes, you'll experience hot springs, energy vortexes, and famous ashrams, all guaranteeing you'll find at least some relaxation if not true spiritual transcendence.

At a Glance

Start: Los Angeles, CA

End: Santa Fe, NM

Miles Traveled: 1,340 miles

Suggested Duration: 8 days

States Visited: Arizona, California, New Mexico

Key Sights: Arcosanti; Cathedral Rock; El Santuario de Chimayó; Joshua Tree National Park; Petrified Forest National Park

Best Time to Go: This trip is doable year-round, but the weather in the region is at its most pleasant in the springtime and autumn. Summers can get very hot.

Day 1: Los Angeles, CA, to Ojai, CA

83 miles (1 hour, 30 minutes without traffic and stops)

From Los Angeles, take Highway 101 north to exit 70B. From here, it's about nine miles up Highway 33 to the bohemian town of Ojai, known for its hot springs and spiritual centers.

ALONG THE WAY

Town: Just north of Santa Monica, the beach town of Malibu boasts 21 miles of sandy ocean beach plus plenty of cute boutiques, cafés, and restaurants. Popular attractions include the sea caves at **El Matador State Beach** (✉ *32350 Pacific Coast Hwy.* ☎ *818/880–0363* ⊕ *www.*

californiabeaches.com) and the surfer-favorite Zuma Beach.

Eat & Drink: Overlooking the Pacific Ocean, **Malibu Farm** restaurant (✉ *23000 Pacific Coast Hwy.* ☎ *310/456–8850* ⊕ *www.malibu-farm.com*) offers a huge, eclectic menu with a solid selection of light seafood dishes alongside tacos, salads, and pizzas. Many of the items here are vegan and/or gluten-free, including some of the desserts.

OJAI

Do: Ojai's biggest draw is perhaps its easy access to natural hot springs. The best known is **Ecotopia** (✉ *2566 Matilija Canyon Rd.* ☎ *805/272–0011* ⊕ *www. ojaiecotopia.com*), a series of five pools located on the banks of the Matilija River. Art lovers will appreciate the **Beatrice Wood Center for the Arts** (✉ *8585 Ojai Rd.* ☎ *805/646–3381* ⊕ *www.beatricewood. com*), while those with an interest in spirituality or Eastern philosophy may want to stop by the **Krishnamurti Educational Center** (✉ *1098 McAndrew Rd.* ☎ *805/646–2726* ⊕ *www.kfa.org*, which frequently holds classes based on the teachings of Indian philosopher Jiddu Krishnamurti.

Eat & Drink: One of the most romantic options in town, the **Ranch House** (✉ *102 Besant Rd.* ☎ *805/646–2360* ⊕ *www. theranchhouse.com*) features New American fine dining and a solid wine menu, served in an enchanting tucked-away garden.

Stay: The twin properties collectively known as the **Iguana Inns of Ojai** (✉ *11794 N. Ventura Ave.* ☎ *805/646–5277* ⊕ *www.blueiguanainn.com*) do a great job of encapsulating the town's whimsical vibes, with art-filled rooms and beautiful gardens. Another quiet option, the **Ojai Retreat and Inn** (✉ *160 Besant Rd.* ☎ *805/646–2536* ⊕ *www.ojairetreat. com*) offers B&B-style rooms and cottages on a peaceful hilltop overlooking the Ojai Valley.

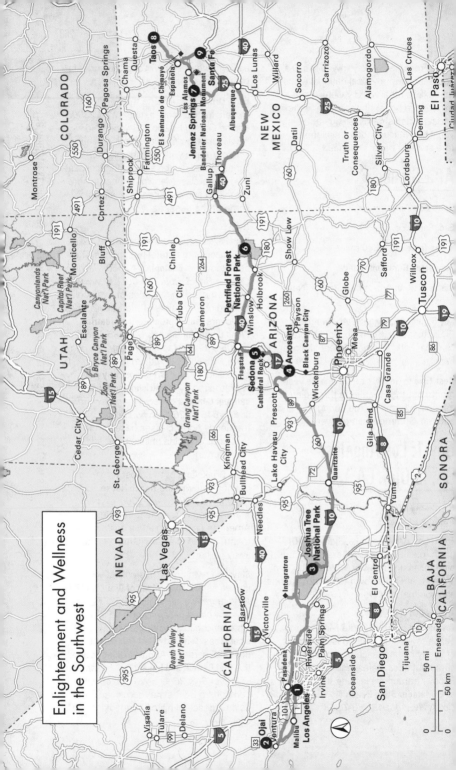

Enlightenment and Wellness in the Southwest

Breakfast: Start your day off at **LO>E. Social Cafe** (✉ 205 N. Signal St. ☎ 805/646–1540 ⊕ www.lovesocialcafe.com), a friendly spot with a large open-air patio and a great breakfast menu offering scrambles, breakfast tacos, baked goods, and all sorts of fancy coffee drinks.

Day 2: Ojai, CA, to Joshua Tree

212 miles (3 hours, 30 minutes without traffic and stops)

Head back toward Ventura, and then east toward Pasadena and on to funky Joshua Tree National Park, checking out some unusual local attractions along the way.

ALONG THE WAY

Town: Pasadena is a good spot to take a break, with its historic, walkable downtown area full of shops and restaurants, many housed in historic buildings. If you have a couple of hours to spare, you may want to check out the **Huntington Library, Art Collections, and Botanical Gardens** (✉ 1151 Oxford Rd. ☎ 626/405–2100 ⊕ www.huntington.org), with its extensive collection of European art and reference materials plus its 16 sprawling themed gardens full of plant life from around the world.

Eat & Drink: Right in Old Town Pasadena, the local branch of L.A.'s beloved **Sage Vegan Bistro** (✉ 1700 Sunset Blvd. ☎ 213/989–1718 ⊕ www.sageveganbistro.com) offers plant-based takes on popular dishes from around the world, plus sandwiches, salads, tacos, and pizzas. Around 90% of the produce here comes from local organic farmers and many of the items are gluten- and nut-free.

Roadside Attraction: Built in the late 1950s by UFOlogist George Van Tassel based on a blueprint he claimed came from extraterrestrial sources, the **Integratron** (✉ 2477 Belfield Blvd., Landers, CA ☎ 760/364–3126 ⊕ www.integratron.

com) is a 38-foot-high white dome that resembles an observatory, albeit one constructed entirely of wood and fiberglass. Today the structure is used primarily for sound bath healings and other special events.

JOSHUA TREE NATIONAL PARK

Do: This area's main draw is **Joshua Tree National Park** (☎ 760/367–5500 ⊕ www.nps.gov/jotr), located at the convergence of the Mojave and Colorado deserts. The 1,235-mile expanse of wilderness is characterized by its otherworldly rock formations popular with rock climbers and its abundance of yucca brevifolia plants, commonly referred to as Joshua trees. The area around the park has drawn free thinkers for decades, as evidenced by some of the more unusual area attractions. The Frank Lloyd Wright–designed **Joshua Tree Retreat Center** (✉ 59700 Twentynine Palms Hwy. ☎ 760/365–8371 ⊕ www.jtrcc.org) is one such spot, and offers spiritual teachings and retreats. Also worth checking out is the **Sky Village Swap Meet** (✉ 7028 Theatre Rd. ☎ 760/365–2104 ⊕ www.skyvillageswapmeet.com) in Yucca Valley, which offers a café and a weekend market, and is home to the Crystal Cave, a whimsical construction built with structural foam and filled with multihue crystals.

Eat & Drink: Housed in an old diner in Yucca Valley, north of Joshua Tree, **La Copine** (✉ 848 Old Woman Springs Rd. ☎ 760/289–8537 ⊕ www.lacopinekitchen.com) offers eclectic fine dining with a menu that changes by the season.

Stay: While you may just want to camp right in the national park, you certainly don't have to—there are plenty of lovely places to stay not far from the park entrance. For a rustic experience with a few more creature comforts, the **Castle House Estate** (✉ 64278 E. Broadway ☎ 323/337–7180 ⊕ www.thecastlehouseestate.com) offers a few shaded campsites as well as fully furnished yurts, a container home, a vintage RV, and a couple of "guard towers," two-story rooms designed to look like castle turrets. If you're a fan of design, consider booking a night at the **Lautner Compound** (✉ *67710 San Antonio St.* ☎ *760/832–5288* ⊕ *www.thelautner. com*), a collection of four vacation rentals designed back in 1947 by famed American architect John Lautner.

Breakfast: Get your first meal of the day in at the **Natural Sisters Cafe** (✉ *61695 Twentynine Palms Hwy.* ☎ *760/366–3600* ⊕ *www.naturalsisterscafe.com*), which offers biscuits and gravy, tofu scrambles, egg dishes, and a variety of healthy smoothies and made-to-order juices.

Day 3: Joshua Tree to Arcosanti, AZ

356 miles (5 hours, 30 minutes without traffic and stops)

Head south to Palm Springs and hop on Interstate 10 until you reach the outskirts of Phoenix before heading north to the township of Arcosanti, which was started in the 1970s as an architectural experiment designed to address urban sprawl.

ALONG THE WAY

Town: Although it's best known for its annual gem-and-mineral show, the largest such conference on earth, Quartzite is a fun stopover year-round, thanks to a few quirky shops and plenty of hiking opportunities. For an unusual bit of history, stop by the **Hi Jolly Monument** (✉ *W. Elsie La. and Hi Jolly La.*). This pyramidical gravestone with a camel silhouette on top is the final resting place of Hadji Ali (nicknamed "Hi Jolly"), a camel driver who came to the United States in the mid-19th century as part of the U.S. Army's Camel Corps.

Eat & Drink: Dating back to 1918, **Rock Springs Café** (✉ *35900 Old Black Canyon Hwy.* ☎ *623/374–5794* ⊕ *www.rock-springs.cafe*) in Black Canyon City is the

Extend Your Trip

From Joshua Tree: The Best of Southern California; California's National Parks *(Ch. 3)*

From Sedona: The Best of Arizona *(Ch. 5)*

From Taos or Santa Fe: The Best of New Mexico *(Ch. 5)*

oldest independent restaurant in Arizona. Here you can chow down on all sorts of comfort food, from burgers to barbecued chicken, but the real draw is the wide variety of pies, from all-American apple pie to chocolate cherry cream varieties.

Photo Op: Just north of Black Canyon City, the Sunset Point rest area offers well-maintained bathrooms and drinking fountains along with a gigantic sundial and great western views out over the desert.

ARCOSANTI

Do: Along with a gift shop full of their signature bells and an outdoor swimming pool, the experimental township **Arcosanti** (✉ *13555 S. Cross L Rd., Mayer, AZ* ☎ *928/632–7135* ⊕ *www.arcosanti. org*) offers one-hour guided tours of the site. They start with a short video in the gift shop/reception center and continue through the grounds; some add an extra hour to focus on architecture.

Eat & Drink: There's a simple café just downstairs from the visitor center, which offers buffet-style meals most days of the week; there are plenty of options for special diets available.

Stay: Arcosanti offers a range of on-site lodging, including simple guest rooms with private or shared bathrooms and a couple of suites that can be reserved via Airbnb. There's also a campsite, and dorm space is available for groups.

Breakfast: A buffet breakfast with toast, tea, coffee, cereal, and usually a hot dish is included with your stay at Arcosanti.

Day 4: Arcosanti, AZ, to Sedona, AZ

53 miles (1 hour without traffic and stops)

Continue north up the I–17 until you reach AZ-179, which will take you right to Sedona, known in New Age communities for its energy vortexes.

ALONG THE WAY

Nature: One of the most recognizable geological formations in the Sedona area is the 12,000-foot-high Cathedral Rock, which is also a great place to take a hike; just wear solid shoes, as the trail can be slippery.

Eat & Drink: Chow down on Mexican fare at Sedona's colorful **Elote Café** (✉ *350 Jordan Rd.* ☎ *928/203–0105* ⊕ *www. elotecafe.com*), named for Mexico's celebrated street corn.

SEDONA

Do: Sedona offers tons to do, from relaxing in one of the ample local spas to browsing crystal shops to taking a guided tour of the area's alleged vortexes. The cliffside Chapel of the Holy Cross is also a must-visit, both for its serene atmosphere and its unusual architecture.

Eat & Drink: At **Mariposa** (✉ *700 AZ-89A* ☎ *928/862–4444* ⊕ *www.mariposase-dona.com*), a Latin-inspired restaurant in one of Sedona's most picturesque spots, you can enjoy tapas, empanadas, and grilled selections with your Red Rocks view.

Stay: For a romantic splurge, it doesn't get more Sedona-chic than **L'Auberge de Sedona** (✉ *301 Little La.* ☎ *800/905–5745*

⊕ *www.lauberge.com*). If your budget is more modest, **Desert Quail Inn** (✉ *6626 AZ-179* ☎ *928/284–1433* ⊕ *www. desertquailinn.com*) is bare-bones but well-maintained.

Breakfast: Its whimsical garden seating is enough to make **Chocolatree** (✉ *1595 AZ-89A* ☎ *928/282–2997* ⊕ *www. chocolatree.com*) a perfect way to start your day, but luckily they also have an extensive menu of gourmet health food, smoothies, espresso drinks, and, if you're in a brunchier mood, cocktails.

Day 5: Sedona, AZ, to Petrified Forest

137 miles (2 hours, 30 minutes without traffic and stops)

Head north along 89A to Flagstaff before joining the Interstate 40, which will take you to the ancient Petrified National Forest.

ALONG THE WAY

Town: Just a short drive from Sedona, Flagstaff is a good place to grab food or supplies. Take a little extra time to wander the Historic Downtown District right on Route 66 or head up to the **Lowell Observatory** (✉ *1400 W. Mars Hill Rd.* ☎ *928/774–3358* ⊕ *www.lowell.edu*) on the western side of town.

Eat & Drink: Sit down for some hearty English fare at the **Cornish Pasty Co.** (✉ *26 S. San Francisco St.* ☎ *928/440–5196* ⊕ *www.cornishpastryco.com*), a pub res-taurant featuring church pew bench–style seating and extensive draft beer options.

PETRIFIED FOREST NATIONAL PARK

Do: Within **Petrified Forest National Park** (☎ *928/524–6228* ⊕ *www.nps.gov/pefo*), petrified logs scattered about a vast pink-hued lunar-like landscape resemble a fairy-tale forest turned to stone. You can easily spend days exploring the park,

Sedona's Cathedral Rock is one of the most recognizable geological formations in the area.

but if you're short on time, make sure to at least spend some time at the Canyon de Chelly (☎ 928/674–5500 ⊕ www.nps.gov/cach), home to more than 7,000 archaeological sites. You may even spot an ancient petroglyph.

Eat & Drink: If you don't want to eat at your hotel, you can save time and money by grabbing a meal at the **Painted Desert Visitor Center Cafeteria** (✉ 1 Park Rd. ☎ 928/524–6228 ⊕ www.nps.gov/pefo).

Stay: Historic **La Posada Hotel** (✉ 303 E. 2nd St., Winslow, AZ ☎ 928/289–4366 ⊕ www.laposada.org) features old-fashioned rooms that exude a 1930s vibe; there's also an excellent on-site restaurant.

Breakfast: Stick around La Posada's **Turquoise Room** (✉ 303 E. 2nd St., Winslow, AZ ☎ 928/289–2888 ⊕ www.theturquoiseroom.net) for breakfast; you can grab your morning meal here.

Day 6: Petrified Forest to Jemez Springs, NM

308 miles (4 hour, 45 minutes without traffic and stops)

Continue along Interstate 40 until Albuquerque, then make your way north to Jemez Springs, known for its mineral-rich thermal waters.

ALONG THE WAY

Town: New Mexico's biggest city is a great spot to stop and stretch your legs or spend an afternoon. Attractions worth stopping for in Albuquerque include the **Petroglyph National Monument** (✉ Western Trail NW ☎ 505/899–0205 ⊕ www.nps.gov), which is among the largest petroglyph sites on the continent, as well as the **Indian Pueblo Cultural Center** (✉ 2401 12th St. NW ☎ 505/843–7270 ⊕ www.indianpueblo.org), an expansive museum committed to preserving Pueblo culture and history.

Eat & Drink: Set in the Edo neighborhood, the **Grove Cafe & Market** (✉ *600 Central Ave. SE* ☎ *505/248–9800* ⊕ *www. thegrovecafemarket.com*) offers a large all-day breakfast menu plus bistro-style salads and sandwiches at lunchtime. Many of the ingredients are sourced from local organic farmers. They also offer French macarons every Friday through Sunday.

JEMEZ SPRINGS

Do: This tiny settlement is a great place to break up your journey for the night; it offers easy access to a mix of developed and wild hot springs. The village's **Bodhi Manda Zen Center** (✉ *1 Bodhi Dr.* ☎ *575/829–3854* ⊕ *www.bmzc.org*) attracts spiritual seekers and offers daily meditations for Zen practitioners as well as occasional retreats. Jemez Springs is also home to the historic **Jemez Historic Site** (✉ *18160 NM-4* ☎ *575/829–3530* ⊕ *www.nmhistoricsites.org*), which features the remains of a 15th-century pueblo and a 17th-century Franciscan mission.

Eat & Drink: Although **Nomad Mountain Café** (✉ *38710 NM-126* ☎ *575/829–3197* ⊕ *nomad-mountain-cafe.business.site*) is best known for its pizza, they also serve everything from salads to prime rib.

Stay: If you'd like to devote some time to soaking, **Jemez Hot Springs** (✉ *40 Abousleman Loop* ☎ *575/829–9175* ⊕ *www. jemezhotsprings.com*) is a good option. While you can come here as a day visitor, booking a stay at one of the on-site cottages is also an option.

Breakfast: Grab a cup of joe and a pastry at **Highway 4 Coffee** (✉ *17502 NM-4* ☎ *575/829–4655*) before you continue on toward Taos.

Day 7: Jemez Springs, NM, to Taos, NM

121 miles (2 hours, 45 minutes without traffic and stops)

Travel via state highways northeast toward Taos, taking a detour to explore Bandelier National Monument along the way.

ALONG THE WAY

Town: The atomic bomb was originally developed in little Los Alamos; learn more about it (and about the region overall) at the **Los Alamos History Museum** (✉ *1050 Bathtub Row* ☎ *505/662–4493* ⊕ *www.losalamoshistory.org*).

Eat & Drink: One of the oldest spots in Los Alamos, **Blue Window Bistro** (✉ *1789 Central Ave.* ☎ *505/662–6305* ⊕ *www. labluewindowbistro.com*) boasts an extensive lunch menu with everything from tacos to calamari.

Detour: A short drive from Los Alamos, **Bandelier National Monument** (✉ *15 Entrance Rd. Los Alamos, NM* ☎ *505/672–3861* ⊕ *www.nps.gov/band*) is worth visiting for its ancient Pueblo dwellings, some dating back almost 1,000 years. Highlights include a visitor's center with displays of ancient artifacts as well as a network of well-maintained trails; the 1.2-mile-long Main Loop Trail will give you access to many of the monument's most important archaeological sites. Ladders are provided for those who want to climb up into a few of the ancient dwellings.

TAOS

Do: The most important site in Taos is **Taos Pueblo** (✉ *120 Veterans Hwy.* ☎ *575/758–1028* ⊕ *www.taospueblo. com*), a UNESCO World Heritage site and one of the oldest continuously inhabited spots in North America, with a history spanning over a millennia. Other not-to-miss spots include the Rio Grande

Gorge Bridge, which offers fantastic views of the basalt canyon below, and the **San Francisco de Asís Mission Church** (✉ *60 St. Francis Plaza* ☎ *575/758–2754* ⊕ *www.sfranchos.org*), an 1816 adobe church that has provided inspiration for the likes of Ansel Adams and Georgia O'Keeffe. If you'd like to unwind at the end of your day, consider attending a meditation session at **Mindful Frontiers** ☎ *575/770–3683* (⊕ *mindfulfrontiers. net/community*) or booking an Ayurvedic treatment at **Auromesa** (✉ *101 Coyote Loop* ☎ *575/776–4263* ⊕ *www.auromesa.com*), both in the Taos suburb of Arroyo Hondo.

Eat & Drink: Housed in a renovated 19th-century chapel, **The Love Apple** (✉ *803 Paseo Del Pueblo Norte* ☎ *575/751–0050* ⊕ *www.theloveapple.net*) offers a seasonal menu with ingredients sourced primarily from local farms. All the meals here are made from scratch, and there are plenty of options for people with dietary restrictions.

Stay: Right in the heart of Taos, overlooking its historic plaza, the luxurious **La Fonda** on the Plaza (✉ *108 S. Plaza* ☎ *575/758-2211* ⊕ *www.lafondataos. com*) features elegant rooms full of local touches and great views from its rooftop terrace restaurant. For an off-the-grid (and offbeat) alternative to staying in town, head a few miles north to the **Earthship Global Visitor Center** (✉ *2 Earthship Way, Tres Piedras, NM* ☎ *575/751–0462* ⊕ *www.earthshopbiotecture. com*), where you can spend the night in a cottage built primarily from upcycled tires and rammed earth, designed to have minimal impact on its natural surroundings. Self-guided tours are also available for day visitors.

Breakfast: Begin your day at **Bent Street Cafe & Delhi** (✉ *120 Bent St.* ☎ *575/758-5787* ⊕ *www.bentstreetdeli.com*), which serves a southwestern-inspired breakfast menu all day plus a smattering of freshly baked pastries.

Day 8: Taos, NM, to Santa Fe, NM

70 miles (1 hour, 30 minutes without traffic and stops)

Make your way south to Santa Fe, stopping at the Hacienda de Guru Ram Das along the way.

ALONG THE WAY

Town: Stop in Espanola to visit the **Hacienda de Guru Ram Das** (✉ *1A Ram Das Guru Pl., Española, NM* ☎ *505/753–6341* ⊕ *www.espanolaashram.com*), run by followers of Sikh Yogi Bhajan (of Yogi Tea fame). A variety of spiritual programs and educational activities are available; check the website for timings and availability. Also check out **Santuario de Chimayó** (✉ *1445 NM-503* ☎ *505/351–4889* ⊕ *www.elsantuariodechimayo.us*).

Eat & Drink: Sit down for New Mexico-style tacos, fajitas, and—of course—sopaipillas at the **Sopaipilla Factory** (✉ *7 W. Gutierrez* ☎ *505/455–2855* ⊕ *www.sopaipillafactoryrestaurant.com*) in northern Santa Fe. This laid-back local favorite in the town of Pojoaque offers abundant outdoor seating and a large vegetarian menu. All dishes are served with a free sopaipilla and a side of honey or honey butter.

Detour: El Santuario de Chimayó is an adobe church that's often touted as the Lourdes of the Southwest. According to legend, a light appeared here on Good Friday in 1810—a hole was subsequently dug and a crucifix was unearthed. The dirt from the hole is believed to have healing properties to this day.

SANTA FE

Do: Santa Fe has a ton of things to see and do, from marveling at the ancient sacred artifacts at the **Museum of International Folk Art** (✉ *706 Camino Lejo, on Museum Hill, Lejo* ☎ *505/476–1200* ⊕ *www.moifa.org*) to wandering through the historic downtown, filled with whimsical shops and independent art galleries. Make sure to leave yourself plenty of time to immerse yourself in the fantastical at **Meow Wolf** (✉ *1352 Rufina Cir.* ☎ *505/395–6369* ⊕ *www.meowwolf. com*), a multimedia art attraction full of kaleidoscopic, interactive exhibits that put a creatively offbeat spin on reality.

Eat & Drink: If you're in the mood for a healthy, tasty meal, make a beeline to **Ras Rody's Jamaican Vegan** (✉ *1312 Agua Fria St.* ☎ *505/385–3011* ⊕ *www.rasrody. com*) food cart, just a few minutes' drive from downtown. Here you'll find an ever-changing menu of richly spiced Jamaican cuisine, fresh fruit juices, and delicious desserts.

Stay: Few properties compare to the **Inn of the Five Graces** (✉ *150 E. De Vargas St.* ☎ *505/992–0957* ⊕ *www.fivegraces.com*), an elegant adobe-style luxury hotel with warm, sumptuous rooms and a mosaic-filled spa offering a range of Ayurveda-inspired massages and treatments. If your budget is a bit more modest, consider retiring to the relaxing **Ojo Santa Fe** (✉ *242 Los Pinos Rd.* ☎ *877/977–8212* ⊕ *ojosantafe.ojospa.com*) on the south side of town, with its contemporary rooms and extensive spa. Don't miss the chance to soak in one of the private mineral-rich "ojito" soaking tubs.

Breakfast: Open for all three meals, **Cafe Pasqual** (✉ *121 Don Gaspar Ave.* ☎ *505/983–9340* ⊕ *pasquals.com*) serves fresh, Latin-inspired fare in a colorful space decorated with Mexican folk art and murals.

The Best of Texas

Written by Kristy Alpert

A road trip through the entire state of Texas may seem like an epic undertaking, and that's because it is. No other state in the United States has as many roadways, ranging from rural ranch-to-market roads lined with wildflowers to high-speed highways—including the fastest road in the nation, Highway 130, where the speed limit is 85 mph. A direct line through the state would stretch a whopping 801 miles between its northern tip in the Panhandle to the southern banks of the Rio Grande River, but the ultimate road trip through Texas isn't quite as linear. This journey through the Lone Star State is a winding route that highlights the state's best sights, cities, and natural scenery. Traverse the terraces of its award-winning wine country, cruise the coastal corridors along the Gulf of Mexico, bathe in the starry night sky above Big Bend National Park, and enjoy the wide-open plains as you discover the warmth and wonder of the "Great State of Texas."

At a Glance

Start: Dallas, TX

End: Dallas, TX

Miles Traveled: 2,587 miles

Suggested Duration: 10 days

States Visited: Texas

Key Sights: The Alamo; Bartons Springs Pool; Big Bend National Park; Houston's Museum District; Marfa Lights Viewing Center

Best Time to Go: Either spring or falls works for optimal weather, but spring is bluebonnet season in Texas and truly a special time to visit the state.

Day 1: Dallas, TX, to Waco, TX

97 miles (1 hour, 30 minutes without traffic and stops)

The most direct route on I–35 E not only saves time, but also passes through some of the most beloved roadside

The Best of Texas

stops along the way. If coming from DFW International Airport, start on John W Carpenter Freeway (TX-114) before merging onto I–35 E near downtown Dallas. Don't forget to stock up on some of the city's famous gas station tacos from **Fuel City** (⊕ 801 S. Riverfront Blvd. ☎ 214/426–0011 ⊕ www.fuelcity.com) near the Convention Center District before leaving town.

ALONG THE WAY

Photo Op: The historic **Ellis County Courthouse** (⊠ 101 W. Main St.) in Waxahachie makes an impressive backdrop for a photo, which is why it has been featured in many films throughout the years, including *Tender Mercies* and *Bonnie and Clyde*. The gingerbread-house-like structure is listed on the National Register of Historic Places and dates back to 1897.

Detour: Between the months of March and April, the wildflowers on the sides of the road bloom in a glorious display of blue. During this "bluebonnet season" in Texas, bypass Waxahachie and head for Ennis instead to drive along the Official Texas Bluebonnet Trail.

Eat & Drink: No true Texan would make the trip between Dallas and Waco without stopping in at the **Czech Stop** (⊠ 104 S. George Kacir Dr. ☎ 254/826-4161 ⊕ www.czechstop.net) in West, Texas, for one of their delicious pastries. The small town of West has been home to a thriving Czech community for over a century, and its downtown is filled with Czech bakeries and antiques stores. But it's hard to beat the convenience of a gas station–and–Czech bakery combination, especially since they make some of the best kolaches in Texas.

WACO

Do: Once simply known as the halfway marker between Dallas and Austin, Waco has seen a resurgence in recent years thanks to its role on the hit HGTV home makeover show *Fixer Upper*. The city is now a mecca for fans of Chip and Joanna

Gaines, where stops include **Magnolia Market at the Silos** (⊠ 601 Webster Ave. ☎ 254/235–0603 ⊕ magnolia.com), Black Oak Art Studio (⊠ 1619 Franklin Ave. ☎ 254/732–1533 ⊕ www.blackoakart. com), and Cottonland Castle (⊠ 3300 Austin Ave.).

Eat & Drink: The cupcakes at **Silos Baking Co.** (⊠ 601 Webster Ave. ☎ 254/235–0603 ⊕ magnolia.com/silos-baking-co) are best eaten alfresco on the grounds of the expansive Magnolia complex, but for an old-school taste of Waco, pull in to dine on your dashboard at **Cupp's Drive Inn** (⊠ 1424 Speight Ave. ☎ 254/753–9364 ⊕ www.cuppsdriveinn.com).

Stay: HGTV fans can live their *Fixer Upper* dreams at the **Magnolia House** (⊠ 323 S. Madison Ave. ☎ 254/235–6111 ⊕ www. magnoliamarket.com) vacation rental 20 minutes outside Waco. In town, the Bed & Breakfast on **White Rock Creek** (⊠ 267 Ruby Dell La. ☎ 254/799–9783 ⊕ www. whiterockcreek.com) is a charming example of Waco's warm hospitality.

Breakfast: Every dish served at Lee Bankston's **Butter My Biscuit Café** (⊠ 1427 S. Valley Mills Dr. ☎ 254/752–2333 ⊕ www. buttermybiscuitcafe.com) is served either on or alongside a fluffy homemade biscuit; be sure to try a bronut (a sweet biscuit doughnut combo), too.

Day 2: Waco, TX, to Austin, TX

102 miles (1 hour, 35 minutes without traffic and stops)

This all-interstate route along I–35 S is the quickest way into Texas's capital city.

ALONG THE WAY

Eat & Drink: Central Texas is often referred to as the Barbecue Belt, where famous barbecue joints like the Salt Lick, Kruez Market, and Franklin Barbeque often have lines that last for hours. **Pit Stop**

Barbecue (✉ *502 S. 1st St.* ☎ *254/458–5059*) in Temple is lesser known, but still favored by locals for its blend of Korean, Cajun, and soul food.

Town: A large, round rock in the low-water crossing section of Bushy Creek gave the town Round Rock its name in the mid-1800s, and the rock is still a reminder of the town's cattle driving past. Today the town is home to a historic downtown shopping area and one of the best parks in the nation, the **Play for All Park** (✉ *151 North A. W. Grimes Blvd.* ☎ *512/218–5400* ⊕ *www.roundrocktexas.gov*), where children of all abilities can play side by side without limitations.

Shop: Spend the afternoon scouring for deals on designer fashions and goods at the 125 stores of the **Round Rock Premium Outlets** (✉ *4401 I–35 N* I ☎ *512/863–6688* ⊕ *www.premiumoutlets.com*).

AUSTIN

Do: Austin's reputation as the "Live Music Capital of the World" rings true with live performances from big-name artists popping up everywhere from **Waterloo Records** (✉ *600 N. Lamar Blvd.* ☎ *512/475–2500* ⊕ *www.waterloorecords.com*) to the **Cactus Café** (✉ *2247 Guadalupe St.* ☎ *512/475–6515* ⊕ *www.cactuscafe.org*). Head to the South Congress (SoCo) District to see firsthand how local businesses strive to "Keep Austin Weird" through its quirky vintage stores, independent bookshops, and funky eateries.

Eat & Drink: Austin takes Tex-Mex to the next level with its own ATX-Mex staples like the Don Juan El Taco Grande breakfast taco at **Juan in a Million** (✉ *2300 E. Cesar Chavez St.* ☎ *512/472–3872* ⊕ *www.juaninamillion.com*) or the Bob Armstrong dip at **Matt's El Rancho** (✉ *2613 S. Lamar Blvd.* ☎ *512/462–9333* ⊕ *www.mattselrancho.com*).

Stay: Snap a picture of the **Austin Motel's** (✉ *1220 S. Congress Ave.* ☎ *512/441–1157* ⊕ *www.austinmotel.com*) red-neon marquee before checking in to see why this quintessential Austin motel was once dubbed the "Phallus Palace." The former roadside motel has since become a playground for Austin's stylish set, where rooms feature retro-chic decor that vibes with the motel's midcentury-modern look.

Breakfast: Breakfast is the most important meal of the day anywhere, but in Austin, it's sacred. **Joe's Bakery & Coffee Shop** (✉ *2305 E. 7th St.* ☎ *512/472–0017* ⊕ *www.joesbakery.com*) has been a favorite for pan de huevo and breakfast tacos since it opened in 1935, while newcomer **Paperboy** (✉ *1203 E. 11th St.* ☎ *512/910–3010* ⊕ *www.paperboyaustin.com*) earned its reputation selling decadent breakfast sandwiches and creative pastries (like strawberry pink peppercorn pop tarts) from a food truck before opening up a brick-and-mortar restaurant in East Austin.

Day 3: Austin, TX, to Houston, TX

162 miles (2 hours, 35 minutes without traffic and stops)

Highway 290 is a straight shot between Austin and Houston, with a short stretch of pay-by-mail tolls. Take exits as wanted, since this flyby road soars past some scenic backroads (like Old Potato Road near Paige) that meander through pastures of rusting oil drilling machinery and pick-your-own blackberry farms.

ALONG THE WAY

Eat & Drink: The 12-inch-platter-sized pancakes are legendary at **Maxine's Café and Bakery** (✉ *905 Main St.* ☎ *512/303–0919* ⊕ *www.maxinescafe.com*) in Bastrop, where you can order them stacked 12 high, but it's the homemade chicken-fried steak and freshly baked pies that keep locals coming back.

Nature: The pine trees at **Lost Pines of Bastrop State Park** (✉ *100 Park Rd. 1A* ☎ *512/321–2101* ⊕ *www.tpwd.state. tx.us*) are unlike any others in the state. These Central Texas loblolly pines were separated by a prehistoric glacier and have adapted to their sandy and gravely soil to thrive in their unique ecosystem alongside white-tailed deer, armadillos, and the endangered Houston toad.

Detour: Round Top is home to one of the best and oldest antiques fairs in the nation, the **Round Top Antiques Fair** (✉ *475 TX-237* ⊕ *www.roundtoptexasantiques. com*). The 30,000 square-foot Big Red Barn is just the start of this 100-per-cent-antiques-and-vintage-only triannual fair, where professional porters and shippers help transport large items for shoppers.

Town: Although you don't have to stop in Brenham to sample homemade Blue Bell Ice Cream (it's available in most grocery stores throughout the state) from **The Little Creamery** (✉ *1101 S. Blue Bell Rd.* ☎ *979/836–7977* ⊕ *www.bluebell.com*) in town, it's best if you do. Every Texan has a favorite Blue Bell flavor, so find yours at the on-site ice cream parlor before heading out for an artsy scavenger hunt to find the elaborate murals hiding just off the town's Main Street

HOUSTON

Do: Houston's world-class arts scene extends from the extensive collection at the **Museum of Fine Arts** (✉ *1001 Bissonnet St.* ☎ *713/639–7300* ⊕ *www. mfah.org*) to the exclusive and highly curated private works on display at the **Menil Collection** (✉ *1533 Sul Ross St.* ☎ *713/525–9400* ⊕ *www.menil.org*). Explore the delicious side of Houston with a stroll through the city's Asiatown or space out on a visit to the **NASA Johnson Space Center** (✉ *2101 E. NASA Pkwy.* ☎ *281/483–0123* ⊕ *www.nasa. gov*) visitor's center.

Extend Your Trip

From Austin or San Antonio: Texas Hill Country *(Ch. 5)*

From San Antonio: Ultimate Cross Country Road Trip South *(Ch. 2)*

Eat & Drink: Everything James Beard Award–nominee and native Houstonian Bobby Heugel touches is gold, and his dining credits in Houston include **Anvil Bar & Refuge** (✉ *1424 Westheimer Rd.* ☎ *713/523–1622* ⊕ *www.anvilhouston. com*). **Ninfa's** on Navigation (✉ *2704 Navigation Blvd.* ☎ *713/228–1175* ⊕ *www.ningas.com*) serves the city's top fajitas, and the dim sum menu at **Fung's Kitchen** (✉ *7320 Southwest Fwy.* ☎ *713/779–2288* ⊕ *www.eatatfungs. com*) is extensive and the service is fast.

Stay: Guests can enjoy sweeping views of the entire city from the **Post Oak Hotel's** (✉ *1600 W. Loop S* ☎ *844/386–1600* ⊕ *www.thepostoakhotel.com*) elegant perch above Uptown Houston.

Breakfast: The servers at **Empire Café** (✉ *1732 Westheimer Rd.* ☎ *713/528–5282* ⊕ *www.empirecafemenu.com*) can be found dolling out hearty breakfast plates with French toast made from rustic Italian bread, crispy roasted potatoes smothered with mozzarella, and handcrafted cappuccinos all from inside these former gas station digs.

Day 4: Houston, TX, to South Padre Island, TX

377 miles (5 hours, 45 minutes without traffic and stops)

Make it to the shoreline in less than six hours by taking the U.S. 59 S and U.S. 77 route between these two cities.

ALONG THE WAY

Town: Victoria is the only county in Texas where all six flags have flown, and the town of Victoria has them all on display at **De Leon Plaza** (✉ *101 N. Main St.*).

Eat & Drink: Victoria is also home to more than five of the BBQ restaurants along the highly underrated Coastal Texas BBQ Trail.

Nature: King Ranch (✉ *2205 TX-141* ☎ *361/592–8055* ⊕ *www.king-ranch. com*) in Kingsville is one of the biggest ranches in the world, where its 825,000 acres make it larger than the entire state of Rhode Island. Book a nature tour to explore the wildlife and rare birds that flock to what is often called "The Last Great Habitat."

SOUTH PADRE ISLAND

Do: This barrier island resort town is a birder's paradise, where a five-story watchtower offers views of migrating birds at the **South Padre Island Birding Nature Center** (✉ *6801 Padre Blvd.* ☎ *956/761–6801* ⊕ *www.spibirding. com*). Assist in a sea turtle release at **Sea Turtle Inc.** (✉ *6617 Padre Blvd.* ☎ *956/761–4511* ⊕ *www.seaturtleinc. org*), charter a boat to cruise for dolphin sightings, or paddleboard nearby the stunning *Cristo de los Pescadores* statue at **Isla Blanca Park** (✉ *33174 State Park Rd.* ☎ *956/761–5494* ⊕ *www.cameron-county.us*).

Eat & Drink: Seafood is served on menus throughout the Gulf Coast, but in South Padre Island, it's "fresh catches only" at grab-and-go **Ceviche Ceviche** (✉ *1004 Padre Blvd.* ☎ *956/772–1555* ⊕ *www. facebook.com/cevichecevichesouthpadreisland*) and the marina-side **Sea Ranch Restaurant and Bar** (✉ *33330 State Park Rd.* ☎ *956/761–1314* ⊕ *www.searanchrestaurant.com*).

Stay: Waterfalls and palm trees dot the landscape throughout **Isla Grand Beach Resort's** (✉ *500 Padre Blvd.* ☎ *956/761–6511* ⊕ *www.islagrand.com*) sprawling 10-acre property, located beachside in the southern portion of the island.

Breakfast: Specialty coffees and freshly baked pastries are available at **Yummies Bistro** (✉ *700 Padre Blvd.* ☎ *956/761–2526* ⊕ *www.facebook.com/yummies. bistro*) for dining in or they can be wrapped or poured in custom tumblers for easy snacking and sipping on the road.

Day 5: South Padre Island, TX, to San Antonio, TX

297 miles (4 hours, 30 minutes without traffic and stops)

Interstate 37 is the fastest way out of town, which is why it's one of the few freeway hurricane evacuation routes for the Texas coast. Start on I-69 E and then follow I-37 N all the way to San Antonio.

ALONG THE WAY

Town: Robstown is the official birthplace of the popular poker game Texas Hold'em, although nowadays you're more likely to see locals holding a create-your-own fruit cup from the retro **Rod 'n' Roll's Treats and Eats** (✉ *324 W. Ave. J* ☎ *361/767–1323* ⊕ *www.rodnrolls.com*) than a deck of cards.

Detour: In April the petite town of Poteet holds its annual Strawberry Festival and has been doing so since April 1948, where carnival rides, live concerts, and strawberry tastings fill the weekend schedule.

The Alamo is still a symbol of Texan state pride.

SAN ANTONIO

Do: Relive history with a visit to the **Alamo**—a pivotal battleground during the Texas Revolution—(✉ *300 Alamo Plaza* ☎ *210/225–1391* ⊕ *www.thealamo.org*) and the four historic missions at the **San Antonio Missions National Historic Park** (✉ *6701 San Jose Dr.* ☎ *210/534–8875* ⊕ *www.nps.gov/saan*). The San Antonio River cuts through the bustling **River Walk promenade** (✉ *849 E. Commerce St.* ☎ *210/227–4262* ⊕ *www.thesanantonioriverwalk.com*), where shoppers stroll alongside landscaped pathways to boutiques and brand-name stores and restaurant goers dine riverside as boats of live music float by.

Eat & Drink: San Antonio is the birthplace of the puffy taco, a messy and crunchy deep-fried taco with all the fixins'. The taco was invented by brothers Henry and Ray Lopez who each now own their own puffy taquerias, **Ray's Drive Inn** (✉ *822 S.W. 19th St.* ☎ *210/432–7171* ⊕ *www. raysdriveinn.net*) and **Henry's Puffy Tacos**

(✉ *6030 Bandera Rd.* ☎ *210/647–8339* ⊕ *www.henryspuffytacos.com*).

Stay: The **Hotel Havana** (✉ *1015 Navarro St.* ☎ *210/222–2008* ⊕ *www.havanassanantonio.com*) is listed on the National Register of Historic Places, but this Cuban-chic boutique hotel has been restored to its grand dame glory with an eclectically modern spin.

Breakfast: Breakfast is served all day at the **Guenther House** (✉ *205 E. Guenther St.* ☎ *210/227–1061* ⊕ *www.guentherhouse.com*), where their exclusive Founders Choice Coffee is brewed fresh and pastries are made from the restaurant's own milled flour.

Day 6: San Antonio, TX, to Marfa, TX

405 miles (5 hours, 45 minutes without traffic and stops)

Drive through the beautiful Texas Hill Country along I–10 W before entering the West Texas desert, where peace and quiet stretches on for miles.

ALONG THE WAY

Shop: The "Hill Country Mile" in Boerne follows the River Road Park and historic Main Street and offers a taste of Hill Country's best in one short, paved stretch of land. Make a quick stop to browse through stores of handcrafted jewelry, shop for homemade jams at the **Boerne Epicure Gourmet Market** (✉ 210 S. Main St. ☎ 830/331–9355 ⊕ www. boerneepicure.com), and pick through authentic antiques (and delicious home-made pickles) at **Fickle Pickles** ✉ 118 S. Main St. ☎ 830/249–9306 ⊕ www. ficklepickles.com.

Town: Kerrville is one of Texas Hill Country's best-kept secrets, where spring-fed creeks trickle through city parks and German heritage lives on through restaurants, food trucks, and annual festivals. Walk along the mighty Guadalupe River in Louise Hays Park before grabbing a sandwich from **Greengrociers Deli** (✉ 225 W. Water St. ☎ 830/257–3354 ⊕ www. greengrocersdeli.com) or a Bavarian pretzel and craft beer at **Pint and Plow Brewing Company** (✉ 332 Clay St. ☎ 830/315–7468 ⊕ www.pintandplow.com).

Roadside Attraction: The stones of **Stonehenge II**—an exact replica of the British structure—(✉ 120 Point Theatre Rd. S, Ingram, TX ☎ 830/367–5121 ⊕ www. hcaf.com) were relocated stone-by-stone to their home along the Guadalupe River in Ingram. This unusual art piece shares space with replicas of Easter Island statues, also created by artist Al Shepperd.

Detour: Visit **Lost Maples Winery** (✉ 34986 RM-187 ☎ 830/966–5131 ⊕ www. lostmapleswinery.com) and Lost Maples State Natural Area in Vanderpool during the fall to catch glimpses of some of the best fall foliage in the state.

MARFA

Do: The entire town of Marfa is a social media post waiting to happen. This unlikely arts destination made headlines when acclaimed minimalist artist Donald Judd left New York City for the high desert of West Texas, where he transformed a former army base into a vibrant art museum now known as the **Chinati Foundation** (✉ 1 Cavalry Row ☎ 432/729–4362 ⊕ www.chinati.org). Today the town is as stylish as it is quirky, where visitors can peruse the galleries at Ballroom Marfa, shop for designer shoes at Cobra Rock Boot Company, and then head out after the sun sets to watch for potential extraterrestrial activity at the **Marfa Lights Viewing Center** (✉ U.S. 90 ☎ 432/729–4772 ⊕ www.visitmarfa.com).

Eat & Drink: Food Shark (✉ 909 W. San Antonio St. ⊕ food-shark.business.site) was the first food truck to get its own emoji, but they're better known for their delicious Mediterranean platters and sandwiches. **Cochineal** (✉ 107 W. San Antonio St. ☎ 432/729–3300 ⊕ www. cochinealmarfa.com) puts a casual spin on fine dining while the wine garden at **Al Campo** (✉ 200 S. Russell St. ☎ 432/729–2068 ⊕ www.alcampomarfa. com) plays with pairing wines with their award-winning queso and tacos.

Stay: Splurge for a stay at the **Saint George Hotel** (✉ 105 S. Highland Ave. ☎ 432/729–3700 ⊕ www.marfasaint-george.com) or give glamping a shot in the bohemian chic tents, teepees, yurts, trailers, and kasitas at **El Cosmico** (✉ 802 S. Highland Ave. ☎ 432/729–1950 ⊕ www.elcosmico.com).

Breakfast: Ramona Tejada has welcomed celebrities (Matthew McConaughey is a fan) and cash-only customers in her home since she converted her kitchen into a breakfast joint off Route 67. She makes everything from scratch at **Marfa Burrito** (✉ 515 S. Highland Ave.), including her salsas and hand-rolled tortillas.

Day 7: Marfa, TX, to Big Bend National Park

129 miles (2 hours, 45 minutes without traffic and stops)

Head South on U.S. 67 S until you reach the border town of Presidio, and then continue along FM-170 (aka River Road) to cruise beside the Rio Grande River along the U.S. and Mexico border through Big Bend Ranch State Park.

ALONG THE WAY

Eat & Drink: Mexican food is a must on this stretch of the drive, and **El Changarrito** (✉ *79845 FM-170* ☎ *432/229–2274* ⊕ *www.facebook.com/ElChangarrito79845*) in Presidio offers some of the best tacos and tortas this side of the border. Try their *tacos de camaron* (shrimp tacos) with a homemade *limonada con frutas* (fruit lemonade).

Town: The colorful characters that reside in Terlingua have breathed new life into this bonafide ghost town, where the quicksilver mines—and the community surrounding them—were abandoned just before WWII. Today the town is home to shipping container markets, quirky desert art installations, and one of the most eccentric chili cook-offs the first Saturday in November, but the most popular attraction is the front porch of the Terlingua Trading Company (✉ *100 Ivey St.* ☎ *432/371–2234* ⊕ *www.facebook.com/TerlinguaTradingCompany*) for a sunset serenade and some good 'ol fashioned talkin' as the sun drips below the desert skyline.

BIG BEND NATIONAL PARK

Do: Big Bend National Park (☎ *432/477–2251* ⊕ *www.nps.gov/bibe*) is jokingly referred to as "Texas's Gift to the Nation," but a visit to the 801,163 acres of native grasses, natural hot springs, and wild stargazing is no joke. Hike Santa Elena Canyon, canoe the Rio Grande River, cruise along the Ross Maxwell Scenic Drive, and take in a sunset from "The Window" before settling in for some celestial entertainment at this International Dark Sky Park–certified gem.

Eat & Drink: The **Mountain View Restaurant** at the Chisos Mountains Lodge (✉ *1 Basin Rural Station* ☎ *432/477–2291* ⊕ *www.chisosmountainslodge.com*) is the only full-service dining option in the park, where nightly specials are served alongside stunning views of the Chisos Basin.

Stay: The curated art and exquisite design of the **Willow House** (✉ *23112 FM-170* ☎ *432/213–2270* ⊕ *www.willowhouse.co*) make this design hotel an oasis in the desert, just six miles outside Big Bend National Park. Each of the hotel's 12 casitas have an unobstructed view of the Chisos Mountain Range, while the Main House is a meeting point for guests to come together for cocktails around a roaring fire.

Breakfast: At **La Posada Milagro Guesthouse's** (✉ *101 Milagro Way* ☎ *424/645–8017* ⊕ *www.laposadamilagro.com*) on-site coffee shop, the name *Espresso Y Poco Mas* translates to "espresso and a little bit more," and the espresso speaks for itself while the "poco mas" ranges from French toast to fresh squeezed orange juice.

Day 8: Big Bend National Park to El Paso, TX

330 miles (5 hours, 15 minutes without traffic and stops)

Although taking TX-118 N to I-10 W isn't the quickest route to El Paso, it's one of the more scenic drives through West Texas, as it passes by the craggy peaks of Mt. Livermore.

ALONG THE WAY

Town: Fort Davis is home to the **McDonald Observatory** (✉ *3640 Dark Sky Dr.* ☎ *432/426–3640* ⊕ *www.mcdonaldobservatory.org*), a research unit of the University of Texas at Austin. Tours begin with participants driving to the summit of Mt. Locke and Mt. Fowlkes, where the 10-meter mirror on the Hobby Eberly Telescope makes the neighboring 1-meter telescopes seem modest.

Eat & Drink: Mom's Kitchen (✉ *403 Laurel St.* ☎ *432/283–2134*) in Van Horn is the last stop in the central time zone, but it's the first choice for authentic homemade Mexican food. Owner Maggie Espinoza pours her heart and soul into the homemade sauces that drench her hearty lunch plates and blanket her handcrafted tacos and burritos.

Detour: Follow U.S. 90 W to catch a glimpse of the famous ***Prada Marfa*** (✉ *14880 U.S. 90* ☎ *432/729–3600* ⊕ *www.ballroommarfa.org*) in Valentine. Despite its retail façade, this Elmgreen & Dragset installation is a permanent land art project where the door is always locked and the interior is forever featuring Prada's fall 2005 collection of bags and shoes.

EL PASO

Do: Discover the many sides of this border town by hiking through the rugged terrain of Franklin Mountains State Park and Huenco Tanks State Park, uncovering new artists at the **El Paso Museum of Art** 's (✉ *1 Arts Festival Plaza* ☎ *915/212–0300* ⊕ *www.elpasoartmuseum.org*) art school gallery, strolling through the bustling downtown markets, or getting lost in the colorful murals of historic El Segundo Barrio Street.

Eat & Drink: L&J Café (✉ *3622 E. Missouri Ave.* ☎ *915/566–8418* ⊕ *www.ljcafe. com*) has been family-owned since 1927 and loved by many just as long for their homemade Mexican food and fresh chile de arbol salsa (be sure to buy some in the gift shop). Afterwards, head to **Elemi** (✉ *313 N. Kansas St.* ☎ *915/532–2090* ⊕ *www.facebook.com/elemieptx*) for cocktails.

Stay: The **Plaza Hotel Pioneer Park** (✉ *106 W. Mills Ave.* ☎ *915/440–7666* ⊕ *www. plazahotelelpaso.com*) is one of the town's most impressive landmarks, where its "Pueblo Deco" architectural façade sets the stage for the 130 guest rooms within. Just a block over, the modern **Stanton House** (✉ *209 N. Stanton St.* ☎ *915/271–3600* ⊕ *www.stanton-house. com*) remains effortlessly cool throughout its chic open-concept common areas and tastefully curated guest rooms.

Breakfast: The perfect temperature for brewing coffee (210 degrees) inspired the name behind **2Ten Coffee Roasters** (✉ *3007 Montana Ave.* ☎ *915/745–8010* ⊕ *www.2tencoffeeroasters.com*). Their single origin and blended beans are roasted in El Paso, where craft coffees are served alongside creative items like breakfast nachos and El Paso toast (a fried egg with chorizo and black beans on a thick slice of toasted bread) at their multiple cafés across town.

Day 9: El Paso, TX, to Lubbock, TX

342 miles (5 hours, 20 minutes without traffic and stops)

Take a short cut through New Mexico along U.S. 62 E to avoid spending more than six hours on the road, and make sure to keep an eye out for the Salt Flats of Texas and Guadalupe Peak—the highest point in Texas—in Guadalupe Mountains National Park before crossing the state line into New Mexico.

ALONG THE WAY

Eat & Drink: The quirky decor and sassy signs in front of the **Cornudas Café** (✉ *180 U.S. 62* ☎ *915/964-2508*) in Cornudas are a fitting welcome to this roadside restaurant, where menus are hand-written on brown paper sacks. You'd be hard-pressed to find a better burger west of the Pecos.

Town: The speed limit doesn't give Salt Flat its due justice (it remains 75 mph throughout the town's limits), but this curious little town is worthy of a slower look. The ancient dry salt pan in Salt Flat once spurred a war (El Paso Salt War), but today is part of the peaceful land-scapes of **Guadalupe Mountains National Park** (☎ 915/828–3251 ⊕ www.nps.gov. gumo).

Photo Op: Stop for a picture in front of the Texas State Line Monument in Carlsbad right before U.S. 62 E continues into New Mexico.

LUBBOCK

Do: This vibrant college town truly shines on game days, when the Goin' Band from Raiderland can be heard miles from the stadium and the tortillas shelves are empty throughout the town (throwing tortillas at Texas Tech football games has been a tradition since 1989). Explore Lubbock's musical past at the **Buddy Holly Center** (✉ 1801 Crickets Ave. ☎ 806/775–3560 ⊕ www.buddyhollycenter.org), dedicated to the Lubbock-born musician, or learn about the WWII glider pilot training program in Lubbock at the Silent Wings Museum (✉ 6202 I–27 Frontage Rd. ⊕ www.ci.lubbock.tx.us).

Eat & Drink: Lubbock is part of the Texas High Plains wine region—the sec-ond-largest AVA in the state—and offers some great chances to taste some of the state's finest vintages. Sip at the **Funky Door Bistro & Wine Room** (✉ 6801 Mil-waukee Ave. ☎ 806/687–0505 ⊕ www. thefunkydoor.com) and **McPherson Cellars Winery** (✉ 1615 Texas Ave. ☎ 806/687–9463 ⊕ www.mcphersoncellars.com) or try a local brew instead at the **Crafthouse Gastropub** (✉ 3131 34th St. ☎ 806/687–1466 ⊕ www.crafthousepub.com).

Stay: The **Cotton Court Hotel** (✉ 1610 Broad-way St. ☎ 806/758–5800 ⊕ www.cotton-courthotel.com) offers the quintessential Lubbock experience, where upscale accommodations and modern motel vibes are matched with curated antiques and industrial farmhouse decor.

Breakfast: The **Cast Iron Grill** (✉ 620 19th St. ☎ 806/771–7690 ⊕ www.castiron-grilllubbock.com) is best known for their sweet southern pies, but between 7 am and 10:45 am, it's all about their hash browns. Omelets at the grill are made with three eggs, but no one's going to judge you for ordering a slice of straw-berry banana split pie with your coffee instead.

Day 10: Lubbock, TX, to Dallas, TX

346 miles (5 hours without traffic and stops)

Notice the subtle changes along I–20 E as the landscape transitions from the high plains of the Panhandle to the prairies and lakes of North Texas along I–30 E.

ALONG THE WAY

Detour: The 10 Cadillacs submerged nose-down at **Cadillac Ranch** (✉ 13651 I–40 Frontage Rd. ☎ 806/848–0764) in Amarillo haven't moved since they were buried as an art installation in 1974 along historic Route 66. They have, however, changed in color, as visitors come armed with spray paint and accessories to leave their mark on this roadside attraction.

Eat & Drink: Owner Jay Stearns not only came up with the amazing recipes at **Jay's BBQ Shack** (✉ 602 S. 11th St. ☎ 325/829–6401 ⊕ www.jaysbbqshack.com) in Abilene, but he designed and made the pit he smokes them in, too. His two-hand-ed barbecue tacos are Texas barbecue at its finest, but don't leave without trying his smoked jalapeno poppers.

Town: Fort Worth is often associated with Dallas (i.e., Dallas/Fort Worth or DFW), but the city stands on its own with a scene that's a little bit western (the daily cattle drives at the **Stockyards National Historic District** ✉ 131 E. Exchange Ave. ☎ 817/626–7921 ⊕ www.fortworth-stockyards.org) and a little bit urban (the vibrant shopping and entertainment throughout Sundance Square). See the only Michelangelo in the Americas at the **Kimbell Art Museum** (✉ 3333 Camp Bowie Blvd. ☎ 817/332–8451 ⊕ www.kimbellart.org), marvel at the largest high-definition screen in the world at the **Texas Motor Speedway** (✉ 3545 Lone Star Cir. ☎ 817/215–8500 ⊕ www.texasmotorspeedway.com), or catch a film at the modern **Coyote Drive-In** on Panther Island (⊕ coyotedrive-in.com/fortworth).

DALLAS

Do: Dallas plays host to the State Fair of Texas—the longest-running state fair in the United States—each September and October in Fair Park but welcomes visitors year-round with its urban parks, unrivaled shopping, and arts district that's been rated the largest arts district in the nation. Unearth the stories surrounding the JFK assassination at the **Sixth Floor Museum** (✉ 411 Elm St. ☎ 214/747–6660 ⊕ www.jfk.org), view the outdoor murals in Deep Ellum, stroll the manicured grounds at the **Dallas Arboretum and Botanical Garden** (✉ 8525 Garland Rd. ☎ 214/515–6615 ⊕ www.dallasarboretum.org), and take in a view of the entire city from the observation deck at **Reunion Tower** (✉ 300 Reunion Blvd. E ☎ 214/712–7040 ⊕ www.reuniontower.com).

Eat & Drink: Get your barbecue fix at **Pecan Lodge** (✉ 2702 Main St. ☎ 214/748–8900 ⊕ www.pecanlodge.com) in Deep Ellum or enjoy the farm-fresh menu at **Petra and the Beast** (✉ 601 N. Haskell Ave. ☎ 318/935–0906 ⊕ www.petraandthebeast.com). For fine dining, head to **Fearing's Restaurant** (✉ 2121 McKinney Ave. ☎ 214/922–4848 ⊕ www.fearingrestaurant.com) to sample bold flavors from local celebrity and author of The Texas Food Bible, chef Dean Fearing.

Stay: Step inside Dallas's most beloved mansion-turned-luxury-hotel at the **Rosewood Mansion on Turtle Creek** (✉ 2821 Turtle Creek Blvd. ☎ 214/559–2100 ⊕ www.rosewoodhotels.com), where sumptuous guest rooms pay an upscale homage to the 1920s former residence. The rooftop pool above the Joule extends past the building's exterior, where swimmers can look out over the downtown streets below from a thick pane of glass.

Breakfast: The home-style breakfast menu is extensive and served all day at **Original Market Diner** (✉ 4434 Harry Hines Blvd. ☎ 214/521–0992 ⊕ www.originalmarketdiner.com). Try their banana bread French toast or opt for a hearty helping of pork chops and eggs.

Texas Hill Country

Written by Kristy Alpert

The Texas Hill Country begins just north of San Antonio and stretches wide across the Edwards Plateau in Central Texas, where granite domes rise above grassy prairies of wildflowers as sparkling rivers ebb and flow along with the natural sway of the land. The pace of life is sweet and slow throughout this region, despite the vibrant energy and creativity from the eclectic mix of Anglo, German, and Spanish cultural influences.

Only in Hill Country are roadside stands just as likely to sell homemade kolaches and sizzling salsas as they are to sell fresh local produce, like the famous Hill Country peaches (in season May through August) and ripe red fruit from the native prickly pear cactus. Soak in the warmth along the windswept limestone hills of the three award-winning American Viticultural Areas of the region (Texas Hill

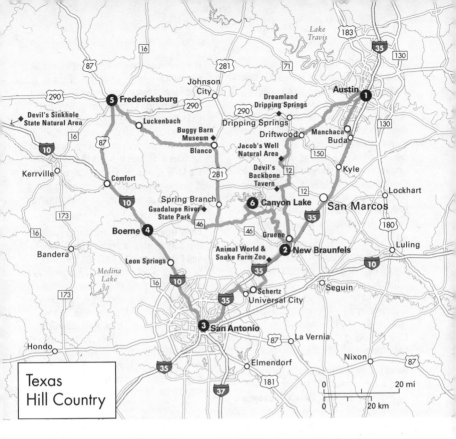

Texas
Hill Country

Country is also known as "Texas Wine Country") or cool down with a cold drink and an inflated tube while floating down the slow-flowing Guadalupe River.

At a Glance

Start: Austin, TX

End: Austin, TX

Miles Traveled: 297 miles

Suggested Duration: 6 days

States Visited: Texas

Key Sights: The Alamo; Barton Springs Pool; The Cave With No Name; Guadalupe River State Park; Wineries of Fredericksburg

Best Time to Go: The colorful blooms of spring (specifically March to May) turn the hillsides into spectacular photo ops, but this route is captivating all year long.

Day 1: Austin, TX, to New Braunfels, TX

63 miles (1 hour, 25 minutes without traffic and stops)

Swap the traffic of I–35 S for the scenic backgrounds of the "Devil's Backbone" (a limestone ridge that runs through parts of Hill Country) by taking TX-1 Loop S to Farm-to-Market Road 1826 toward Driftwood and then Ranch Road 12 to Wimberley. Then follow Purgatory Road (FM-306) as it winds through Gruene and crosses the Guadalupe River into New Braunfels.

ALONG THE WAY

Eat & Drink: The family recipes at **Salt Lick BBQ** (18300 Farm to Market Rd. 1826 512/858–4959 www.saltlickbbq. com) were first tested over hot coals on a pit made with rocks during the wagon trains of the mid-1800s and have been perfected over a similar, impressively constructed permanent pit in Driftwood. The barbecue here is famous throughout Texas, and the outdoor picnic seating beneath the shade of live oak trees fills up quickly on sunny afternoons.

Nature: The spring-fed swimming hole at **Jacob's Well Natural Area** (✉ 1699 Mt. Sharp Rd. ☎ 512/214–4593 ⊕ www. hayscountytx.com) allows swimmers—by reservation only between May 1 and September 30—into its crystal clear waters and mystic underwater caves. Hiking around the area is free year-round and offers some challenging trails.

Detour: Devil's Backbone is regarded as the most haunted stretch of Texas highway, and the **Devil's Backbone Tavern** (✉ 4041 Farm to Market Rd. 32, Fischer, TX ☎ 830/964–2544 ⊕ www. devilsbackbonetavern.com), an authentic honky-tonk near Canyon Lake, is where ghostly tales and local legends are discussed below the sounds of the jukebox.

Town: The historic town of Gruene (pronounced "green") looks much like it did when German cotton farmers settled in during the late 1870s. Visit the oldest dance hall in Texas (Gruene Hall), shop for souvenirs and candy at the General Store, or enjoy a meal on a patio overlooking the Guadalupe River at the **Gristmill River Restaurant** (✉ 1287 Gruene Rd. ☎ 830/625–0684 ⊕ www.gristmill-restaurant.com).

NEW BRAUNFELS

Do: Taking its name from its German founder, Prince Carl of Solms-Braunfels, New Braunfels sits at the confluence of the Comal and Guadalupe rivers, where visitors can float lazily down either

river with rentals from countless local outfitters during warmer months or *próst* with the town at the annual Wurstfest in November. Cool down at **Schlitterbahn Waterpark** (✉ 400 N. Liberty Ave. ☎ 830/625–2351 ⊕ www.schlitterbahn. com) or stay dry with a retro night out at **Stars & Stripes Drive-In Movie Theater** (✉ 1178 Kroesche La. ☎ 830/620–7469 ⊕ www.driveinusa.com) after strolling the shops, museums, and restaurants of downtown New Braunfels.

Eat & Drink: The atmosphere is lively and the schnitzel is crispy at **Kraus's Café and Biergarten** (✉ 148 S. Castell Ave. ☎ 830/625–2807 ⊕ www.krausecafe. com), where the beer menu features local craft brews and imported German beers. Afterward, grab a seat in the outdoor living room at **Huisache Grill and Wine Bar** (✉ 303 W. San Antonio St. ☎ 830/620–9001 ⊕ www.huisache.com) or sample your way through a tasting flight at **New Braunfels Brewing Company** (✉ 180 W. Mill St. ☎ 830/261–3463 ⊕ new-braunfels-brewing-company. mybigcommerce.com).

Stay: Sleep inside a National Historic Landmark at the **Faust Hotel and Brewing Co.** (✉ 240 S. Seguin Ave. ☎ 830/625–7791 ⊕ www.fausthotel.com) in downtown New Braunfels or sneak just outside of town to the opulent accommodations at **Gruene Mansion Inn** (✉ 1275 Gruene Rd. ☎ 830/629–2641 ⊕ www. gruenemansioninn.com).

Breakfast: Edouard Naegelin Sr. arrived in New Braunfels from Alsace-Lorraine in 1868 with a sack of flour and loads of ambition. His namesake bakery, **Naegelin's Bakery** (✉ 129 S. Seguin Ave. ☎ 830/625–5722 ⊕ www.naegelins.com), is the oldest bakery in Texas and the best place in town to grab a hot cup of coffee and a handcrafted pastry.

Day 2: New Braunfels, TX, to San Antonio, TX

34 miles (40 minutes without traffic and stops)

Today's quick ride breezes by on this interstate stretch along I–35 S.

ALONG THE WAY

Roadside Attraction: The **Animal World & Snake Farm Zoo** (✉ *5640 I–35 S* ☎ *830/608–9270* ⊕ *www.awsfzoo.com*) boasts one of the most diverse collections of snakes in the country, including a green anaconda and a black mamba.

Town: The town of Schertz winds its way from Randolph Air Force Base to the edge of the highway, where one of the largest flea markets in the United States is held weekends at **Bussey's Flea Market** (✉ *18738 N. I–35 Frontage Rd.* ☎ *210/651–6830* ⊕ *www.busseysfm. com*). Picnic on the banks of Cibolo Creek or spend the afternoon walking the trails at Crescent Bend Nature Park.

Eat & Drink: Military members know how to pick a sandwich joint, and you'll notice the armed forces support by the patches that line the walls at **Youz Guyz** (✉ *316 Pat Booker Rd.* ☎ *210/659–8930* ⊕ *www. youzguyscheesesteaks.com*) in Universal City. The cheesesteaks at this unsuspecting location are on par with the best in Philly, and that's likely due to the fact that Joey Vento, of world-famous Geno's Steaks, is Youz Guyz's godfather.

SAN ANTONIO

Do: The San Antonio River breathes life into this vibrant city, flowing through the quaint pedestrian shops and restaurants of the **River Walk** (✉ *849 E. Commerce St.* ☎ *210/227–4262* ⊕ *www.thesanantonioriverwalk.com*) and continuing on to the five UNESCO missions in the city (including Mission San Antonio de Valero, better known as **The Alamo** ✉ *300 Alamo Plaza* ☎ *210/225–1391*

⊕ *www.thealamo.org*). Walk the Skywalk on the Land Bridge at **Phil Hardberger Park Conservancy** (✉ *1021 Voelcker La.* ☎ *210/492–7472* ⊕ *www.philhardberger-park.org*) or discover why the city was designated a UNESCO Creative City of Gastronomy with **SA Food Tours** (✉ *711 Navarro St.* ☎ *210/764–9467* ⊕ *www. safoodtours.com*).

Eat & Drink: The carnitas tacos served at **Carnitas Lonjas** (✉ *1107 Roosevelt Ave.* ☎ *210/455–2105* ⊕ *carnitas-lonja.square. site*) are slow-cooked to perfection and best enjoyed with a cold *cerveza* at any of the no-frills picnic tables surrounding this South Side taqueria. The **Bottling Dept. Food Hall** (✉ *312 Pearl Pkwy., Bldg. 6* ☎ *210/564–9140* ⊕ *www.atpearl.com*) in the historic Pearl neighborhood puts a spotlight on local chefs serving international flavors at restaurants like Mi Roti and Brasserie Mon Chou Chou.

Stay: Hotel Emma's (✉ *136 E. Grayson St.* ☎ *210/488–8300* ⊕ *www.thehotelemma.com*) chic quarters once housed a brewery, but now this riverfront hotel is home to 145 guest rooms and suites, as well as some of the top dining options in town. This boutique hotel's location in the Pearl area gives guests easy access to the city's best restaurants, bars, cafés, and shops, not to mention the Pearl's twice-weekly farmer's market.

Breakfast: Brothers José and David Caceres have come a long way from selling their mother's prized pastries on the streets of Mexico City. Their restaurant, **La Panaderia Bakery Café** (✉ *301 E. Houston St.* ☎ *210/592–6264* ⊕ *www. lapanaderia.com*), has multiple locations throughout the city, all selling their exquisite *pan dulces* (sweet breads) and other handmade breads, like their tequila almond croissants and breakfast *tortas* (cakes) made with freshly baked birote bread.

Day 3: San Antonio, TX, to Boerne, TX

32 miles (40 minutes without traffic and stops)

The quickest route between San Antonio and Boerne on I–10 W takes you past the massive Six Flags Fiesta Texas theme park.

ALONG THE WAY

Town: The small town of Leon Springs takes travelers back in time with three historic buildings along its Historic District. The town was the site of the first officer training camp (established May 8, 1917) and the birthplace of the first ever Macaroni Grill Restaurant franchise.

Eat & Drink: Stop in for a bite at the **Flagstop Café** (✉ 28425 I–10 ☎ 830/981–4413 ⊕ www.flagstop.com) just outside Boerne. Their burgers are legendary in these parts, but you can't go wrong with anything fried.

BOERNE

Do: Explore Boerne's historical side at the **Kuhlmann-King Historical House**—an impressive 1880s home built by a German settler (✉ 402 E. Blanco Rd.)—or at the **Dienger Trading Co.** (✉ 210 N. Main St. ☎ 830/331–2225), which now operates a boutique, bakery, and bistro from its carefully restored 1884 building. Soak in the sunshine at the **Cibolo Nature Center** (✉ 140 City Park Rd. ☎ 830/249–4616 ⊕ www.cibolo.org) and create an urban scavenger hunt out of the town's **Art al Fresco trails** (⊕ www.ci.boerne. tx.us/1386/Art-Al-Fresco) before heading underground at the Cave Without a Name (✉ 325 Kreutzberg Rd. ☎ 830/537–4212 ⊕ www.cavewithoutaname.com).

Eat & Drink: Peggy's on the Green (✉ 128 W. Blanco Rd. ☎ 830/572–5000 ⊕ www. peggysonthegreen.com) serves Southern food with an upscale twist inside an historic 19th-century stagecoach stop, while

Extend Your Trip

From Austin or San Antonio: The Best of Texas *(Ch. 5)*

From San Antonio: The Ultimate Cross Country Road Trip South *(Ch. 2)*

Compadres Hill Country Cocina (✉ 209 Lohmann St. ☎ 830/331–2198) specializes in smoked meats and Tex-Mex eats. Monday nights are for fish-and-chips at **Cibolo Creek Brewing** (✉ 448 S. Main St. ☎ 830/816–5275 ⊕ www.ciblolocreek-brewing.com), where plates are paired with pitchers of Boerne's finest craft brews.

Stay: The rooms at **The William** (✉ 170 S. Main St. ☎ 361/420–1270 ⊕ www. thewillamboerne.com) all feature New Orleans-style balconies that look out over Boerne's Main Street, while each of the rooms at **The Kendall** (✉ 128 W. Blanco Rd. ☎ 830/249–2138 ⊕ www.thekendalltx.com) tells a unique story from the town's past, like the St. John's Suite inside a former chapel.

Breakfast: Set inside an historic building on Main Street, **The Boerne Grill** (✉ 141 S. Main St. ☎ 830/249–4677 ⊕ www. facebook.com/theboernegrill) serves Hill Country coffee with local breakfast staples like smothered biscuits, *migas* (corn chips and eggs), and breakfast tacos.

Day 4: Boerne, TX, to Fredericksburg, TX

39 miles (40 minutes without traffic and stops)

Follow I–10 W through Comfort before turning on to U.S. 87 N and traveling almost due north to Fredericksburg.

ALONG THE WAY

Town: Antiques shopping is almost a sport between Comfort's Front Street and High Street. At **The 8th Street Market** (✉ 523 8th St. ☎ 830/201–0214 ⊕ www. the8thstreetmarket.com) inside the old 1940s-era Ford dealership, old and unexpected treasures line the interior as the smell of roasted coffee from the Comfort Coffee Co. wafts through the air. For an actual sporting experience, head to Flat Rock Ranch for an afternoon of mountain biking.

Eat & Drink: Grab a glass of local Hill Country wine at **Bending Branch Winery** (✉ 142 Lindner Branch Rd. ☎ 830/995–2948 ⊕ www.bendingbranchwinery.com) in Comfort to sample some of Texas's award-winning vintages.

Detour: Venture out around sundown to Rocksprings to explore the **Devil's Sinkhole** (☎ 830/683–2287 ⊕ www.tpqd. state.tx.us), the largest single-chamber cavern in the state, and watch in awe as more than three million Mexican free-tailed bats pour out from the eerie cavern (May through October).

FREDERICKSBURG

Do: Famous for its wine, wildflowers, shopping, and German heritage, Fredericksburg offers the chance to unwind or venture out into the heart of Hill Country with its easy access to Enchanted Rock, the **Lyndon B. Johnson National Historical Park** (✉ 1048 Park Rd. ☎ 830/868–7128 ⊕ www.nps.gov/lyjo), and the trails at **Wildseed Farms** (the nation's largest working wildflower farm [✉ 100 Legacy Dr. ☎ 830/990–1393 ⊕ www.wildseedfarms. com]). Brush up on your WWII history at the **National Museum of the Pacific War** (✉ 311 E. Austin St.), shop around the boutiques of Main Street, pick your own peaches at **Jenschke Orchards** (✉ 8301 U.S. 290 ☎ 830/997–8422 ⊕ www. bestfredericksburgpeaches.com), and taste your way through Hill Country at **Becker Vineyards** (✉ 464 Becker Farms Rd. ☎ 830/644–2681 ⊕ www.

beckervineyards.com) and **Narrow Path Vineyards** (✉ 6331 S. Ranch Rd. ☎ 830/998–1916 ⊕ www.narrowpath-winery.com).

Eat & Drink: The wines at **Southold Farm + Cellar** (✉ 330 Minor Threat La. ☎ 512/829–1650 ⊕ www.southhold-farmandcellar.com) are made from indigenous yeasts while the winemakers at **William Chris Vineyards** (✉ 10352 U.S. 290 ☎ 830/998–7654 ⊕ www.william-chriswines.com) remain committed to pre-industrial methods of winemaking (i.e., open-air fermentation) from Texas-grown grapes. Feast on German fare made with local ingredients at **Otto's German Bistro** (✉ 316 E. Austin St. ☎ 830/307–3336 ⊕ www.ottosfbg.com) and stop in for samples at **Das Peach Haus** (✉ 1406 S. U.S. 87 ☎ 830/997–8969 ⊕ www.jelly.com), home to Fischer & Wieser products like the locally beloved Original Roasted Raspberry Chipotle Sauce.

Stay: Named after Texas legend (who is also the great-great-great-grandfather of current owner Alice Adair) James L. Trueheart, **The Trueheart Hotel's** (✉ 201 N. Llano St. ☎ 830/992–3489 ⊕ www. thetruehearthotel.com) charming rooms are outfitted in a style that blends retro pop with western chic. Just down the road, the luxury bed-and-breakfast **Hoffman Haus** (✉ 608 E. Creek St. ☎ 830/997–6739 ⊕ www.hoffmanhaus.com) boasts 23 rooms, each with the distinctly Hill Country aesthetic of crisp white linens and lavender bath products.

Breakfast: Breakfasts at **Nury's Restaurant** (✉ 714 S. Washington St. ☎ 830/992–3217 ⊕ www.nuryscuisine.com) range from classic pancakes and eggs to huevos divorciados, where two eggs are separated in neighboring sauces of homemade ranchero (red) and homemade tomatillo (green). Don't be shy about ordering pie for breakfast at the **Fredericksburg Pie Company** (✉ 108 E. Austin St.), where they serve locally roasted

Visit Texas Hill Country in springtime so you can see the gorgeous Texas bluebonnets in bloom.

coffees like Texas Hill Country Pecan and the Fredericksburg Pie Company House Blend.

Day 5: Fredericksburg, TX, to Canyon Lake, TX

65 miles (1 hour, 20 minutes without traffic and stops)

Drive past the historic dance halls and hilly vineyards along U.S. 290 and RM-1888 before crossing the Blanco River and continuing along U.S. 281 S toward Canyon Lake.

ALONG THE WAY

Town: The slogan "Everybody's Somebody in Luckenbach" can be found on bumper stickers and T-shirts throughout this quirky town. Best known for its 1887 dance hall—which still hosts regular dances and concerts and has become a rite of passage for many Texas musicians—the original general store and

"feed lot" food stand are both worthy of a visit before continuing on.

Eat & Drink: The **Chess Club Café** (✉ *1020 U.S. 281* ☎ *830/833–4930* ⊕ *www. chessclubcafe.com*) in Blanco is only open 8 am to 2 pm Wednesday through Sunday, so come early and come hungry for specials like chicken-fried steak and scratch-made biscuits.

Roadside Attraction: The **Buggy Barn Museum** (✉ *1915 Main St.* ☎ *830/833–5708* ⊕ *www.buggybarnmuseum.com*) in Blanco is as niche as they come. More than 200 restored buggies, carriages, and wagons are on display, many of which have appeared in films like *True Grit*, *Abraham Lincoln: Vampire Hunter*, and *There Will Be Blood*.

Nature: There are 13 miles of hiking and biking trails throughout **Guadalupe River State Park** (✉ *3350 Park Rd.* ☎ *830/438– 2656* ⊕ *www.tpwd.state.tx.us*), although most visitors are more focused on the four miles of river frontage. Toss a tube in the river for a peaceful float or hop in for a refreshing dip on a hot day.

CANYON LAKE

Do: Often referred to as the "Jewel of Texas Hill Country," Canyon Lake is a nature lover's playground, with hiking trails, boat docks, and campsites. Kayak on the lake, take a tour through the Canyon Lake Gorge, or explore the region's prehistoric past at **The Heritage Museum of the Texas Hill Country** (✉ 4831 FM-2673 ☎ 830/899–4542 ⊕ www.theheritagemuseum.com).

Eat & Drink: The tasting room at **La Cruz de Comal Wines** (✉ 7405 FM-2722 ☎ 713/725–4260 ⊕ www.lacruzdecomalwines.com) at the vineyards of Canyon Lake has a "Provence meets Texas Hill Country" feel, but the wines are purely Texan, with 100% of the grapes grown on the estate. Grab one of the healthy meal replacement shakes at the **Nutrition Shack** (✉ 14128 FM-306 ☎ 214/732–0295 ⊕ www.goherbalife.com) with delicious twists like the Fruity Pebble Protein Oats or the Sopapilla Cheesecake Shake, or head to **Canyon City Grill** (✉ 14601 FM-306 ☎ 830/964–3640 ⊕ www.canyoncitygrill-tx.com) for burgers and their famous "Texas Tots" beneath the oak trees.

Stay: The views from the lodge suites and the cathedral cabins at **Canyon Lakeview Resort** (✉ 872 Ledgerock Dr. ☎ 210/787–1770 ⊕ www.canyonlakeviewresort.com) offer panoramic views of the resort's 80 miles of shoreline around Canyon Lake. Days at this lakefront property are spent on the water, while evenings are spent around the boulder-lined fire pits soaking in the warmth of the area long after the sun goes down.

Breakfast: Inspired by the wild game and fresh-baked goods that mark the menu, **Wildflour Artisan Bakery & Grill** (✉ 2000 FM-2673 ☎ 830/964–2159 ⊕ www.wildflourbakeryandgrill.com) offers an authentic taste of Hill Country. Popular breakfast items include their whole-hog

Essential Listening

Waylon Jennings put this town on the map with his song "Luckenbach, Texas," and his longtime friend Willie Nelson has played the song for fans onstage at the Luckenbach Dance Hall.

sausages and homemade biscuits with Paw Paw Bill's sausage gravy.

Day 6: Canyon Lake, TX, to Austin, TX

65 miles (1 hour, 15 minutes without traffic and stops)

Cross the Guadalupe River one final time before turning on to I-35 N for a quick drive back into Austin.

ALONG THE WAY

Town: Named for the nearby watering hole Manchaca Springs (referred to as "Manshack Springs"), where Tejano army officer-turned-Texas-legend José Antonio Menchaca once camped, the town of Manchaca is very much still a watering hole along the route to Austin. Grab a drink at the **Manchaca Springs Saloon** (✉ 793–727 FM-1626 ☎ 512/436–1016 ⊕ www.facebook.com/ManchacaSpringsSaloon) or taste some craft brews at **Texas Keeper Cider** (✉ 12521 Twin Creek Rd. ☎ 512/910–3409 ⊕ www.texaskeeper.com).

Eat & Drink: Miguel Vidal puts his signature twist on Texas barbecue from his celebrated barbecue-and-taco truck, **Valentina's Tex-Mex BBQ** (✉ 11500 Menchaca Rd. ☎ 512/221–4248 ⊕ www.valentinastexmexbbq.com), just north of Manchaca. He slow smokes his meats and hand-rolls his tortillas to create a delicious base for homemade salsas and sauces.

Detour: For a long time, **Dreamland** (✉ 2770 U.S. 290 ☎ 512/827–1279 ⊕ www.dreamlanddstx.com) in Dripping Springs was just that: a dream. The outdoor entertainment, recreation, and arts venue now puts sustainability first (rainwater collection tanks, Tesla charging stations, etc.), followed closely by their immense array of fun activities like lawn games, eccentric art installations, and a family-friendly beer garden.

AUSTIN

Do: With an average of more than 300 sunny days each year and live-music venues that range from parks to patios, getting outside in Austin is the best way to soak in this capital city's vibe. Walk the 10-mile urban trail around Lady Bird Lake, swim in the spring-fed waters of **Barton Springs** (✉ Barton Springs Rd. ☎ 512/974–6300 ⊕ www.austintexas.gov), peruse the galleries at **Jack S. Blanton Museum of Art** at the University of Texas at Austin (✉ 200 E. Martin Luther King Jr. Blvd. ☎ 512/471–5482 ⊕ www.blantonmuseum.org), and get entertained at the many bars, restaurants, and venues along Austin's famous Sixth Street.

Eat & Drink: Asking an Austinite where to get the best tacos in Austin will lead to a lengthy debate, which you'll likely be discussing while in line—which can last up to four hours—for the award-winning brisket at **Franklin Barbecue** (✉ 900 E. 11th St. ☎ 512/653–1187 ⊕ www.franklinbarbecue.com). But save yourself the debate (still get the brisket though; it's worth the wait!) and head to **Veracruz All Natural** (✉ 111 E. Cesar Chavez St. ☎ 512/665–2713 ⊕ www.veracruzallnatural.com), because their handmade tacos have a spot on everyone's "taco top 10."

Stay: Austin's **Proper Hotel** (✉ 600 W. 2nd St. ☎ 512/628–1500 ⊕ www.properhotel.com), a member of Design Hotels, is quintessential Austin at its finest, with local textiles and textures layered smartly inside its 244 modern rooms. For a fresh look into Austin's past, book a room inside the luxuriously restored 1928 mansion at the **Commodore Perry Estate**, an Auberge Resort (✉ 4100 Red River St. ☎ 512/817–5200 ⊕ www.aubergeresorts.com).

Breakfast: Not only is the coffee at **Greater Goods Coffee Roasters** (✉ 2501 E. 5th St. ☎ 512/382–9857 ⊕ www.greatergoodsroasting.com) some of the best in the nation, but this do-gooder microroaster gives back a portion of the sales from each of their coffees to one of four local Texas nonprofits.

Chapter 6

THE MIDWEST AND THE PLAINS

WELCOME TO
THE MIDWEST AND THE PLAINS

TOP REASONS TO GO

★ **Badlands National Park:** This dramatic South Dakota landscape is home to steep canyons, bison, bighorn sheep, and stunning scenic viewpoints.

★ **The Cherokee Heritage Center:** Visit this museum and historical society to learn more about the history and culture of the Cherokee Nation of Oklahoma.

★ **Wisconsin's Door County:** Located on a scenic peninsula between Green Bay and Lake Michigan, Door County is one of the Midwest's most charming regions, with outdoor adventures, antique shops, and boutique wineries galore.

★ **Detroit:** Michigan's biggest city comes with fascinating museums, rich history, and lively food and art scenes.

★ **Mackinac Island:** For the ultimate Great Lakes experience, visit this island in the middle of Lake Huron, with nature trails, historic forts, and the often filmed Grand Hotel.

1 The Best of the Dakotas. Two of the country's least-visited states have an unexpected amount to offer.

2 Native American Homelands of the Great Plains. Explore Oklahoma, Kansas, and Nebraska through the tribes that live there today.

3 The Best of the Ozarks. The Ozark Mountains offer beautiful vistas and plenty of outdoor adventures in Arkansas, Missouri, Kansas, and Oklahoma.

4 The Best of the Heartland. Experience the ultimate Midwestern charm as you travel through the farmlands, lakes, and cities that make up Minnesota, Wisconsin, and Iowa.

5 Underrated Cities of the Midwest. See for yourself all the culture the Midwest has to offer, including incredible museums, delicious food scenes, and hip art communities.

6 All the Great Lakes. Hit up all five of the Great Lakes in one unforgettable trip.

7 A Frank Lloyd Wright Tour. From Chicago to Philadelphia, visit some of the famous architect's best works.

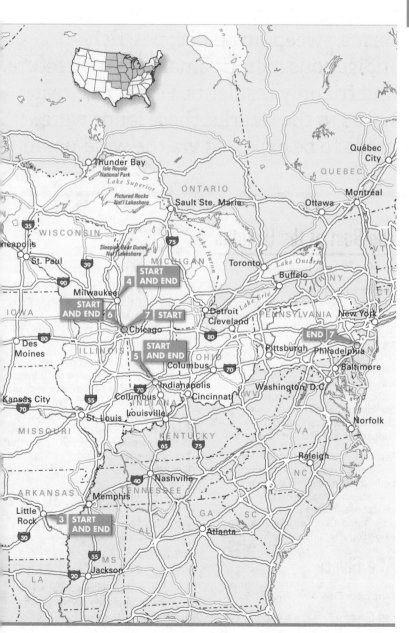

An expansive region covering the entire middle of the country, the Midwest and the Great Plains are lands of rolling farms, sweeping landscapes, rich Indigenous history, amazing architecture, and friendly residents. From the Great Lakes to the Ozarks, these lands were made to be explored via the wide-open road.

The Best of the Dakotas

Written by Cassandra Brooklyn

Collectively known as "The Dakotas," the supremely underrated states of North and South Dakota truly have something for everyone: rolling hills, underground cave systems, Wild West history, rich Native American culture, and national and state parks brimming with hiking, biking, kayaking, and wildlife-viewing. From rustic cabins and campgrounds to chic glamping sites and upscale hotels, the Dakotas have accommodations for every budget and every type of traveler, too.

Though this road trip itinerary visits seven cities in seven days, know that both North and South Dakota are over-flowing with parks, museums, public art instillations, historic sites, and incredible eateries, so it's not a bad idea to consider extending your trip if possible.

At a Glance

Start: Sioux Falls, SD

End: Sioux Falls, SD

Miles Traveled: 1,240 miles

Suggested Duration: 7 days

States Visited: North Dakota, South Dakota

Key Sights: Badlands National Park; Crazy Horse National Memorial; Mount Rushmore; Theodore Roosevelt National Park; Wind Cave National Park

Best Time to Go: If you're hoping to do a lot of outdoor activities, spring and summer are the best times to take advantage of the stunning weather, as many destinations close for the winter. That being said, if you're a leaf-peeping connoisseur or winter sports buff, fall and early winter provide their own unique offerings in the Dakotas.

Day 1: Sioux Falls, SD, to Badlands National Park

275 miles (4 hours without traffic and stops)

Today's drive is a straight shoot across Highway 90, including several optional stops at quirky roadside attractions.

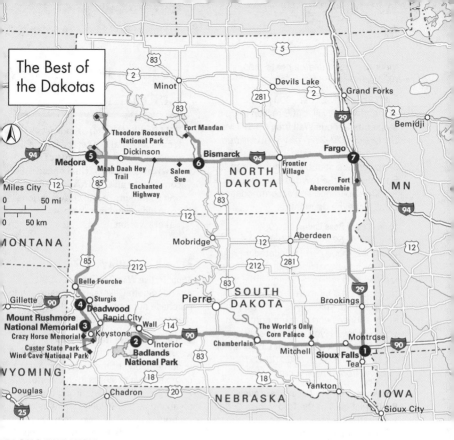

The Best of the Dakotas

ALONG THE WAY

Roadside Attraction: Stop at the **World's Only Corn Palace** (✉ *604 N. Main St.* ☎ *605/995–8430,* ⊕ *www.cornpalace. com*) in Mitchell at the beginning of your route (70 miles from Sioux Falls) and at the six-ton Giant Prairie Dog at the end (20 miles before Wall).

Photo Op: The town of Chamberlain is the home of the impressive *Dignity of Earth and Sky* **sculpture** (☎ *605/347–5776* ⊕ *www.lampherestudio.com/dignity*), a statue dedicated to the Lakota and Dakota people of South Dakota. The sculpture depicts a 50-foot Lakota woman with a traditional star quilt.

Detour: Just north of I-90 in the town of Wall (the gateway town to Badlands National Park) is **Wounded Knee: The Museum** (✉ *207 10th Ave.* ☎ *605/279–2573* ⊕ *www.woundedkneemuseum.org*), a memorial to the Sioux people killed at the infamous Wounded Knee Massacre.

BADLANDS NATIONAL PARK

Do: You can drive the 39-mile Scenic Byway within **Badlands National Park** (☎ *605/433–5361* ⊕ *www.nps.gov/badl*) in about an hour, but you'll want to spend the most time along Sage Creek Rim Road (on the western edge of the loop), as it's one of the best places to see bison, bighorn sheep, pronghorns, and prairie dogs. The remoteness of the park makes it perfect for backcountry hikers and campers who want to escape the crowds and explore the wilderness far from trails and roads. Badlands bike tours can also be arranged. There's also almost no light pollution here, so the astronomy and night sky viewing is also incredible. If you're a fan of astronomy, plan your visit for July, when the area hosts the annual Badlands Astronomy Festival.

Eat & Drink: Fewer than 800 people live in the town of Wall, but 2 million people stop at its famous **Wall Drug** (✉ *510 Main St.* ☎ *605/279–2175* ⊕ *www.walldrug. com*) each year for food, photos, and shopping. It's about 10 minutes from the Badlands, so the town is a popular place for affordable food and accommodations. Don't miss the doughnuts.

Stay: Cedar Pass Lodge (✉ *20681 SD–240* ☎ *605/433–5460* ⊕ *www. cedarpasslodge.com*) is located within Badlands National Park, but it books up fast, so plan ahead. Staying within the park may be a bit more expensive, but it's worth the splurge, as it allows you to enjoy sunrises and sunsets right from your window. If you prefer to stay outside the park, check out **Frontier Cabins Motel** (✉ *1101 Glenn St.* ☎ *888/200–8519* ⊕ *www.frontiercabins.net*) in Wall.

Breakfast: Head to **Cedar Pass Lodge Restaurant** (part of the Cedar Pass Lodge) and try the fry bread topped with *wojapi*, a Native American berry sauce.

Day 2: Badlands National Park to Mount Rushmore

75 miles (1 hour, 30 minutes without traffic and stops)

Today is a relatively quick drive, but if you're a photographer and want to get the best light, be sure to get to Mount Rushmore before 11 am. Another good option is to drive 50 miles south of Mount Rushmore to explore Wind Cave National Park for the first half of the day, before heading north to check out Mount Rushmore for the last half.

Essential Listening

KILI Radio (90.1 FM) broadcasts from a local Lakota reservation, so you can hear old tribal music from powwows, modern tribal music, community affairs broadcasting, and commentary and conversations from elders and members of the Lakota Nation.

ALONG THE WAY
Shop: Native West Trading Co., near Interior, South Dakota, is a great place to purchase authentic, handcrafted items made by local Native artists.

Detour: Wind Cave National Park (☎ *605/745–4600* ⊕ *www.nps.gov/wica*) is home to one of the longest and most complex cave systems in the world. Aboveground there are hiking trails and an abundance of wildlife; while below-ground, explore the cave, its maze of passages, and its unique honeycomb-like boxwork formations via candlelit tours. You could spend a couple of hours here before or pay it a visit after exploring Mount Rushmore (it's about an hour drive each way).

Eat & Drink: If you want to enjoy lunch in Wind Cave National Park, be sure to pack your own meal, because other than vending machines, the only dining venues inside park boundaries are the two picnic areas, one near the visitor center and the other at Elk Mountain Campground.

MOUNT RUSHMORE
Do: Hike the half-mile Presidential Trail to take in views of the iconic **Mount Rushmore National Memorial** (✉ *13000 SD–244, Keystone, SD* ☎ *605/574–2523* ⊕ *www.nps.gov/moru*). The Nature Trail also connects to the Presidential Trail and takes you to the Carver's Studio, where you can find the tools and models used

in the construction of Mount Rushmore. From May through September, Mount Rushmore puts on evening light and music ceremonies that go through the history of the site.

Eat & Drink: While at Mount Rushmore, swing by the **Memorial Team Ice Cream** (✉ 13000 SD–244 ☎ 605/574–2515 ⊕ www.mtrushmorenationalmemorial. com) and treat yourself to Thomas Jefferson's ice cream, made with the original recipe used in 1780 by America's third president. Jefferson is credited with bringing the first recipe for ice cream to what would become the United States. For a more substantial meal, **Skogen Kitchen** (✉ 29 N 5th St. ☎ 605/673–2241 ⊕ www.skogenkitchen.com) in nearby Custer, is a Nordic-theme restaurant offering gourmet food that's typically hard to find in this area. Despite the high-end fare, the food is affordable and the restaurant has a casual outdoor patio that is pet-friendly.

Stay: **Under Canvas Glamping** (✉ Presidio, 24342 Ranch Rd. ☎ 888/496–1148 ⊕ www.undercanvas.com) is just a few miles from Mount Rushmore and has on-site programming like yoga, nature walks, and bike tours.

Breakfast: Grapes & Grinds (✉ 609 U.S. 16A ☎ 605/666–5142 ⊕ www.grapes-grinds.com) in Keystone offers the best of both worlds: coffee and wine. Start your day with a bagel and brew, and grab a bottle of wine for later.

Day 3: Mount Rushmore to Deadwood, SD

50 miles (1 hour, 10 minutes without traffic and stops)

You can spend the first half of the day exploring Custer State Park and/or the Crazy Horse Memorial, which are both not too far from Mount Rushmore. Then you'll head north to Deadwood, and no

Extend Your Trip

From the Badlands: Ultimate Cross Country Trip North (*Ch. 2*)

From Mount Rushmore or Sioux Falls: The Ultimate Wild West Road Trip (*Ch. 4*)

matter which route you take, the drive is beautiful, but the most spectacular route would be to take a detour along the Spearfish Canyon byway. That will add about an hour to the drive, but you'll pass beautiful waterfalls and gorgeous landscapes. This route is particularly stunning when the leaves are changing in autumn.

ALONG THE WAY

Detour: Visit the rolling hills of **Custer State Park** (✉ 13438 U.S. 16A ☎ 605/255–4514 ⊕ www.gfp.sd.gov), where roaming bison and towering granite spires line the route. The park is famous for its herd of 1,300 bison, which you can spot along the Wildlife Loop Road. It's the largest publicly owned bison herd in the country and the experience is similar to what you'd encounter in Yellowstone National Park. Each September, the park hosts its annual Buffalo Roundup, where wranglers on horseback round up the park's herd to be sorted and vaccinated. The park also offers mountain biking, fishing, paddle boating, mountain climbing, and some of the best hiking in the Black Hills. You could spend anywhere from a few hours to a few days hiking in the park.

Eat & Drink: For lunch, head to **Black Hills Burger and Bun Co.** (✉ 441 Mt. Rushmore Rd. ☎ 605/673–3411 ⊕ www.blackhillsburgerandbun.com) in Custer, which serves homemade burgers, salads, and fun sides (think cheese curds and fried green tomatoes) using minimally processed ingredients.

Detour: Explore the living history and culture of South Dakota's Native American tribes at the **Crazy Horse Memorial** (✉ 12151 Ave. of the Chiefs, Crazy Horse, SD ☎ 605/673–4681 ⊕ www.crazyhorsememorial.org). Designed to be the world's largest work of art (the face alone is 87 feet tall), this tribute depicts Crazy Horse, the legendary Lakota leader who helped defeat General Custer at Little Bighorn. A work in progress, thus far the warrior's head has been carved from the mountain, and the colossal head of his horse is beginning to emerge. It's worth spending a few bucks to take the bus to the base of the memorial. Also, don't miss the Native American Museum on-site, which is included with the admission to Crazy Horse.

DEADWOOD

Do: Explore the ultimate Wild West town of Deadwood, where real-life (and HBO) legends Wild Bill Hickcock and Calamity Jane called home. Wander the old streets where actors perform shoot-outs, tour the town in an old stagecoach, and try your hand at gold panning at the old **Broken Boot Mine** (✉ 1200 Pioneer Way ☎ 605/578–9997 ⊕ www.brokenbootgoldmine.com). The town is also known for rodeos, music jams, and all sorts of festivals, so check out special programming at Outlaw Square (✉ 703 Main St. ☎ 605/578–1876 ⊕ www.outlawsquare.com) to find out what's going on.

Eat & Drink: For dinner, order a local craft beer and burger at **Deadwood's Saloon #10** (✉ 657 Main St. ☎ 800/952–9398 ⊕ www.saloon10.com), where Wild Bill was famously shot during a poker game. You can even pay your respects at his grave, found in the town's Mount Moriah cemetery. Upstairs at the Saloon, you'll find the Deadwood Social Club, offering a finer dining experience.

Stay: Deadwood has loads of accommodations at different price points and offering different amenities. If you want to stay in town, **SpringHill Suites by Marriott**

Deadwood (✉ 322 Main St. ☎ 605/559–1600 ⊕ www.marriott.com) is a good bet (it's connected to the Cadillac Jack casino and within walking distance to museums), but if you want to stay in nature, book a lodge (two-to-seven bedrooms) at the **Black Hills Executive Lodging** (✉ 11842 U.S. 14 ALT, Sturgis, SD ☎ 605/578–3555 ⊕ www.executive–lodging.com).

Breakfast: While you're picking up coffee, pastries, and sandwiches at the **Pump House** (✉ 73 Sherman St. ☎ 605/571–1071 ⊕ www.mindblownstudio.com), check out the blown glass art being made next door at Mind Blown Studio.

Day 4: Deadwood, SD, to Medora, ND

220 miles (3 hours, 45 minutes without traffic and stops)

Enjoy beautiful rolling hills and wide-open prairie landscapes as you drive into North Dakota. About 30 minutes outside Deadwood, you will pass through the community of Belle Fourche, pronounced as "Bell Foosh." This town is considered to be along the geographic center of the United States (excluding Hawaii and Alaska).

ALONG THE WAY

Town: Stop by Sturgis, a sleepy town that livens up for three weeks of rallies during the annual **Sturgis Motorcycle Rallies**

(⊕ www.sturgismotorcyclerally.com) each August. If you're not there for the rally, pop into the Motorcycle Museum (⌧ 999 Main St. ☎ 605/347–2001 ⊕ www. sturgismuseum.com) to learn a bit about the town's motorcycle culture.

Eat & Drink: Much of the Belle Fourche area's economy is built on cattle, and when local ranchers and other residents want a good steak, they go to the **Branding Iron** (⌧ 19079 U.S.–85 ☎ 605/892–2503). This is a no-nonsense, saloon-style facility with wood paneling on the walls, a bar, pool tables, lots of seating, and big food portions.

Detour: The 150-mile **Maah Daah Hey Trail** (☎ 701/225–5796 ⊕ www.mdhta.com) is an epic single-track trail carved through the North Dakota Badlands, showcasing some of the country's most unique and breathtaking terrain. Majestic plateaus, large expanses of rolling prairie, and rivers intertwine to offer any outdoors lover a taste of pure, unadulterated badlands.

MEDORA

Do: Medora is an outdoor enthusiast's dream, offering road biking, hiking, and camping, along with a downtown area full of shops and restaurants. Be sure to get to town by 7 pm so you can attend the live *Medora Musical* (⌧ 3422 Chateau Rd. ☎ 800/633–6721 ⊕ www.medora. com).

Eat & Drink: Dinner at the **Pitchfork Steak Fondue** (⌧ 3422 Chateau Rd. ☎ 800/633–6721 ⊕ www.medora.com) is a must. Here chefs load steaks onto a pitchfork and "fondue" them western style—basically, they're deep–fried in a vat of hot oil. Steaks are served with various sides, desserts, and drinks, and vegetarians can order a "Just the Fixin's" plate.

Stay: Luxury meets western charm at the **Historic Rough Riders Hotel** (⌧ 301 3rd Ave. ☎ 701/623–4444 ⊕ www.medora. com) in downtown Medora, but if you're looking for something more economical or pet-friendly, check out the "tiny-house

style" lodges at **Elkhorn Quarters** (⌧ 400 E. River Rd. S ☎ 800/633–6721 ⊕ www. medora.com).

Breakfast: Start your day with a cup of joe and fresh baked goods at the **Hidden Springs Java** (⌧ 350 4th St. ☎ 701/623–4700 ⊕ www.facebook.com/ HiddenSpringsJava) or grab a proper breakfast at the **Cowboy Café** (⌧ 215 4th St. ⊕ 701/623–4343).

Day 5: Medora, ND, to Bismarck, ND

130 miles (2 hours without traffic and stops)

Today's route is an easy drive on I–94, with several potential detours and photo ops.

ALONG THE WAY

Nature: Bison, deer, prairie dogs, wild horses, and eagles are plentiful in **Theodore Roosevelt National Park** (☎ 701/623–4466 ⊕ www.nps.gov/thro), and a loop ride in the South Unit gets you up close with the wildlife. The park's 70,400 acres of breathtaking badlands are full of hiking trails, scenic overlooks, picnic spots, and campsites.

Photo Op: The best places for photo ops in Theodore Roosevelt National Park are Buck Hill and Wind Canyon. Also stop at the Painted Canyon for one last look (and a quick pic) of the park as you exit and head to Bismarck.

Eat & Drink: Pop into **Fluffy Fields Vineyard and Winery** (⌧ 2708 21st St E ☎ 701/483–2242 ⊕ www.fluffyfields.com) in Dickinson, North Dakota's first year-round winery, for a glass of wine on the patio to pair with the daily lunch and dessert specials (just keep in mind that the winery is closed Monday and Tuesday).

Detour: Beginning at Exit 72 on I–94 near Gladstone is the Enchanted Highway, a 32-mile stretch that ends in the small

One of South Dakota's most stunning drives takes you through Badlands National Park.

town of Regent. Beginning with the *Geese in Flight* sculpture at Exit 72, large metal sculptures are placed along the county highway, each with a parking area and kiosk. Some of the sculptures include *World's Largest Tin Family*, *Teddy Rides Again*, *Pheasants on the Prairie*, and *Grasshoppers in the Field*.

Roadside Attraction: About 30 miles before Bismarck, you'll pass *Salem Sue*, the "World's Largest Holstein Cow."

Detour: About 40 minutes north of Bismarck is **Fort Mandan** (✉ 838 28th Ave. SW, Washburn, ND ☎ 701/462–8535 ⊕ www.parkrec.nd.gov), where Lewis and Clark met up with Sacagawea on their famous expedition. You can tour the historic site and walk in the footsteps of these legendary explorers.

BISMARCK

Do: Explore the art scene in downtown Bismarck, North Dakota's capital, by visiting several art galleries and colorful alley art in between Broadway and Main Avenue. Next, check out some of the outdoor attractions along the Missouri River walking path, which include the eagle sculptures, Steamboat Park, and **Chief Looking's Village Historic Site** (✉ 2023 Burnt Boat Rd. ☎ 701/222–6455). The grounds at the State Capitol building have an arboretum trail with 75 species of trees, shrubs, and flowers. To learn about the state's geological, agricultural, industrial, and Native American history, visit the **North Dakota Heritage Center and State Museum** (✉ 612 E. Boulevard Ave. ☎ 701/328–2666 ⊕ www.statemuseum.nd.gov).

Eat & Drink: Bismarck is packed with great food and drink options. Grab a burger and brew at **Peacock Alley** (✉ 422 E. Main Ave. ☎ 701/221–2333 ⊕ www.peacock–alley.com) or sample the bison medallions at the **Pirogue Grille** (✉ 121 N. 4th St. ☎ 701/223–3770 ⊕ www.piroquegrille.com). The brewery scene is also hoppin' and **Laughing Sun Brewing** (✉ 1023 E. Front Ave. ☎ 701/751–3881 ⊕ www.laughingsunbrewing.com) has plenty of options to tempt your palate and can also provide a tour.

Stay: Many standard and upscale hotels exist in the city, but for a unique lodging experience, head to **Fort Abraham Lincoln State Park** (✉ *4480 Fort Lincoln Rd.* ☎ *701/667–6340* ⊕ *www.parkrec. nd.gov*), where you can overnight in a cabin or a teepee and wake up next to hiking trails.

Breakfast: Stop in at the **Terra Nomad** (✉ *514 E. Main Ave.* ☎ *701/751–2070* ⊕ *www.terranomadcompany.com*), a unique café in downtown Bismarck offering a holistic experience (and Instagram-worthy meals) to guests.

Day 6: Bismarck, ND, to Fargo, ND

245 miles (3 hours, 40 minutes without traffic and stops)

You may notice the flattened topography and fields that abound as you enter North Dakota's Red River Valley.

ALONG THE WAY

Town: Visit **Frontier Village** (✉ *404 Louis Lamour La.* ☎ *800/222–4766* ⊕ *www. discoverjamestownnd.com*) in the town of Jamestown to take a picture with the "World's Largest Buffalo" and to visit the **National Buffalo Museum** (✉ *500 17th St. SE* ☎ *800/807–1511* ⊕ *www.buffalomuseum.com*), where you can learn about the history and preservation of buffalo and even see an albino bison.

Eat & Drink: If you're ever going to try a bison burger, Jamestown is the perfect place to do it. Try one at the **Frontier Fort Bar & Grill** (✉ *1838 3rd Ave. SE* ☎ *701/252–7492*).

Photo Op: Stop by the **Fargo-Moorhead Convention and Visitors Bureau** (✉ *2001 44th St. S* ☎ *701/282–3653* ⊕ *www. fargomoorhead.org*) to take a picture with the original woodchipper from the movie *Fargo*. Also, if North Dakota is your last state to check off your bucket list (it seems like this happens a lot), you can join the "Saved the Best for Last" club at the visitor center; you get a commemorative T-shirt, an official certificate, and sometimes a round of applause from the staff.

FARGO

Do: While it might have gotten the most hype from the Coen Brothers' movie and television series of the same name, Fargo is North Dakota's largest city and visitors will find a lively cultural scene here. Art lovers will enjoy the unconventional **Plains Art Museum** (✉ *704 1st Ave. N* ☎ *701/551–6100* ⊕ *www.plainsart. org*) and the interactive and mural art spread across the city. Catch a live show at the **Fargo Theatre** (✉ *314 Broadway N* ☎ *701/239–8385* ⊕ *www.fargotheatre. org*), then head over to **Unglued** (✉ *408 Broadway N* ☎ *701/205–1597* ⊕ *www. ungluedmarket.com*), a draft market with 300 local artists.

Eat & Drink: Start with fried pickles at **Toasted Frog** (✉ *305 Broadway N* ☎ *701/478–7888* ⊕ *www.toastedfrog. com*), then enjoy bacon–wrapped bison meat loaf at **Mezzaluna** (✉ *309 Roberts St. N* ☎ *701/364–9479* ⊕ *www.dinemezzaluna.com*) in downtown Fargo.

Stay: The **Hotel Donaldson** (✉ *101 Broadway N* ☎ *701/478–1000* ⊕ *www. hoteldonaldson.com*) is definitely the most unique place to stay, as the rooms are designed around the work of regional artists and the hotel includes art galleries and hosts literary, artistic, and musical performances.

Breakfast: Jump-start your day at the **Twenty Below Coffee Co.** (✉ *14 Roberts St. N* ☎ *701/566–0977* ⊕ *www.20below.coffee*) in downtown Fargo, where you can get poached eggs, homemade bread, and killer coffee.

Day 7: Fargo, ND, to Sioux Falls, SD

245 miles (3 hours, 40 minutes without traffic and stops)

Today is an easy drive along I–29 so you'll have plenty of time to explore Sioux Falls when you arrive.

ALONG THE WAY

Detour: Explore **Fort Abercrombie** (✉ 935 Broadway N ☎ 701/553–8513 ⊕ www. history.nd.gov), the first permanent U.S. military fort that was once known as "the Gateway to the Dakotas."

SIOUX FALLS

Do: Summer is the best time to catch free concerts and festivals in South Dakota's largest city, but public art installations, including the Sculpture Walk and Arc of Dreams, can be enjoyed year-round. On the first Friday of each month in summer (known as First Fridays), downtown streets come alive with music, discounts, and drink specials at restaurants, bars, and shops. You can also explore **Falls Park** (✉ 131 E. Falls Park Dr. ☎ 605/367–7430 ⊕ www. siouxfalls.org), where the Big Sioux River runs through a series of rock faces; don't miss the observation tower and the ruins of an old mill.

Eat & Drink: Named after the shish kebab–like grilled meat that is popular across southeastern South Dakota, **Urban Chislic** (✉ 431 W. 85th St. ☎ 605/275–6328 ⊕ www.urbanchislic.com) is a fun, casual restaurant and bar. They specialize in chislic, but also have a full menu of burgers, sandwiches, and fun appetizers. For a sweet treat, head to **CH Patisserie** (✉ 309 S. Phillips Ave. ☎ 605/275–0090 ⊕ www.chpastries.com), owned by world champion pastry chef Chris Hanmer.

Stay: Housed within a restored bank from 1918, **Hotel On Phillips** (✉ 100 N. Phillips Ave. ☎ 605/274–7445 ⊕ www. hotelonphillips.com) is Sioux Falls's first boutique hotel; it combines classic charm with modern and elegant guest rooms.

Breakfast: At the **Phillips Avenue Diner** (✉ 121 S. Phillips Ave. ☎ 605/335–4977 ⊕ www.phillipsavenuediner.com), you can enjoy classic breakfast dishes in a retro diner.

Native American Homelands of the Great Plains

Written by Shoshi Parks

Crisscrossed by rivers and rich with bison and waterfowl, the American prairie was once, and still remains, a place of essential Indigenous heritage and culture. Even before the Native nations of the Southeast were removed from their homelands en masse to Oklahoma along the Trail of Tears, the Pawnee, Osage, Comanche, Omaha, Ponca, Sac, Fox, and more called this land home. Although the people of the Plains fought hard against the westward expansion of the United States, one by one they succumbed to the brutal, genocidal tactics brandished by the U.S. Army and land-seeking settlers. But while the region's Indigenous people have been forced into reservations and faced the attempted destruction of their language, culture, and heritage, dozens of tribes remain, from Oklahoma and Kansas to Missouri and Nebraska. This road trip is a look at the heart of Indian Country: what was, what is, and what could have been.

At a Glance

Start: Oklahoma City, OK

End: Omaha, NE

Miles Traveled: 1,374 miles

Suggested Duration: 9 days

States Visited: Kansas, Missouri, Nebraska, Oklahoma

Key Sights: Cherokee Heritage Center; First Americans Museum; The Five Civilized Tribes Museum; Genoa Indian Industrial School; Osage Nation Museum

Best Time to Go: This trip can be taken at any time of the year, but to get the most out of the region's wild, open spaces, travel between April and November.

Day 1: Oklahoma City, OK, to Sallisaw, OK

160 miles (2 hours, 30 minutes without traffic and stops)

After landing at Will Rogers Airport, today's drive will take you east through the heart of Indian Country via I–40. Set the tone for your trip with a stop at the **First Americans Museum** (✉ *659 American Indian Blvd.* ☎ *405/ 594–2100* ⊕ *www.famok.org*) before leaving town. The architecturally stunning gallery shares the heritage, culture, and artwork of the 39 Native American nations in modern-day Oklahoma.

ALONG THE WAY
Town: Just outside OKC, stop by the **Citizen Potawatomi Nation Cultural Heritage Center** (✉ *1899 S. Gordon Cooper Dr.* ☎ *405/878–5830* ⊕ *www.potawatomiheritage.com*) in Shawnee, which tells the story of the Potawatomi. The tribe was forced out of the Great Lakes region by the Indian Removal Act, first to Kansas and then on to Oklahoma, where they established their new nation in the 1870s.

Eat & Drink: Fill up on Nishnawbe fry bread tacos stuffed with meat, beans, and plenty of spice at **Firelake Frybread Tacos** in Shawnee (✉ *1568 S. Gordon Cooper Dr.* ☎ *405/273–0108* ⊕ *www.facebook.com/frybreadtaco*).

Roadside Attraction: In Okemah, the birthplace of legendary folk musician Woody Guthrie, you'll find what's left of his boyhood home, the London House, and a mural to his legacy. His anthem "This Land Is Your Land" is just one example of how Indigenous people have been erased from the narrative of who belongs in America.

Nature: Six miles south of Vian, alligator snapping turtles, bald eagles, and waterfowl gather at the convergence of the Arkansas and Canadian rivers in the **Sequoyah National Wildlife Refuge** (✉ *107993 S. 4520 Rd.* ☎ *918/773–5251* ⊕ *www.fws.gov*). Ancient Native American campsites found within the sanctuary date back almost 1,000 years.

SALLISAW
Do: Once part of the Cherokee Nation, Sallisaw today maintains a monument to the creator of the tribe's written language, Sequoyah. Visit his oneroom cabin, a National Literary Landmark, built in 1829 and now called **Sequoyah's Cabin Museum** (✉ *470288 OK–101* ☎ *918/775–2413* ⊕ *www.visitcherokeenation.com*). Southeast of town on the Arkansas River, you'll find **Spiro Mounds** (✉ *18154 N. 1st St.* ☎ *918/962–2062* ⊕ *www.okhistory.org*), the remains of an ancient settlement that dates back to 800 CE.

Eat & Drink: Head just south of town for some serious barbecue with a 55-year pedigree at **Wildhorse Mountain BBQ** (✉ *Kerr Blvd.* ☎ *918/775–9960* ⊕ *www.wildhorsemountainbbqco.com*).

Stay: Sallisaw is light on lodging and what's there isn't great. Either get a cheap room at the **Quality Inn** (✉ *710 S. Kerr Blvd.* ☎ *918/774–0400* ⊕ *www.choicehotels.com*) or try the even more affordable, slightly nicer W alnut Inn (✉ *824 S. Paw Paw Rd.* ☎ *918/427–6600*), 15 miles away in Roland.

Breakfast: Stop by **Ruger's Grill** (✉ *118 E. Cherokee Ave.* ☎ *918/571–0391*) where

Native American Homelands
of the Great Plains

classic breakfast favorites are served hot and fast every morning starting at 7 am.

Day 2: Sallisaw, OK, to Tahlequah, OK

76 miles (1 hour, 30 minutes without traffic and stops)

Head back west on I–40 then north on Highway 351 to pass through the Muscogee (Creek) Nation before continuing on to the capital of the Cherokee Nation, Tahlequah.

ALONG THE WAY

Town: When the Five Civilized Tribes (the Cherokee, Chickasaw, Choctaw, Muscogee [Creek], and Seminole) were forced from their eastern homeland in the 1830s, the Muscogee (Creek) Nation settled here around modern-day Muskogee. The **Five Civilized Tribes Museum** (✉ *1101 Honor Heights Dr.* ☎ *918/683–1701* ⊕ *www.fivetribes.org*), in the original Indian Agency building from that era, tells the story of their history and displays the work of modern Native artists.

Eat & Drink: Nibble on sandwiches, salads, and cinnamon rolls inside the 100-year-old downtown Muskogee home that now holds the **Harmony House Lunch & Bakery** (✉ *208 S. 7th St.* ☎ *918/687–8653* ⊕ *www.harmonyhouse4lunch.com*).

Detour: Just 10 miles northeast of Muskogee, the Cherokee Nation operates the **Fort Gibson Historic Site** (✉ *907 N. Garrison Ave.* ☎ *918/478–4088* ⊕ *www.okhistory.org*). In the mid-19th century, the log fort served a prominent role in the forced relocation of Native tribes and the battle for the West.

TAHLEQUAH

Do: Here in the capital of the Cherokee Nation, there are several museums dedicated to the heritage and practices of the tribe, including the **Cherokee Heritage Center** (✉ *21192 S. Keeler Dr.* ☎ *918/456–60077* ⊕ *www.cherokeeheritage.org,*), the **Cherokee National Prison Museum** (✉ *124 E. Choctaw St.* ☎ *918/207–3640* ⊕ *www.visitcherokeenation.com*), and the **Cherokee National Supreme Court Museum** (✉ *122 E. Keetoowah St.* ☎ *918/207–3508* ⊕ *www.visitcherokeenation.com*).

Eat & Drink: Indulge in catfish etouffee, sausage gumbo, and po' boys at **Linney Breaux's Cajun Eatery** (✉ *1716 Muskogee Ave.* ☎ *918/708–9461* ⊕ *www.linneybreauxs.com*). After dinner stop by **Dewain's Place** (✉ *303 S. Water Ave.* ☎ *918/458–9736*), where the cocktails are strong and there's karaoke, live music, and plenty of games to keep you entertained.

Stay: In Tahlequah, chain hotels are the only option. Try the **Best Western NSU Inn** (✉ *101 Reasor St.* ☎ *918/431–0600* ⊕ *www.bestwestern.com*) or splurge on one of the priciest joints in town, the **Holiday Inn Express and Suites** (✉ *2142 Mahaney Ave.* ☎ *918/506–4545* ⊕ *www.ihg.com*).

Breakfast: Wake up with coffee and a crepe at **Drip** (✉ *900 E. Will Rogers Blvd.* ☎ *918/923–3555* ⊕ *www.facebook.com/dripbeveragelab*).

Essential Listening

Empire of the Summer Moon by S. C. Gwynne is a sweeping historical account of the 40-year struggle of the Comanche Nation to maintain control of their Oklahoma territory in the 19th century.

Day 3: Tahlequah, OK, to Tulsa, OK

66 miles (1 hour, 15 minutes without traffic and stops)

Today's drive takes you through Sequoyah State Park, over the waters of Fort Gibson Lake, and on to Tulsa. Once known as the "oil capital of the world," Tulsa has more art deco architecture than almost anywhere else in the country. In the mid-19th century, it was at the crossroads of territory granted for three tribes removed from their eastern lands: the Muscogee (Creek), Cherokee, and Osage.

ALONG THE WAY

Nature: At **Sequoyah State Park** (✉ *17131 Park 10, Hulbert, OK* ☎ *918/772–2046* ⊕ *www.travelok.com*), named for the great Cherokee chief, you can cruise Fort Gibson Lake in a paddle boat, play a round of golf, or book a trail ride at the Sequoyah Riding Stables.

Eat & Drink: Right on the lakeshore in Sequoyah State Park, you'll find tasty eats like Monte Cristo sandwiches, hillbilly queso fries, and sweet tea–glazed chicken at **Swadley's Foggy Bottom Kitchen** (✉ *120 Old N. Park Dr.* ☎ *580/494–3009* ⊕ *www.foggybottomkitchens.com*).

TULSA

Do: In Tulsa, stop by the **Gilcrease Museum** (✉ *1400 N. Gilcrease Museum Rd.* ☎ *918/596–2700* ⊕ *www.gilcrease.org*), which has an all-encompassing collection of art and artifacts from throughout North America, including work from hundreds of Indigenous cultures. At the **Gathering Place** (✉ *2650 S. John Williams Way E* ☎ *918/779–1000* ⊕ *www.gatheringplace.org*), arguably one of the best city parks in the United States, there are a variety of delightful trails, art installations, and playgrounds for visitors of all ages. As you travel through the city, keep an eye out for remnants of the golden age of Route 66 (like the 21-foot-tall space

cowboy Buck Atom), especially along 11th Street.

Eat & Drink: Splurge on an eclectic menu of beautifully adorned meats and hearty vegetarian fare at the **Palace Café** (✉ *1301 E. 15th St.* ☎ *918/582–4321* ⊕ *www.palacetulsa.com*) or try the best Vietnamese in town at the beloved **Lone Wolf Banh Mi** (✉ *203 E. Archer St.* ☎ *918/728–7778* ⊕ *www.lonewolftulsa.com*). Sip carefully crafted cocktails at the classy-cool **Hodges Bend** (✉ *823 E. 3rd St.* ☎ *918/398–4470* ⊕ *www.hodges-bend.com*) or, for a more laid-back vibe, head to **Fassler Hall's** (✉ *304 S. Elgin Ave.* ☎ *918/576–7898* ⊕ *www.fasslerhall.com*) biergarten for a pint and a plate of mind-blowing duck-fat fries with gouda.

Stay: Spend the night in the chic hotel **The Mayo** (✉ *115 W. 5th St.* ☎ *918/582–6296* ⊕ *www.themayohotel.com*), which also has a popular roof deck bar. On old Route 66, try **The Campbell Hotel** (✉ *2636 E. 11th St.* ☎ *855/744–5500* ⊕ *www.thecampbellhotel.com*).

Breakfast: Grab breakfast in the modern brick-walled diner **Chimera** (✉ *212 N. Main St.* ☎ *918/779–4303* ⊕ *www.chimeratulsa.com*), where the breakfast tacos are served all day long, or check out **Cirque Coffee** (✉ *1317 E. 6th St.* ☎ *918/933–4489* ⊕ *www.cirquecoffee.com*), a roaster with some of the best lattes and cold brews in town.

Day 4: Tulsa, OK, to Kansas City, KS

275 miles (4 hours, 40 minutes without traffic and stops)

Today's drive is the longest of your trip. Follow Highway 75 north out of Tulsa, skirting the eastern edge of the Osage Nation. Break for bison at the Woolaroc Museum and Wildlife Preserve then continue north on Highway 123 across the Kansas border and through the prairies to Kansas City.

ALONG THE WAY

Nature: At the **Woolaroc Museum and Wildlife Preserve** (✉ *1925 Woolaroc Ranch Rd.* ☎ *918/336–0307* ⊕ *www.woolaroc.org*) in Bartlesville, buffalo roam a 3,700-acre wildlife preserve just as they did before their near-eradication thanks to the westward expansion of America. A museum on the property houses Native American art and artifacts, along with other collections that pay tribute to the West.

Detour: About 20 miles northwest of Barnsdall, veer off course for a visit to the **Osage Nation Museum** (✉ *819 Grandview Ave.* ☎ *918/287–5441* ⊕ *www.osagenation–nsn.gov*) in Pawhuska. In addition to featuring beautiful and fascinating art and artifacts, the museum is an active cultural and educational center for the tribe.

Town: See Laura Ingalls Wilder's famous books brought to life at the **Little House on the Prairie Museum** (✉ *2507 County Rd. 3000* ☎ *620/289–4238* ⊕ *www.little-houseontheprairiemuseum.com*) on the southern edge of Independence, Kansas.

Eat & Drink: Feast on fajita nachos and enchiladas rancheras at **El Pueblitos Mexican Restaurant** (✉ *112 W. Duke St.* ☎ *580/317–8081*) in Independence.

KANSAS CITY

Do: One of the largest cities in the Midwest, you'll find only a few remnants of Native people here. South of the city's center is the **Shawnee Indian Mission State Historic Park** (✉ *3403 W. 53rd St.* ☎ *913/262–0867* ⊕ *www.kshs.org*), what remains of a short-lived Native American residential school that forcibly re-educated children of the Shawnee, Delaware, and other Native nations in the mid-1800s. In Riverview near downtown, visit the Huron Indian Cemetery, all that remains of the territory granted to the Wyandotte Nation in the 1840s.

Eat & Drink: Kansas City loves its barbecue. Do like the locals do and head to one of the city's best. Try **Joe's Kansas City Barbeque** (✉ *3002 W. 47th Ave.* ☎ *913/722–3366* ⊕ *www.joeskc.com*) or the classic **Gates BBQ** (✉ *1325 Emanuel Cleaver II Blvd.* ☎ *816/531–7522* ⊕ *www.gatesbbq.com*). Wash down dinner with live music and a drink at **Red Eye** (✉ *6102 State Ave.* ☎ *913/334–6700* ⊕ *www.red-eye-page.io*) or funeral home–turned–dive bar **Fat Matt's Vortex** (✉ *411 N. 6th St.* ☎ *913/296–7142*).

Stay: After a long day of driving, get a good night's rest at the boutique **Crossroads Hotel** (✉ *2101 Central St.* ☎ *816/897–8100* ⊕ *www.crossroadshotelkc.com*) or the Gothic Revival **Hotel Kansas City** (✉ *1228 Baltimore Ave.* ☎ *816/685–1228* ⊕ *www.hotelkc.com*), a former private social club for hobnobbing with presidents.

Breakfast: Wake up to salmon toast and Spanish tortillas at the **Happy Gillis Cafe & Hangout** (✉ *549 Gillis St.* ☎ *816/471–3663* ⊕ *www.happygillis.com*).

Day 5: Kansas City, KS, to Nebraska City, NE

160 miles (2 hours, 45 minutes without traffic and stops)

Take I-29 out of St. Louis to Highway 273, then head north on Highway 59 through St. Joseph, before getting back on I-29 to Nebraska City. Most of the

In Tahlequah, the Cherokee Heritage Center offers opportunities to learn more about the tribe.

drive travels the eastern bank of the Missouri River through the eponymous state. Before hitting Nebraska City, you'll briefly dip in and out of Iowa's southwest corner.

ALONG THE WAY

Photo Op: Make a pit stop at **O'Malley's Pub** (✉ 540 Welt St. ☎ 816/640–5235 ⊕ www.westonirish.com) in Weston, Missouri's oldest bar, which is hidden underground within a moodily lit limestone brewery.

Nature: Walk the 1–mile Gosling Lake Trail loop in **Lewis and Clark State Park** (✉ 801 Lakecrest Blvd. ☎ 816/579–5564 ⊕ www.mostateparks.com) on the Missouri River. The famed explorers passed through in 1804, some of the first white Americans to travel through the Native nations of the West.

Detour: It's less than a 10-minute detour from I–29 north of Weston to Atchison, home of the **Amelia Earhart Birthplace Museum** (✉ 223 N. Terrace St. ☎ 913/367–4217 ⊕ www.ameliaearhartmuseum.

org) and the Amelia Earhart Earthworks, where the aviator's face is etched into a hillside overlooking Warnick Lake.

Town: In St. Joseph, Missouri, you'll find two memorials to things long gone: the **Jesse James Home Museum** (✉ 1201 S. 12th St. ⊕ jesse–james–home.edan.io), where the outlaw was famously gunned down by Robert Ford in 1882, and the **Pony Express National Historic Trail and Museum** (✉ 914 Penn St. ☎ 816/279–5059 ⊕ www.ponyexpress.org), which is dedicated to the short-lived mail route that once connected the East to the West in the late 1850s and early 1860s.

Eat & Drink: In St. Joseph, dine at **Belle Epoque** (✉ 1141 Frederick Ave. ☎ 816/676–1529 ⊕ www.facebook.com/thecafebelleepoque), a sweet little café with European vibes.

Roadside Attraction: The Presbyterian **Iowa and Sac & Fox Mission** (✉ 1737 Elgin Rd. ⊕ www.kshs.org) in Highland served as a school for the tribe's children until they were moved off the land in the 1860s.

NEBRASKA CITY

Do: The **Arbor Day Farm** (✉ 2611 Arbor Ave. ☎ 402/873–8717 ⊕ www.arbordayfarm. org) combines a state historical park, amusement park, and plenty of opportunities to commune with nature in the birthplace of America's tree-planting holiday. At the **Kregel Windmill Factory Museum** (✉ 1416 Central Ave. ☎ 402/873–1078 ⊕ www.kregelwindmillfactorymuseum. org), learn about the forgotten minutiae of early-20th-century technology.

Eat & Drink: Enjoy charbroiled pork loin and baby back ribs at **Ladybug BBQ** (✉ 610 S. 11th St. ☎ 402/873–1148).

Stay: Spend the night in a Victorian home surrounded by more than 6 acres of pine trees at the **Whispering Pines Bed and Breakfast** (✉ 610 S. 11th St. ☎ 402/873–1148) or in the attractive Lied Lodge (✉ 2700 Sylvan Rd. ☎ 402/73–8733 ⊕ www.arbordayfarm.org), a relaxing hotel evocative of its natural surroundings.

Breakfast: Omelets, skillets, and biscuits and gravy await at the **Downtowner Casual Cafe** (✉ 715 1st Corso ☎ 402/713–5424.

Day 6: Nebraska City, NE, to Kearney, NE

180 miles (2 hours, 45 minutes without traffic and stops)

Today's drive is a mostly straight shot west across the plains on I–80 with a stop in the hometown of the University of Nebraska–Lincoln.

ALONG THE WAY

Town: In Lincoln, visit the **Pioneer Park Nature Center** (✉ 3201 S. Coddington ☎ 402/441–7895 ⊕ www.lincoln.ne.gov) where the native beasts of the prairie, buffalo and elk, roam on more than 600 acres. The **International Quilt Museum** (✉ 1523 N. 33rd St. ☎ 402/472–6549 ⊕ www.internationalquiltmuseum.org)

on the university campus has the world's largest collection of quilts, including those created by Indigenous quilters from around the United States.

Eat & Drink: In Lincoln, enjoy a burger at **Honest Abe's Burgers and Freedom** (✉ 126 N. 14th St. ☎ 402/261–4904 ⊕ www. grounduprestaurants.com) or grab a slice and a pint at **Yia Yia's Pizza and Beer** (✉ 1423 O St. ☎ 402/477–9166 ⊕ www. yiayiapizzandbeer.com).

KEARNEY

Do: The multimedia exhibit at the imposing **Great Platte River Road Archway** (✉ 3060 E. 1st St. ☎ 308/237–1000 ⊕ www.archway.org) tracks how white Americans expanded westward across the plains. At the **Fort Kearny State Historical Park** (✉ 1020 V Rd. ☎ 308/865–5305 ⊕ www.outdoornebraska.gov), one of the stops on the Oregon Trail, you can learn more about the pioneers, Pony Express riders, gold prospectors, and Pawnee scouts who spent time at the site.

Eat & Drink: Find tasty bar-and-grill fare at **Cunningham's Journal** (✉ 610 Talmadge St. ☎ 308/237–5122 ⊕ www.cunninghams–journal.com) or steak and seafood at upscale **Coppermill Steakhouse** (✉ 421 Talmadge St. ☎ 308/455–4580 ⊕ www. coppermillsteakhouse–kearney.com). After dinner pop into **Gillies** (✉ 1822 Central Ave. ☎ 308/236–9393 ⊕ www. facebook.com/gillieslive), a dive with cheap drinks and an outdoor patio.

Stay: The regional chain **New Victorian Inn & Suites** (✉ 903 2nd Ave. ☎ 308/237–5858 ⊕ www.newvictorianinn.com) offers cleanliness and comfort for great value.

Breakfast: Start the day with a hearty homestyle breakfast at the **Breakfast Cart** (✉ 2524 1st Ave. ☎ 308/238–4210 ⊕ www.breakfastcartandcatering.com).

Day 7: Kearney, NE, to Niobrara, NE

209 miles (3 hours, 45 minutes without traffic and stops)

Head east along the Platte River, the banks of which attract hundreds of thousands of sandhill cranes each year. Past Grand Island, you'll travel north on Highway 281 then stagger-step your way east and north to Royal then on to Niobrara and the beautiful Niobrara River.

ALONG THE WAY

Town: Wood River's the **Crane Trust** (✉ 9325 S. Alda Rd. ☎ 308/382–1820 ⊕ www.cranetrust.org) is dedicated to the conservation of the majestic sandhill crane, which migrates through the region every spring. Even if you're visiting in a different season, the Crane Trust's nature center is worth a visit.

Eat & Drink: In Grand Island, stop in at the cozy **Farmer's Daughters Cafe** (✉ 105 N. Walnut St. ☎ 308/382–9794) for coffee and a "brownbox" lunch.

Roadside Attraction: Encounter 12-million-year-old wildlife at the **Ashfall Fossil Beds State Historic Park** (✉ 86930 517th Ave. ☎ 402/893–2000 ⊕ www.ashfall.unl.edu) in Royal where paleontologists are still at work uncovering the fossils left by a deadly volcanic ash fall.

NIOBRARA

Do: Native to the Niobrara River Valley region, the **Ponca Tribe** (✉ 2548 Park Ave. ☎ 402/857–3519 ⊕ www.poncatribe–ne.org) operates a museum and educational trail in Niobrara. If you're traveling in August, don't miss their annual powwow, an extravaganza of dance and Native American heritage. While in Niobrara, have an adventure on its namesake river, where you can rent a canoe, tube, or kayak on your own or with a paddle guide.

Eat & Drink: Get a burger, cheese curds, and a stiff drink at the **Sportsmen's Bar** (✉ 25411 Park Ave. ☎ 402/857–3340) or a patty melt and chicken-fried steak at the sweetly cozy Country Cafe (✉ 89141 NE-14 ☎ 402/857–3544 ⊕ www.eatcountrycafe.com).

Stay: Stay the night at the **Whitetail River Lodge** (✉ 89140 NE-14 ☎ 402/857–3564 ⊕ www.whitetailriverlodge.com), an Amish-built log cabin B&B. If you're visiting between May and October, snagging a campsite or cabin at Niobrara State Park is well worth the effort.

Breakfast: Just south of Niobrara in Verdigre, dig into Czech pastries and homestyle café classics at **Cozy Corner** (✉ 223 S. Main St. ☎ 402/668–2313 ⊕ cozy–corner–cafe–verdigre.edan.io).

Day 8: Niobrara, NE, to Seward, NE

170 miles (3 hours without traffic and stops)

Travel south to Norfolk, the hometown of legendary comedian and Tonight Show host Johnny Carson, then on to Genoa, where a former residential school for re-educating Native American children has been preserved as a museum. Continue on to Seward via Highway 81 or Highway 34.

ALONG THE WAY

Town: In Norfolk, there's the **Norfolk Arts Center** (✉ 305 N. 5th St. ☎ 402/371–7199 ⊕ www.norfolkartscenter.org) with an outdoor sculpture garden. While in Johnny Carson's childhood hometown, get a look at where he grew up: 306 South 13th Street.

Eat & Drink: While in Norfolk, get a sandwich, salad, or flatbread pizza at local favorite **Black Cow Fat Pig** (✉ 702 W. Norfolk Ave. ☎ 402/316–4315 ⊕ www.blackcowfatpig.com).

Roadside Attraction: In the 19th and early 20th centuries, the U.S. government worked to eradicate Native people by forcing their children to attend brutal boarding schools. Opened in 1884, the **Genoa Indian Industrial School** (✉ 209 E. Webster Ave. ⊕ www.genoaindianschoolmuseum.org) now operates as a museum dedicated to shedding light on this shameful chapter of American history.

Photo Op: At the end of today's road waits the largest time capsule in the world, a 45-ton vault buried in Seward in 1975.

SEWARD

Do: Seward has a charming historic downtown core lined with boutiques, galleries, and antique shops. If you're visiting between May and September, stop in the **Inner Maker Art Village** (✉ 1693 224th Rd. ☎ 402/540–6929 ⊕ www.innermaker.com), which features jewelry and art crafted by members of local tribes and an assortment of books on Native American history.

Eat & Drink: Get dinner at **Rue 6** (✉ 123 S. 6th St. ☎ 402/646–9150), a gastropub with craft cocktails, flatbread pizzas, and skillet mac and cheese, or find corned beef and burgers at the bowling alley/karaoke bar, **Sparetime Lounge & Grill** (✉ 123 S. 4th St. ☎ 402/643–3898). Thursday through Saturday, the **Bottle Rocket Brewery** (✉ 230 S. 5th St. ☎ 402/641–4314 ⊕ www.bottlerocketbrewing.com) pulls draughts until well after dark.

Stay: Spend the night in **Liberty House** (✉ 441 N. 5th St. ☎ 402/643–2555 ⊕ www.libertybbantiques.com), a quaint bed-and-breakfast, or get a room at the convenient **Cobblestone Hotel & Suites** (✉ 2575 Progressive Rd. ☎ 402/646–1004 ⊕ www.staycobblestone.com).

Breakfast: Fill up on breakfast sandwiches and Texas toast n' gravy at the homey **JD's Coffee Shop** (✉ 522 Seward St. ☎ 402/643–2739 ⊕ www.jdscoffeeshop.com).

Essential Listening

Listen to Conor Oberst's *Upside Down Mountain*. The Omaha-raised singer-songwriter and frontman of Bright Eyes runs two record labels and a bar, Pageturners Lounge, in town.

Day 9: Seward, NE, to Omaha, NE

78 miles (1 hour, 15 minutes without traffic and stops)

Pass once more through Lincoln then hop on I–80 headed for your final destination, Omaha (with a worthwhile last stop at the Wildlife Safari Park just off the interstate on Highway 66). When it's time to catch your flight, you'll find the airport, OMA, on the city's northeast edge, along with major rental car companies.

ALONG THE WAY

Eat & Drink: Stop for burgers, melts, and root beer floats at the family-owned roadside diner **HoneyCreek** (✉ 13631 Energy Way ☎ 402/786–3838 ⊕ www.honeycreekdining.com) in Greenwood.

Nature: Drive a 4-mile track through **Ashland's Wildlife Safari Park** (✉ 16406 292nd St. ☎ 402/944–9453 ⊕ www.wildlifesafaripark.com), where North American bison, wolves, pelicans, and more roam freely.

Photo Op: The beautifully designed **Holy Family Shrine** (✉ 23132 Pflug Rd. ☎ 402/332–4565 ⊕ www.hfsgretna.org) in Gretna is an Instagram-worthy stop.

OMAHA

Do: In this city of almost half a million, there's plenty to do, including visits to the **Durham** (✉ 801 S. 10th

St. ☎ 402/444–5071 ⊕ www.durham-museuml.org), a history museum in a repurposed art–deco train station, and the **Joslyn Art Museum** (2200 Dodge St. 402/342–3300 www.joslyn.org). At the headquarters of the **Lewis and Clark Trail** (✉ 601 Riverfront Dr. ☎ 402/661–1804 ⊕ www.nps.gov/lecl), learn more about the Native people with whom the Corps of Discovery communed, including the Omaha on whose homeland the city now sits.

Eat & Drink: Dine on comfort food made from local, seasonal ingredients at **Kitchen Table** (✉ 1415 Farnam St. ☎ 402/933–2810 ⊕ www.kitchentableomaha.com), then toast to your last night at **Kaitei** (✉ 6109 1/3 Maple St.), a speakeasy downstairs from a ramen shop in Benson, or the tiki bar **Laka Lono Rum Club** (✉ 1204 Howard St. ☎ 402/786–8640) in the Old Market District.

Stay: Rest up at one of Omaha's stylish downtown hotels, like the **Magnolia** (✉ 1615 Howard St. ☎ 402/341–2500 ⊕ www.magnoliahotels.com).

Breakfast: Soak up your last night's celebration with banana bread French toast and a kimchi omelet at the hip **Saddle Creek Breakfast Club** (✉ 1540 N. Saddle Creek Rd. ☎ 402/932–5970 ⊕ www.facebook.com/SCBCOmaha).

The Best of the Ozarks

Written by Kristy Alpert

Often shadowed by the midwestern metropolises that surround it, the Ozark Mountains were once defined by their isolation; today that's one of the region's greatest assets. The hills of the Ozarks roll up from the beds of sparkling rivers and peak as the grand oak and hickory trees seem to sway on the ledge of limestone bluffs. The region winds its way through the southern portions of Missouri and into northern Arkansas and eastern Oklahoma, just barely touching the edge of southeastern Kansas. The air is as pure as the hearts of the people in the region, where mom-and-pop shops thrive alongside boutique hotels, chef-driven restaurants, and world-renowned art museums. A road trip through the region offers the chance to uncover the charming folklore, natural beauty, and undiscovered gems of the Ozarks.

At a Glance

Start: Little Rock, AR

End: Little Rock, AR

Miles Traveled: 1,388 miles

Suggested Duration: 9 days

States Visited: Arkansas, Kansas, Missouri, Oklahoma

Key Sights: Crystal Bridges Museum of National Art; Elephant Rocks State Park; Hot Springs National Park; the Lake of the Ozarks; Thorncrown Chapel

Best Time to Go: Travel in spring or autumn to see the Ozark foliage in all its true glory.

Day 1: Little Rock, AR, to Bentonville, AR

215 miles (3 hours, 10 minutes without traffic and stops)

The Clinton National Airport in Little Rock is the area's biggest airport, and where you'll be able to pick up a rental car to start your trip. Although the backroads between Little Rock and Bentonville pass through the heart of the Ozark National Forest, the highway route on I–40 and I–49 gets you there in less time and takes you through Arkansas's little-known wine country.

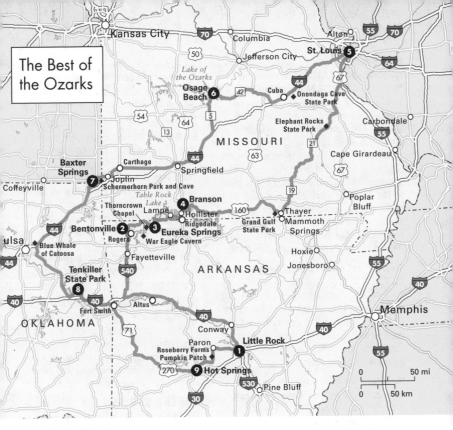

The Best of the Ozarks

ALONG THE WAY

Town: Take the exit on AR64 to venture deep into the Arkansas Wine Trail in Altus, Arkansas. The region reminded immigrants Jacob Post and Johann Wiederkehr so much of their home German and Swiss wine regions that they settled in and began growing grapes in the late 1880s. Their wineries are still there today, along with about a dozen other wineries. A drive through the region is stunning, but a short lunch break or tasting makes this stop truly memorable.

Eat & Drink: Just 4 miles off the road in the heart of the Arkansas Wine Trail in Atlus, you'll find winemaker and master sommelier Audrey House's award-winning **Chateau Aux Arc Vineyard and Winery** (✉ 8045 AR-186 ☎ 479/468–4400 ⊕ www.chateauauxarc.com). In the tasting room, visitors can sample complex blends, dry reds, and House's signature Cynthiana wines (which she pioneered to become the state grape of Arkansas).

BENTONVILLE

Do: Sam Walton put Bentonville on the map when he opened **Walton's 5&10** (✉ 105 N. Main St. ☎ 479/277–8493 ⊕ www.walmartmuseum.com) in 1951, which would later inspire the world's first Walmart. The five-and-dime store is still there, attached to an authentic soda fountain that serves arguably the best butter pecan ice cream around. More recently, another member of the Walton family, Alice Walton, helped to open the architecturally stunning **Crystal Bridges Museum of American Art** (✉ 600 Museum Way ☎ 479/418–5700 ⊕ www.crystalbridges.org) and the family-friendly **Amazeum** (✉ 1009 Museum Way ☎ 479/696–9280 ⊕ www.amazeum.org).

Eat & Drink: Join James Beard Award–nominated chef Matt McClure inside the Hive at the **21C Museum Hotel** (✉ *200 N.E. A St.* ☎ *479/286–6575* ⊕ *www.thehivebentonville.com*) for a culinary journey through farm-fresh regional cuisine with many rotating dishes that give a nod to the Indian and Hmong families that have settled in Bentonville. For an ethereal eating experience, book a table at **The Preacher's Son** (✉ *201 N.W. A St.* ☎ *479/445–6065* ⊕ *www.thepreachers-son.com*) for a gluten-free meal inside a renovated church that includes a speakeasy downstairs for after–dinner drinks.

Stay: The **21C Museum Hotel Bentonville** (✉ *200 N.E. A St.* ☎ *479/286–6500* ⊕ *www.21cmuseumhotels.com*) sits just off the main town square of downtown Bentonville and would be on the list of must–see places within the city even if you're not spending the night, thanks to its rotating gallery of art.

Breakfast: The biscuits are huge and the coffee is strong at the **Buttered Biscuit** (✉ *1403 S.E. Moberly La.* ☎ *479/319–4822* ⊕ *www.thebutteredbiscuit.co*); the strawberry cheesecake pancakes are a true indulgence.

Day 2: Bentonville, AR, to Eureka Springs, AR

44 miles (1 hour, 10 minutes without traffic and stops)

Arkansas's scenic Highway 12 is without a doubt one of the most stunning drives in the state. The road doesn't stop winding once you pass Rogers, but you'll pass beneath canopied trees and over sparkling rivers.

ALONG THE WAY

Town: The boutiques and antiques stores of historic downtown Rogers alone are worth a stop, but now the town's brick-lined streets lead to an award-winning craft brewery, the **Ozark Beer Co.**

(✉ *109 N. Arkansas St.* ☎ *479/636–2337* ⊕ *www.ozarkbeercompany.com*), and the headquarters for locally beloved **Onyx Coffee Lab** (✉ *101 E. Walnut St.* ☎ *479/899–6750* ⊕ *www.onyxcoffeelab.com*).

Eat & Drink: A short drive from downtown Rogers will put you face-to-face with Arkansas's only working watermill. The **War Eagle Mill** (✉ *11045 War Eagle Rd.* ☎ *866/492–7324* ⊕ *www.wareaglemill.com*) is a working gristmill (buy organic grain, cereal, and flour on-site), and its restaurant serves one of the best brunches in the state (breakfast and lunch are also available). Visit the third weekend in October for the mill's celebrated arts-and-craft fair.

Nature: War Eagle Cavern (✉ *21494 Cavern Dr.* ☎ *479/789–2909* ⊕ *www.wareagle-cavern.com*) is just a 2-mile drive off the main road, where you'll find the only lakeside cavern entrance in the state. Cave tours are available and take you deep within the caverns of this historic spot.

EUREKA SPRINGS

Do: More than 60 natural springs bubble and spring from this quirky Victorian town, where a series of winding staircases guide visitors up and down the steep terrain to boutique shops, family-owned restaurants (chain stores and restaurants are frowned upon), and miles of hiking trails. An active artist enclave colors the town with an artsy vibe, but it's the underground catacombs and sinister story behind the town's largest hotel that keeps intrigue alive.

Eat & Drink: A bicycle sits on top of the marquee at **Sparky's Roadhouse Café** (✉ *147 E. Van Buren* ☎ *479/253–6001* ⊕ *www.sparkysroadhouse.com*), which is the first sign of this 1950s style diner's funky decor. Come prepared to sign a waiver if you plan to sample their Stupid Hott Burger with homemade ghost chili salsa, or simply lounge with a cold beer on the open-air patio.

Stay: Known as "The Grand Ol' Lady of the Ozarks," the 1886 **Crescent Hotel and Spa** (✉ *75 Prospect Ave.* ☎ *855/725–5720* ⊕ *www.crescent–hotel.com*) features 72 guest rooms and 4 luxury lodges on its stunningly landscaped perch overlooking Eureka Springs. The hotel is known as the most haunted hotel in America, where nightly ghost tours uncover the hotel's haunting past.

Breakfast: The **Eureka Springs Coffee House** (✉ *11 N. Main St.* ☎ *479/239–2010* ⊕ *www.eurekaspringcoffee.com*) serves freshly baked cinnamon rolls and muffins alongside a variety of specialty coffee drinks made from Onyx Coffee Lab's signature roasts.

Day 3: Eureka Springs, AR, to Branson, MO

53 miles (1 hour, 10 minutes without traffic and stops)

The top end of what Arkansans call "the Pig Trail," AR23 is one of the state's most scenic drives, with wildflowers in the spring and autumn colors shimmering in the fall. The road connects with the fastest way to get to Branson via 86E and 65N.

ALONG THE WAY

Detour: Before leaving Eureka Springs, take a detour to the **Thorncrown Chapel** (✉ *12968 U.S. 62* ☎ *479/253–7401* ⊕ *www.thorncrown.com*). The chapel is in the opposite direction from Branson, but the short detour to see this hidden glass chapel in the woods is worth it. The 48–foot chapel is one of three glass chapels in Arkansas, all designed by E. Fay Jones. The walk is short from the parking lot at the base of the hill, but the views are spectacular inside and outside of this absolutely inspiring structure.

Town: Ridgedale, Missouri is home to the Top of the Rock, a scenic overlook at **Big Cedar Lodge** (✉ *190 Top of the Rock*

Extend Your Trip

From St. Louis: Route 66 *(Ch. 2)*; Along the Mississippi *(Ch. 2)*; Underrated Cities of the Midwest *(Ch. 6)*

6

Rd. ☎ *417/335–2777* ⊕ *www.bigcedar.com*) that offers four levels of viewing balconies to gaze out upon the Ozark Mountains and Table Rock Lake. Spend an hour or two soaking in the views before continuing on toward Branson.

Eat & Drink: The Buffalo Bar at Big Cedar Lodge offers the best views from its outdoor patio, where classic pub fare and wood–fired pizzas fill the lunch menu.

BRANSON

Do: Branson offers authentic American small-town charm like few other towns can even imagine. Pies are sweeter in Branson, shopping is friendlier, and the entertainment is as clean as the streets of its historic downtown.

Eat & Drink: Branson Landing (✉ *100 Branson Landing Blvd.* ☎ *417/239–3002* ⊕ *www.bransonlanding.com*) is where the nightlife action happens in town, but for an authentic Branson meal, head to the **Farmhouse Restaurant** (✉ *119 W. Main St.* ☎ *417/334–9701* ⊕ *www.farmhouserestaurantbranson.com*) to fill up on chicken-fried steak, fried okra, and their famous blackberry cobbler.

Stay: The Branson Hotel (✉ *214 W. Main St.* ☎ *417/544–9814* ⊕ *www.thebransonhotel.com*) features nine rooms inside a renovated 1903 historic buildings and is reserved only for adults. For a more family-friendly option, check out the lakefront condos at **Still Water Resort** (✉ *21 Stillwater Trail* ☎ *800/777–2320* ⊕ *www.stillwaterresort.com*) overlooking Branson's Table Rock Lake.

Breakfast: Breakfast is served all day at **Billy Gail's Café** (✉ *5291 State Hwy. 265* ☎ *417/338–8883* ⊕ *www.billygailsrestaurant.com*), where their Billion Dollar Bacon is hearty enough to be an entrée itself.

Day 4: Branson, MO, to St. Louis, MO

345 miles (6 hours, 15 minutes without traffic and stops)

Stick close to the border of Missouri and Arkansas along Route 160 E to MO-19 N before heading up U.S. 67 N for the chance to stop and explore Grand Gulf State Park and Elephant Rocks State Park.

ALONG THE WAY

Town: Thayer, Missouri, is just 10 miles from **Grand Gulf State Park** (☎ *417/264–7600* ⊕ *www.mostateparks.com*), which is more commonly known as the "Little Grand Canyon." The gulf itself stretches for a mile between canyon walls reaching 130-feet tall, where natural bridges and collapsed caves leave much to be explored.

Eat & Drink: Cross back over the border to Mammoth Springs, Arkansas, to dine alfresco by the mighty Spring River at Wood's **Riverbend Restaurant** (✉ *80 Main St.* ☎ *870/625–9357* ⊕ *riverbend–restaurant.business.site*). Breakfast is served all day long, but their barbecued ribs will keep you satisfied all the way to St. Louis.

Roadside Attraction: Elephant Rocks State Park (✉ *7390, 7406, MO-21* ☎ *573/546–3454* ⊕ *www.mostateparks.com*) is home to giant red granite boulders that have taken the shape of elephants. Use your imagination to make out the elephant shapes or simply climb to the top of the 27-foot-tall Dumbo rock for the ultimate bragging rights.

ST. LOUIS

Do: Set along the west bank of the Mississippi River, St. Louis is home to the only **National Blues Museum** (✉ *615 Washington Ave.* ☎ *314/925–0016* ⊕ *www.nationalbluesmuseum.org*) in the country and offers amazing photo ops from either the bottom or top of the city's famous **Gateway Arch** (✉ *11 N. 4th St.* ☎ *314/655–1600* ⊕ *www.nps.gov/gaar*). St. Louis is naturally suited for adventures, with its **Citygarden** (✉ *801 Market St.* ☎ *314/241–3337*), **Meramec Caverns** (✉ *1135 Hwy. W, Sullivan, MO* ☎ *573/468–2283* ⊕ *www.americascave.com*), and nature reserves.

Eat & Drink: It's the local wild cherry wood used to smoke the meat at **The Shaved Duck** (✉ *2900 Virginia Ave.* ☎ *314/776–1407* ⊕ *www.theshavedduck.com*) that makes all the difference at this award-winning St. Louis barbecue joint. You won't go wrong with anything from the smoker, but make sure to leave room for their decadent sides.

Stay: Each of the four rooms takes the name of a beautiful St. Louis location at the 19th-century **Fleur-de-Lys Mansion** (✉ *3500 Russell Blvd.* ☎ *314/773–3500* ⊕ *www.thefleurdelys.com*).

Breakfast: Breakfast is included with your stay at Fleur-de-Lys, and consists of freshly baked breads and locally roasted coffee from Thomas Coffee.

Day 5: St. Louis, MO, to Osage Beach, MO

166 miles (2 hours, 50 minutes without traffic and stops)

Not only does this route along I-44 put you on historic Route 66 for part of the trip, but you'll also pass right by Onondaga Cave State Park, a National Natural Landmark.

Hot Springs National Park is home to the most celebrated thermal waters in the country.

ALONG THE WAY

Town: Check Cuba off your list ... well, at least Cuba, Missouri; this small town is loaded with charisma. Drive along Cuba's Historic Route 66 for an outdoor art gallery of sorts as you pass by the town's 14 outdoor murals depicting famous moments in history.

Eat & Drink: Shelly's Route 66 Café (✉ 402 S. Lawrence St. ☎ 573/885–6000) in Cuba hasn't changed much since it first opened during the historic route's heyday. This classic diner serves hearty breakfasts and daily specials for lunch.

Photo Op: The dramatic stalagmites and impressive underground ponds within **Onondaga Cave State Park** (✉ 7556 Hwy. H ☎ 573/245–6576 ⊕ www.mostateparks. com) are just as photogenic as the Vilander Bluff natural area that sits above them; although you don't need to wait for a guide to access the panoramic views of the Meramec River at the top of Vilander Bluff.

OSAGE BEACH

Do: Osage Beach is just one of the quaint towns surrounding Lake of the Ozarks, where everything revolves around the water. Speedboats, pontoons, fishing boats, and Jet Skis can all be rented at an hourly rate, and even the local spas offer floating therapies.

Eat & Drink: Enjoy excellent views and casual bites at the **Redhead Lakeside Grill and Yacht Club** (✉ 1700 Yacht Club Dr. ☎ 573/693–1525 ⊕ www.redheadlake-sidegrill.com); you can even spend the day in the lakeside pool. Or enjoy drinks and bar food at **Shorty Pants Lounge and Marina** (✉ 1680 Autumn La. ☎ 573/302–1745 ⊕ www.shortypantslounge.com).

Shop: There are more than 35 stores mapped out along the **Osage Beach Outlet Marketplace** (✉ 4540 Osage Beach Pkwy. ☎ 573/348–6065 ⊕ www.premiumout-lets.com), where shoppers can score deals on designer handbags or grab a stylish swimsuit for the lake.

Stay: The **Inn at Harbour Ridge** (✉ *6334 Red Barn Rd.* ☎ *573/302–0411* ⊕ *www. harbourridgeinn.com*) is located just outside the city limits of Osage Beach on a lakefront property nearby a community dock and swimming platform.

Breakfast: At the Inn at Harbour Ridge, gourmet breakfasts of cheddar omelets or baked cinnamon French toast and peach-smothered sausages fuel guests for a day of adventuring around the lake.

Day 6: Osage Beach, MO, to Baxter Springs, KS

170 miles (2 hours, 45 minutes without traffic and stops)

This long stretch of highway on I-44 goes by fast and ends with a stop along historic Route 66.

ALONG THE WAY

Eat & Drink: Set along Route 66, 1950s-style **Iggy's Diner** (✉ *2400 Grand Ave.* ☎ *417/237–0212* ⊕ *www.iggysdiner. com*) in Carthage, Missouri, serves breakfast, lunch, and dinner, and hand-dips the ice cream for their famous floats, malts, and shakes.

Roadside Attraction: Designed by Precious Moments creator Samuel J. Butcher, the **Precious Moments Chapel** (✉ *4321 S. Chapel Rd.* ☎ *800/543–7975* ⊕ *www. preciousmomentschapel.org*) in Carthage is a standalone chapel devoted entirely to the Precious Moments characters the artist created decades ago. Sistine Chapel–style murals line the inside of the building, while a gift shop sells everything from exclusive figurines to wedding accessories.

Nature: A long viewing platform at the **Schermerhorn Park and Cave** (✉ *3501 S. Main St.* ☎ *620/783–2373*) lets visitors peek inside this half-mile-long cave, where rare species of salamander are protected by the EPA. The park is part

of the 55 square miles that comprise the Ozarks of Kansas, and this little slice of the state is ripe with caves, sinking streams, and sinkholes.

BAXTER SPRINGS

Do: The historic town of Baxter Springs is just a few miles from the OK-KS-MO Tri-State Marker (you can stand in three places at one time!), where it sits along Route 66 with preserved gas stations and vintage service buildings. The town's Native American and Route 66 history are explored within the **Baxter Springs Heritage Center & Museum** (✉ *740 East Ave.* ☎ *620/856–2385* ⊕ *www.baxter-springsmusuem.org*), where visitors can begin a self-guided drive to 12 different sites along the town's Civil War trail, including **Fort Blair** (✉ *198 E. 6th St.* ☎ *620/856–2385* ⊕ *www.baxterspring-smusuem.org*).

Eat & Drink: Weston's **Route 66 Café** (✉ *1737 Military Ave.* ☎ *620/856–4414*) offers comfort diner food with friendly service.

Stay: The three bedrooms inside the **Rose Cottage** (✉ *221 E. 9th St.* ☎ *620/856–2524* ⊕ *www.rosecottagekansas.com*) along Route 66 encompass both floors of the 1899 Victorian home.

Breakfast: Breakfast is where **Weston's Café** (✉ *1737 Military Ave.* ☎ *620/856–4414*) really shines: the coffee is hot, the biscuits are drenched in gravy, and pies are made fresh daily.

Day 7: Baxter Springs, KS, to Tenkiller State Park, OK

58 miles (2 hours, 35 minutes without traffic and stops)

Continue along Route 66 as you pass over the Kansas border into Oklahoma toward the Blue Whale of Catoosa (one of the kitschier roadside attractions along the route). From there you'll begin to weave your way back and forth over the Arkansas River before arriving in the state park.

ALONG THE WAY

Town: The **Blue Whale of Catoosa** (✉ *2600 U.S. Rte. 66* ☎ *918/266–2505*) may sound like a mythical creature, but in the town of Catoosa, it's a local legend. Made from metal and cement, the whale was built in a pond as a surprise anniversary gift in the 1970s but became a secret swimming hole along Route 66. Swimming is no longer allowed, but the spot is a popular picnic area.

Eat & Drink: While in Catoosa, grab a pineapple whip (or a snow cone topped with Nerds and a Ring Pop) from the **Oh Mighty Ices** (✉ *603 S. Cherokee St.* ☎ *918/693–1852*) seasonal food truck and enjoy your treat around the colorful picnic tables set up by the whale.

TENKILLER STATE PARK

Do: There are more than 130 miles of shoreline surrounding Lake Tenkiller at **Tenkiller State Park** (✉ *448159 E. 979 Dr., Vian, OK* ☎ *918/489–5641* ⊕ *www.travelok.com*). Along with watersports and fishing, the clear waters of the lake provide ideal conditions for scuba diving to the lake's sunken treasures, including an airplane fuselage, a school bus, a helicopter, and two boats.

Eat & Drink: Boats and Jet Skis can pull right up to the floating deck at **Clearwater Café** (✉ *Lake Tenkiller State Park, Vian, OK* ☎ *918/489–5655* ⊕ *www.facebook.com/clearwater.tenkiller*) at Pine Cove Marina on Tenkiller Lake, where steaks are cooked to order and onion rings come stacked a foot high.

Stay: RV and tent campgrounds line the park grounds, but it's the state park's 38 cabins that offer the best views along the lake.

Breakfast: There are few things sweeter than **Sweet Nana's Donuts** (✉ *207 E. Schley* ☎ *918/773–5003* ⊕ *www.facebook.com/sweetnanasdonuts*), other than maybe Nana herself. This mom–and–pop bakery serves full breakfasts (bacon, eggs, breakfast burritos, hot coffee, etc.), but the specialty doughnuts, maple bacon bars, and sausage rolls are among their best sellers.

Day 8: Tenkiller State Park, OK, to Hot Springs, AK

175 miles (3 hours, 30 minutes without traffic and stops)

Follow I–40 through Oklahoma and, just before crossing the Arkansas River, veer onto U.S. 71 S into Fort Smith, Arkansas, where you'll soon be driving out of the Ozarks and into Ouachita National Forest.

ALONG THE WAY

Town: Fort Smith is the third–most–populated city in Arkansas, and this quirky town offers everything from an amusement park ride in the middle of its downtown to a museum dedicated entirely to the spot where Elvis Presley got his first buzz cut when joining the army on March 25, 1958.

Eat & Drink: The cranberry pecan bread at **The Bread Box** (✉ *7004 S. Fresno St.* ☎ *479/424–1200* ⊕ *www.thebreadbox-andmore.com*) in Fort Smith is legendary around Arkansas. Sandwiches are the specialty at this family-run bakery, so try the chicken salad sandwich on cranberry pecan bread or the Amy Joe grown-up grilled cheese with melted cheddar and swiss cheeses on grilled spinach feta bread topped with tomatoes, sliced pickles, and jalapenos.

HOT SPRINGS

Do: In Central Arkansas's Ouachita Mountains, Hot Springs is home to some of the most prized thermal waters in the country (143 degrees and packed full of minerals). Run the bases around one of the first MLB Spring Training fields in the United States or soak in the gangster history inside **Hot Springs National Park** (✉ *369 Central Ave.* ☎ *501/620–6715* ⊕ *www.nps.gov/hosp*) at Bathhouse Row, where many of these historic hot spring bathhouses are still operational (they were once a favorite vacation spot for legendary criminals Al Capone, Lucky Luciano, and Bugsy Siegel).

Eat & Drink: Inside a renovated bathhouse, **Superior Bathhouse Brewery** (✉ *329 Central Ave.* ☎ *501/624–2337* ⊕ *www.superiorbathhouse.com*) serves upscale pub food and craft beers brewed from the thermal waters of the national park. Former speakeasy and mobster hangout, **The Ohio Club** (✉ *336 Central Ave.* ☎ *501/627–0702* ⊕ *www.theohioclub.com*) is still a hot spot for nightlife in Hot Springs.

Stay: The chic **Hotel Hale** (✉ *341 Central Ave.* ☎ *501/760–9010* ⊕ *www.hotel-hale.com*) operates inside a renovated bathhouse along Bathhouse Row, where the boutique property features nine modern guest rooms with thermal water bathtubs.

Breakfast: Kollective Coffee and Tea (✉ *110 Central Ave.* ☎ *501/701–4000* ⊕ *www.facebook.com/kollectivecoffeetea*) is one of the top third-wave coffee shops in Arkansas, serving organic and local specialties (vegan options available) alongside locally roasted coffee.

Day 9: Hot Springs, AR, to Little Rock, AR

62 miles (1 hour, 25 minutes without traffic and stops)

Keep an eye out for roadside stands selling quartz crystals as you drive along Arkansas's scenic Highway 7 toward Owensville, then cross through the last stretches of the Ouachita National Forest on AR-9 toward Paron before taking the scenic route into Little Rock on Kanis Road.

ALONG THE WAY

Nature: During a fall road trip, stop in at the **Roseberry Farms Pumpkin Patch** (✉ *12223 AR-9* ☎ *501/722–8545* ⊕ *www.roseberry–farms.com*) for an authentic Arkansas hayride and s'mores around the fire.

LITTLE ROCK

Do: Arkansas's capital is a city of tales and trails. The tales begin with **Little Rock Central High School**, a National Historic Site (✉ *2120 W. Daisy L. Gatson Bates Dr.* ☎ *501/374–1957* ⊕ *www.nps.gov/chsc*) on the U.S. Civil Rights Trail, and the trails begin with the **Big Dam Bridge** (✉ *4000 Cook's Landing Rd.* ⊕ *www.bigdambridge.com*) that connects to 14 miles of winding trails along the city's River Trail system. The trail connects Little Rock's bustling River Market District to countless breweries and restaurants, and even provides pedestrian/cyclist access to the **Clinton Presidential Center** (✉ *1200 President Clinton Ave.* ☎ *501/374–4242* ⊕ *www.clintonlibrary.gov*).

Eat & Drink: Set inside a repurposed gas station, **The Fold: Botanas & Bar** (✉ *3501 Old Cantrell Rd.* ☎ *501/916–9706* ⊕ *www.thefoldlr.com*) serves modern Ark-Mex at its finest. The decor is retro chic and the tacos are served on handmade tortillas and filled with locally sourced ingredients. Order a ground-bison burrito and a homemade lemonade for the full experience.

Stay: The Empress of Little Rock (✉ *2120 S. Louisiana St.* ☎ *501/374–7966* ⊕ *www.theempress.com*) is listed on the National Register of Historic Places for its pure representation of Victorian architecture.

Breakfast: Out in the Argenta Arts District, Saturdays are for pancakes over at **Mugs Café** (✉ *515 Main St.* ☎ *501/379–9101* ⊕ *www.mugscoffeecompany.com*). During the week, the hipster coffeehouse serves breakfast starting at 7 am and locally roasted coffee all day long.

The Best of the Heartland

Written by Kristine Hansen

America's heartland—a more appropriate nickname for the oft-labeled "flyover country" since midwesterners really are the nicest people you'll ever meet—may be flush with farmland, but it's also a supremely underrated destination for the arts, dining, and nature. On this nine-day trip, you'll explore a mix of college towns and metropolises that provide the perfect balance of nightlife and small-town charm. Get ready to paddle, bike, and stroll across the great states of Wisconsin, Iowa, and Minnesota, all while finding out what makes this region so unique.

At a Glance

Start: Milwaukee, WI

End: Milwaukee, WI

Miles Traveled: 1,655 miles

Suggested Duration: 9 days

States Visited: Iowa, Minnesota, Wisconsin

Key Sights: Apostle Islands National Lakeshore,;Grant Wood's American Gothic House & Center; Milwaukee Art Museum; Rock Island State Park; Voyageurs National Park

Best Time to Go: Unless you want to snowmobile or cross-country ski, it's best to stick to a season free of snow and hazardous driving conditions. Spring and fall mean fewer crowds, but even then, you may need to pack a winter jacket, so summer is your best bet.

Day 1: Milwaukee, WI, to Madison, WI

80 miles (1 hour, 20 minutes without traffic and stops)

You literally cannot get lost driving between Wisconsin's two largest cities: the only way to travel on I-94 is west (Lake Michigan is a dead end to the east). Pick up your rental car at General Mitchell International Airport, a quick 15-minute drive north of downtown Milwaukee.

ALONG THE WAY

Detour: Built by Chicagoans during the turn of the last century, Lake Geneva (population 8,000) is Wisconsin's Lake Como (there's even a nearby lake called Lake Como) with the type of grand historic estates you'd find in Newport, Rhode Island. The 26-mile path around the namesake lake might seem daunting, but you'll get a good view from Horticultural Hall, with its red-tile roof.

Eat & Drink: Don't knock the truck stop at the **Pine Cone Travel Plaza** (✉ *685 Linmar La.* ☎ *920/699–2766* ⊕ *www.pineconetravelplazamenu.com*) in Johnson Creek. The cream puffs are nearly the size of your head and there's an actual cheese department.

Nature: Even today, Wisconsin is home to a significant portion of the country's Native American population. At **Aztalan State Park** (✉ *N6200 County Rd. Q* ☎ *608/873–9695* ⊕ *www.dnr.wisconsin.gov*), a National Historic Landmark in Jefferson, you can view remnants and a reconstruction of a Middle Mississippian village (from between AD 1000 and 1300) on a short walk.

MADISON

Do: Wander into the century-old **State Capitol building** (✉ *2 E. Main St.* ☎ *608/266–0382* ⊕ *www.wisconsin.gov*) for a free, self-guided tour (it actually has one of the largest domes in the world). Then

ogle a genuine Thai pavilion (a gift from the Thai government to the University of Wisconsin, and the only such example in the continental United States) at the 16-acre **Olbrich Botanical Gardens** (✉ *3330 Atwood Ave.* ☎ *608/246–4550* ⊕ *www. olbrich.org*).

Eat & Drink: You're in the Dairy State for a reason, right? At Memorial Union on the University of Wisconsin campus, enjoy a scoop of ice cream at **Daily Scoop** (✉ *800 Langdon St.* ☎ *608/262–5959* ⊕ *www. union.wisc.edu*). It's crafted on campus and paired with a view of Lake Mendota from the sprawling terrace. For dinner, **The Old Fashioned** (✉ *23 N. Pinckney St.* ☎ *608/310–4545* ⊕ *www.theoldfash-ioned.com*) is a tourist hot spot, but its cheese curds and beer cheese soup don't miss; it's the perfect place to try a Wisconsin Old Fashioned, too (which replaces whiskey with brandy).

Stay: Because you're only here for one night, the view is a nonnegotiable amenity. Check into **The Edgewater** (✉ *1001 Wisconsin Pl.* ☎ *608/535–8200* ⊕ *www. theedgewater.com*), a full-service resort towering above Lake Mendota. Deep-fried cheese curds at Statehouse are a must, as is a walk on the hotel's pier.

Breakfast: As with every college town, Madison is loaded with coffee shops. On State Street (which connects the University of Wisconsin campus with Capitol Square), you'll find **Michelangelo's Coffee House** (✉ *114 State St.* ☎ *608/251–5299* ⊕ *www.michelangeloscoffeehouse.com*), a café-style concept with a black-and-white domed awning out front.

Day 2: Madison, WI, to Iowa City, IA

175 miles (3 hours without traffic and stops)

Leaving Wisconsin and taking U.S. 151 S all the way, you'll cut through the country's highest concentration of organic farms (in Vernon County, including the town of Viroqua) and cross the glorious Mississippi River in Dubuque, Iowa.

ALONG THE WAY

Eat & Drink: Wollersheim Winery, Distillery, and Bistro (✉ *7876 WI-188* ☎ *608/643–6515* ⊕ *www.wollersheim.com*) in Prairie du Sac, Wisconsin is where Hungarian Agoston Haraszthy planted grapevines in the 1840s before founding California's oldest commercial winery, Buena Vista Winery in Sonoma.

Detour: Baraboo is home to Wisconsin's most popular state park, **Devil's Lake State Park** (✉ *S5975 Park Rd.* ⊕ *www.dnr.wi.gov*). Rock climbers love it and so do swimmers. Even with just an hour to spare you can still fit in a hefty hike.

Roadside Attraction: Trust us, you have not seen anything like the quirky, weird, and wonderful **House on the Rock** (✉ *5754 WI-23* ☎ *608/935–3639* ⊕ *www.thehouseontherock.com*) in the town of Spring Green, Wisconsin. Alex Jordan—an admirer of then local architect Frank Lloyd Wright, whose homestead (Taliesin) is just up the road—built this in 1960; it's cantilevered atop a rock and contains the world's largest indoor carousel.

IOWA CITY

Do: Ninety minutes southwest of Iowa City, you'll find the **American Gothic House & Center** (✉ *300 American Gothic St.* ☎ *641/652–3352* ⊕ *www.americangothichouse.org*), the house in one of America's most famous paintings (*American Gothic* by Grant Wood, an Iowan painter). There's even a costume closet of denim

and pitchforks so you can emulate the farming couple. Back in Iowa City, find out why UNESCO named it a City of Literature, in part due to the University of Iowa's Writers' Workshop (the nation's best creative writing program). Take a stroll on the "ped mall" (car-free street) or take a tour of the two university museums, the **Stanley Museum of Art** (✉ *125 N. Madison St.* ☎ *319/335–1727* ⊕ *www.stanleymuseum.uiowa.edu*) and the **Museum of Natural History** (✉ *17 N. Clinton St.* ☎ *319/335–0480* ⊕ *www.mnh.uiowa.edu*).

Eat & Drink: You can count on a college town to go beyond burgers, and that's exactly what draws locals to **Thai Spice** (✉ *1210 S. Gilbert St.* ☎ *319/351–2581* ⊕ *www.facebook.com/thaispiceiowacity*) for comfort food or **Szechuan House** for spicy Chinese dishes (✉ *320 E. Burlington St.* ☎ *319/338–6788* ⊕ *www.szechuanhouseia.com*).

Stay: Despite Iowa's appreciation for the arts, funky and artsy hotels haven't quite arrived here yet. Dovetailing the tiny-house trend, bunk at the 700-square-foot Milk House at **Lucky Star Farm** (✉ *2625 Hwy. 1 SW* ☎ *319/683–4042* ⊕ *www.theluckystarfarm.com*), an Airbnb located between Iowa City and Kalona in Johnson County. On the 20–acre working farm, you'll find llamas, goats, a chicken coop, a pond (borrow a stand-up paddleboard), and a fire pit.

Breakfast: In downtown Iowa City, the "Macpullman" at the **Pullman Bar & Diner** (✉ *17 S. Dubuque St.* ☎ *319/338–1808* ⊕ *www.pullmandiner.com*) is a delicious riff on a fast-food favorite: sausage, egg, and cheese on an English muffin, topped with chipotle aioli.

Day 3: Iowa City, IA, to Eau Claire, WI

282 miles (5 hours without traffic and stops)

You have two options to head north out of Iowa City: I–380 N (the freeway) or the more scenic IA-1. Taking the latter option drops you along the Mississippi River on U.S. 151 N.

ALONG THE WAY

Attraction: Learn more about Grant Wood at the **Grant Wood Studio and Museum** (✉ 810 2nd Ave. SE ☎ 319/366–7503 ⊕ www.crma.org/grant–wood/grant–wood–studio) in Cedar Rapids, Iowa.

Eat & Drink: If you're lucky, you might hook up with a pizza farm (a unique phenomenon where pizzas are baked on a farm that grows nearly all of the ingredients) from **A to Z Produce and Bakery** (✉ N2956 Anker La. ☎ 715/448–4802 ⊕ www.atozproduceandbakery.com) in Stockholm, Wisconsin. But if not, **Stockholm Pie & General Store** (✉ N2030 Spring St. ☎ 715/442–5505 ⊕ www.stockholmpieandgeneralstore.com) will satisfy.

EAU CLAIRE

Do: Rent a bicycle to further explore one of the Midwest's best examples of a renaissance. Check out **Tangled Up in Hue** (✉ 505 S. Barstow St. ☎ 715/855–0090 ⊕ www.tangledupinhue.com), with works by 100 artists, and the vibrant taproom at the **Brewing Projekt** (⊕ 1807 N. Oxford Ave. ☎ 715/598–1836 ⊕ www.thebrewingprojekt.com). Don't miss the **Pablo Center at the Confluence** (✉ 128 Graham Ave. ☎ 715/832–2787 ⊕ www.pablocenter.org), an arts center along the Chippewa River with live performances and rotating art exhibits.

Eat & Drink: Since its 1994 debut, **Mona Lisa's** (✉ 428 Water St. ☎ 715/839–8969 ⊕ www.monalisas.biz) in downtown Eau Claire has ranked high with locals for its artistically plated Italian dinners that are a mix of surf and turf.

Stay: Owned and operated by Justin Vernon (the Grammy Award–winning artist also known as Bon Iver), **The Oxbow Hotel** (✉ 516 Galloway St. ☎ 715/839–0601 ⊕ www.theoxbowhotel.com) lets you borrow records to play back in your room and also hosts a farm-to-fork restaurant with outdoor seating and live music.

Breakfast: Whether you want to grab one of six signature croissants to go or dine in over egg entrées with a twist (like the Green Goddess or smoked salmon scramble), **The French Press** (✉ ☎ 715/598–7017 ⊕ www.thefrenchpressauclaire.com) is a little taste of Europe.

Day 4: Eau Claire, WI, to St. Cloud, MN

156 miles (2 hours, 30 minutes without traffic and stops)

Follow I–94 W to the Twin Cities (Minneapolis and St. Paul), then on to St. Cloud, named after Saint–Cloud, a city near Paris, France.

ALONG THE WAY

Photo Op: The **Minneapolis Sculpture Garden** (✉ 725 Vineland Pl. ☎ 612/375–7600 ⊕ www.walkerart.org), part of the **Walker Art Center in Minneapolis**, is a great spot to stretch your legs and take in some art,

Extend Your Trip

From Madison, Milwaukee, or Iowa City: Underrated Cities of the Midwest *(Ch. 6)*

From Door County: All the Great Lakes *(Ch. 6)*

including its most famous piece: a spoon cradling a cherry.

Eat & Drink: You can have a decent lunch, with a malt, at the three locations of **Snuffy's Malt Shop** (⊕ www.snuffysmalt-shops.com)—in Minnetonka, Edina, or Bloomington—for a fun dip back into the 1950s.

Town: A perennial pick for one of the most beautiful small towns in America, Stillwater, Minnesota, sits on the west bank of the St. Paul River. Check out the river and the town via the River City Sculpture Tour or pop in and out of antiques shops on Main Street.

ST. CLOUD

Do: If you like to kayak or canoe, the Beaver Islands (30 very small islands in the Mississippi River) are a fun outing. Prefer to keep dry and on land? The **Munsinger Clemens Gardens** (⊠ 1515 Riverside Dr. SE ☏ 320/257–5959 ⊕ www.ci.stcloud.mn.us) have been blooming and thriving since the 1930s on the banks of the Mississippi River. The White Garden is inspired by the famous Sissinghurst Castle Garden in Kent, England.

Eat & Drink: You'll find a range of options in St. Cloud, from Indian at **Star of India** (⊠ 2812 W. Division St. ☏ 320/281–3388 ⊕ www.starofindiamn.com) to Mongolian at **Mongo's Grill** (3701 W. Division St. 320/253–2695 www.mongosgrill.com). **Jules' Bistro** (⊠ 921 W. St. Germain St. ☏ 320/252–7125 ⊕ www.julesbistrostcloud.com), serving contemporary American cuisine, is a fine option, too.

Stay: Although St. Cloud's hotel cluster is dominated by chains, a suitable alternative is **Pillar Inn** (⊠ 419 Main St. ☏ 320/685–3828 ⊕ www.thepillarinn.com) in nearby Cold Spring. Just three rooms are tucked into the Queen Anne beauty.

Breakfast: Skip Starbucks and go to **Rock Creek Coffeehouse** (⊠ 214 2nd Ave. N ☏ 320/281–5713 ⊕ www.

rockcreekcoffeehouse.com) in nearby Sauk Rapids. It opens at 6 am, which is useful to know, as Voyageurs National Park is your next stop and you'll want lots of time to explore.

Day 5: St. Cloud, MN, to Voyageurs National Park, MN

247 miles (4 hours, 20 minutes without traffic and stops)

You're going to need nearly the full day at **Voyageurs National Park** (☏ 218/283–6600 ⊕ www.nps.gov/voya) as this natural paradise spanning 220,000 acres is not a drive-in type of park like Yellowstone or Yosemite. Fill up your coffee mug and get going early.

ALONG THE WAY

Eat & Drink: Hibbing is one of the few towns you'll pass through on MN–65 N and U.S. 53 N. Skip the breweries and pizza joints for more appropriate morning food: pastries at the fourth-generation-owned **Sunrise Bakery** (⊠ 2601 1st Ave. ☏ 218/263–4985 ⊕ www.sunrisebakery.com).

VOYAGEURS NATIONAL PARK

Do: This isn't a park where you can pull up to the visitor center, grab a map, and head off on a quick hike. Guided boat tours (which take about two hours) are the recommended way to experience the vast park. Tours depart daily in the high season from Rainy Lake and Kabetogama visitor centers. For a deeper immersion, hire a local guide who can show you the park through overnight camping.

Eat & Drink: As remote as this park is, you can actually have lunch without leaving it at the **Kettle Falls Hotel** (⊠ 12977 Chippewa Trail ☏ 218/240–1724 ⊕ www.kettlefallshotel.com), accessible only by water. Otherwise, it's recommended you pack your own food in.

Wisconsin's Door County is especially scenic during the fall.

Stay: If your time is limited but you still want to see as much of the park as possible, then **Ebel's Voyageur Houseboats** (✉ *10326 Ash River Trail, Orr, MN* ☎ *218/374–3571* ⊕ *www.ebels.com*) allows you to squeeze in more time along—and above—the water. Or stay at **The Nomad Motel** (✉ *10 Riverview Blvd, International Falls, MN* ☎ *218/302–1096* ⊕ *www.thenomadmotel.com*), a 1950s-era motel with design details in the guestrooms like caneback bedframes and sunburst mirrors.

Breakfast: Regardless of where you end up staying, packing your own breakfast or stopping at a fast food stop once you hit the road is your best bet.

Day 6: Voyageurs National Park, MN, to Bayfield, WI

227 miles (4 hours without traffic and stops)

Once you hit Duluth, you'll drive around the rim of Lake Superior for the rest of the trip on U.S. 53 S and then again on State Highway 13 S.

ALONG THE WAY

Detour: To properly experience Boundary Waters Canoe Area Wilderness (just over 1 million acres in size) would take several days, but you can still get a sneak peek, particularly of the surrounding towns like Grand Marais, by traveling north on MN 61 N. Just be sure to allow enough time to get back on the route to Bayfield. From Duluth to Grand Marais is about four hours round–trip.

Eat & Drink: Gronk's Grill & Bar (✉ 4909 E. 2nd St. ☎ 715/398–0333 ⊕ www.gronksgrill.com) in Superior, Wisconsin, hits you with humor before you've even taken your first bite. First, there's the faux sign for a "fish camp" on the log cabin exterior. Then, you'll see the His and Hers burgers (Gronk Burger is a breaded burger stacked with bacon and barbecue sauce while Ms. Gronk Burger is topped with deep-fried pickles).

BAYFIELD

Do: Thankfully it's possible to experience the **Apostle Islands National Lakeshore** (✉ 415 Washington Ave. ☎ 715/779–3397 ⊕ www.nps.gov/apis) on a day trip, even if you don't sail or have a kayak (although those can be rented in town if you wish to explore the caves). The Madeline Island Ferry Line takes you from Bayfield to Madeline in 25 minutes while the 2½-hour Grand Tour from **Apostle Islands Cruises** (✉ 2 Front St. ☎ 715/779–3925 ⊕ www.apostleisland.com) coasts by nearly all of islands on a 55-mile sail.

Eat & Drink: For a progressive, orchard-driven feast, Bayfield is loaded with options, including **Blue Vista Farm** (✉ 34045 S. Hwy. J ☎ 715/779–5400 ⊕ www.bluevistafarm.com), **North Wind Organic Farm** (✉ 86760 Valley Rd. ☎ 715/779–3254 ⊕ www.northwindorganicfarm.org), and **Erickson's Orchard** (✉ 86600 Betzold Rd. ☎ 715/913–0717 ⊕ www.ericksonorchard.com). The farm stands sell baked goods and cider, along with produce and fruit. For something more substantial, try a Lake Superior–caught whitefish sandwich at **Morty's Pub** (✉ 108 Rittenhouse Ave. ☎ 715/779–3996 ⊕ www.mortyspub.com), a block from the lake.

Stay: Wild Rice Retreat (✉ 84860 Old San Rd. ☎ 715/779–0178 ⊕ www.wildriceretreat.com) is the kind of wellness stay you might find in Sedona, Arizona, but with that Great Lakes friendliness. You can sign up for a guided retreat or create your own Zen with yoga classes.

Essential Listening

Listen to the audiobook of Wisconsin memoirist Michael Perry's *Population 485*, a raw portrait of a small town (New Auburn, Wisconsin) told through the lens of his experiences as a volunteer firefighter.

Accommodations are in the Treehaus, the Ricepod, or the Nest, all examples of modern architecture carved into a woodsy backdrop. With an expansive porch overlooking Lake Superior, **Rittenhouse Inn** (✉ 301 Rittenhouse Ave. ☎ 715/779–5111 ⊕ www.rittenhouseinn.com) is an historic B&B in downtown Bayfield that has won over many travelers.

Breakfast: Wonderstate Coffee (✉ 117 Rittenhouse Ave. ☎ 715/913–0330 ⊕ www.wonderstate.com) is the Bayfield outpost for the Viroqua-based coffee roaster. Along with coffee, they sell a variety of locally baked pastries.

Day 7: Bayfield, WI, to Green Bay, WI

279 miles (4 hours, 45 minutes without traffic and stops)

It's exciting to think you're in one of the northernmost areas of the United States, isn't it? Canada is, well, just to the north, separated from the continental United States by Lake Superior. Today you'll drive U.S. 51 S for the majority of the route, cutting through what Wisconsinites call "the North Woods" or simply "Up North."

ALONG THE WAY

Roadside Attraction: Wisconsin Concrete Park (✉ *8236 State Hwy. 13* ☏ *715/339–7282* ∰ *www.wisconsinconcretepark.org*) in Phillips may be a bit of a detour, but if you like the slightly weird, and wish to understand one of Wisconsin's most overlooked art traditions (outsider art), it's worth the journey. On its 18 acres, you'll find 237 embellished mixed-media and concrete statues by the late Fred Smith.

Eat & Drink: Just outside the Menomonie Indian Reservation, **Jake's Supper Club** (✉ *E5690 County Rd.* ☏ *715/235–2465* ∰ *www.jakessupperclub.com*) on Tainter Lake is an introduction to another Wisconsin tradition: the supper club. Portions are huge and the service is leisurely, so keep in mind that this is not an option if you're short on time. And despite the name, they open at 3:30 pm on weekdays and serve brunch on weekends.

GREEN BAY

Do: With only about 100,000 residents, Green Bay is a real anomaly for its size: it hosts an NFL team—the Green Bay Packers, who have earned 13 National Champion titles)—along with the **Green Bay Botanical Garden** (✉ *2600 Larsen Rd.* ☏ *920/490–9457* ∰ *www.gbbg.org*), the **NEW Zoo & Adventure Park** (✉ *4378 Reforestation Rd.* ☏ *920/434–7841* ∰ *www.newzoo.org*), the charmingly old-fashioned **Bay Beach Amusement Park** (✉ *1313 Bay Beach Rd.* ☏ *920/448–3365* ∰ *greenbaywi.gov/445/Bay–Beach*), and the 700-acre **Bay Beach Wildlife Sanctuary** (✉ *1660 E. Shore Dr.* ☏ *920/391–3671* ∰ *www.baybeachwildlife.com*).

Eat & Drink: Even if you're not a Green Bay Packers fan, grab lunch or dinner at Lambeau Field's **1919 Kitchen & Tap** (✉ *1265 Lombardi Ave.* ☏ *920/965–6970* ∰ *www.1919kitchenandtap.com*). You can also sign up for a guided tour to learn more about the NFL's only community-owned team, tour the Packers Hall of Fame, and shop in the pro shop, with its staggering amount of NFL-inspired items.

Stay: Downtown Green Bay's gem is **Hotel Northland** (✉ *304 N. Adams St.* ☏ *920/393–7499* ∰ *www.marriott.com*), a restored historic property originally opened in the 1920s. Dinner is served in the Walnut Room with a bar that looks right out of *The Great Gatsby*.

Breakfast: The Creamery Downtown (✉ *114 Pine St.* ☏ *920/489–8437* ∰ *www.thecreamerycafe.com*) serves everything from homemade chai tea to Bloody Marys to get your day started, along with menu items such as a Benedict Flight or truffle scrambled eggs.

Day 8: Green Way, WI, to Door County, WI

44 miles (45 minutes without traffic and stops)

This is your easiest and shortest driving day, but that's only because once you arrive in Sturgeon Bay, you'll be driving along the peninsula to experience the glory of Door County, an area similar in beauty and stature to New England's Nantucket. From Sturgeon Bay (the county seat to Northpoint (the northernmost tip), it's about a one hour drive covering 45 miles.

ALONG THE WAY

Eat & Drink: In Ephraim since 1906, **Wilson's Restaurant & Ice Cream** (✉ *9990 Water St. S* ☏ *920/854–2041* ∰ *www.wilsonsicecream.com*) is across the street from Green Bay (the body of water, not the city). It's where you can score an ice-cream cone or basket of greasy fare like burgers and fries.

Shop: People come to Door County to shop their hearts out, thanks to the region's many antique stores. **Summer Camp Antiques** (✉ *11996 WI-42* ☏ *920/854–8081* ∰ *www.summercampantiques.com*) in Ellison Bay is highly curated and worth a stop if you don't like to dig too much.

Nature: Washington Island is home to two lavender fields—**Fragrant Isle** (✉ *1350 Airport Rd.* ☎ *920/847–2950* ⊕ *www. fragrantisle.com*) and **Island Lavender** (✉ *1309 Range Line Rd.* ☎ *920/737–1531* ⊕ *www.islandlavender.com*). Be sure to pick up some dried lavender for the rest of your journey. Both companies also feature lavender-laden gardens you can stroll.

DOOR COUNTY

Do: Bypass the throngs of tourists in Door County for a two-ferry trip to **Rock Island State Park** (✉ *1924 Indian Point Rd.* ☎ *920/847–2235* ⊕ *www.dnr.wisconsin. gov*). First, you need to get to Washington Island: hop the Washington Island Car Ferry from the northern tip of Door County's peninsula, then the passenger ferry from there. On Rock Island is Pottawatomie Lighthouse, dating back to 1836 and open for tours daily between Memorial Day and Columbus Day. Just note that cars and bicycles are not allowed on Rock Island.

Eat & Drink: On Washington Island, **Red Cup Coffee House** (✉ *1885 Detroit Harbor Rd.* ☎ *920/847–3304* ⊕ *www.redcupkillercoffee.com*) is a nice stop to fuel up. Fair Isle, selling fair-trade trinkets and gifts, is adjacent.

Stay: Outside of Sturgeon Bay, the county's largest town, you won't find a single chain hotel. Through Airbnb, you'll find gems like a modernized pioneer log cabin built in 1909 in Ridges Sanctuary's backyard. Its owners invite guests to dine at their restaurant, **Roots Inn & Kitchen** (✉ *2378 Maple Dr.* ☎ *920/854–5107* ⊕ *www.rootsinnandkitchen.com*) in Sister Bay, at a discount.

Breakfast: Is that a goat on the roof? Yep, it is. **Al Johnson's** (✉ *10698 N. Bay Shore Dr.* ☎ *920/854–2626* ⊕ *www.aljohnsons. com*) is a nod to Door County's Swedish heritage, serving thin pancakes topped with lingonberries. If there's a wait for a table, shop in the attached boutique; you might find a sweater or pair of socks imported from Sweden or Norway.

Day 9: Door County, WI, to Milwaukee, WI

165 miles (2 hours, 30 minutes without traffic and stops)

The fastest way back to Milwaukee is to take I-43 S, but then you'd miss another glimpse of Lake Michigan. Leaving Sturgeon Bay, instead take WI-42 S through towns like Kewaunee and Algoma until you hit Manitowoc.

ALONG THE WAY

Town: An hour north of Milwaukee, Sheboygan is in the middle of a renaissance thanks to its fabulous art museums like the Art Preserve of the **John Michael Kohler Arts Center** (✉ *3636 Lower Falls Rd.* ☎ *920/453–0346* ⊕ *www.jmkac.org*), which celebrates the state's outsider artists. A Sheboygan-style brat (this city is the brat capital of the world) can be sampled at **Al & Al's Steinhaus** (✉ *1502 S. 12th St.* ☎ *920/452–5530* ⊕ *www.alnals. com*) or you can pick some up for later at **Johnsonville Marketplace** (✉ *N6877 Rio Rd.* ☎ *920/453–5678* ⊕ *www.johnsonville.com*).

Eat & Drink: Port Washington is so famous for its smoked fish—try the spread at **Ewig Bros. Fish Company** (✉ *121 S. Wisconsin St.* ☎ *262/284–2236* ⊕ *www. ewigsmokedfish.com*)—that it hosts Fish Day the third Saturday of every July.

MILWAUKEE

Do: Take some time to explore the **Milwaukee Art Museum** (✉ *700 N. Art Museum Dr.* ☎ *414/224–3200* ⊕ *www. mam.org*), the **Harley Davidson Museum** (✉ *400 W. Canal St.* ☎ *414/287–2789* ⊕ *www.h-dmuseum.com*), and the **Pabst Mansion** (✉ *2000 W. Wisconsin Ave.* ☎ *414/931–0808* ⊕ *www.pabstmansion. com*), former home of Frederick Pabst, founder of Pabst Brewing. Milwaukee is a big beer town after all, so be sure to spend some time checking out its many breweries, including **Lakefront Brewery**

(✉ *1872 N. Commerce St.* ☎ *414/372–8800* ⊕ *www.lakefrontbrewery.com*) and **Miller Brewery** (✉ *4251 W. State St.* ☎ *414/931–2337* ⊕ *www.millerbrewery-tour.com*).

Eat & Drink: At the **Milwaukee Public Market** (✉ *400 N. Water St.* ☎ *414/336–1111* ⊕ *www.milwaukeepublicmarket.org*), vendors sell a wide variety of food, from plant-based meals served out of a converted VW bus to Middle Eastern cuisine. West Allis Cheese & Sausage Shoppe sells "orphans" (mini-wedges of Wisconsin cheese).

Stay: The sophisticated **Kimpton Journeyman Hotel** (✉ *310 E. Chicago St.* ☎ *888/536–9008* ⊕ *www.journeymanhotel.com*) has a hip rooftop bar with views of the city.

Breakfast: A rare daytime-only bar, **Uncle Wolfie's Breakfast Tavern** (✉ *234 E. Vine St.* ☎ *414/763–3021* ⊕ *www.unclewolfies.com*) serves a hip brunch menu, with options like bananas foster oatmeal and biscuits and gravy.

Underrated Cities of the Midwest

Written by Kristine Hansen

Sure, everyone knows Chicago, but what about those "second cities" of the Midwest—places like Milwaukee, Indianapolis, St. Louis, and Louisville? This trip will take you to some of the most underrated spots in the region, including smaller towns like Madison, Iowa City, Grand Rapids, and Fort Wayne that deliver on college-town chill and big-city fun on a smaller scale. From regional foods, craft beer, and lesser-known art museums and cultural institutions to natural spaces like parks, lakes, and rivers and quaint Main Streets for eclectic shopping, it's time to experience what many dub "flyover country" with new eyes and a fresh

perspective to stop those naysayers in their haughty tracks.

At a Glance

Start: Indianapolis, IN

End: Indianapolis, IN

Miles Traveled: 1,462 miles

Suggested Duration: 9 days

States Visited: Indiana, Iowa, Kentucky, Michigan, Missouri, Ohio, Wisconsin

Key Sights: Arab American National Museum; the Gateway Arch; Indianapolis Motor Speedway; Motown Museum; Muhammad Ali Center

Best Time to Go: Because this is the Upper Midwest, weather needs to be on your side, and if you opt for spring or fall, expect an even more vibrant aesthetic (fields of flowers or fall foliage) for your drive through the landscape.

Day 1: Indianapolis, IN, to Louisville, KY

115 miles (1 hour, 45 minutes without traffic and stops)

Fly into the Indianapolis International Airport and pick up a rental car before starting your road trip. On your first day, it's a straight shot down I-65 S. Between the two cities are rural areas and small towns for a nice easy day of driving.

ALONG THE WAY

Town: Love architecture? Columbus, Indiana, is home to a surprising number of modernist works, including three by Eero Saarinen: Miller House and Garden, North Christian Church, and the Irwin Bank Building.

Eat & Drink: Zaharakos (✉ *329 Washington St.* ☎ *812/378–1900* ⊕ *www.zaharakos.com*), in Columbus, has been in business since around 1900 and continues to

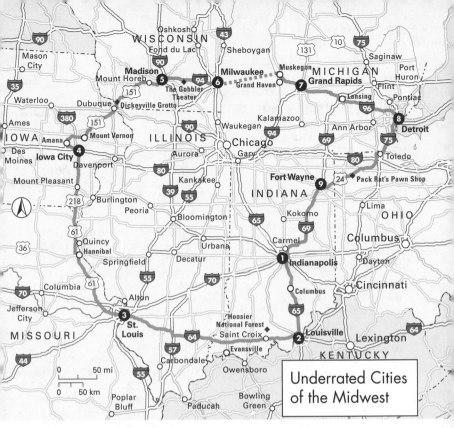

Underrated Cities of the Midwest

be a popular ice-cream shop for locals today. Before or after ordering, check out the second-floor museum's antique soda-fountain finds, dating back to the 1800s.

LOUISVILLE

Do: At night, walk over the **Big Four Bridge** (✉ 1101 River Rd. ☎ 502/574–3768 ⊕ www.louisvillewaterfront.com) above the Ohio River, connecting Kentucky with Indiana; this converted railroad bridge is pedestrian-only and lit up at night. Even if you're not a sports fan, diving into the history of baseball-bat manufacturing at **Louisville Slugger Museum & Factory** (✉ 800 W. Main St. ☎ 877/775–8443 ⊕ www.sluggermuseum.com) or learning about the late boxer Muhammad Ali at the **Muhammad Ali Center** (✉ 144 N. 6th St. ☎ 502/584–9254 ⊕ www.alicenter. org) is captivating.

Eat & Drink: Local chef (and former Top Chef contestant) Edward Lee has morphed into a celebrity in recent years, but you may be lucky and snag a reservation at **610 Magnolia** (✉ 610 W. Magnolia Ave. ☎ 502/636–0783 ⊕ www.610magnolia. com) or **Whiskey Dry** (✉ 412 S. 4th St. ☎ 502/749–7933 ⊕ www.whiskeydryres-taurant.com).

Stay: Tucked into 19th-century warehouses, the 91-room **21C Museum Hotel** (✉ 700 W. Main St. ☎ 502/217–6300 ⊕ www.21cmusuemhotels.com) is part art museum, part sweet stay, with sculptures and installations everywhere you look. Keep an eye out for a golden replica of Michelangelo's David.

Breakfast: Tres Leches Pancakes and Dulce Leche French Toast. Need we say more? **Con Huevos** (✉ 2339 Frankfort Ave.

☎ 502/384–3027 ⊕ www.conhuevos.com) is a Louisville favorite.

Day 2: Louisville, KY, to St. Louis, MO

260 miles (3 hours, 50 minutes without traffic and stops)

I–64 W takes you directly west to St. Louis. You'll pass through Evansville, Indiana, a college town (home to the University of Southern Indiana and University of Evansville). Look for the Gateway Arch as you're cruising into and around St. Louis.

ALONG THE WAY

Nature: The southern section of the **Hoosier National Forest** (✉ 811 Constitution Ave. Bedford, IN ☎ 812/275–5987 ⊕ www.fs.usda.gov) overlaps with I–64 W. To reach it, exit in Saint Croix, Indiana, and take IN37 S to IN62 E for an easy 1-mile hike on the Celina Interpretive Trail, departing from the Celina boat ramp.

Eat & Drink: You'll find the most variety of non-chain restaurants in Evansville, Indiana. Craving a sweet snack? Be **Happy Pie Company** (✉ 2818 B Mt. Vernon Ave. ☎ 812/449–7718 ⊕ www.behappypiecompany.com) is one option, with five-inch pies and "pie bites" more suitable for one or two people.

ST. LOUIS

Do: St. Louis's 1,300-acre Forest Park (that's bigger than New York City's Central Park!) is home to the totally free-to-enter **Saint Louis Art Museum** (✉ 1 Fine Arts Dr. ☎ 314/721–0072 ⊕ www.slam.org). Two other sculpture parks link nature with art (and, again, are free): **Laumeier Sculpture Park** (✉ 12580 Rott Rd., Sappington, MO ☎ 314/615–5278 ⊕ www.laumeiersculpturepark.org) and **Citygarden Sculpture Park** (✉ 801 Market St. ☎ 314/241–3337 ⊕ www.

citygardensstl.org). To feel like a kid again, check out **City Museum** (✉ 750 N. 16th St. ☎ 314/231–2489 ⊕ www.citymuseum.org), an artful indoor reuse project that involves slides, climbing, and other interactive fun for all ages in a century-old warehouse.

Eat & Drink: If you're craving Italian, find toasted ravioli (breaded and deep-fried), a signature St. Louis dish, in The Hill neighborhood's restaurants, such as **Mama's on the Hill** (✉ 2132 Edwards St. ☎ 314/776–3100 ⊕ www.mamasonthehill.com). For a latte break, drop into **Kaldi's Coffee** (✉ 700 De Mun Ave. ☎ 314/727–9955 ⊕ www.kaldiscoffee.com), adjacent to Citygarden Sculpture Park with an equally artsy interior.

Stay: Angad Arts Hotel (✉ 3550 Samuel Shepard Dr. ☎ 314/561–0033 ⊕ www.angadartshotel.com) is the only hotel out there that will ask you what your mood is upon check-in … and then send you to a room awash in a color that matches.

Breakfast: Don't even think about leaving without sampling gooey butter cake. **The Mud House** (✉ 2101 Cherokee St. ☎ 314/776–6599 ⊕ www.themudhousestl.com)—a café in the cute and historic Cherokee District—features it on their menu, along with the signature "Mud Slinger" (vegetarian black bean chili, roasted potatoes, red onion, and cheddar) and a spicy tofu scramble.

Day 3: St. Louis, MO, to Iowa City, IA

260 miles (4 hours without traffic and stops)

U.S. 61 N takes you directly north to Iowa. You may even find the temperature drops.

ALONG THE WAY

Town: Near Hannibal, Missouri, you'll find quite a few breweries and wineries with tasting rooms. **Cave Hollow West Winery** (⊠ *217 Cave Hollow Rd.* ☎ *573/231–1000* ⊕ *www.cavehollow.westwinery.com*) makes wine inspired by Mark Twain's books while **Mark Twain Brewing Company** (⊠ *422 N. Main St.* ☎ *573/406–1300* ⊕ *www.marktwainbrewingcompany.com*), across the street from Twain's boyhood home, is another ode to him.

Eat & Drink: Mount Pleasant, Iowa, is a nice place to stop for lunch, perhaps at **Sanity Coffee House** (⊠ *104 S. Iris St.* ☎ *319/931–9594* ⊕ *www.facebook.com/Sanitycoffee*), which serves espresso drinks, paninis, milk shakes, and whoopie pies.

IOWA CITY

Do: Not every city has a pedestrian mall as pleasant as Iowa City: check out **Prairie Lights Books & Cafe** (⊠ *15 S. Dubuque St.* ☎ *319/337–2681* ⊕ *www.prairielights.com*) for reading material and **Artifacts** (⊠ *331 E. Market St.* ☎ *319/358–9617* ⊕ *www.artifacts-iowacity.com*) for unique vintage finds, from clothes to furnishings. About 15 minutes west of Iowa City is the **Herbert Hoover Presidential Library and Museum** (⊠ *210 Parkside Dr.* ☎ *319/643–5301* ⊕ *www.hoover.archives.gov*). On the University of Iowa campus is the **Stanley Museum of Art** (⊠ *125 N. Madison St.* ☎ *319/335–1727* ⊕ *www.stanleymuseum.uiowa.edu*) and the **Museum of Natural History** (⊠ *17 N. Clinton St.* *319/335–0480* ⊕ *www.mnh.uiowa.edu*).

Extend Your Trip

From Louisville: The Great American Whiskey Road Trip *(Ch. 7)*

From St. Louis: Route 66 *(Ch. 2)*; Along the Mississippi *(Ch. 2)*; The Best of the Ozarks *(Ch. 6)*

From Iowa City, Madison, or Milwaukee: The Best of the Heartland *(Ch. 6)*

From Grand Rapids: A Frank Lloyd Wright Tour *(Ch. 6)*

Eat & Drink: College towns are full of casual, global-eating opportunities, such as **Oasis Falafel** (⊠ *206 N. Linn St.* ☎ *319/358–7342* ⊕ *www.oasisfalafel.com*) or **Szechuan House** (⊠ *320 E. Burlington St.* ☎ *319/338–6788* ⊕ *www.szechuanhouseia.com*). Close out the night with a drink at the **Vue Rooftop** (⊠ *328 S. Clinton St.* ☎ *319/519–4650* ⊕ *www.vuerooftop-ic.com*), on the 12th floor of the Hilton Garden Inn Iowa City, with amazing views and a big-city vibe.

Stay: The modern suites at **Hotel Vetro** (⊠ *201 S. Linn St.* ☎ *319/337–4961*) are the perfect, pampering spot to crash after a day on the go.

Breakfast: Stick a fork into soul food infused with midwestern ingredients at **Bluebird Diner** (⊠ *330 E. Market St.* ☎ *319/351–1470* ⊕ *www.thebluebird-diner.com*), where the breakfast menu includes the Rajun Cajun omelet and Oeufs Louis XIV (eggs scrambled with black truffles).

Day 4: Iowa City, IA, to Madison, WI

175 miles (3 hours without traffic and stops)

Today you'll travel along the Great River Road, a 250-mile chunk of gorgeous scenery that includes Dickeyville, Wisconsin. Be sure to also take photos of the Mississippi River when you pass over it in Dubuque, Iowa.

ALONG THE WAY

Shop: The German-founded **Amana Colonies** (✉ *622 46th Ave., Amana, IA* ☎ *319/622–7622* ⊕ *amanacolonies.com*) are a locals' favorite day-trip destination for its gift shops, bakery, and café. Pick up a loaf of German dill or German black bread.

Detour: Mt. Vernon, Iowa, is a supercute small town and home to Cornell College.

Roadside Attraction: Dickeyville Grotto (✉ *255–377 Great River Rd.* ☎ *608/568–3119* ⊕ *www.dickeyvillagegrotto.com*) in Dickeyville, Wisconsin, lies along U.S. 61 and is like nothing you've ever seen. Established by a priest between 1925 and 1930, it's a great example of the state's outsider art, where untrained artists used found objects (wood, rocks, and shells in this case) to create beautiful spaces.

Eat & Drink: In Mount Horeb, Wisconsin's Norwegian influence pops up in a few restaurants, including **Sjolind's Chocolate House** (✉ *219 E. Main St.* ☎ *608/437–0233* ⊕ *www.sjolinds.com*), which also serves pastries and sipping chocolate.

MADISON

Do: You didn't come all this way to not try cheese. **Fromagination** (✉ *12 S. Carroll St.* ☎ *608/255–2430* ⊕ *www.fromagination. com*) is a Parisian-inspired cheese shop on Capitol Square. Stroll State Street (its small collection of independent shops sell fair-trade goods and unique finds) to the University of Wisconsin–Madison and enjoy ice cream at **Memorial Union's Daily Scoop** (✉ *800 Langdon St.* ☎ *608/262–5959* ⊕ *www.union.wisc.edu*) from its outdoor terrace hugging Lake Mendota. Then check out the continental United States's only Thai pavilion at **Olbrich Botanical Gardens** (✉ *3330 Atwood Ave.* ☎ *608/246–4550* ⊕ *www.olbrich.org*) in Monona.

Eat & Drink: L'Etoile (✉ *1 S. Pinckney St.* ☎ *608/251–0500* ⊕ *www.letoile–restaurant.com*) is a farm-to-fork, finer-dining institution (founder Odessa Piper shopped the Dane County Farmers' Market across the street back in the 1970s) while its more casual sibling, **Graze** (✉ *1 S. Pinckney St.* ☎ *608/251–2700* ⊕ *www.grazemadison.com*), is a block away.

Stay: Located a block off State Street and a few blocks from UW–Madison's Memorial Union, **Graduate Madison** (✉ *601 Langdon St.* ☎ *608/257–4391* ⊕ *www.graduatehotels.com*) merges preppy-chic with laid-back fun. Enjoy drinks with cheese curds on the rooftop lounge.

Breakfast: Mickie's Dairy Bar (✉ *1511 Monroe St.* ☎ *608/256–9476* ⊕ *www.mickiesdairybar.com*) on Monroe Street is a classic, no-frills breakfast institution, with omelets, shakes, and root-beer floats.

Day 5: Madison, WI, to Milwaukee, WI

79 miles (1 hour, 15 minutes without traffic and stops)

Once you're on I–94 E, just enjoy the drive and notice the quaint red barns and rolling green hills. Rarely is there traffic between Madison and Milwaukee, except for the towns bordering each.

ALONG THE WAY

Photo Op: No, that's not a space ship: the saucer-shaped building at the Johnson Creek exit (Exit 267) off I–94

Detroit has an impressive art scene, with the Detroit Institute of Art leading the way.

is the former Gobbler supper-club restaurant. Now it's a theater with live performances.

Eat & Drink: It may not be state fair season, but you can still snag the biggest cream puffs you've ever seen at the **Pine Cone Travel Plaza** (⌧ 685 Linmar La. #C, Johnson Creek, WI ☎ 920/699–2766 ⊕ www.pineconetravelplazamenu.com), also at Exit 267.

MILWAUKEE

Do: With its soaring white wings over Lake Michigan, the Santiago Calatrava–designed Quadracci Pavilion of the **Milwaukee Art Museum** (⌧ 700 N. Art Museum Dr. ☎ 414/224–3200 ⊕ www.mam.org) is a stunner. Rent a shared bike from **Bublr** (⌧ 275 W. Wisconsin Ave. ☎ 414/931–1121 ⊕ www.bublrbikes.org) and cruise up Lincoln Memorial Drive along the lake. **Milwaukee Kayak Company** (⌧ 318 S. Water St. ☎ 414/301–2240 ⊕ www.milwaukeekayak.com) rents out kayaks and canoes at its Harbor District locale, providing a great way to experience the skyline from the Milwaukee River.

Eat & Drink: Food halls are where it's at here, either the mostly Black-owned eateries at **Sherman Phoenix** (⌧ 3536 W. Fond Du Lac Ave. ☎ 262/228–6021 ⊕ www.shermanphoenix.com) or the **Milwaukee Public Market** (⌧ 400 N. Water St. ☎ 414/336–1111 ⊕ www.milwaukeepublicmarket.org). Close down the night with a Pink Squirrel at a classic Milwaukee cocktail lounge like **At Random** (⌧ 2501 S. Delaware Ave. ☎ 414/481–8030 ⊕ www.atrandommke.com). Frozen custard is also a must here, either at **Leon's Frozen Custard** (⌧ 3131 S. 27th St. ☎ 414/383–1784 ⊕ www.leonsfrozencustard.us) or one of three locations of **Kopp's** (⊕ www.kopps.com).

Stay: Milwaukee is called Brew City for a reason: beer barons emigrated from Germany to here. Bunk at the 90-room **Brewhouse Inn & Suites** (⌧ 1215 N. 10th St. ☎ 414/810–3350 ⊕ www.brewhousesuites.com), within the former Pabst Brewery complex and home to antique copper kettles once used to make beer.

Breakfast: Since the 1970s, **Beans & Barley** (✉ *1901 E. North Ave.* ☎ *414/278–7878* ⊕ *www.beansandbarley.com*) on the East Side has managed to fuse Mexican with vegan and organic for all-day dining, along with old-fashioned pie slices and killer coffee in a sunny, high-ceilinged diner. Pick up snacks and a magazine for the ferry in the attached market.

Day 6: Milwaukee, WI, to Grand Rapids, MI

128 miles, including Lake Express Ferry across Lake Michigan (3 hours, 45 minutes without traffic and stops)

Today you're leaving part of the drive to the Lake Express ferry captain. The high-speed car ferry departs from the Port of Milwaukee (just south of the Hoan Bridge in Bay View) and drops you off in Muskegon, Michigan. From there, it's an easy 45-minute trip along I–96 E.

ALONG THE WAY

Photo Op: Be sure to scale a flight of stairs to the ferry's roof, but bring a jacket: it's cold and windy up there.

Detour: Grand Haven, Michigan (22 miles from the ferry terminal), along the Lake Michigan shoreline, is that quintessential summer beach town with a boardwalk.

Eat & Drink: Rebel Pies (✉ *360 W. Western Ave.* ☎ *231/375–5382* ⊕ *www.rebelpies.com*) in downtown Muskegon can hook you up with a pizza (signature pies carry names like "Polynesian Farmer" and "The Jack White") and a craft beer, thanks to its co-tenant Unruly Brewing.

GRAND RAPIDS

Do: Called the GRAM by locals, the superb **Grand Rapids Art Museum** (✉ *101 Monroe Center St. NW* ☎ *616/831–1000* ⊕ *www.artmuseumgr.org*) has rotating exhibitions and a collection spanning eras. Stretch your legs at **Frederik Meijer Botanical Gardens & Sculpture Park** (✉ *1000 E. Beltline Ave. NE* ☎ *616/957–1580* ⊕ *www.meijergardens.org*) or learn about a past president at **Gerald R. Ford Presidential Library & Museum** (✉ *1000 Beal Ave.* ☎ *734/205–0555* ⊕ *www.fordlibrarymuseum.gov*).

Eat & Drink: Opt for a local craft beer (Grand Rapids is nicknamed "Beer City USA") with dinner at **Stella's Lounge** (✉ *53 Commerce Ave. SW* ☎ *616/742–4444* ⊕ *www.stellaslounge.com*), known for its stuffed burgers, beer-battered avocados, and vintage arcade games. Afterwards, grab a drink at **Brewery Vivant** (✉ *925 Cherry St. SE* ☎ *616/719–1604* ⊕ *www.breweryvivant.com*), located within a former funeral chapel.

Stay: The **CityFlats Hotel** (✉ *83 Monroe Center St. NW* ☎ *616/608–1720* ⊕ *www.cityflatshotel.com*) has an eco-friendly mantra and a downtown location near shops, restaurants, and the GRAM.

Breakfast: That Early Bird (✉ *1445 Lake Dr. SE* ☎ *616/258–8350* ⊕ *www.thatearlybird.com*) serves breakfast nachos, curry hash, and horchata lattes—a fun switch on American-style breakfasts.

Day 7: Grand Rapids, MI, to Detroit, MI

157 miles (2 hours, 15 minutes without traffic and stops)

I–96 E takes you from Grand Rapids to Detroit, curling around the State Capitol of Lansing.

ALONG THE WAY

Eat & Drink: A tad southwest of Grand Rapids lies **Moelker Orchards** (✉ *9265 Kenowa Ave. SW* ☎ *616/453–2585* ⊕ *www.moelkerorchards.com*), where a family has been growing apples, peaches, and cherries since 1907. The market sells farm-fresh produce and sweet treats, including pies and apple dumplings.

Town: Jump off I–96 E to spot the Michigan Capitol Building in Lansing and perhaps snap a photo from the car. Guided hour-long tours are offered weekdays and Saturdays.

DETROIT

Do: Once famous for its car manufacturing, now it's the art scene here that attracts new residents and visitors alike. Spend some time gallery-hopping or visiting the **Detroit Institute of Art** (✉ *5200 Woodward Ave.* ☎ *313/833–7900* ⊕ *www.dia.org*). The **Motown Museum** (✉ *2648 W. Grand Blvd.* ☎ *313/875–2264* ⊕ *www.motownmuseum.org*) and the **Arab American National Museum** (✉ *13624 Michigan Ave., Dearborn, MI* ☎ *313/429–2535* ⊕ *www.arabamericanmuseum.org*) in nearby Dearborn are two completely unique experiences you won't find elsewhere and that help tell the region's full story.

Eat & Drink: You've heard of Detroit-style pizza (rectangular with a thick, chewy crust), so now's the time to try it; any Jet's (www.jetspizza.com) location will do. For a more upscale yet eclectic experience, book a table at **Grey Ghost Detroit** (✉ *47 Watson St.* ☎ *313/262–6534* ⊕ *www.greyghostdetroit.com*). And don't go to bed without slipping into a booth at the vintagey Candy Bar, inside **The Siren Hotel** (✉ *1509 Broadway St.* ☎ *313/277–4736* ⊕ *www.thesirenhotel.com*).

Stay: The Siren Hotel is a delightful throwback experience with its midcentury, golden-age-of-Hollywood decor. It's home to **Karl's** (✉ *1509 Broadway St.* ☎ *313/855–2757* ⊕ *www.karlsdetroit.com*), run by one of the city's most celebrated chefs, Kate Williams.

Breakfast: Detroit's West Village is home to Lisa Ludwinski's wildly popular **Sister Pie** (✉ *8066 Kercheval Ave.* ☎ *313/447–5550* ⊕ *www.sisterpie.com*) where breakfast as well as bakery items are available each morning.

Day 8: Detroit, MI, to Fort Wayne, IN

162 miles (2 hours, 35 minutes without traffic and stops)

From Detroit, I–75 S cuts through Toledo, Ohio, and weaves down to Fort Wayne.

ALONG THE WAY

Eat & Drink: It's rare to find a Hungarian restaurant in these parts, which is why you should pull over for lunch at Tony Packo's Café (✉ *1902 Front St.* ☎ *419/691–6054* ⊕ *www.tonypacko.com*) in Toledo, Ohio, since 1932. Enjoy the signature Hungarian hot dogs, perogies, chicken paprikas, or an apple or cherry strudel.

Roadside Attraction: In Defiance, Ohio, you'll find a stack of five 1960s-era VW Bugs at Pack Rat's Pawn Shop (✉ *1938 E. 2nd St.* ☎ *419/782–7287* ⊕ *www.packratpawnshop.com*), each decorated with further pizazz.

FORT WAYNE

Do: An outdoor sculpture park called **Promenade Park** (✉ *202 W. Superior St.* ☎ *260/427–6000* ⊕ *www.fortwayneparks.org*) is a great place to chill and people-watch, with kayak rentals, canal boats, and swings. Love street art? Check out the Fort Wayne tourism website (⊕ *www.visitfortwayne.com*) for a handy interactive map that points you to the city's best.

Eat & Drink: For a town of only 267,000 residents, Fort Wayne is packed with such quality dining you may want to create a progressive meal during your short stay, ending with an Extreme Shake at **Just Cream** (✉ *338 E. Dupont Rd.* ☎ *260/489–3002* ⊕ *www.icecreamboutiquefw.com*).

Stay: The Bradley (✉ *204 W. Main St.* ☎ *260/428–4018* ⊕ *www.provenancehotels.com/the-bradley*) is a Vera Bradley–themed hotel (a well-loved design shop in these parts). As you might expect, the brand's signature fabrics are on nearly every soft surface.

Breakfast: Duck into the tiny, 1950s-style **Cindy's Diner** (✉ 230 W. Berry St. ☎ 260/422–1957) for all-day breakfast and what's called "garbage" (hash browns, eggs, onions, cheese, and ham, all grilled together).

Day 9: For Wayne, IN, to Indianapolis, IN

126 miles (2 hours without traffic and stops)

For the final leg of the trip, it's an easy two-hour cruise south along I–69 S, an artery that connects the state's two largest (by population) cities.

ALONG THE WAY

Eat & Drink: Why wait until you reach Indianapolis to start the Indy Ice-Cream Trail? In business since 1870, **Graeter's** (✉ 338 E. Dupont Rd. ⊕ www.graeters. com) is the only commercial ice-cream manufacturer to use French Pot freezers. Taste the frozen goodness for yourself at its location just north of Indy in Carmel.

INDIANAPOLIS

Do: Either stroll or rent a bike to experience a portion of the 8-mile-long Indianapolis Cultural Trail (www.indyculturaltrail. org), rimmed with art sculptures. Learn more about the Indy 500 at the **Indianapolis Motor Speedway Museum** (✉ 4750 W. 16th St. ☎ 317/492–6784 ⊕ www. imsmuseum.org), located at the famed track itself, or browse the collection (with works by Rembrandt, Hopper, Matisse, Picasso, and O'Keeffe) at the **Indianapolis Museum of Art** (✉ 4000 N. Michigan Rd. ☎ 317/923–1331 ⊕ www.discovernewfields.org), on the 152-acre Newfields campus.

Eat & Drink: At the state's oldest bar, the **Slippery Noodle Inn** (✉ 372 S. Meridian St. ☎ 317/631–6974 ⊕ www.slipperynoodle. com), you'll be able to tick off live blues music and dinner (from wings to pasta, plus burgers, subs, and salads) in one swoop.

Stay: Explore the nightlife in Indiana's largest city by booking a room downtown. **The Alexander** (✉ 333 S. Delaware St. ☎ 317/624–8200 ⊕ www.thealexander.com) has a great location and Instagram-worthy, mouth-blown glass pendant lighting at its on-site lounge, Plat 99.

Breakfast: The omelets at **Café Patachou** (✉ 225 W. Washington St. ⊕ www. cafepatachou.com) carry sassy names like "The Hippie with a Benz" while "broken yolks" are over-easy eggs on toast with a side of arugula salad. For a to-go treat for your plane ride, order a "Compost Cookie," inspired by Milk Bar owner Christina Tosi.

All the Great Lakes

Written by Kristine Hansen

If you grew up near a Great Lake, you were likely drilled with the HOMES acronym in grade school to keep them straight: Huron, Ontario, Michigan, Erie, and Superior. Filled with folklore (hello, shipwrecks!) and rimmed with lighthouses, cultural landmarks, and resort towns (not to mention a thriving surfing culture and wine regions), these five freshwater lakes easily marvel first-time visitors. No, you cannot see across the lakes and, yes, these waters are deep. Ticking off five lakes in 10 days might seem ambitious, but it's not impossible. Using this carefully crafted route, all the Great Lakes are seamlessly woven into an easy-to-follow itinerary packed with signature regional eats, blissful hikes, and natural wonders (like Niagara Falls and Indiana Dunes National Park).

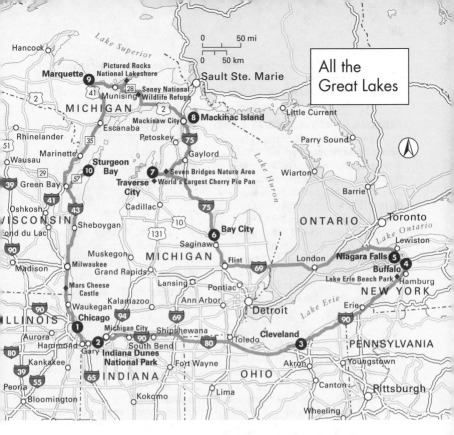

At a Glance

Start: Chicago, IL

End: Chicago, IL

Miles Traveled: 1,734 miles

Suggested Duration: 10 days

States Visited: Illinois, Indiana, Ohio, Michigan, New York, Wisconsin

Key Sights: The Chicago Art Institute; Indiana Dunes National Park; Lake Erie Islands; Mackinac Island; Niagara Falls

Best Time to Go: Since this is the northernmost side of the country, avoid winter unless you get a kick out of frozen lakeshores. Summer is, of course, when the weather is best, but late spring or early fall only mean layers of clothing and thinner crowds.

Day 1: Chicago, IL, to Indiana Dunes National Park

45 miles (1 hour without traffic and stops)

Your first day is also your easiest driving day, a quick one-hour trip traveling I–90 E toward Indiana. Flights into Chicago's O'Hare International Airport, one of the world's largest, are easy to come by and cars can be rented at the airport.

ALONG THE WAY

Eat & Drink: It's pretty much a sea of truck stops and fast-food drive-thrus along this route, but at the Calumet Avenue exit you will find a refreshing treat at **Jodi's Italian Ice Factory** (✉ *7322 Calumet Ave.*

☎ 219/902–5661 ⊕ www.jodisice.com) in Hammond, Indiana, as well as at **Dairy Belle** (✉ 7102 Calumet Ave. ☎ 219/931–4550), a vintage ice-cream stand.

INDIANA DUNES NATIONAL PARK

Do: Whether you're a trailblazer or stroller, **Indiana Dunes National Park** (✉ 1050 N. Mineral Springs Rd. ☎ 219/395–1882 ⊕ www.nps.gov/indu) offers both. Hugging 15 miles of Lake Michigan shoreline, its 15,000 acres include 50 miles of trails. If you're into biking, pack the bikes to explore the Calumet and Porter Brickyard Bike Trails. On the northern tip of the park, **Old Lighthouse Museum** (✉ 1 Washington St. ☎ 219/872–6133 ⊕ www.old-lighthousemuseum.org) in Michigan City is the state's oldest remaining lighthouse.

Eat & Drink: Don't be fooled: although not as slick and spacious as, say, Goose Island's Chicago taproom, **Burn'Em Brewing** (✉ 718 Freyer Rd. ☎ 219/210–3784 ⊕ www.burnembrewing.com) in Michigan City is a nice surprise for sipping its craft beer in a down-home environment, with a small outdoor patio.

Stay: With a restaurant and wine/martini bar, and a five-minute walk to a private beach, the 1924 **Duneland Beach Inn** (✉ 3311 Pottawattomie Trail ☎ 219/874–7729 ⊕ www.farinasupperclub.com) in Michigan City, also home to **Farina's Supper Club**, is a posh place to spend the night.

Breakfast: Inspired by regions around the world, **Third Coast Spice Café** (✉ 761 Indian Boundary Rd. ☎ 219/926–5858 ⊕ www.thirdcoastspice.com) in Chesterton serves breakfast dishes like Buffalo Hot Hash and fun drinks like Cinnamon Toast Latte.

Day 2: Indiana Dunes National Park to Cleveland, OH

293 miles (4 hours, 40 minutes without traffic and stops)

Buckle up for your nearly five-hour ride to what many call the North Coast, following I–90 E all the way.

ALONG THE WAY

Town: Michigan City, Indiana's Uptown Arts District is worth a peek before you get back on the road.

Eat & Drink: Most people know South Bend, Indiana, for the University of Notre Dame (and presidential candidate, former mayor, and now Secretary of Transportation Pete Buttigieg) but the city also has delicious restaurants, making it the perfect spot to stop for lunch with options like **Fiddler's Hearth** (✉ 127 N. Main St. ☎ 574/232–2853 ⊕ www.fiddlershearth. com) and **West End Bakery** (✉ 414 W. 7th St., Mishawaka, IN ☎ 574/225–1267 ⊕ www.facebook.com/WestEndBakery-Mishawaka) in nearby Mishawaka, open since 1928.

Shop: Shipshewana, Indiana, off I–90 E south of Exit 101, is America's largest Amish community. Pull over to browse not only baked goods but also hand-crafted furniture at **Brandenberry Amish Furniture** (✉ 1045 IN 5 ☎ 260/768–3270 ⊕ www.brandenberryamishfurniture. com) and **Dutchman Log Furniture** (✉ 7275 W. 200 N ☎ 260/366–0702 ⊕ www.dutchmanlogfurniture.com). If shabby-chic is more your style, check out **Cherry Pickers** (✉ 160 Morton St. ☎ 574/612–4569 ⊕ www.cherrypick-ersinc.com) and **2 Chicks and a Chair** (✉ 155 Harrison St. ☎ 574/536–6575 ⊕ www.facebook.com/2ChicksandaChair) for reclaimed finds.

CLEVELAND

Do: Few people know that Cleveland has beaches and—gasp!—islands (hop a ferry from Sandusky, an hour west of Cleveland, to Lake Erie Islands, the chain of 19 islands within Ohio; others in the archipelago are in Canada, Michigan, New York, and Pennsylvania). Stroll Lake Erie's shoreline or just chill on the sand at **Edgewater Park** (☎ 216/635–3200 ⊕ www.clevelandmetroparks.com). If you're a music fan, don't miss the **Rock & Roll Hall of Fame** (✉ 1100 E. 9th St. ☎ 216/781–7625 ⊕ www.rockhall.com).

Eat & Drink: Michael Symon (of ABC's The Chew and five Food Network shows, including Iron Chef America) is Cleveland's most famous chef. Check out his food at **Mabel's BBQ** (✉ 2050 E. 4th St. ☎ 216/417–8823 ⊕ www.mabelsbbq.com) in downtown Cleveland—don't miss the banana cream pie.

Stay: Since the goal of this road trip is to see the Great Lakes, book a room with a Lake Erie view at **The Schofield Hotel** (✉ 2000 E. 9th St. ☎ 216/357–3250 ⊕ www.theschofieldhotel.com), a boutique hotel in a 1902 building that's a short walk to the lakefront.

Breakfast: Stray from the downtown area to the super cute **Luna Bakery & Cafe** (✉ 2482 Fairmount Blvd. ☎ 216/231–8585 ⊕ www.lunabakerycafe.com) in Cleveland Heights, for everything from a flaky, buttery croissant to a breakfast burrito or smoked salmon toast.

Day 3: Cleveland, OH, to Buffalo, NY

189 miles (3 hours without traffic and stops)

I–90 E takes you the entire way there, with a few tolls en route. You also pass through Pennsylvania.

Essential Listening

Milwaukee writer Dan Egan's The Death and Life of the Great Lakes reads like a novel, pulling you into environmental problems like zebra-mussel invasions, but also the history of port traffic.

ALONG THE WAY

Nature: Angola on the Lake, New York, is a popular vacation hamlet and second-home community, adjacent to **Lake Erie Beach Park** (✉ www.lunabakerycafe.com ✉ 9568 Lake Shore Rd., Angola, NY ☎ 716/549–0970 ⊕ www.townofevans.org). It's the perfect spot to stretch your legs and sink your toes in the sand.

Eat & Drink: Just before you hit Buffalo are several lakefront options, including an extensive lunch menu (including Maryland crab cakes, signature burgers, and Alaskan snow-crab legs) at **Rodney's** (✉ 4179 Lake Shore Rd. ☎ 716/627–5166 ⊕ www.rodneysonthelake.com) in Hamburg, right on the shoreline with outdoor seating.

BUFFALO

Do: The Frank Lloyd Wright–designed **Graycliff** (✉ 6472 Old Lake Shore Rd., Derby, NY ☎ 716/947–9217 ⊕ www.experiencegraycliff.org) hugs Lake Erie's bluffs in nearby Derby, 30 minutes south of downtown Buffalo. It offers four different tours, with the hour-long standard tour best for those pressed for time.

Eat & Drink: It's a fact: Buffalo's chicken wings are famous and delicious. There's even a Buffalo Wing Trail. Looking for something else that's tasty and quick? **West Side Bazaar** (✉ 25 Grant St. ☎ 716/783–8489 ⊕ www.westsidebazaar.com) is a project providing recent immigrants a boost for their food stands or artisans' booths.

Stay: One of the most intriguing hotels in Buffalo is also among its finest. The **Hotel Henry** (✉ *444 Forest Ave.* ☎ *716/882–1970* ⊕ *www.hotelhenry. com*) is set on 42 sprawling acres in a Romanesque-style building that was once an asylum.

Breakfast: Flapjacks drizzled with New York maple syrup or mini-doughnuts and omelets at the vintage-y **Swan Street Diner** (✉ *700 Swan St.* ☎ *716/768–1823* ⊕ *www.swanstreetdiner.com*)—tucked into a 1937 former diner car—will get you fueled for another day of driving.

Day 4: Buffalo, NY, to Niagara Falls, NY

20 miles (25 minutes without traffic and stops)

Don't be fooled by the short drive along I–190 N; you'll need all that extra time to explore Niagara Falls, which straddles the United States and Canada, and where Lake Erie drains into Lake Ontario. Don't forget to pack your passport if you plan to cross the border so you can return to New York with ease. If you'd rather leave the car behind, book a one-day tour with **Gray Line** (☎ *877/285–2113* ⊕ *www.graylineniagarafalls.com*), which offers three different tours.

ALONG THE WAY

Eat & Drink: Tiny Lewiston, New York, is along the drive and boasts **Orange Cat Coffee Co.** (✉ *703 Center St.* ☎ *716/754–2888*), perfect if you plan to depart Buffalo early in the day. Just look for the white house with the black shutters.

NIAGARA FALLS

Do: Two of the three famous falls are in the United States: Bridal Veil Falls and American Falls. The other (Horseshoe Falls, also called Canadian Falls, and the largest) lies in Ontario, Canada. **Niagara Falls State Park** (✉ *332 Prospect St.* ☎ *716/278–1794* ⊕ *www.*

Extend Your Trip

From Buffalo or Niagara Falls: The Best of New York State *(Ch. 8)*

From Sturgeon Bay: The Best of the Heartland *(Ch. 6)*

From Chicago: The Great American Baseball Road Trip *(Ch. 2)*; A Frank Lloyd Wright Tour *(Ch. 6)*

niagarafallsstatepark.com)—the country's oldest state park and championed into preservation by Frederick Law Olmsted—offers a mix of overlooks as well as trails to hike. Drop by the visitor center to get your bearings. Old Falls Street, USA is a three-block shopping and entertainment district lined with Adirondack chairs and food vendors. Every Friday night during summer is a live music concert.

Eat & Drink: The Kasbah (✉ *6130 Dunn St.* ☎ *905/357–1000* ⊕ *www.thekasbah.ca*) is a farm-to-table Greek, Italian, and Armenian restaurant owned by an Armenian émigré and boasting a patio. Leave decisions to the chef with the Kasbah Combo dinner menu. In a sea of chains, **Milestones on the Falls** (✉ *6755 Fallsview Blvd., Niagara Falls, ON, Canada* ☎ *905/358–4720* ⊕ *www.milestonesonthefalls.com*) is refreshing, with views of the falls, bistro-type fare for lunch and dinner, and a nice wine list featuring Niagara selections.

Stay: Given that Niagara Falls is a popular group-tour spot and also attracts honeymooners, the lodging stock is a mix of quaint inns and chains. **Old Stone Inn Boutique Hotel** (✉ *6080 Fallsview Blvd., Niagara Falls, ON, Canada* ☎ *905/357–1234* ⊕ *www.oldstoneinnhotel.com*), a former flour mill dating back to 1904, lies somewhere between, with a chic restaurant and bar flaunting steampunk décor.

There are no cars allowed on peaceful Mackinac Island (you'll have to park your car overnight at a lot by the ferry dock).

Breakfast: Linger over three-egg omelets and Belgian waffles at the **Flying Saucer** (✉ *6768 Lundy's La., Niagara Falls, ON, Canada* ☎ *905/356–4553* ⊕ *www.flyingsaucerrestaurant.com*), a quirky alternative to IHOP and Denny's with the same diner-like location.

Day 5: Niagara Falls, NY, to Bay City, MI

300 miles (4 hours, 50 minutes without traffic and stops)

Bypassing Detroit—via I–69 W in Michigan—to pass through Canada and reach this cozy town along Lake Huron's Saginawa Bay is a decision you won't regret. You'll pass through many charming towns, like Frankenmuth with its Bavarian-style architecture, on this easy-to-drive route relatively free of traffic congestion.

ALONG THE WAY

Eat & Drink: You can't leave Canada without sampling poutine. **Smoke's Poutinerie London** (✉ *551 Richmond St. Unit 2.*) ☎ *519/679–2873* ⊕ *smokespoutinerie.com/store/smokes-poutinerie-london/*) in London, Ontario, is a quick in-and-out option.

Town: The **Flint Institute of Arts** (✉ *1120 E. Kearsley St.* ☎ *810/234–1695* ⊕ *www.flintarts.org*) in Flint, Michigan, is the state's second-largest art museum with paintings by Mary Cassatt and John Singer Sargent, as well as ancient Asian objects dating as far back as the 11th century.

BAY CITY

Do: With just 33,000 residents, Bay City has a small-town vibe and access to beaches like **Bay City State Park** (✉ *3582 State Park Dr.* ☎ *989/684–3020* ⊕ *www2.dnr.state.mi.us/parksandtrails/Details.aspx?type=SPRK&id=437*), home to Tobico Marsh, the largest remaining freshwater coastal wetlands along the Great Lakes. Craving some culture?

Saginaw Art Museum (✉ *1126 N. Michigan Ave.* ☎ *989/754–2491* ⊕ *www.saginawartmuseum.org*), in nearby Saginaw, is a hidden gem.

Eat & Drink: Tucked into the former city hall, **Old City Hall Restaurant** (✉ *814 Saginaw St.* ☎ *989/892–4140* ⊕ *www.oldcityhallrestaurant.com*) flaunts an incredible wine list and 23 beers on tap, many from Michigan.

Stay: The **Historic Webster House** (✉ *900 5th St.* ☎ *989/316–2552* ⊕ *www.historicwebsterhouse.com*) is a Victorian-era bed-and-breakfast featuring stone walls, fireplaces, and Jacuzzi tubs. Each night there's a free wine-and-cheese reception for guests.

Breakfast: Although the brunch menu at **Harless + Hugh** (✉ *1003 Washington Ave.* ☎ *989/385–1657* ⊕ *www.harlessandhugh.com*) is tiny, it's done well. Choose from items like avocado toast, house waffles, and breakfast burritos with roasted-tomato chutney. Mimosas, pour-over coffee, and cappuccinos are also served.

Day 6: Bay City, MI, to Traverse City, MI

146 miles (2 hours, 25 minutes without traffic and stops)

I–75 N to M-72 W takes you to Traverse City, passing through a series of small towns along the way.

ALONG THE WAY

Nature: The 314-acre Seven Bridges Nature Area in Kalkaska offers easy hiking trails within a wetlands area, plus the remains of an 1882 sawmill.

Eat & Drink: Just before you reach Traverse City, **The Cottage** (✉ *472 Munson Ave.* ☎ *231/947–9261* ⊕ *www.cottagecafetc.com*) offers the ultimate in comfort food: all-you-can-eat fried perch.

TRAVERSE CITY, MI

Do: If you love wine, Traverse City is your jam, as it's the state's most developed (and revered) wine region with two AVAs (American Viticultural Areas): Old Mission Peninsula AVA and Leelanau Peninsula AVA. The town of 16,000 residents also hugs Lake Michigan along the shores of Grand Traverse Bay. Tasting rooms are akin to Napa and Sonoma with food-pairing packages, vineyards on-site, and grand tasting rooms. **Green Bird Organic Cellars** (✉ *9825 E. Engles Rd.* ☎ *231/386–5636* ⊕ *www.greenbirdcellars.com*) is a cute winery stop; it's on a 67-acre organic farm and the owners produce both estate wines and hard ciders.

Eat & Drink: This town offers a lot of diverse dining but you shouldn't drive away without sampling locally grown cherries, woven into dinner entrées and desserts alike. Do a taste-around at **The Little Fleet** (✉ *448 E. Front St.* ☎ *231/943–1116* ⊕ *www.thelittlefleet.com*), a food-truck yard. Or opt for a water view at **Harrington's By the Bay** (✉ *13890 S.W. Bay Shore Dr.* ☎ *231/421–9393* ⊕ *www.harringtonsbythebay.com*) or the **Boathouse Restaurant** (✉ *14039 Peninsula Dr.* ☎ *231/223–4030* ⊕ *www.boathouseonwestbay.com*) for an upscale dinner , paired with local wine. And don't leave without sampling cherry pie at either of the two cafés run by **Grand Traverse Pie Company** (⊕ *www.gtpie.com*).

Stay: Switch things up on your trip by bunking at a winery's guesthouse, like the **Inn at Chateau Grand Traverse** (✉ *12301 Center Rd.* ☎ *231/938–6120* ⊕ *www.cgtwines.com*), located at a winery dating back to 1974.

Breakfast: Jump on over to France (or at least its cuisine) via **Brasserie Amie** (✉ *160 E. Front St.* ☎ *231/753–3161* ⊕ *www.brasserieamie.com*) with a croque madame or croque monsieur, crêpes, or tarte flambée for an elegant brunch.

Day 7: Traverse City, MI, to Mackinac Island, MI

117 miles (2 hours without traffic and stops)

Leaving Traverse City, travel north on I–75 N or U.S. 31 N to Mackinaw City, driving through the Gaylord State Forest Area. You'll hop on the Star Line Mackinac Island Ferry to car-free Mackinac Island. The ferry trip takes 18 minutes and parking is available near the ferry's departure point.

ALONG THE WAY

Eat & Drink: Gaylord is an outdoorsy community with many restaurants as well as **Big Buck Brewery** (✉ *550 S. Wisconsin Ave.* ☎ *989/448–7072* ⊕ *www.bigbuckbrewery.com*) with its robust menu of salads, burgers, and pizza.

Roadside Attraction: Just outside downtown Traverse City is "the world's largest cherry pie pan." Find it at the **Sara Lee Bakery Group** at ✉ *3424 Cass Road.*

MACKINAC ISLAND

Do: Even if you aren't staying at **Grand Hotel** (✉ *286 Grand Ave.* 800/334–7263 ⊕ *www.grandhotel.com*), pop over for a self-guided tour of the 1887 grand estate, one of Mackinac Island's most photographed buildings. Two lighthouses are on the island: McGulpin Point Lighthouse and Old Mackinac Point Lighthouse. A horse-drawn carriage tour is a fun way to explore the island in less than a day. Fudge crafted on the island is a favorite souvenir.

Eat & Drink: Frequent island visitors love **Millie's on Main** (✉ *7294 Main St.* ☎ *906/847–9901* ⊕ *www.milliesonmain. com*) for pub fare and drinks at **Pink Pony Bar** (✉ *7221 Main St.* ☎ *906/847–3341* ⊕ *www.pinkponymackinac.com*), perched above the water and with cute pink umbrellas outdoors. Pink Pony serves also breakfast, lunch, and dinner.

Stay: The **Inn on Mackinac** (✉ *6896 Main St.* ☎ *855/784–3846* ⊕ *www.innonmackinac.com*) is a vibrantly colored Victorian inn in the historic Marina District.

Breakfast: Lucky Bean (✉ *7383 Market St.* ⊕ *www.luckybeanmi.com*) is a sleek and modern coffeehouse serving not only coffee and espresso drinks, but also bagels, pastries, and oatmeal to start your day off right.

Day 8: Mackinac Island, MI, to Marquette, MI

162 miles (2 hours, 50 minutes without traffic and stops)

Today you'll cross into Michigan's UP (Upper Peninsula) and drive through Seney National Wildlife Refuge on M-77 N.

ALONG THE WAY

Nature: Pictured Rocks National Lakeshore (✉ *N8391 Sand Point Rd.* ☎ *906/387–3700* ⊕ *www.nps.gov/piro*)—named for the mineral stains on its sandstone cliffs—in Munising hugs the South Shore of Lake Superior.

Eat & Drink: Smoked fish is a delicacy in these parts. Try for yourself at **Cap'n Ron's Smoked Fish** (✉ *1336 Commercial St.* ☎ *906/202–0960* ⊕ *capn-rons.square. site*) in Munising, which sells smoked whitefish, smoked fish dip, and smoked fish "sausage" to go as well as pasties (another signature food of the UP).

MARQUETTE

Do: This college town along Lake Superior (across the water from Thunder Bay, Ontario) has a vibrant downtown lined with a natural foods co-op and vintage stores. It's also surrounded by protected forests—including **Hiawatha National Forest** (☎ *906/428–5800* ⊕ *www.fs.usda.gov*) and Presque Isle Park—for easy day hikes. Stroll to the end of downtown for a neat glimpse at the mouth of Lake Superior.

346

Eat & Drink: Tucked into a former movie theater in downtown Marquette, **Delft Bistro** (⊠ 139 W. Washington St. ☎ 906/273–2455 ⊕ www.thedelftbistro. com) is a chic, fun lunch and dinner spot while **Lagniappe** (⊠ 145 Jackson Cut Aly ☎ 906/226–8200 ⊕ marquettecajun.com) offers a taste of Cajun cuisine. There's even a Voodoo Bar, pouring 20 Michigan craft beers.

Stay: Most of Marquette's lodging choices are chains, but the **Landmark Inn** (⊠ 230 N. Front St. ☎ 906/228–2580 ⊕ www.thelandmarkinn.com) is a good nonchain option. The inn also has a restaurant/pub and frames views of Lake Superior.

Breakfast: Café Bodega (⊠ 517 N. 3rd St. ☎ 906/226–7009 ⊕ www.bodegamqt. com) serves all-day breakfast every day of the week with a special focus on vegan/vegetarian cuisine and locally sourced ingredients.

Day 9: Marquette, MI, to Sturgeon Bay, WI

217 miles (3 hours, 45 minutes without traffic and stops)

U.S. 41 S traces the western shoreline of Green Bay through Wisconsin until you hit the city of Green Bay, before curling northeast to Sturgeon Bay. This is the largest city in Door County, a resort community popular with Chicagoans and Milwaukeeans, located on its southern portion between Green Bay and Lake Michigan.

ALONG THE WAY
Eat & Drink: Pick up Mexican lunch at **Blue Bike Burrito** (⊠ 2020 Hall Ave. ☎ 715/735–9889 ⊕ www.bluebikeburrito. com) in Marinette, Wisconsin, and find a spot along the waterfront to dine.

STURGEON BAY
Do: Learn more about the region's shipbuilding industry and Swedish heritage with a visit to **Door County Maritime Museum** (⊠ 120 N. Madison Ave. ☎ 920/743–5958 ⊕ www.dcmm. org). Door County is also home to five state parks with easy hikes and stunning water views. Closest to Sturgeon Bay are **Whitefish Dunes State Park** (⊠ 3275 Clarks Lake Rd. ☎ 920/823–2400 ⊕ www.dnr. wi.gov), on the Lake Michigan side, and **Potawatomi State Park** (☎ 920/746–2890 ⊕ dnr.wisconsin.gov/topic/parks/potawatomi), on the Green Bay side.

Eat & Drink: The to-go sandwiches at **Door County Creamery** (⊠ 10653 N. Bay Shore Dr. ⊠ 920/854–3388 ⊕ www.doorcountycreamery.com) are heavenly and you can enjoy them right next door at Sister Bay Beach, along Green Bay's shoreline in Sister Bay. The goat-cheese producer also sells gelato and cheese. Fish boils are a local tradition: try one out at **Old Post Office Restaurant** (⊠ 10040 N. Water St. ☎ 920/854–4034 ⊕ www.oldpostoffice-doorcounty.com) in Fish Creek for dinner. Numerous farm stands sell fresh or frozen cherries, depending on the season, along with cherry pies and other desserts.

Stay: Sturgeon Bay is loaded with cute inns and B&Bs, including **Holiday Music Motel** (⊠ 30 N. 1st Ave. ☎ 920/743–5571 ⊕ www.holidaymusicmotel.com), a laid-back music-themed motel with its own radio station, and **White Lace Inn** (⊠ 16 N. 5th Ave. ☎ 920/743–1105 ⊕ www. whitelaceinn.com), a romantic B&B walking distance to downtown.

Breakfast: It's worth the half-hour drive north of Sturgeon Bay to view goats grazing on the grass roof at **Al Johnson's** (⊠ 10698 N. Bay Shore Dr. ☎ 920/854–2626 ⊕ www.aljohnsons.com in Sister Bay. You might even have time to stay for the Swedish pancakes. Across the street is Green Bay (the water, not the city).

Day 10: Sturgeon Bay, WI, to Chicago, IL

245 miles (4 hours without traffic and stops)

I–43 S takes you straight to Chicago (merging with I–94 S just south of downtown Milwaukee), but for a route that rims Lake Michigan, take Wisconsin Highway 42 S through the towns of Kewaunee and Two Rivers, before switching to I–43 S in Manitowoc.

ALONG THE WAY

Town: In Milwaukee, Lincoln Memorial Drive is where you can soak up Lake Michigan at its glory as you dodge dog-walkers, bicyclists, and runners along its paved paths. You'll also get a view of the Santiago Calatrava–designed **Milwaukee Art Museum** (⌂ *700 N. Art Museum Dr.* ☎ *414/224–3200* ⊕ *www.mam.org*).

Eat & Drink: Stop by the **Milwaukee Public Market** (⌂ *400 N. Water St.* ☎ *414/336–1111* ⊕ *www.milwaukeepublicmarket. org*), where a variety of vendors serve an eclectic mix of food and beverages.

Roadside Attraction: You can't miss the castle-motif **Mars Cheese Castle** (⌂ *2800 W. Frontage Rd.* ☎ *855/352–6277* ⊕ *www.marscheese.com*) in Kenosha County, right on I–94 S at Exit 340. About 400 varieties of Wisconsin cheese are sold here.

CHICAGO

Do: As the biggest city ringing the Great Lakes, Chicago has an incredible amount of sights and culture. Take a boat tour down the Chicago River and then a stroll along Lake Shore Trail and Lake Michigan, which leads to the **Field Museum** (⌂ *1400 S. Lake Shore Dr.* ☎ *312/922–9410* ⊕ *www.fieldmuseum.org*) and **Shedd Aquarium** (⌂ *1200 S. Lake Shore Dr.* ☎ *312/939–2438* ⊕ *www.sheddaquarium.org*). The **Art Institute of Chicago** (⌂ *111 S. Michigan Ave.* ☎ *312/443–3600* ⊕ *www.artic.edu*) is another must-see.

Eat & Drink: You can't leave Chicago without trying deep-dish pizza. **Lou Malnati's** (⌂ *805 S. State St.* ☎ *312/786–1000* ⊕ *www.loumalnatis.com*) is a local institution. Afterwards, head north to the hip Lincoln Park neighborhood and its collection of bars, like dive bar **Delilah's** (⌂ *2771 N. Lincoln Ave.* ☎ *773/472–2771* ⊕ *www.delilahschicago.com*) and blues music institution **B.L.U.E.S.** (⌂ *2519 N. Halsted St.* ☎ *773/528–1012* ⊕ *www. chicagobluesbar.com*).

Stay: On the city's Gold Coast, understated luxury abounds at the **Park Hyatt Chicago** (*800 N. Michigan Ave.* ☎ *312/335–1234* ⊕ *www.hyatt.com*), which dominates the skyline high above the old Water Tower. The views are spectacular from many of its oversized rooms.

Breakfast: Old-school **Eleven City Diner** (⌂ *1112 S. Wabash Ave.* ☎ *312/212–1112* ⊕ *www.elevencitydiner.com*) attracts locals looking for all-day breakfast and deli staples.

A Frank Lloyd Wright Tour

Written by Kristine Hansen

One of the world's most famous architects, Frank Lloyd Wright's masterful buildings are scattered all across the country (38 states hold at least one of his designs), but the best of the best lie between Chicago and Philadelphia. This trip will take you through small towns, major metropolises, and pastoral paradises, including the Mayan-inspired Unity Temple in Oak Park, Illinois; Fallingwater in rural Pennsylvania; and the recently restored Martin House in Buffalo, New York.

The godfather of Prairie School organic-style architecture may have been born in Wisconsin (in 1867), but Wright's adult years were spent in Oak Park, a Chicago suburb that today is home to the world's largest concentration of Wright-designed projects, including his home and studio. Wright enthusiastically took on residential and commercial commissions (from churches to cottages) during his 70-year career until his death at the age of 92 (in 1959). Buckle up and get ready for this highly immersive study into why Wright garnered a cult following worldwide.

At a Glance

Start: Chicago, IL

End: Philadelphia, PA

Miles Traveled: 1,245 miles

Suggested Duration: 7 days

States Visited: Illinois, Indiana, Michigan, New York, Pennsylvania

Key Sights: Beth Sholom Synagogue House; Fallingwater; Frank Lloyd Wright Home and Studio; Polymath Park; Unity Temple

Best Time to Go: Since some attractions are closed during the winter months, stick to spring and fall, which provide glimpses of flora and fauna, and fewer crowds.

Day 1: Chicago, IL, to Oak Park, IL

9 miles (20 minutes without traffic or stops)

The Chicago area is serviced by two major airports: O'Hare International Airport and Midway International Airport. Both are accessible to Oak Park and downtown Chicago via the "L" aboveground trains operated by the Chicago Transit Authority. You can also rent a car at each airport. Oak Park borders the city of Chicago on its west side, off I–290 (the Eisenhower Expressway), a 20-minute drive from downtown.

ALONG THE WAY

Town: Slow down your pace to properly take in the world's largest concentration of Wright projects in Oak Park's Frank Lloyd Wright–Prairie School of Architecture Historic District, on the National Register of Historic Places since 1973. Choose from a self-guided audio walking tour (sold in the home and studio's gift shop) or two-hour bicycle tour (weekends between May and October). The houses are easy to find: look for hipped roofs, angular turrets, overhanging eaves, and disguised front doors.

Photo Op: Two blocks from Frank Lloyd Wright's home and studio is **Austin Gardens** (✉ *167 Forest Ave.* ☎ *708/524–2050* ⊕ *www.pdop.org*)—wrapped in an iron gate with a bronze bust of Wright at the south end of Forest Avenue.

OAK PARK

Do: Get a lesson in Wright's artistry (before he moved deeper into his boxy, Prairie-style design) via a 60-minute guided tour of the shingle-style **Frank Lloyd Wright Home and Studio** (✉ *951 Chicago Ave.* ☎ *312/994–4000* www.flwright.org), in his namesake Historic District, home to dozens of residential commissions completed between 1896 and 1913. With UNESCO World Heritage site status, the modern, reinforced-concrete **Unity Temple** (✉ *875 Lake St.* ☎ *708/848–6225* ⊕ *www.unitytemple.org*) is a nod to Wright's Unitarian upbringing.

Eat & Drink: From Indiana rabbit to Maine lobster, all prepared by a chef whose culinary roots are in the Caribbean and Boston, **Hemmingway's Bistro** (✉ *211 N. Oak Park Ave.* ☎ *708/524–0806* ⊕ *www.hemmingwaysbistro.com*) is a nod to Oak Park's other famous former resident: author Ernest Hemingway. For a sweet treat, dip back a century at **Petersen's Ice Cream** (✉ *1100 Chicago*

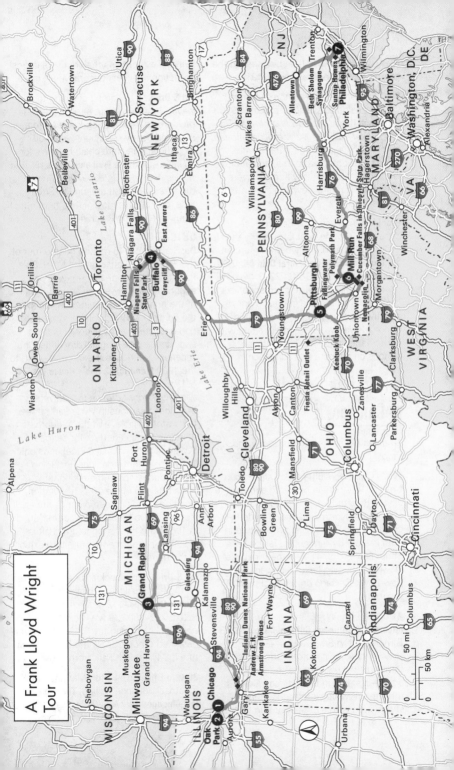

Ave. ☎ *708/386–6131)*, in business at the same Oak Park address since 1919.

Stay: Immerse yourself more fully in a Wright design by waking up in the 1915 **Emil Bach House** (✉ *7415 N. Sheridan Rd.* ☎ *773/654–3959* ⊕ *www.emilbachhouse. com*) in Chicago's Rogers Park, with three bedrooms, two baths, and a full kitchen in the two-story home. Slivers of Lake Michigan are viewable from many rooms.

Breakfast: Ask any Emil Bach House docent where the best latte is and their eyes will get all dreamy before mentioning **Charmers Food and Floral Café** (✉ *1500 W. Jarvis Ave.* ☎ *773/743–2233* ⊕ *www. charmerscafe.com*). The plant shop/café brews coffee and espresso drinks, plus the most indigo shade of lavender lemonade you've ever sipped, along with homemade "pop tarts" and the locally famous chimichurri egg sandwich.

Day 2: Oak Park, IL, to Chicago, IL

18 miles (35 miles without traffic and stops)

While your two sights today are both in Chicago, they are at opposite ends of the city: in Rogers Park just south of Evanston on the North Side and in Hyde Park on the South Side. Travel time between both is around 40 minutes. Taking Lake Shore Drive (U.S. 41 S) is the most scenic view, hugging Lake Michigan, with downtown Chicago on the final third of the route.

ALONG THE WAY

Photo Op: At **Chicago Cultural Center** (✉ *78 E. Washington St.* ☎ *312/744–6630* ⊕ *www.cityofchicago.org*), the Louis Comfort Tiffany's handcrafted windows—a staple in the Arts and Crafts movement, which informed Wright's styles—are works of beauty. Fun fact: the

Windy City contains the country's largest collection of Tiffany decorative-art glass.

Eat & Drink: You weren't planning to leave Chicago without a relish- and mustard-coated hot dog tucked into a steamed poppy-seed bun, were you? Skip the cult-favorite chain Portillo's for an indie stand like **Fred and Jack's** (✉ *7600 S. Yale Ave.* ☎ *773/783–9700* ⊕ *www. orderfredandjacks.com*) on the South Side, one of Chicago's oldest, born out of a pushcart during the 1940s.

CHICAGO

Do: Start with a 45-minute guided tour of the Emil Bach House on the North Side. Its Cream City brick exterior was used abundantly in Milwaukee around the time of the home's 1915 construction, and the Frank Lloyd Wright Trust's restoration emulated nearly every furnishing and sconce from original drawings for a Japanese tea house. Next, head south to the 1909 **Frederick C. Robie House** (✉ *5757 S. Woodlawn Ave.* ☎ *312/994–4000* ⊕ *www.flwright.org*) on the University of Chicago campus in Hyde Park; three tours are available, and the in-depth, 90-minute one is perfect for serious Wright fans (Fridays and weekends only). Tenets of Wright's designs, including embedded lamps in the dining table, were retained in the 2009 restoration. Crushed you didn't see Wright's Imperial Hotel in Tokyo before it was demolished in 1967? The hotel's signature chair is included in a permanent furniture exhibit in the house.

Eat & Drink: Sip a cocktail or enjoy oysters on the half shell at the beach house-like **Cindy's Rooftop** (✉ *12 S. Michigan Ave.* ☎ *312/792–3502* ⊕ *www.cindysrooftop. com*) while viewing the Sir Anish Kapoor-designed *Cloud Gate* ("The Bean") sculpture in Millennium Park from above.

Stay: In Chicago's Fulton Market, where meatpackers once sizzled, **The Hoxton, Chicago** hotel (✉ *200 N. Green St.* ☎ *312/761–1700* ⊕ *www.thehoxton.*

com) hosts *Top Chef* champion Stephanie Izard's rooftop Cabra Cevicheria.

Breakfast: Chicago diners are the real deal, like **Lou Mitchell's** (⌧ *565 W. Jackson Blvd.* ☎ *312/939–3111* ⊕ *www.loumitchells.com*) in the Loop. Cram into a vinyl booth, close your eyes, and take a whiff of fluffy eggs, malted waffles, and silver-dollar pancakes—plus bottomless cups of coffee to fuel your ride.

Day 3: Chicago, IL, to Grand Rapids, MI

217 miles (3 hours, 25 minutes without traffic and stops)

Once you're out of Chicagoland (be prepared for traffic), it's a smooth, easy ride up to Michigan along I–94 E, often just a few miles inland from the Lake Michigan shoreline.

ALONG THE WAY

Photo Op: A quick drive-by of the 1939 **Andrew F. H. Armstrong House** (⌧ *43 Cedar Trail*) in Ogden Dunes, Indiana, will remind you of Wright's talent of merging his buildings with the landscapes; the screened porch is nestled in a forested paradise.

Nature: With its new national park status, the 15,000-acre **Indiana Dunes National Park** (☎ *219/395–1882* ⊕ *www.nps.gov/indu*) in Porter, Indiana, flaunts 15 miles of shoreline on Lake Michigan's southern edge. Slip into hiking boots to explore its 50 miles of trails snaking through the namesake dunes along with wetlands, forests, and prairies.

Eat & Drink: These days the exit signs off I–94 tout wineries and CBD dispensaries, but locals know **Bit of Swiss** bakery (⌧ *4333 Ridge Rd.* ☎ *269/429–1661* ⊕ *www.bitofswiss.com*) in Stevensville—pardon the pun—rises above with its grab-and-go mini cream cakes, fruit tortes, almond croissants, and cinnamon

rolls. Outdoor café-style seating makes the cabin structure that much more charming.

Detour: While official tours do not take place, **The Acres** (⌧ *Hawthorne Dr.*), a 70-acre subdivision in tiny Galesburg, just south of Grand Rapids, boasts four homes—plus a fifth built by Taliesin architect Francis "Will" Willsey a year after Wright's death—commissioned during the 1940s and 1950s by Upjohn pharmaceutical scientists. In 2004, it landed on the National Register of Historic Places and is worth a drive through.

GRAND RAPIDS

Do: The 3,600-square-foot 1909 **Meyer May House** (⌧ *450 Madison Ave. SE* ☎ *616/246–4821* ⊕ *www.meyermayhouse.steelcase.com*) is an exquisite expression of Wright's Prairie style; it's owned by Steelcase, a local company contracted to make Wright's furnishings for the Johnson Wax Administration Building in Racine, Wisconsin. See George Mann Niedecken's signature chair "hoofs" and a mural unearthed during a late-1980s restoration. Because it's tucked into one of the country's largest historic districts (Heritage Hill), be sure to bring your walking shoes.

Eat & Drink: Along nearby Cherry Street are enough coffee shops, bars, and bakeries to get you wired or tanked. Book an, ahem, visitation at **Brewery Vivant** (⌧ *925 Cherry St. SE* ☎ *616/719–1604* ⊕ *www.breweryvivant.com*), tucked into a converted funeral home's redbrick chapel and serving lunch and dinner items like poutine, duck nachos, and bratwurst (with house-brewed Belgian- and French-style beer, of course).

Stay: Seeing even just a small percentage of Heritage Hill's 1,300 homes—representing nearly every architectural style from 1844 on—might seem impossible, but staying overnight puts a serious dent in the effort. The **Leonard at Logan House** (⌧ *440 Logan St. SE* ☎ *616/308–6585*

⊕ www.leonardatlogan.com), with just eight rooms, puts you in the thick of the action, serving a full breakfast in its 1914 storybook-like interiors. Otherwise, count yourself lucky if you snag a reservation at the Wright-designed, Usonian-style Samuel and Dorothy Eppstein House in Galesburg (available on Airbnb).

Breakfast: Despite its name, **Wealthy Street Bakery** (✉ 610 Wealthy St. SE ☎ 616/301–2950 ⊕ www.wealthystreet-bakery.com) is not at all snooty. Heavy on pastries and loaded with gluten-free offerings, the bakery-café's menu includes seven breakfast sandwiches served on homemade ciabatta.

Day 4: Grand Rapids, MI, to Buffalo, NY

389 miles (6 hours without traffic and stops)

The fastest way to get to Buffalo is on I–69 E to Highway 402 through Canada's Southern Ontario province (bonus: Niagara Falls pit-stop!), crossing over the border on the Blue Water Bridge that links Port Huron, Michigan, with Sarnia, Ontario.

ALONG THE WAY

Nature: Straddling the U.S.-Canada border is **Niagara Falls State Park** (✉ 332 Prospect St., Niagara Falls, NY ☎ 716/278–1794 ⊕ www.niagarafallsstatepark.com), the country's oldest state park. Even if you only have time for a brief visit, the Observation Tower and four clearly marked Niagara Gorge hiking trails (stretch those legs!) are suitable orientations to this natural wonder.

Eat & Drink: At **Flip Burger** (✉ 305 Prospect St. ☎ 716/278–1111 ⊕ www.flipburger-inc.com) in Niagara Falls, you can enjoy classic burgers and milk shakes on the seasonal patio.

Essential Listening

A lot of books have been written about Wright, but most are nonfiction. Lose yourself in T. C. Boyle's *The Women: A Novel*, fictitiously chronicling—while staying true to history—the four female loves of Wright.

BUFFALO

Do: When you reach Buffalo, buckle up for three off-beat, Wright-designed, posthumous landmarks based on his drawings. Modeled after the University of Wisconsin crew team's boathouse (which was never built), Wright apprentice Tony Puttnam unveiled the Prairie-style **Fontana Boathouse** (✉ 1 Rotary Row ☎ 716/362–3140 ⊕ www.wrightsboathouse.org) along the Niagara River in 2007. At home among dozens of antique cars in the **Buffalo Transportation Pierce-Arrow Museum**, the 2014 Buffalo Filling Station (✉ 263 Michigan Ave. ☎ 716/853–0084 ⊕ www.pierce-arrow.com) features a fireplace, deck, copper roof with twin totem poles, and salmon-hued concrete exterior. Finally, in Frederick Law Olmstead's Delaware Park (home to Forest Lawn Cemetery) lies the **Blue Sky Mausoleum** (✉ 972–990 W. Delavan Ave. ⊕ www.blueskymausoleum.com), built in 2004.

In addition, Isabel and Darwin Martin's former 15,000-square-foot home (built between 1903 and 1905) at the **Martin House Complex** (✉ 125 Jewett Pkwy. ☎ 716/856–3858 ⊕ www.martinhouse.org) saw one of the most extensive renovations of any Wright home (costing $52 million), right on down to the Tree of Life stained glass windows.

Eat & Drink: Immigrant food vendors at the **West Side Bazaar** (✉ 25 Grant St. ☎ 716/783–8489 ⊕ www.westsidebazaar.

Fallingwater is on every architecture buff's bucket list.

com) are partially funded by a local economic-development initiative, bringing their cuisine to this grab-and-go marketplace that also sells crafts. **Hutch's** (✉ *1375 Delaware Ave.* ☎ *716/885–0074* ⊕ *www.hutchsrestaurant.com*) whisks you to France with dinner delicacies like soft-shell crabs, prime rib, Faroe Island salmon, and Nova Scotia halibut.

Stay: Hotel Henry (✉ *444 Forest Ave.* ⊕ *www.hotelhenry.com*), located within the historic Richardson Olmsted Campus and once an insane asylum, shows off the prowess of one of America's most famed architects, H. H. Henry Richardson. The **Albright-Knox Art Gallery** (✉ *1285 Elmwood Ave.* ☎ *716/882–8700* ⊕ *www. albrightknox.org*) (reopening in 2022 as the Buffalo Albright Knox Gundlach Art Museum), home to works by artists like Willem de Kooning, Mark Rothko, Jackson Pollock, and Lee Krasner, is a quick stroll away.

Breakfast: The concentration of Wright projects in Buffalo is daunting and takes two days to explore—but you can check

the memory of one off (the building perished in a 1950 fire) over eggs and bacon at **Swan Street Diner** (✉ *700 Swan St.* ☎ *716/768–1823* ⊕ *www.swanstreet-diner.com*), tucked into a fully restored, 1937 Sterling Company diner car and located across the street from the Larkin Administration Building.

Day 5: Buffalo, NY, to Pittsburgh, PA

275 miles (4 hours, 25 minutes without traffic and stops)

Taking I–90 W out of Buffalo, you'll travel southwest to Erie before connecting with I–79 S shortly after entering Pennsylvania. The landscape along I–79 S and I–76 E is gorgeous; picture lots of rolling green hills that likely inspired Wright's designs.

ALONG THE WAY

Attraction: The Martins' sprawling property just outside Buffalo in Derby—dubbed **Graycliff** (✉ *6472 Old Lake Shore Rd.* ☎ *716/947–9217* ⊕ *www.experiencegraycliff.org*)—is perched above Lake Erie. The two-hour tour is a deeper immersion into the late 1920s estate designed by Wright.

Eat & Drink: East Aurora, New York, may be the location for many Hallmark holiday films, but the village's roots are in the **Roycroft Campus** (✉ *31 S. Grove St.* ☎ *716/655–0261* ⊕ *www.roycroftcampuscorp.com*), a utopian society founded by Elbert Hubbard in 1895, where craftspeople churned out Morris chairs and other Arts-and-Crafts designs within the guild. Tour the campus and enjoy lunch at the 1905 **Roycroft Inn** (✉ *40 S. Grove St.* ☎ *716/652–5552* ⊕ *www.roycroftinn.com*).

Detour: If you collect Fiestaware, you can easily spend an hour digging through selections in the **Fiesta Retail Outlet** (✉ *6th and Harrison St.* ☎ *304/387–1300* www.fiestafactorydirect.com) in Newell, West Virginia, where every colorful crock and mug has been made since 1907.

PITTSBURGH

Do: Pittsburgh itself doesn't have too many connections to Wright, but it's a good stopping point to prepare yourself for all the Pennsylvania-based Wright buildings you'll be seeing tomorrow. That doesn't mean the city itself is lacking in architecture. Just as it sounds, **Pittsburgh's "Millionaire's Row"** (✉ *5th Avenue in Shadyside*) is where steel barons in this Rust Belt city built their Victorian-era mansions. Between 1830 and 1930, Pittsburgh had more millionaires than any U.S. city.

Eat & Drink: Since 1933, **Primanti Bros.** (✉ *46 18th St.* ☎ *412/263–2142* ⊕ *www.primantibros.com*) has stuffed its sandwiches with fries, and thankfully there are nine locations across Pittsburgh

today. Head to the founding one in the Strip District, a neighborhood settled by Italian immigrants, and where the aroma of roasted garlic still reigns due to its many eateries and delis.

Stay: At the 8,000-square-foot 1870 **Parador Inn** (✉ *939 Western Ave.* ☎ *412/231–4800* ⊕ *www.theparadorinn.com*) in Pittsburgh's North Shore, breakfast is served with reggae music by owner Ed Menzer. At the **Calvary United Methodist Church** (✉ *971 Beech Ave.* ☎ *412/231–2007* ⊕ *www.calvarypgh.com*) across the street, a trio of Louis Comfort Tiffany glass windows are among the world's largest.

Breakfast: Former New Yorkers opened **Pear and the Pickle** (✉ *1800 Rialto St.* ⊕ *www.pearandpickle.com*) to serve the breakfast sandwiches they missed from their local bodega; sample them along with lox and bagels and coffee brewed from Redstart Roasters' responsibly sourced beans.

Day 6: Pittsburgh, PA, to Mill Run, PA

67 miles (1 hour, 15 minutes without traffic and stops)

Today's quick route will take you to some of Wright's most famous designs. Conveniently, three of Wright's Pennsylvania projects (Kentuck Knob, Polymath Park, and Fallingwater) are within a tight radius: Kentuck Knob and Fallingwater are 7 miles apart while Polymath Park is about 45 minutes away. These are winding country roads, a nice change from the freeway.

ALONG THE WAY

Attraction: Tom and Heather Papinchak's **Polymath Park** (✉ *187 Evergreen La.* ☎ *877/833–7829* ⊕ *www.polymathpark.com*) in Acme relocates Wright homes from other parts of the country (yes, really) to this 130-acre subdivision. See interiors of Mäntylä (formerly in Minnesota) and Duncan (once in Lisle, Illinois), plus Balter (designed by Wright apprentice Peter Berndston) on the Wright House Collection tour. For an even more intimate experience, you can even stay the night at one of the homes.

Eat & Drink: Of course, you've had a McDonald's Big Mac at least once in your life, but you probably haven't ordered one at the **McDonald's** (✉ *575 Morgantown St.*) where it was first served, in Uniontown. That was in 1967 and a sign proves it. Otherwise you can pack a picnic to enjoy on the grounds of Polymath Park or Kentuck Knob—the latter has beautiful art sculptures.

Attraction: The Usonian-style **Kentuck Knob** (✉ *723 Kentuck Rd.* ☎ *724/329–1901* ⊕ *www.kentuckknob.com*) is located on 73 acres in Chalk Hill, Pennsylvania. Current owner Peter Palumbo overheard people talking about its need for a buyer while touring Fallingwater in 1985. He snapped up the elegant property but lives in another home nearby, leaving the house open for 90-minute in-depth and 45-minute standard tours.

Nature: Cucumber Falls in Ohiopyle State Park (✉ *124 Main St.* ☎ *724/329–8591* ⊕ *www.dcnr.state.pa.us*) in Ohiopyle is a popular day trip for Pittsburgh residents—you'll understand why once you spot the glorious 30-foot waterfall. It's only three minutes from Kentuck Knob. Park in the lot at the Cucumber Falls trailhead off Chalk Hill Road and climb down a few steps to the lookout point.

MILL RUN

Do: We've saved the best for last in this region. Even non-Wright fans will likely have heard of **Fallingwater** (✉ *1491 Mill Run Rd.* ☎ *724/329–8501* ⊕ *www.fallingwater.org*), a weekend home in Mill Run designed in 1935 for Liliane and Edgar Kaufmann, owners of Kaufmann's Department Store in Pittsburgh. *Smithsonian Magazine* named the gorgeous

home—perched on top of a waterfall—among 28 places to see before you die. There are daily self-guided and guided hourlong architectural tours, as well as three-hour brunches and sunset experiences.

Eat & Drink: Treetops Restaurant (✉ *187 Evergreen La.* ☎ *877/833–7829* ⊕ *www.treetoprestaurant.net*) at Polymath Park is appropriately named for its treehouse-like location, an organic-architecture concept Wright would surely approve. Enjoy its vegan, vegetarian, and gluten-free meals (don't fret: there's also filet mignon).

Stay: The 2,220-acre **Nemacolin** (✉ *1001 Lafayette Dr.* ☎ *866/344–6957* ⊕ *www.nemacolin.com*) property holds three spectacular hotels: the Lodge, a Rockefeller's former hunting lodge; the Chateau, modeled after the Ritz Paris, and Falling Rock, a bucket-list item for any Wright fan. While there, go art-hopping at Reflection (a contemporary-art museum), wander through the Hardy family's 900-piece art collection, or observe the artist-in-residence's working studio.

Breakfast: Smoothies, breakfast sandwiches, and pastries at **Ohiopyle Bakery & Sandwich Shoppe** (✉ *85 Main St.* ☎ *724/329–2253* ⊕ *www.ohiopylebakery.com*), just minutes from Fallingwater in the whitewater-rafting mecca of Ohiopyle, are served by a farming family and paired with coffee.

Day 7: Mill Run, PA, to Philadelphia, PA

270 miles (4 hours without traffic and stops)

I–76 E is a great way to see nearly all of Pennsylvania's southern half, as you drive from the southwest part to the southeast tip. Philadelphia is serviced by Philadelphia International Airport, where rental cars can easily be returned.

356

ALONG THE WAY

Eat & Drink: It's one thing to pull over for ice cream. But **Igloo Soft Freeze** (✉ *462 E. Main St.* ☎ *814/652–2442* ⊕ *www.theiglooicecream.com*) in Everett, Pennsylvania, is literally inside an ice-cream-cone-shaped building.

Detour: At the **Allentown Art Museum** (✉ *31 N. 5th St.* ☎ *610/432–4333* ⊕ *www.allentownartmuseum.org*), in Allentown, Pennsylvania, is the Francis Little House II, a reconstruction of the Wright-designed library that was demolished in 1971 along Lake Minnetonka in Minnesota. The library's two other sections are in the Metropolitan Museum of Art in New York City and the Minneapolis Institute of Art.

PHILADELPHIA

Do: Wright was 85 years old in 1954 when he designed the **Beth Sholom Synagogue** (✉ *8231 Old York Rd.* ☎ *215/887–1342* ⊕ *www.bethsholomcongregation.org*), a Mayan Revival synagogue in Elkins Park, Pennsylvania (just 9 miles and 40 minutes north of Philly). It opened five months after his 1959 death. See the modern marvel—including a 40-foot concrete monolith, a riff on Moses's stone tablets—on an hourlong Guided Architectural Building Tour. For a quick drive-by, check out the only other Wright-designed project near Philly: the **Suntop Homes** (✉ *152–154 Sutton Rd.*). Built in 1939 in nearby Ardmore as a Usonian twist on row homes, the houses were designed to coax city people to the suburbs. Although two dwellings were destroyed in two separate fires, the last two remain.

Eat & Drink: One of the country's first food halls, **Reading Terminal Market** (✉ *51 N. 12th St.* ☎ *215/922–2317* ⊕ *www.readingterminalmarket.org*) has continuously operated since 1893 in downtown Philly's Historic Landmark building. Even Pennsylvania Dutch cuisine is represented (by three vendors, including Hatville Deli, known for its Lebanon bologna and smoked-cheddar sandwich on Amish bread).

Shop: When you visit one of the country's oldest cities, the antiques shopping is bound to be epic. At **Architectural Antiques** (✉ *721 N. 2nd St.* ☎ *215/922–3669* ⊕ *www.architecturalantiques.com*) in the Northern Liberties neighborhood, you might score anything from vintage pub decor to a newel post for your next home-remodeling project.

Stay: The **Lokal Hotel** (✉ *139 N. 3rd St.* ☎ *267/702–4345* ⊕ *www.staylokal.com*), in Old City, is a supercute, modern refresh on a historic building, featuring six apartment-style rooms. For a step further back in history, book a room at the **Morris House Hotel** (✉ *225 S. 8th St.* ☎ *215/922–2446* ⊕ *www.morrishousehotel.com*), a 1787 building within Philadelphia's Historic District where rates include breakfast and afternoon tea. Both are a short walk from the Liberty Bell and Independence Hall.

Breakfast: The **Bourse Food Hall** (✉ *111 S. Independence Mall E* ☎ *215/625–0300* ⊕ *www.theboursephilly.com*), located inside the Victorian-era Bourse Building, is where Menagerie Coffee grinds Dogwood coffee beans daily. Grab a breakfast sandwich or yogurt and granola parfait, too.

Chapter 7

THE SOUTHEAST AND FLORIDA

WELCOME TO THE SOUTHEAST AND FLORIDA

TOP REASONS TO GO

★ **Asheville:** A highlight of any Carolinas visit, Asheville wows with its arts, crafts, food, beer, and music scenes.

★ **Great Smoky Mountains National Park:** Even as the country's most visited national park, there is still more than enough beauty and deserted woodland for everyone to enjoy a peaceful communion with nature.

★ **Kentucky's Bourbon Trail:** Thirty-seven distilleries, including some of the world's best, make up the famed Kentucky Bourbon Trail.

★ **Martin Luther King Jr.** National Historic Park: As the home of MLK, Atlanta was a hub of the civil rights movement, and you can retrace his life by visiting this historic park along with his childhood home and burial place.

★ **Everglades National Park:** More than 1.5 million acres of South Florida's 4.3 million acres of subtropical, watery wilderness are part of Everglades National Park, one of the country's largest national parks.

1 **The Blue Ridge Parkway.** This famous drive takes you through scenic parts of North Carolina and Virginia.

2 **The Best of the Carolinas.** History, food, and gorgeous landscapes are everywhere in North and South Carolina.

3 **National Parks of the Southeast.** Experience the beauty of four national parks, including Great Smoky Mountains.

4 **The Great American Whisky Tour.** Visit distilleries along Kentucky's Bourbon Trail and beyond.

5 **The Civil Rights Tour.** Retrace the Civil Rights movement through key sites in the South.

6 **The Great American Music Road Trip.** From New Orleans to Nashville, see how the history of American music mirrors the history of America.

7 **The Best of Northern and Central Florida.** The Atlantic and Gulf coasts of the Sunshine State offer beaches, history, and good eats.

8 **The Best of Southern Florida.** From Miami to Key West, you can see some of the most unique and stunning landscapes in the country.

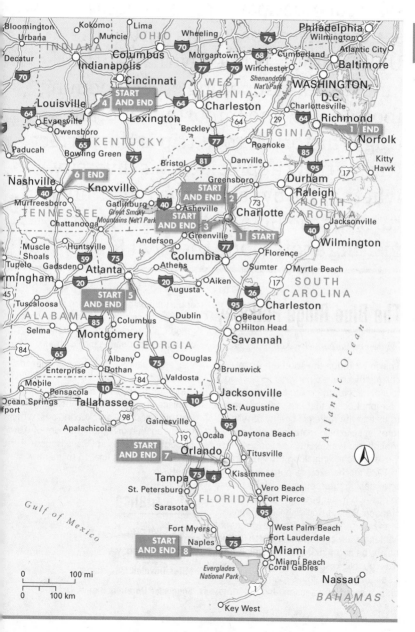

From the southern reaches of the Appalachian Mountains to the swamplands spanning the country's southeastern coast, this part of the United States is filled with beautiful landscapes, happening cities, booming food scenes, and important, if often tragic, history. A road trip is the perfect way to truly appreciate this diversity, whether it's by taking the twists and turns of the Blue Ridge Parkway or visiting spots along the Civil Rights Trail.

The Blue Ridge Parkway

Written by Barbara Noe Kennedy

Snaking through the southern Appalachians, this classic parkway forces you to slow down, thanks to a speed limit of 45 mph. Luckily that just makes it easier to take in the majestic beauty of wild forests, splashing waterfalls, and misty mountains, with plenty of hiking, camping, and picnicking along the way. Started in 1935 for the express purpose of showcasing the mountains, the parkway winds 465 miles between Shenandoah National Park at Rockfish Gap, Virginia, in the north and Great Smoky Mountains National Park at Cherokee, North Carolina, in the south. Safe from development, it's a bucolic respite where black bears, deer, and other animals roam, lavish flora changes with the season, and outdoorsy opportunities abound. There are some facilities along the way, including three lodges, six restaurants, several visitor centers, and multiple picnic areas.

While the parkway has provided decades of family fun and road-trip memories, it's important to remember that its creation displaced many residents, including the Eastern Band of Cherokee Indians, who fought against giving up the right-of-way through their lands at Qualla Boundary, the parkway's final 15 miles near Cherokee.

At a Glance

Start: Charlotte, NC

End: Richmond, VA

Miles Traveled: 767 miles

Suggested Duration: 6 days

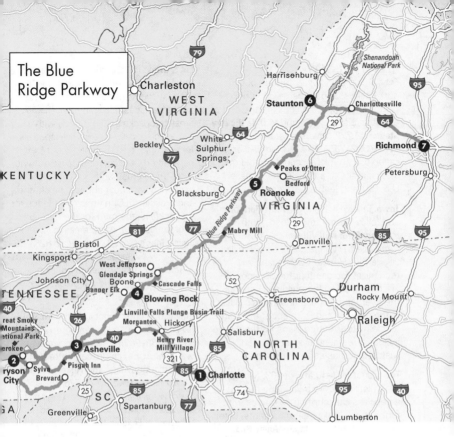

The Blue Ridge Parkway

States Visited: North Carolina, Virginia

Key Sights: Biltmore House and Estate; Blowing Rock; Great Smoky Mountains National Park; Museum of the Cherokee Indian; Brevard waterfalls

Best Time to Go: Springtime is glorious with blooming flowers while summer's wildflowers and autumn's multihued leaves are always gorgeous. Keep in mind the parkway is not maintained in winter and may close due to inclement weather year-round, particularly in the late fall through early spring.

Day 1: Charlotte, NC, to Bryson City, NC

180 miles (3 hours, 30 minutes without traffic and stops)

The trip begins in big-city Charlotte, which is quite a ways away from the Blue Ridge Parkway, but is a good starting point for anyone who needs to fly in and pick up a rental car. On your first day, you'll travel mostly fast highways—I-85, U.S. 321, and I-40—getting ever closer to the mountains. At Clyde, hop onto U.S. 74 for the final scenic push into Bryson City.

ALONG THE WAY

Eat & Drink: Cauliflower fritters, pulled-pork nachos, and burgers with smoked Gouda and tobacco onions are the sort of delicious dishes you'll find at **Olde Hickory Station** (✉ 232 Government Ave. SW ☎ 828/322–2356 ⊕ www.oldehickorystation.com), which occupies an old train station in the heart of Hickory, where U.S. 321 and I–40 meet.

Town: Take Exit 119 off I–40 at Hildebran and follow Henry River Road south to **Henry River Mill Village** (⊕ www.henryrivermillvillage.com), an old milling village that Hunger Games fans will recognize. You can tour the abandoned village, including the buildings used as the Everdeens' house and Peeta's Bakery in the movies, and learn about the state's textile history. Future plans for the village include a restaurant, museum, and restored homes as vacation rentals.

Town: Just off I–40 at Exit 103, Morganton's historic downtown, centered on a neoclassical courthouse, buzzes with funky shops, galleries, restaurants, cafés, and the popular **Adventure Bound Books** (✉ 120 N. Sterling St. ☎ 828/475–6955 ⊕ www.adventureboundbooks.com). It's also where you'll find "Sacred Dance and the Muses," one of the Ben Long frescoes (⊕ www.romanticasheville.com/fresco) located on the ceiling of the **City of Morganton Municipal Auditorium**; anyone can pop in and take a look.

BRYSON CITY

Do: This walkable, outdoorsy town on the edge of **Great Smoky Mountains National Park** (☎ 865/436–1200 ⊕ www.nps.gov/grsm) offers a relaxing vibe along the Tuckasegee River. Check out the petite downtown, and find outfitters that will help you fish, kayak, and/or paddleboard. The national park is within a hiking boot's distance, with plenty of trails to head out and explore, including the 4-mile Deep Creek Loop, which takes in two pretty waterfalls.

Eat & Drink: The Bistro at the **Everett Hotel** (✉ 16 Everett St. ☎ 828/488–1934 ⊕ www.theeveretthotel.com) is hands-down the nicest place in town. It's small but packs a lot of punch with a fresh, eclectic menu and daily specials: for example, bacon-draped meat loaf, pan-seared Carolina mountain trout with a cornmeal crust, and a chicken breast sandwich with goat cheese, fig chutney, and prosciutto. Don't miss the handcrafted cocktails (the mint for the mint juleps is grown locally). A more casual choice is **Jimmy Mac's** (✉ 121 Main St. ☎ 828/488–4700 ⊕ www.facebook.com/jimmymacsrestaurant), an all-American grill on Main Street featuring hand-cut steaks, fresh seafood, pasta, and a cavalcade of TVs.

Stay: Good choices include the **McKinley Edwards Inn** (✉ 208 Arlington Ave. ☎ 828/488–9626 ⊕ www.mckinleyedwardsinn.com), an upscale retreat in a landmark building; the **Folkestone Inn** (✉ 101 Folkestone Rd. ☎ 828/488–2730 ⊕ www.folkestoneinn.com), originally a 1920s mountain farmhouse; and **Lakeview at Fontana** (✉ 171 Lakeview Lodge Dr. ☎ 800/742–6492 ⊕ www.lakeviewfontana.com), a spa retreat with basic rooms tucked into a gorgeous mountainscape.

Breakfast: Grab a coffee, bagels with signature spreads, and light fare at **La Dolce Vita** (✉ 191 Everett St. ☎ 828/488–5888 ⊕ www.dolcebryson.com).

Day 2: Bryson City, NC, to Asheville, NC

97 miles (2 hours, 40 minutes without traffic and stops)

Wind through the mountain landscapes via U.S. 19 and U.S. 441 south to Cherokee, where, just north, you'll finally jump onto the Blue Ridge Parkway at its southernmost terminus.

ALONG THE WAY

Nature: Drag yourself out of bed early to arrive just after sunrise at the **Oconauftee Visitor Center** (✉ *1194 Newfound Gap Rd.* ☎ *828/497–1904* ⊕ *www.nps.gov/ grsm*) in Cherokee, near the Blue Ridge Parkway's southern terminus, where elk calmly graze in the meadows. You'll also find the **Mountain Farm Museum** (☎ *828/497–1904* ⊕ *www.nps.gov*), an authentic Smokies log homestead. And you can't miss the **Museum of the Cherokee Indian** (✉ *589 Tsali Blvd.* ☎ *828/497– 3481* ⊕ *www.cherokeemuseum.com*), which delves into Cherokee culture and history, including a full-scale reproduction of an Oconaluftee Indian village.

Photo Op: Be sure to spend some time in **Great Smoky Mountains National Park** (☎ *865/436–1200* ⊕ *www.nps. gov/grsm*) before striking out on the parkway. If nothing else, drive to the top of Clingmans Dome, the park's loftiest peak at 6,643 feet. Hike a half mile to the observation tower and gulp in the refreshing mountain air as you take in the 360-degree views of blue-hued peaks marching off into the distance.

Town: Drop off the parkway at Balsam Gap (mile marker 443.1), where U.S. 23/74 leads to the town of Sylva. The all-American main street has one-of-a-kind eats, activity outfitters, multiple bookstores, and four breweries (to stock up for later, of course). You could stay for an hour, enjoying coffee and homemade pie at the **Coffee Shop** (✉ *385 W. Main St. Sylva, NC* ☎ *828/586–2013*), or remain all day, enjoying the area's outdoorsy offerings. Go fly-fishing on the **WNC Fly Fishing Trail** (☎ *800/962–1911* ⊕ *www.flyfishing-trail.com*), with local outfitters available to take you out to the best fishing holes, or hike on the rugged 7-mile **Pinnacle Park Trail** (⊕ *www.discoverjacksonnc.com/out-doors/trails/pinnacle-park-trail*), offering supreme mountain panoramas.

Detour: Located about 15 miles south of Wagon Road Gap (mile marker 402) via

Essential Listening

Old Crow Medicine Show's *Volunteer* album is a folksy, spirited ode to Americana bluegrass, the perfect companion as you make your way through the hills and dales of Appalachia.

U.S. 276, Brevard is not only a cute town, with retail favorites like the **White Squirrel Shoppe** (✉ *6 W. Main St.* ☎ *828/877–3530* ⊕ *www.whitesquirrelshoppe.com*), but it's at the heart of North Carolina's "land of waterfalls." There are 250-plus cascades nearby, some small, some large, some famous (a couple were featured in *The Hunger Games* and *Last of the Mohicans*), some not so much, but all beautiful.

Eat & Drink: Pisgah Inn (✉ *408 Blue Ridge Pkwy.* ☎ *828/235–8228* ⊕ *www.pisga-hinn.com*), at mile marker 408 in Canton, sits 5,000 feet above the surrounding rugged terrain, providing spectacular mountain views to accompany your rainbow trout, fried chicken, and baked chicken pot pie.

ASHEVILLE

Do: Browse the art galleries, Appalachian craft shops, indie coffee shops, bookstores, and breweries (there are over 60 of them) in this funky, laid-back, music-and-beer-filled mountain town. The town's most famous site is the **Biltmore House and Estate** (✉ *1 Lodge St.* ☎ *800/411–3812* ⊕ *www.biltmore.com*), George Vanderbilt's 250-room Gilded-Age mansion, which remains the nation's largest private house and is open with a variety of tours.

Eat & Drink: It's hard to pick out just one or two places to dine in this hub of foodie creativity; stroll the downtown streets and it's guaranteed you'll find something to your liking. **Smoky Park Supper Club** (✉ *350 Riverside Dr.* ☎ *828/350–0315* ⊕ *www.smokypark.com*) offers wood-fired pork chops, trout, New York strip, and more along the French Broad River while **The Montford** (✉ *199 Haywood St.* ☎ *828/505–8750* ⊕ *themonford.com*) has small bites and craft cocktails (not to mention spectacular mountain sunsets from its rooftop perch). With 50 breweries and counting, don't forget to sample some beers in this epicenter of craft brewing; among the voluminous offerings are **Turgua Brewing Co.** (✉ *3131 Cane Creek Rd.* ☎ *828/338–0218* ⊕ *www.turguabrewing.com*), a small farmhouse brewery on a 5-acre farm in Fairview, and **Whistle Hop** (✉ *1288 Charlotte Hwy.* ☎ *828/338–9447* ⊕ *www.whistlehop.com*), with its train-caboose taprooms.

Stay: The classic parkway experience demands something retro. Try **JuneBug Retro Resort** (✉ *355 Clarks Chapel Rd.* ☎ *828/208–1979* ⊕ *www.junebugretro-resort.com*), a 50-acre property sprinkled with restored 1950s campers, or **Log Cabin Motor Court** (✉ *330 Weaverville Rd.* ☎ *828/645–6546* ⊕ *www.theashevillecabins.com*), where rustic revival-style cabins celebrate the golden age of the American road trip.

Breakfast: Early Girl Eatery (✉ *8 Wall St.* ☎ *828/259–9292* ⊕ *www.earlygirleatery.com*) is the place to go for Southern comfort food created from fresh local ingredients, with locations in Downtown, North Asheville, and West Asheville.

Day 3: Asheville, NC, to Blowing Rock, NC

89 miles (2 hours, 30 minutes without traffic or stops)

Today you'll follow the Blue Ridge Parkway's sinuous turns to Blowing Rock.

ALONG THE WAY

Eat & Drink: The homey **Switzerland Café** (✉ *9440 NC-226A* ☎ *828/765–5289* ⊕ *www.switzerlandcafe.com*) in Little Switzerland is a favorite stop on the North Carolina Barbecue Society Historic Barbecue Trail, though there are plenty of homemade nonbarbecue options as well. The tomato basil soup is a specialty.

Nature: The 1.75-mile (round-trip) **Linville Falls Plunge Basin Trail** (⊕ *www.nps.gov/blri/planyourvisit/linville-falls-trails.htm*), starting at the Linville Falls Visitor Center, is a gorgeous waterfall trek along Linville Gorge.

Detour: At 3,739 feet above sea level, Banner Elk is a historic alpine town near Grandfather Mountain, about 15 minutes off the parkway via NC-105 and NC-184. Visit the **Banner House Museum** (✉ *7990 Hickory Nut Gap Rd.* ☎ *828/898–3634* ⊕ *www.bannerhousemuseum.org*), showcasing 19th-century Blue Ridge life; wine-taste at **Banner Elk Winery** (✉ *60 Deer Run* ☎ *828/898–9090* ⊕ *www.bannerelkwinery.com*); sample local brews at the spectacularly situated **Beech Mountain Brewing Co.** (✉ *1007 S. Beech Mountain Pkwy.* ☎ *828/387–2011* ⊕ *www.beechmountainbrewingco.com*) or simply stretch your legs and poke into the shops and galleries in the charming downtown.

BLOWING ROCK

Do: In this cute, nature-loving town , you'll find upscale shops, galleries, cafés, and the **Blowing Rock Art & History Museum** (✉ *159 Ginny Stevens La.* ☎ *828/295–9099* ⊕ *www.blowingrockmuseum.org*), perfect for hanging out after a day of driving. You'll also find plenty of opportunities for hiking, fishing, and communing with nature in the surrounding wildlands.

Eat & Drink: The Speckled Trout (✉ *922 Main St.* ☎ *828/295–9819* ⊕ *www.thespeckledtrout.com*) offers a fresh take on Appalachian standards, with innovatively prepared North Carolina trout and more. The Devilish Eggs, with house-smoked trout and roasted red pepper sauce, are, well, devilishly good. The adjacent bottle shop has a breathtaking selection of local brews.

Stay: The **Green Park Inn** (✉ *9239 Valley Blvd.* ☎ *828/414–9230* ⊕ *www.green-parkinn.com*) is a Victorian dream, with live music in the lobby on Friday and Saturday night and a made-to-order breakfast every morning. Another option, right on Main Street, is **Montainaire Inn and Log Cabins** (✉ *827 Main St.* ☎ *828/295–7991* ⊕ *www. mountainaireinn.com*), with standard but clean rooms—splurge for a cabin.

Breakfast: The Village Café (✉ *146 Green-way Ct.* ☎ *828/295–3769* ⊕ *www.the-cafevillage.weebly.com*) offers waffles, crepes, omelets, and other delectable breakfast goods in a historic house.

Day 4: Blowing Rock, NC, to Roanoke, VA

173 miles (4 hours without traffic or stops)

Today you'll stay on the Blue Ridge Parkway the entire way.

ALONG THE WAY

Nature: An easy, half-mile interpretive loop trail from mile marker 272.5 leads to the magnificent Cascade Falls.

Detour: Jump off the parkway at mile marker 260 to take a twisty, 30-mile loop via NC-163, U.S. 221, and NC-16 to West Jefferson and Glendale Springs, enjoying some spectacular natural beauty along the way. In both hamlets, you'll find tiny chapels adorned with Italian-style frescoes, the 20th-century masterpieces of Ben Long, who studied in Florence.

Eat & Drink: Since opening in 1949, the **Bluffs Restaurant** (✉ *45338 Blue Ridge Pkwy.* ⊕ *www.bluffsrestaurant.org*) in Laurel Springs has been legendary for its southern menu, notably its ham biscuits, fried chicken, and berry cobbler. After being shuttered for a decade, this

Extend Your Trip

From Charlotte or Asheville: The Best of the Carolinas *(Ch. 7)*

From Charlotte or Great Smoky Mountains National Park: National Parks of the Southeast *(Ch. 7)*

From Richmond: Civil War Battle-fields and History *(Ch. 2)*

parkway favorite is once again *the* place to savor sweet potato pancakes in a booth overlooking the parkway.

Photo Op: It's hard to imagine a more picturesque mill than Mabry Mill with its reflective pond and surrounding forest that's downright stunning in autumnal display. You'll find it at mile marker 176.

ROANOKE

Do: The largest city along the parkway has the culture, fine eats, and lodgings that go with urban living, but here the mountains always loom in the distance. Check out the neon **Roanoke Star** (✉ *2000 J. B. Fishburn Pkwy.* ☎ *540/953–2000* ⊕ *www.playroanoke.com*) atop Mill Mountain (and hike the Star Trail); find treasures at **Black Dog Salvage** (✉ *902 13th St. SW* ☎ *540/343–6200* ⊕ *www. blackdogsalvage.com*), home of the TV show *Salvage Dawgs*; and browse the historic **Roanoke City Market** (✉ *Market Square SE* ☎ *540/342–2028* ⊕ *www. downtownroanoke.org*), in operation since 1862. **Center in the Square** (✉ *1 Mar-ket Square SE* ☎ *540/342–5700* ⊕ *www. centerinthesquare.org*) is home to the city's art, science, and history museums, along with live theater, dance, and opera. **Explore Park** (✉ *56 Roanoke River Pkwy.* ☎ *540/427–1800* ⊕ *www.explorepark. org*), right off the parkway, is another must-stop, with a museum, ziplines, hiking and biking trails, and more.

Fall is one of the best times to experience the Blue Ridge Parkway.

Eat & Drink: In the city market, **Caribbica Soul** (✉ *215 Market St. SE* ☎ *540/330–2345* ⊕ *www.caribbicasoul.com*) has fragrant, smoky jerk chicken, while the extensive menu at **Martin's Downtown Bar & Grill** (✉ *413 1st St. SW* ☎ *540/985–6278* ⊕ *www.martinsdowntown.com*) features ribs, tacos, salads, wraps, and more—Monday night is half-price-hamburger night.

Stay: The luxe **Hotel Roanoke** (✉ *110 Shenandoah Ave. NE* ☎ *540/985–5900* ⊕ *www.hilton.com*), dating from 1882, has hosted presidents, rock stars, and celebrities, while Roanoke Boutique Hotel (✉ *539 Day Ave. SW* ☎ *540/420–4455* ⊕ *www.roanokeboutiquehotel. com*) occupies an 1890 Italianate home in Roanoke's historic district, with nature-loving hosts who can point you to the best of the area's outdoor activities.

Breakfast: Downshift Bikes and Beer (✉ *210 4th St. SW* ☎ *540/739–2453* ⊕ *www. downshiftbikes.com*) has breakfast bowls and one-of-a-kind peanut butter coffee; it's a cool bike shop/restaurant combo.

Day 5: Roanoke, VA, to Staunton, VA

120 miles (3 hours, 30 minutes without traffic or stops)

The drive continues along the Blue Ridge Parkway to its northernmost terminus at Rockfish Gap. From here, hop onto I-81 for an hour and 20 minutes to Staunton, a bucolic drive through the Shenandoah Valley even though it's all interstate highway.

ALONG THE WAY

Nature: The spectacular Peaks of Otter area at mile marker 85.6, with its tree-covered peaks towering above bucolic Abbott Lake, is worth a stop for several hours of exploring or even to stay overnight. Several hikes lead up the peaks and to a waterfall, and the **Peaks of Otter Lodge** (⊕ *www.peaksofotter. com*) has a restaurant famed for its fried chicken.

Town: Located 10 miles east of the parkway at mile marker 86, Bedford is a charming little town that's home to the **National D-Day Memorial** (✉ *3 Overlord Cir.* ☎ *540/586–3329* ⊕ *www.ddayorg.com*). The town lost 19 men on that fateful day in 1944. In addition, the 470-acre **Claytor Nature Study Center** (✉ *1844 Woods Rd.* ☎ *434/544–8360* ⊕ *www.lynchburg.edu*) is a bird-filled, trail-laced oasis.

Eat & Drink: Jump off the parkway at Indian Gap, at mile marker 47, for a 5-mile detour to **JJ's Meat Shak** (✉ *1607 Magnolia Ave.* ☎ *540/261–1489* ⊕ *www. jjsmeatshak.com*), a family-owned barbecue joint that started in a 20-foot trailer.

STAUNTON

Do: In this quintessential Shenandoah Valley small town, you can take an architectural walking tour of one of six historic districts filled with a panoply of buildings by esteemed architect T. J. Collins (Beverley Street is a good place to start). Visit the **Woodrow Wilson Birthplace and Library** (✉ *20 N. Coalter St.* ☎ *540/885–0987* www.woodrowwilson. org), attend a Shakespeare play at the **Blackfriars Playhouse** (✉ *10 S. Market St.* ☎ *877/682–4236* ⊕ *www.american-shakespearecenter.com*), the world's only re-creation of Shakespeare's indoor theater that was destroyed in the 1666 Great Fire of London, or go wine and beer tasting.

Eat & Drink: In this foodie town, try the always-packed **Shack** (✉ *105 S. Coalter St.* ☎ *540/490–1961* ⊕ *www.theshackva. com*) or **Zynodoa** (✉ *115 E. Beverly St.* ☎ *540/885–7775* ⊕ *www.zynodoa.com*), with its inspired southern cuisine.

Stay: Hotel 24 South (✉ *24 S. Market St.* ☎ *540/885–4848* ⊕ *www.hotel24south. com*) opened its gracious doors in 1924 and remains a stylish retreat. Other interesting options include **Gibson's Warehouse** (1 ✉ *9 Middlebrook Ave.* ☎ *540/324– 5050* ⊕ *www.gibsonwarehouse.com*),

a beautifully renovated 1905 warehouse-turned-apartment-rental designed by T. J. Collins, and the **Blackburn Inn** (✉ *301 Greenville Ave.* ☎ *540/712–0601* ⊕ *www.blackburn-inn.com*), which occupies a former mental hospital dating from 1828.

Breakfast: Cranberry's Grocery & Eatery (✉ *7 S. New St.* ☎ *540/885–4755* ⊕ *www.gocranberrys.com*) serves breakfast all day, with dishes created using local ingredients; malt yeast waffles with fruit and whipped cream are a favorite.

Day 6: Staunton, VA, to Richmond, VA

108 miles (1 hour, 40 minutes without traffic or stops)

You've left the Blue Ridge Parkway behind, so your last day consists of a leisurely drive east toward Richmond, home to the closest major airport in the area.

ALONG THE WAY

Town: Charlottesville is Thomas Jefferson's town, home to his breathtaking residence of **Monticello** (✉ *931 Thomas Jefferson Pkwy.* ☎ *434/984–9800* ⊕ *www.monticello.org*). But even without Jefferson, the city is a standout destination with lauded regional cuisine, a noteworthy music scene, and local vineyards that range among Virginia's best. Make a visit to Monticello or stroll the grounds of Jefferson's neoclassical masterpiece, the University of Virginia.

Eat & Drink: Take a seat at one of the outdoor tables at the fun and festive **Red Pump Kitchen** (✉ *401 E. Main St.* ☎ *434/202–6040* ⊕ *www.redpump-kitchen.com*) in the Downtown Mall area to enjoy Tuscan-style fare like gourmet pizzas fresh from the wood-burning oven, seafood, and homemade pastas.

RICHMOND

Do: Virginia's capital city is also one of the oldest cities in America, making it the perfect place to soak up history and culture. Its museum scene is excellent—don't miss the **Virginia Museum of Fine Arts** (✉ 200 N. Arthur Ashe Blvd, ☎ 804/340–1400 ⊕ www.vmfa.museum) and the **Black History Museum and Cultural Center of Virginia** (✉ 122 W. Leigh St. ☎ 804/780–9093 ⊕ www.blackhistorymuseum.org); if you have time, visit the **Edgar Allen Poe Museum** (✉ 1914 E. Main St. ☎ 804/648–5523 ⊕ www.poemuseum.org). And don't forget to take a walk past **St. John's Church** (✉ 2401 E. Broad St.), the spot where Patrick Henry famously said, "Give me liberty or give me death."

Eat & Drink: If you want to splurge, book a table at **Lemaire** (✉ 101 W. Franklin St. ☎ 804/649–4629 ⊕ www.lemairerestaurant.com), named after Etienne Lemaire, maître d'hôtel to Thomas Jefferson from 1794 until the end of his presidency. The farm-to-table menu serves regional southern cuisine with small plates and entrées that feature local produce and regional meats and fishes. For something more low-key, **Lunch Supper** (✉ 1215 Summit Ave. ☎ 804/353–0111 ⊕ www.lunchorsupper.com) serves elevated southern pub food in a hip space.

Stay: A 70-foot-high ceiling with a stained-glass skylight and 10 of the original Louis Comfort Tiffany stained-glass windows, rich tapestries, and replicas of traditional Victorian furniture make the **Jefferson Hotel** (✉ 101 W. Franklin St. ☎ 804/788–8000 ⊕ www.jeffersonhotel.com) the most elegant hotel in Richmond.

Breakfast: Be prepared to wait in line to check out Richmond's favorite diner, **Millie's Diner** (✉ 2603 E. Main St. ☎ 804/643–5512 ⊕ www.milliesdiner.com). This is the place for brunch, serving everything from huevos rancheros to the signature Devil's Mess kitchen-sink omelet.

The Best of the Carolinas

Written by Stratton Lawrence

In a single day of exploring the Carolinas, you can stand at the highest point east of the Mississippi River and paddle through the Lowcountry, where the horizon across the flat coastal plains feels infinite. Few regions possess both the geographic and cultural diversity of the Carolinas. Appalachian culture and dialects persist in Blue Ridge hamlets, worlds away from the fishing- and water-sports-based lifestyle of the Outer Banks or the rich architectural history and food culture of Charleston.

A drive through North and South Carolina is a microcosm of America, from sleepy, centuries-old port towns like Beaufort to the forward-thinking, tech-focused Triangle cities of Durham, Chapel Hill, and Raleigh. On this road trip, you'll scale soaring peaks, stand at the edge of the continental shelf on Ocracoke Island, and dine on some of the country's finest seafood in downtown Charleston.

At a Glance

Start: Charlotte, NC

End: Charlotte, NC

Miles Traveled: 1,238 miles

Suggested Duration: 10 days

States Visited: North Carolina, South Carolina

Key Sights: Biltmore Estate; Conagee National Park; Fort Sumter Military Park; Jockey's Ridge State Park; Mt. Mitchell

Best Time to Go: During spring and fall, you'll avoid icy roads in the mountains, bitter cold winds at the beach, and summer's sweltering heat in the midlands. There's also the added bonus of fall colors and the spring bloom.

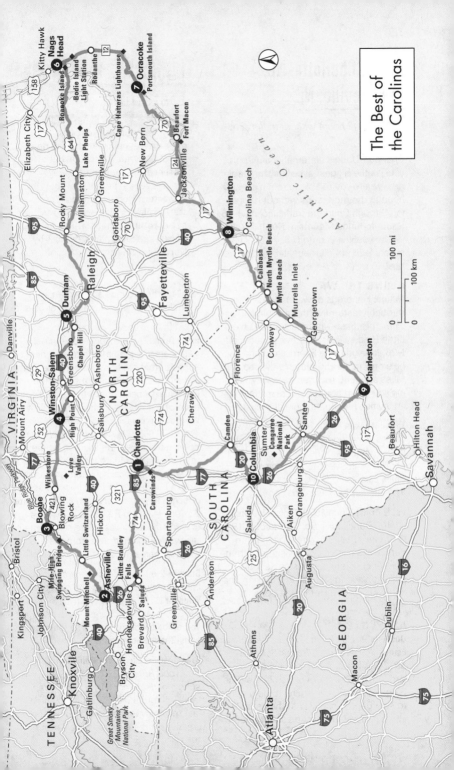

The Best of
the Carolinas

Day 1: Charlotte, NC, to Asheville, NC

130 miles (2 hours without traffic and stops)

Charlotte/Douglas International Airport (CLT) is the biggest airport in the Carolinas, where you're able to rent a car and head to the mountains without navigating through Charlotte traffic. Follow I–85 South to Kings Mountain, North Carolina, where you'll veer onto U.S. 74 until it meets I–26 in Columbus, taking you the final 30 miles to Asheville.

ALONG THE WAY

Nature: Hundreds of waterfalls cascade through western North Carolina, and one of the prettiest—and most accessible—is Little Bradley Falls, just five minutes off I-26 at Saluda. The 2.4-mile out-and-back hike only gains 150 feet in elevation and takes about 40 minutes each way, leading you to a magical triple cascade with an inviting swimming hole at the base.

Town: It takes about 60 seconds to walk across downtown Saluda, but every step is charming, from the train tracks that parallel Main Street to the charming **Purple Onion** café (✉ *16 E. Main St.* ☎ *828/749– 1179* ⊕ *purpleonionsaluda.com*).

Eat & Drink: Since 1979, **Piggy's Ice Cream** (✉ *102 Duncan Hill Rd.* ☎ *828/692–1995* ⊕ *www.harrysandpiggys.com*) in Hendersonville has drawn in visitors with the herd of concrete animals on its roof. It's a perfect place to sit back in a rocking chair and wolf down a Hot Fudge Bonanza sundae.

ASHEVILLE

Do: Asheville's crown jewel is the **Biltmore Estate** (✉ *1 Approach Rd.* ☎ *800/411– 3812* ⊕ *www.biltmore.com*), George Vanderbilt's 250-room palace in the Blue Ridge Mountains. If you're in the mood to splurge, you can stay at the estate's inn, but either way, spend an afternoon

Essential Listening

About an hour into your first day's drive, you'll start to pick up WNCW 88.7, an FM station out of Isothermal Community College that serves as the cultural glue of western North Carolina. The station plays a diverse, bluegrass-heavy rotation that features new releases and live performances by North Carolina artists.

strolling the grounds and garden, including a tour of the mansion or on-site winery.

Eat & Drink: The brewery scene in Asheville is among the nation's best—there's a reason that big-time brewers like Sierra Nevada and New Belgium set up their East Coast operations in this area. For a taste of the city's best local suds, visit **Wedge Brewing Co.** (✉ *37 Paynes Way* ☎ *828/505–2792* ⊕ *www.wedgebrewing. com*) in the River Arts District, where fermenters share square footage with working studios for local sculptors and artists. Grab a bite from the food trucks on-site, or scoot to your reservation at **The Admiral** (✉ *400 Haywood Rd.* ☎ *828/252–2541* ⊕ *www.theadmiralasheville.com*), where the weekly menu draws from the best of the local harvest.

Stay: In the heart of downtown, walkable to Asheville nightlife and shops, **The Windsor** (✉ *36 Broadway St.* ☎ *844/494– 6376* ⊕ *www.windsorasheville.com*) lets you enjoy modern luxury in a restored early-20th-century hotel.

Breakfast: Get to **Sunny Point Café** (✉ *626 Haywood Rd.* ☎ *828/252–0055* ⊕ *www. sunnypointcafe.com*) by 9 am to grab a table without a wait. This healthy breakfast mainstay is the city's favorite spot for creative morning entrées like carrot hot cakes and huevos rancheros with black bean cakes and cilantro crema.

Day 2: Asheville, NC, to Boone, NC

90 miles (2 hours without traffic and stops)

Today is all about the scenic drive, much of it along the iconic Blue Ridge Parkway. After summitting Mt. Mitchell, continue on the parkway to Linville, where you'll take NC-105 the last 20 miles to Boone.

ALONG THE WAY

Detour: At 6,684 feet, Mt. Mitchell is the highest mountain in eastern North America, and the road to its summit—including the approach along the Blue Ridge Parkway—is one of the country's most scenic drives. After winding to the apex, walk the quarter-mile paved trail to the observation deck to take in the astounding views in every direction. Bring a picnic for lunch when you reach the top.

Town: Perched on a ridge along the Blue Ridge Parkway, Little Switzerland charms with its Alpine architecture, sweeping views of the valley below, and celebratory square dancing on summer Saturday evenings at Geneva Hall.

Photo Opp: In the shadow of Grandfather Mountain, the 228-foot **Mile-High Swinging Bridge** (✉ 2050 Blowing Rock Hwy. ☎ 800/468–7325 ⊕ www.grandfather. com) stretches over a lush valley, offering visitors the chance to step out into the void.

BOONE

Do: In this charming mountain town, **Tweetsie Railroad** (✉ 300 Tweetsie Railroad La. ☎ 828/264–9061 ⊕ www. tweetsie.com) is pure kitsch and pure fun. Ride the 3-mile circuit, pulled by a historic steam locomotive. There are also live shows, an amusement park for kids, and a petting zoo.

Eat & Drink: For a true taste of mountain flavors like local boar, venison, and trout cooked over fire, **Gamekeeper** (✉ 3005 Shulls Mill Rd. ☎ 828/963–7400 ⊕ www. gamekeeper-nc.com) specializes in preparations of less common meats, including emu and antelope.

Stay: An early-20th-century car dealership and department store is now **The Horton Hotel** (✉ 611 W. King St. ☎ 828/832–8060 ⊕ www.thehorton.com), a charming property that's in walking distance of the Appalachian State University campus, and next door to a Mast General Store.

Breakfast: On the way out of town, grab a croissant and a cup of joe from **Hatchet Coffee Roasters** (✉ 150A Den Mac Dr. ☎ 828/278–7505 ⊕ www.hatchetcoffee.com).

Day 3: Boone, NC, to Winston-Salem, NC

90 miles (1 hour, 30 minutes without traffic and stops)

You're headed due east on U.S. 421 today, descending from the Appalachian highlands into the foothills.

ALONG THE WAY

Town: The twin downtowns of Wilkesboro and North Wilkesboro straddle the Yadkin River, creating two walkable strips of shops and restaurants. This is the hometown of bluegrass great Doc Watson (and the festival he founded, MerleFest); a mural featuring the blind flatpicker graces a wall downtown.

Eat & Drink: Glenn's (✉ 800 River St. ☎ 336/838–2541 ⊕ www.glennsrestaurantwilkesboronc.com) isn't fancy—this cash-only Wilkesboro diner has been dishing out burgers and dogs to musical legends in town for concerts, including Dolly Parton, for half a century. But you're here for one thing: livermush. This regional sausage-like specialty is made from ground pig liver, offal, and cornmeal. Put a slice or two in a buttermilk biscuit for a savory taste of the NC foothills.

Roadside Attraction: Love Valley is like no other town in the Carolinas, partly because cars are not allowed; this is cowboy country, built by a couple in the 1950s to emulate the Wild West. Park just outside the small downtown and step into the Western-inspired stores while watching cowpokes tie up their steeds to the hitching post. Saturday nights get a little rowdy here, so unless you're ready to join the party, visit during daylight hours.

WINSTON-SALEM

Do: Before Winston-Salem was the home of Camel cigarettes, the original town of Salem was a Moravian settlement, and the streets of the **Old Salem Museums & Gardens** (✉ *900 Old Salem Rd.* ☎ *336/721-7350* ⊕ *www.oldsalem. org*) today are reminiscent of Williamsburg, Virginia, but not nearly as heavily trafficked. Walking the brick sidewalks of this incredibly well-preserved, living village takes you back in time.

Eat & Drink: Gourmet taco shops are not hard to find, but **Crafted** (✉ *527 N. Liberty St.* ☎ *336/955-2458* ⊕ *www.eatatcrafted.com*) rises above the rest with homemade flour tortillas (and chips), excellent margaritas, and the perfect appetizer: a grilled avocado filled with queso, pico, and chorizo.

Stay: The 55-acre **Graylyn Estate** (✉ *1900 Reynolda Rd.* ☎ *336/758-2600* ⊕ *www. graylyn.com*) is worthy of a leisurely multiday stay. Rooms in the castle-like stone mansion are beautifully furnished. In the evenings, read in the stately library or play pool in the billiards room—it's like staying in a real-life game of Clue, minus the murder mystery.

Breakfast: You may stop in to **Krankies** (✉ *211 E. 3rd St.* ☎ *336/722-3016*

⊕ *www.krankiescoffee.com*) for their delicious iced coffees, flavored with homemade syrup, but you can't leave without indulging in a chicken biscuit doused in honey and hot sauce.

Day 4: Winston-Salem, NC, to Durham, NC

80 miles (1 hour, 30 minutes without traffic and stops)

You're heading due east on I-40 for most of the drive today—a nearly straight shot.

ALONG THE WAY

Roadside Attraction: If you swing through High Point on your way out of Winston-Salem, the **World's Largest Chest of Drawers** (✉ *508 N. Hamilton St.*) is a fascinating piece of the town's furniture-industry lore.

Town: Spend a few hours in Chapel Hill, walking Franklin Street and the campus of the University of North Carolina at Chapel Hill. Stroll through the **Coker Arboretum** (✉ *399 E. Cameron Ave.* ☎ *919/962-0522* ⊕ *www.ncbg.unc.edu*) before visiting the Carolina Basketball Museum (✉ *450 Skipper Bowles Dr.* ☎ *919/962-6000* ⊕ *www.goheels.com*), featuring jerseys and mementos from all-time greats who wore the Carolina Blue, including Michael Jordan and Vince Carter.

Eat & Drink: Grab a rooftop table at **Top of the Hill** (✉ *100 E. Franklin St.* ☎ *919/929-8676* ⊕ *www.thetopofthehill.com*) in Chapel Hill, a brewery and restaurant at the center of town, overlooking Franklin Street.

Photo Op: Chapel Hill's **Old Well** (✉ *E. Cameron Ave.*) is a simple blue-domed rotunda with a water fountain, but it's one of the most photographed and recognizable landmarks in the state.

DURHAM

Do: During baseball season, the Durham Bulls are the hottest ticket in town. They may be the nation's most well-loved minor league team, and the downtown **Durham Bulls Athletic Park** (⊠ *409 Blackwell St.* ☎ *919/687–6500* ⊕ *www.milb.com/durham*) helps keep them a vital part of the city. If it's not a game day, stroll through the **American Tobacco Campus** (⊠ *300 Blackwell St.* ⊕ *www.americantobaccocampus.com*) next door, a former cigarette company warehouse district that's been revitalized with shops, restaurants, and the headquarters of Burt's Bees.

Eat & Drink: In an elegant but relaxed dining room downtown, **Mothers & Sons** (⊠ *107 W. Chapel Hill St.* ☎ *919/294–8247* ⊕ *www.mothersandsonsnc.com*) serves some of the South's best Italian fare. Choose from the bruschetta selection, then move on to the divine eggplant parm. Save room for ice cream, around the corner at the **Parlour** (⊠ *117 Market St.* ☎ *919/564–7999* ⊕ *www.theparlour.co*).

Stay: Downtown's coolest spot to lay your head is **Unscripted Durham** (⊠ *202 Corcoran St.* ☎ *984/329–9500* ⊕ *www.unscriptedhotels.com*), a once-decrepit motor lodge that's been refurbished into a hip motel that features a pool and bar overlooking the city center. **The Durham Hotel** (⊠ *315 E. Chapel Hill St.* ☎ *919/768–8830* ⊕ *www.thedurham.com*), just round the corner, is equally trendy, with its own rooftop bar pouring craft cocktails and local beers.

Breakfast: Monuts (⊠ *1002 9th St.* ☎ *919/286–2642* ⊕ *www.monutsdonuts.com*) makes Durham's best donuts, but their stellar menu ranges from hefty breakfast burritos to the "Guac Dirty to Me" biscuit.

Extend Your Trip

From Asheville or Charlotte: The Blue Ridge Parkway *(Ch. 7)*

From the Outer Banks: The East Coast's Best Beaches *(Ch. 2)*

From Charleston: The Civil Rights Trail *(Ch. 7)*; Civil War History and Battlefields *(Ch. 2)*

From Columbia: National Parks of the Southeast *(Ch. 7)*

Day 5: Durham, NC, to Nags Head, NC

220 miles (3 hours, 30 minutes without traffic and stops)

Head down I-40 to Raleigh, where you'll pick up U.S. 64, taking you 200 miles to the Outer Banks.

ALONG THE WAY

Nature: Lake Phelps, accessible via **Pettigrew State Park** (⊠ *2252 Lake Shore Rd.* ☎ *252/797–4475* ⊕ *www.ncparks.gov*), stands out among large lakes in the Carolinas because it's not man-made. Alligators and black bears abound in this region, and tall cypress trees line the banks. It's a glimpse of a primordial ecosystem that still persists in sparsely populated eastern North Carolina.

Town: Start your drive in the morning, allowing for several hours to explore the town of Manteo on Roanoke Island, where the "Lost Colony" settlers disappeared after establishing a settlement in 1587. Their (imagined) story is told via a live drama in an outdoor theater fronting Albemarle Sound (Andy Griffith got his start here, playing the role of Sir Walter Raleigh). While touring the site of the colony, visit the ornate Elizabethan

Gardens, a walled garden built in honor of the queen.

Eat & Drink: After the morning drive, recharge with a rockfish wrap or turkey Reuben from **Poor Richard's Sandwich Shop** (✉ 305 Queen Elizabeth St. ☎ 252/473–3333 ⊕ www.poorrichards-manteo.com). Order it to go and eat by the waterfront in Manteo.

NAG'S HEAD

Do: At sunset, hike up the towering dunes (the tallest on the East Coast) at **Jockey's Ridge State Park** (✉ 300 W. Carolista Dr. ☎ 252/441–7132 ⊕ www.ncparks.gov), a barren expanse of sand that feels like trekking across the desert, and affords stunning views of the ocean and the sound from its ridge.

Eat & Drink: In the Outer Banks, you often choose between the view and the quality of your meal. Spend the sunset outside before dipping into the strip mall confines of **Blue Moon Beach Grill** (✉ 4104 S. Virginia Dare Tr. ☎ 252/261–2583 ⊕ www.bluemoonbeachgrill.com), where the humble environs belie the care put into the fish tacos and seafood bucatini.

Stay: The most impressive thing about **First Colony Inn** (✉ 6715 S. Croatan Hwy. ☎ 252/441–2343 ⊕ www.firstcolonyinn.com) is its lawn; spread across a full acre, staying here feels like crashing at a friend's private estate. The second is that this massive wooden building was moved to this location, salvaging the structure after hurricanes and real estate prices forced it off the beachfront. First Colony mixes little luxuries with rustic authenticity, and the sea breezes and rocking chairs on the full-length porches don't hurt.

Breakfast: Grab a waterfront picnic table and breathe in the salt air while you enjoy a smoothie and multigrain banana pancakes at **Freshfit Café** (✉ 7531 S. Virginia Dare Tr. ☎ 252/715–6444 ⊕ www.obxfreshfitcafe.com).

Day 6: Nags Head, NC, to Ocracoke, NC

90 miles (2 hours, 30 minutes without traffic and stops)

The drive down NC-12, through several oceanfront towns and a national seashore, is one of the country's greatest drives. Take your time, but keep in mind that the drive ends with a ferry to Ocracoke, which leaves every 15-to-30 minutes; depending on time of year, traffic can back up, forcing you to wait through several cycles to board.

ALONG THE WAY

Town: The drive through the Outer Banks alternates between undeveloped wildlife refuge and national seashore and the small towns pocketed between them. Rodanthe stands out for its **Chicamacomico Life-Saving Station** historic site (✉ 23645 NC-12 ☎ 252/987–1552 ⊕ www.chicamacomico.org), a small village of buildings from the days before the U.S. Coast Guard, when the U.S. Life-Saving Service remained at the ready to aid shipwrecked boats on the shoals off the Outer Banks.

Eat & Drink: In Rodanthe, **Taqueria Las Ahumaderas** (✉ 24594 NC-12 ☎ 252/548–9145) serves a surprisingly large variety of seafood-based Mexican fare from a waterfront food truck. Eat your enchiladas while watching the kitesurfers soar through the air along the sound.

Photo Op: You'll pass two lighthouses on today's drive, and each is worth a visit. The **Bodie Island Light Station** (✉ 8210 Bodie Island Lighthouse ☎ 252/441–5711 www.nps.gov/caha) is clearly visible from NC-12, and known by mariners for its black-and-white-striped pattern. Even more famous is the spiral pattern of the **Cape Hatteras Lighthouse** (✉ 46379 Lighthouse Rd., Buxton, NC ☎ 252/473–2111 www.nps.gov/caha), which reaches

Hip Asheville is filled with trendy bars and restaurants.

210 feet and can be climbed during the summer.

OCRACOKE

Do: The island of Ocracoke feels trapped in time, and one of its charms is a slow pace of life that lets you do nothing but lie in a hammock, take a walk on the isolated beach, or browse the quaint craftsman shops that circle Silver Lake, the harbor that anchors the village. But if you have time, the 20-minute private ferry to Portsmouth Village is an amazing, eye-opening experience. Portsmouth's last residents moved away in 1971, leaving this once-bustling port abandoned. It's a true coastal ghost town, reachable only by boat, with buildings like the Methodist church and life-saving station maintained by the National Park Service and open for tours.

Eat & Drink: 1718 Brewing not only produces the best beer in the Outer Banks (try the Coffee Kölsch or Mexican Chocolate), but their **Plum Pointe Kitchen** (✉ *1129 Irvin Garrish Hwy.* ☎ *252/928–7586*

⊕ *plum-pointe-kitchen.business.site*) cranks out specialties like a crab-stuffed pretzel that elevates sunsets on its rooftop deck.

Stay: Ocracoke offers several upscale inns and bed-and-breakfast options, including the lovely **Ocracoke Harbor Inn** (✉ *144 Silver Lake Dr.* ☎ *252/928–5731* ⊕ *www.ocracokeharborinn.com*). For a real taste of Ocracoke culture and history, get a room at **Blackbeard's Lodge** (✉ *111 Back Rd.* ☎ *252/928–3421* ⊕ *www. blackbeardslodge.com*), a rustic but compelling inn spread over several buildings, interconnected by winding walkways and rooftop passageways.

Breakfast: Order from the window in the side of the house at **Magic Bean Coffee Bazaar** (✉ *35 School Rd.* ☎ *252/588–2440* ⊕ *www.facebook.com/MagicBeanOcracoke*), then relax in a lawn chair while sipping on a butterbeer coffee or a satisfying smoothie.

Day 7: Ocracoke, NC, to Wilmington, NC

160 miles (5 hours, 30 minutes without traffic and stops)

It's only 160 miles to Wilmington, but the trip today takes over five hours because it begins with a ferry ride. During the middle of the open-water trip, land is not visible in any direction. You're deposited at Cedar Island and then you drive on U.S. 70 through the "Down East" island communities of this isolated region, taking in sweeping vistas across the marsh for the first hour. After passing through Beaufort, take NC-24 along the coast to U.S. 17 in Jacksonville, for the final push back to civilization in Wilmington.

ALONG THE WAY

Town: The waterfront homes in Beaufort, North Carolina, each have a plaque with the year they were constructed, and all are part of a self-guided walking tour offered by the **Beaufort Historic Site** (⊕ beauforthistoricsite.org). Tour on foot or via a double-decker red English bus.

Eat & Drink: Set on (and over) the water in Beaufort, **Moonrakers** (⊠ 326 Front St. ☎ 252/838–0083 ⊕ www.moonrakers-beaufort.com) brings the local catch to perfection in its wood-fired grill. The first floor is casual, while upstairs is a bit fancier, with slightly better views. But head straight for the roof, where the smaller menu is worth the sacrifice for the clear vista at the Sky Deck bar.

Detour: It's only slightly out of the way to cruise across the bridge to Atlantic Beach, where **Fort Macon** (☎ 252/726–3775 ⊕ www.ncparks.gov) has guarded the approach to Beaufort since the 1830s. The brick fortification, an important Civil War site, is built into a giant dune, and from its cannons, the views toward Shackleford Banks and Cape Lookout make it clear why this point was such strategic land to hold.

WILMINGTON

Do: Downtown Wilmington invites long walks, both through its shops and restaurant district on Water Street, fronting the Cape Fear River, and along 3rd Avenue, where historic mansions line the road for several blocks. Stroll through the gardens at the **Burgwin-Wright House** museum (⊠ 224 Market St. ☎ 910/762–0570 ⊕ www.burgwinwrighthouse.com), and if you're a train aficionado, leave an hour to take in the **Wilmington Railroad Museum** (⊠ 505 Nutt St. ☎ 910/763–2634 ⊕ www.wrrm.org), which holds the world record for the longest model train ever assembled.

Eat & Drink: Wilmington's dining scene has three all-stars: **Manna** (⊠ 123 Princess St. ☎ 910/763–5252 ⊕ www.mannaavenue.com), **PinPoint** (⊠ 114 Market St. ☎ 910/769–2972 ⊕ www.pinpointrestaurant.com), and **Seabird** (⊠ 1 S. Front St. ☎ 910/769–5996 ⊕ www.seabirdnc.com), each taking pride in locally sourced seafood. Consider a progressive dinner, with raw oysters and cocktails at Seabird, lobster bruschetta at PinPoint, and speckled trout at Manna.

Stay: Along the river, **Hotel Ballast** (⊠ 301 N. Water St. ☎ 910/763–5900 ⊕ www.hilton.com) has an imposing presence in Wilmington, but that also means spectacular views of the river and city from its modern, comfortable rooms.

Breakfast: Bespoke Coffee (⊠ 202 Princess St. ☎ 910/769–4088 ⊕ www.bespokecoffeenc.com) serves the city's best cup of joe, but if you're hankering for substantial grub, visit **The Basics** (⊠ 319 N. Front St. ☎ 910/343–1050 ⊕ www.thebasicswilmington.com) for the impressive build-your-own biscuit menu.

Day 8: Wilmington, NC, to Charleston, SC

180 miles (3 hours, 30 minutes without traffic and stops)

There are no turns on today's drive: just stick to Highway 17 all the way down the coast to the "Holy City."

ALONG THE WAY

Eat & Drink: Restaurants along the entire Carolina coast advertise Calabash seafood, and today you'll pass through the real border town of Calabash, North Carolina. If you want to shamelessly indulge in a generous platter of fried seafood, do it at the **Boundary House** (✉ *1045 River Rd.* ☎ *910/579–8888* ⊕ *www.boundaryhouserestaurant.com*).

Photo Op: North Myrtle Beach is where the shag, South Carolina's state dance, originated, and its clubs still fill up on Saturday nights with couples, old and young, sliding across the dance floor. Step into **Fat Harold's Beach Club** (✉ *212 Main St.* ☎ *843/249–5779* ⊕ *www.fatharolds. com*), take in the historic room and black-and-white photos on the wall, and then take a few turns on the legendary dance floor yourself.

Town: You'll spend over an hour of today's drive passing the pancake houses and putt-putt courses of Myrtle Beach, South Carolina. The entire Grand Strand is tourist-driven, but there are a few hidden gems. It's worth stopping along the way for a round of mini-golf—where else can you putt from the top of a 50-foot volcano or down the deck of a pirate ship?

CHARLESTON

Do: Charleston's unique peninsular geography is best appreciated from the water, and the best way to get onto Charleston Harbor is via a ferry to **Fort Sumter** (☎ *843/883–2123* ⊕ *www.nps.gov/*

fosu). Tour the fort—perhaps the most important coastal fortification during the Civil War—before returning to the Battery for a leisurely walk through the South of Broad neighborhood, home to countless historic mansions and the photogenic Rainbow Row. Finish the evening with a walk through the City Market, which stays open at night on summer weekends and during the holidays.

Eat & Drink: Charleston is a city where you can eat a five-star meal three times a day for weeks on end and never retrace your steps. For the pinnacle of the local catch, splurge on the seafood tower at **The Ordinary** (✉ *544 King St.* ☎ *843/414–7060* ⊕ *www.eattheordinary.com*). Other options include stopping into the **Bar at Husk** (✉ *76 Queen St.* ☎ *843/577–2500* ⊕ *www.huskrestaurant.com*) for their famous cheeseburger, or scarfing down the addictive okonomiyaki at **Xiao Bao Biscuit** (✉ *224 Rutledge St.* ⊕ *www. xiaobaobiscuit.com*).

Stay: Just far enough off the City Market to feel relaxed but still close to the action, **Emeline** (✉ *181 Church St.* ☎ *843/577–2644* ⊕ *www.hotelemeline. com*) combines the best of a big hotel (terrific restaurants and thoughtful amenities like filtered sparkling water) with the charm and creative perks of a boutique hotel (classic vinyl and an in-room record player).

Breakfast: Local miller Greg Johnsman knows how to stir up the perfect pot of grits, a skill he puts to use at **Millers All Day** (✉ *120 King St.* ☎ *843/501–7342* ⊕ *www.millersallday.com*), a King Street breakfast café with a throwback-soda-fountain feel.

Day 9: Charleston, SC, to Columbia, SC

115 miles (2 hours without traffic and stops)

Take I–26 west from Charleston to Columbia, and you'll steadily see hills start to form as you gently leave the Lowcountry behind.

ALONG THE WAY

Eat & Drink: Fill up your plate with pulled pork, mac-and-cheese, and collard greens at one of the three rustic buildings, all adorned with decades of memorabilia, at **Lone Star BBQ & Mercantile** (✉ *2212 State Park Rd.* ☎ *803/854–2000* ⊕ *www. destination-bbq.com*) in Santee.

COLUMBIA

Do: Many of the world's oldest and largest cypress trees stand deep in the swamp at South Carolina's only national park, **Congaree National Park** (☎ *803/776–4396* ⊕ *www.nps.gov.cong*), just 20 minutes from Columbia. A 2-mile boardwalk loop delivers you into woods and is accessible at all but the highest flood stages. When the Congaree River overflows its banks, this park can be almost entirely underwater, but when waters recede, hiking trails allow access deep into a primitive, wild ecosystem where deer, owls, and wild boar are a regular sight.

Eat & Drink: Set in a former auto-parts warehouse, **Motor Supply Company Bistro** (✉ *920 Gervais St.* ☎ *803/256–6687* ⊕ *www.motorsupplycobistro.com*) was ahead of its time when it opened in 1989, and it continues to set trends with its butcher program, local farmer sourcing, and approach to detail in everything from its infused cocktails to hand-mixed salad dressings.

Stay: Local beer on tap at check-in is just the first perk at **Hotel Trundle** (✉ *1224 Taylor St.* ☎ *803/722–5000* ⊕ *www. hoteltrundle.com*), a trendy, bohemian downtown boutique that puts you in walking distance of the statehouse and the University of South Carolina campus.

Breakfast: Just outside the capitol building, **Immaculate Consumption** (✉ *933 Main St.* ☎ *803/799–9053* ⊕ *www.immaculate-consumption.com*) fuels legislative sessions with macchiatos, pastries, and a menu of sandwiches suitable for packing a picnic to go.

Day 10: Columbia, SC, to Charlotte, NC

90 miles (1 hour, 30 minutes without traffic and stops)

On your last day of driving, head due north on I–77, direct to the "Queen City."

ALONG THE WAY

Town: If you're up for taking back roads, detour to Camden, South Carolina, where the historic neighborhood of mansions and estates remains unpaved to allow for a gentler tread on horses' feet. This is thoroughbred country, and it's also an important Revolutionary War site and early Colonial settlement.

Roadside Attraction: At the state border, you'll pass one of the Southeast's biggest theme parks, **Carowinds** (✉ *14523 Carowinds Blvd.* ☎ *704/588–2600* ⊕ *www.carowinds.com*). This is a roller coaster lover's dream park—among the dozen high-speed coasters is Fury 325, which soars 325 feet in the air and reaches 95 miles per hour.

CHARLOTTE

Do: At the **U.S. National Whitewater Center** (✉ *5000 Whitewater Center Pkwy.* ☎ *704/391–3900* ⊕ *www.whitewater. org*), you can paddle a kayak or raft through intense rapids, free-climb high in the air over a pool, soar through the air on a massive zipline, or mountain bike through central North Carolina's most challenging trails.

Eat & Drink: In a restored church in the hip Plaza Midwood neighborhood, **Supperland** (✉ *1212 The Plaza* ☎ *704/817–7514* 🌐 *www.supper.land*) encourages leisurely, shared meals with its menu of steaks, pot roast, and rich southern sides. Or opt for the crowd-pleasing options at **Optimist Hall** (✉ *1115 N. Brevard St.* ☎ *980/701–0040* 🌐 *www.optimisthall. com*), a sprawling food hall with plenty of international flair.

Stay: For your last night in the Carolinas, enjoy true southern luxury at the **Duke Mansion** (✉ *400 Hermitage Rd.* ☎ *704/714–4400* 🌐 *www.dukemansion. com*), where the grounds and gardens are as thoughtfully maintained as the comfortable rooms.

Breakfast: Amelie's (✉ *2424 N. Davidson St.* ☎ *704/376–1781* 🌐 *www.ameliesfrenchbakery.com*), a French bakery with locations around Charlotte, is a local staple for coffee and breakfast sandwich croissants. Of course, if you opt for a preflight Bo-berry biscuit, the decadent sweet treat from Bojangles (founded in Charlotte in 1977), nobody will judge you.

National Parks of the Southeast

Written by Stefanie Waldek

The American West might lay claim to some of the country's most famous national parks, but the Southeast has four of its own that are well deserving of a visit. Best of all, you can visit them in a single weeklong road trip. This adventure takes you to the iconic Skyline Drive of Shenandoah National Park in Virginia, the dramatic cliffs of New River Gorge National Park in West Virginia, the waterfalls of Great Smoky Mountains National Park (the most visited national park in America) in Tennessee and North Carolina, and the swamps of Congaree National Park in South Carolina. Along the way, you'll discover quirky roadside attractions, historic homes and hotels, and impressively good food.

At a Glance

Start: Charlotte, NC

End: Charlotte, NC

Miles Traveled: 1,120 miles

Suggested Duration: 7 days

States Visited: North Carolina, South Carolina, Tennessee, Virginia, West Virginia

Key Sights: Congaree National Park; Great Smoky Mountains National Park; Luray Caverns; New River Gorge National Park; Shenandoah National Park

Best Time to Go: While all the parks are open year-round, some facilities are seasonal, so it's best to take this road trip in the spring, summer, or fall.

Day 1: Charlotte, NC, to Meadows of Dan, VA

130 miles (2 hours, 30 minutes without traffic and stops)

Your journey begins at Charlotte Douglas International Airport—fly in, grab a rental car, and hit the road. It's a pretty short drive from Charlotte to Meadows of Dan as you head north via I–85 and U.S. 52, a route that brings you through Winston-Salem and past Pilot Mountain.

ALONG THE WAY

Eat & Drink: Stop for lunch in Winston-Salem, where you'll have plenty of options to satisfy even the pickiest eaters. Try **Sweet Potatoes** (✉ *607 Trade St. NW* ☎ *336/717–4844* 🌐 *www.sweetpotatoes.ws*) for southern food or the **Katharine Brasserie + Bar** (✉ *401 N. Main*

National Parks
of the Southeast

St. ☎ *336/761–0203* ⊕ *www.katharine-brasserie.com*) for French cuisine.

Photo Op: As you leave Winston-Salem and drive north on U.S. 52, you'll spot an unusual rocky "knob" atop a hill—this is Pilot Mountain, a geologic icon in North Carolina. You can drive to the summit to snap photos of the panoramic views.

Town: The historic town of Mt. Airy is a must-visit for Andy Griffith fans, where there's a museum dedicated to the actor. Griffith was born and raised here, and he likely used the location as inspiration for the fictional setting of Mayberry, from his eponymous show.

MEADOWS OF DAN

Do: Meadows of Dan isn't so much of a destination in itself, but its **Primland Resort** (✉ *2000 Busted Rock Rd.* ☎ *855/876–6593* ⊕ *www.aubergeresorts.com*) certainly is. Book an overnight stay so you can spend the afternoon riding horses, going shooting, or driving RTVs across the 12,000-acre grounds; there's an outdoor adventure for everyone. At night, visit the resort's observatory for a stargazing session.

Eat & Drink: There are two dinner options at Primland: the fine dining **Elements Restaurant** and the casual **19th Pub** (☎ *276/222–6966* ⊕ *aubergeresorts.com/primland/dine*).

Stay: Accommodations at Primland range from hotel-style rooms in the main lodge with classic wilderness-resort vibes to luxe private houses scattered across the property.

Breakfast: Breakfast is served at the resort, but if you'd like to eat on the road, drop by **Mabry Mill Restaurant & Gift Shop** (✉ *266 Mabry Mill Rd. SE* ☎ *276/952–2947* ⊕ *www.mabrymillrestaurant.com*) just off the property for its signature oatmeal pancakes.

Day 2: Meadows of Dan, VA, to Shenandoah

170 miles (3 hours without traffic and stops)

The directions are simple today: drive north on I–81, then east on I–64 to get to the southern entrance of Shenandoah National Park.

ALONG THE WAY

Town: Stretch your legs in Roanoke, Virginia, where you can grab a bite to eat or do a little sightseeing. Make a pit stop at the **Roanoke Pinball Museum** (✉ *1 Market Sq. SE* ☎ *540/342–5746* ⊕ *www.roanokepinball.org*) or browse the antiques shop **Black Dog Salvage** (✉ *902 13th St. SW* ☎ *540/343–6200* ⊕ *www.blackdogsalvage.com*), made famous by the TV show *Salvage Dawgs*.

Eat & Drink: You can take a trip to Germany without ever leaving Virginia by stopping for lunch at **Edelweiss German Restaurant** (✉ *19 Edelweiss La.* ☎ *540/337–1203* ⊕ *www.edelweissvirginia.com*) in Staunton, a favorite of locals and road-trippers alike.

Detour: History buffs might want to take a side trip to Charlottesville, Virginia, to tour Thomas Jefferson's **Monticello** (✉ *931 Thomas Jefferson Pkwy.* ☎ *434/984–9800* ⊕ *www.monticello.org*) and James Monroe's **Highland** (✉ *2050 James Monroe Pkwy.* ☎ *434/293–8000* ⊕ *www.highland.org*). The town is about a 45-minute drive past Shenandoah National Park.

SHENANDOAH NATIONAL PARK

Do: Cruise the winding Skyline Drive, which runs 105 miles through the length of **Shenandoah National Park** (☎ *540/999–3500* ⊕ *www.nps.gov.shen*). It'll take at least three hours to make the full trip one-way, and that doesn't include stops at the scenic overlooks. Don't forget to make time for a few hikes,

Shenandoah National Park offers superb sunrises over the Blue Ridge Mountains.

too, like Blackrock Summit, an hourlong, 1-mile-loop hike that hugs the mountain following along the Appalachian Trail.

Eat & Drink: Dine in the park at the **Pollock Dining Room** at Skyland (✉ *Skyland Dr., Upper Loop, mile 41* ☎ *877/847–1919* ⊕ *www.goshenandoah.com*), then follow with drinks at the Mountain Taproom in the same location. Just keep in mind that they're both only open seasonally. Head to Circa '31 at the **Mimslyn Inn** (✉ *401 W. Main St.* ☎ *540/743–5105* ⊕ *www.mimslyninn.com*) in Luray, Virginia, for dining all yearlong (and be sure to grab a cocktail at the speakeasy).

Stay: There are two seasonal hotels within the park's borders, **Skyland** (✉ *Skyline Dr., mile 41.7–42.5*) and **Big Meadows Lodge** (✉ *Skyline Dr., mile 51* ☎ *977/847–1919* ⊕ *www.goshenandoah. com*), as well as multiple cabins and campsites. For year-round stays, try the boutique **Hotel Laurance** (✉ *2 S. Court St.* ☎ *540/742–7060* ⊕ *www.hotellaurance. com*) in Luray.

Breakfast: Grab a coffee and a pastry at **Gathering Grounds Pâtisserie & Café** (✉ *24 E. Main St.* ☎ *540/743–1121* ⊕ *www. ggrounds.com*) in Luray to start your day.

Day 3: Shenandoah to New River Gorge

210 miles (4 hours without traffic and stops)

You'll do a little backtracking south along I-81 before heading west on I-64.

ALONG THE WAY

Nature: The largest cave system in the eastern U.S.—that we know of, anyway—is **Luray Caverns** (✉ *101 Cave Hill Rd.* ☎ *540/743–6551* ⊕ *www.luraycaverns.com*), located just outside Shenandoah National Park. Impressively, the caverns are step-free, making the site completely accessible.

Town: Your drive today will bring you through White Sulphur Springs, home of famous resort the **Greenbrier** (✉ *101*

W. Main St. ☎ 844/837–2466 ⊕ www.
greenbrier.com), noted for its bold decor
by interior designer Dorothy Draper. The
destination has been frequented for its
therapeutic natural pools since the 18th
century, but the Greenbrier has since
turned it into a dining, shopping, and
gambling hot spot. Oh, and there's a
massive Cold War–era bunker beneath
the hotel that you can tour, too—it was
designed to house all members of Congress in the event of a catastrophe.

Eat & Drink: Fancy a not-so-fancy bite?
Embrace a road-trip classic: a burger
at **Jim's Drive In** (✉ 479 Washington St.
☎ 304/645–2590 ⊕ www.facebook.com/
jimsdrivein) in Lewisburg, West Virginia,
which has been fueling motorists since
the 1950s.

NEW RIVER GORGE NATIONAL PARK

Do: Established in 2020, **New River Gorge
National Park** (☎ 304/465–0508 ⊕ www.
nps.gov/neri) is best known for its adventure activities—namely whitewater rafting on New River and rock climbing the
steep cliff faces of the gorge. For more
low-key fun, drive across the 876-foot-tall
New River Gorge Bridge or visit the coal
mining ghost town of Thurmond, West
Virginia, where the former train depot
now serves as a visitor's center and
museum for the national park.

Eat & Drink: There are no dining facilities
within the park. Instead, enjoy a casual
dinner of pizza and beer at **Pies and Pints**
(✉ 219 W. Maple Ave. ☎ 304/574–2200
⊕ www.piesandpints.net) in Fayetteville,
West Virginia.

Stay: Camping is permitted in the park,
but for a more comfortable stay, there's
the **Historic Morris Harvey House Bed-
and-Breakfast** (✉ 201 W. Maple Ave.
☎ 304/250–7090 ⊕ www.morrisharvey-
house.com) in Fayetteville, which has
five cozy rooms.

Breakfast: Enjoy the all-day breakfast
at **Cathedral Café** (✉ 134 S. Court St.

☎ 304/574–0202 ⊕ www.thecathedral-
cafe.com), which is housed in—you
guessed it—an old church. It's also a
bookstore, so you can pick up a new read
for the road.

Day 4: New River Gorge to Gatlinburg, TN

*275 miles (4 hours, 30 minutes without
traffic and stops)*

Buckle up for a long drive today. You'll
start off traveling south on I-77, then
once you reach Wytheville, Virginia, you'll
head west on I-81. Finally, you'll take U.S.
441 south to Gatlinburg, Tennessee.

ALONG THE WAY

Roadside Attraction: Before you start
driving south, take a quick 15-minute
detour north on WV-17 to the kitschy
Mystery Hole (✉ 16724 Midland Trail
☎ 304/658–9101 ⊕ www.mysteryhole.
com) in Ansted, West Virginia. Started
in the 1970s by a man claiming the area
contains a mysterious force that bends
the laws of gravity, the spot is now the
ultimate in roadside silliness, leaning into
its sideshow-esque reputation.

Eat & Drink: On New Year's Day in 1953,
country crooner Hank Williams died in
his Cadillac, reportedly in the parking lot
of the Skyline Drive-In in Hilltop. Today
that eatery is known as **Hank's Last Stop**
(✉ 6329 Legends Hwy. ☎ 304/469–1025),
and if you're hankering for a hot dog, this
is the place to get one.

Town: Wytheville, Virginia, the hometown
of first lady Edith Bolling Wilson, is the
perfect place for a pit stop. You can visit
Mrs. Wilson's birthplace (✉ 145 E. Main
St. ☎ 276/223–3484 ⊕ www.edith-
bollingwilson.org), which is not only a
museum but also the home of Skeeter's
World Famous Hot Dogs. Wytheville has
plenty of local shops for you to peruse or
you can head just outside of town to pet
alpacas at **Cobb Hill Alpacas** (✉ 448 Turley

Farm Rd. ☎ 276/780–1690 ⊕ www.
cobbhillalpacas.com).

Roadside Attraction: Interred at the Mountain View Cemetery in Rural Retreat, Virginia, is Dr. Charles Taylor Pepper, who is theorized to be the namesake of the soda that bears his name. (There's not much hard evidence to support this, but it's a big part of local lore.) If you really love Dr. Pepper, stop by to pay your respects.

GATLINBURG

Do: Gatlinburg is one of the gateways to Great Smoky Mountains National Park, and it's filled to the brim with entertainment. Ascend the **Gatlinburg Space Needle** (✉ 115 Historic Nature Trail ☎ 865/436–4629 ⊕ www.gatlinburgspaceneedle. com), take in the views from the aerial tramway at the **Ober Gatlinburg Ski Area and Amusement Park** (✉ 1001 Parkway ☎ 865/436–5423 ⊕ www.obergatlinburg.com), or peruse the displays at the **Museum of Salt and Pepper Shakers** (✉ 461 Brookside Village Way ☎ 865/430–5515 ⊕ www.thesaltandpeppershakermuseum.com).

Eat & Drink: After eating hot dogs all day, you might want a lighter dinner. Head to Pigeon Forge, and try one of **Local Goat's** (✉ 2167 Parkway ☎ 865/366–3035 ⊕ www.localgoatpf.com) fresh salads or just give in and have a burger.

Stay: There are accommodations of all kinds (and all price points) in Gatlinburg, from the historic **Gatlinburg Inn** (✉ 755 Parkway ☎ 865/436–5133 ⊕ www. gatlinburginn.com) to the tropical-themed **Margaritaville Resort** (✉ 539 Parkway ☎ 865/430–4200 ⊕ www.margaritavilleresortgatlinburg.com). Many travelers also opt to rent self-service cabins.

Breakfast: Brave the crowds at the **Log Cabin Pancake House** (✉ 327 Historic Nature Trail ☎ 865/436–7894 ⊕ www. logcabinpancakehouse.com); you might have to wait a bit for a table, but it's worth every minute.

Day 5: Great Smoky Mountains National Park

As the most visited national park in the United States, Great Smoky Mountains National Park deserves a full day of your time. Today you have the entire day to explore the park from your base in Gatlinburg.

Do: Great Smoky Mountains (☎ 865/436–1200 ⊕ www.nps.gov/grsm) has more than 300 miles of scenic drives, so take the day to cruise them, including the 11-mile Cades Cove Loop Road (arguably the most scenic part of the Smoky Mountains) and the 14-mile Newfound Gap Road. And don't skip hiking—there are many waterfalls in the park, many of which are accessible by easy trails, like the 5-mile Abrams Falls Trail. If you don't need a full day in the park, you could backtrack to nearby Pigeon Forge, just 15 minutes north of Gatlinburg, which is home to **Dollywood** (✉ 2700 Dollywood Parks Blvd. ☎ 800/365–5996 ⊕ www. dollywood.com), Dolly Parton's amusement park. If you head back to Gatlinburg early, make a visit to **Ripley's Aquarium of the Smokies** (✉ 88 River Rd. ☎ 865/430–8808 ⊕ www.ripleysaquariums.com) or the shops of the **Great Smoky Arts & Crafts Community** (✉ 668 Glades Rd. ☎ 865/436–6921 ⊕ www.gatlinburg-crafts.com).

Eat & Drink: Dining options are limited inside the park, so either bring your own picnic or take a break from the outdoors for lunch at the **Wild Plum Tea Room** (✉ 555 Buckhorn Rd. ☎ 865/436–3808 ⊕ www.wildplumtearoom.com) in Gatlinburg; it has limited operating hours, so be sure to plan ahead. The eclectic lunch spot serves seasonal fare made with local ingredients. For dinner, splurge on a meal at the **Peddler Steakhouse** (✉ 820 River Rd. ☎ 865/436–5794 ⊕ www. peddlergatlinburg.com), a perfect spot for a romantic date in Gatlinburg.

Stay: Stay put at your hotel or vacation rental from last night.

Breakfast: Tennessee Jed's (✉ 631 Parkway ☎ 865/412–1131 ⊕ www.tennesseejeds.net) is quick, easy, and delicious. Order a hearty breakfast sandwich, then finish your meal with the brown butter minicake. Who says you can't have dessert in the morning?

Day 6: Great Smoky Mountains to Congaree

240 miles (4 hours without traffic and stops)

Take US-321 east to I–40, then connect to I–26 near Asheville, North Carolina, and head south.

ALONG THE WAY

Town: Though today's route technically skirts by Asheville, North Carolina, it's worth making a brief detour to visit this funky mountain town. Visit the impressive **Biltmore Estate** (✉ 1 Approach Rd. ☎ 800/411–3812 ⊕ www.biltmore.com), peruse the city's many art galleries and studios, or pick up some honey at the **Asheville Bee Charmer** gift shop (✉ 32 Broadway St. ☎ 828/505–7736 ⊕ www. ashevillebeecharmer.com).

Eat & Drink: Break for lunch at **Downtown Deli & Donuts** (✉ 147 E. Main St. ☎ 864/707–5585 ⊕ www.downtowndelianddonuts.com) in Spartanburg, North Carolina, where you can order salads, sandwiches, and doughnuts, of course.

Roadside Attraction: Stop for a quick photo with the world's largest fire hydrant in Columbia, South Carolina, a 40-foot-tall, 675,000-pound behemoth known as **Busted Plug Plaza** (✉ 1404 Taylor St.).

CONGAREE NATIONAL PARK

Do: This swampy national park (☎ 803/776–4396 ⊕ www.nps.gov/cong) is known for its meandering boardwalk trails and its old-growth forest with some

Extend Your Trip

From Gatlinburg: The Great American Music Road Trip (Ch. 7)

From Congaree or Charlotte: The Best of the Carolinas (Ch. 7)

of the tallest trees east of the Mississippi. If you're seeking a little more adventure, rent a canoe and hit the water. Just be sure to pack plenty of bug spray. And speaking of bugs, one of the most spectacular sights in Congaree is the annual synchronous fireflies festival, during which thousands (maybe millions!) of the luminescent critters synchronize their flash patterns in one of nature's most mysterious shows. The event takes place between mid-May and mid-June, and tickets are awarded via a lottery system.

Eat & Drink: There are no dining options within the park, so pack a picnic for lunch, and then enjoy dinner and drinks at **929 Kitchen & Bar** (✉ 929 Gervais St. ☎ 803/764–3825 ⊕ www.929kitchen. com) in nearby Columbia, where the menu features "upscale modern" Korean fare.

Stay: South Carolina's capital, Columbia, is the place to stay near Congaree; you can stay at boutique hotels like **Graduate Columbia** (✉ 1619 Pendleton St. ☎ 803/779–7779 ⊕ www.graduatehotels.com) or **Hotel Trundle** (✉ 1224 Taylor St. ☎ 803/722–5000 ⊕ www.hoteltrundle.com).

Breakfast: As a college town, Columbia is home to some stellar breakfast establishments serving greasy hangover cures. **Cafe Strudel** (✉ 300 State St. ☎ 803/794–6634 ⊕ www.cafestrudel.com) is no exception—order its famous Hangover Hash Browns.

Day 7: Congaree to Charlotte, NC

90 miles (1 hour, 30 minutes without traffic and stops)

The final leg of your journey is an easy one—straight north on I–77 to catch your flight home.

ALONG THE WAY

Detour: To be perfectly honest, this is a pretty quiet stretch of the road trip, which is why you should make a little detour to Winnsboro, South Carolina, located about 10 miles off I–77. It's home to the **South Carolina Railroad Museum** (✉ *110 Industrial Park Rd.* ☎ *803/712–4135* ⊕ *www.scrm.org*), a historic town clock that's been running for more than a century, and a quaint main street with restaurants and shops.

Eat & Drink: Stop in Rock Hill, South Carolina, for a quick lunch at **Amélie's French Bakery & Café** (✉ *157 E. Main St.* ☎ *803/403–9409* ⊕ *www.ameliesfrench-bakery.com*), where you can enjoy light bites like sandwiches and soups. Be sure to grab a few pastries or macarons to go as a snack on your flight home.

The Great American Whiskey Tour

Written by Brandon Schultz

Bourbon doesn't always come from Kentucky, but it does originate in the United States and is the country's only federally legislated spirit, making it one of the most beloved whiskies in America and the centerpiece of any whiskey trail trip. Louisville is, and probably always will be, the heart of Bourbon Country so it's the perfect place to begin and end your eight-day, six-state whirlwind road trip. On this epic adventure, you will not just sample Kentucky bourbon (traveling along the famed Bourbon Trail) and Tennessee whiskey, but spirits from Virginia, Ohio, Indiana, and more, as whiskey distilling booms across all 50 states.

It goes without saying, but we'll say it anyway: it's especially important to drink responsibly throughout this itinerary and never drink and drive. There's plenty of time built into this trip to linger at each distillery, and remember that these are tastings, not ragers, so sip and savor thoughtfully.

At a Glance

Start: Louisville, KY

End: Louisville, KY

Miles Traveled: 2,040 miles

Suggested Duration: 8 days

States Visited: Indiana, Kentucky, Ohio, Tennessee, West Virginia, Virginia

Key Sights: Jack Daniels Distillery; Jim Beam American Stillhouse; Keeneland Race Course; Maker's Mark Distillery; Mammoth Cave National Park

Best Time to Go: Spring and fall offer ideal temperatures for this journey, and mid-to-late fall brings the added bonus of fewer visitors at the distilleries.

Day 1: Louisville, KY, to Lexington, KY

85 miles (1 hour, 40 minutes without traffic and stops)

Today's drive is a simple start and the shortest leg of the trip, traveling an easy 80 miles eastward. Don't get too late of a start, though; you'll want plenty of time at the three distilleries along the way.

ALONG THE WAY

Town: Stop in Shelbyville, about 45 minutes from Louisville, and check out the **Bulleit Distilling Co. Visitor Experience**

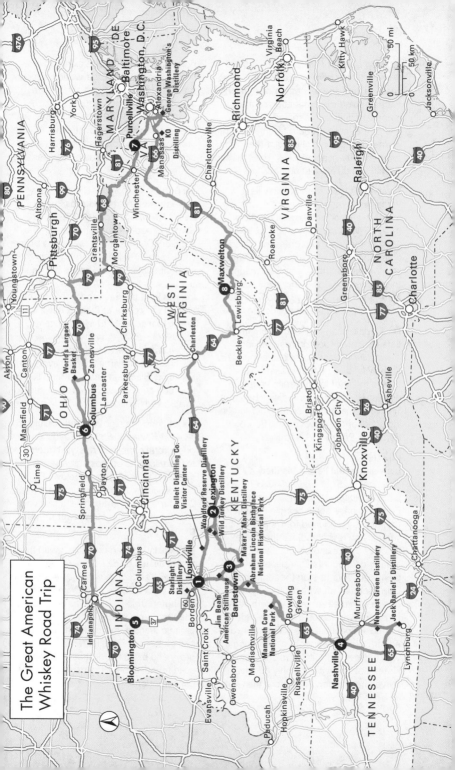

The Great American Whiskey Road Trip

(✉ *3464 Benson Pike* ☎ *502/647–5799* ⊕ *www.bulleit.com*). Here, where sustainability and technology are driving forces behind the production of the brand's traditional rye recipe, you'll find one of the more modern facilities on your journey and catch a shiny glimmer of the future of American whiskey. The tour and tasting will take about an hour.

Town A half hour from Shelbyville is Versailles, where you'll want to stop to explore **Woodford Reserve Distillery** (✉ *7785 McCracken Pike* ☎ *859/879–1812* ⊕ *www.woodfordreserve.com*) for a far more traditional approach to whiskey making. Bourbon was first made on this property in 1812, and you'll feel (and taste) the history everywhere. The tour and tasting will take an hour or so.

Eat & Drink: Snag lunch at **Glenn's Creek Café** (⊕ *www.woodfordreserve.com/our-distillery/glenns-creek-cafe-menu/*) at the Woodford Reserve Distillery, where the chef in residence whips up distillery-inspired favorites, like Bourbon Trail Chili (made-from-scratch cornbread included) or the slow-cooked Bourbon Barbecue Pulled-Pork Sammich.

LEXINGTON

Do: Visit the **Old Pepper Distillery** (✉ *1228 Manchester St.* ☎ *859/309–3230* ⊕ *www.jamesepepper.com*), where James E. Pepper is once again being distilled after the lot sat abandoned for more than 50 years. Now revitalized, it's the centerpiece of the Lexington Distillery District, featuring 25 acres of shops, eateries, and plenty of spots to stop for additional sips. Don't venture off without touring the distillery's small yet fascinating history museum, where you'll learn that the Old Fashioned cocktail was allegedly invented for Colonel Pepper himself during a visit to New York City's Waldorf Astoria Hotel. Naturally, it's the only cocktail served here today. With more than 400

horse farms in the city, Lexington is the "horse capital of the world," so you may want to check out a stately site like *Keeneland Race Course* (✉ *4201 Versailles Rd.* ☎ *859/254–3412* ⊕ *www.keeneland.com*) to enjoy the beautiful grounds, scope some stellar horses, or catch a Thoroughbred race. It's open daily to the public.

Eat & Drink: Grab a few slices of New York–style pizza at **Goodfellas Pizzeria** (✉ *110 N. Mill St.* ☎ *859/281–1101* ⊕ *www.goodfellaspizzeria.com*) in the Distillery District, just a few steps from Old Pepper Distillery. There's plenty of outdoor seating (and a bocce ball court), but be sure to poke around the industrial interior for a bit. Save room for dessert around the corner at **Crank & Boom Ice Cream Lounge** (✉ *1210 Manchester St.* ☎ *859/288–2176* ⊕ *www.crankand-boom.com*), where local ingredients are churned into small-batch flavors like Kentucky Blackberry and Buttermilk and Bourbon and Honey. Feel free to upgrade to a Spiked Scoop.

Stay: Spend the night at **Origin Lexington** (✉ *4174 Rowan* ☎ *859/245–0400* ⊕ *www.originhotel.com*), where stylish rooms feature accents of moss green, soft gray, and leathery brown below alluring black ceilings. If you won't make it to the 24-hour fitness center, have a free yoga kit (mat, block, and strap) sent to your room.

Breakfast: Get ready for Day 2 with breakfast at **Josie's** (✉ *821 Chevy Chase Pl.* ☎ *859/523–8328* ⊕ *www.josiesky.com*) in the Chevy Chase neighborhood of Lexington. This breakfast-all-day spot has a lighter fare, like egg white omelets and organic granola, for the health-conscious, and gluttonous, heavier fare, like sausage gravy and biscuits, for those setting a solid foundation for the day's whiskey consumption.

Day 2: Lexington, KY, to Bardstown, KY

120 miles (2 hours, 45 minutes without traffic and stops)

Today's goal is only about 60 miles southwest of Lexington, but it's smack between two classic distilleries you won't want to miss, so you'll need to shun the straight line and embrace a somewhat circuitous route just this once.

ALONG THE WAY

Town: Just over a half hour from Lexington, Lawrenceburg is home to **Wild Turkey Distillery** (✉ *1417 Versailles Rd.* ☎ *502/839–2182* ⊕ *www.wildturkeybourbon.com*), where the world's longest-tenured master distiller continues to oversee whiskey traditions that predate Prohibition. You'll also find Matthew McConaughey's favorite bourbon, Longbranch, here (he created it). The tour and tasting will take about one hour.

Photo Op: Just outside the entrance of Wild Turkey is a giant mural of, well... a wild turkey (you'll recognize it from the bottle). It's a perfect spot for an amusing pose to commemorate your wild whiskey wanderlust.

Eat & Drink: Have lunch at Star Hill Provisions at **Maker's Mark Distillery** (✉ *3350 Burks Spring Rd.* ☎ *270/865–2099* ⊕ *www.makersmark.com*). The chef in residence prepares seasonal menus of local Kentucky ingredients with hearty sandwiches and flavorful salads. The star of the menu is the Maker's and Ale-8-One Slushie, ideal for dessert.

Town: Stop in Clermont to tour the home of the world's best-selling whiskey at **Jim Beam American Stillhouse** (✉ *568 Happy Hollow Rd.* ☎ *502/543–9877* ⊕ *www. jimbeam.com*). Jim Beam is aged twice as long as the legal requirement for bourbon, and the tour lasts a little longer than your typical distillery walkthrough,

Essential Listening

Before entering Bardstown, listen to Stephen Foster's "My Old Kentucky Home, Good Night." This antislavery song was inspired in part by visits to Federal Hill, which you can visit when you arrive. The other assumed inspiration for this song was Harriet Beecher Stowe's groundbreaking antislavery novel, *Uncle Tom's Cabin*, which you might also listen to as an audiobook, but that one will take about 20 hours.

too, so you may have time to safely snag an extra sip at the Jim Beam Bourbon Bar and linger a little at your last stop of the day. The tour and tasting take around 90 minutes.

BARDSTOWN

Do: Bardstown is more than a place to crash for the night. Depending on how early you get started today, you should be able to visit at least one or two of its main attractions, including the **Oscar Getz Museum of Whiskey History** (✉ *114 N. 5th St.* ☎ *502/348–2999* ⊕ *www.oscargetzwhiskeymuseum.com*), **Women's Civil War Museum** (✉ *204 E. Broadway St.* ☎ *502/349–0291* ⊕ *www.civil-war-museum.org*), and **My Old Kentucky Home** mansion (✉ *501 E. Stephen Foster Ave.* ☎ *502/348–3502* ⊕ *www.visitmyoldkyhome.com*). There are even a couple distilleries in town if you're up for more tasting (you're done driving for the day, so go for it).

Eat & Drink: Embrace Kentucky cuisine with dinner at **Kurtz Restaurant** (✉ *418 E. Stephen Foster Ave.* ☎ *502/348–8964* ⊕ *www.kurtzrestaurant.com*), where family recipes have been served in this historic house since 1937. Start with Kentucky country ham or skillet-fried chicken, but save room for sampling the scrumptious pies and cobblers for dessert.

Stay: Book a room in **The Talbott Inn** (✉ 101 W. Stephen Foster Ave. ☎ 502/348–3494 ⊕ www.talbottinn. com) for a convenient stay in the center of downtown Bardstown, steps from the quaint town's restaurants and shops. You'll find modern rooms in a historic 1913 building and you can't beat the price or location. If you're up for some potential spook factor, you could check into the neighboring **Talbott Tavern** (✉ 107 W. Stephen Foster Ave. ☎ 502/348–3494 ⊕ www.talbotts.com) bed-and-breakfast, built in 1779. Here you'll also find the world's oldest bourbon bar.

Breakfast: Day 3 comes with considerably more driving time, so pop into **Fresh** (✉ 114 N. 3rd St. ☎ 502/331–6345 ⊕ www.freshcoffeebardstown.com) for a to-go breakfast. Grab some Good Folks coffee and a big ole pastry or two from this zero-waste kitchen with a locally sourced menu that changes weekly (and sometimes daily).

Day 3: Bardstown, KY, to Nashville, TN

300 miles (5 hours without traffic and stops)

Start fairly early today as the first leg of this journey takes you 3½ hours south to your first stop before about-facing northward toward Nashville.

ALONG THE WAY

Nature: If you can pull yourself out of bed even earlier, a slight detour of about 15 minutes in each direction will bring you to **Mammoth Cave National Park** (☎ 270/758–2180 ⊕ www.nps.gov/maca), home of the world's longest known cave system, just over an hour from Bardstown. The visitor center opens at 8 am, but if you want to spend the recommended three

hours exploring the park, you may need to cut a distillery from your day.

Attraction: Leave Kentucky bourbon behind (for now) and move on to Tennessee whiskey today with a tour of **Jack Daniel's Distillery** (✉ 280 Lynchburg Hwy. ☎ 931/759-6357 ⊕ www.jackdaniels. com) in Lynchburg, Tennessee. Theme tours range from 70 to 90 minutes for more traditional experiences and three hours for a filling tour that culminates in a country meal.

Eat & Drink: Have lunch in Lynchburg at **Miss Mary Bobo's** (✉ 295 Main St. ☎ 931/759–7394 ⊕ www.missmarybobos.com), where Southern hospitality has been the hallmark of every hearty meal since Miss Mary Bobo opened her kitchen in 1908 and ran it for more than 60 years. Now owned by the Jack Daniel's Distillery, the family-style restaurant has expanded to nine dining rooms serving more than 200 hungry patrons daily so you'll want to make reservations for this one.

Attraction: Relearn your whiskey history with a visit to **Nearest Green Distillery** (✉ 3125 U.S. 231 N ☎ 931/773–3070 ⊕ www.unclenearest.com) in Shelbyville, where Uncle Nearest Premium Whiskey is produced. Uncle Nearest was the world's first African-American master distiller and the man who taught a young Jack Daniel to filter his whiskey through sugar maple charcoal. The tour takes 90 minutes.

NASHVILLE

Do: You'll trip over things to do in Nashville, but make sure one of them is a visit to **Nelson's Green Brier Distillery** (✉ 1414 Clinton St. ☎ 615/913–8800 ⊕ www.greenbrierdistillery.com). With a dramatic history including shipwreck and lost family fortune on the way to seeking the American dream, Charles Nelson went from soapmaker to grocer to distiller, becoming one of the pioneers of whiskey bottling before Prohibition closed the business. Generations later, his descendants rediscovered the distillery and relaunched the brand exactly 100 years after it had closed. The tour and tasting will take about 45 minutes.

Eat & Drink: Stay on theme with dinner at **Whiskey Kitchen** (✉ *118 12th Ave. S* ☎ *615/254–3029* ⊕ *www.mstreet-nashville.com*). Alongside the city's largest collection of whiskeys, you'll find delicious pub fare like the Fried Green Tomato BLT, Low Country Pulled Pork Sandwich, and a city staple, Nashville Hot Fried Chicken.

Stay: Slip into Nashville's new urban style with a stay at **Fieldhouse Jones** (✉ *811 Main St.* ☎ *615/650–9075* ⊕ *www. fieldhousejones.com*) in the city's artsy East Nashville neighborhood. Uniquely designed accommodations range from traditional and deluxe rooms and suites to legitimately cool bunk bed combos, and the public spaces are a social media star's dream come true.

Breakfast: Try something new this morning by heading to **Yeast Nashville** (✉ *805 Woodland St.* ☎ *615/678–4592* ⊕ *www.yeastnashville.com*) and ordering a tongue-twisting Tex-Czech Kolache with your morning tea. Traditional Czech kolaches are like superthick danishes of brioche-y dough filled with fruit, poppyseed, or cheese, but a Tex-Czech version embraces the tradition of the 19th-century Texas Czechs who started stuffing them with meat.

Day 4: Nashville, TN, to Bloomington, IN

275 miles (4 hours, 40 minutes without traffic and stops)

Head north on I–65 N through Kentucky and into Indiana. It's a long drive, but a fairly direct route today.

Extend Your Trip

From Lexington or Nashville: The Great American Music Road Trip *(Ch. 7)*

From Nashville: The Civil Rights Trail *(Ch. 7)*

From Louisville: Underrated Cities of the Midwest *(Ch. 6)*

ALONG THE WAY

Detour: Just under two hours into your drive, American history buffs will want to hop off I–65 in Kentucky for a 20-minute detour to **Abraham Lincoln Birthplace National Historic Park** (✉ *2995 Lincoln Farm Rd.* ☎ *270/358–3137* ⊕ *www.nps. gov/abli*). The first memorial to Lincoln, 56 steps lead up the knoll to where he was born to commemorate his 56 years of life, and a humble replica of his one-room cabin can be found within the stately memorial at the top.

Detour: Pay a visit to **Starlight Distillery** (✉ *19816 Huber Rd.* ☎ *812/923–9463* ⊕ *www.starlightdistillery.com*) at Huber's Orchard, Winery & Vineyards in Borden, Indiana, about an hour from the Abe Lincoln detour or three hours direct from Nashville. While originally launched to distill brandies from the vineyards' grapes, Starlight also produces a few single-barrel bourbons and ryes, and even a blackberry whiskey worth a taste. The distillery tour and tasting will take just 30 minutes, so you may want to tack on the 30-minute wine tour and tasting, too, for a broader understanding of the whole operation.

Eat & Drink: While road tripping through small-town USA, have an all-American lunch of a burger and fries at **Norma Jean's Ice Cream** (✉ *302 E. Water St.* ☎ *812/967–2663*

⊕ norma-jeans-ice-cream.business. site) during your stop in Borden. Order from the window and chow down at the creekside picnic tables. You should finish this meal with some scoops of ice cream, and are encouraged to venture into flavors like Fat Elvis, Zanzibar Chocolate, and Orange Pineapple.

BLOOMINGTON

Do: Just an hour south of Indianapolis, Bloomington is a quaint city near Lake Monroe with equal helpings of nature and culture. Downtown has plenty of shops and galleries, like the popular Fountain Square shop collective and the **I Fell** (⊠ 415 W. 4th St. ☎ 812/361–6719 ⊕ www.ifellbloomington.wordpress. com) community art center with studios, shops, and a bakery. Check out the **Eskenazi Museum of Art** (⊠ 1133 E. 7th St. ☎ 812/855–5445 ⊕ www.artmuseum. indiana.edu) and the **Wylie House Museum** (⊠ 307 E. 2nd St. ☎ 812/855–6224 ⊕ www.libraries.indiana.edu) for indoor activities, or head to **McCormick's Creek State Park** (⊠ 250 McCormick Creek Park Rd. ☎ 812/829–2235 ⊕ www.in.gov) or **Hoosier National Forest** (⊠ 811 Constitution Ave, Bedford, IN ☎ 812/275–5987 ⊕ www.fs.usda.gov) for outdoor time.

Eat & Drink: Visit Bloomington's first craft distillery, **Cardinal Spirits** (⊠ 922 S. Morton St. ☎ 812/202–6789 ⊕ www.cardinal-spirits.com), for dinner, drinks, and a tour. You're halfway through your whirlwind whiskey odyssey now, so take a break to appreciate sips of Cardinal's vodka, gin, or rum—these are the specialties here. For dinner, try the Truffle Chicken with mashed potatoes or the Salmon Breeze with broccolini and maitake mushrooms.

Stay: Check in to the **Showers Inn Bed & Breakfast** (⊠ 430 N. Washington St. ☎ 812/334–9000 ⊕ www.showersinn. com) for a cozy stay in the center of town. The historic Showers-Graham house is outfitted with modern conveniences and upscale amenities at reasonable rates with complimentary parking.

Breakfast: Take advantage of the included breakfast buffet at the Showers Inn. In addition to the standards like fruit, yogurt, and cereal, you'll find homemade specialties like corned beef hash and poached eggs, spinach and Gruyère strata, and lemon poppyseed pound cake.

Day 5: Bloomington, IN, to Columbus, OH

230 miles (3 hours, 50 minutes without traffic and stops)

Head north to Indianapolis before venturing east along I–70 E for the majority of today's shorter drive. A stop in Indianapolis will keep the second leg just over 2½ hours, and there are no other major stops along the way, so feel free to take a later start and aim to be in Indy for lunch.

ALONG THE WAY

Town: Indianapolis is your sole stop before Columbus, so you'll have plenty of time to explore Indiana's capital city. If you can't wait until the evening for today's dose of whiskey, stop by **Westfork Whiskey Co.** (⊠ 1660 Bellefontaine St. ☎ 317/672–7468 ⊕ www.westforkwhiskey.com) for smooth sips of distilled Indiana grains in the tasting room. Other options include checking out the **Eiteljorg Museum** (⊠ 500 W. Washington St. ☎ 317/636–9378 ⊕ www.eiteljorg.org) for Native American and western art, the **Kurt Vonnegut Museum and Library** (⊠ 543 Indiana Ave. ☎ 317/423–0391 ⊕ www. vonnegutlibrary.org), and, of course, the **Indianapolis Motor Speedway** (⊠ 4790 W. 16th St. ☎ 317/492–8500 ⊕ www.indianapolismotorspeedway.com).

Eat & Drink: It may not look like much from the outside, but if you ask a local for a lunch recommendation, you'll probably be directed to **Lockerbie Pub** (⊠ 631 E. Michigan St. ☎ 317/631–9545 ⊕ lockerbie-pub.business.site). You'll find everything from fried pickles to burgers

Did You Know?

Now one of America's most popular names in bourbon, the Beam family first began producing whiskey in 1795. James Beam rebuilt the distillery after it closed during Prohibition, opening the Clermont space that officially became Jim Beam in 1935.

at this inexpensive dive, but the breaded tenderloins are what keep business strong (well, that and the beer).

COLUMBUS

Do: If you've had enough of museums from earlier today, check out outdoor Columbus by toddling around German Village, taking pics in **Topiary Park** (✉ *480 E. Town St.* ☎ *614/645–0197* ⊕ *www. columbus.gov*) or the **Columbus Park of Roses** (✉ *3901 N. High St.* ☎ *614/645– 3391* ⊕ *www.parkofroses.org*), or admiring nature at **Hayden Falls Park** (✉ *4326 Hayden Run Rd.* ☎ *614/645–3300* ⊕ *www.columbus.gov*). Toward the end of your exploration, tour **Middle West Spirits** (✉ *1230 Courtland Ave.* ☎ *614/299– 2460* ⊕ *www.middlewestspirits.com*), where it's all about appreciating the good life as one cofounder describes a sip here as an "everyday special occasion." Try the ryes, including dark pumpernickel, and remember that bourbon doesn't have to be made in Kentucky—it's just a myth—so give it a go, perhaps in a cocktail at Service Bar on-site.

Eat & Drink: Service Bar (✉ *1230 Courtland Ave.* ☎ *614/947–1231* ⊕ *www. servicebarcolumbus.com*) is the spot to stay for dinner, whether you went for that bourbon cocktail after your tour or not. Expect serious upgrades of familiar plates, like Crispy Ribs with fried broccoli in a hibiscus Commander Tso's sauce or Roasted Potato Gnocchi with oxtail, kabocha squash, and truffle. Go overboard with not Tres but Cinco Leches Cake for dessert.

Stay: Although **The Blackwell** (✉ *2110 Tuttle Park Pl.* ☎ *614/247–4000* ⊕ *www. theblackwell.com*) caters to more of a business crowd and the austere exterior may not spark much joy, you'll love the four-star accommodations and service that come with this surprisingly affordable reservation.

Breakfast: Take one last bite of Columbus's German heritage with breakfast at **Valters at the Maennerchor** (✉ *976 S. High St.* ☎ *614/444–3531* ⊕ *www.valtersat-themaennerchor.com*), founded more than 150 years ago by a dozen German immigrants. Here you'll find skillets loaded with hearty helpings (including bratwurst, of course); you can even grab a traditional soft pretzel for the road on your way out.

Day 6: Columbus, OH, to Purcellville, VA

350 miles (6 hours, 40 minutes without traffic and stops)

Today's drive is the longest of the trip clocking in at just over 6½ hours traveling west into northeast Virginia. If you want to shave a little time off, you can buy back a half hour by skipping today's stops and taking a slightly more streamlined route.

ALONG THE WAY

Roadside Attraction: If six straight days of whiskey is turning you into something of a basket case, you'll want to stop for a photo with the World's Largest Basket on Main Street in the little town of Dresden, Ohio. It's 48 feet wide, 11 feet long, and 23 feet high, making it larger than some houses.

Eat & Drink: Since you'll want to get to Purcellville early enough to explore, you can stop at any service station along the route for lunch, but if you prefer something a little quainter, pop into **The Casselman** (✉ *113 Main St.* ☎ *301/895–5055* ⊕ *www.thecasselman.com*) in Grantsville, Maryland, four hours into your drive. You'll find simple, country food with Pennsylvania Dutch and Amish influences, especially in the bakery downstairs, where there's also an antiques shop.

PURCELLVILLE

Do: You may be surprised to learn that Virginia is the birthplace of American whiskey. Visit **Catoctin Creek Distilling Company** (✉ *120 W. Main St.* ☎ *540/751–8404* ⊕ *www.catoctincreekdistilling.com*) to tour the facility, try a whiskey flight, and snag a bottle of Virginia's most awarded whiskey, Roundstone Rye, to take home. A tour-and-tasting combo here will take about an hour. You're clearly in town for Catoctin Creek, but this is wine country, so you may want to check out one or two of the many surrounding wineries, too. For a less alcohol-induced activity, there aren't many spots more charming than **Blooming Hill Lavender Farm** (✉ *19929 Telegraph Springs Rd.* ☎ *703/431–0779* ⊕ *www.bloominghillva.com*), open to the public for strolling and shopping.

Eat & Drink: Don't be fooled by the barn location; **Magnolia at the Mill** (✉ *198 N. 21st St.* ☎ *540/338–9800* ⊕ *www.magnoliasmill.com*) is the best spot in town for a chic dinner on the more comfortable side of upscale. You'll find filet mignon, seared salmon with lump crab, and shrimp and grits served on white-linen cloths, but you're also in luck if you're looking for hickory-grilled burgers or brick-oven pizzas.

Stay: Springdale Village Inn (✉ *18348 Lincoln Rd.* ☎ *540/751–8686* ⊕ *www.springdalevillageinn.com*) is the bed-and-breakfast for you in Purcellville. Colonial cottage–decorated rooms provide cozy accommodations in the Federal-style estate house believed to be one of the last stops on the Underground Railroad, just 14 miles from the border to freedom. The five acres of bucolic bliss are well worth wandering, too.

Breakfast: Sit down early to Springdale Village Inn's daily farm-to-table breakfast and load up properly for the two-distillery day with a considerable drive between.

Day 7: Purcellville, VA, to Maxwelton, WV

320 miles (5 hours, 20 minutes without traffic and stops)

Head a bit farther east today before looping back westward toward Kentucky. You'll make it just about halfway, stopping in West Virginia for a little more whiskey and a good night's sleep.

ALONG THE WAY

Town: Your first whiskey stop today may be a surprising one. An hour east of Purcellville, stop at **George Washington's Distillery** (✉ *5514 Mount Vernon Memorial Hwy.* ☎ *703/780–3383* ⊕ *www.mountvernon.org*) at Mount Vernon in Alexandria to tour a re-creation of one of the nation's earliest large-scale whiskey distilleries, and one of the most profitable ventures on Washington's estate. Washington's recipe is once again being produced, in very limited batches, since the distillery's reopening in 2007.

Town: Sample one last taste of Virginia whiskey at **KO Distilling** (✉ *10381 Central Park Dr.* ☎ *571/292–1115* ⊕ *www.kodistilling.com*) in Manassas, about 45 minutes west of Alexandria. Try a flight of Bare Knuckle whiskeys, including straight bourbon, wheat, and rye, from this relative newcomer to the craft distilling scene. A tour before your tasting will take about 30 minutes.

Eat & Drink: Have lunch in Manassas before the final 3½-hour haul to Maxwelton. At **The Bone BBQ** (✉ *9420 Battle St.* ☎ *703/330–3820* ⊕ *www.thebonebbq.com*), you'll find pulled pork, hickory-smoked chicken, smoked turkey, brisket, and more, served with sweet potato fries, mac n cheese, and baked potato on a menu that also includes specialty sandwiches like a brisket-and-pulled-pork po'boy and a few juicy burgers.

MAXWELTON

Do: Get a taste of Appalachian whiskey at **Smooth Ambler Spirits** (✉ 745 Industrial Park Rd. ☎ 304/497–3123 ⊕ www.smoothambler.com) in the West Virginia mountains, where they believe their clean water, crisp air, and ideal climate produce some of the country's top spirits. Smooth Ambler specializes in bourbon whiskies, so be sure to take some comparison sips before returning to limestone-laced Kentucky tomorrow.

Eat & Drink: Most of the area action is in Lewisburg, five minutes from Maxwelton, and it's here that you'll find **Food & Friends** (✉ 878 Washington St. ☎ 304/645–4548 ⊕ www.foodandfriendslewisburgwv.com), a neighborhood favorite for a good meal and equally good atmosphere. Check out the chargrilled menu for brisket, pecan-crusted chicken, baby back ribs, or bourbon-glazed salmon.

Stay: Maxwelton/Lewisburg isn't exactly a tourism area, so you won't be staying in town. Luckily, there's a sweet little hotel in nearby White Sulphur Springs, about 15 minutes away, and you'll spend a comfortable night here at **Howard's Creek Inn** (✉ 50 E. Main St. ☎ 304/667–9863 ⊕ www.howardscreekinn.com).

Breakfast: Back in Lewisburg, hit up **The Wild Bean** (✉ 1056 E. Washington St. ☎ 304/645–3738 ⊕ www.thewildbrew.com) for a dependable breakfast of huevos rancheros or the Papas Plato of home fries, fajita veggies, and avocado topped with buttermilk crema and salsa. You can also try the scrambled eggs menu, with plenty of add-ins like black beans, jalapeños, spinach, or sautéed peppers and onions.

Day 8: Maxwelton, WV, to Louisville, KY

360 miles (5 hours, 30 minutes without traffic and stops)

Your last day on the road is as easy as it gets—just hop on I–64 W and take it back to Louisville.

ALONG THE WAY

Town: Stop in West Virginia's capital city of Charleston to stretch your legs. Take a walk along the Kanawha River and check out Haddad Riverfront Park before strolling down Capitol Street in town. Make your way to **Capitol Market** (✉ 800 Smith St. ☎ 304/344–1905 ⊕ www.capitolmarket.net) on Smith Street to peruse the vibrant indoor-outdoor market and grab lunch before hitting the road again.

Eat & Drink: It's been a fairly meat-forward trip, as you'd expect from this barbecue-loving region, so step back from the pit for the afternoon and try some Cajun pasta with shrimp or good old-fashioned spaghetti and meatballs in spicy puttanesca sauce at **Soho's Capitol Market** (✉ 800 Smith St. ☎ 304/720–7646 ⊕ www.sohoscrw.com).

LOUISVILLE

Do: There is a ton of whiskey and bourbon to be had here. The great news is you can walk to many of the distilleries (or their outposts) in town, so you can taste a little more enthusiastically than when you were driving. Three spots you must hit are **Old Forester Distilling Co.** (✉ 119 W. Main St. ☎ 502/779–2222 ⊕ www.oldforester.com), home of America's first bottled bourbon; **Angel's Envy Distillery** (✉ 500 E. Main St. ☎ 502/890–6300 ⊕ www.angelsenvy.com), finished in port wine casks; and **Rabbit Hole Distillery** (✉ 711 E. Jefferson St. ☎ 502/561–2000 ⊕ www.rabbitholedistillery.com), a hypermodern outfit with an art collection as covetable as its spirits.

Eat & Drink: Have one last carnivorous feast at **Steak & Bourbon** (✉ *1321 Herr La.* ☎ *502/708–2196* ⊕ *www.steak-bourbon. com*) where, as you'd guess, large slabs of beef and an even larger bourbon collection (about 70 varieties) are the specialties. Potatoes are particularly prized here, too, with their own section on the menu.

Stay: The Louisville hotel scene is small but surprisingly strong. End your trip on a provocative note with a stay at **Vu Guest-house** (✉ *822 S. Floyd St.* ☎ *502/785–0815* ⊕ *www.vuguesthouselouisville. com*), a boutique with mystique to spare. Inside an old tobacco warehouse in the Smoketown neighborhood, the luxury boutique is equal parts sexy and gaudy. Whether it takes itself seriously is anyone's guess, but it's comfortable, fun, and an unbeatable backdrop for some memorable last-night-of-the-trip photos.

Breakfast: For your final meal of the journey, head to **Highland Morning** (✉ *1416 Bardstown Rd.* ☎ *502/365–3900* ⊕ *www.highlandmorning.com*) for big portions of biscuits and gravy, crab cake Benedict, or a bacon-and-fried-egg sandwich on an English muffin. If you want to treat yourself, indulge in the sinful pancake menu, where Dreamsicle, Key West Key Lime, and Strawberry Shortcake are just a few of the tempting varieties available.

The Civil Rights Trail

Written by Chanté LaGon

Spanning over 100 locations across 15 states, the U.S. Civil Rights Trail retraces the fight for Black American civil rights during the pivotal civil rights movement of the 1950s and 1960s. On this road trip, you'll see a selection of these essential sights as you travel through the American South's wow-inducing mountains and Spanish moss–covered public squares. From the hustle of Atlanta, "the city too busy to hate" to the old-world charm of Charleston, you'll find everything from monuments honoring Martin Luther King Jr. and other heroes of the movement to glimpses and remnants of African culture from long ago.

At a Glance

Start: Atlanta, GA

End: Atlanta, GA

Miles Traveled: 1,660 miles

Suggested Duration: 7 days

States Visited: Alabama, Georgia, Mississippi, South Carolina, Tennessee

Key Sights: Edmund Pettus Bridge; Martin Luther King Jr. National Historic Park; National Center for Civil and Human Rights; National Civil Rights Museum at Lorraine Motel; Rosa Parks Museum

Best Time to Go: This Southern road trip offers pleasant driving weather year-round, but expect bonus activities—and bigger crowds—around the time of the Martin Luther King Jr. national holiday (the third Monday in January) or during Black History Month in February.

Day 1: Atlanta, GA, to Nashville, TN

250 miles (3 hours, 45 minutes without traffic and stops)

Hartsfield-Jackson Atlanta International Airport is home to Delta Air Lines so finding a convenient flight is quite easy. The world's busiest airport offers an expansive selection of car rental options, too, but there are outposts throughout the convention-hosting metro area if you're not flying in. Once you hit the road, motor up I–75 past Atlanta's heavy downtown traffic and about 30 minutes north, get a preview of the roadside mountains to come. You'll know you're more than

The Civil Rights Trail

halfway there when the highway winds through the Appalachian Mountains and over the Tennessee River in Chattanooga, along with some tight lanes that you'll have to share with big rigs pumping their breaks during the descent.

ALONG THE WAY

Photo Op: Before you hit the road, head to **State Farm Arena** (✉ 1 State Farm Dr.) and take a picture near Centennial Olympic Park Drive. With the building's big "Atlanta" sign in the background, you'll feel as if you've officially stepped into one of the city's infamous reality TV shows.

Eat & Drink: The site of militia training during the Civil War, **Marietta Square** (✉ 99 S. Park Sq. NE ⊕ www.mariettaga.gov) in Marietta, Georgia, is now home to quaint shops and a variety of restaurants, from Australian meat pies and barbecue to hot dogs and Mexican.

Roadside Attraction: Marietta's **The Big Chicken** (✉ 12 Cobb Pkwy. SE) is just what it sounds like. Built in 1963 as part of a KFC, the drive-thru is optional, but a drive-by of the landmark (complete with moving beak and eyes) is a must.

Town: Before Atlanta's Georgia Aquarium became a must-see, the **Tennessee Aquarium** (✉ 1 Broad St. ☎ 423/265–0695 ⊕ www.tnaqua.org) in Chattanooga drew visitors from throughout the region, and remains impressive with its two buildings and an IMAX 3-D theater. The **Chattanooga Zoo** (✉ 301 N. Holtzclaw Ave. ☎ 423/697–1322 ⊕ www.chattzoo.org) and its more than 500 animals welcome visitors who prefer their exhibits on dry land. Rest your feet and view the city from above on the mile-long and 72%-steep grade **Lookout Mountain Incline Railway** (✉ 3917 St. Elmo Ave. ☎ 423/821–4224 ⊕ www.

ridetheincline.com), in operation for more than 125 years.

NASHVILLE

Do: To best appreciate the city's civil rights history, center your visit in the downtown area, with easy access to the **National Museum of African American Music** (✉ *510 Broadway* ☎ *615/301–8724* ⊕ *www.nmaam.org*) and the **Davidson County Courthouse** (✉ *1 Public Sq.*). The Public Works Administration's modern courthouse is grand enough to take in on its own, but be sure to stroll through its plaza and to the nearby **Witness Walls** (⊕ *www.witnesswalls.com*), commemorating protests led by civil rights leaders C. T. Vivian and Diane Nash in response to the bombing of a civil rights attorney's home in 1960. After the bombing, Nashville's laws segregating lunch counters began to loosen; make a visit to **Woolworth on 5th** (✉ *221 5th Ave. N* 615/891–1361 ⊕ *www.woolworthonfifth.com*), designated as a historic landmark in honor of the sit-ins that kicked off the city's civil rights movement.

Eat & Drink: For a taste of the spicy specialty born here, head to **Hattie B's Hot Chicken** (✉ *112 19th Ave. S* ☎ *615/678–4794* ⊕ *www.hattieb.com*). Music City lives up to its name, with storefront after storefront on Broadway piping music out its doors. Duck into any of the bars for a nightcap, or to get the night started.

Stay: What's better than fine art, fine meals, and comfortable, modern rooms? **21c Museum Hotel Nashville** (✉ *221 2nd Ave. N* ☎ *615/610–6400* ⊕ *www.21cmuseumhotels.com*) has all three. You'll feel as if you've stepped back in time at the **Fairlane Hotel** (✉ *401 Union St.* ☎ *615/988–8511* ⊕ *www.fairlanehotel.com*), but the service and amenities will match your present-day expectations.

Breakfast: At **417 Union** (✉ *417 Union St.* ☎ *615/401–7241* ⊕ *www.417union.com*), the service is attentive and friendly, with delicious breakfast basics such as

shrimp and grits and chicken and waffles served in a lively spot filled with military memorabilia. Plus, there's a full bar for noteworthy Bloody Marys.

Day 2: Nashville, TN, to Memphis, TN

212 miles (3 hours without traffic and stops)

It's all "Music Highway" heading southwest to Memphis, the bluesy sister to Nashville's country and pop heritage. You'll cross the Tennessee River once more, and see more woodlands along the way, including a cut through the Hatchie National Wildlife Refuge.

ALONG THE WAY

Nature: Natchez Trace State Park's (✉ *24845 Natchez Trace Rd.* ☎ *731/968–3742* ⊕ *www.tnstateparks.com*) 48,000 acres of public lands and lakes offer hiking, fishing, and pontoon cruises.

Town: Hit the halfway mark at Lexington, Tennessee, for a stretch and brief rest from the road. Explore the Civil War battleground at nearby **Parkers Crossroads** (☎ *731/968–1191* ⊕ *www.parkerscrossroads.org*), which is convenient for its self-guided driving tour.

Eat & Drink: A top-secret rub is just one reason **Bozo's Hot-Pit Bar-B-Q** (✉ *342 U.S. 79* ☎ *901/294–3400* ⊕ *www.bozoshotpitbar-b-q.com*) in Mason has been around for nearly 100 years. Make sure to get a piece of the homemade pie-of-the-day to go, and hope it's the unbeatable pecan pie.

MEMPHIS

Do: Start your stay on a high note along Beale Street. The area started as a commercial and entertainment hub for the area's African Americans around the time of the Civil War, and was reborn half a century later as the incubator for the Memphis blues sound, courtesy of Muddy Waters and B. B. King.

The **Mason Temple** (✉ *930 Mason St.* ☎ *901/947–9300* ⊕ *www.cogic.org*), home base for the Church of God in Christ denomination, was where Martin Luther King Jr. gave his "I've been to the mountaintop" speech in 1968, foreshadowing his untimely death. Just one day after his speech, he was assassinated at the Lorraine Motel; today it's one of the buildings that make up the must-see **National Civil Rights Museum** (✉ *450 Mulberry St.* ☎ *901/521–9699* ⊕ *www. civilrightsmuseum.org*).

Eat & Drink: Memphis is a barbecue town. You can't go wrong with the ribs or the chopped pork sandwich at **Interstate Barbecue** (✉ *2265 S. 3rd St.* ☎ *901/775–2304* ⊕ *www.interstatebarbecue.com*). The shop's barbecue spaghetti may seem out of place, but it's a pasta-and-pork showstopper.

Stay: The **Guesthouse at Graceland** (✉ *3600 Elvis Presley Blvd.* ☎ *800/238–2000* ⊕ *www.guesthousegraceland.com*) is a destination hotel, complete with a music venue, so there's plenty to do and see on-site. But if you're an Elvis fan, the biggest perk is being within steps of the Graceland Mansion where The King lived.

Breakfast: From fancy lemon ricotta pancakes to basic buttermilk, **Staks** (✉ *4615 Poplar Ave.* ☎ *901/509–2367* ⊕ *www. stakspancakes.com*) makes them all. Or you can griddle them yourself, with a "Pour Your Own" option.

Day 3: Memphis, TN, to Jackson, MS

209 miles (3 hours without traffic and stops)

Head south into the Magnolia State from Tennessee, pausing for authentic southern food and to explore the Natchez Trace Parkway and the Ross Barnett Reservoir Overlook.

Extend Your Trip

From Nashville or Memphis: The Great American Music Road Trip *(Ch. 7)*

From Memphis: Along the Mississippi *(Ch. 2)*

From Charleston or Atlanta: Civil War Battlefields and History *(Ch. 2)*

ALONG THE WAY

Detour: Add about an extra half hour to your travel time today to visit the small town of Sumner, MS, home to the **Emmett Till Interpretive Center** (✉ *120 N. Court St.* ☎ *662/483–1231* ⊕ *www.emmett-till. org*). In 1955, 14-year-old Till was brutally murdered by two white men in the town of Money, 30 miles south of Sumner. The two men were eventually acquitted of his murder, which became a symbol of the horrific treatment of Black people in the American South.

Town: The scenic Natchez Trace Parkway runs through Ridgeland, MS, about 15 minutes north of Jackson. You may catch sight of an alligator at Ross Barnett Reservoir, with views of the 33,000-acre lake at the overlook.

Eat & Drink: The fried catfish at **Cock of the Walk** (✉ *141 Madison Landing Cir.* ☎ *601/856–5500* ⊕ *www.cockofthewalkrestaurant.com*) in Ridgeland is lauded by locals and offers a view of Ross Barnett Lake to boot.

JACKSON

Do: Center your visit to Jackson around a tour of the **home of Medgar Evans** (✉ *2332 Margaret W. Alexander Dr.* ☎ *601/345–7211* ⊕ *www.nps.gov/memy*), Mississippi's first NAACP field secretary and a civil rights activist who was assassinated in front of his home in 1963. **Tougaloo College** (✉ *500 W. County Line Rd.*

☎ 601/977–7700 ⊕ www.tougaloo.edu), a historically black college and university (HBCU) that served as a stopping place for the Freedom Riders, is also worth a visit. The campus was instrumental as a gathering place for the burgeoning civil rights movement. If you have time, make a visit to **the Mississippi Civil Rights Museum** ✉ (222 North St. ☎ 601/576–6800 ⊕ www.mscivilrightsmuseum.com) to learn more about the Mississippi activists who made the movement possible.

Eat & Drink: Sit down to a hearty dish of angel hair pasta with lump crabmeat or the smoked salmon pizza at **Bravo!** (✉ 4500 I–55 N ☎ 601/982–8111 ⊕ www.bravobuzz.com) The award-winning Italian restaurant has been around for more than 20 years, likely due to its generous portions and lively but comfortable environment.

Stay: You'll do fine in any one of the city's major hotel chains, but for something different, the historic **Old Capitol Inn** (✉ 226 N. State St. ☎ 601/359–9000 ⊕ www.oldcapitolinn.com) is the city's sole boutique hotel, with uniquely decorated rooms and a rooftop bar to unwind in after a day on the road.

Breakfast: The pies may take center stage here, but for a rotating menu of freshly baked scones, muffins, and sausage rolls you can grab and take to go, head over to **Urban Foxes** (✉ 826 North St. ☎ 769/572–5505 ⊕ www.urbanfoxesjxn.com).

Day 4: Jackson, MS, to Montgomery, AL

247 miles (4 hours without traffic and stops)

Pay homage as you travel between these two anchors of the civil rights movement, with the small but mighty Selma along the way. The 50th anniversary of the march at Edmund Pettus Bridge was honored in 2015 with a visit by President Obama.

ALONG THE WAY

Town: Selma is home to the iconic **Edmund Pettus Bridge** (☎ 800/457–3562 ⊕ www.selma-al.gov), where the late Senator John Lewis and others were brutally attacked on "Bloody Sunday" in early March 1965 for pushing to secure the right to vote. The **National Voting Rights Museum and Institute** (✉ 6 U.S. 80 E ☎ 334/526–4340 ⊕ www.nvrmi.com) captures the effort from the start, with photos and stories of the foot soldiers who took part in the marches and exhibits of what a jail cell and voting booth looked like at the time.

Eat & Drink: The wood-cabin environment of **Tally-Ho** (✉ 509 Mangum Ave. ☎ 334/872–1390 ⊕ www.tallyhoselma.com) in Selma is as much a draw as the steaks. **Lannie's Bar-B-Q Spot** (✉ 2115 Minter Ave. ☎ 334/874–4478) is far from fancy, but the pulled-pork sandwich and fried okra are local favorites. Both are under 10 minutes away from the Edmund Pettus Bridge.

MONTGOMERY

Do: You may have a hard time choosing among the wealth of civil rights movement exhibits here. No matter what, be sure to visit the **Rosa Parks Museum** (✉ 252 Montgomery St. ☎ 334/241–8615 ⊕ www.troy.edu)—situated where the icon was arrested for not sitting on the back of a bus—and the **Civil Rights Memorial Center** (✉ 400 Washington Ave. ☎ 334/956–8439 ⊕ www.splcenter.org). Both offer unique and deeply moving perspectives that encourage self-reflection. If you have time, other spots include the **Freedom Riders Museum** (✉ 210 S. Court St. ☎ 334/414–8647 ⊕ www.ahc.alabama.gov), the **Legacy Museum** (✉ 115 Coosa St. ☎ 334/386–9100 ⊕ www.museumandmemorial.eji.org), and the **National Memorial for Peace and Justice** (✉ 417 Caroline St.).

Eat & Drink: Treat yourself to **Vintage Year** (✉ 405 Cloverdale Rd. ☎ 334/819–7215 ⊕ www.vymgm.com), and make sure to order from the thoughtful wine list; the restaurant started as the city's only wine shop. You'll find everything from expertly cooked steaks to crab cakes to pasta dishes here.

Stay: Red Bluff Cottage (✉ *551 Clay St.* ☎ *334/264–0056* ⊕ *www.redbluffcottage.com*) is a four-room Old South–style bed-and-breakfast within blocks of many historic sites, including the Alabama State Capitol building.

Breakfast: Stop by **Cahawba House** (✉ *31 S. Court St.* ☎ *334/356–1877* ⊕ *www.cahawbahouse.com*) for cinnamon beignets and biscuits, served with locally sourced honey and jams. Top your biscuit with Conecuh sausage, an Alabama staple.

Day 5: Montgomery, AL, to Savannah, GA

334 miles (5 hours, 30 minutes without traffic and stops)

Head into Georgia's first city by way of college towns important to the civil rights movement, like Tuskegee in Alabama.

ALONG THE WAY

Town: You won't get too far into today's drive before reaching **Tuskegee University** (✉ *1200 W. Montgomery Rd., Tuskegee, AL* ☎ *334/727–8011* ⊕ *www.tuskegee.edu*), the HBCU that hosted training for the Tuskegee Airmen, and can claim Booker T. Washington, George Washington Carver, and the first African American National Book Award winner, Ralph Ellison, among its alumni. Take a few hours to tour the campus—the only one to have a National Historic Site designation—including a museum and grounds dedicated to its iconic graduates.

Roadside Attraction: Get in touch with your inner school kid at the **Lunch Box Museum** (✉ *3218 Hamilton Rd.* ☎ *706/653–6240* ⊕ *www.therivermarketantiques.com*) in

Columbus, Georgia. If you'd rather stay in the car, the **Museum of Wonder: Drive-Thru** (✉ *970 AL-169, Seale, AL* ⊕ *www.museumofwonder.com*) about 15 minutes south of Columbus, offers a 24-7 opportunity to get a glimpse of hundreds of oddities and art, some spooky and some kooky.

Eat & Drink: Hefty sandwiches served in an old train depot make the **Railroad Café** (✉ *117 Lowe St.* ☎ *478/821–5252* ⊕ *www.rrcafe.biz*) in Fort Valley, Georgia, a worthwhile stop. After lunch, get a proper welcome to the Peach State at **Lane Southern Orchards** (✉ *50 Lane Rd.* ☎ *800/277–3224* ⊕ *www.lanesouthernorchards.com*). You can't go wrong with the peach ice cream or a peach cobbler.

SAVANNAH

Do: While Savannah isn't huge on civil rights history, it makes a nice stopping point before Charleston. As one of the United States's first planned cities, you'll find plenty of history here, including its connected squares and famed **Forsyth Park** (✉ *2 W. Gaston St.* ☎ *912/351–3841* ⊕ *www.savannahga.gov*). Get a lay of the land with a trolley tour, hopping on and off to explore historic sites such as the **First African Baptist Church** (✉ *23 Montgomery St.* ☎ *912/233–6597* ⊕ *www.firstafricanbc.com*), the **Owens-Thomas House & Slave Quarters** (✉ *124 Abercorn St.* ☎ *912/790–8889* ⊕ *www.telfair.org*), and the **Cathedral of St. John the Baptist** (✉ *222 E. Harris St.* ☎ *912/233–4709* ⊕ *www.savannahcathedral.org*), one of the nation's largest Catholic churches in the South. The shops along River Street make for easy souvenir hunting. The area can get lively at night as visitors take advantage of the historic district's open container laws.

Eat & Drink: For dinner, make reservations at the James Beard Award–winning **Grey** (✉ *109 Martin Luther King Jr. Blvd.* ☎ *912/662–5999* ⊕ *www.thegreyrestaurant.com*). Later, walk to the Perry Hotel for a delicious rooftop cocktail at the **Peregrin** (✉ *256 E. Perry St.* ☎ *912/559–8333*

www.peregrinsavannah.com). For something less sceney but with more of a party vibe, any bar along Bay Street, River Street, or at the city market will do.

Stay: The **Hyatt Regency Savannah** (✉ 2 W. Bay St. ☎ 912/238–1234 ⊕ www.hyatt. com) and the **Westin Savannah Harbor Golf Resort & Spa** (✉ 1 Resort Dr. ⊕ www. marriott.com) offer relaxing views of the Savannah River, and are perfectly situated for walking around downtown and River Street. Gorgeous Airbnb rentals in historic homes abound here, too.

Breakfast: Enjoy fresh pastries, a perfect cappuccino, and dreamy macarons at **Café M** (✉ 128 E. Bay St. ☎ 912/712–3342 ⊕ www.cafemsavannah.com), an authentic Parisian bistro.

Day 6: Savannah, GA, to Charleston, SC

107 miles (2 hours without traffic and stops)

These cities may look familiar in landscape, with cobblestone streets and Spanish moss hanging from the trees, but Charleston's got a Lowcountry flavor all its own, distinguished by shrimp and grits, she-crab soup, and Frogmore stew.

ALONG THE WAY

Eat & Drink: Beaufort's **Dockside** (✉ 71 Sea Island Pkwy. ☎ 843/379–3288 ⊕ www. docksidebeaufort.com) overlooks the water and serves just about any kind of seafood you may want. While their version of Frogmore stew is called by its more common name, Lowcountry boil, the key ingredients are all there: big shrimp, smoked sausage, corn on the cob, and potatoes. Paired with their hush puppies, it's a delicious combination.

Detour: The **Gullah Geechee Cultural Heritage Corridor** (⊕ www.gullahgeecheecorridor.org) is a 12,000-square-mile stretch that acknowledges the culture,

language, and history of the West African descendants who were enslaved across the coastlands of South Carolina, North Carolina, Georgia, and Florida. You'd be remiss not to visit at least one of the history centers or museums dedicated to the centuries-old culture while you're in the area. Hilton Head Island, Johns Island, James Island, or Beaufort are stops that won't take you too far out of your way.

CHARLESTON

Do: You may be tempted to just stroll the city's charming historic downtown—and by all means do—but be sure to make a trip to the **Charleston City Market** (✉ 188 Meeting St. ☎ 843/937–0920 ⊕ www. thecharlestoncitymarket.com) for a handwoven basket while you're here. Pay tribute to the nine parishioners who lost their lives as a result of a shocking hate crime in 2015 at **Emanuel African Methodist Episcopal** (✉ 110 Calhoun St. ☎ 843/722–2561 ⊕ www.motheremanuel.com), the oldest AME church in the South.

Eat & Drink: If you can get a dinner reservation at **Husk** (✉ 76 Queen St. ☎ 843/577–2500 ⊕ www.huskrestaurant. com), you'll be wowed with its foodie-worthy elevations of common South Carolina staples—think Carolina rice, catfish, cornbread, and locally sourced vegetables.

Stay: There's an abundance of boutique hotels and historic-building accommodations in Charleston, so you have plenty of options. The most luxurious of the set, like the **French Quarter Inn** (✉ 166 Church St. ☎ 843/722–1900 ⊕ www.fqicharleston.com), can set you back more than $500 a night. If it's more about the sights than it is the stay, you may find that an Airbnb in one of the historic homes is your best bet.

Breakfast: Hit **The Daily** (✉ 652 King St. ☎ 843/619–0151 ⊕ www.shopthedaily. com) for creative coffee creations, squeezed-on-the-spot juices, and a

The Eternal Flame at the Martin Luther King Jr. National Historic Site symbolizes the continuing efforts to realize Dr. King's dreams of equality.

rotating cast of freshly baked pastries and take-out options.

Day 7: Charleston, SC, to Atlanta, GA

300 miles (5 hours without traffic and stops)

It's not the most scenic route, but as you head north, look for the lush golf greens of Augusta and get ready for the multilane metropolis where speedy driving belies any reputation about the "slow" South.

ALONG THE WAY

Town: Augusta boasts more than just the Masters Tournament. It sits on the banks of the Savannah River, so a stroll along the riverwalk is a low-key way to get a view of the town. Swamp life abounds at the **Phinizy Center** (✉ *1858 Lock and Dam Rd.* ☎ *706/828–2109* ⊕ *www.phinizy-center.org*); kids will get a kick out of river otter and turtle sightings.

Eat & Drink: Abel Brown (✉ *491 Highland Ave.* ☎ *706/738–6491* ⊕ *www.abel-brownaugusta.com*) in Augusta is where to go for oysters. The Johnny cake served with pimento cheese is a slice of savory southern charm.

ATLANTA

Do: The **National Center for Civil and Human Rights** (✉ *100 Ivan Allen Jr. Blvd.* ☎ *678/999–8990* ⊕ *www.civilandhuman-rights.org*) is a three-level, 43,000-square-foot, interactive, multisensory immersion into both the U.S. civil rights movement and global human rights efforts, complete with handwritten journals and personal items from Martin Luther King Jr. Speaking of King, stop by the Sweet Auburn district for a visit to **M.L.K.'s childhood home** (✉ *501 Auburn Ave. NE*), the **King National Historic Park** (✉ *450 Auburn Ave. NE* ☎ *404/331–5190* ⊕ *www.nps.gov/malu*), the **Ebenezer Baptist Church** (✉ *101 Jackson St. NE* ☎ *404/688–7300* ⊕ *www.ebenezeratl.org*), and the **King Center** (✉ *449 Auburn Ave. NE* ☎ *404/526–8900* ⊕ *www.thekingcenter*.

org), which is where Dr. King and Coretta Scott King are buried.

Eat & Drink: Get a delicious meal and a craft beer or cocktail, then work it all off with a few games at **Ponce City Market** (⊠ *675 Ponce De Leon Ave. NE* ☎ *404/900–7900* ⊕ *www.poncecitymarket.com*). The massive food court will have something for everyone, whether it's Hop's Chicken, the award-winning H&F Burger, or a handy slice at Pizza Jeans. The rooftop midway is the perfect blend of adult amusement with classics like skee ball and mini-golf and a full bar.

Stay: Hotel Clermont (⊠ *789 Ponce De Leon Ave. NE* ☎ *470/485–0485* ⊕ *www. hotelclermont.com*) is within walking distance of Ponce City Market, and as a former "motor hotel," it only makes sense to book a night or two to close out your road trip. You'll fancy the midcentury-modern decor and boho-chic vibe of the lobby. The French brasserie-style Tiny Lou's is worth a visit for dinner, too, but if you're still full from the PCM food court, make sure to at least get a nightcap on the hotel's rooftop or Lobby Bar.

Breakfast: "Relax, It's Just Eggs" reads one of the signs at **Thumbs Up Diner** (⊠ *573 Edgewood Ave. SE* ☎ *404/223–0690* ⊕ *www.thumbsupdiner.com*). And the vibe here is indeed a good kind of laid-back. Don't get antsy while you wait for a table; if the bar is available, go for it. The potato-packed skillets, fish and grits, and generous omelets make it all worthwhile.

The Great American Music Road Trip

Written by Katherine Chou

From Motown to hip-hop to grunge, American music is a cultural institution, spanning time periods and genres, reflecting the nation's social concerns, fashions,

and current events. Every region in the country seems to have its own musical influence, but when you focus on what truly makes American music what it is, it all comes down to its southern roots. Namely, every American genre has its foundation in at least one of three roots: blues, jazz, and Appalachian music.

This road trip is a journey through that family tree of American music. You'll explore the three root genres and their origin stories, visiting New Orleans for jazz, the Mississippi Delta for blues, and Appalachia for its eponymous music. Then you'll trace some of their descendants, including rockabilly and soul in Memphis and country in Nashville, while also visiting other areas with an important musical legacy, including northern Alabama and eastern Kentucky.

But this trip isn't just about the dusty past. Music arose in these centers because of their culture and creative energy, which continue to inspire musicians today. This itinerary has live music almost nightly, so you'll not only see a glimpse of the past of American music, but also where it's heading.

At a Glance

Start: New Orleans, LA

End: Nashville, TN

Miles Traveled: 1,882 miles

7

The Southeast and Florida THE GREAT AMERICAN MUSIC ROAD TRIP

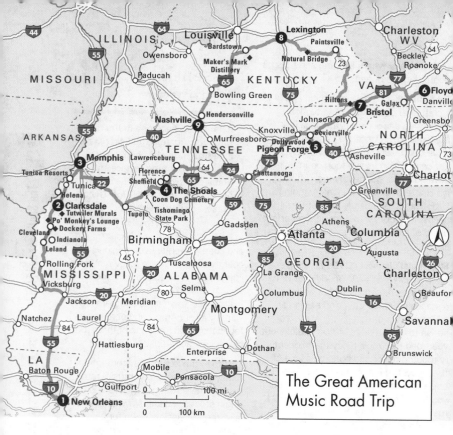

Suggested Duration: 11 days

States Visited: Alabama, Arkansas, Kentucky, Louisiana, Mississippi, Tennessee, Virginia

Key Sights: Dollywood; Graceland; the Grand Ole Opry; Muscle Shoals Recording Studios; Preservation Hall

Best Time to Go: This trip is doable year-round, but beware that summers are sweltering in New Orleans and Mississippi, and hurricane season in New Orleans stretches from June to November. Overall, spring balances the pros and cons best.

Day 1: New Orleans, LA

The trip starts with a focus on jazz, in the city often considered its birthplace. New Orleans has a lot to experience, so spend an extra day or two here if you can. Louis

Armstrong New Orleans International Airport is located 11 miles west of downtown. Rental cars are available at the airport, but parking around town is a hassle and tickets are common. Rent a car when you're ready to hit the road instead.

At the turn of the 20th century, jazz first gained popularity in the city, with elements adopted from different groups, like layered rhythms, a call-and-response format, and expressive voicing from West African enslaved people; chords, the piano, and brass instruments from Europeans; and the "tresillo" rhythm (used in second-line funeral music) from Cubans. Brass bands were already popular in the late-19th century nationwide, then came ragtime, and a new sound evolved to combine the two, with the addition of improvisation. When Louis Armstrong and Jelly Roll Morton added "swing" notes (which sounds like a note swinging into the next), jazz was born.

By the 1920s, most of the city's jazz players left for Chicago and other cities, so the genre continued to evolve outside of New Orleans. Most notably, Louis Armstrong pioneered the shift from collective improvising to solo improvising. With this new emphasis on individual style, jazz broke off into many subgenres, including swing, bebop, cool jazz, fusion, and jazz rock.

Do: Start at the **New Orleans Jazz Historical Park Visitor Center** (✉ 916 N. Peters St. ☎ 504/589–4841 ⊕ www.nps.gov/jazz), where jazz musicians who double as park rangers give lively demos and performances that shed insight into the city's musical heritage. The Old U.S. Mint location houses the **New Orleans Jazz Museum** (✉ 400 Esplanade Ave. ☎ 504/568–6993 ⊕ www.nolajazzmuseum.org), which features rotating exhibits, plus one permanent display at the end, which is—spoiler alert—Louis Armstrong's first cornet. Be sure to spend some time wandering the French Quarter, stopping at Jackson Square to watch musicians perform on the pedestrian mall and in front of St. Louis Cathedral.

The adjacent Tremé neighborhood, where Louis Armstrong's childhood home and Black Storyville once stood, is the cradle of jazz. **Louis Armstrong Park** (✉ 701 N. Rampart St. ☎ 504/658–3200 ⊕ www.nola.gov) celebrates the city's musical heritage and its most important landmark is Congo Square, the ancestral birthplace of New Orleans music. Most enslaved people spent their one day off each week here, drumming, dancing, singing, and chanting together, their polyrhythms laying the groundwork for jazz. These days, drummers can be found jamming in the square most Sunday afternoons. Perseverance Hall No. 4 is another landmark within the park; it was a society dance hall where jazz musicians played.

Other must-see musical sights in the city include the **Backstreet Cultural Museum** (✉ 1116 Henriette Delille St. ☎ 504/657–6700 ⊕ www.backstreetmuseum.org), whose spotlights on the city's African American culture and traditions tie into jazz; **Jelly Roll Morton's home** (✉ 1443 Frenchmen St.) in the Seventh Ward; **Fats Domino's home** (✉ 1208 Caffin Ave.) in the Ninth Ward; and **Music Box Village** (✉ 4557 N. Rampart St. ⊕ www.musicboxvillage.com) in the Bywater, a playground of sonic exploration where houses and their interiors are the instruments; it embodies New Orleans's experimental spirit today.

Finally, if you see a marching band trailed by dancing revelers, it's a "second line" and you should join. While other groups also paraded to commemorate the dead, African Americans turned these into joyous celebrations, which also influenced jazz. Second lines most commonly occur for weddings now. Sunday afternoons in the French Quarter and Tremé are your best bet for catching one.

Shop: Louisiana Music Factory (✉ 421 Frenchmen St. ☎ 504/586–1094 ⊕ www.louisianamusicfactory.com) stocks rare records from regional artists that only a local shop would have. It's hailed as the best record store in town.

Eat & Drink: For lunch, **Parkway Tavern** (✉ 538 Hagan Ave. ☎ 504/482–3047 ⊕ www.parkwaypoorboys.com) in Mid-City created New Orleans's iconic po'boy sandwich and remains a top choice to sample one. For dinner, **Gumbo Shop** (✉ 630 Saint Peter St. ☎ 504/525–1486 ⊕ www.gumboshop.com) in the French Quarter serves traditional Creole dishes, including a Best of New Orleans–poll gumbo. Afterward, live music is an absolute must, and **Preservation Hall** (✉ 726 Saint Peter St. ⊕ www.preservationhall.com) should be at the top of your list. Opened in 1961 to preserve traditional jazz, it's among the world's top music landmarks. If you can't get a ticket, other spots dedicated to jazz are **Fritzel's Jazz Club** (✉ *733 Bourbon St.* ☎ *504/586–4800* ⊕ *www.fritzelsjazz.net*), the city's oldest club, and the legendary **Tipitina's** (✉ *501 Napoleon Ave.* ☎ *504/895–8477* ⊕ *www.tipitinas.com*).

Stay: The **Soniat House** (✉ *1133 Chartres St.* ☎ *504/522–0570* ⊕ *www.soniathouse.com*) in the French Quarter is a perennial favorite with old-world elegance and antiques throughout. On the other end of the design spectrum, the **Old No. 77 Hotel & Chandlery** (✉ *535 Tchoupitoulas St.* ☎ *504/527–5271* ⊕ *www.old77hotel.com*) in the Central Business District (CBD) has a chic, contemporary look punctuated by industrial accents from the building's warehouse past.

Breakfast: A beignet and chicory café au lait at **Café du Monde** (✉ *800 Decatur St.* ☎ *504/525–4544* ⊕ *www.cafedumonde.com*) is a must, for breakfast or otherwise. They're open 24 hours, so you have no excuses. If you have more time, indulge in a jazz brunch like one at the ritzy **Commander's Palace** (✉ *1403 Washington Ave.* ☎ *504/899–8221* ⊕ *www.commanderspalace.com*) in the Garden District.

Day 2: New Orleans, LA, to Clarksdale, MS

347 miles (5 hours, 40 minutes without traffic and stops)

It's all about the blues today. After a stint on I-55, you'll reach the Mississippi Delta and Highway 61, aka the Blues Highway. It's a full day with a nearly five-hour haul to the first major stop, so be prepared.

The Delta blues is like the bassline of American popular music—you don't always notice it, but it's there, laying the foundation. It was born in the cotton fields along Highway 61, with the music of enslaved people at its core: spirituals (European hymns that enslaved people

Extend Your Trip

From Clarksdale or Memphis: Along the Mississippi *(Ch. 2)*

From Memphis or Nashville: The Civil Rights Trail *(Ch. 7)*

From Pigeon Forge: National Parks of the Southeast *(Ch. 7)*

From Lexington: The Great American Whisky Tour *(Ch. 7)*

adapted to reflect their lives) and work songs and field hollers (group and individual vocalizations and songs in a call and response pattern, mirroring the rhythms of their labor). Facing similar struggles despite their eventual freedom, the descendants of these enslaved people continued to use music as an emotional outlet, but in modern ways. Now equipped with guitars, they modified the call and response to a lone singer calling and their guitar responding, its sound distorted by sliding a bottleneck to mimic the human voice. Once the blues left the Delta, it combined with other music to spawn just about every modern genre we know.

ALONG THE WAY

Eat & Drink: Pop in to local favorite **Chuck's Dairy Bar** (✉ *20668 U.S. 61* ☎ *662/873–4021*) in Rolling Fork, Mississippi, for a Chuckburger—starring the dynamic duo of chili and slaw—and a chocolate shake.

Town: Stop in Leland, Mississippi, for the small **Highway 61 Museum** (✉ *307 N. Broad St.* ☎ *662/686–7646* ⊕ *www.highway61blues.com*), which spotlights area stars like Son Thomas. Then visit the nearby **Birthplace of Kermit the Frog Museum** (✉ *415 S Deer Creek Dr. E* ☎ *662/686–7383* ⊕ *www.birthplaceofthefrog.com*). No, it's not music related, although Kermit does play a mean banjo

Essential Listening

This is one road trip where a premade playlist is a necessity. Here are some must-plays.

"West End Blues" by Louis Armstrong

"Sweet Sixteen" by B. B. King

"Cross Road Blues" by Robert Johnson

"Try a Little Tenderness" by Otis Redding

"Hound Dog" and "Suspicious Minds" by Elvis Presley

"Hey Jude" by Wilson Pickett

"Next Girl" by The Black Keys

"Nobody Knows You When You're Down and Out" by Bessie Smith

"I Will Always Love You" and "Jolene" by Dolly Parton

"Can the Circle Be Unbroken" by the Carter Family

"Coal Miner's Daughter" by Loretta Lynn

"Uncle Pen" by Bill Monroe and His Blue Grass Boys

"Highwayman" by The Highwaymen (Johnny Cash, Waylon Jennings, Kris Kristofferson, Willie Nelson)

in "Rainbow Connection." Jim Henson grew up in Leland, and the frogs at nearby Deer Creek allegedly inspired him to create Kermit. An original Kermit puppet lives in the exhibit, banjo in hands.

Town: Indianola's stellar **B. B. King Museum** (✉ 400 2nd St. ☎ 662/887–9539 ⊕ www.bbkingmuseum.org) honors the hometown legend. Check out rare artifacts, play with high-tech exhibits, and meet a bunch of Lucilles (King's guitars).

Attraction: Seven miles east of Cleveland, MS, is **Dockery Farms** (✉ 229 Hwy. 8 ☎ 662/719–1048 ⊕ www.dockeyfarms.org), which many consider the birthplace of the blues because so many early greats lived and played here, including Father of the Delta Blues Charley Patton, Son House, Howlin' Wolf, and Robert Johnson.

Town: In the college town of Cleveland, the modern and interactive **GRAMMY Museum Mississippi** (✉ 800 W. Sunflower Rd. ☎ 662/441–0100 ⊕ www.grammymuseumms.org) isn't specifically about the blues, but it does have a section where Keb' Mo' teaches you to write a song with him, which you can then mix and save.

Photo Op: Juke joints arose as unofficial drinking/gambling/blues dens during the Jim Crow era. **Po' Monkey's Lounge** (✉ 99 Po Monkey Rd.) in Merigold was one of the Delta's last rural ones and unlike any other, thanks to its colorful owner Willie "Po' Monkey" Seaberry. It shut down after Seaberry's death in 2016, but the shack is still standing, at least for now.

CLARKSDALE

Do: You'll arrive late, so visit Clarksdale's sights the next morning. The **Delta Blues Museum** (✉ 1 Blues Alley ☎ 662/627–6820 ⊕ www.deltabluesmuseum.org) houses a critical marker on the blues timeline: Muddy Waters's cabin. Two seminal Library of Congress recordings were made here in 1941–42 and, after hearing just how good he sounded, spurred Waters to move to Chicago, changing the trajectory of music forever. **The Blues Crossroads** (✉ 599 N. State St.), marked by three guitars, is the Delta blues photo. Robert Johnson was the most influential bluesman of all time, but legend has it that he sold his soul to the devil for his mind-blowing guitar skills, right at these very crossroads.

Shop: In Clarksdale, pick up records, art prints, souvenirs, and insider information on everything Clarksdale and the blues at the eclectic **Cat Head Delta Blues & Folk Art** shop (✉ *252 Delta Ave.* ☎ *662/624–5992* ⊕ *www.cathead.biz*).

Eat & Drink: Kill two birds with one stone and chow down at **Ground Zero** (✉ *387 Delta Ave.* ☎ *662/621–9009* ⊕ *www. groundzerobluesclub.com*) while enjoying live blues. Try the fried catfish, a Delta staple, or fried chicken.

Stay: Fancy it's not, but the **Shack Up Inn** (✉ *001 Commissary Cir Rd.* ☎ *662/624–8329* ⊕ *www.shackupinn.com*) is the closest you'll get to the Delta blues in your sleep. The converted sharecropper cabins, corrugated tin roof and all, also contain some welcome anachronisms like air-conditioning. In the town center, the **Travelers Hotel** (✉ *212 3rd St.* ☎ *662/483–0693* ⊕ *www.stayattravelers.com*) is a modern option with an artsy vibe.

Breakfast: Head to **Our GrandMa's House of Pancakes** (✉ *115 3rd St.* ☎ *662/592–5290*) for a classic breakfast, delivered with a smile.

Day 3: Clarksdale, MS, to Memphis, TN

101 miles (2 hours without traffic and stops)

It's more blues today, plus a little bit of soul. It's a short and straightforward drive along Highway 61 with a detour to Arkansas, a stop in Tunica, and then on to Memphis.

ALONG THE WAY

Detour: Sixteen miles south of Clarksdale on Route 49 are the **Tutwiler Murals**. They depict the pivotal moment when composer W. C. Handy first heard the blues, performed by a man who sang about a dog and played guitar with a knife. Confused? So was Handy. But he was intrigued enough to later adapt and compose the first commercially successful blues song ("Memphis Blues"). The murals also pay tribute to Tutwiler's Sonny Boy Williamson and to Delta landscapes.

Town: Take a 30-minute-return trip off Highway 61 to Helena, Arkansas, to watch the renowned King Biscuit Time radio show broadcast at the Delta Cultural Center. They've aired live performances by the top blues artists since 1941, making it the oldest daily show in America. It runs from 12:15 pm to 12:45 pm on weekdays. The **Delta Cultural Center** (✉ *141 Cherry St.* ☎ *870/338–4350* ⊕ *www.deltaculturalcenter.com*) also has a worthwhile interactive exhibit on the region's blues, gospel, and country history.

Eat & Drink: Follow the blues legends of yore and the locals of today into the **Blue & White Restaurant** (✉ *1355 U.S. 61* ☎ *662/363–1371* ⊕ *www.blueandwhiterestaurant.com*) in Tunica to try their Delta Fried Green Tomatoes.

Town: The Gateway to the **Blues Museum** (✉ *13625 U.S. 61* ⊕ *www.tunicatravel. com*) in Tunica Resorts is housed in a photogenic rustic train depot from 1895. The well-designed museum tells stories about the blues pioneers, and also connects their impact to later musicians from different genres, including the British Invasion bands. You can even assess the Delta blues' impact on you by recording your own blues song here.

MEMPHIS

Do: The **Stax Museum of American Soul Music** (✉ *926 E. McLemore Ave.* ☎ *901/261–6338* ⊕ *www.staxmuseum. com*) is easiest to reach by car. After Motown, Stax was the second-biggest soul music studio and was instrumental in the "Memphis sound" of stars like Otis Redding and Booker T & the MGs. Be sure to cut loose on the museum's disco floor and gawk at Isaac Hayes's

1972 Cadillac Eldorado with 24K gold accents and shag-fur carpeting. Downtown, the **National Civil Rights Museum** (✉ *450 Mulberry St.* ☎ *901/521–9699* ⊕ *www.civilrightsmuseum.org*) is located at the Lorraine Motel, where Martin Luther King Jr. was assassinated. While it's a must-see for obvious reasons, it also traces the African American struggle for equality, giving context to the evolution of not just soul music, which was connected to the civil rights movement, but also the blues, gospel, and all other music rooted in the African American experience.

Shop: On Beale Street, the **A. Schwab general store** (✉ *163 Beale St.* ☎ *901/523–9782* ⊕ *www.a-schwab.com*) is the last original Beale Street business standing (c. 1876). An old-school soda fountain upstairs adds to the nostalgia, and a museum shows the area's history. Downstairs is packed with souvenirs and odd novelty items.

Eat & Drink: Barbecue in Memphis is a serious business. Local opinions can be divided, but two excellent choices are Charlie Vergos' **Rendezvous** (✉ *52 S. 2nd St.* ☎ *901/523–2746* ⊕ *www.hogsfly. com*) for dry-rubbed ribs and **Central BBQ** (✉ *147 E. Butler Ave.* ☎ *901/672–7760* ⊕ *www.eatcbq.com*) for pulled pork. Barbecue nachos at the latter are also popular. For live music, head to Beale Street, the home of the blues. After the Civil War, the street became a southern hub for Black entertainment, attracting musicians from all over. B. B. King led the Memphis blues sound, so it's fitting that his eponymous club, **BB King's Blues Club** (✉ *143 Beale St.* ☎ *901/524–5464* ⊕ *www.bbkings.com*) remains a top destination for live music here.

Stay: The boutique **Hu. Hotel** (✉ *79 Madison Ave.* ☎ *833/585–0030* ⊕ *www. huhotelmemphis.com*) has a sleek midcentury-modern look and a trendy vibe (that period in their name is not a typo). The rooftop bar is also perfect for watching sunsets and the Mighty Lights show on the Hernando De Soto Bridge. For upscale history, the **Peabody Hotel** (✉ *149 Union Ave.* ☎ *901/529–4000* ⊕ *www.peabodymemphis.com*) has welcomed the fanciest of folks since 1869, and also the fanciest of ducks since the 1930s. The daily Peabody Duck March is worth a look. They waddle out to spend the day splashing in the lobby fountain before retreating for the evening to their $200,000 penthouse.

Breakfast: Sunrise Memphis (✉ *670 Jefferson Ave.* ☎ *901/552–3168* ⊕ *www. sunrise901.com*) loves biscuit sandwiches and they load them up with creative southern goodness. The setting is equally fun, as are the beermosas (Miller Genuine Draft and orange juice).

Day 4: Memphis

Memphis deserves a full day of your time, and today you'll explore its rockabilly and soul history. If you'd rather not drive today, a free shuttle (with entrance ticket) takes you between Sun Studio, Graceland, and the Rock 'n' Soul Museum.

For much of the 20th century, Memphis was a hotbed of musical innovation. Artists came from across the region, including B. B. King, Howlin' Wolf, Jerry Lee Lewis, Johnny Cash, Elvis Presley, Otis Redding, and Al Green. Their various musical styles mixed with Memphis's urban flavor in a massive melting pot and recombined into dynamic new genres.

Elvis Presley, who frequented Beale Street and Black gospel churches growing up, ignited a cultural revolution with his blend of blues and country that defined rockabilly. It was characterized by a driving beat, expressive vocals, guitar-break solos, and Sam Phillips's echo effect at Sun Studio. While it fizzled out by the end of the 1950s, it led directly to rock and roll, then punk, heavy metal,

New Wave, and emo. Delta blues also transformed in Memphis, going electric with an upbeat tempo, jazz elements, and a band (sometimes with horns). B. B. King led the way with his expressive vibrato and note bending, which paved the way for rock's lead guitarists. Soul grew as a secular form of gospel, equally wrought with emotion that voiced the African American experience, but mixed with rhythm and blues (which, to over-simplify, combined blues and swing jazz). In Memphis, soul, led by Al Green, took on a purer, more gospel-leaning sound, often backed by radiant horns. By the 1970s, soul gave way to funk, disco, rap, hip-hop, neo soul, and contemporary R&B.

Do: Start at **Sun Studio** (✉ 706 Union Ave. ☏ 800/441–6249 ⊕ www.sunstudio.com), the birthplace of rock and roll. Outtakes from sessions and behind-the-scenes stories about the legends who got their big breaks here (including B. B. King, Ike Turner, and the "Million Dollar Quartet" rockabilly artists) keep the tour captivating. Plus you can stand on the X where a 19-year-old Elvis recorded his debut single, "That's All Right." Follow the King's footsteps to **Graceland** (✉ Elvis Presley Blvd. ☏ 901/332–3322 ⊕ www.graceland.com) next. This sprawling shrine to Elvis takes on average three-to-four hours to visit. Even if you're not an Elvis fan, don't be surprised if you become one by the end; in addition to the eye-popping design of the rooms, a wealth of personal artifacts and exhibits offer glimpses into the human side of the icon. Back on Beale Street, the Smithsonian's **Memphis Rock 'n' Soul Museum** (✉ 191 Beale St. ☏ 901/205–2533 ⊕ www.memphisrocknsoul.org) tracks the stories of these two influential genres. Well-stocked jukeboxes highlight each decade and tell the stories in song.

Eat & Drink: For lunch, **Coletta's Pizzeria** (✉ 1063 South Pkwy. E ☏ 901/948–7652 ⊕ www.colettas.net) is out by Stax;

don't miss their barbecue pizza. For dinner, **Bar-B-Q-Shop** (✉ 1782 Madison Ave. ☏ 901/272–1277 ⊕ www.thebar-b-qshop.com) near Overton Square has barbecue spaghetti, along with the usual barbecue favorites done their way. For live music with fewer tourists than Beale Street, **Wild Bill's** (✉ 1580 Vollintine Ave. ☏ 901/206–3272 ⊕ www.wildbillmemphis.com) is a venerable juke joint in Midtown.

Breakfast: As the oldest diner in Memphis, the **Arcade** (✉ 540 S. Main St. ☏ 901/526–5757 ⊕ www.arcaderestaurant.com) is worth a visit whether you pick the Elvis booth or not. If you do sit there, you almost have to order the peanut butter and banana sandwich; if you resist, the sweet potato pancakes are a near-delicacy.

Day 5: Memphis, TN, to The Shoals, AL

203 miles (3 hours, 30 minutes without traffic and stops)

Today's drive gives you some more Elvis history, then takes you to northern Alabama, where two small studios in the middle of nowhere pumped out a distinct, genre-spanning sound. Take I–69 from Memphis via I–69 to I–269 N and I–22 E to Tupelo. From there, U.S. 45 connects you to the scenic Natchez Trace Parkway, which is a peaceful, forested drive through lands rich in Native American and American history.

FAME Studios in tiny Muscle Shoals pioneered the signature Muscle Shoals sound that defined southern soul in the 1960s. Often described as swampy, it's a mix of country, gospel, and rhythm and blues generated by the studio's session musicians. Artists like Aretha Franklin, Wilson Pickett, and Etta James recorded here initially, but as those records charted, artists across all genres came (and continue to come) seeking that special sauce. In 1969, FAME's rhythm-section session musicians broke off and opened Muscle Shoals Sound Studio in Sheffield, still with that calling-card sound. They, too, were successful, drawing the likes of the Rolling Stones ("Brown Sugar" and "Wild Horses" were recorded here), Bob Dylan, Willie Nelson, and many more.

ALONG THE WAY

Town: At the **Elvis Presley Birthplace** (✉ 306 Elvis Presley Dr. ☎ 662/841–1245 ⊕ www.elvispresleybirthplace.com) in Tupelo, see a slice of Elvis's life long before the sideburns, gold lamé suits, and jungle room. You can peek inside the humble shotgun house he entered the world. **Tupelo Hardware Co.** (✉ 114 Main St. ☎ 662/842–4637 ⊕ www.tupelohardware.com) is where Elvis bought his first guitar and the spot he stood to make the purchase is marked.

Eat & Drink: Johnnie's Drive-In (✉ 908 E. Main St. ☎ 662/842–6748) is Tupelo's oldest restaurant (1945) and a local favorite (of a teenaged Elvis, too). Get a dough burger, also known as a slug burger elsewhere in northern Mississippi. Johnnie's version has a combo of dough and secret ingredients mixed into the meat.

Nature: If you're missing nature, the Natchez Trace Parkway is studded with opportunities for a walk. In **Tishomingo State Park** (☎ 662/438–6914 ⊕ www.mdwfp.com), the 1.8-mile Bear Creek Nature Trail has views over the valley and includes a suspension-bridge crossing and scenic rock formations.

Roadside Attraction: Visiting the **Coon Dog Cemetery** (✉ 4945 Coondog Cemetery Rd. ☎ 256/383–0783 ⊕ www.coondogcemetery.com) requires a rerouting, but when else will you visit one? Never, because this is the only one. Beloved raccoon-hunting dogs rest here permanently, their spots marked by often hand-chiseled headstones. Turn off Natchez Trace Parkway at Maud Road to get here.

THE SHOALS

Do: Both **FAME Studios** (✉ 603 Avalon Ave. ☎ 256/381–0801 ⊕ www.fame2.com) and **Muscle Shoals Sound Studio** (✉ 3614 N. Jackson Hwy. ☎ 256/978–5151 ⊕ www.muscleshoalssoundstudio.org) can be toured. The original Muscle Shoals Sound Studio has even been restored to its 1970s state. Other spots include the **Alabama Music Hall of Fame** (✉ 617 U.S. 72 W ☎ 256/381–4417 ⊕ www.alamhof.org) and the **W. C. Handy Museum and Library** (✉ 620 W. College St. ☎ 256/760–6434 ⊕ www.wchandymuseum.org), which dives into this Father of the Blues' successful career as a bandleader, composer, businessman, and groundbreaker.

Eat & Drink: The nearby town of Florence has a creative—some might say hipster—vibe. For upscale, farm-to-table southern dishes with international flair, try **Odette's** (✉ 120 N. Court St. ☎ 256/349–5219 ⊕ www.odettealabama.com). For dessert, stop by old-school **Trowbridge's** (✉ 316 N. Court St. ☎ 256/764–1503) for their legendary orange-pineapple ice cream. For live music, just outside town, there's the novelty of **Tuscumbia's Rattlesnake Saloon** (✉ 1292 Mt. Mills Rd. ☎ 256/370–7220 ⊕ www.rattlesnakesaloon.net), inside a large cave, which was also a former hog pen.

Stay: The industrial chic **GunRunner Boutique Hotel** (✉ 310 E. Tennessee St. ☎ 855/269–4724 ⊕ www.gunrunnerhotel.com) in Florence features 10 luxury suites draped in local pride. Themed rooms include Muscle Shoals Sound, Sam Phillips, and Single Lock.

Breakfast: Stagg Grocery (✉ 1424 Huntsville Rd. ☎ 256/764–7382) is all about the basics—eggs, grits, sausage, bacon, biscuits, etc.—and they do it well. But if you're here on a Friday morning, snag the biscuit with chocolate gravy because it only appears then.

7

The Southeast and Florida THE GREAT AMERICAN MUSIC ROAD TRIP

Day 6: The Shoals, AL, to Pigeon Forge, TN

338 miles (6 hours without traffic and stops)

Enjoy a mix of southern gospel, rock, and blues today. It's a long drive and you'll lose an hour with the time-zone change. Take U.S. 43 N to Lawrenceburg, then U.S. 64 E and I-24 E to Chattanooga. I-75 N, I-40 E, and TN-66 S take you to Pigeon Forge.

Although they developed concurrently and influenced each other, the so-called southern gospel of white southerners was different from the gospel of Black southerners. Black gospel had far-reaching influences on popular music, from soul to rock, and was characterized by choirs and the shared experience, with emotive singing, improvisation, and a call-and-response format. White gospel also played a role in later genres, especially country, but it focused on the individual's search for salvation and featured male quartets singing in harmony. Some artists, like Elvis, were deeply influenced by both styles.

ALONG THE WAY

Town: The **James D. Vaughan Gospel Music Museum** (✉ *31 Public Sq.* ☎ *931/762–8991*) in Lawrenceburg, Tennessee, explores a father of southern gospel's contributions to the genre, which included popularizing it by sponsoring the first professional quartets and founding a record company. The small museum is inside the Chamber of Commerce. Ask at the second-floor office during business hours to gain entry.

Town: In Chattanooga, channel your inner rocker at the **Songbirds Experience** (✉ *35 Station St.* ☎ *423/531–2473* ⊕ *www.songbirdsfoundation.org*) to explore everything electric guitar. Hands-on exhibits invite you to, among other things, build a guitar, experiment with

amps, and learn to play. Then head to the **Bessie Smith Cultural Center and Chattanooga African American Museum** (✉ *200 E. Martin Luther King Blvd.* ☎ *423/266–8658* ⊕ *www.bessiesmithcc.org*) for a small exhibit on Bessie Smith. The Chattanooga native, often considered the greatest blues singer of all time, was a pioneer among the female blues singers who were all the rage in the 1920s.

Eat & Drink: Chattanooga's culinary scene focuses on creative, fresh, and natural. The local favorite for gourmet burgers (also with veggie options) is **Urban Stack** (✉ *12 W. 13th St.* ☎ *423/475–5350* ⊕ *www.urbanstack.com*). Go for the fried green tomato burger.

Photo Op: Now's your chance to snag a photo with Dolly Parton, and she won't blink. Sevierville's beloved daughter is immortalized in a statue in front of the **Sevier County Courthouse** (✉ *125 Court Ave.*).

PIGEON FORGE

Do: This Great Smoky Mountains town is famous for one thing: **Dollywood**, Dolly Parton's amusement park (✉ *2700 Dollywood Parks Blvd.* ☎ *800/365–5996* ⊕ *www.dollywood.com*). Not only is Dollywood a shrine to one of country's (and the country's) greatest music icons, but it's also an homage to the Great Smoky Mountains of her childhood. While there are museums that showcase Dolly's personal items, her tour bus, and a replica of the cabin she grew up in, there are also opportunities to watch craftspeople forge iron, blow glass, and more, keeping the area's heritage alive. Since this is Dolly's park, there's plenty of live music, too, including Appalachian, southern gospel, pop, oldies, and even a musical that chronicles Dolly's life, with some of her family members performing. And don't miss the roller coasters either; the Lightning Rod launches you up the hill at 45 mph, before dropping you at a 73-degree angle at 73 mph. Depending on what time you arrive in Pigeon Forge,

Elvis Presley lived at Graceland from 1957 until his death in 1977.

it might be best to save Dollywood for the next morning and afternoon.

Eat & Drink: Just so there are no surprises, Pigeon Forge is like kitsch on steroids. Most restaurants are chains or fast food, but if you roll into town on an empty stomach, **Local Goat** (✉ 2167 Parkway ☎ 865/366–3035 ⊕ www. localgoatpf.com) is a locally sourced, made-from-scratch New American restaurant with just enough oddball gourmet burgers to keep things interesting. They also have local craft beers on tap and craft cocktails.

Stay: Dollywood's own **DreamMore Resort** (✉ 2525 DreamMore Way ☎ 800/365–5996 ⊕ www.dollywood.com) is a comfortable and clean option. But the perks are the best part: free shuttle to the park or free parking, complimentary TimeSaver pass that lets you jump the line for most rides and get reserved seating at shows, discounted park tickets, and VIP treatment with a special entrance to the park.

Breakfast: Stick to the kitsch by visiting **Frizzle Chicken Farmhouse Café** (✉ 2785 Parkway ☎ 865/774–7707 ⊕ www. frizzlechickenfarmhousecafe.com). The breakfast is southern-style and the place is filled with 100 animatronic singing chickens.

Day 7: Pigeon Forge, TN, to Floyd, VA

233 miles (3 hours, 40 minutes without traffic and stops)

It's all about Appalachian music on this leg of the drive. If it's a Friday (which is when Floyd's Friday Night Jamboree takes place), head straight for Floyd to maximize time. Festivities start at 6:30 pm. From Pigeon Forge, head out to I–40 E, then I–81 N and VA-8 S to get to Floyd.

Along with blues and jazz, the third root genre of American music is Appalachian music (also called old-time or mountain music), which is characterized by acoustic string instruments and vocal harmonies. It was a product of various immigrant musical traditions brewing together in the isolated mountains. The most prominent components came from Irish, English, and Scottish settlers, who brought storytelling ballads about everyday struggles, hymns, jig and reel dancing, and the fiddle. Carrying on traditions from their enslaved ancestors, African Americans contributed a call-and-response structure and a precursor to the banjo, a Muslim African instrument that enslaved people re-created with hollowed-out gourds. The distinctive combination of fiddle and banjo was the driving force of this new music, as was a strong element of community.

ALONG THE WAY

Eat & Drink: If you spend the first half of the day at Dollywood, be sure to eat there before hitting the road. Dollywood's food has won awards in the amusement park world, like best pork barbecue at **Hickory House BBQ** (✉ *Craftsman's Valley* ⊕ *www.dollywood.com*). Whatever you do, don't skip the park's legendary cinnamon bread, whose flour comes from Dollywood's own grist mill. Another treat is the banana pudding, made from Dolly's personal recipe.

Town: Stop at the **Blue Ridge Music Center** (✉ *700 Foothills Rd.* ☎ *276/236–5309* ⊕ *www.blueridgemusiccenter.org*) in Galax, Virginia, to explore the evolution of Appalachian music. Fun, interactive exhibits let you mix mountain music and write lyrics.

FLOYD

Do: Floyd is a delightful small town where music, art, and farming live happily ever after. Join the community at the Friday Night Jamboree for the age-old Appalachian tradition of gathering for music and dance. **Floyd Country Store** (✉ *206 S. Locust St.* ☎ *540/745–4563* ⊕ *www. floydcountrystore.com*) has hosted this

version since the 1980s. The lineup is southern gospel for the first hour, followed up with two rollicking sets by traditional string bands. The music isn't just on the stage, though—performances spill onto the streets. If you can't work a Friday evening in Floyd into your itinerary, the Floyd Country Store also hosts Americana Afternoons on Saturdays at noon, which is acoustic roots music ranging from blues to jazz to bluegrass. Then the Sunday Music Jam runs practically all afternoon, with old-time music at 1:30 pm and bluegrass at 4 pm.

Eat & Drink: If you're attending the jamboree, grab a quick bite at the Floyd Country Store. They serve American classics, both old and new, and source from local farms as much as possible. For live music on non-jamboree days, both **Dogtown Roadhouse** (✉ *302 S. Locust St.* ☎ *540/745–6836* ⊕ *www. dogtownroadhouse.com*) and **Buffalo Mountain Brewery** (✉ *332 Webbs Mill Rd. N* ☎ *540/745–2491* ⊕ *www.buffalomountainbrewery.com*) host performances on weekend nights.

Stay: In the town center, **Floyd Hotel** (✉ *300 Rick Lewis Way* ☎ *540/745–6080* ⊕ *www.hotelfloyd.com*) is eco-friendly and artsy with small-town charm. For something different, Floyd Yurt Lodging (✉ *379 Parkway La. S* ☎ *540/505–4586* ⊕ *www.floydyurtlodging.com*) has one 30-foot yurt, complete with an indoor bathroom and a skylight view of the stars.

Breakfast: Many of the town's lodgings include breakfast, but if not, the **Pharmhouse Pharmacy & Café** (✉ *311 E. Main St.* ☎ *540/745–3333* ⊕ *www.thepharmhouse-rx.com*) serves the regulars, along with breakfast tacos in creative combinations.

Day 8: Floyd, VA, to Bristol, TN

164 miles (3 hours without traffic and stops)

From Floyd, take U.S. 221 S to Galax, VA. Then connect to I-77 N and I-81 S to get to Bristol, which is in both Tennessee and Virginia.

Country music emerged in 1927 at the Bristol recording sessions, dubbed the Big Bang of Country Music. With compelling artists and new audio technology producing better sound, records and radio beamed this new music far beyond the local communities. The biggest stars to emerge from the sessions were the Carter Family and Jimmie Rodgers, respectively known as the First Family and Father of Country Music. The Carter Family's music was rooted in traditional Appalachian ballads, but it was also progressive, particularly Maybelle Carter's guitar style. Known as the Carter scratch, Maybelle simultaneously played bass, rhythm, and melody, which was revolutionary at the time and continues to be emulated today. Mississippi-born Rodgers was also an innovator. His music incorporated different styles that he was exposed to as a traveling railroad worker, including blues and Swiss yodeling.

ALONG THE WAY

Eat & Drink: In downtown Galax, **Creekside Café** (✉ *1007 S. Main St.* ☎ *276/238–0407* ⊕ *www.facebook.com/creeksidecafegalax*) is a good old country diner that the locals love.

Detour: If it's a Saturday, the **Carter Family Fold** (✉ *3449 A. P. Carter Hwy.* ☎ *276/594–0676* ⊕ *www.carterfamilyfold.org*) in Hiltons, Virginia, hosts a weekly evening concert and dance party (Appalachian-style, of course, with flatfooting and clogging). On-site and open for viewing before the concert are A. P. Carter's original general store, which houses a museum about the family, and the cabin that A. P. was born in, which was relocated here.

BRISTOL

Do: Visit the well-designed, Smithsonian-affiliated **Birthplace of Country Music Museum** (✉ *101 Country Music Way* ☎ *423/573–1927* ⊕ *www.birthplaceofcountrymusic.org*) to learn about the Bristol sessions and their continued impact. Among the engaging exhibits, many of which are interactive, are curious facts about early audio technology, an audio appearance by Nirvana, and opportunities to sing along and dance. A good photo op is the Bristol Sessions murals, depicting many of the sessions' artists. It's on the Tennessee side of State Street (which is also the Virginia–Tennessee border).

Eat & Drink: Southern Craft BBQ in the **Sessions Hotel** complex (✉ *833 State St.* ☎ *276/285–5040* ⊕ *www.sessionshotel.com*) does gourmet takes on southern favorites, plus tacos with a barbecue treatment. There isn't much live music in town on a regular basis, but **Bloom Café & Listening Room** (✉ *606 State St.* ☎ *423/573–1602* ⊕ *www.bloomcafebristol.com*) hosts shows multiple nights a week. For straight-up drinking, Bristol has several craft breweries, including **Bristol Station Brews & Taproom** (✉ *41 Piedmont Ave.* ☎ *276/608–1220* ⊕ *www.bristolbrew.com*).

Stay: The Sessions Hotel, set in a complex of revitalized factories, features creative, industrial chic rooms that nod to the city's musical heritage. If the hard miles on the road have gotten to you, they also have an on-site spa and a relaxing rooftop bar.

Breakfast: Blackbird Bakery (✉ *56 Piedmont Ave.* ☎ *276/645–5754* ⊕ *www.blackbirdbakerybristol.com*) is a local favorite for their array of made-from-scratch doughnuts, pastries (including jalapeno bacon kolaches), pies, baklava, brownies, bread, and more.

Day 9: Bristol, TN, to Lexington, KY

271 miles (5 hours, 10 minutes without traffic and stops)

Today the focus is on country and bluegrass. From I–81 N, head to U.S. 23 N, the Country Music Highway. This National Scenic Byway snakes through the green mountains of eastern Kentucky, a region that has produced more country hitmakers per capita than any other. Homegrown stars include, from south to north, Patty Loveless, Loretta Lynn, Stapleton, Billy Ray Cyrus, and the Judds. Keep an eye out for road signs announcing whose hometown is coming up. This itinerary leaves U.S. 23 after Staffordsville (Chris Stapleton), so if you're looking for signs of Billy Ray or the Judds, detour to go farther north. After U.S. 23, head west for Lexington.

Bluegrass descended from Appalachian music, but with elements of blues and especially jazz mixed in. The whole genre boils down to one man: Bill Monroe, from western Kentucky. He started out playing mandolin in traditional string bands, but as his career progressed, he experimented with different sounds and musicians until he found a combination that became (and remains) the standard for bluegrass. The name for this new genre was even taken from his band, which was called the Blue Grass Boys. The instruments were upright bass, guitar, mandolin, banjo, and fiddle. The key components—and main differences from Appalachian music—were a lightning-fast tempo, a distinctive three-pick banjo style innovated by Earl Scruggs (now known as the Scruggs style), improvisation and soloing (jazz influences), and the characteristic "high, lonesome sound."

ALONG THE WAY

Eat & Drink: Some eastern Kentucky staples to look out for as you travel Route 23 are soup beans (pork-stewed pinto beans) with cornbread, salmon patties, and country ham. **Music Highway Grill** at Jenny Wiley State Resort Park (⌧ *419 Jenny Wiley Dr.* ☎ *606/889–1790* ⊕ *www.parks.ky.gov*) in Prestonsburg has all three, plus other Kentucky favorites.

Town: In Paintsville, the **U.S. 23 Country Music Highway Museum** (⌧ *100 Stave Branch Rd.* ☎ *606/297–7823* ⊕ *www. paintsvilletourism.com*) showcases the stars that hail from this region, with a memorabilia-filled display for each. It's small, but a nice homage to local heroes.

Nature: Stretch your legs with a short walk to 65-foot-high and 78-foot-long **Natural Bridge** (⌧ *2135 Natural Bridge Rd., Slade, KY* ☎ *606/663–2214* ⊕ *www. parks.ky.gov*). The shortest trail is 0.75 miles and you can walk to the top of bridge (be careful up there).

LEXINGTON

Do: Although Lexington isn't specifically a bluegrass hub, there's live bluegrass nearly every night somewhere in town, either formally or in a jam. Among these are two radio broadcasts you can attend. *Woodsongs Old-Time Radio Hour* broadcasts around the world from the historic **Lyric Theater** (⌧ *300 E. 3rd St.* ☎ *859/280–2201* ⊕ *www.lexingtonlyric.com*) on Monday nights while Red Barn Radio spotlights artists inspired by Appalachian Americana music; they broadcast on Wednesday nights from **ArtsPlace** (⌧ *161 N. Mill St.* ☎ *859/255–2951* ⊕ *www.lex-arts.org*). Both shows include live music and chats with the artists.

Eat & Drink: Blue Door Smokehouse (⌧ *226 Walton Ave.* ☎ *859/252–4227* ⊕ *www. bluedoorsmokehouse.com*) has such good barbecued brisket and other meaty favorites that they often sell out, so go early. Just note they're only open in the (early) evening on weekends; otherwise they close in the midafternoon.

Stay: Staying at the sleek **21c Museum Hotel** (✉ *167 W. Main St.* ☎ *859/899–6800* ⊕ *www.21cmuseumhotels.com*) is like spending the night at the MoMA, but legal. With four contemporary art galleries and art in every room and in the public spaces, there's always something that'll catch your eye.

Breakfast: Organic and locally sourced when possible, **Doodles** (✉ *262 N. Limestone* ☎ *859/317–8507* ⊕ *www. doodleslex.com*) is both fresh and creative. Try the Pigs & Puffs or the Dirty Shrimp & Grits. The Kentucky Hot Brown Quesadilla gets an honorable mention for its morning twist on an iconic Louisville creation.

Day 10: Lexington, KY, to Nashville, TN

225 miles (3 hours, 45 minutes without traffic and stops)

On today's drive, you'll go from bluegrass back to country. The route is straightforward with the Bluegrass Parkway taking you to Bardstown, then I-65 runs south all the way to Nashville, with a short detour in the suburbs of Hendersonville.

ALONG THE WAY
Town: With a downtown that looks like the classic American main street, Bardstown, Kentucky, has been hailed the Most Beautiful Small Town in America. If you're looking for a break, it's a nice place for a stroll.

Eat & Drink: Mammy's Kitchen (✉ *116 W. Stephen Foster Ave.* ☎ *502/350–1097* ⊕ *mammys-kitchen.business.site*) in Bardstown has a devoted local following, a space with personality, and home-cooked country food. You're in bourbon country, so try the bourbon Cinnabon flapjacks or the bourbon burger.

Detour: Bourbon tends to pop up in country songs a lot and you have to visit at least one distillery while in Bourbon Country. **Maker's Mark** (✉ *3350 Burks Spring Rd.* ☎ *270/865–2099* ⊕ *www. makersmark.com*) in Loretto has an old-timey setting with preserved mid-19th century distilling techniques. This detour adds less than 30 minutes to the day's drive.

Town: Around 20 miles outside Nashville, Hendersonville will always be home to Johnny and June Carter Cash. You can pay your respects to country's royal couple at **Hendersonville Memory Gardens** (✉ *353 Johnny Cash Pkwy.*), where they're buried.

NASHVILLE
Do: If you're not planning to attend a show at the **Grand Ole Opry** (✉ *2804 Opryland Dr.* ☎ *615/871–6779* ⊕ *www.opry.com*), stop in for the daytime backstage tour on your way into town. Sometimes they'll let you stand in the performers' spot onstage—in the famed wooden circle that was cut from the Ryman Auditorium stage. Downtown, the **Johnny Cash Museum** (✉ *119 3rd Ave. S* ☎ *615/256–1777* ⊕ *www. johnnycashmuseum.com*) houses an extensive collection of both public and private artifact offering different perspectives on his life. Upstairs, but under a separate ticket, is the **Patsy Cline Museum** (✉ *119 3rd Ave. S* ☎ *615/454–4722* ⊕ *www. patsymuseum.com*). Vignettes of her life are presented, along with artifacts. It's a relatively small exhibit, but provides a good look into her life.

Eat & Drink: Near downtown, family-owned **Peg Leg Porker's** (✉ *903 Gleaves St.* ☎ *615/829–6023* ⊕ *www.pegleg-porker.com*) hickory-smoked dry rubbed ribs are a favorite, as are the pulled-pork platter and fried pie. A night out at Lower Broadway's honky tonks is a must, preferably with boots on, which you can actually buy at one of the honky tonks. Stop in at **Tootsie's Orchid Lounge** (✉ *422 Broadway* ☎ *615/726–0463* ⊕ *www.tootsies.*

net) to soak up some history. It's across the alley from Ryman, so Opry stars used to sneak out the back after their set to wind down (or up?) at Tootsie's. **Robert's Western World** (✉ *416 Broadway B* ☎ *615/244–9552* ⊕ *www.robertswesternworld.com*) is the aforementioned boot seller, and also the honky tonk that locals tend to recommend most. **Nudie's Honky Tonk** (✉ *409 Broadway* ⊕ *www.nudieshonkytonk.com*) is another gem—Nudie was the rhinestone-tailor extraordinaire to music's biggest stars. His bold creations line the walls, including Elvis's famous gold lamé suit. Finally, for hardcore line dancing with plenty of space to freestyle, **Wildhorse Saloon** (✉ *120 2nd Ave. N* ☎ *615/902–8200* ⊕ *www.wildhorsesaloon.com*) awaits.

Stay: For a historical experience, sleep in the former Nashville train station, which is now the **Union Station Hotel** (✉ *1001 Broadway* ☎ *615/726–1001* ⊕ *www.unionstationhotelnashville.com*). The 120-year-old building exudes old-world glamour with a 65-foot barrel-vaulted lobby ceiling, stained glass windows, and crystal chandeliers, but the recently renovated rooms have a sophisticated midcentury-modern style.

Breakfast: Start your day at **Biscuit Love** (✉ *316 11th Ave. S* ☎ *615/490–9584* ⊕ *www.biscuitlove.com*) in the Gulch with a simple bonut (a biscuit doughnut dressed up with much more) or go all in with a decadent biscuit pairing that runs the gamut from hot chicken to bananas foster.

Day 11: Nashville

Your final day is all about country. Nashville International Airport is 8 miles east of downtown. Around town, parking can be expensive or difficult to find. Unless you're leaving right away, consider returning the car when you arrive and taking the shuttle bus or taxi to the airport.

After the Bristol Sessions, radio broadcasts like the Grand Ole Opry spread the new country music, catalyzing transformations, especially out West, where the "western" of "country and western" began to develop. These western forms were particularly influenced by Jimmie Rodgers, with his bluesy sound and yodeling. Gene Autry introduced the singing cowboy genre while Texan Bob Wills fronted the dance-hall western swing genre. But the most significant development spun off western swing after World War II, led by Ernest Tubb. It featured just a core rhythm section with a steel guitar and fiddle out front, a slower beat, twangy vocals, and glum, personal lyrics about heartbreak, adultery, and drinking. This new genre was honky-tonk, with Hank Williams at the forefront, becoming the foundation of all country music.

Honky-tonk became so popular that rockabilly combined it with the blues to dominate American culture. Nashville countered rockabilly's rise and honky-tonk's demise with the antithesis of honky-tonk—a pop and jazz-infused sound with smooth vocals, backup singers, and a string orchestra without a single fiddle or steel guitar. Patsy Cline was a flagbearer of this Nashville sound. By the late 1960s and 1970s, traditionalists rebelled against this mainstream style, with Merle Haggard leading the Bakersfield sound, a western swing–rock hybrid, and Willie Nelson and Waylon Jennings leading outlaw country, which revived honky-tonk and merged it with blues, rockabilly, and rock. Since then, country has continued to swing back and forth between old-school honky-tonk and crossover pop.

Do: Start at the **Country Music Hall of Fame and Museum** (✉ *222 Rep. John Lewis Way S.* ☎ *615/416–2001* ⊕ *www.countrymusichalloffame.org*) for a primer on the genre's legacy. Rotating exhibits elevate this museum far beyond just a (fascinating) directory of country stars, so budget at least a couple of hours, if not more. Also, get your ticket to the perennial favorite **RCA Studio B** (✉ *1611 Roy Acuff Pl.* ☎ *615/416–2001* ⊕ *www.studiob. org*) tour here, and book early because time slots can sell out. Inside RCA Studio B, you'll magically turn up in the 1950s, when the studio was cranking out the slick Nashville sound. Inside-scoop stories about icons who recorded there, including Elvis and Dolly Parton, bring the studio to life.

Back downtown, **Ryman Auditorium** (✉ *116 5th Ave. N* ☎ *615/889–3060* ⊕ *www. ryman.com*) was built as a bona fide tabernacle. Then once the Grand Ole Opry rolled in, it became known as the Mother Church of Country Music. But this building isn't just for country fans; the biggest stars across all genres, and even some cows, have stood on that hallowed stage. Take the tour to learn more about its wild history. And if you're able to snag a ticket for a show here, any show, do it. Finally, the **National Museum of African American Music** (✉ *510 Broadway* ☎ *615/301–8724* ⊕ *www.nmaam.org*) is an expansive exploration of the African American impact on American culture through music. While you've explored pieces of that story on this road trip, this museum lays all the pieces out to form a comprehensive picture.

Eat & Drink: Prince's Hot Chicken, a legendary purveyor of a legendary Nashville dish (hot chicken), now has a food truck downtown for lunch (✉ *423 6th Ave. S* ⊕ *www.princeshotchicken. com*). Have a light (in volume) dinner at the **Grilled Cheeserie** (✉ *2003 Belcourt Ave.* ☎ *615/203–0351* ⊕ *www.grilledcheeserie.com*). With their ingenious concoctions—like macaroni and cheese inside the grilled cheese, plus bacon bits—you'll never be tempted to order a grilled cheese from a kid's menu again. After dinner, the **Bluebird Café** (✉ *4104 Hillsboro Pike* ☎ *615/383–1461* ⊕ *www. bluebirdcafe.com*) is a visit … if you can get in. Singer-songwriters, ranging from not-yet-known artists to mega-stars, perform and tell stories about the songs in this intimate showcase. Buy tickets online in advance or try your luck with the walk-up line.

Breakfast: While the **Pancake Pantry** (✉ *1796 21st Ave. S* ☎ *615/383–9333* ⊕ *www.thepancakepantry.com*) in Hillsboro isn't only about pancakes, with 19 different varieties, they're still very much about pancakes. These range from workhorse silver dollars to the pancake with three sausage links tucked inside ("Pigs in a Blanket").

The Best of North and Central Florida

Written by Mark Sullivan

Orlando is usually a visitor's first (and often only) introduction to Florida, but for anyone who wants to expand their horizons beyond the theme parks, the city makes a great starting point to explore the rest of the state. Drive for an hour or two in any direction and you'll encounter a different Florida, one that's quite rich in historical sites and natural wonders.

This itinerary starts in Orlando, then travels up the Atlantic Seaboard, across the center of the state, and down the Gulf Coast. Along the way it passes through some of Florida's most fascinating destinations: windswept beaches, unique geological formations, and crystal clear springs teeming with wildlife.

At a Glance

Start: Orlando, FL

End: Orlando, FL

Miles Traveled: 675 miles

Suggested Duration: 8 days

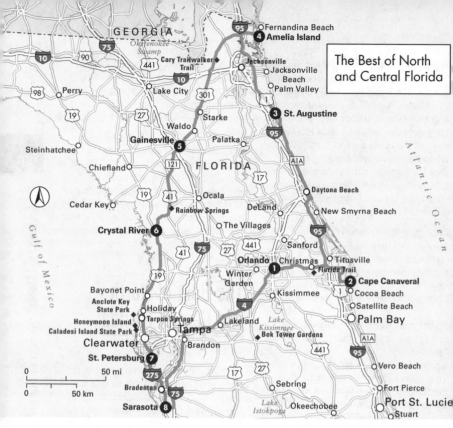

The Best of North and Central Florida

States Visited: Florida

Key Sights: Cocoa Beach; Daytona Beach; Disney Springs; Kennedy Space Center; St. Augustine

Best Time to Go: The Sunshine State is an all-season destination. School breaks and holidays tend to be the most crowded (especially Orlando) while summer sees the least amount of crowds.

Day 1: Orlando, FL, to Cape Canaveral, FL

55 miles (50 minutes without traffic and stops)

Land in Orlando, where you can pick up a rental car from the airport and ignore the urge to make a quick visit to Disney World. Once you take FL-408 east from Orlando, you'll notice a lot less congestion. FL-50 passes through protected lands, including the St. Johns National Wildlife Refuge. FL-405 across the Indian River takes you directly to Kennedy Space Center.

ALONG THE WAY

Nature: If you want to stretch your legs a bit, a section of the Florida Trail, the wildest of the 11 national scenic trails across the United States, can be accessed near the community of Christmas.

CAPE CANAVERAL

Do: One of Florida's most enduring attractions (it's been around longer than Walt Disney World or any of the other area theme parks) is the Kennedy Space Center. Explore its history at the **Kennedy Space Center Visitor Center Complex** (✉ Space Commerce Way, Merritt Island, FL ☎ 855/433–4210 ⊕ www.

kennedyspacecenter.com), where you can pay tribute to the men and women who've gone into space at the *Heroes & Legends* exhibit. If you can't wait to get some sun, Cocoa Beach is one of the prettiest stretches of sand in the area. Beachfront **Alan Shepard Park** (✉ *299 E. Cocoa Beach Causeway* ☎ *321/868–3258* ⊕ *www.cityofcocoabeach.com*) is named after an astronaut and is a favorite spot for watching rocket launches.

Eat & Drink: There are plenty of dining options in and around Cape Canaveral, but the food doesn't get any fresher than at **Seafood Atlantic** (✉ *520 Glen Cheek Dr.* ☎ *321/784–1963* ⊕ *www.seafoodatlantic.org*), a fish market with an alfresco dining room.

Stay: An oceanfront hotel, the **Inn at Cocoa Beach** (✉ *4300 Ocean Beach Blvd.* ☎ *321/799–3460* ⊕ *www.theinnatcocoabeach.com*) has a laid-back vibe and spectacular views.

Breakfast: As you're driving up the coast, stop in Titusville at **Le Crave** (✉ *2520 S. Washington Ave.* ☎ *321/292–7373* ⊕ *www.lecravecafe.com*) known for its delicious crepes and other savory and sweet breakfast treats.

Day 2: Cape Canaveral, FL, to St. Augustine, FL

128 miles (2½ hours without traffic and stops)

Today you'll head north up Florida's beautiful Atlantic coast. I-95 to FL-207 is the quickest way up the coast, getting you to St. Augustine in just under two hours. But since this is a road trip, you should cut over to the more scenic, two-lane coastal route of A1A north of Daytona Beach.

ALONG THE WAY

Eat & Drink: With an unbeatable location right on the pier, Daytona Beach's outpost of **Joe's Crab Shack** (✉ *1200 Main St.* ☎ *386/238–4050* ⊕ *www.joescrabshack.com*) is a local favorite. Grab a seat on the rooftop terrace and enjoy king crab legs (the specialty) served with potatoes and corn.

Photo Opp: Billed as the "World's Most Famous Beach," Daytona Beach is one of the few in the country where you can drive your car right onto the sand, meaning there are a lot of tailgate parties in progress. (Alcohol is officially prohibited, but no one is actually checking.) It's 23 miles long, so the farther you get from the "Strip" near International Speedway Boulevard, the sparser the crowds.

ST. AUGUSTINE

Do: Straddling the sparkling Matanzas River is St. Augustine, the nation's oldest city. The gargantuan **Castillo de San Marcos National Monument** (✉ *1 S. Castillo Dr.* ☎ *904/829–6506* ⊕ *www.nps.gov/casa*), a fort built by the Spanish in 1695, proved surprisingly strong against British cannonballs. More petite is **Fort Matanzas National Monument** (✉ *8635 A1A S* ☎ *904/471–0116* ⊕ *www.nps.gov/foma*), which defended the city's southern borders beginning in 1742. That makes the colonial-style **Cathedral Basilica of St. Augustine** (✉ *38 Cathedral Pl.* ☎ *904/824–2806* ⊕ *www.thefirstparish.org*), built in 1795, a relatively recent addition to the city.

Eat & Drink: In a charming house in the Historic District, **Collage** (✉ *60 Hypolita St.* ☎ *904/829–0055* ⊕ *www.collagestaug.com*) has a menu that's completely dependent on what the fishermen bring in that day. **The Floridian** (✉ *72 Spanish St.* ☎ *904/829–0655* ⊕ *www.thefloridianstaug.com*) is known for its vegetarian fare, but its menu of farm-to-table dishes satisfies even devoted meat eaters.

The Rocket Garden is one of the Kennedy Space Center's most populat attractions.

Stay: A stone's throw from the water, the luxe **Bayfront Marin House Historic Inn** (✉ 142 Av. Menendez ☎ 904/824–4301 ⊕ www.bayfrontmarinhouse.com) lets you gaze out at the playful dolphins in the Intracoastal Waterway.

Breakfast: Actually located on Cordova Street in the Historic District, the **Maple Street Biscuit Company** (✉ 39 Cordova St. ☎ 904/217–7814 ⊕ www.maplestreet-biscuits.com) serves tasty breakfast sandwiches and other early-morning fare.

Day 3: St. Augustine, FL, to Amelia Island, FL

70 miles (1 hour, 20 minutes without traffic and stops)

Head to Amelia Island in the northeastern corner of Florida. As usual there's the fast way—U.S. 1 to I–295 to I–95 to FL-200—and the much more scenic route along the coast that detours onto A1A.

ALONG THE WAY

Town: Jacksonville may not be a tourist destination, but it has its charms. One of its highlights is **MOCA Jacksonville** (✉ 333 N. Laura St. ☎ 904/366–6911 ⊕ www.mocajacksonville.unf.edu), housed in a stately downtown building that was once the headquarters of the Western Union Telegraph Company. The loftlike space is filled with modern art that's smart yet accessible. Even if you think you're not a zoo person, the **Jacksonville Zoo and Gardens** (✉ 370 Zoo Pkwy. ☎ 904/757–4463; ⊕ www.jacksonvillezoo.org) may win you over with large-scale exhibits of tigers, penguins, and venomous snakes. Don't miss Wild Florida, which showcases the state's surprisingly varied wildlife.

Eat & Drink: The sophisticated **Bistro Aix** (✉ 1440 San Macro Blvd. ☎ 904/398–1949 ⊕ www.bistrox.com), south of downtown on San Marco Boulevard, has classic French dishes like onion soup and steak frites, as well as homemade pastries.

AMELIA ISLAND

Do: Amelia Island is one of Florida's gems, with a beautiful coastline lined by massive sand dunes. There are seven parks that make up **Talbot Island State Parks** (✉ *A1A North* ☎ *904/251–2320* ⊕ *www.floridastateparks.org*), and three of them have beautiful beaches. Big Talbot, with its Boneyard Beach of wind-twisted trees, is a photographer's paradise, and Little Talbot is popular for swimming and beachcombing, while Amelia Island State Park is popular for its beachfront horseback riding. There are several must-see sights, including **Fort Clinch State Park** (✉ *2601 Atlantic Ave.* ☎ *904/277-7274* ⊕ *www.floridastateparks.org*), home to one of the most perfectly preserved 19th-century brick forts in the country. It was built to dissuade the English from invading after the War of 1812.

Eat & Drink: In the historic town of Fernandina Beach, **Sliders Seaside Grill** (✉ *1998 S. Fletcher Ave.* ☎ *904/277–6652* ⊕ *www.slidersseaside.com*) lives up to its name. The relaxed restaurant overlooks a surf break, so watching locals ride the waves is part of the fun. So is the menu, filled with dishes that pile on the seafood, like the crab-topped flounder.

Stay: Located on more than 1,300 acres of shoreline, the **Omni Amelia Island Resort** (✉ *39 Beach Lagoon Rd.* ☎ *904/261–6161* ⊕ *www.omnihotels.com*) couldn't have a better location. The palm-shaded pool is the best place to take in the unobstructed ocean views. The last word in luxury, the **Ritz Carlton Amelia Island** (✉ *4750 Amelia Island Pkwy.* ☎ *904/277–1100* ⊕ *www.ritzcarlton.com*) has indulgent rooms, superb service, and top-flight amenities like the Surrender Spa. Don't miss a meal at its top-rated restaurant, simply called Salt.

Breakfast: The garden bagel at **Amelia Island Coffee** in Fernandina Beach (✉ *207 Centre St.* ☎ *904/321-2111* ⊕ *www.ameliaislandcoffee.com*) won't win over New Yorkers, but the combo of cream cheese, hummus, avocado, tomato, and onion is undeniably tasty.

Day 4: Amelia Island, FL, to Gainesville, FL

97 miles (1 hour, 50 minutes without traffic and stops))

U.S. 301 takes you most of the way to Gainesville. Take a slight right at Waldo, and FL-24 takes you the last few miles.

ALONG THE WAY

Nature: If you need a break to stretch your legs, the 1.4-mile **Cary Trailwalker Trail** (✉ *7400 Pavilion Rd.* ⊕ *www.alltrails.com*) is a loop through some unspoiled terrain. The trailhead is near the town of Bryce on U.S. 301.

GAINESVILLE

Do: Gainesville is the home of the University of Florida, but there's more to do in and around this college town than cheer on the home team, including plenty of natural wonders. Scientists believe the sinkhole at the center of **Devil's Millhopper Geological State Park** (✉ *4732 Millhopper Rd.* ☎ *352/955–2008* ⊕ *www.floridastateparks.org*) formed thousands of years ago. After you descend past several waterfalls, you reach a subtropical paradise 12 stories below the surface. The **Prairie Paynes Preserve State Park** (✉ *100 Savannah Blvd., Micanopy, FL* ☎ *352/466–3397* ⊕ *www.floridastateparks.org*), about 10 miles south of the city, is home to herds of wild horses. If that's not unusual enough, it also has free-roaming bison. Take it all in from the 50-foot-high observation tower.

Eat & Drink: The dining room at the storefront **Paramount Grill** (✉ *12 S.W. 1st Ave.* ☎ *352/378–3398* ⊕ *www.paramountgrill.com*) is surprisingly simple, letting the artistry of the food take center stage. All the dishes take advantage of the best local produce of the area.

Stay: Painted a sunny shade of yellow, **The Laurel Oak Inn Bed & Breakfast** (✉ *221 S.E. 7th St.* ☎ *352/373–4535* ⊕ *www.laureloakinn.com*) is an exquisitely restored Queen Anne–style Victorian showplace. Breakfast is a home-cooked meal, which becomes an extravaganza on the weekends with "Sweetness on Sunday."

Breakfast: As the name suggests, **Uppercrust** (✉ *4118 N.W. 16th Blvd.* ☎ *352/376–7187* ⊕ *www.uppercrustgnv. com*) is a bakery focusing on croissants and other perfectly executed pastries. It's located on Northwest 16th Boulevard, just outside the university area.

Day 5: Gainesville, FL, to Crystal River, FL

62 miles (1 hour, 25 minutes without traffic or stops)

Take Fl-121 south to Williston, then U.S. 41 south past Rainbow Springs. County Road 491 delivers you to Crystal Springs.

ALONG THE WAY

Nature: Humans first visited **Rainbow Springs** (✉ *19158 S.W. 81st Place Rd., Dunnellon, FL* ☎ *352/465–8555* ⊕ *www. floridastateparks.org*) more than 10,000 years ago. Stone tools made by the Timucua people reveal the area's rich history. Today people head to the springs for a dip in the remarkably clean waters. There are three beautiful waterfalls—a rarity in Florida. They're all man-made, remnants from when this was a tourist attraction.

CRYSTAL RIVER

Do: Crystal River isn't undiscovered by any means, but it still remains a bit off the typical tourist trail. The six Native American burial mounds at **Crystal River Archaeological State Park** (✉ *3400 N. Museum Point* ☎ *352/795–3817* ⊕ *www.floridastateparks.com*) make this

one of the longest continually occupied regions of the state. Head to the top of the Temple Mound for sweeping views of the nearby marshes. At **Crystal River National Wildlife Refuge** (✉ *1502 S.E. Kings Bay Dr.* ☎ *352/563–2088* ⊕ *www. fws.gov*), manatees congregate in large numbers from November to March. Make your way to Three Sisters Springs, part of the refuge, where you can spot dozens of the gentle giants in the remarkably clear water.

Eat & Drink: There's nothing fancy at the **Crab Plant** (✉ *201 N.W. 5th St.* ☎ *352/795–4700* ⊕ *www.crabplant. com*), a fish market on 5th Street in Crystal River. But the dining room has two big pluses: the freshest seafood you'll find in these parts and a view of the waters of King Bay. Stone crab, the specialty here, comes right off the owner's boat. Local shrimp is also caught right at the dock outside.

Stay: On the shore of Kings Bay, the **Plantation on Crystal River** (✉ *9301 W. Fort Island Trail* ☎ *352/795–4211* ⊕ *www. plantationoncrystalriver.com*) is an eco-friendly resort located on 232 acres near all of the area's nature preserves. The resort's on-site dive shop has daily snorkeling excursions.

Breakfast: The name doesn't do this place justice. Sure, but **Breakfast Station #9** (✉ *1676 S.E. U.S. 19* ☎ *352/228–4077* ⊕ *www.breakfaststationcentral.com*) serves stick-to-your-ribs morning meals, and it's an equally good lunch stop if you get a late start.

Day 6: Crystal River, FL, to St. Petersburg, FL

91 miles (1 hour, 45 minutes without traffic and stops)

Head south on U.S. 98, then merge onto U.S. 19 for the rest of the drive to St. Petersburg.

ALONG THE WAY

Nature: There are many stretches of sand in this area that are worth an hour or two of your time, but these two state parks—both of which require a bit of effort to get there—are something special. A ferry from Honeymoon Island takes you to **Caladesi Island State Park** (✉ *Offshore Island* ☎ *727/469–5918* ⊕ *www.floridastateparks.org*), the perfect place to kayak along a 3-mile route among the mangroves. Even more remote is Anclote Key State Park, three miles offshore from the town of **Tarpon Springs** (☎ *727/638–4447* ⊕ *www.floridastateparks.org*). After the ferry ride, hike to the lighthouse dating back to 1887 or find a remote spot on the sand all to yourself.

ST. PETERSBURG

Do: Enjoy your time in St. Petersburg, where the swaying palm trees and gentle bay breezes might get you to stay a little longer than you expected to. The big attraction in this arts colony is **The Dalí** (✉ *One Dali Blvd.* ☎ *727/823–3767* ⊕ *www.thedali.org*), an homage to famed Spanish painter Salvador Dalí. It has a surprising number of his works, including some from earlier in his career when he was still finding his signature surreal style. One of Florida's old-school tourist attractions, **Sunken Gardens** (✉ *1825 4th St. N* ☎ *727/551–3102* ⊕ *www.stpete. org*) is today a cool oasis in St. Petersburg's concrete jungle.

Eat & Drink: In the stunning 1920s Birchwood Hotel, **Birch & Vine** (✉ *340 Beach Dr. NE* ☎ *727/896–1080* ⊕ *www. thebirchwood.com*) is the see-and-be-seen spot in St. Petersburg, whether you're sitting in a banquette in the elegant dining room or outside on the patio. It ups the ante on all of its dishes, adding creative flourishes to local seafood.

Stay: Dating from 1933, the **Hollander Hotel** (✉ *421 4th Ave. N* ☎ *727/873–7900* ⊕ *www.hollanderhotel.com*) has a distinctive Old Florida vibe. Rooms have lots of historic touches, and the pretty pool and the surrounding patio are party central on the weekends.

Breakfast: Often called the best breakfast in St. Petersburg by locals and tourists alike, the **Wooden Rooster** (✉ *104 2nd Ave. NE* ☎ *727/822–7373* ⊕ *www.thewoodenrooster.com*) has a hip vibe and serves a smooth cup of coffee.

Day 7: St. Petersburg, FL, to Sarasota, FL

37 miles (45 minutes without traffic or stops)

From St. Petersburg, I–275 sweeps you across the wide expanse of Tampa Bay. U.S. 19 and U.S. 301 then take you south to downtown Sarasota. Even nicer is the coastal route down FL-289 through Longboat Key.

ALONG THE WAY

Town: The **De Soto National Memorial** (✉ *8300 Desoto Memorial Hwy.* ☎ *941/792–0458* ⊕ *www.nps.gov/deso*) remembers the story of Spanish Conquistador Hernando de Soto, who came ashore with his men and a team of horses near what is now the town of Bradenton in 1539. The memorial also includes much about the Native people who were living here at the time.

Eat & Drink: Bradenton's **Beach Bistro** (✉ *6600 Gulf Dr.* ☎ *941/778–6444* ⊕ *www.beachbistro.com*) lives up to its name as a seaside spot with gorgeous views, especially at sunset. The award-winning cuisine includes creative fare like "lobstercargots," large chunks of buttery lobster.

SARASOTA

Do: There is a string of barrier islands just west of Sarasota just waiting to be explored. Siesta Key is home to Siesta Beach, a gorgeous stretch of sand fronting 40 acres of nature trails. Also on Siesta Key is Turtle Beach, which is a little more secluded than most nearby spots. But Sarasota isn't just about the beaches. Built by John Ringling (of Ringling Brothers Circus fame), the **John and Mabel Ringling Museum of Art** (✉ 5401 Bay Shore Rd. ☎ 941/359–5700 ⊕ www.ringling.org) is set within an Italian Renaissance-style palazzo. It originally housed Ringling's own encyclopedic collection of art, and now includes everything from Old Master paintings to modernist masterpieces. Also located on the museum grounds is Ringling's home, Ca' d'Zan, built to resemble the Doge's Palace in Venice.

Eat & Drink: In St. Armond's Circle, a beautiful ring of elegant restaurants and other upscale businesses on St. Armand's Key, you'll find **Café L'Europe** (✉ 431 St. Armand's Cir. ☎ 941/388–4415 ⊕ www.cafeleurope.net). It's elegant in a slightly old-fashioned way, as are the dishes; think sole meuniere, potato-crusted grouper, and chateaubriand. North of St. Armand's Key is Longboat Key, home to **Euphemia Haye** (✉ 5540 Gulf of Mexico Dr. ☎ 941/383–3633 ⊕ www.euphemiahaye.com), a tucked-away cottage whose menu focuses on beef and lamb.

Stay: On Lido Key, the upscale **Lido Beach Resort** (✉ 700 Benjamin Franklin Dr. ☎ 941/388–2161 ⊕ www.lidobeachresort.com) has two free-form pools, three hot tubs, and a perfectly manicured beach with perfectly spaced lounge chairs. Many of the elegant rooms have their own full kitchens, making them great for longer stays.

Breakfast: On Main Street in Sarasota, **First Watch** (✉ 1395 Main St. ☎ 941/954–1395 ⊕ www.firstwatch.com) is close to the causeway that leads to St. Armand's Key. It's focused on breakfast, brunch, and lunch with savory dishes like a carnitas omelet.

Day 8: Sarasota, FL, to Orlando, FL

131 miles (2 hours without traffic or stops)

On your last day, an easy drive on I–75 and I–4 take you back to Orlando, where you'll have some time to explore before your flight home the next day.

ALONG THE WAY

Roadside Attraction: Stop in Lake Wales to stroll around the grounds of **Bok Tower Gardens** (✉ 1151 Tower Blvd. ☎ 863/676–1408 ⊕ www.boktowergardens.org). At its center is an art deco carillon set on 50 acres crisscrossed with paths and dotted with benches. It's old-timey Florida, and it's wonderful.

ORLANDO

Do: When locals spend the day at Disney, it's most often at **Disney Springs** (✉ 1486 Buena Vista Dr., Lake Buena Vista ☎ 407/939–5277 ⊕ www.disneysprings.com) a massive shopping, dining, and entertainment complex. The attractions are endless, from floating above the waterfront in a hot-air balloon to speeding over the waves in a boat that looks like a vintage automobile. The best views are from a Mississippi River–style paddle wheeler.

Eat & Drink: There are a lot of dining options at Disney Springs—perhaps the most fun is **The Edison** (✉ 1570 E. Buena Vista Dr., Lake Buena Vista ☎ 407/560–9288 ⊕ www.theedisonfla.com), a 1920s-style speakeasy. (It's Disney, so it's the kind of speakeasy where you can bring the kids.) This isn't a theme park grab-and-go meal, so expect entrées like pan-seared salmon, blackened mahimahi, and a delectable queen-cut prime rib. Be sure to reserve ahead of time here and at all of the Disney Springs sit-down eateries.

Stay: Disney's Saratoga Springs Resort and Spa (✉ *1960 Broadway, Lake Buena Vista* ☎ *407/939–5277* ⊕ *disneyworld.disney. go.com/resorts/saratoga-springs-resort-and-spa*) has it all, including a splendid spa where you can soak your troubles away. This lodging transports you to Upstate New York, where for more than a century people have enjoyed "taking the waters" at the natural hot springs.

Breakfast: Southern-style cooking at its most extravagant, **Chef Art Smith's Homecomin'** (✉ *1602 E. Buena Vista Dr., Lake Buena Vista* ☎ *407/560–0100* ⊕ *www. homecominkitchen.com*) takes your usual offerings and adds something unexpected. Why have run-of-the-mill eggs Benedict when you could have it with hush puppy cakes and grilled chicken tenders?

The Best of Southern Florida

Written by Jessica Poitevien

Flat Florida may not be top of mind when it comes to road trips, but what it lacks in topography, it makes up for in abundant wildlife, vibrant cities, and a uniquely diverse mixture of cultures. South Florida, in particular, is a relatively small area—the longest you'll drive in one day is only four hours—but it's brimming with adventures of all kinds from its glamorous nightlife and ever-growing art scene to its natural beauty and foodie hot spots. On this six-day itinerary, you'll find out why Miami is known as Magic City before diving into Florida's wild side with visits to three national parks, including the only place on Earth where both alligators and crocodiles co-exist. Throughout the week, you'll walk in Ernest Hemingway's shoes, share the sidewalk with a rooster or two, get a taste of slow-paced living, and much more.

People say Florida is strange, and perhaps it is, but this road trip will leave you with an appreciation for what makes the Sunshine State that perfect kind of weird.

Extend Your Trip

For either Florida itinerary, connect Cocoa Beach with Miami to combine the two trips to create an ultimate Best of Florida experience.

At a Glance

Start: Miami, FL

End: Miami, FL

Miles Traveled: 430 miles

Suggested Duration: 7 days

States Visited: Florida

Key Sights: Biscayne National Park; Dry Tortugas National Park; Everglades National Park; Southernmost Point of the Continental United States; Wynwood Art District

Best Time to Go: With year-round sunshine and consistently warm temperatures, a visit to South Florida is always a good idea. But for optimal conditions, plan your visit for winter or early spring (December through April). That's when humidity is low, rainy days are sparse, and those pesky mosquitoes have mostly retreated.

Day 1: Miami (South Beach and Downtown Miami)

Miami aka Magic City aka the Capital of Latin America has enough to keep you entertained for a week or even more, but if you're short on time, there's plenty you can accomplish in two days. Pick up a rental car at Miami International Airport, then head north on I–95 to the infamous

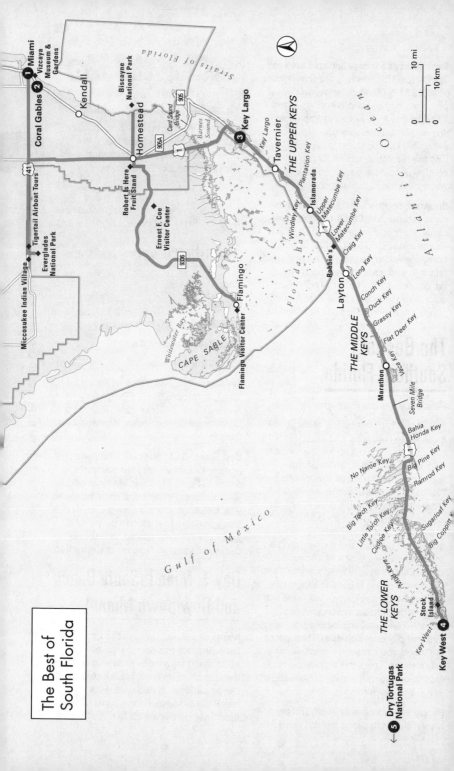

The Best of South Florida

1 Miami
Vizcaya Museum & Gardens

2 Coral Gables

Kendall

Biscayne National Park

Homestead

Robert Is Here Fruit Stand

Tigertail Airboat Tours

Miccosukee Indian Village

Everglades National Park

Ernest F. Coe Visitor Center

Flamingo

Flamingo Visitor Center

Whitewater Bay

CAPE SABLE

Gulf of Mexico

Straits of Florida

Card Sound Bridge

Barnes Sound

3 Key Largo

Key Largo

Tavernier

THE UPPER KEYS

Plantation Key

Windley Key

Islamorada

Upper Matecumbe Key

Lower Matecumbe Key

Robbie's

Craig Key

Long Key

Layton

Conch Key

Duck Key

Grassy Key

THE MIDDLE KEYS

Flat Deer Key

Vaca Key

Marathon

Seven Mile Bridge

Florida Bay

Atlantic Ocean

Bahia Honda Key

No Name Key

Big Pine Key

Ramrod Key

Big Torch Key

Little Torch Key

Cudjoe Key

Sugarloaf Key

Big Coppitt

THE LOWER KEYS

Key West

Stock Island

4 Key West

5 Dry Tortugas National Park

905

905A

1

41

SR36

10 mi

10 km

South Beach. That'll be your home base as you discover the many neighborhoods that make up Miami.

Do: The miles of beach are the main draw at South Beach, but this tourist favorite is also a hub for shopping, decadent dining, buzzing nightlife, and even a bit of art. Be sure to stroll down Lincoln Road for a taste of it all. Before nightfall, admire the distinct 1930s architecture of the Art Deco District before it transforms into party central. Although Downtown Miami isn't the most popular place to hang out, museum lovers will find plenty to do here. For an overview of South Florida history, there's the **HistoryMiami Museum** (✉ 101 W. Flagler St. ☎ 305/375–1492 www.historymiami.org), while admirers of art flock to the **Pérez Art Museum Miami** (✉ 1103 Biscayne Blvd. ☎ 305/375–3000 ⊕ www.pamm.org), and science buffs should make their way to the **Phillip and Patricia Frost Museum of Science** (✉ 1101 Biscayne Blvd. ☎ 305/434–9600 ⊕ www.frostscience.org). To take in the skyline views, you can meander around **Bayfront Park** (✉ 301 Biscayne Blvd. ☎ 305/358–7550 ⊕ www.bayfrontparkmiami.com), shop 'til you drop at **Bayside Marketplace** (✉ 401 Biscayne Blvd. ☎ 305/577–3344 ⊕ www.baysidemarketplace.com), or go for a whirl on the **Skyviews Miami Observation Wheel** (✉ 401 Biscayne Blvd. ☎ 786/529–7177 ⊕ www.skyviewsmiami.com).

Eat & Drink: In South Beach, treat yourself to casual Italian fare at the chic but cozy **Osteria Morini** (✉ 1750 Alton Rd. ☎ 305/918–1037 ⊕ www.osteriamorini.com), or take your taste buds on a world tour at **Juvia** (✉ 1111 Lincoln Rd. ☎ 305/763–8272 ⊕ www.juviamiami.com), which combines French, Japanese, and Peruvian cooking styles. For several dining options in one area, head to the waterfront **Sunset Harbour** (✉ 1900 Bay Rd.).

Photo Op: Was that photo taken in Miami or Spain? Your friends will never know the difference when you snap a pic at

Española Way in South Beach, a quaint, pedestrian-only street paved with cobblestones and lined with restaurants on both sides.

Stay: There are plenty of luxury getaways in Miami, but the **W South Beach** (✉ 2201 Collins Ave. ☎ 305/938–3000 ⊕ www.marriott.com) is an icon for many reasons, including its guest rooms that guarantee an ocean view. If you'd rather stay in the heart of all the action, the **Stiles Hotel** (✉ 1120 Collins Ave. ☎ 305/674–7800 ⊕ www.thestileshotel.com) is a great choice.

Breakfast: Quick but tasty breakfast sandwiches are par for the course at **A Simple Eggstaurant** (✉ 1516 Washington Ave. ☎ 305/497–9082 ⊕ www.ordersimpleggstaurant.com/#/), but for a healthy morning pick-me-up, **Delicious Raw Kitchen Juice Bar** (✉ 1828 Bay Rd. ☎ 786/461–1786 ⊕ www.delraw.com) offers smoothies, açai bowls, and more.

Day 2: Miami (Wynwood Art District and Little Havana)

Your second day in Miami leaves the chaos of South Beach and heads to two less hopping, but just as essential Miami neighborhoods.

Do: There are over 50 blocks of murals lining the streets of Wynwood, so take your time roaming around and admiring your favorites. **The Wynwood Walls** (2520 N.W. 2nd Ave. ☎ 305/531–4411 ⊕ www.museum.thewynwoodwalls.com) enclosure is the epicenter of all the street art, but don't forget to stop by a few of the galleries nestled between boutiques, bars, and restaurants. There's no doubt that the Cuban population has helped shape Miami into what it is today, so take a guided walking tour of Little Havana to learn about the neighborhood's history.

A stop at **Domino Park** (801 S.W. 15th Ave. ☎ *305/859–2717* ⊕ *www.miamigov. com*) is also a must to see the *viejitos* (old men) playing the park's namesake game. If you're lucky, you might even get to join in. Meanwhile, art aficionados will appreciate a visit to **Cubaocho Museum & Performing Arts Center** (1465 S.W. 8th St. ☎ *305/285–5880* ⊕ *www.cubaocho. com*) thanks to its collection of 19th- and 20th-century Cuban art.

Eat & Drink: For a sweet snack while in Wynwood, head to the **Salty** (50 N.W. 23rd St. ☎ *305/639–8501* ⊕ *www.sal-tydonut.com*) for doughnuts and coffee or **Fireman Derek's Bake Shop** (2818 N. Miami Ave. ☎ *786/703–3623* ⊕ *www. firemandereks.com*) for rich cakes, cookies, and pies, but your main meals of the day should be reserved for Little Havana. When it comes to Cuban food, **Versailles** (3555 S.W. 8th St. ☎ *305/444–0240* ⊕ *www.versaillesrestaurant.com*) is a restaurant that never disappoints. A sweet finish is not too far away at **Azucar Ice Cream Company** (1503 S.W. 8th St. ☎ *305/381–0369* ⊕ *www.azucaricecream.com*) with its Cuban-inspired flavors like sweet plantain and caramel flan. Next, sip on mojitos and Cuba libres while dancing to—or at least admiring—some live salsa music at **Ball & Chain** (1513 S.W. 8th St. ☎ *305/643–7820* ⊕ *www.ballandchainmiami.com*), which has been a Little Havana staple since it first opened in 1935.

Stay: It's best to stay put at wherever you spent your first night in Miami.

Breakfast: You'll find an Anthony Bourdain–approved, southern-style breakfast at **Yardbird Southern** (1600 Lenox Ave. 305/538–5220 ⊕ *www.runchickenrun. com*).

Day 3: Miami to Everglades National Park to Coral Gables

80 miles (1 hour, 45 minutes without traffic and stops)

Today's adventures are all about getting a glimpse of what South Florida looked like before developers created the cities we know today. You'll drive out west on U.S. 41, surrounded by flat marshes and canals, to visit Everglades National Park, then head back east to Coral Gables, a good jumping-off point for tomorrow's activities.

ALONG THE WAY

Nature: Everglades National Park (☎ *305/242–7700* ⊕ *www.nps.gov.ever*) is huge, so keep your trip focused around the **Shark Valley Visitor Center** (✉ 36000 S.W. 8th St., Miami, FL). Once you're in the park, keep your eyes peeled for alligators, herons, egrets, deer, turtles, and more as you hike, bike (rentals are available), or take the tram tour around the 15-mile loop trail. At the halfway point, you'll find the 45-foot-tall Shark Valley Observation Tower with panoramic views that stretch as far as 20 miles.

Detour: Although you'll have to drive a bit past the Everglades National Park entrance to reach the **Miccosukee Indian Village** (⊕ *www.village.miccosukee.com*), this stop enriches the overall experience by giving more context to the Native people who have lived in the area for centuries. This replica village showcases the tribe's traditional way of life and features a museum with interactive exhibits, a gift shop, and an alligator demonstration area where you can expect to see brave Miccosukee men sticking their heads inside the mouth of a gator.

Roadside Attraction: A trip to the Everglades would be incomplete without hopping on an airboat ride to get a different perspective on this unique ecosystem. For smaller group experiences, opt for one of the four airboat companies within the Miccosukee Indian Reservation. In particular, guides with **Tigertail Airboat Tours** (☎ 305/439–2745 ⊕ www. tigertailairboattours.com) share their knowledge not only of the landscape and wildlife, but also of the Miccosukee tribal history.

Eat & Drink: Only light snacks and beverage vending machines are available at the Shark Valley Visitor Center. Be sure to pack some food or eat before entering the park. You can also head to one of the Miccosukee restaurants near the park entrance. Just keep an eye out for signs pointing the way to fry bread, and you can't go wrong.

CORAL GABLES

Do: You'll probably arrive in Coral Gables exhausted from a day out in the Florida sun, but a post-nap, leisurely stroll down Miracle Mile is well worth it for some window shopping at the boutiques, as well as grabbing dinner and drinks. Literature lovers should swing by **Books & Books** (✉ 265 Aragon Ave. ☎ 305/442–4408 ⊕ www.booksandbooks.com), a locally owned, indie bookstore with a café that also offers flavorful meals.

Eat & Drink: Serving South Florida's carnivore community since 1962, **Graziano's** (✉ 2301 Galiano St. ☎ 305/460–0001 ⊕ www.grazianosgroup.com) whips up Argentinian-style meals that are all about succulent cuts of beef, chorizo, and of course, perfectly paired wines.

Stay: There's a different kind of luxury that comes with a stay in Coral Gables—one that's classy, subdued, timeless, and not at all flashy. No place exudes that feeling more than the **Biltmore Hotel** (✉ 1200 Anastasia Ave. ☎ 305/445–1926 ⊕ www. biltmorehotel.com), which opened in 1926 and still features its Spanish, Italian, and Moorish-inspired architecture in a truly grand setting.

Breakfast: Head to **Threefold Cafe** (✉ 141 Giralda Ave. ☎ 305/704–8007 ⊕ www. threefoldcafe.com) to check out the only Aussie restaurant in town and enjoy a hearty breakfast that puts a twist on your usual morning favorites, like fried French toast with Nutella.

Day 4: Coral Gables to Biscayne National Park to Key Largo

84 miles (2 hours without traffic and stops)

Today deserves an early start, so you can fit in all the essential detours needed to truly experience this area. Once you leave the garden-meets-city vibes of Coral Gables, it's a fairly uneventful drive down the Ronald Reagan Turnpike to reach Biscayne National Park. Then a mostly two-lane drive awaits as you continue south to Key Largo, the first of the Florida Keys.

ALONG THE WAY

Detour: The European influences of Coral Gables continue at the **Vizcaya Museum & Gardens** (✉ 3251 S. Miami Ave. ☎ 305/250–9133 ⊕ www.vizcaya.org) in Coconut Grove, backtracking a bit to Miami, where you'll find a stunning Mediterranean-style villa with an impressive collection of centuries-old art. Explore the rooms of this home, but be sure to save plenty of time for the perfectly manicured waterfront gardens, a favorite photo shoot spot for both professionals and smartphone-wielding amateurs.

An airboat tour is one of the most popular ways to see Everglades National Park.

Eat & Drink: There are only light snacks and premade cold sandwiches available at Biscayne's Dante Fascell Visitor Center so it's best to eat before you reach the park. For an early lunch, head to South Miami, where you'll find **Cracked by Chef Adrianne** (✉ 7400 S.W. 57th Ct. ☎ 305/665–5820 ⊕ www.igotcracked. com), which focuses on free-range and organic ingredients on the vegetarian-friendly menu.

Nature: Since 95% of **Biscayne National Park** (☎ 305/230–1144 ⊕ www.nps.gov/bisc) is covered in water, you'll need some help exploring. Luckily, Biscayne National Institute (the tour operator arm of the park) offers plenty of guided adventures so you can sail, snorkel, paddle, or kayak your way around. Customized private tours are also available. If you're a scuba diver, don't miss out on the park's Maritime Heritage Trail, which showcases six of the many shipwrecks in the area.

Detour: On the second half of today's journey, you can also take a detour to the other entrance of Everglades National Park, via the **Ernest F. Coe Visitor Center** (✉ 40001 State Hwy. 9336, Homestead, FL). Hiking enthusiasts may appreciate the more natural trails of this side of the Everglades. And a chance to see crocodiles in the only place where they coexist with alligators, head to the southernmost tip of the park near the **Flamingo Visitor Center** (✉ 1 Flamingo Lodge Hwy., Homestead, FL).

Roadside Attraction: After all these outdoorsy adventures, head to the **Robert Is Here Fruit Stand** (✉ 19200 S.W. 344th St., Homestead, FL ☎ 305/246–1592 ⊕ www.robertishere.com) for the perfect afternoon pick-me-up. It's a slight detour west, but absolutely worth it to try the milkshakes and smoothies made with not-so-typical fruits like guanabana, black sapote, mamey, and more.

KEY LARGO

Do: The gateway to the Florida Keys, Key Largo is all about getting out onto the water, with diving and snorkeling being its most popular activities. Nobody comes to Key Largo without visiting **John Pennekamp Coral Reef State Park** (✉ 102601 Overseas Hwy. ☎ 305/451–6300 ⊕ www.floridastateparks.org), one of the jewels of the state park system. Watersports enthusiasts head to the adjacent Key Largo National Marine Sanctuary, which encompasses about 190 square miles of coral reefs, seagrass beds, and mangrove estuaries. If you've never tried diving, Key Largo is the perfect place to learn. Dozens of companies will be more than happy to show you the ropes, like **Quiescence Diving Services** (✉ 103680 Overseas Hwy. ☎ 305/451–2440 ⊕ www.keylargodiving.com).

Eat & Drink: The only thing more enticing than the cute and quirky environment of **Mrs. Mac's Kitchen** (✉ 99336 Overseas Hwy. ☎ 305/451–3722 ⊕ www.mrsmacskitchen.com), the most popular restaurant in Key Largo, is its full menu of fresh seafood. If you make it in time to watch the sunset, then you'll want to dine or get a drink at **Sundowners** (✉ 103900 Overseas Hwy. ☎ 305/451–4502 ⊕ www.sundownerskeylargo.com), which offers incredible views over Florida Bay as you munch on their menu of steak, hearty sandwiches, and local seafood.

Stay: Baker's Cay Resort (✉ 97000 Overseas Hwy. ☎ 305/852–5553 ⊕ www.hilton.com) offers the ultimate in luxury stays with its serene waterfront location and optional all-inclusive packages that are customizable to your needs. **Kona Kai Resort & Gallery** (✉ 97802 Overseas Hwy. ☎ 305/852–7200 ⊕ www.konakairesort.com) also welcomes guests to a waterfront location but in a more intimate, kids-free setting. Don't forget to enjoy a stroll around the resort's botanical garden and sophisticated art gallery.

Breakfast: Check out **Doc's Diner** (✉ 99696 Overseas Hwy. ☎ 305/451–2895 ⊕ www.docsdiner.com) for all your American breakfast favorites, along with highly rated (and highly sweet) French toast, pancakes, and waffles.

Day 5: Key Largo to Key West

97 miles (2 hours, 15 minutes without traffic and stops)

Today you'll figure out why the southernmost segment of U.S. 1 is nicknamed the Overseas Highway as you cross more than 40 bridges through the Florida Keys before reaching Key West. The one- (at times two-) lane road can be frustrating, but the beautiful views are distracting enough, especially after you pass Marathon Key and find yourself on the Seven Mile Bridge, the longest in all the Florida Keys.

ALONG THE WAY

Town: Besides Key West, Islamorada is one of the most popular places to visit in the Florida Keys. When you see a giant statue of a lobster, be sure to pull over and go shopping at **Rain Barrel Village** (✉ 86700 Overseas Hwy. ☎ 305/521–2043 ⊕ www.rainbarrelvillage.com), where the work of more than 500 artists is on display and you can buy a variety of souvenirs, handmade crafts, and more. Just down the road is the **History of Diving Museum** (✉ 82990 Overseas Hwy. ☎ 305/664–9737 ⊕ www.divingmuseum.org), featuring one of the world's largest collections of diving helmets, armored suits, and scuba gear, plus tons of diving memorabilia.

Shop: While there's no shortage of places offering the region's most famous dessert (sweet-but-tart Key lime pie), the award-winning version from the **Blond Giraffe Key Lime Pie Factory** (✉ *92220 Overseas Hwy.* ☎ *305/922–2400* ⊕ *www.blondgiraffe.com*) in Tavernier is among the best of the best.

Eat & Drink: For a late lunch, stop in Stock Island—about 15 minutes from Key West—for a fresh seafood meal at **Hogfish Bar & Grill** (✉ *6810 Front St.* ☎ *305/293–4041* ⊕ *www.hogfishbar.com*). People flock here for the creamy lobster bisque, the many preparations of locally caught fish, and the famous piña colada bread pudding, which can only be made in limited quantities and often sells out.

KEY WEST

Do: Aimlessly wandering the streets of Key West is entertaining enough with its plethora of shops, art galleries, and bars, but you'll want to go in with a game plan to make the most of your time. Float through the bright and airy greenhouse of the **Key West Butterfly and Nature Conservatory** (✉ *1316 Duval St.* ☎ *305/296–2988* ⊕ *www.keywestbutterfly.com*), where you'll find yourself totally surrounded by hundreds of birds and butterflies who aren't shy about landing on your shoulder. Less than a half mile away, the **Ernest Hemingway Home and Museum** (✉ *907 Whitehead St.* ☎ *305/294–1136* ⊕ *www.hemingwayhome.com*) tells the story of the prolific writer's time in the area, with some Key West history sprinkled in. As the sun begins to set, don't miss out on the biggest party in Key West at **Mallory Square** (✉ *400 Wall St.* ☎ *305/809–3700* ⊕ *www.mallorysquare.com*), where everyone gathers to watch the sunset alongside musicians, food vendors, and street performers.

Photo Op: Between the rogue roosters roaming the roads and the picture-perfect homes with wraparound verandahs, Key West is chock-full of photo ops, but there are two in particular that you can't leave the Keys without: the southernmost point of the continental United States monument, **Southernmost Point Buoy** (✉ *Whitehead St. and South St.*) and the mile marker 0 sign, signaling the start of the Overseas Highway.

Eat & Drink: Grab a bite at **Pepe's Cafe Key West** (✉ *806 Caroline St.* ☎ *305/294–7192* ⊕ *www.pepeskeywest.com*), which is believed to be the oldest eatery in the area and where steak and seafood are the specialties. No matter where you have dinner, end the night with a sweet treat at **Better Than Sex** (✉ *926 Simonton St.* ☎ *305/296–8102* ⊕ *www.betterthansexdesserts.com*), a dessert restaurant, followed by barhopping on Duval Street.

Stay: Teleport to the olden days of Key West with a stay at the **Curry Mansion Inn** (✉ *301–305 Duval St.* ⊕ *www.currymansion.com*), a historic home turned bed-and-breakfast that's the perfect combination of cozy accommodations and central location. For a really unique stay, check out Airbnb's floating boat homes known as the Tiki Suites.

Breakfast: Fill up on seafood eggs Benedict, homemade banana bread, and more with the most "heavenly" breakfast in Key West, served at **Blue Heaven** (✉ *729 Thomas St.* ☎ *305/296–8666* ⊕ *www.blueheavenkw.com*).

Day 6: Dry Tortugas National Park

Don't expect to drive much today because there are only two ways to get to Dry Tortugas National Park: via a flight with **Seaplane Adventures** (✉ *3471 S. Roosevelt Blvd.* ☎ *305/293–9300* ⊕ *www.keywestseaplanecharters.com*), the only company that flies to the park, or via a boat on the **Yankee Freedom III ferry** (✉ *100 Grinnell St.* ☎ *305/294–7009* ⊕ *www.drytortugas.com*).

Do: No matter how you arrive at **Dry Tortugas National Park** (☎ *305/242–7700* ⊕ *www.nps.gov/drto*), you must explore Fort Jefferson, whether on a guided tour or on your own. Then you'll have plenty of time to lounge on the beach, enjoy some world-class snorkeling fit for both beginners and experts, and go birding to spot the nearly 300 species that have been recorded in the area. Those who come on the ferry will have a fully narrated 45-minute tour of Fort Jefferson included in the price of their ticket, while seaplane guests have access to complimentary snorkeling gear.

Eat & Drink: There are no opportunities to purchase food while at Dry Tortugas National Park, so plan accordingly. If you choose to go on a day trip aboard the Yankee Freedom III ferry, a breakfast snack and box lunch are included, but you still might want to bring some extra snacks. Seaplane Adventures provides their guest with water and soft drinks, but no food. If you head back to Key West at the end of the day, enjoy dinner at **Half Shell Raw Bar** (✉ *231 Margaret St.* ☎ *305/294–7496* ⊕ *www.halfshellrawbar.com*) known for its conch ceviche and other fresh seafood.

Stay: If you're feeling adventurous, there are campsites available for overnight stays at Dry Tortugas National Park. Otherwise, head back to the comfort of your Key West home base.

Breakfast: Tasty bites in a eclectic surroundings are offered by the **Koffie House** (✉ *602 Greene St.* ☎ *305/890–1794* ⊕ *www.koffiehouse.com*), while those in need of a quick breakfast with a side of photo ops can head to **Cuban Coffee Queen** (✉ *284 Margaret St.* ☎ *305/292–4747* ⊕ *www.cubancoffeequeen.com*), where a small *Greetings from Key West* mural can be found on the side of the building.

Day 7: Key West to Miami

164 miles (3 hours, 10 minutes without traffic and stops)

Today's drive will be the longest one of the trip as you make your way back to Miami to return your rental and say goodbye to the Sunshine State. As on the way down, you'll spend most of your time on the narrow Overseas Highway (U.S. 1) before crossing into the bigger cities of South Florida. Today's pit stops will be all about checking out the things you didn't see on your way down to Key West.

ALONG THE WAY

Town: Every key in the Florida Keys chain has something different to offer, and Marathon is no exception. Stop here to spend time at the **Turtle Hospital** (✉ *2396 Overseas Hwy.* ☎ *305/743–2552* ⊕ *www.turtlehospital.org*), where daily educational tours show guests how they rehabilitate and release turtles back into the wild. The **Dolphin Research Center** (✉ *58901 Overseas Hwy.* ☎ *305/289–1121* ⊕ *www.dolphins.org*) is also nearby, offering visitors the chance to learn about these adorable mammals with an educational tour and even swim with them.

Roadside Attraction: Robbie's (✉ *77522
Overseas Hwy.* ☎ *305/664–8070*
⊕ *www.robbies.com*) in Islamorada is a
full-service marina with kayaking tours,
parasailing adventures, sunset cruises,
and more, but it's the tarpon feedings
that made this place famous. For a few
dollars, you'll get a bucket of fish that
you can feed to the giant tarpon fish (also
known as silver kings) who hang out by
the dock. With a fish in hand, lower yourself toward the water and wait for them
to jump up and grab the bait with their
mouths wide open. Just watch out for
the nearby pelicans also waiting to steal
your fish. Robbie's also has a few shops
with handcrafts, antiques, souvenirs, and
more. It's also a great place to stop for
lunch or even just coffee and ice cream.

Chapter 8

THE NORTHEAST

WELCOME TO THE NORTHEAST

TOP REASONS TO GO

★ **Niagara Falls:** The three magnificent waterfalls that make up Niagara Falls have been attracting visitors for centuries.

★ **Harriet Tubman Byway:** This 125-mile route takes you through Maryland's eastern shore to over 30 key spots in the legendary abolitionist's life.

★ **Cape May:** The crowning jewel of the northeastern coast, Cape May is a charming throwback to Victorian resort towns.

★ **The White Mountains:** Offering spectacular hiking and skiing, these dramatic peaks and notches are unforgettable.

★ **Acadia National Park:** The Northeast's only national park, Acadia's 49,000 acres of protected forests, beaches, mountains, and rocky coastline can't be missed.

★ **Cape Cod National Seashore:** Thirty miles of superb beaches, great rolling sand dunes, swamps, marshes, wetlands, and pitch-pine and scrub-oak forest make up one of Cape Cod's most defining areas.

1 **The Best of the Chesapeake Bay.** Explore the coasts of Maryland and Virginia while experiencing one of America's most unique ecosystems.

2 **The Best of New York State.** The Empire State is filled with mountain landscapes, cool cities, historic spots, and scenic wineries galore.

3 **The Best of Long Island and the Jersey Shore.** Escape NYC by retreating to its charming neighbors to the east and south, and their beaches, wineries, and museums.

4 **The Best of New England.** Visit all six states that make up this region in one trip packed with culture, history, and New England charm.

5 **New England's Great Outdoors.** Experience the best of New England's lakes, mountains, and national and state parks.

6 **Coastal New England.** Embrace the area's seafaring history by hitting up its best beach towns.

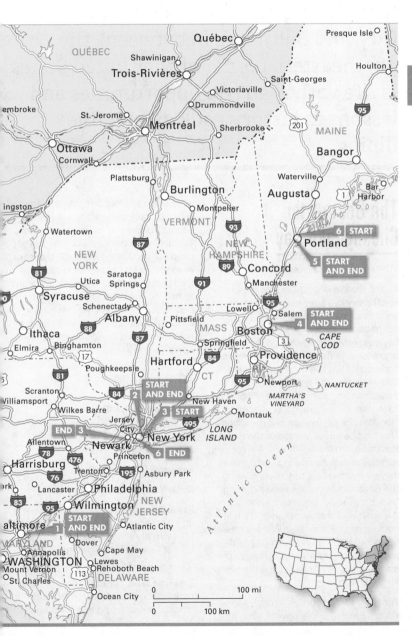

From the deep woods of New England to the lively beaches of the Mid-Atlantic (and the big cities of Boston, New York City, and Baltimore in between), the northeastern corner of the United States is rife with road trip opportunities and lessons in history, geology, and fine dining.

The Best of the Chesapeake Bay

Written by Barbara Noe Kennedy

As the world's largest estuary, the Chesapeake Bay is a salty realm of historic waterfront villages, charming lighthouses, migrating birds, refined inns, and bayside restaurants serving the region's impressive seafood bounty. First reconnoitered by Captain John Smith some 350 years ago, the historic domain of the watermen and women who still harvest its waters retains a bygone, peaceful vibe ideal for exploration and relaxation. This loop begins at the top of the Bay in Baltimore, a historic city with a surprising number of cultural offerings, and makes its way south on country byways along the Bay's western edge before curving back north along its eastern side. Along the way you'll discover Maryland's first colonial capital; trail-laced Westmoreland State Park; George Washington's birthplace; the refined waterside villages of Irvington and St Michaels; and the nearly forgotten Smith Island.

The drive's latter portion through Maryland's Eastern Shore unveils several sites related to freedom fighter Harriet Tubman, particularly along the Harriet Tubman Underground Railroad Byway. Tubman was born near Cambridge and used her knowledge of the Chesapeake's marshes, fields, and rivers in her quest to lead people north to freedom. In addition to historic sites, the area is filled with bed-and-breakfasts in genteel historic buildings, crab shacks, open-air seafood restaurants, and idyllic sunset-watching spots.

At a Glance

Start: Baltimore, MD

End: Baltimore, MD

Miles Traveled: 647 miles

Suggested Duration: 5 days

States Visited: Maryland, Virginia

Key Sights: American Revolution Museum; Annapolis Naval Academy; Baltimore Museum of Art; Historic St. Mary's City; Harriet Tubman Underground Railroad National Historic Site

Best Time to Go: Summer is prime beach time (although be prepared to deal with crowds), while spring and fall bring bird migration and gorgeous foliage (and fewer people). Oyster season is October through March, while blue crabs are harvested April through mid-December.

Day 1: Baltimore, MD, to Annapolis, MD

32 miles (40 minutes without traffic or stops)

Your first day is a perfunctory highway drive via I-97 and U.S. 50 southeast to Annapolis.

ALONG THE WAY

Nature: The paved Baltimore and Annapolis (B&A) Trail rumbles along an old railroad track for 13 miles between Glen Burnie and Annapolis, and it is beloved by walkers and bikers alike. A ranger station in Severna Park occupies an 1889 general store and has a small museum.

Detour: Sandy Point State Park (✉ *1100 E. College Pkwy.* ⊕ *www.dnr.maryland. gov*), 10 miles east of Annapolis via U.S. 50, gives you your first gorgeous glimpse of the Chesapeake Bay. The sandy beach is good for swimming, and you can also fish, crab, picnic, soak in some rays, and take in views of the stunning Chesapeake Bay Bridge.

ANNAPOLIS

Do: Maryland's capital is a leafy, walkable, boat-loving town filled with historic buildings that house boutiques, galleries, restaurants, inns, and museums. At the top of town sits the State Capitol, the nation's oldest continuously working statehouse. From there, stroll down adorable Main Street toward Ego Alley at the harbor with its bougie yachts. The nearby grounds of the **Annapolis Naval Academy** (✉ *121 Blake Rd.* ☎ *410/293–1000* ⊕ *www.usna.edu*) are another tree-shaded place to stroll (don't miss the tomb of Revolutionary War naval commander John Paul Jones). You can also tour the **Thomas Shoal Point Lighthouse**

(☎ *301/440–8763* ⊕ *www.thomaspoint-lighthouse.org*), the Bay's only active screwpile lighthouse, accessible by boat.

Eat & Drink: Take a water taxi from City Dock (or walk across Spa Creek Bridge) to Eastport, Annapolis's lively maritime neighborhood, where several local restaurants comprise Restaurant Row. Divine choices include **Boatyard Bar & Grill** (✉ *400 4th St.* ☎ *410/216–6206* ⊕ *www.boatyardbarandgrill.com*), a nautical-theme place to go for oysters on the half shell and Maryland's official state dessert, Smith Island Cake; **Carrol's Creek Café** (✉ *410 Severn Ave.* ☎ *410/263–8102* ⊕ *www.carrolscreek.com*), serving local seafood overlooking Spa Creek; and **Galway Bay** (✉ *63 Maryland Ave.* ☎ *410/263–8333* ⊕ *www.galwaybaymd. com*), a fun Irish pub. **Chick & Ruth's Delly** (✉ *165 Main St.* ☎ *410/269–6737* ⊕ *www.chickandruths.com*), on Main Street, serves downhome breakfast, lunch, and dinner—it's a favorite spot to spy politicians.

Stay: You'll have your pick of charming inns and B&Bs here. The **Inn at Horn Point** (✉ *534 Burnside St.* ☎ *410/268–1126* ⊕ *www.innathornpoint.com*) in the historic maritime district has water views; **Annapolis Inn** (✉ *144 Prince George St.* ☎ *410/295–5200* ⊕ *www.annapolisinn. com*) conveys sumptuous living from bygone days; and the **Historic Inns of Annapolis** (✉ *58 State Cir.* ☎ *410/263–2641* ⊕ *www.historicinnsofannapolis. com*) offers three boutique inns in meticulously restored historic buildings near the statehouse.

Breakfast: Miss Shirley's Café (✉ *1 Park Pl.* ☎ *410/268–5171* ⊕ *www.missshirleys. com*) is a popular Southern-inspired breakfast spot, while **Iron Rooster** (✉ *12 Market Space* ☎ *410/990–1600* ⊕ *iron-roosterallday.com*) has homemade pop tarts and all-day breakfast.

The Best of Chesapeake Bay

Day 2: Annapolis, MD, to St. Marys City, MD

70 miles (1 hour, 40 mins without traffic or stops)

Follow winding, tree-shaded MD-2 and MD-4 south to California, Maryland. From there, hop on MD-237 and MD-5 for the last scenic stretch into St. Mary's City.

ALONG THE WAY

Nature: A 4-mile out-and-back hike through **Calvert Cliffs State Park** (✉ *10540 H. G. Trueman Rd.* ☎ *443/975–4360* ⊕ *www.dnr.maryland.gov*) leads to the Chesapeake Bay, where you can hunt for fossilized shark's teeth.

Eat & Drink: Attached to the mainland via a bridge, Solomons Island is a humming boat-centric village with several waterfront restaurants, including **Zahniser's Dry Dock** (✉ *251 C St.* ☎ *410/326–4817* ⊕ *www.zahnisers.com*) and Stoney's Kingfishers Seafood Bar & Grill (✉ *14442 Solomons Island Rd. S* ☎ *410/394–0236* ⊕ *www.stoneysseafoodhouse.com*).

ST. MARY'S

Do: Maryland's first settlers arrived from England in 1634 and built a now long-vanished city along the St. Mary's River near the Chesapeake Bay. Today an outdoor living history museum and archaeological site, **St. Mary's** (✉ *18751 Hogaboom La.* ☎ *240/895–4990* ⊕ *www.hsmcdigshistory.org*) showcases the (rebuilt) town center with a stocked mercantile, a tobacco plantation, a Woodland Indian hamlet, and a replica of the *Dove*, the English merchant ship that brought the original colonists.

Eat & Drink: For fresh seafood, head to **Ruddy Duck Seafood and Alehouse** (✉ *16810 Piney Point Rd.* ☎ *301/994–9944* ⊕ *www.ruddyduckseafood.com*) in Piney Point, overlooking the Potomac River and St. George Creek.

Stay: The **Inn at Brome Howard** (✉ *18281 Rosecroft Rd.* ☎ *240/434–3209* ⊕ *www.bromehoward.com*), the only lodging within St. Mary's City, occupies a 19th-century farmhouse that has charming porches overlooking St. Mary's River. Other nearby options include the **Quarters at Pier 450** (✉ *48342 Wynne Rd., Ridge, MD* ☎ *301/679–3900* ⊕ *www.pier450.com*), a restored 1940s fishing camp, and the welcoming **Swanendele Inn at St. Mary's** (✉ *49946 Airedele Rd., Ridge, MD* ☎ *301/576–9910* ⊕ *www.swanendeleinn.com*). And if you're a group, consider the **Cove Point Lighthouse** (✉ *3500 Lighthouse Blvd.* ☎ *410/326–2042* ⊕ *www.calvertmarinemuseum.com*) in Lusby, a historic lighthouse keeper's quarters with two rental units.

Breakfast: Good spots for homestyle favorites include **Linda's Café** (✉ *21779 Tulagi Pl., Lexington Park, MD* ☎ *301/862–3544* ⊕ *www.facebook.com/lindascafelpcity*) in Lexington Park and the **Grille Leonardtown** (✉ *25470-C Point Lookout Rd.* ☎ *301/690–2105* www.leonoardtowngrille.net) in Leonardtown.

Day 3: St. Marys, MD, to Irvington, VA

120 miles (2 hours, 30 minutes without traffic or stops)

Take a leisurely drive on MD-5 and MD-234 to U.S. 301. From there, amble south on two-lane country roads to Irvington through Virginia's Northern Neck.

ALONG THE WAY

Attraction: George Washington was born in 1732 at what's now the **George Washington Birthplace National Monument** (✉ *1732 Popes Creek Rd.* ☎ *804/224–1732* ⊕ *www.nps.gov/gewa*), just off VA-3 near Colonial Beach. The house where Mary Ball gave birth burned down long ago, but within the 538 peaceful

The lively city of Baltimore even has its own Washington Monument.

acres, you'll find a typical 18th-century home that conveys the mood of rural colonial life.

Nature: Oak- and maple-shaded trails lace **Westmoreland State Park** (✉ 145 Cliff Rd. ☎ 804/493–8821 ⊕ www.dcr.virginia. gov), a hidden gem off VA-3 near Montross. Look for bald eagles along the path down to Fossil Beach.

IRVINGTON

Do: A laid-back Tidewater town, Irvington is ideal for strolling, browsing unique boutiques, and slurping oysters. You can peek into the past at the **Steamboat Era Museum** (✉ 156 King Carter Dr. ☎ 804/438–6888 ⊕ www.steamboateramuseum.org) and **Historic Christ Church** (✉ 420 Christ Church Rd. ☎ 804/438–6855 ⊕ www.christchurch1735.org), dating from 1735. Other activities include fishing, golfing, or sailing.

Eat & Drink: Options for trying oysters including **Fish Hawk Oyster Bar** (✉ 480 King Carter Dr. ☎ 804/438–4489 ⊕ www. tidesinn.com), or if you're up for a short drive, **Rappahannock Oyster Co.** (✉ 784 Locklies Creek Rd. ☎ 804/204–1709 ⊕ www.rroysters.com) in nearby Topping, a working oyster farm with a riverfront restaurant, Merroir Tasting Room. The **Dog and Oyster Vineyard** (✉ 170 White Fences Dr. ☎ 804/438–9463 ⊕ www. dogandoyster.com) produces wines that pair delectably with local oysters.

Stay: The **Tides Inn** (✉ 480 King Carter Dr. ☎ 804/438–5000 ⊕ www.tidesinn.com) is a classic retreat with gorgeous Bay views at every turn and even has its own Virginia Oyster Academy, where you can harvest and cook oysters (plenty of other activities include sailing, paddleboarding, wine-and-cheese sunset cruises, and an excellent spa).

Breakfast: **The Local** (✉ 4337 Irvington Rd. ☎ 804/438-9356 ⊕ www.thelocal-blend.com), a community-based coffee shop, offers a tempting menu that includes breakfast sandwiches, açai bowls, and crab muffins.

Day 4: Irvington, VA, to St. Michaels, MD

265 miles (5 hours without traffic or stops)

Wander through Northern Neck country on VA-3 east to I–64, which shuttles across the York River and James River at the southernmost end of Chesapeake Bay. From Virginia Beach, follow U.S. 13 north, which sweeps you above (and beneath) the Chesapeake Bay via the 20-mile Chesapeake Bay Bridge-Tunnel. On the other side, follow U.S. 50 north to MD-33, which brings you into St. Michaels.

ALONG THE WAY

Attraction: The United States won the American Revolution in 1781 at Yorktown, where today you can visit the historic battlefield. Don't miss the state-of-the-art **American Revolution Museum** (✉ *200 Water St.* ☎ *757/253–4838* ⊕ *www.historyisfun. org*) with living-history experiences that include a re-created Continental Army encampment and a Revolution-era farm. You'll also find here the **Watermen's Museum** (✉ *309 Water St.* ☎ *757/887–2641* ⊕ *www.watermens.org*), celebrating the hardworking men and women who make a living off the Chesapeake's waters.

Eat & Drink: The Museum of the American Revolution has a café with Colonial-inspired dishes, or you can try **Water Street Grille** (✉ *323 Water St.* ☎ *757/369–5644* ⊕ *www.waterstreetgrilles.net*), which serves seafood, pasta, and tapas with a York River view.

Detour: One of the Chesapeake's low-lying isles, **Smith Island** (⊕ *smithisland.org*) is accessible via a 50-minute passenger-ferry ride from Crisfield, Maryland. The island lives on the age-old ways of its watermen-and-women, who still make a living harvesting oysters and crabs from the Bay's watery depths. Explore the three villages, bird-watch, sample Smith Island cake, and listen for the Elizabethan accents left over from the original English colonists.

Nature: Migrating birds flock to **Blackwater National Wildlife Refuge** (✉ *2145 Key Wallace Dr.* ☎ *410/228–2677* ⊕ *www. fws.gov*), a marshy sanctuary with hiking, kayaking, and the largest breeding population of bald eagles on the East Coast north of Florida. In addition, archaeologists recently discovered a historic homestead within the refuge that was owned by Ben Ross, Harriet Tubman's father; Tubman likely spent time here as a child and lived here as a teenager.

Attraction: Harriet Tubman's famous escapes north started in the Cambridge area, where she spent her childhood. Her story is told in depth at the 17-acre **Harriet Tubman Underground Railroad National Historical Site** (✉ *4068 Golden Hill Rd.* ☎ *410/221–2290* ⊕ *www.nps.gov/hatu*). The 125-mile Harriet Tubman Underground Railroad Byway, linking historic sites related to Tubman's life, starts here. For even more insight into Tubman's life, a bit farther north in Cambridge you'll find the **Harriet Tubman Museum and Educational Center** (✉ *424 Race St.* ☎ *410/228–0401* ⊕ *www.harriettubmanorganization.com*).

ST. MICHAELS

Do: Once a thriving Colonial seaport, this quintessential Chesapeake village is built for casual ambling, with one-of-a-kind shops, galleries, and restaurants along Talbot Street and open-air seafood restaurants and inns snuggling its harbor. It's also home to the esteemed **Chesapeake Bay Maritime Museum** (✉ *213 N. Talbot St.* ☎ *410/745–2916* ⊕ *www.cbmm. org*), a working shipyard with generational shipbuilders, hands-on activities, and the 1879 Hooper Strait Lighthouse. Be sure to get on the water at some point; *Selina II* (✉ *101 N. Harbor Rd.* ☎ *410/726–9400* ⊕ *www.sailselina.com*), a luxury sailing yacht, and **Patriot Cruises** (☎ *410/745–3100* ⊕ *www.patriotcruises.com*), with its narrated river cruises, are two possibilities.

Eat & Drink: The Chesapeake's bounty is served boiled, steamed, and grilled at **St. Michaels Crab & Steak House** (✉ *305 Mulberry St.* ☎ *410/745–3737* ⊕ *www. stmichaelscrabhouse.com*), in the historic harbor area. For something fancier but still local, try **Stars Restaurant** (✉ *308 Watkins La.* ☎ *443/258–2228* ⊕ *www. innatperrycabin.com/dining-areas/stars*) within the Inn at Perry Cabin on the town's western edge.

Stay: St. Michaels has tons of options for upscale B&Bs and inns. **Aida's Victoriana Inn** (✉ *205 Cherry St.* ☎ *410/745–3368* ⊕ *www.victorianainn.com*) overlooks the harbor; the **Parsonage Inn** (✉ *210 N. Talbot St.* ☎ *410/745–8383* ⊕ *www.parson-age-inn.com*), in a splendid Victorian, dates from 1883; and the **Inn at Perry Cabin** (✉ *308 Watkins La.* ☎ *410/745–2200* ⊕ *www.innatperrycabin.com*) is an elegant splurge.

Breakfast: Crepes by the Bay (✉ *413 S. Talbot St.* ☎ *410/745–8429* ⊕ *crepes-by-the-bay.business.site*) serves crepes with crab and spinach, artichokes and smoked salmon, and other creative twists.

Day 5: St. Michaels, MD, to Baltimore, MD

160 miles (3 hours, 30 minutes without traffic or stops)

Take country roads east to Preston and north to Denton, along the Harriet Tubman Underground Railroad Byway (for those interested in exploring the Byway further, a self-guided driving tour can be downloaded online). Then head north to I–95 via MD-404 and MD-213. From there, it's a straight shot back to Baltimore via I–95, which gives you time to explore one of America's most under-rated cities.

ALONG THE WAY

Attraction: Hop on the Harriet Tubman Underground Railroad Byway between Preston and Denton, which showcases a total of 36 Tubman-related sites, including **Linchester Mill** (✉ *3390 Linchester Rd.* ☎ *410/673–7929* ⊕ *www.prestonmary-land.us*), a re-created 19th-century village in Preston offering a glimpse into life during Tubman's times; the restored, hand-hewn **James H. Webb Cabin** (✉ *Grove Rd.* ⊕ *harriettubmanbyway.org/webb-cabin*) in Preston, representing typical housing for most free African Americans in the 1800s; and **Tuckahoe Neck Friends Meeting House** (✉ *24820 Meeting House Rd.* ⊕ *www.carolinehistory.org*) in Denton, one of five Quaker meeting houses whose members maintained a local Underground Railroad network.

Eat & Drink: Shore Gourmet (✉ *512 Franklin St.* ☎ *410/479–2452* ⊕ *www.shoregour-metmarket.com*) in Denton, housed in a century-old schoolhouse, is a fun place to stop for a healthy, fresh bite with ingredients form local farmers and producers.

Photo Op: Colonial buildings pack the historic village of **Chestertown,** with spectacular sunsets fanning out over its picture-perfect harbor.

Town: The graceful Chesapeake City Bridge offers a soaring view over the genteel village of **Chesapeake City**, a working canal town packed with restaurants and shops occupying 19th-century buildings.

Roadside Attraction: Duck decoys are an art form throughout the Chesapeake region, with the little town of Havre de Grace as the centerpiece. Decoy carvers have whittled away here for decades, a legacy celebrated at the **Havre de Grace Decoy Museum** (✉ *215 Giles St.* ☎ *410/939–3739* ⊕ *www.decoymuseum. com*).

BALTIMORE

Do: In this thriving harborside metropolis, you'll find world-class museums, booming art scenes, historical sites, and excellent restaurants and bars. **The Walters Art Museum** (✉ 600 N. Charles St. ☎ 410/547–9000 ⊕ www.thewalters. org), the **Baltimore Museum of Art** (✉ 10 Art Museum Dr. ☎ 443/573–1700 ⊕ www. artbma.org), and the **American Visionary Art Museum** (✉ 800 Key Hwy. ☎ 410/244–1900 ⊕ www.avam.org) are gems for art lovers while the **National Aquarium** (✉ 501 E. Pratt St. ☎ 410/576–3800 ⊕ www. aqua.org) is considered one of the country's best. Fort McHenry (✉ 2400 E. Fort Ave. ☎ 410/962–4290 ⊕ www. nps.gov/fomc) commemorates Francis Scott Key's writing of the "Star-Spangled Banner." Or you can simply take in the waterfront scenes of historic Fell's Point and the Inner Harbor, both hopping with restaurants, shops, and galleries.

Eat & Drink: Peter's Inn in Fell's Point (✉ 504 S. Ann St. ☎ 410/675–7313 ⊕ www.petersinn.com), once a gritty biker bar, serves classy farm-to-market fare in a cozy space. For true Chesapeake flavor, try **Bertha's Restaurant and Bar** (✉ 734 S. Broadway ☎ 410/327–5795 ⊕ www. berthas.com) in Fell's Point; **Faidley's Seafood** (✉ 203 N. Paca St. ☎ 410/727–4898 ⊕ www.faidleyscrabcakes.com) in the historic Lexington Market, famed for its jumbo lump crab cakes; or beachy **Nick's Fish House** (✉ 2600 Insulator Dr. ☎ 410/347–4123 ⊕ www.nicksfishhouse. com), with wooden decks overlooking the water.

Stay: Luxurious **Sagamore Pendry** (✉ 1715 Thames St. ☎ 443/552–1400 ⊕ www. pendry.com) in Fell's Point occupies the city's vintage Recreation Pier. The **Ivy Hotel** (✉ 205 E. Biddle St. ☎ 410/514–6500 ⊕ www.theivybaltimore.com) is another sumptuous option, in a historic mansion in the Mount Vernon neighborhood. The landmark **Lord Baltimore Hotel** (✉ 20 W. Baltimore St. ☎ 410/539–8400 ⊕ www.lordbaltimorehotel.com), built downtown in 1928, has an old world–style lobby.

Breakfast: Blue Moon Café (✉ 1621 Aliceanna St. ☎ 410/522–3940 ⊕ www. bluemoonbalitmore.com) in Fell's Point is bright and funky with hearty dishes like scrapple-and-egg sandwiches and crab-and-bacon Benedicts.

The Best of New York State

Written by Mark Sullivan

You'll be surprised how quickly the skyscrapers and apartment towers of Manhattan can give way to the countryside once you head upstate. Within a couple of hours you'll be traversing rolling hills and majestic stands of evergreen trees.

After leaving New York City, this trip takes you through some of the favored vacation destinations for city residents and out-of-towners alike. The Hudson Valley, the Catskills, the Adirondacks, and the Finger Lakes draw those who want to experience a slower pace of life and the state's spectacular scenery. There are plenty of alternate routes to choose, many taking you past waterfalls or through beautifully restored covered bridges.

At a Glance

Start: New York City, NY

End: New York City, NY

Miles Traveled: 1,162 miles

Suggested Duration: 9 days

States Visited: New York

Key Sights: Central Park; Finger Lakes wineries; Franklin D. Roosevelt National Historic Site; Niagara Falls; Storm King Arts Center

8

The Northeast THE BEST OF NEW YORK STATE

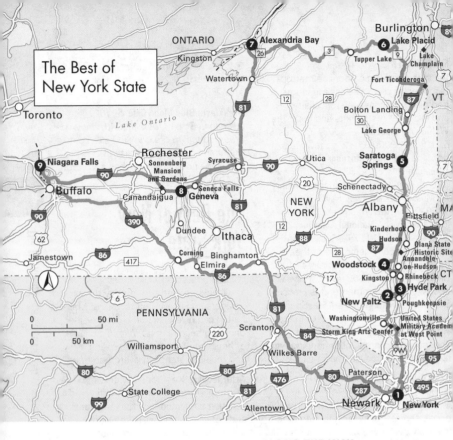

The Best of
New York State

Best Time to Go:

Best Time to Go: New York City shines no matter what season you visit. Unless you're in search of winter sports, Upstate New York is definitely more of a warm-weather destination. With so many outdoor activities, this itinerary is ideal to follow from late spring to fall.

Day 1: New York City, NY, to New Paltz, NY

92 miles (2 hours without traffic or stops)

Day one takes you north of the city into the heart of the Hudson Valley, heading up the scenic Palisades Parkway to the charming town of New Paltz.

ALONG THE WAY

Attraction: Perched on a picturesque spot overlooking the Hudson River, the **United States Military Academy at West Point** (✉ *2107 New South Post Rd.* ☎ *845/938-2638* ⊕ *www.westpoint.edu*)—more commonly known as just West Point—is a short detour off 9W along NY-218. Stop by for a tour of the West Point Museum in one of the handsome stone buildings that make up the complex. Fort Putnam, a key strategic point in the Revolutionary War, has been carefully restored.

Attraction: Spread out over 500 acres of fields and forests, **Storm King Arts Center** (✉ *1 Museum Rd., New Windsor, NY* ☎ *845/534-3115* ⊕ *stormking.org*) is an impressive array of dozens of large-scale sculptures created by some of the best artists in the world, including David Smith, Alexander Calder, and Isamu

Noguchi. A free shuttle takes you past the sculptures or you can walk through the grounds and find the perfect spot for a picnic lunch (and an art selfie).

Eat & Drink: Dating back to 1839 and claiming to be America's oldest winery, the stone buildings of **Brotherhood Winery** (✉ *100 Brotherhood Plaza Dr.* ☎ *845/496-3661* ⊕ *www.brotherhood-winery.com*) are a short drive west from Storm King in Washingtonville. After dining on country-style French fare at the restaurant, enjoy a tour and tasting.

NEW PALTZ

Do: The Shawangunk Mountains are the top destination in these parts, and 21,000 acres of this rocky terrain is in **Minnewaska State Park Preserve** (✉ *5281 Route 44-55, Kerhonkson, NY* ☎ *845/255-0751* ⊕ *www.parks.ny.gov*). The jewel here is Lake Minnewaska itself, easily reachable from the Lake Minnewaska Visitor Center off NY-44.

Eat & Drink: It's no surprise that a university town like New Paltz would have such a diverse dining scene. One of the best eateries is **A Tavola** (✉ *46 Main St.* ☎ *845/255-1426* ⊕ *www.atavolany.com*), a sophisticated trattoria on Main Street.

Stay: Nothing can prepare you for the jumble of towers, turrets, and chimneys that make **Mohonk Mountain House** (✉ *1000 Mountain Rest Rd.* ☎ *845/795-3286* ⊕ *www.mohonk.com*) such an awe-inspiring sight. Even better is its location on a rocky outcropping over a crystal-blue mountain lake. To get here from New Paltz, take Mountain Rest Road west.

Breakfast: On Main Street, **Mudd Puddle** (✉ *Walter St. Market, 10 Main St.* ☎ *845/255-3436* ⊕ *www.muddpuddlecoffee.com*) is where locals congregate in the morning for coffee and conversation. The pastries are great, too.

Day 2: New Paltz, NY, to Hyde Park, NY

25 miles (47 minutes without traffic and stops)

Today take the Mid-Hudson Bridge to the eastern side of the Hudson Valley, exploring some of the region's most charming stops along the way. The day's final destination is Hyde Park, which was a relaxing retreat for the very presidential Roosevelt family. Both Theodore and Franklin spent time here, and Franklin's wife, Eleanor, turned it into a hub for her political organizing.

ALONG THE WAY

Town: The riverside community of Poughkeepsie is home to **Vassar College** (✉ *124 Raymond Ave.* ☎ *845/437-7000* ⊕ *www.vassar.edu*), founded in 1865 as a women's college. The 1,000-acre campus is well worth a stroll, especially if you duck into the striking Frances Lehman Loeb Art Center, designed by world-famous architect César Pelli.

Eat & Drink: On Poughkeepsie's Main Street, **Brasserie 292** (✉ *292 Main St.* ☎ *845/473-0292* ⊕ *www.brasserie292.com*) is a classic bistro down to its pressed-copper ceilings and red-leather banquettes.

Photo Op: The world's longest pedestrian bridge, the 1¼-mile **Walkway Over the Hudson** (✉ *61 Parker Ave.* ☎ *845/834-2867* ⊕ *www.walkway.org*) runs from Highland in the west to Poughkeepsie in the east. It has some of the best views of New York's famous river.

HYDE PARK

Do: As it runs through Hyde Park, NY-9 becomes Albany Post Road. The thoroughfare is quite charming, lined with Dutch-colonial-style buildings made of golden fieldstone. Your first stop along the road should be the **Franklin D. Roosevelt National Historic Site** (✉ *4079*

Niagara Falls is made up of American Falls and Bridal Veil Falls in New York and Horseshoe Falls in Canada.

Albany Post Rd. ☎ *845/486–7770* ⊕ *www.fdrlibrary.org*), the birthplace of the 32nd president. It's also home to his presidential library, the first such library to be constructed and designed by the president it honors. The only National Historic Site dedicated to a first lady, the **Eleanor Roosevelt National Historic Site** (✉ *106 Valkill Park Rd.* ☎ *845/229–9422* ⊕ *www.nps.gov/elro*) is at Val-Kill Cottage, the home she maintained about two miles from the family home. While the Roosevelt homes were family places, the **Vanderbilt Mansion** (✉ *119 Vanderbilt Park Rd.* ☎ *845/229–9115* ⊕ *www.nps.gov/vama*) was made for aristocratic living. It's considered one of the architectural treasures on the Northeast and can be explored by visitors today.

Eat & Drink: Just off Albany Post Road, the **Culinary Institute of America** (✉ *1946 Campus Dr.* ☎ *845/452–9600* ⊕ *www.ciachef.edu*) has an eye-popping location in a former Jesuit monastery. The most respected culinary school on the East Coast, it has five student-run restaurants. The best might be Bocuse, which serves classic French fare.

Stay: Across from the entrance to the Vanderbilt Mansion on Albany Post Road, the **Journey Inn** (✉ *1 Sherwood Pl.* ☎ *845/229–8972* ⊕ *www.journeyinn.com*) is a lovely bed-and-breakfast filled with treasures from the owner's travels. The lovely Vanderbilt Suite has two rooms done up in shades of ivory and gold.

Breakfast: On the grounds of the Culinary Institute of America, the **Apple Pie Bakery Café** (✉ *Culinary Institute of America, 1946 Campus Dr.* ☎ *845/905-4500* ⊕ *www.applepiebakerycafe.com*) has soaring arched windows letting in lots of sunlight. The sweet and savory dishes are standouts.

Day 3: Hyde Park, NY, to Woodstock, NY

35 miles (55 minutes without traffic or stops)

Head north on NY-9G, crossing the Hudson once again on your way to the hippie (and more and more these days, hipster) Catskills hangout of Woodstock.

ALONG THE WAY

Town: Often topping the list of the country's most charming small towns, Rhinebeck is bisected by NY-9, which is called Mill Street as it passes by the area's beautifully preserved century-old homes. Just outside town is **Wilderstein** (✉ 330 Morton Rd. ☎ 845/876-4818 ⊕ www.wilderstein.org), a dazzling display of Victorian exuberance with a five-story-tall turret. Rhineback shines on summer weekends when there are air shows at the **Old Rhineback Aerodrome** (✉ 9 Norton Rd., Red Hook, NY ☎ 845/752–3200 ⊕ www.oldrhineback. org). For a different but no less charming vibe, head directly across the river to explore up-and-coming Kingston, a historic city (it was New York State's first capital) with an artistic bent and family-friendly.

Eat & Drink: You can't do better for lunch than **Terrapin** (✉ 6426 Montgomery St. ☎ 845/876–3330 ⊕ www.terrapin-restaurant.com), just off Mill Street on Montgomery Street in Rhinebeck. Its location in an 1825 church makes it one of the region's most memorable restaurants. Or try **Outdated Café** (✉ 314 Wall St. ☎ 845/331–0030 ⊕ www.outdatedcafe. com) in Kingston, a quirky café set within an antiques shop that serves coffee, sandwiches, and pastries made from scratch.

Detour: It's well worth a short detour up NY-9G to Annandale-on-Hudson, which is pretty much synonymous with the 540-acre campus of **Bard College** (✉ 30 Campus Rd. ☎ 845/758–6822 ⊕ www. bard.edu). Its parklike surroundings make it one of the loveliest spots in the Hudson Valley.

Nature: One of the region's most rewarding hikes is at **Poet's Walk** (✉ 776 River Rd., Red Hook, NY ☎ 845/473–4440 ⊕ www.scenichudson.org), an easy 2.2-mile trail within a 120-acre park with sweeping views of the Hudson River in the foreground and the Catskill Mountains in the distance.

WOODSTOCK

Do: Although it might have a countercultural reputation thanks to a certain music festival, the town of Woodstock is actually pretty mellow. The Catskills Mountains' community is perfect for an afternoon of window-shopping, and you can't do better than duck into its boutiques, bookshops, and art galleries or stop for a cup of coffee at one of its numerous cafés. There are two standout cultural havens: the **Woodstock Artists Association and Museum** (✉ 28 Tinker St. ☎ 845/679–2940 ⊕ www.woodstockart.org) and the **Center for Photography at Woodstock** (✉ 59 Tinker St. ☎ 845/679–9957 ⊕ www. cpw.org).

Eat & Drink: In a rambling farmhouse on Mill Hill Road, **Cucina** (✉ 109 Mill Hill Rd. ☎ 845/679–9800 ⊕ www.cucinawoodstock.com) serves the area's best Italian fare. A charming storefront on Tinker Street is home to **Shindig** (✉ 1 Tinker St. ☎ 772/684–7091 ⊕ www.woodstock-shindig.com), which offers comfort food along with ciders, ales, and all manner of craft beers.

Stay: "Hippie chic" might be the best way to describe the **Hotel Dylan** (✉ 320 Maverick Rd. ☎ 846/684–5422 ⊕ www. thehoteldylan.com), a boutique hotel with surprisingly sophisticated rooms. It's on Maverick Road, six minutes from downtown.

Breakfast: On Tinker Street, long-time favorite **Oriole 9** (✉ *17 Tinker St.* ☎ *845/679–5763* ⊕ *www.oriole9.com*) is the breakfast spot people rave about, especially because most of the produce comes from the owner's organic farm. Lunch is tasty, too. Or take a slight detour a bit west of Woodstock to sample the highly rated yet simple breakfasts at the **Phoenician Diner** (✉ *5681 NY-28, Phoenicia, NY* ☎ *845/688–9957* ⊕ *www.phoeniciadiner.com*); specialties include corned beef hash and chicken and waffles.

Day 4: Woodstock, NY, to Saratoga Springs, NY

99 miles (2 hours without traffic or stops)

Your destination today is Saratoga Springs, where people have gone to "take the waters" for hundreds of years. You can take I–87 most of the way there, passing into the Adirondack Mountains and its gentle hills and evergreen forests along the way.

ALONG THE WAY

Town: With its more than 100 antique shops, hipster haven Hudson is the perfect place to pass an hour or two. About four miles south of town on NY-9G is **Olana State Historic Site** (✉ *5720 State Rte. 9G* ☎ *518/751–0344* ⊕ *www.olana. org*), a 37-room Moorish-style castle built in the 1870s by Hudson River School artist Frederic Church. Looking like a temple crossed with a railroad station, it's unforgettable.

Eat & Drink: In a fickle community that's always looking for the next big thing, Hudson's **Swoon Kitchenbar** (✉ *340 Warren St.* ☎ *518/822–8938* ⊕ *www.swoonkitchenbar.com*) has stood the test of time. It's farm-to-table fare that stands up to the hype.

Town: The tiny village of Kinderhook has two outsized attractions. On Old Post

Road is the **Martin Van Buren National Historic Site** (✉ *1013 Old Post Rd.* ☎ *518/758–9689* ⊕ *www.nps.gov.mava*), a Federal-style mansion owned by the country's eighth president. And of the best surviving examples of 18th-century Dutch-colonial style is the handsome **Luykas Van Alen House** (✉ *2589 NY-9H* ☎ *518/758–9265* www.cchsny.org).

SARATOGA SPRINGS

Do: On the National Register of Historic Places, 2,200-acre **Saratoga Spa State Park** (✉ *19 Roosevelt Dr.* ☎ *518/584–2535* ⊕ *www.parks.ny.gov*) is a year-round draw, with walking trails in warmer weather and cross-country skiing in winter. This is also where you'll find the Roosevelt Baths and Spa. On the grounds of Saratoga Raceway, the **Saratoga Harness Racing Museum and Hall of Fame** (✉ *352 Jefferson St.* ☎ *518/587–4210*) is a celebration of the region's Thoroughbred horse racing tradition. Yaddo is a highly regarded artists' colony, and it's a treat to wander through the formal gardens.

Eat & Drink: In a coveted corner spot on Phila Street in Saratoga Springs, **Ravenous** (✉ *21 Phila St.* ☎ *518/581–0560* ⊕ *www.ravenouscrepes.com*) is famous for its sweet and savory crepes. If you're looking for more refined fare, your best choice is the elegant **15 Church** (✉ *15 Church St.* ☎ *518/587–1515* ⊕ *www.15churchrestaurant.com*).

Stay: For a taste of what visitors a century ago experienced when they came to Saratoga Springs for a relaxing retreat, book a stay at the **Gideon Putnam Resort and Spa** (✉ *24 Gideon Putnam Rd.* ☎ *866/890–1171* ⊕ *www.gideonputnam. com*). It has a perfect spot inside the borders of Saratoga Spa State Park.

Breakfast: It bills itself as a bakery, but **Mrs. London's** (✉ *464 Broadway* ☎ *518/581–8100* ⊕ *www.mrslondonbakery.com*) is also the perfect spot for a cup of coffee and an oven-fresh pastry.

Day 5: Saratoga Springs, NY, to Lake Placid, NY

125 miles (2 hours, 40 minutes without traffic or stops)

It's a pretty simple route—I-87 to NY-9N to NY-73—that leads directly to Lake Placid, a wintertime destination that might just be ever more beautiful in the summer. Veer off onto NY-9N to take in beautiful Lake George and Lake Champlain along the way.

ALONG THE WAY

Photo Op: New York's Route 9 N runs alongside the western shores of Lake George and Lake Champlain, making it one of the most scenic drives in the region.

Eat & Drink: On Main Street in the lakeside community of Bolton Landing, family-run **Cate's Italian Garden** (✉ 4952 Lake Shore Dr. ☎ 518/644-2041 ⊕ www.catesitaliangarden.com) offers a wide range of classic dishes.

Attraction: Originally named Fort Carillon, this structure built by the French in 1755 was captured by the British in 1759 and renamed **Fort Ticonderoga** (✉ 102 Fort Ti Rd. ☎ 518/585-2821 ⊕ www.fortticonderoga.org). It fell into the hands of colonists in 1775, but only until the British realized they could put cannons atop nearby Mount Defiance.

LAKE PLACID

Do: Built for the 1932 Olympic Games, the **Olympic Center** (✉ 2634 Main St. ☎ 518/523-1655 ⊕ www.lakeplacidolympicsites.com) was home to the "Miracle on Ice," where the American men's ice hockey team took the gold medal away from the seemingly unbeatable Soviets. Feel the thrill of victory with bobsled and luge rides on the competition track.

Eat & Drink: Located within the Mirror Lake Inn, **The View** (✉ 77 Mirror Lake Dr.

Extend Your Trip

From Saratoga: Retracing the American Revolution *(Ch. 2)*

From Niagara Falls: All the Great Lakes *(Ch. 6)*; A Frank Lloyd Wright Tour *(Ch. 6)*

From New York City: The Best of Long Island and the Jersey Shore *(Ch. 8)*; Coastal New England *(Ch. 8)*

☎ 518/253-2544 ⊕ www.mirrorlakeinn.com) lives up to its name with floor-to-ceiling windows overlooking the sparkling waters below and the tallest peaks of the Adirondacks in the distance.

Stay: The region's only waterfront resort, the posh **Lake Placid Lodge** (✉ 144 Lodge Way ☎ 518/523-2700 ⊕ www.lakeplacidlodge.com) makes the most of its location with stunning views from almost everywhere, including your room. Expect extras like crackling fireplaces and hand-hewn furnishings.

Breakfast: Fluffy flapjacks topped with locally made maple syrups are the specialty at the **Farmhouse Café** (✉ 2726 Main St. ☎ 518/523-3139) on Main Street.

Day 6: Lake Placid, NY, to Alexandria Bay, NY

132 miles (2 hours, 45 minutes without traffic and stops)

Due west from Lake Placid, mostly along NY-3 and NY-26, is Alexandria Bay. This stretch of shoreline along the St. Lawrence River is known for its "castles" built by wealthy New Yorkers as weekend retreats.

ALONG THE WAY

Eat & Drink: A great place to refuel is the **Pine Grove** (✉ *166 Main St.* ☎ *518/359–3669* ⊕ *pine-grove-restaurant.business.site*), where comfort foods take pride of place in the menu. It's on Main Street in Tupper Lake.

Roadside Attraction: In Tupper Lake, the **Wild Center** (✉ *45 Museum Dr.* ☎ *518/359–7800* ⊕ *www.wildcenter.org*) lets you stroll above the treetops on a series of wooden walkways.

ALEXANDRIA BAY

Do: The Thousands Islands region has attracted wealthy vacationers for more than a century. George C. Boldt, proprietor of The Waldorf Astoria hotel in New York, began building the 120-room **Boldt Castle** (✉ *1 Heart Island* ☎ *315/482–9724* ⊕ *www.boldtcastle.com*) in 1900. It remained unfinished for more than 70 years, when it was finally completed in spectacular fashion. Modest in comparison is the 28-room **Singer Castle** (✉ *1136 Country Rte. 6, Chippewa Bay, NY* ☎ *315/324–3275* ⊕ *www.singercastle.com*), built in 1905 as a summer home for Frederick C. Bourne, president of Singer Co. Ltd. of sewing machines' fame. Take a boat tour to either castle from Alexandria Bay.

Eat & Drink: There are plenty of waterfront eateries in Alexandria Bay, but the Kitchen at the **Captain Visger Inn** (✉ *2 Church St.* ☎ *315/681–3422* ⊕ *www.captainvisgerhouse.com*) is special, especially if you can snag a table in the garden and take in the sunset views.

Stay: Just north of Alexandria Bay, the **Harbor Hotel** (✉ *16 N. Franklin St., Watkins Glen, NY* ☎ *607/535–6116* ⊕ *www.watkinsglenharborhotel.com*) sits right on the edge of the St. Lawrence River and has lovely views from the guest rooms.

Breakfast: Locals rave about the quiches at **Coffee Pot Cathy's** (✉ *3 James St.* ☎ *315/482–0818*), a favorite in Alexandria Bay.

Day 7: Alexandria Bay, NY, to Geneva, NY

145 miles (2 hours, 20 minutes without traffic or stops)

On day six, you're headed to the Finger Lakes, New York's top wine region. I–81 takes you down to Syracuse, and then I–90 skirts across the northern tips of the long, slender lakes that give the region its name.

ALONG THE WAY

Town: A college town, Syracuse is filled with institutes of higher learning. But the **Erie Canal Museum** (✉ *318 Erie Blvd. E* ☎ *315/471–0593* ⊕ *www.eriecanalmuseum.org*) just feels like fun, with a replica of a canal boat in a handsome 1850s building that once served as a weigh station.

Eat & Drink: Once a darling of the biker crowd, Syracuse's **Dinosaur Bar-B-Que** (✉ *246 W. Willow St.* ☎ *315/476–4937* ⊕ *www.dinosaurbarbque.com*) is now known throughout the state for its barbecued ribs and salt potatoes.

Town: Just before you reach Geneva, you'll pass by the town of Seneca Falls, famous as the location for the first women's rights convention in the United States in 1848, considered the beginning of the suffrage movement. Today you can visit the **Women's Rights National Historical Park** (✉ *136 Fall St.* ☎ *315/568–0024* ⊕ *www.nps.gov/wori*) and the **National Women's Hall of Fame** (✉ *1 Canal St.* ☎ *315/568–8060* ⊕ *www.womenofthehall.org*).

GENEVA

Do: New York's best-known wine region, the Finger Lakes encompasses 11 extremely long, narrow bodies of water created 10,000 years ago when the glaciers receded. There's not really a main town of the Finger Lakes, but Geneva, on the northern tip of Seneca

Lake, has a bustling downtown and lots of cultural activities. The main activity, though, is visiting wineries. A longtime favorite is **Fox Run Vineyards** (⌧ *670 NY-14, Penn Yan, NY* ☎ *315/536–4616* ⊕ *www. foxrunvineyards.com*), on NY-14 south of Geneva. It's housed in a converted Civil War–era dairy barn. On Route 76 near the town of Hammondsport is **Heron Hill Winery** (⌧ *9301 CR 76* ☎ *607/868–4241* ⊕ *www.heronhill.com*), known for its beautiful views of Keuka Lake. Also on Keuka Lake is **Dr. Konstantin Frank Vinifera Wine Cellars** (⌧ *9749 Middle Rd.* ☎ *800/320–0735* ⊕ *www.drfrankwines. com*), founded by a Ukrainian immigrant who is considered the father of vini-culture in the region. Be sure to drive responsibly as you visit the wineries, or sign up for a winery tour that does the driving for you.

Eat & Drink: In the town of Dundee, half-way between Geneva and Watkins Glen, is **FLX Wienery** (⌧ *5090 NY-14* ☎ *607/243–7100* ⊕ *www.flxwienery.com*), where you'll find homemade brats, chorizo, and other types of sausage. Dundee's Glenora Wine Cellars is home to the farm-to-table favorite **Veraisons** (⌧ *5435 NY-14* ☎ *800/243–5513* ⊕ *www.glen-dora.com*), which is inspired by produce from local purveyors. In a space that was once a convenience store on Geneva's West Lake Road, **Ports Café** (⌧ *4432 W. Lake Rd.* ☎ *315/789–2020* ⊕ *www. portscafe.com*) is now a chic eatery with a globe-trotting menu.

Stay: Built in 1889, the massive **Belhurst Castle** (⌧ *4069 W. Lake Rd.* ☎ *315/781–0201* ⊕ *www.bellhurst.com*) is on the National Register of Historic Places. It sits outside the town of Geneva on the northwestern shore of Seneca Lake, pro-viding sweeping views from many of its rooms. An understated elegance imbues **Mirbeau Inn & Spa** (⌧ *851 W. Genesee Street Rd.* ☎ *877/647–2328* ⊕ *www. mirbeau.com*), on Genesee Street Rd. in the town of Skaneateles.

Breakfast: On NY-414 in Hector, the beloved **Stonecat Café** (⌧ *5315 NY-414* ☎ *607/546–5000*) is the best place to stop for breakfast or brunch. Ingredients come from local farms like Lively Run Goat Dairy.

Day 8: Geneva, NY, to Niagara Falls, NY

121 miles (2 hours without traffic and stops)

Today I–90 will take you to New York's northwest corner, which holds the city of Buffalo and the treasured American icon that is Niagara Falls.

ALONG THE WAY

Attraction: A few miles west of Geneva is **Sonnenberg Mansion and Gardens** (⌧ *151 Charlotte St.* ☎ *585/394–4922* ⊕ *www. sonnenberg.org*) in the town of Canandai-gua. The 52-acre grounds are a magnif-icent example of late-Victorian garden design.

Eat & Drink: In downtown Canandaigua, the storefront **Patty's Place** (⌧ *33 N. Main St.* ☎ *585/396–9470*) is an idea place to fuel up for the drive. The breakfast pizza, piled with sausage, bacon, mozzarella, and cheddar, is a crowd pleaser.

NIAGARA FALLS

Do: Once you arrive in the city of Buffalo, you're going to want to visit its most famous feature. Misty mornings are per-haps the best time to visit Niagara Falls—made up of American Falls and Bridal Veil Falls in New York and Horseshoe Falls across the border in Ontario, Canada—but there's not really a bad time to visit. Take it all in from **Niagara Falls State Park** (⌧ *332 Prospect St.* ☎ *716/278–1794* ⊕ *www.niagarafallsstatepark.com*), established in 1885 to protect the pub-lic's access to the falls.

Eat & Drink: On Buffalo's Rhode Island Street, the **Left Bank** (⌧ *511 Rhode Island*

St. ☎ 716/882–3509 ⊕ www.leftbankres-taurant.com) is a dimly lit bistro with a friendly bar and a relaxed back garden. A far-reaching wine list doesn't overlook the best New York vintages at Wine on Third (✉ 501 3rd St. ☎ 716/589–9463 ⊕ www.wineonthird.com), a long, narrow eatery that's not far from the falls, but away from the crowds.

Stay: The classic choice is the **Red Coach Inn** (✉ 2 Buffalo Ave. ☎ 716/282–1459 ⊕ www.redcoach.com), on Buffalo Street in Niagara Falls. Rooms are individually decorated in English country house style.

Breakfast: You'll rub elbows with plenty of locals at **Betty's in Buffalo** (✉ 370 Virginia St. ☎ 716/362–0633 ⊕ www.bettysbuffalo.com), a modern take on the classic diner. Try the Scrambled Mess, which is a pile of fresh vegetables and asiago cheese over eggs, accompanied by home fries.

Day 9: Niagara Falls, NY, to New York City, NY

388 miles (6 hours, 30 minutes without traffic and stops)

The last day of the trip is the most driving-heavy as you head back through the Finger Lakes toward New York City. The long journey is still quite scenic as you drive through the heart of New York's farming communities. Depending on if you make stops, you might only have one night in NYC to take in what the city has to offer, so it might be best to expand your trip if possible.

ALONG THE WAY

Town: Considered by its residents to be "America's Most Fun Small Town," Corning is a southern Finger Lakes town that's home to the unique **Corning Museum of Glass** (✉ 1 Museum Way ☎ 607/937–5371 ⊕ www.cmog.org), the world's largest museum of glass and glass artifacts. Corning's past and

present is steeped in glassmaking, which you can see from the many art galleries, boutiques, and studios lining its streets.

Eat & Drink: Carey's Brewhouse (✉ 58 Bridge St. ☎ 607/377–5651 ⊕ www.careysbrewhouse.com) in Corning serves a collection of local and international brews as well as your standard pub grub.

NEW YORK CITY

Do: It's a bit insane to recommend only one day in what is considered by many to be the best city in the world, but if you can't expand your trip by a few days, it's still possible to see the highlights. Don't miss wandering around **Central Park** (☎ 212/310–6600 ⊕ www.centralparknyc.org) and a visit to one of the major museums—both the **Metropolitan Museum of Art** (✉ 1000 5th Ave. ☎ 212/353–7710 ⊕ www.metmuseum.org) and the **American Museum of Natural History** (✉ 200 Central Park West ☎ 212/769–5100 ⊕ www.amnh.org) are right next to Central Park, albeit on opposite sides. Afterward, wander south to the Theater District to catch a Broadway show.

Eat & Drink: New Yorkers will never agree on where to get the best slice of pizza in New York City, but luckily you have plenty of options to choose from. Take the subway downtown to the West Village for a pie (no slices) at **John's of Bleecker St.** (✉ 278 Bleecker St. ☎ 212/243–1680 ⊕ www.johnsofbleecker.com) or try a slice at **Patsy's Pizzeria** (✉ 61 W. 74th St. ☎ 212/579–3000 ⊕ www.patsyspizzeria.us) on the Upper West Side near the Museum of Natural History. If you went downtown, end your night with some bar-hopping through the Village; don't miss a cocktail at **Employees Only** (✉ 510 Hudson St. ⊕ www.employeesonlynyc.com). If you decide to stick with uptown, try a cookie at **Levain Bakery** (✉ 351 Amsterdam Ave. ☎ 917/464–3782 ⊕ www.levainbakery.com).

Stay: Midtown is filled with overpriced and teeny-tiny hotels, but the elegant suites at the **Conrad New York Midtown** (✉ 151 W. 54th St. ☎ 212/307–5000 ⊕ www.hilton.com) are spacious and worth the money. Or head to NoMad to spend the night at the hip **Made Hotel** (✉ 44 W. 29th St. ☎ 212/213–4429 ⊕ www.madehotels.com). The rooftop bar has excellent city views.

Breakfast: The best bagel in the city is another hotly contested disagreement among New Yorkers. We say take your pick between **Russ & Daughters** (✉ 179 E. Houston St. ☎ 212/475–4880 ⊕ www.russanddaughters.com) on the Lower East Side or **Tal Bagels** (✉ 2446 Broadway ☎ 212/712–0171), which has several locations across Manhattan.

The Best of Long Island and the Jersey Shore

Written by Stefanie Waldek

Sure, it's easy to fill a New York City vacation with plenty of activities—after all, it's one of the greatest cities in the world. But if you've already checked most of the boxes on your to-do list there, it's time to consider what else to see in the region. Whether you're an out-of-towner extending your trip or a local looking for a getaway, this itinerary brings you to the best of Long Island and New Jersey, from quintessential summer hot spot, the Hamptons and the wineries of the North Fork, to the mega-resorts of Atlantic City and Victorian-era Cape May.

At a Glance

Start: New York, NY

End: Jersey City, NJ

Miles Traveled: 600 miles

Suggested Duration: 6 days

States Visited: New Jersey, New York

Key Sights: Atlantic City Boardwalk; Cape May Lighthouse; Montauk Point Lighthouse; Shelter Island; The Stone Pony

Best Time to Go: Beaches abound in this itinerary, so traveling in summer is a no-brainer. That said, summer does mean larger crowds, and hotels often book up far in advance. The shoulder seasons offers great deals, and winters at the beach can be magical in their own right.

Day 1: New York City, NY, to Montauk, NY

120 miles (2 hours, 30 minutes without traffic and stops)

New York City has plenty of spots to pick up rental cars, including at its two major airports, JFK and LaGuardia. As you head east out of the city into Long Island, you'll want to listen to your traffic apps—there are multiple highways that traverse Long Island, and you'll want to take whichever one has the least traffic.

ALONG THE WAY

Town: There's a lot to see and do at the far eastern end of Long Island, so try making it all the way to Southampton before stopping. Stretch your legs by strolling through the charming village (where you can stop at the various boutiques and restaurants), and visit the **Parrish Art Museum** (✉ 279 Montauk Hwy., Water Mill, NY ☎ 631/283–2118 ⊕ www.parrishart.org).

Eat & Drink: In Amagansett, stop for lunch at the original location of **Hampton Chutney Co.** (✉ 12 Amagansett Sq. ☎ 631/267–3131 ⊕ www.hamptonchutney.com), which serves dosas (a crepe-like wrap) stuffed with South Indian and American fillings, from masala potatoes to smoked turkey.

The Best of Long Island and the Jersey Shore

CONNECTICUT

Hartford

Waterbury

New London

New Haven

Bridgeport

Westport

Darien

Long Island Sound

Pollock-Krasner House

Greenport ③

114

Montau...

Shelter Island

Sag Harbor

Amagansett

Riverhead

Hither Hil... State Par...

Southampton

LONG ISLAND

Newburgh

Woodbury

Peekskill

NEW YORK

Hamburg

Lafayette

Andover

Paterson

Hackensack

City Island

Fort Totten

Passaic

Morristown

Hoboken

Newark

New York

Washington

Elizabeth

Jersey City

Plainfield

New Brunswick

Perth Amboy

Keansburg

Highlands

Lambertville

Matawan

Monmouth Beach

Princeton

Eatontown

Long Branch

Trenton

9

④ **Asbury Park**

195

NEW JERSEY

Point Pleasant Beach

Mantoloking

Toms River

Seaside Heights

206

Double Trouble State Park

Barnegat Light

Ocean Acres

Surf City

Hammonton

Long Beach Island

Beach Haven

40

Pleasantville

Brigantine

Lindwood

⑤ **Atlantic City**

Somers Point

Lucy the Elephant

Ocean City

9

Rio Grande

Wildwood

⑥ **Cape May**

Atlantic Ocean

| 0 | 20 mi |
| 0 | 20 km |

Nature: Prefer a more natural stop for a driving break? Take a short hike in Montauk's **Hither Hills State Park** (☎ 631/668–2554 ⊕ www.parks.ny.gov), where you can climb the Walking Dunes, 80-foot-tall sand dunes that "move" through the woods and swallow everything in their path—incredibly slowly, of course.

MONTAUK

Do: Montauk is a go-to summer hot spot for well-to-do New Yorkers, with a slightly more laid-back vibe than its glitzier neighbors in the Hamptons. The beach beckons here, but be sure to carve time out from your sunbathing and surfing sessions to visit **Montauk Point Lighthouse** (✉ 2000 Montauk Hwy. ☎ 631/668–2544 ⊕ www.montauklighthouse.com), hike through a former World War II military base at **Camp Hero State Park** (✉ 1898 Montauk Hwy. ☎ 631/668–3781 ⊕ www.parks.ny.gov), and stop for a beer at Montauk Brewing Co. (✉ 62 S. Erie Ave. ☎ 631/668–8471 ⊕ www.montaukbrewingco.com)

Eat & Drink: The **Surf Lodge** (✉ 183 Edgemere St. ☎ 631/483–5045 ⊕ www.thesurflodge.com) is the life of the party in Montauk—it's the place to eat, drink, and listen to music, from the afternoon until the early hours of the morning.

Stay: As Montauk's popularity has grown, so have its hotel options. You still can't go wrong with the classics: book a stay at Montauk icon **Gurney's** (✉ 290 Old Montauk Hwy. ☎ 631/668–2345 ⊕ www.gurneyresorts.com), lauded for its spa. But if you want to try a newer option, luxury hotel **Marram** (✉ 21 Oceanview Terr. ☎ 631/668–2050 ⊕ www.marrammontauk.com) is a great choice.

Breakfast: Start your day with a wholesome breakfast from health café **Naturally Good** (✉ 779 Montauk Hwy. ☎ 631/668–9030 ⊕ www.naturallygoodcafe.com).

Extend Your Trip

From Cape May: The East Coast's Best Beaches (Ch. 2)

From New York City: The Best of New York (Ch. 8); Coastal New England (Ch. 8)

Day 2: Montauk, NY, to Greenport, NY

30 miles (1 hour, 30 minutes without traffic and stops)

Backtrack down NY-27 W before turning north on NY-114 as you make your way to the heart of Long Island wine country. Although you can keep heading west on NY-27 and then north on County Road 48 to reach Greenport, the more fun route is to take a ferry to spend some time on idyllic Shelter Island. A second ferry on the other side of the island will take you right to Greenport. Both ferries allow cars.

ALONG THE WAY

Detour: If you have time for a detour, make a stop at the **Pollock-Krasner House** (✉ 830 Springs Fireplace Rd. ☎ 631/324–4929 ⊕ www.stonybrook.edu), the home and studio of famed American artists Jackson Pollock and Lee Krasner. In the village of Springs, the farmhouse is only about 10 minutes out of your way.

Town: Before you hop on the South Ferry to Shelter Island, explore the village of Sag Harbor. Pick up coffee and a snack at **Grindstone Coffee & Donuts** (✉ 7 Main St. 6 ☎ 31/808–3370 ⊕ www.grindstonedonuts.com), peruse the exhibits at the **Sag Harbor Whaling & Historical Museum** (✉ 200 Main St. ☎ 631/725–0770 ⊕ www.sagharborwhalingmuseum.org), and browse the many antiques shops in town.

Cape May is filled with grand Victorian mansions.

Eat & Drink: When you make it over to Shelter Island, stop for lunch at **Shelter Island Seafood** (✉ *87 N. Ferry Rd.* ☎ *631/765–8181* ⊕ *www.shelterisland-seafood.com*) for fresh catches.

Nature: One of Long Island's best natural gems is the **Mashomack Preserve** (✉ *79 S. Ferry Rd.* ☎ *631/749–1001* ⊕ *www.nature.org*) on Shelter Island, covering 2,039 acres of forests, marshes, and beaches. Take a quick hike or bring your binoculars to go birding.

GREENPORT

Do: Use Greenport as your base camp for touring the wineries and breweries of the North Fork. Some of the area's best include **Bedell Cellars** (✉ *36225 Main Rd., Cutchogue, NY* ☎ *631/734–7537* ⊕ *www.bedellcellars.com*), **Borghese Vineyard** (✉ *17150 Middle Rd., Cutchogue, NY* ☎ *631/734–5111* ⊕ *www.borghese-vineyard.com*), and **Greenport Harbor Brewery** (✉ *42155 Main Rd., Peconic, NY* ☎ *631/477–1100* ⊕ *www.greenportbrew.com*). When you've had your fill, head to the beach for a leisurely afternoon, kayak at **Orient Beach State Park** (✉ *40000 Main Rd.* ☎ *631/323–2440* ⊕ *www.parks.ny.gov*), or go shopping in town.

Eat & Drink: **Claudio's** (✉ *111 Main St.* ☎ *631/477–0627* ⊕ *www.claudios.com*) is a Greenport legend, serving seafood since 1870—the institution has since branched out to open several other local eateries and bars, including a pizza spot.

Stay: Book a stay at the 16-room boutique hotel **The Menhaden** (✉ *207 Front St.* ☎ *631/333–2777* ⊕ *www.themenhaden.com*), which blends modern design with traditional coastal elegance. Be sure to have a cocktail at the rooftop bar to enjoy views of the harbor.

Breakfast: Family-owned diner **Crazy Beans** (✉ *2 Front St.* ☎ *631/333–2436* ⊕ *www.crazybeansrestaurant.com*) opened in 2016, but it has plenty of 1950s flair.

Day 3: Greenport, NY, to Asbury Park, NJ

160 miles (2 hours, 45 minutes without traffic and stops)

Again, let the traffic apps pick your route across Long Island. But as you approach New York City, take the Cross Island Parkway over the Throgs Neck Bridge, then I-95 across the George Washington Bridge into New Jersey. Eventually, you'll head south on the Garden State Parkway and over to one of the hippest towns on the famed Jersey Shore.

ALONG THE WAY

Roadside Attraction: Fort Totten (⊠ *Totten Ave. and 15th Rd.* ☎ *718/352–4793* ⊕ *www.nycgovparks.org*) in Queens is home to an interesting Civil War–era fortress. If you have the time, take a ranger-guided tour to learn about the site's history.

Detour: Did you know you can get a taste of New England–seaside charm right in New York City? The Bronx's City Island feels a world apart from the bustle of Manhattan. Stop by for a seafood lunch at **City Island Lobster House** (⊠ *691 Bridge St.* ☎ *718/885–1459* ⊕ *www.cilolobsterhouse.com*) or **Sammy's Fish Box** (⊠ *41 City Island Ave.* ☎ *718/885–0920* ⊕ *www.sammysfishbox.com*).

Eat & Drink: If you'd prefer to hold out for lunch, head to **Evan's Restaurant** (⊠ *8 Cliffwood Ave. W.* ☎ *732/566–9122* ⊕ *www.evansrestaurant.com*) in Matawan, New Jersey, a classic family-owned Greek diner.

ASBURY PARK

Do: Asbury Park has a long and storied history as a Jersey Shore resort town. Although it went through some hard times at the end of the 20th century, it has since come roaring back as a hip weekend getaway. It's perhaps best known for the legendary concert hall **The Stone Pony** (⊠ *913 Ocean Ave.* ☎ *732/502–0600* ⊕ *www.stoneponyonline.com*), where Jersey icons Bruce Springsteen and Jon Bon Jovi both got their start. But at its heart, Asbury Park is a beach getaway, so be sure to spend some time at Asbury Park Beach and its historic boardwalk, now lined with buzzy restaurants and bars.

Eat & Drink: Drop by the **Wonder Bar** (⊠ *1213 Ocean Ave.* ☎ *732/455–3767* ⊕ *www.wonderbarasburypark.com*) for Yappy Hour, a dog-friendly happy hour, then stay for dinner and a concert. Or head to the **Asbury Festhalle & Biergarten** (⊠ *527 Lake Ave.* ☎ *732/997–8767* ⊕ *www.asburybiergarten.com*) for German dishes and beer, plus live music.

Stay: Boutique hotels abound in Asbury Park. Favorites include the retro-chic **Asbury Hotel** (⊠ *210 5th Ave.* ☎ *732/774–7100* ⊕ *www.theasburyhotel.com*) in a former Salvation Army building and the luxurious **Asbury Ocean Club** (⊠ *1101 Ocean Ave.* ☎ *732/825–6000* ⊕ *www.asburyoceanclub.com*).

Breakfast: New Jersey is renowned for its diners, and in Asbury Park, **Toast** (⊠ *516 Cookman Ave.* ☎ *732/776–5900* ⊕ *www.asburypark.toastcitydiner.com*) is the go-to for breakfast.

Day 4: Asbury Park, NJ, to Atlantic City, NJ

80 miles (1 hour, 30 minutes without traffic and stops)

Today's route is pretty simple: just continue south on the Garden State Parkway. If you're traveling in the summer, just be ready for some serious beach traffic, especially on Saturdays (when most of the weekly summer rentals change owners).

ALONG THE WAY

Road Attraction: Even if you know nothing about the Jersey Shore, you've probably heard of the hit MTV show that brought worldwide fame (or maybe infamy) to the region. The house where the party happened (✉ *1209 Ocean Terr.* ⊕ *www. shorestore.com*) is still there, Italian flag on the garage and all (You can even rent it out.). Make a stop in Seaside Heights to snap a photo and take a stroll on the nearby, equally as famous, boardwalk.

Eat & Drink: A gas station chain for lunch? Look, Wawa isn't just any old roadside fuel-up spot—stopping for lunch here is practically a rite of passage on the Jersey Shore. You'll find plenty along today's route, but the one in **Barnegat** (✉ *945 W. Bay Ave.*) is right off the Parkway and just before your Long Beach Island detour. Order a hoagie, make a milk shake, and grab a few snacks for the road.

Detour: Let's be honest—you're not going to Atlantic City for the beach. So if you want an afternoon in the sun, take a quick detour to low-key Long Beach Island, better known as LBI.

Photo Op: If you've made the LBI detour, make a quick stop at **Barnegat Light** (✉ *208 Broadway* ☎ *609/494–2016* ⊕ *www.state.nj.us*) to photograph the picturesque lighthouse.

ATLANTIC CITY

Do: Despite its interesting history (it inspired the board game Monopoly and had quite the role in the Prohibition era), today Atlantic City is known for one thing, and one thing only: gambling. But if hitting the slots is not your thing, you can also roam the boardwalk (which is the oldest and longest in the United States), catch one of the big headliner shows, or go shopping at the **Tanger Outlets** (✉ *2014 Baltic Ave.* ☎ *800/405–9555* ⊕ *www.tangeroutlet.com*).

Eat & Drink: Celebrity chef restaurants go hand in hand with big casinos, but it's the local spots that really showcase AC's

charm. **Chef Vola's** (✉ *111 S. Albion Pl.* ☎ *609/345–2022* ⊕ *www.chefvolas.com*) is a traditional BYOB Italian spot, while Dock's Oyster House (✉ *2405 Atlantic Ave.* ☎ *609/345–0092* ⊕ *www.docksoysterhouse.com*) offers seafood galore.

Stay: If you're going the casino route, the **Borgata** (✉ *1 Borgata Way* ☎ *609/317–1000* ⊕ *www.theborgata.com*) is one of the city's best, though it is located off the boardwalk. For something totally different, stay at the **Chelsea Inn** (✉ *8 S. Morris Ave.* ☎ *609/345–4700* www.thechelseainn.com*), a Victorian-style B&B established in 1880.

Breakfast: Bagels are a must when in New Jersey. In Atlantic City, grab one for the road from **Hot Bagels and More** (✉ *212 Pacific Ave.* ☎ *609/541–3488* ⊕ *www.hotbagelsandmore.com*).

Day 5: Atlantic City, NJ, to Cape May, NJ

50 miles (1 hour without traffic and stops)

It's back on the Parkway again, as you take it all the way down to Exit 0 and the end of the Jersey Shore (and to one of the best beach destinations on the East Coast).

ALONG THE WAY

Roadside Attraction: Take the scenic route back to the Parkway (drive south along Atlantic Avenue to Margate City) to see **Lucy the Elephant** (✉ *9200 Atlantic Ave.* ⊕ *www.lucytheelephant.org*), a 65-foot-tall landmark built in 1881. According to the *New York Times*, Lucy is "the oldest surviving example of zoomorphic architecture on Earth."

Eat & Drink: Stop for lunch at Lindwood's **Bakeria 1010** (✉ *2110 New Rd.* ☎ *609/927–5812* www.bakeria1010.com*), a pizzeria-bakery combo known for its incredible bread.

Town: It's a fairly short drive today, so right before you reach Cape May, make a pit stop in Wildwood to explore its famous 38-block-long boardwalk (plus three amusement park piers). The town is also a hub for midcentury architecture, particularly the Doo Wop style. Visit the **Doo Wop Preservation League** museum (✉ 4500 Ocean Ave. ☎ 609/523–1975) to learn more.

CAPE MAY

Do: Dotted with Victorian mansions and lined with a family-friendly boardwalk, Cape May is the southernmost point on the shore and one of the country's oldest seaside resorts. Go shopping at the Washington Street Mall (a pedestrian-only strip in the center of town), climb the **Cape May Lighthouse** (✉ 215 Light House Ave. ☎ 609/224–6066 ⊕ www. capmaymac.org), or simply hit the beach. At night, take a ghost tour by lantern light—the historic town has quite a few spooky legends.

Eat & Drink: Start with dinner at harborfront **Lobster House** (✉ 906 Schellengers Landing Rd. ☎ 609/884–8296 ⊕ www. thelobsterhouse.com), then move on to beers at the Rusty Nail (✉ 205 Beach Ave. ☎ 609/884–0017 ⊕ www.caperesorts.com). For cocktails, try the Prohibition-style Brown Room at Congress Hall.

Stay: Dive into Cape May's Victorian past at one of the many B&Bs or book a room at historic **Congress Hall** (✉ 200 Congress Pl. ☎ 888/944–1816 ⊕ www.caperesorts.com), originally opened in 1816. For something more contemporary, there's **Lokal** (✉ 5 Stockton Pl. ☎ 609/536–9157 ⊕ www.staylokal.com), a boutique "micro-resort" with eight stylish rooms.

Breakfast: Uncle Bill's Pancake House (✉ 261 Beach Ave. ☎ 609/884–7199 ⊕ www.unclebillspancakehouse.com) is a Cape May institution that satisfies diners with warm, fluffy stacks of pancakes and other breakfast items.

Day 6: Cape May, NJ, to Jersey City, NJ

154 miles (2 hours, 30 minutes without traffic and stops)

Retrace your steps north on the Parkway, then take I–278 into the New York metro area. But before ending your trip, spend your last night in Jersey City, NYC's underrated neighbor across the Hudson. You can still easily take a flight back from JFK or LGA, or the even-closer Newark International Airport.

ALONG THE WAY

Nature: You might've heard of New Jersey's Pine Barrens, a 1.1 million-acre ecosystem that's the reported home of the Jersey Devil. Take a hike through them at **Double Trouble State Park** (✉ 581 Pinewald Keswick Rd., Bayville, NJ ☎ 732/341–4098 ⊕ www.state.nj.us). Jersey Devil sightings not guaranteed.

Eat & Drink: Stop for a quirky diner lunch at **Shut Up and Eat** (✉ 804 Main St. ☎ 732/349–4544 ⊕ www.shutupandeat-tr.com) in Toms River, where the waitstaff famously don pajamas instead of a uniform.

Town: Get your last fill of New Jersey's boardwalks in Point Pleasant Beach— **Jenkinson's Boardwalk** (✉ (300 Ocean Ave. ☎ 732/892–0600 ⊕ www.jenkinsons. com) has an aquarium, rides, an arcade, and mini-golf. If you're still hungry, stop for a bite at the original Jersey Mike's Subs while you're here.

JERSEY CITY

Do: Located right across the Hudson River from NYC, Jersey City has long been regaled to bridge-and-tunnel-status, but as the most diverse city in all of America, it more than deserves your love. Explore **Liberty State Park** (✉ 200 Morris Pesin Dr. ☎ 201/915–3403 ⊕ www.visithudson.org) and visit **Liberty Science Center** (✉ 222 Jersey City Blvd. ☎ 201/200–1000

⊕ www.lsc.org); you can even take a ferry to Liberty Island and the Statue of Liberty (which any Jersey local will tell you is actually in New Jersey). Or just take a stroll on the 18½-mile **Hudson River Waterfront Walkway,** which gives you perhaps the best views of New York City you'll find anywhere.

Eat & Drink: You might have heard some choice food critics declare that the best New York pizza is actually in New Jersey. See what the fuss is about at **Razza** (✉ 275 Grove St. ☎ 201/356–9348 ⊕ www.razzanj.com), which serves wood-fired pies that regularly top best-pizza lists. Or head to India Square, home to the highest concentration of Indian Americans in the Western Hemisphere. You have plenty of incredible Indian restaurants to choose from here, but **Rasoi** (✉ 810 Newark Ave. ☎ 201/222–8850 ⊕ www.rasoi123. com) is one of the best. Afterwards, grab a drink at **dullboy** (✉ 364 Grove St. ☎ 201/795–1628 ⊕ www.dullboybar. com), a vaguely literary-themed cocktail bar with some serious speakeasy vibes.

Stay: The boutique hotel trend hasn't quite made it to Jersey City yet, so spend your last night at the **Hyatt Regency** (✉ 2 Exchange Pl. ☎ 201/469–1234 ⊕ www. hyatt.com), which offers unmatched city views.

Breakfast: Head 10 minutes north to Hoboken (Frank Sinatra's hometown) to grab a Taylor ham-egg-and-cheese bagel sandwich (another Jersey must-eat) at **Bagels on the Hudson** (✉ 802 Washington St. ☎ 201/798–2221 ⊕ www.bagel-sonthehudson.com).

The Best of New England

Written by Jen Rose Smith

From high peaks and beach breaks to swimming holes and art museums, this New England adventure loops through the best of the region in eight packed days. Luckily for any traveler, the Northeast offers epic road-tripping on a miniature scale: a few hours behind the wheel can take you from sea level to the highest point in the northeastern United States.

Along the way, duck into picture-post-card towns for clam shacks, craft beer, and maple syrup shots. Take plenty of covered-bridge and lighthouse selfies to shore up your Yankee cred. And it's not all small town life—in Portland, Providence, and Boston, soak up the history and culture that keep New England a creative hotbed.

At a Glance

Start: Boston, MA

End: Boston, MA

Miles Traveled: 695 miles

Suggested Duration: 8 days

States Visited: Connecticut, Massachusetts, Maine, New Hampshire, Vermont, Rhode Island

Key Sights: The Breakers Mansion; The Freedom Trail; Mark Twain House; Massachusetts Museum of Contemporary Arts; Mount Washington

Best Time to Go: Razzle-dazzle foliage displays make autumn a spectacular time to travel through this region, and sunny weather can easily stretch through mid-October. But if you want to maximize beach time and swimming hole stops,

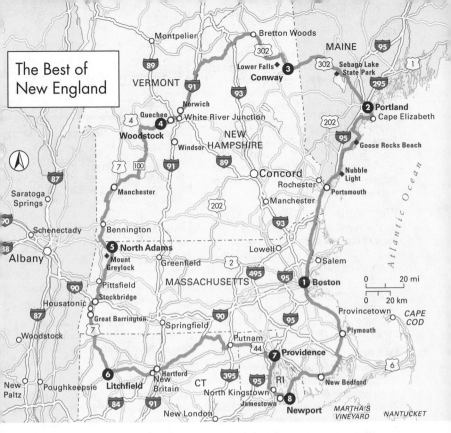

join the summer crowds that flock to the shore and mountains in July and August.

Day 1: Boston, MA, to Portland, ME

112 miles (1 hour, 45 minutes without traffic and stops)

Hop between two maritime heavyweights on your way from Boston to Portland, pausing to explore historic houses, waterside seafood joints, and islands with a spine-chilling history.

ALONG THE WAY

Town: In Portsmouth, you can stroll the brick-lined downtown to the edge of the Piscataqua River, where restaurant decks jut out over the bustling waterway. You could spend a morning among the historic houses at the **Strawbery Banke Museum** (✉ *14 Hancock St.* ☎ *603/433–1100* ⊕ *www.strawberybanke.org*), and this is also the starting point for boat trips to the storied Isles of Shoals (a history of piracy, murder, and ghosts suffuses these small islands, long populated by an independent lot who, according to many, hadn't the sense to winter on the mainland.)

Photo Op: Pretty in white, red, and black, picture-perfect **Nubble Light** (✉ *Sohier Park Rd.* ☎ *207/363–1040* ⊕ *www. nubblelight.org*) in York, Maine, is among the most photographed lighthouses in the world.

Nature: Just north of the tony Kennebunks is the 3-mile-long **Goose Rocks Beach** (✉ *Dyke Rd.* ☎ *207/967–3465* ⊕ *www.kporttrust.org/*

goose-rocks-beach), among the prettiest stretches of sand in southern Maine.

Eat & Drink: Just before you arrive in Portland, duck off the road for classic Maine lobster rolls or fried clams at **The Lobster Shack at Two Lights** (✉ 225 Two Lights Rd. ☎ 207/799–1677 ⊕ www.lobstershacktwolights.com) in Cape Elizabeth. Outdoor picnic tables here have views of the nearby lighthouse.

PORTLAND

Do: Wander the I. M. Pei–designed **Portland Museum of Art** (✉ 7 Congress St. ☎ 207/775–6148 ⊕ www.portlandmuseum.org), home to many works by Maine artist Winslow Homer, then hop on a schooner for a sunset cruise of Casco Bay. Craft breweries are big here, but there are also chic cocktail bars and ultrabrowsable Old Port boutiques.

Eat & Drink: Seafood gets center stage at **Eventide Oyster Co.** (✉ 86 Middle St. ☎ 207/774–8538 ⊕ www.eventideoysterco.com), where Maine oysters are displayed on a mammoth, ice-field chunk of granite just inside the door. The brown butter lobster roll, served in a steamed bun, is a New England legend. After dinner, head to the funky basement bar **Maps** (✉ 64 Market St.), which is just a few blocks away.

Stay: Budget hotels are scarce in Portland, and it's worth staying in a central location to enjoy the city at night. Splurge for a room at **The Press Hotel** (✉ 119 Exchange St. ☎ 207/808–8800 ⊕ www.thepresshotel.com), where you'll spend the night in the former home of the Portland Press Herald newspaper, with typewriter art on the walls to prove it.

Breakfast: The justifiably famous **Standard Baking Co.** (✉ 75 .Commercial St. ☎ 207/773–2112 ⊕ www.standardbakingco.com) is the place to go for buttery morning buns, fluffy scones, and top-quality joe using beans from Portland's Coffee by Design.

Extend Your Trip

From Portland: New England Great Outdoors (Ch. 8)

From Boston: Retracing the American Revolution (Ch. 2)

Day 2: Portland, ME, to Conway, NH

61 miles (1 hour, 30 minutes without traffic and stops)

Go from Portland's salty air to the heart of New Hampshire's White Mountains, passing thick forests broken by glassy lakes.

ALONG THE WAY

Town: Stretch your legs while exploring the lakeshore of Casco, Maine's **Sebago Lake State Park** (✉ 11 Park Access Rd. ☎ 207/693–6231 ⊕ www.maine.gov), where you'll find locals fishing from the boat launch, a tangle of hiking trails, and excellent swimming right off the beach.

Eat & Drink: Keep driving past Conway to have lunch at the grand **Omni Mount Washington Resort** (✉ 310 Mt. Washington Hotel Rd. ☎ 603/278–1000 ⊕ www.omnihotels.com) in Bretton Woods, New Hampshire, which has gorgeous sunset views of Mount Washington. Cocktails on the shady back porch—or scones in the old-fashioned tearoom—will make the 45-minute side trip worth your while.

CONWAY

Do: A base camp for year-round adventures in the White Mountains, Conway leads to steep hiking trails and wild scenery. From here you can drive to the top of Mount Washington, ride the historic cog railway, or pick one of many nearby trailheads for a long walk through the woods.

Eat & Drink: Irish pub food at **May Kelly's Cottage** (✉ *3002 White Mountain Hwy.* ☎ *603/356–7005* ⊕ *www.maykellys.com*) is ideal as hearty post-trail fare, with live-music sessions on some weekend nights.

Stay: The friendly **White Mountains Hostel** (✉ *36 Washington St.* ☎ *866/902–2521*) is the place to meet fellow adventurers and get trailhead advice. For a few more creature comforts, try the **Red Elephant Inn Bed and Breakfast** (✉ *28 Locust La.* ☎ *603/356–3548* ⊕ *www.redelephantinn.com*), with eight cozy rooms and friendly hosts.

Breakfast: Upstairs tables at the **Stairway Café** (✉ *2649 White Mountain Hwy.* ☎ *603/356–5200* ⊕ *www.stairwaycafe. com*) make for prime people-watching in downtown Conway, and all-day breakfasts include fat stacks of pancakes, homemade hash, and venison sausage.

Day 3: Conway, NH, to Woodstock, VT

111 miles (2 hours, 30 minutes without traffic and stops)

Watch the peaks close in as you follow the famously scenic Kancamagus Highway across White Mountain National Forest. Follow the lush Connecticut River Valley right into Vermont to discover Woodstock's picture-perfect, miniature town center.

ALONG THE WAY

Nature: Located near the 7-mile marker on the Kancamagus Highway, **Lower Falls** (✉ *Kancamagus Hwy.* ☎ *603/536–6100* ⊕ *www.fs.usda.gov*) is a broad, beautiful swimming hole in the Swift River that's ideal for cooling off on hot days.

Town: Just across the river from Dartmouth College, Norwich was founded in 1765, making this one of Vermont's oldest European communities. It's home

to the excellent **Montshire Museum of Science** (✉ *1 Montshire Rd.* ☎ *802/649–220* ⊕ *www.montshire.org*) and the flagship location of **King Arthur Flour** (✉ *135 U.S. 5 S* ☎ *802/649–3361* ⊕ *www.kingarthurflour.com*).

Eat & Drink: Savory meat and vegetable pies are the draw at beloved local café **Piecemeal Pies** (✉ *5 S. Main St.* ☎ *802/281–6910* ⊕ *www.piecemealpies. com*) in White River Junction, but there's also quirky homemade sodas, moreish desserts, and a hard-cider bar with bottles sourced from all across Vermont.

Photo Op: Just before you get to Woodstock, duck into tiny Quechee to snap a photo of **Simon Pearce** (✉ *1760 Quechee Main St.* ☎ *802/295–1470* ⊕ *www. simonpearce.com*), a glass-blowing studio in a restored woolen mill by the Ottauquechee River. Just downriver is a pretty covered bridge, built after the historic original was shattered by tropical storm Irene.

WOODSTOCK

Do: Wander Woodstock's pretty town center, then meet a dairy herd of Jersey cows at **Billings Farm and Museum** (✉ *69 Old River Rd.* ☎ *802/457–2355* ⊕ *www. billingsfarm.org*). Even if it's not the springtime maple season, it's worth a visit to **Sugarbush Farm** (✉ *591 Sugarbush Farm Rd.* ☎ *802/457–1757* ⊕ *www. sugarbushfarm.com*), where you can sample syrup made from sap collected in the surrounding forest.

Eat & Drink: At casual pub **Worthy Kitchen** (✉ *442 Woodstock Rd.* ☎ *802/457–7281* ⊕ *www.worthyvermont.com*), an immense drinks menu featuring local craft beers is scrawled onto the wall. The hearty plates of fried chicken, burgers, and salads are sourced from Vermont farms.

Stay: Friendly staff and updated rooms elevate the basic, 1960s-style **Sleep Woodstock Motel** (✉ *4324 Woodstock Rd.* ☎ *802/332–6336* ⊕ *www.*

Riding the cog railway to the top of Mount Washington rewards you with stunning vistas.

sleepwoodstock.com), easily the best budget option in a town known for high-end accommodations. Upgrade to the historic **Jackson House Inn** (✉ *43 Senior La.* ☎ *802/457-2065* ⊕ *www.jacksonhouse.com*) for a huge farmhouse breakfast, and ultracomfy rooms in a restored building.

Breakfast: Excellent cappuccinos arrive alongside breakfast burritos, avocado bagels, and maple syrup–drenched pancakes at Mon Vert Café (✉ *28 Central St.* ☎ *802/457-7143* ⊕ *www.monvertcafe.com*), a local hangout in the town center.

Day 4: Woodstock, VT, to North Adams, MA

97 miles (2 hours, 15 minutes without traffic and stops)

Follow scenic Route 100 through a lineup of verdant valleys, then duck into historic Manchester on your way to arty North Adams.

ALONG THE WAY

Town: New Englanders have vacationed in Manchester, Vermont, since before the Civil War, in grand mansions that are now gently faded. Before moving on, visit the **Museum of Fly Fishing** (✉ *4070 Main St.* ☎ *802/362-3300* ⊕ *www.amff.org*) or check out **Hildene** (✉ *1005 Hildene Rd.* ☎ *802/362-1788* ⊕ *www.hildene.org*), the former home of Robert Todd Lincoln.

Eat & Drink: At **Depot Café** (✉ *515 Depot St.* ☎ *802/366-8181* ⊕ *www.depot62.com*) in Manchester, who can resist a lunch of pizza and Mediterranean food served in the back of a furniture store?

Roadside Attraction: Tucked behind the staid-looking Wilburton Inn in Manchester is the **Museum of the Creative Process** (✉ *Wilburton Dr.* ☎ *802/445-5280* ⊕ *www.museumofthecreativeprocess.com*), an eccentric museum dedicated to the unconscious, conflict resolution, and the creative process. In practice, that means lots of giant sculptures.

Shop: Bennington Potters (✉ *324 County St.* ☎ *800/205–8033* ⊕ *www.bennnig-tonpotters.com*) in—you guessed it—Bennington, Vermont, has been making heavy, glazed stoneware dishes for more than 70 years.

Detour: Drive to **Mount Greylock** (✉ *30 Rockwell Rd., Lanesborough, MA* ☎ *413/499–4262* ⊕ *www.mass.gov*), the highest point in Massachusetts, adding an extra 18 miles to your day's road time. Up at the top of the mountain, enjoy big views across the Berkshires and pause for a drink at the historic **Bascom Lodge** (✉ *N. Adams Rd.* ☎ *413/743–1591* ⊕ *www.bascomlodge.net*). It's also a great place to stay after visiting North Adams.

NORTH ADAMS

Do: In the heart of the Berkshires, the city of North Adams is a haven for artists and art lovers. Visit the vast **Massachusetts Museum of Contemporary Arts** (✉ *1040 Mass MoCA Way* ☎ *413/662–2111* ⊕ *www.massmoca.org*) to see one of the finest art collections in the Northeast.

Eat & Drink: Seriously nothing-fancy **Jack's Hot Dog Stand** (✉ *12 Eagle St.* ☎ *413/664–9006* ⊕ *www.jackshotdog-stand.com*) has the feel of a gritty, small-town classic. (Not actually a stand, it's a hole-in-the-wall restaurant.) For more contemporary tastes, head to **Public Eat + Drink** (✉ *34 Holden St.* ☎ *413/664–4444* ⊕ *www.publiceatanddrink.com*), then check out the microbrews at **Bright Ideas Brewing** (✉ *111 Mass MoCA Way* ☎ *413/346–4460* ⊕ *www.brightideas-brewing.com*).

Stay: Perched on the summit of nearby Mount Greylock is the Arts and Crafts–style **Bascom Lodge** (✉ *N. Adams Rd.* ☎ *413/743–1591* ⊕ *www.bascomlodge.net*), which has very basic rooms and spectacular views. Right by Mass MoCA is the utterly stylish **Porches Inn** (✉ *231 River St.* ☎ *413/664–0400* ⊕ *www.porches.com*), where rooms are stocked with vintage finds and art you can buy.

Breakfast: In Mass MoCA itself is **Tunnel City Coffee** (✉ *87 Marshall St.* ☎ *413/398–5304* ⊕ *www.tunnelcitycoffee.com*), with house-roasted beans and a lineup of delicious pastries.

Day 5: North Adams, MA, to Litchfield, CT

76 miles (1 hour, 50 minutes without traffic and stops)

Follow scenic U.S. 7 all the way through the Berkshires, then slip into the green hills of northwestern Connecticut.

ALONG THE WAY

Town: It's easy to see why Norman Rockwell decided to live and paint in the picture-perfect historic town of Stock-bridge. Take a break to stroll the Main Street shops, check out the **Norman Rockwell Museum** (✉ *9 Glendale Rd. (MA-183)* ☎ *413/298–4100* ⊕ *www.nrm.org*), or explore the beautiful house-museum **Chesterwood** (✉ *4 Williamsville Rd.* ☎ *413/298–3579* ⊕ *www.chesterwood.org*). Afterward, head to Great Barrington, where an old church has been converted into the **Guthrie Center** (✉ *2 Van Deusenville Rd.* ☎ *413/258–1955* ⊕ *www.guthriecenter.org*), a shrine to Arlo Guthrie's career that holds regular jam sessions.

Eat & Drink: Rubiner's Cheesemongers and Grocers (✉ *264 Main St.* ☎ *413/528–0488* ⊕ *www.rubiners.com*) in Great Barring-ton is a cheese lovers' paradise that combines a fantastic cheese shop with a small café specializing in grilled-cheese sandwiches. If you'd rather picnic, grab a cheese wedge to go with a fresh whole-grain loaf from **Berkshire Mountain Bakery** (✉ *367 Park St.* ☎ *413/274–1313* ⊕ *www.berkshiremountainbakery.com*) in Housatonic.

Shop: Antiques are business in the Berkshires, and the section of U.S. 7 from Great Barrington to Sheffield is called "Antiques Alley."

LITCHFIELD

Do: Quiet and upscale Litchfield is one of the country's finest examples of a late-18th-century New England town. Promenade around the gracious Litchfield Green, where you'll find a classic white-steepled church and the **Litchfield Historical Society** (✉ 7 South St. ☎ 860/567–4501 ⊕ www.litchfieldhistoricalsociety.org), which organizes tours of the nearby **Tapping Reed House** (✉ 82 South St. ☎ 860/567–4501 ⊕ www. litchfieldhistoricalsociety.org).

Eat & Drink: Sip small-batch spirits from **Litchfield Distillery** (✉ 569 Bantam Rd. ☎ 860/361–6503 ⊕ www.litchfielddistillery.com), then head to the festive West Street Grill (✉ 43 West St. ☎ 860/567–3885 ⊕ www.weststreetgrill. com) for refined takes on American bistro fare.

Stay: Accommodations are pricy around these parts. The **Litchfield Inn** (✉ 432 Bantam Rd. ☎ 860/567–4503 ⊕ www. litchfieldinnct.com) is a comfortable favorite, with updated rooms and an impressive breakfast spread. If you're ready to splash out and want something with more personality, snag the 780-square-foot treehouse at high-end **Winvian Farm** (✉ 155 Alain White Rd., Morris, CT ☎ 860/567–9600 ⊕ www. winvian.com).

Breakfast: Drive 7 minutes west of town for coffee, pastries, or a breakfast sandwich at **Arethusa a Mano** (✉ 833 Bantam Rd., Bantam, CT ☎ 860/567–5722 ⊕ www.arethusafarm.com), set on beautiful Arethusa Farm.

Essential Listening

The podcast *Crimetown* is a fascinating tale of mob corruption at the height of the bad old days in Providence.

Day 6: Litchfield, CT, to Providence, RI

104 miles (2 hour, 30 minutes without traffic and stops)

Wind through the quietest corners of Connecticut and past state capital Hartford, then touch down in Rhode Island's creative, gritty, quirky capital.

ALONG THE WAY

Eat & Drink: Just before Hartford, you'll find the one-time industrial powerhouse of New Britain, which today is home to a high population of Polish immigrants; enjoy a lunch of pierogi and kielbasa at **Staropolska** (✉ 252 Broad St. ☎ 860/612–1711 ⊕ www.staropolska.net) on Broad Street.

Town: The capital of Connecticut gets a bad rap, but Hartford is worth a stop to discover the homes of **Harriet Beecher Stowe** (✉ 77 Forest St. ☎ 860/522–9258 ⊕ www.harrietbeecherstowecenter.org) and **Mark Twain** (✉ 385 Farmington Ave. ☎ 860/247–0998 ⊕ www.marktwainhouse.org), which are right next to each other. And art lovers could spend hours in the **Wadsworth Atheneum** (✉ 600 Main St. ☎ 860/278–2670 ⊕ www.thewadsworth. org), the oldest art museum in America.

Shop: The "quiet corner" of northeast Connecticut is overflowing with antiques shops. The **Antiques Marketplace** (✉ 109 Main St. ☎ 860/928–0442 ⊕ www.facebook/antiquesmarketplace) in Putnam draws the finest goods from hundreds of vendors; nearby **Jeremiah's Antiques Shops** (✉ *26 Front St.* ☎ *860/928–0666* ⊕ *www. jeremiahsantiques.com*) is another favorite.

PROVIDENCE

Do: As Rhode Island's capital, Providence proves itself as a quirky city with lots of history, good eats, and a strong arts scene. Browse from ancient to contemporary works at the **Rhode Island School of Design Museum of Art** (✉ *20 N. Main St.* ☎ *401/454–6500* ⊕ *www.risdmuseum. org*), then check out the plethora of galleries and shops downtown. Duck into the Greek Revival **Providence Atheneum** (✉ *251 Benefit St.* ☎ *401/421–6970* ⊕ *www.providenceathenaeum.org*) and say hello to the bust of local horror writer H. P. Lovecraft.

Eat & Drink: It's all about sausage at the casual **Wurst Kitchen** (✉ *960 Hope St.* ☎ *401/421–4422* ⊕ *www.chez-pascal. com*); for a taste of Italian-American heritage in Providence, head to tiny **Enoteca Umberto** (✉ *256 Atwells Ave.* ☎ *401/272–8466* ⊕ *enotecaumberto. restaurantwebexpert.com*) and eat fresh pasta with fabulous wine pairings. Afterward, walk through a lingerie shop to enter the speakeasy-style bar **Justine's** (✉ *11 Olneyville Sq.* ☎ *401/454–4440*).

Stay: In a city that loves design, the most stylish option is **The Dean** (✉ *122 Fountain St.* ☎ *401/455–3326* ⊕ *www.thedean-hotel.com*), which combines a modern aesthetic with vintage furnishings. Meet other budget-minded travelers at **Esperanto Providence Hostel & Guesthouse** (✉ *62 Nolan St.* ☎ *401/216–8807* ⊕ *www. providencehostel.com*), with clean, cozy shared rooms that are a 15-minute walk from downtown.

Breakfast: Pick up truly excellent single-origin coffee and pastries at **The Shop** (✉ *460 Wickenden St.* ☎ *401/684–1140* ⊕ *www.theshopfoxpoint.com*), or stay for savory breakfasts using whole-grain

bread from the famed **Seven Stars Bakery** (✉ *820 Hope St.* ☎ *401/521–2200* ⊕ *www.sevenstarsbakery.com*). Of course, you can also go straight to the source—Seven Stars Bakery also has a full line of pastries that are among the best in New England.

Day 7: Providence, RI, to Newport, RI

33 miles (45 minutes without traffic and stops)

A quick drive to Newport leaves more time for beach lounging, mansion exploring, and taking in the vibe of a town that's all about summer vacation.

ALONG THE WAY

Shop: Before you leave Providence, duck into **Lovecraft Arts & Sciences** (✉ *65 Weybosset St.* ☎ *401/264–0838* ⊕ *www. weirdprovidence.org*), a shop dedicated to weird fiction, horror, and all things H. P. Lovecraft.

Eat & Drink: There are outlets of **Del's Lemonade** (✉ *6525 Post Rd.* ☎ *401/885–2225* ⊕ *www.delsnk.com*), a frozen-lemonade joint, all around the state, but it just feels right to pick up a frosty, green-and-yellow cup in North Kingstown to enjoy as you roll over the bridge into Newport.

Town: Blink and you'll miss the island of Jamestown, which is located between the mainland and Newport itself. Duck off the main road, though, and you can climb the tower at the **Jamestown Lighthouse Museum** (✉ *Beavertail Rd.* ☎ *401/423–3270* ⊕ *www.beavertaillight.org*), with gorgeous views into Block Island Sound.

NEWPORT

Do: Grand, historic mansions like **The Breakers** (✉ *44 Ochre Point Ave.* ☎ *401/847–1000* ⊕ *www.newportmansions.org*) are glimpses of the Gilded Age excess that made Newport a prime vacation destination for the rich in the early-20th century; walking the beautiful **Cliff Walk** (☎ 401/845–5802 ⊕ www.cliffwalk.com) lets you peer into their backyards. Another highlight is the austere and beautiful Touro Synagogue (⊠ 85 Touro St. ☎ 401/847–4794 ⊕ www.tourosynagogue.org), the oldest in the United States. Don't let all that history keep you from the beach, where there's surfing, sunbathing, and a total scene.

Eat & Drink: Chowder at **The Black Pearl** (⊠ 30 Bannister's Wharf ☎ 401/846–5264 ⊕ www.blackpearlnewport.com) is something of a Newport tradition, or you can head to **Flo's Clam Shack** (⊠ 4 Wave Ave. ☎ 401/847–8141 ⊕ www.flosclamshacks.com) in nearby Middleton for Rhode Island–style clam cakes. Dessert is an Awful Awful ice-cream shake (that stands for "awful big, awful good") at **Newport Creamery** (⊠ 181 Bellevue Ave. ☎ 401/846–6332 ⊕ www.newportcreamery.com). At night, head down to the waterfront, where you'll find bustling pubs on Bannister's Wharf.

Stay: With a close-to-the-water location and shockingly good prices, the **Crow's Nest at Seamen's Church Institute** (⊠ 18 Market Sq. ☎ 401/847–4260 ⊕ www.crowsnestnewport.com) is the town's best bargain (they used to cater to passing sailors!). Prices skyrocket from there, but if you can afford it, the **Castle Hill Inn** (⊠ 590 Ocean Dr. ☎ 888/466–1355 ⊕ www.castlehillinn.com) on Ocean Drive is a waterfront stunner.

Breakfast: Flat whites, Australian meat pies, and sausage rolls make **Meg's Aussie Milk Bar** (⊠ 111 Bellevue Ave. ☎ 401/619–4811 ⊕ www.megsmilkbar.com) a favorite for breakfast in town.

Day 8: Newport, RI, to Boston, MA

101 miles (2 hours without traffic and stops)

Return to the mainland on your way back to Boston via the historic seaside towns of New Bedford and Plymouth.

ALONG THE WAY

Town: Discover why Herman Melville set his epic novel *Moby-Dick* in New Bedford at the **New Bedford Whaling Museum** (⊠ 18 Johnny Cake Hill ☎ 508/997–0046 ⊕ www.whalingmuseum.org), and wander the shops in the restored historic district.

Eat & Drink: Sip maritime-themed ales and lagers on the sunny patio at **Moby Dick Brewing Co.** (⊠ 16 S. Water St. ☎ 774/202–6961 ⊕ www.mobydickbrewing.com) in New Bedford while enjoying lunch from a menu of pub favorites. Or make a final seafood fueling stop at laid-back **Wood's Seafood** (⊠ 15 Town Wharf ☎ 508/746–0261 ⊕ www.woodsseafoods.com) in Plymouth, which is located right on the town wharf.

Town: Plymouth is where the Mayflower passengers finally disembarked, a history on display at the excellent **Plimoth Plantation** (⊠ 137 Warren Ave. ☎ 508/746–1622 ⊕ www.plimoth.org). While some sights in town glorify pilgrim history at the expense of the people who lived here before they arrived, Plimoth Plantation is all about engaging with both Colonial and Wampanoag history.

BOSTON

Do: New England's biggest city has plenty to keep visitors occupied. Walk the **Freedom Trail** (☎ 617/357–8300 ⊕ www.thefreedomtrail.org) all the way from Boston Common to Charlestown, then hop the ferry back to downtown. Just as fascinating is the excellent Black

Heritage Trail, which includes the **Museum of African American History** (⊠ *46 Joy St.* ☎ *617/725–0022* ⊕ *www.maah.org*).

Eat & Drink: Eat your way through the Italian American North End, choosing from enormous subs at **Monica's Mercato** (⊠ *130 Salem St.* ☎ *617/742–4101*), brick-oven-baked pies at **Regina Pizzeria** (⊠ *11½ Thacher St.* ☎ *617/227–0765* ⊕ *www. pizzeriaregina.com*), or updated seafood classics at **Neptune Oyster** (⊠ *63 Salem St.* ☎ *617/742–3474* ⊕ *www.neptuneoyster. com*). For dessert, try the cannoli at two rival bakeries: **Mike's Pastry** (⊠ *300 Hanover St.* ☎ *617/742–3050* ⊕ *www. mikespastry.com*) and **Modern Pastry** (⊠ *257 Hanover St.* ☎ *617/523–3783* ⊕ *www.modernpastry.com*). Nightlife is wildly varied, with options that range from jazz at **Wally's Café** (⊠ *427 Massachusetts Ave.* ☎ *617/828-1764* ⊕ *www. wallyscafe.com*) to the Colonial-era **Warren Tavern** (⊠ *2 Pleasant St., Charlestown, MA* ☎ *617/241–8142* ⊕ *www.warrentavern.com*).

Stay: Channel salty-sailor energy with a berth on the houseboats or yachts at **Green Turtle Floating Bed & Breakfast** (⊠ *1 Pier 8, 13th St., Charlestown, MA* ☎ *617/337–0202* ⊕ *www.greenturtlebb. com*) in the Charlestown Navy Yard. A rock-and-roll vibe at **The Verb** (⊠ *1271 Boylston St.* ☎ *617/566–4500* ⊕ *www. theverbhotel.com*) makes the Fenway-area hotel a standout, and there always seems to be a party down by the pool.

Breakfast: Sticky buns, lemon tarts, and brioche from **Flour Bakery** (⊠ *131 Clarendon St.* ☎ *617/437–7700* ⊕ *www. flourbakery.com*) are worth the hype. For something heartier, try the cafeteria-style brunch at **The Paramount** (⊠ *44 Charles St.* ☎ *617/720–1152* ⊕ *www.paramountboston.com*) in Beacon Hill, but be prepared to line up for this popular spot.

New England's Great Outdoors

Written by Jen Rose Smith

Pack your hiking boots to experience the wild side of a region best known for history and culture. Scenic beauty waits around every turn on this nature-seeking, seven-day adventure through New England's national parks, mountain peaks, scenic lakes, and river valleys.

In between stops to follow hiking trails and animal tracks, duck into outdoorsy communities dedicated to active adventures. This route begins and ends on the coast, but you'll take in some of America's most fascinating mountain ranges, from New Hampshire's White Mountains to the low-lying Taconics of Vermont. Get ready for fresh air and freedom.

At a Glance

Start: Portland, ME

End: Portland, ME

Miles Traveled: 1,000 miles

Suggested Duration: 8 days

States Visited: Maine, New Hampshire, Vermont

Key Sights: Acadia National Park; Ben & Jerry Factory; Mount Katahdi; Lake Winnipesaukee; Smuggler's Notch

Best Time to Go: Peak travel destinations hum with crowds and energy in the summer months, when there's ideal weather for swimming in lakes and rivers. But if hiking, scenery, and wildlife-watching are your main goals, consider traveling in the fall. Early October means colorful foliage at high elevations with a good chance for sunny, warm days at sea level.

New England's
Great Outdoors

Day 1: Portland, ME, to Bar Harbor, ME

164 miles (3 hours, 20 minutes without traffic and stops)

Travel scenic Highway 1 and take in views across quiet coves, hidden beaches, and patches of deeply shaded evergreen forests. In between, bustling tourist towns serve lobster rolls and a good-timing, vacationland spirit. You'll eventually reach Mount Desert Island, a laid-back yet sophisticated hideaway that's home to its main town, Bar Harbor, and Acadia National Park, the only national park in the Northeast.

ALONG THE WAY

Nature: Stroll a curve of sandy beach at **Birch Point Beach State Park** (✉ 459 S. Shore Dr., Owls Head, ME ☎ 207/941–4014 ⊕ www.maine.gov) to find views of the Mussel Ridge Islands that dot Mussel Ridge Channel in Penobscot Bay.

Town: A fishing town–turned–artistic hub, **Rockland** brings together old and new Maine. Find paintings by Maine legend Andrew Wyeth at the **Farnsworth Art Museum** (✉ 16 Museum St. ☎ 207/596–6457 ⊕ www.farnsworthmuseum.org) or walk the 1-mile Rockland Breakwater to a sturdy brick lighthouse that guides in passing schooners. This is also home to the Audubon Society's **Project Puffin Visitor Center** (✉ 311 Main St. ☎ 207/596–5566 ⊕ www.projectpuffin.audubon.org), which offers boat tours to see the comeback puffin colony at Eastern Egg Rock.

Eat & Drink: Tiny Rockport is home to the sunlight-filled restaurant **Nina June** (✉ 24 Central St. ☎ 207/236–8880 ⊕ www.ninajunerestaurant.com), where chef Sara Jenkins has won accolades for her Mediterranean fine dining using local ingredients.

Photo Op: Traditional sailboats called windjammers spend summers tied up in the beautiful **Camden harbor,** so pause to snap a photo of their wooden masts bobbing in the current.

BAR HARBOR

Do: Hop a free shuttle bus from Bar Harbor into **Acadia National Park** (☎ 207/288–3338 ⊕ www.nps.gov.acad), where the one-way Park Loop Road offers access to a series of scenic viewpoints and hiking trails. This 47,000-acre wonderland of seaside cliffs, forested mountains, and pristine beaches is one of the East Coast's most jaw-droppingly scenic sports. For an easy stroll, follow a path along Jordan Pond; a more challenging trek is the rocky climb up the Beehive, using ladder rungs sunk right into the granite. At low tide, a path leads right from Bar Harbor to Bar Island, but timing is key: the sand spit linking the town and the island is only exposed for a few hours each day.

Eat & Drink: Oversized popovers at **Jordan Pond House** (✉ 2928 Park Loop Rd., Seal Harbor, ME ☎ 207/276–3781 ⊕ www.jordanpondhouse.com) are a Mount Desert Island tradition, best eaten on the lawn with a generous side of strawberry jam and sweet butter. For dinner, though, a lobster dinner is essential. With picnic tables overlooking the water, **Stewman's Lobster Pound** (✉ 35 West St. ☎ 207/288–0346 ⊕ www.stewmanlobsterpound.com) serves old-school feasts.

Stay: A rooftop infinity pool sets the chic **West Street Hotel** (✉ 50 West St. ☎ 207/288–0825 ⊕ www.theweststreethotel.com) apart in a town that leans toward old-fashioned style; the water views over Frenchman's Bay means you can catch a fabulous sunrise without getting dressed. Ten minutes outside Bar Harbor is rustic **Emery's Cottages on the Shore** (✉ 181 Sand Point Rd. ☎ 207/288–3432 ⊕ www.emeryscottages.com), where cozy, stand-alone cottages are a short walk from the beach.

Breakfast: Stacks of blueberry pancakes with Maine maple syrup give you a reason to linger at **Two Cats Restaurant** (✉ *130 Cottage St.* ☎ *207/288–2808* ⊕ *www. twocatsbarharbor.com*), but the lobster Benedict is memorable, too.

Day 2: Bar Harbor, ME, to Millinocket, ME

121 miles (2 hours, 15 minutes without traffic and stops)

Leave the coast behind as you head north toward Maine's highest summit: Mount Katahdin. *Katahdin* means "Greatest Mountain" in the Penobscot language, and anyone who sees the awe-inspiring sight will immediately understand the name.

ALONG THE WAY

Town: Lined in stolid brick and brimming with history, Bangor is a former lumber hub with a slightly haunted, frontier feel. Get in the spirit by taking a ghost-themed walking tour or just stroll by the novelist Stephen King's house—the front gates are decorated, fittingly, with spiders and bats.

Eat & Drink: The homey **Harvest Moon Deli** (✉ *72 Columbia St.* ☎ *207/947–3354* ⊕ *www.harvestmoondeli.com*) is a local favorite for sandwiches and salads. Eat in the small dining room or get a take-out meal you can eat at the nearby Bangor waterfront.

Roadside Attraction: A plaque mounted on Bangor's 31-foot *Paul Bunyan* statue (✉ *519 Main St.* ☎ *207/947–0307* ⊕ *www.bangormaine.gov*) hedges its bets by declaring itself "reputed to be the largest statue of Paul Bunyan in the world." Competition aside, this is a famous Maine landmark that's not to be missed.

MILLINOCKET

Do: Mount Katahdin is the centerpiece of **Baxter State Park** (✉ *64 Balsam Dr.* ☎ *207/723–9616* ⊕ *www.baxterstatepark.org*), whose Togue Pond Gate entrance is 25 minutes beyond downtown Millinocket. Climbing the mountain itself requires a high level of physical fitness and a full day of hiking, but there's plenty of ways to experience the park if you're only spending a day here. Spot bog plants on the stroll from the Togue Pond Gatehouse to Cranberry Pond or rent a canoe on-site for a paddle around Togue Pond itself. Designated a national monument by President Obama, nearby **Katahdin Woods and Waters** (✉ *Hauling Rd. 1* ☎ *207/456–6001* ⊕ *www.nps.gov/kaww*) is far less well-known than Baxter. While the facilities are still rustic here, there's a handful of great hiking and biking trails that depart from the monument's Katahdin Loop Road.

Eat & Drink: Rub shoulders with through-hikers at the **Appalachian Trail Café** (✉ *210 Penobscot Ave.* ☎ *207/723–6720* ⊕ *www.facebook.com/ATCafeMillinocket*)—hundreds of AT "finishers" have autographed the ceiling here. The big burritos, burgers, and sandwiches are perfect trail-recovery fare.

Stay: A wooden sauna and guest canoes make the **New England Outdoor Center** (✉ *30 Twin Pines Rd.* ☎ *207/723–5438* ⊕ *www.neoc.com*) a great place to relax after a day on the trail (or on the road). Camping, cabins, and lodge accommodations are comfortable and friendly, with hearty, American-style meals available on-site at the River Driver's Restaurant.

Breakfast: Millinocket is a small town that doesn't have too many food options, so Appalachian Trail Café is a favorite for breakfast, too, with plates weighed down under piles of home fries and scrambled eggs.

Acadia National Park has plenty of hiking options.

Day 3: Millinocket, ME, to Franconia, NH

278 miles (5 hours, 10 minutes without traffic and stops)

The woods turn deeper and darker as you cross the vastness of western Maine before the White Mountain peaks erupt into jagged-rock summits. If you don't mind the extra driving time, an alternative route follows smaller Highway 2 past a series of mill and logging towns past their heyday.

ALONG THE WAY

Town: Augusta, Maine's quiet capital city, lines up on both sides of the Kennebec River, and the British-era **Old Fort Western** (✉ *16 Cony St.* ☎ *207/626–2385* ⊕ *www. oldfortwestern.org*) is preserved right at the edge of the water. Guided tours of the grounds tell stories of the 18th-century French and Indian War, and some spaces are filled with period furniture and artifacts.

Eat & Drink: Just before you reach the New Hampshire border, little Bethel is the place to stop for pub fare and microbrews at the **Sunday River Brewing Company** (✉ *29 Sunday River Rd.* ☎ *207/824–4253* ⊕ *www.sundayriver-brewingcompany.com*). Start with homemade pretzels dunked in beer sauce, then tuck into sandwiches, burgers, or the house-specialty gourmet mac and cheese.

FRANCONIA

Do: Gorge walls climb high above the pathway at **Flume Gorge** (✉ *852 Daniel Webster Hwy.* ☎ *603/745–8391* ⊕ *www. nhstateparks.org*), where kids (and grown-ups) can dart over and around a jumble of boulders. Get a more expansive view of things from the **Cannon Mountain Aerial Tramway** (✉ *260 Tramway Dr.* ☎ *603/823–8800* ⊕ *www.cannonmt. com*) that leads to an observation deck atop the peak. There's a short trail on the summit, or you could hike up via the 3.8-mile Kinsman Ridge Trail and hop the tram back down.

Eat & Drink: A short drive from Franconia is the charming, genteel dining room at **Sugar Hill Inn** (✉ *116 NH-117, Sugar Hill Rd.* ☎ *603/823–5621* ⊕ *www.sugarhill-inn.com*), where evenings are lit with candles and, if it's cold, a roaring fire. The four-course, fixed-price menu is worth the splurge, but European-influenced dishes are available à la carte, too.

Stay: Rooms at the Sugar Hill Inn are delightful, especially when drifting off after a rich dinner. Or if you're unable to stay for longer than one night (there's a two-night minimum), consider driving a few minutes west to **Rustic Log Cabins** (✉ *1450 Sugar Hill Rd.* ☎ *603/838–6761* ⊕ *www.rusticlogcabins.com*) in Lisbon, where seven buildings set along Salmon Hole Brook are equipped with kitchens, wood-burning fireplaces, and outdoor fire pits.

Breakfast: Polly's Pancake Parlor (✉ *672 Sugar Hill Rd.* ☎ *603/823–5575* ⊕ *www.pollyspancakeparlor.com*) is famed for—you guessed it—fat stacks of flapjacks. At this James Beard Award–winning joint, they come in oatmeal buttermilk, buckwheat, and whole wheat, add-ins are generous, and each meal comes with a sugar coma–inducing tray of maple syrup, maple spread, and maple sugar.

Day 4: Franconia, NH, to Stowe, VT

74 miles (1 hour, 30 minutes without traffic and stops)

After a gentle dive into the Connecticut River Valley, climb back into the rolling terrain of Vermont's Green Mountains. It's all two-lane roads and small towns as you meander across the rural state on the way to a historic resort community.

ALONG THE WAY

Town: Grand old houses with peeling paint hint that **St. Johnsbury, VT's** glory days are in the past, but you still can explore remnants of the era when St. J was flying high. The remarkable **St. Johnsbury Athenaeum** is an essential stop ✉ *91171 Main St.* ☎ *802/748–8291* ⊕ *www.stjathenaeum.org*); it's a library-cum-art gallery with canvases by notable Hudson River School artists. Just down the street is the **Fairbanks Museum & Planetarium** (✉ *1302 Main St.* ☎ *802/748–2372* ⊕ *www.fairbanksmuseum.org*), a natural-history museum with such treasures as a mosaics made from beetles, 19th-century dioramas, and plentiful taxidermy.

Eat & Drink: In Vermont, soft-serve ice creams are called creemees, and the finest creemees are made with maple syrup. **Tootsie's Ice Cream** (✉ *5847 VT-15* ☎ *802/563–2152*) in Danville is a contender for the most beloved maple creemee around.

Roadside Attraction: The **American Society of Dowsers** (✉ *184 Brainerd St.* ☎ *802/684–3417* ⊕ *www.dowsers.org*)—the folks who use sticks to find water—is based in Danville. Stop by their bookstore to browse titles such as *A Pocket Guide to Spirit Animals* and *Energy Medicine: The Essential Techniques*.

Shop: Continue a few more miles to the **Hastings Store** (✉ *2748 U.S. 2* ☎ *802/684–3398*) in West Danville. It's a classic country store, the kind that sells both candy bars and farm equipment, and it's also the place to bet on next spring's "ice-out." That's when the ice on nearby Joe's Pond finally breaks up—for a dollar a pop, fill out a ticket with the date and time you think it will happen. The proceeds are split between the winner and the teeny town's general fund, so it's for a good cause. (And if you need some pointers before committing, there's a list of past ice-outs at the cash register.)

STOWE

Do: Stop to wander the cute shops in Stowe village, then rent a bike for a leisurely ride along the 5.3-mile Stowe

Rec Path. In between river crossings and meadows, it wanders past great refreshment spots, such as **Idletyme Brewing Company** (✉ *1859 Mountain Rd.* ☎ *802/253–4765* ⊕ *www.idletymebrewing.com*). To get views of Mount Mansfield, Vermont's highest peak, take Route 108 until it narrows to a ribbon of road winding between boulders and cliffs. The narrow pass is called Smuggler's Notch, popular with climbers and hikers who follow trails into the surrounding forest.

Eat & Drink: The bartenders at **Doc Pond's** (✉ *294 Mountain Rd.* ☎ *802/760–6066* ⊕ *www.docponds.com*) spin vintage vinyl to a laid-back crew in this gourmet pub, where the patio and fire pit are a favorite hangout on summer evenings. Tucked onto the sprawling property of the Von Trapp family (yes, the people from *The Sound of Music*), you'll find the **Von Trapp Brewery and Bierhall** (✉ *1333 Luce Hill Rd.* ☎ *802/253–5750* ⊕ *www.vontrappbrewing.com*), a cavernous space with homemade Austrian beers, sausages, pretzels, and very respectable burgers.

Stay: Modern design features summer camp–inspired flourishes at **Field Guide Lodge** (✉ *433 Mountain Rd.* ☎ *802/253–8088* ⊕ *www.fieldguidestowe.com*), with an outdoor pool and hot tub that are blissful after a day of driving. Mountain bikers will rejoice, because the Cady Hill Forest trails pass right through the property's backyard.

Breakfast: Find the best espresso in town at **PK Coffee** (✉ *1940 Mountain Rd.* ☎ *802/585–7711* ⊕ *www.pkcoffee.com*), along with breakfast sandwiches and a smattering of locally baked pastries.

Day 5: Stowe, VT, to Burlington, VT

48 miles (1 hour without traffic and stops)

The landscape flattens as you descend into the Champlain Valley. At the end of the last glacial period, this was the bottom of the great, inland Champlain Sea. Perched on the edge of lovely Lake Champlain is the artsy, outdoorsy college town of Burlington, a perfect starting point for getting out on the water.

ALONG THE WAY

Town: Stop for fresh doughnuts and apple cider at **Cold Hollow Cider Mill** (✉ *3600 Waterbury Stowe Rd.* ☎ *800/327–7537* ⊕ *www.coldhollow.com*) in Waterbury on your way to Waterbury Reservoir, where you can rent a canoe for a paddle along the forested shoreline. Watch for loons at dawn and dusk, but keep your distance, as mating pairs are sensitive to disturbance.

Eat & Drink: A stop at the **Ben & Jerry's ice-cream factory** (✉ *1281 Waterbury-Stowe Rd.* ☎ *866/258–6877* ⊕ *www.benjerry.com*) in Waterbury is all but obligatory. Grab a cone, snap a selfie with the original ice-cream van, and don't forget to visit the Flavor Graveyard, where headstones honor dearly departed ice cream varieties.

Detour: A quick jaunt south takes you to genteel Shelburne, where the grand Vanderbilt-Webb estate is now open to the public as **Shelburne Farms** (✉ *1611 Harbor Rd.* ☎ *802/985–8686* ⊕ *www.shelburnefarms.org*). A 2-mile stroll takes you from the visitor center past grazing sheep and cows to the lakefront. Next, visit the eclectic Shelburne Museum to find everything from fine art to a full-size paddle-wheel boat on the rambling, indoor-outdoor grounds.

BURLINGTON

Do: Browse the shops and galleries along pedestrian-only Church Street, then head down to the Burlington Waterfront for views of the Adirondack Mountains across the water. From there, a bike path extends along the shoreline—the 10.9-mile trail continues north through neighborhoods and forests, then continues for four miles on a narrow causeway raised up above the water that's part of the Island Line Rail Trail. On summer weekends, you can go even farther, as a tiny bicycle ferry links the causeway with the island of South Hero.

Eat & Drink: A tempting array of creative, locally sourced dishes at **Hen of the Wood** (✉ 55 Cherry St. ☎ 802/540-0534 ⊕ www.henofthewood.com) make this a favorite place for special dinners—the inventive cocktails are also a highlight of dining here. If you can't snag a table, stroll south past City Hall Park to **Pizzeria Verità** (✉ 156 St. Paul St. ☎ 802/489-5644 ⊕ www.pizzeriaverita.com), whose blistered, Neapolitan pies are best followed by a bitter, Italian digestif from the restaurant's extensive amaro menu. Craft beers are huge in Burlington, too, so end your night with a visit to **Citizen Cider** (✉ 316 Pine St. ☎ 802/448-3278 ⊕ www.citizencider.com) to sample their hard ciders (several of which are hard to find in stores).

Stay: Walking distance from the waterfront and downtown landmarks, **Hotel Vermont** (✉ 41 Cherry St. ☎ 802/651-0080 ⊕ www.hotelvt.com) has a great location and a fresh take on all things Vermont. Simply styled rooms are stocked with locally made wool blankets and Vermont art, and the downstairs Juniper Bar carries every single Vermont-made spirit.

Breakfast: Friendly and usually packed, **Penny Cluse** (✉ 169 Cherry St. ☎ 802/651-8834 ⊕ www.pennycluse.com) is a Burlington institution for hearty breakfasts both sweet and savory. If the gingerbread pancakes don't hit the spot, the breakfast burritos surely will. Or you can grab a bagel sandwich at popular **Myer's Bagel Bakery** (✉ 377 Pine St. ☎ 802/863-5013 ⊕ www.myersbagels.com), which sells Montreal-style bagels.

Day 6: Burlington, VT, to Manchester, VT

100 miles (2 hours, 20 minutes without traffic and stops)

Wind between orchards and low mountains in one of Vermont's most scenic and uncrowded regions, as you make your way to a historic town that's been a fresh-air escape for hikers, anglers, and artists since the Civil War.

ALONG THE WAY

Eat & Drink: In little Vergennes, **lu•lu ice cream** (✉ 185 Main St. ☎ 802/777-3933 ⊕ www.luluvt.com) dishes out delightful scoops of "farm-to-spoon" ice cream, with a rotating lineup of flavors that range from classic cookies-and-cream to vegan dragonfruit sorbet. If you're arriving later in the day, **Bar Antidote** (✉ 35 Green St. ☎ 802/877-2555 ⊕ www.barantidote.com) has pub food with appealing vegetarian options and beers provided by on-site Hired Hand Brewing Co.

Town: A rambling spread of carefully tended farmland, Shoreham's valley-floor location is prime for growing. Sample the goods at Champlain Orchards, whose farm store has apples by the peck, apple pies, apple cider, cider syrup, and well, you get the idea. The orchard's more than 140 varieties of apples go from Japanese Akane to the Minnesota-bred Zestar!, with opportunities to pick your own during harvest season.

MANCHESTER

Do: The Battenkill River has long drawn anglers to this community, where there's fine—if challenging—trout fishing up and down the valley. It's also, a little surprisingly, a major hub for fishing gear; tour the Orvis rod factory and you'll get an up close look at a process that's both high-tech and artistic. Just next door is the small but fascinating **American Museum of Fly Fishing** (✉ 4070 Main St. ☎ 802/362–3300 ⊕ www.amff.org). There's also an Orvis fly-fishing school if you want to give it a try. Or you can try out one of the many hikes through the surrounding forest. The 2-mile walk to Lye Brook Falls is a favorite, or you can take the steep, 5.8-mile round-trip trek to the summit of Equinox Mountain, the highest peak in the Taconic mountain range.

Eat & Drink: Sample Vermont's only Burmese cuisine at **Moonwink** (✉ 4479 Main St. ☎ 802/768–8671 ⊕ www.facebook.com/moonwinkvt), with treats including green-mango salad, curries, and noodles swimming in rich, fishy broth. If you can snag a reservation and you're in the mood for something special, the six-table **Silver Fork** (✉ 48 West Rd. ☎ 802/768–8444 ⊕ www.thesilverforkvt.com) is a delight for nuanced but unfussy food with Caribbean and European influences.

Stay: The old-fashioned and welcoming **Wilburton Inn** (✉ 257 Wilburton Dr. ☎ 802/362–2500 ⊕ www.wilburtoninn.com) is perched on a hilltop spot with excellent views. Rooms are comfortable, if a little dated, and there's an outdoor pool for lolling about in the afternoon sunshine. The on-site Museum of the Creative Process is scattered across the lawn, with odd, towering statues and musings from the émigré intellectual who founded the family-owned inn.

Breakfast: With a cute coffee-pot sign to mark the spot, homey café **Up for Breakfast** (✉ 4935 Main St. ☎ 802/362–4204) is the place to pile on eggs, home fries, and French toast before hitting the road.

Day 7: Manchester, VT, to Meredith, NH

132 miles (2 hours, 50 minutes without traffic and stops)

Head once more across the Green Mountains, then drive north along the Connecticut River back into New Hampshire via scenic NH-104. The road takes you to the state's central Lakes Region, where the largest, Lake Winnipesaukee, has 180 miles of coastline.

ALONG THE WAY

Photo Op: Small town Cornish, New Hampshire, is best known for its covered bridges and for having been the home of the late reclusive author J. D. Salinger. Don't miss a postcard-worthy photo of the Cornish-Windsor Bridge, the 460-foot bridge that connects New Hampshire to Vermont across the Connecticut River. Erected in 1866, it is the longest covered wooden bridge in the United States.

Eat & Drink: Home to Dartmouth College, Hanover, New Hampshire, offers an impressive collection of eateries meant to appeal to Ivy Leaguers. Stop for lunch at **Murphy's on the Green** (✉ 11 S. Main St. ☎ 603/643–4075 ⊕ www.murphysonthegreen.com), a wildly popular pub with walls lined with shelves of old books. The varied menu features burgers and salads as well as meat loaf, lobster mac and cheese, and vegetarian dishes like crispy-tofu pad Thai and house-smoked tofu street tacos.

MEREDITH

Do: For many years a workaday mill town with relatively little tourism appeal, Meredith has become a popular summer getaway thanks largely to the transformation in recent years of several historic downtown buildings into Mill Falls, now a cluster of hotels, restaurants, and shops overlooking Lake Winnipesaukee. Your time here will be all about exploring Lake Winnipesaukee, so at **Ekal Activity Center**

(✉ 285 Daniel Webster Hwy. ☎ 603/677–8646 ⊕ www.ekalactivitycenter.com), rent stand-up paddleboards, kayaks, canoes, Aqua-Cycles, and bicycles.

Eat & Drink: Just up the road in Center Harbor, the boathouse-inspired bistro **Canoe** (✉ 232 Whittier Hwy. ☎ 603/253–4762 ⊕ www.canoecenterharbor.com) sits high above Lake Winnipesaukee. It's known for seafood, including wood-fired, bacon-wrapped scallops and a creamy, entrée-size haddock chowder topped with herbs and crushed Ritz Crackers.

Stay: Choose from four lodgings at **Mill Falls at the Lake** (✉ 312 Daniel Webster Hwy. ☎ 844/745–2931 ⊕ www.millfalls.com): relaxing Church Landing and Bay Point are both on the shore of Lake Winnipesaukee while convivial Mill Falls—with a pool—and Chase House are across the street, next to a 19th-century mill that houses shops and restaurants.

Breakfast: With big windows overlooking the lake and timber posts and ceiling beams, **Lakehouse Grille** (within the Church Landing accommodations at Mill Falls at the Lake) captures the rusticity of an old-fashioned camp dining room. Feast on classic American favorites with interesting twists, such as eggs Benedict topped with Maine lobster.

Day 8: Meredith, NH, to Portland, ME

82 miles (2 hours without traffic and stops)

On your last day, travel along the northern reaches of the Lakes Region into a low-key but still lovely part of Maine that takes you to its biggest city.

ALONG THE WAY
Town: With Squam Lake to the west, Lake Winnipesaukee to the south, and the Sandwich Mountains to the north, Center Sandwich offers one of the prettiest environments in the Lakes Region. At the 200-acre **Loon Center** (✉ 183 Lees Mill Rd., Moultonborough, NH ☎ 603/476–5666 ⊕ www.loon.org), you can learn about the progress made in helping restore the state's loon population; vantage points on the Loon Nest Trail overlook the spot resident loons sometimes occupy in late spring and summer. If you're visiting in the fall, a hike up Red Hill is a must. The 2,030-foot mountain really does turn red in autumn. At the top of the moderately steep 1.7-mile Fire Tower Trail, you can climb a fire tower for 360-degree views of Lake Winnipesaukee and Squam Lake, as well as the White Mountains beyond.

Eat & Drink: In a converted barn adorned with paintings by local artists, rustic **Corner House Inn** (✉ 22 Main St. ☎ 603/284–6219 ⊕ www.cornerhouserestaurantandbar.com) is in an 1840s building in charming Center Sandwich village, serving classic American fare.

PORTLAND
Do: When the weather's good, everyone in Portland heads outside, whether for boating on the water, lounging on a beach, or walking and biking the promenades. Between the city's two promenades, the Eastern Promenade, often overlooked by tourists, has by far the best view. Gracious Victorian homes, many now converted to condos and apartments, border one side of the street. On the other is 68 acres of hillside parkland that includes Ft. Allen Park and, at the base of the hill, the Eastern Prom Trail and tiny East End Beach and boat launch.

Eat & Drink: Small, hip **Duck Fat** (✉ 43 Middle St. ☎ 207/774–8080 ⊕ www.duckfat.com) is always packed, even in midafternoon. The focus here is everyday farm-to-table fare: the signature Belgian fries are made with Maine potatoes cooked, yes, in duck fat and served in paper cones. Afterwards, find your way into no-fuss, basement speakeasy

Lincolns (✉ *36 Market St.* ⊕ *www.face-book.com/LincolnsPortlandMaine*) where all drinks cost only $5 (here's your only hint on finding the location: enter through the red doors at 36 Market St. and head downstairs).

Stay: In the beautifully restored Mellen E. Bolster House, **The Francis** (✉ *747 Congress St.* ☎ *207/772-7485* ⊕ *www. thefrancismaine.com*) is a charming boutique hotel with a midcentury-modern vibe that seamlessly compliments the building's immaculately preserved historical design elements.

Breakfast: Don't pass up a chance to try the sweet and savory, all-natural, Maine potato-based doughnuts at **Holy Donut** (✉ *194 Park Ave.* ☎ *207/874-7774* ⊕ *www.theholydonut.com*). Standards are glazed in flavors such as dark chocolate–sea salt, maple, pomegranate, triple berry, and chai, or stuffed with delicious fillings like bacon and cheddar, or ricotta. There are always new inventions, too, such as salted chocolate caramel and Key lime pie.

The New England Coast

Written by Jen Rose Smith

Soak up salt air and sea views on a coast-hugging route through New England's finest beach towns. Wandering between clam shacks and surf breaks, you'll hit peak vacation mode in classic Yankee style, with plenty of time to stretch out on your own patch of sand.

In between beach stops, soak up the region's fascinating culture at museums and historic sites, then catch postcard-worthy sunsets while perched at dockside cafés. This nine-day route goes from blue-blood New England to an LGBTQ+ nightlife mecca, then on to the home stretch of the south-facing coast, finding seafaring communities where

harpooneers once strolled the cobblestones and schooners ruled the waves.

At a Glance

Start: Portland, ME

End: New York City, NY

Miles Traveled: 561 miles

Suggested Duration: 8 days

States Visited: Connecticut, Maine, Massachusetts, New Hampshire, New York, Rhode Island

Key Sights: Cape Cod National Seashore; Coney Island; Mystic Seaport Museum; Salem Witch Trials Memorial; Yale University

Best Time to Go: Vacationing crowds energize the peak summer months of July and August, when joining the throng is all part of the fun. But just keep in mind that means there will be crowds (and traffic) and often lodging in these areas books up far in advance (and many rentals only rent in one-week increments). Plan your trip for June or September to balance warm weather with lower prices and uncrowded beaches. And if you prefer ocean views under moody autumn skies, an October trip is perfect for blustery seaside strolls.

Day 1: Portland, ME, to Kennebunkport, ME

29 miles (40 minutes without traffic and stops)

A short day between Portland and Kennebunkport leaves plenty of time for exploring Maine's coastal havens, which range from nautical kitsch to preppy chic.

ALONG THE WAY

Photo Op: If you think Maine's oldest lighthouse looks familiar, it's because **Portland Head Light** (✉ *12 Captain Strout Cir., Cape*

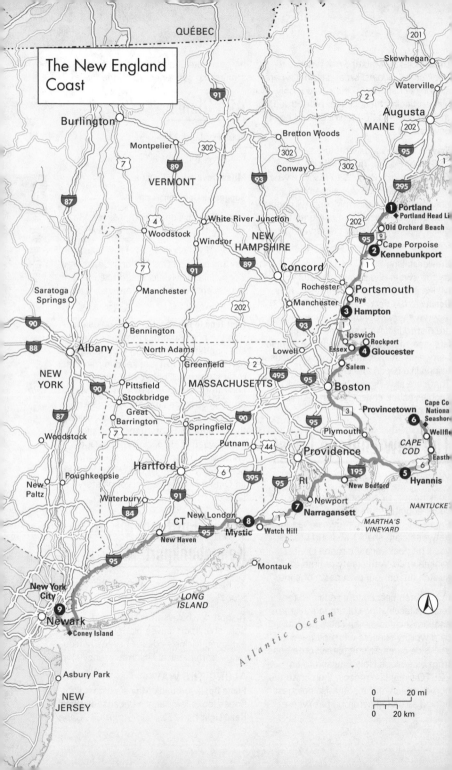

Elizabeth, ME ☎ 207/799–2661 ⊕ www.
portlandheadlight.com) stars on calendars and postcards in every souvenir shop. Snap that essential photo from nearby rocks, then take the time to stroll around surrounding Fort Williams Park, which includes disused gun batteries built between 1896 and 1906.

Town: A seven-mile beach fronts the summer town of **Old Orchard Beach, ME,** but it's the classic pier and boardwalk that make it an essential detour. Give in to the neighboring amusement park and you could while away the day here.

Eat & Drink: Take quiet Route 9 from Old Orchard Beach to Kennebunkport, and you'll hit tiny Cape Porpoise just before arriving. There fishing nets and buoys deck the **Ramp Bar and Grill** (⊠ 77 Pier Rd., Kennebunkport, ME ☎ 207/967–8500 ⊕ www.pier77restaurant.com) in nautical hues. The beachy menu's lobster rolls and mussels earn raves from locals.

KENNEBUNKPORT

Do: The Kennebunks—especially Kennebunkport—provide the complete Maine Coast experience: white-clapboard houses, rocky shorelines, sandy beaches, quaint downtowns, lobster boat–packed harbors, and seafood restaurants of every type. Browse the tony souvenir shops flanking Dock Square, then continue along Ocean Avenue, which parallels the Kennebunk River. From June through September, **First Chance Whale Watch** (⊠ 4 Western Ave. ☎ 207/967–5507 ⊕ www.
firstchancewhalewatch.com) shuttles visitors to summer feeding grounds that attract finbacks, humpbacks, minkes, and the occasional blue whale.

Eat & Drink: Sunset drinks and seafood on the dock at **Arundel Wharf** (⊠ 43 Ocean Ave. ☎ 207/967–3444 ⊕ www.
arundelwharf.com) are a Kennebunkport tradition; you'll get a front-row seat for watching boats nose along the Kennebunkport River. Follow it up with sweet treats at **Rococo Artisan Ice Cream** (⊠ 6

Extend Your Trip

From New York City: Best of Long Island and the Jersey Shore *(Ch. 8)*; Best of New York State *(Ch. 8)*

8

The Northeast THE NEW ENGLAND COAST

Spring St. ☎ 207/835–1049 ⊕ www.
rococoicecream.com), specializing in quirky flavors including goat cheese–blackberry and spicy rocky road.

Stay: Well-appointed glamping tents at **Sandy Pines Campground** (⊠ 277 Mills Rd. ☎ 207/967–2483 ⊕ www.sandypines-camping.com) are full of breezy style, and family-friendly amenities include a playground and saltwater pool. (There are regular tent sites, RV sites, and cottages, too.) And while it's a bit time-worn, the budget-friendly **Seaside Inn** (⊠ 80 Beach Ave. ☎ 207/967-4461 ⊕ www.kenne-bunkbeachmaine.com) has an unbeatable location on Gooch's Beach, reached via a private, sandy path.

Breakfast: Walking distance from Dock Square, **Mornings in Paris** (⊠ 21 Western Ave. ☎ 207/204–0032 ⊕ www.morn-ingsinparis.com) is ideal for picking up a fresh-baked chocolate croissant or melty croque monsieur sandwich before hitting the road.

Day 2: Kennebunkport, ME, to Hampton, NH

41 miles (50 minutes without traffic and stops)

Cross the Piscataqua River on your way to New Hampshire's pint-sized seacoast, where you'll find a lineup of clam shacks, arcades, and partiers flanking the state's only big sandy beach.

ALONG THE WAY

Town: Just past the historic merchant town of Portsmouth is tiny Rye, where the **Seacoast Science Center** (✉ *570 Ocean Blvd.* ☎ *603/436–8043* ⊕ *www.seacoastsciencecenter.org*) has aquariums and kid-pleasing touch tanks. Stretch your legs exploring the surrounding Odiorne Point State Park, a patchwork of salt marshes, rocky shores, and green space.

Eat & Drink: Old-timey lunch wagon **Gilley's Diner** (✉ *175 Fleet St.* ☎ *603/431–6343* ⊕ *www.gilleysdiner.com*), in Portsmouth, offers nostalgia, steamed hot dogs, and unpretentious fast food in a converted 1940s trolley car.

HAMPTON BEACH

Do: Much of the fun in Hampton is just soaking up the sun-and-sand crowd along the sandy-beach waterfront, where gaggles stroll between fried-dough stands and open-air bars. Pinball and Skee-Ball enthusiasts should make a pilgrimage to **Funarama** (✉ *169 Ocean Blvd., Hampton* ☎ *603/926–2381*) and **Playland Arcade** (✉ *211 Ocean Blvd.* ☎ *603/926–3831* ⊕ *www.hamptonbeach.org*), located 500 feet apart on Ocean Boulevard.

Eat & Drink: Enormous slabs of fried dough the length of your arm, usually topped with cinnamon sugar or powdered sugar, are a meal unto themselves and a Hampton Beach tradition—there are shops everywhere, but **Blink's Fry Doe** (191 Ocean Blvd. ☎ *603/926–8933* ⊕ *www.facebook.com/BlinksFrydoe*) is a perennial favorite. Or join the all-day crowds on the decks at **Sea Ketch Restaurant** (✉ *127 Ocean Blvd.* ☎ *603/926–0324* ⊕ *www.seaketch.com*), a favorite for hurricane-glass drinks and sunset views.

Nature: It's not just cruising and cocktails in Hampton Beach. Just north of town is the wonderful **Hampton Salt March Conservation Area,** an estuary with very fine bird-watching opportunities.

Stay: A little removed from the noise along the strip, **Atlantic Breeze Suites** (✉ *429 Ocean Blvd.* ☎ *603/967–4781* ⊕ *www.atlanticbreezesuites.com*) outshines the rather shabby alternatives in the more crowded core. All rooms have kitchenettes, and many have balconies that overlook the ocean or salt marsh.

Breakfast: Sip coffee under a fleet of model airplanes in the **Airfield Café** (✉ *9A Lafayette Rd., North Hampton, NH* ☎ *603/964–1654* ⊕ *www.theairfieldcafe.com*), a North Hampton diner located at the edge of Hampton Airfield. Even better, snag an outdoor picnic table and enjoy house-specialty crab cake Benedict with views of the small planes coming in for a landing.

Day 3: Hampton, NH, to Gloucester, MA

33 miles (1 hour without traffic and stops)

Go from the wild beach-party scene to a working harbor town as you follow a gently curving coast toward the rocky outline of Cape Ann.

ALONG THE WAY

Eat & Drink: Among Massachusetts fried-clam aficionados, the **Clam Box of Ipswich** (✉ *246 High St.* ☎ *978/356–9707* ⊕ *www.clamboxipswich.com*) earns some of the region's highest marks. Pay more for the "native clams," which are whole-bellied alternatives to the more processed strips.

Town: Quiet today, Essex, Massachusetts, was once a 17th-century shipbuilding powerhouse, a history that's on display at the small **Essex Shipbuilding Museum** (✉ *66 Main St.* ☎ *978/768–7541* ⊕ *www.essexshipbuilding.org*). After that, stretch your legs on the four-mile-long **Crane Beach** (✉ *Ipswich, MA* ⊕ *www.thetrustees.org*), flanked by pristine dunes and a maritime pitch pine

Cape Cod National Seashore is one of the most beautiful places on the New England coast.

forest. This pretty spot is one of the world's most important nesting places for piping plovers.

Detour: A 10-minute drive beyond Gloucester is pretty Rockport, an artist colony overflowing with souvenir shops and art galleries. Don't miss snapping a photo of the bright-red replica fishing shack called Motif No. 1; once you see the rebuilt 1840 landmark, you'll find it everywhere, from paintings to calendars to postcards.

GLOUCESTER

Do: While Cape Cod gets all the fame, Massachusetts's northern beaches are quite charming, and Gloucester comes with a particularly interesting maritime history. Browse a tangle of working fishing boats in the harbor on your way to the **Maritime Gloucester** (✉ 23 Harbor Loop ☎ 978/281-0470 ⊕ www. maritimegloucester.org), a museum and aquarium where you'll see wooden boats being restored and displays on the town's seafaring past.

Eat & Drink: Octopus salad and Portuguese soup at the beloved **Azorean Restaurant & Bar** (✉ 133 Washington St. ☎ 978/283-5500 ⊕ www.azoreanrestaurant.com) are reminders that many Gloucester fishermen have Portuguese roots by way of the Azores. For great burgers and corner-bar energy, **Stone's Pub and Eatery** (✉ 242 Main St. ☎ 978/515-7366 ⊕ www.stonespubandeatery.com) is a friendly option with a long list of beers on tap.

Stay: Basic rooms overlooking Smith's Cove are the draw at **Rocky Neck Accommodations** (✉ 43 Rocky Neck Ave. ☎ 978/381-9848 ⊕ www.rockyneckaccommodations.com), located within the historic Rocky Neck artist colony. Each has access to a private or rooftop deck, and there are a handful of restaurants and attractions within walking distance.

Breakfast: Grab a seat at the counter of **Two Sisters Coffee Shop** (✉ 27 Washington St. ☎ 978/281-3378) for hearty breakfasts and homemade bread. Fluffy stacks of French toast are a favorite, or try fish cakes if your appetite for seafood is still going strong.

Day 4: Gloucester, MA, to Hyannis, MA

106 miles (1 hour, 55 minutes without traffic and stops)

Duck into witch-mad Salem on your way to Cape Cod, where the Massachusetts landscape curls into a tendril of historic towns, sandy beaches, and dunes.

ALONG THE WAY

Town: Famed for its history of persecuting so-called witches, **Salem** eventually turned tragedy into a bit of a sideshow, complete with a boatload of spooky legends and witchy souvenirs; today the town is filled with both kitschy and hip shops selling herbs, crystals, and fortunes (if you're going to get your Tarot cards read anywhere, do it here). The town's **Witch Trials Memorial** (⊠ *24 Liberty St.* ⊕ *www.salemweb.com*) is more sober, and located a short distance from the excellent **Peabody Essex Museum** (⊠ *161 Essex St.* ☎ *978/745–9500* ⊕ *www.pem.org*), with a fine, permanent exhibit of maritime art. After that, stroll to the 75 open-air murals that make up the **Punto Urban Art Museum** (⊠ *91-1 Peabody St.* ☎ *978/745–8071* ⊕ *www.puntourbanartmuseum.org*).

Eat & Drink: Pick up brittle and fudge at **Ye Olde Pepper Companie** (⊠ *122 Derby St.* ☎ *978/745–2744* ⊕ *www.oldepeppercandy.com*), which claims to be the oldest candy company in America, or stop by **Far From the Tree** (⊠ *108 Jackson St.* ☎ *978/224–2904* ⊕ *www.farfromthetreecider.com*) to sample homemade hard ciders make with local apples. If you're craving something more substantial, you can't beat the black-blistered, wood-fired pizza pies from **Bambolina** (⊠ *288 Derby St.* ☎ *978/594–8709* ⊕ *www.bambolinarestaurant.com*).

HYANNIS

Do: This bustling Cape Cod hub is a long-time base for the Kennedy family, and home to the thoughtfully curated **John F. Kennedy Hyannis Museum** (⊠ *397 Main St.* ☎ *508/790–3077* ⊕ *www.jfkhyannismuseum.org*); stop there to take in period photos of the former president and Jackie O. In the evening, join a sunset sailing cruise on the harbor by Bay Spirit Tours, or—if your timing is right—catch a Hyannis Harbor Hawks game at **McKeon Park** (⊠ *120 High School Rd.* ⊕ *www.mckeon-park.lany.io*). They're part of the Cape Cod Baseball League, where some of the country's most promising college athletes spend summers playing for intimate crowds.

Eat & Drink: The fried cauliflower and gourmet hot dogs are tempting, but the real draw at **Finn's Craft Beer Tap House** (⊠ *16 Barnstable Rd.* ☎ *508/534–9756* ⊕ *www.finnscraftbeertaphouse.com*) is the truly impressive lineup of brews from across New England. On warm nights, try snagging a spot on the enclosed patio.

Stay: Meet fellow travelers in the **Hyannis Hostel** (⊠ *111 Ocean St.* ☎ *508/775–7990* ⊕ *www.hiusa.org*), which offers a low-key environment, private rooms, and budget-friendly dorms. Breakfast and parking are included, but the hostel only operates from May through September.

Breakfast: Classics like blueberry pancakes and home fries are prepared with largely local ingredients at **Spoon and Seed** (⊠ *12 Thornton Dr.* ☎ *774/470–4634* ⊕ *www.spoonandseed.com*), a homey, family-run breakfast-and-lunch joint worth the short drive from downtown.

Day 5: Hyannis, MA, to Provincetown, MA

48 miles (1 hour without traffic and stops)

Follow the Cape as it wraps back to what locals call "the end of the world"—aka fishing village–turned–LGBTQ+ hot spot, Provincetown—pausing for seaside villages, fresh oysters, and some of the finest beaches in New England.

ALONG THE WAY

Nature: The broad beaches at **Cape Cod National Seashore** (✉ *99 Marconi Site Rd., Wellfleet, MA* ☎ *508/255–3421* ⊕ *www. nps.gov/caco*) seem nearly endless, inviting long walks between the water's edge and crumbling coastal cliffs. Find wild roses blooming in the dunes here, and spot seals, turtles, whales, and the occasional great white shark in the chilly Atlantic water. Start at the **Salt Pond Visitor Center** (✉ *50 Nauset Rd.* ☎ *508/255–3421* ⊕ *www.nps.gov/caco*) in Eastham, where you'll find schedules for ranger-led tours and talks.

Town: The tiny town of **Wellfleet** is famed for delicious oysters and an artsy community. Most shops carry free maps of the community's art galleries, which are mostly clustered in a walkable stretch of Commercial Street.

Eat & Drink: Sample oysters fresh from the sea at **Wellfleet Bookstore & Restaurant** (✉ *50 Kendrick Ave., Wellfleet, MA* ☎ *508/349–3154* ⊕ *www.wellfleetoyster. com*); the family-run spot has its own oyster farm located just across the road. BYOB **Moby Dick's Restaurant** (✉ *3225 Rte. 6, Wellfleet, MA* ☎ *508/349–9795* ⊕ *www.mobys.com*) is a favorite in the New England snack-shack tradition, with great clams and chowder served amid fishing-themed flotsam and jetsam.

Roadside Attraction: Find quirky memorabilia at **Wellfleet Flea Market** (✉ *51 U.S.*

Essential Listening

You're not going to make it through the whole book, but taking in the first chapter of the *Moby-Dick* audiobook will get you in the mood for whaling town lore as you travel through Bedford.

6 ☎ *508/349-0541* ⊕ *www.wellfleetcinemas.com*), a weekend event that takes over the daytime hours of the Wellfleet Drive-In Theatre. Bring plenty of cash to trade for shell art, old clothes, and treasures unearthed from Cape Cod's many historic homes.

PROVINCETOWN

Do: Wander the galleries and score tickets to a drag show on Commercial Street, where you can soak up the castaway feel of a town that's a long way from anywhere. This is the first place the Pilgrims touched down in North America, an event marked at the **Pilgrim's Monument** (✉ *1 High Pole Hill Rd.* ☎ *508/487–1310* ⊕ *www.pilgrim-monument.org*), which has views across the end of the Cape. There's plenty of wild nature here, too, whether you're on a whale-watching boat tour to Stellwagen Bank or wandering trails that lead from the **Province Lands Visitor Center** (✉ *171 Race Point Rd.* ☎ *508/487–1256* ⊕ *www.nps.gov/caco*) into Cape Cod National Seashore.

Eat & Drink: Nostalgic grilled cheese meets classic takes on seafood at casual spot **The Canteen** (✉ *225 Commercial St.* ☎ *508/487–3800* ⊕ *www.thecanteenptown.com*), but their most popular item is an excellent rendition of fish-and-chips. Built into a former sea captain's home, **Strangers and Saints** (✉ *404 Commercial St.* ☎ *508/487–1449* ⊕ *www.strangersandsaints.com*) has a nautical theme and a menu that melds cuisines from every corner of the Mediterranean.

Stay: Within walking distance of the Commercial Street bars is the friendly (and historic) **Pilgrim House** (✉ *336 Commercial St.* ☎ *508/487–6424* ⊕ *www.pilgrimhouseptown.com*), which boasts Henry David Thoreau as a past guest. If you're up for staying out of town, the **HI Truro Hostel** (✉ *111 N. Pamet Rd., Truro, MA* ☎ *508/349–3889* *www.hiusa.org*) is a budget-friendly, seasonal option that's walking distance from a breezy Atlantic-facing beach.

Breakfast: Pick up fried-dough malasadas or caramelized egg tarts from **Provincetown Portuguese Bakery** (✉ *299 Commercial St.* ☎ *508/487–1803* ⊕ *www.provincetownportuguesebakery.com*), a particularly sweet part of the Cape's rich Portuguese heritage. The best espresso is from **Kōhi Coffee Company** (✉ *199 Commercial St.* ☎ *774/538–6467* ⊕ *www.kohicoffee.com*), conveniently located a five-minute walk away.

Day 6: Provincetown, MA, to Narragansett, RI

134 miles (2 hours, 35 minutes without traffic and stops)

Hopscotch across the fractured southern coasts of Massachusetts and Rhode Island to reach a good-time surf town with matchless sunsets.

ALONG THE WAY
Town: Once a whaling capital, **New Bedford, Massachusetts,** sent hundreds of sailing ships around the world. Explore that history at the **New Bedford Whaling Museum** (✉ *33 William St.* ☎ *508/996–4095* ⊕ *www.nps.gov/nebe*), then visit Seamen's Bethel, a church where a salty congregation once heard sermons ringing out from a pulpit shaped like the prow of a ship. Both are part of the New Bedford Whaling National Historic Park, which

curates downloadable, self-guided tours of the historic city.

Eat & Drink: Old-school Italian American favorites are the stars at **Ma Raffa's Italian Restaurant** (✉ *85 Rockdale Ave., New Bedford, MA* ☎ *508/992–8467* ⊕ *www.maraffas.com*), whose menu features spaghetti and meatballs, subs, thin-crust pizza, and all things red sauce. Solid pub food at **Moby Dick Brewing Co.** (✉ *16 S. Water St, New Bedford, MA* ☎ *774/202–6961* ⊕ *www.mobydickbrewing.com*) pairs well with the homemade micro-brews; the Quick Eternity American IPA is a local favorite.

NARRAGANSETT
Do: South-facing beaches attract some of Rhode Island's best surf waves, and Narragansett Town Beach is the place to be on sunny days. Rent a board in the parking lot and paddle into the lineup, or just spread out your towel and enjoy the show. To see a less-crowded side of this jigsaw coast, rent a boat or board from **Narrow River Kayaks** (✉ *94 Middlebridge Rd.* ☎ *401/789–0334* ⊕ *www.narrowriverkayaks.com*) to explore **John H. Chaffee National Wildlife Refuge** (✉ *43 Crest Ave.* ☎ *401/364–9124* ⊕ *www.fws.gov*) via the slow-moving Narrow River.

Eat & Drink: Enjoy panoramic ocean views from the deck at the **Coast Guard House** (✉ *40 Ocean Rd.* ☎ *401/789–0700* ⊕ *www.thecoastguardhouse.com*), an old standby for early-evening drinks; feel free to enjoy a can of Narragansett beer, but keep in mind the actual brewery is about 40 minutes north in Pawtucket. The food at Coast Guard House isn't great, so head over to the **Bike Stop Café** (✉ *148 Boon St.* ☎ *401/284–1414* ⊕ *www.facebook.com/TheBikeStopCafe*), a cycling-themed hangout with great pizza and tacos.

Stay: Boutique style in 16 rooms sets the **Break Hotel** (✉ *1208 Ocean Rd.* ☎ *401/363–9800* ⊕ *www.thebreakhotel.com*) apart from the crowd in

Narragansett, where accommodations lean generic. A heated, outdoor saltwater pool is flanked by comfy loungers, where you can order from the hotel restaurant menu; breakfast is a lineup of sweet and savory small plates.

Breakfast: If you're skipping hotel fare, stop by **Meldgie's Diner** (✉ *120 Knowlesway Ext.* ☎ *401/789–1122* ⊕ *www.meldgies.com*) for a classic American-style breakfast on your way to **Point Judith Lighthouse** (✉ *1460 Ocean Rd.* ☎ *401/789–0444* ⊕ *www.uscg.mil*), where the morning light is ideal for photographs across Block Island Sound.

Day 7: Narragansett, RI, to Mystic, CT

36 miles (50 minutes without traffic and stops)

A short day's drive leaves time to wander sandy beaches, sip champagne cocktails, and step into the world of a 19th-century seafarer.

ALONG THE WAY

Town: The upscale enclave of Watch Hill has one of Rhode Island's finest beaches, **Napatree Point** (✉ *Fort Rd. Westerly, RI* ☎ *401/315–5399* ⊕ *www.thewatchhillconservancy.org*); it's a curving, sandy spit with frilly dune grass and plenty of shore birds. If you're traveling with kids in tow, this is a must for the 19th-century **Flying Horse Carousel** (✉ *151–153 Bay St., Watch Hill, RI* ⊕ *ww.merrygoroundbeach.com*), an easy stop on your way to the **Watch Hill Lighthouse and Museum** (✉ *14 Lighthouse Rd., Westerly, RI* ⊕ *www.watchhilllighthousekeepers.org*).

Eat & Drink: Located within the famed Ocean House hotel, the **Secret Garden champagne bar** (✉ *1 Bluff Ave., Watch Hill, RI* ☎ *401/584–7000* ⊕ *www.oceanhouseri.com*) is the place to sip Veuve Clicquot cocktails and nibble an orange marmalade crepe. It's fancy but fun, and

open from May through October. Find something more substantial at **Ten** (✉ *98 Bay St., Westerly, RI* ☎ *401/315–2620* ⊕ *www.tensandwiches.com*), with its all-organic menu of sandwiches, salads, and espresso.

MYSTIC

Do: Sprawling along the Mystic River, the **Mystic Seaport Museum** (✉ *75 Greenmanville Ave.* ☎ *860/572–0711* ⊕ *www.mysticseaport.org*) recreates life in a 19th-century seaport, complete with ringing blacksmiths' hammers, costumed interpreters, and real historic vessels. It's easy to get caught up in the old-time spirit, even if you're not a seafaring buff. This is the largest maritime museum in the United States, and it's easy to spend a whole day here. Nearby is the excellent **Mystic Aquarium** (✉ *55 Coogan Blvd.* ☎ *860/572–5955* ⊕ *www.mysticsquarium.org*), home to beluga whales, sea lions, and penguins.

Eat & Drink: Yes, the Julia Roberts movie is based on a real-life eatery called **Mystic Pizza** (✉ *56 W. Main St.* ☎ *860/536–3700* ⊕ *www.mysticpizza.com*) where locals and visitors slide into homey booths for pizza and fried pickles. Big, fresh salads and soups from **Mystic Salad Co.** (✉ *12 Cottrell St.* ⊕ *www.facebook.com/myssaladco*) are perfect to-go lunches; find a spot by the nearby Mystic River to watch boat traffic drifting by.

Stay: A series of historic buildings are updated with nautical flair at **The Whaler's Inn** (✉ *20 E. Main St.* ☎ *860/536–1506* ⊕ *www.whalersinnmystic.com*), whose convenient downtown location is ideal for walking to restaurants and bars.

Breakfast: Pick up classic French treats, including sweet and savory croissants, at **Sift Bake Shop** (✉ *5 Water St.* ☎ *860/245–0541* ⊕ *www.siftbakeshopmystic.com*), and snag a sourdough baguette to munch in the car when you hit the road.

Day 8: Mystic, CT, to New York City, NY

134 miles (2 hours, 45 minutes without traffic and stops)

Watch the Connecticut coast rear up into America's most famous city, and where Coney Island is a people-pleasing taste of seaside nostalgia served NYC-style.

ALONG THE WAY

Town: Tours of New Haven's **Yale University** (☎ 203/432–4771 ⊕ www.yale.edu) take in several libraries and the campus's gorgeous Gothic architecture. Save time for additional visits to the **Yale University Art Gallery** (✉ 1111 Chapel St. ☎ 203/432–0600 ⊕ www.artgallery.yale.edu), the **Yale Collection of Musical Instruments** (✉ 15 Hillhouse Ave. ☎ 203/432–0822 ⊕ www.collection.yale.edu), and **Yale Center for British Art** (✉ 1080 Chapel St. ☎ 203/432–2800 ⊕ www.britishart.yale.edu), each free to the public. Another highlight is the **Peabody Museum of Natural History** (✉ 170 Whitney Ave. ☎ 203/432–8987 ⊕ www.peabody.yale.edu), with a famed collection of dinosaur skeletons.

Eat & Drink: New Haven–style pizza is called "apizza," a pie that's whisper thin and crisped in coal-fired ovens. The two heavyweights for apizza are **Frank Pepe's Pizzeria Napoletana** (✉ 157 Wooster St. ☎ 203/865–5762 ⊕ www.pepespizzeria.com), famed for its white-clam pizza, and **Sally's Apizza** (✉ 237 Wooster St. ☎ 203/624–5271 ⊕ www.sallysapizza.com), a favorite for red-sauce versions; they're located on the same street only a few doors apart—go with whomever has the shorter wait.

NEW YORK CITY

Do: Close out a tour of seaside towns by exploring NYC's own beachy vacation spot: **Coney Island.** It's not hard to love the bustle of old-fashioned amusement park rides, hot dog stands, and other diversions along a long, sandy beach in Brooklyn. The area's wild history is on display at the **Coney Island Museum** (✉ 1208 Surf Ave., Brooklyn, NY ☎ 718/372–5159 ⊕ www.coneyisland.com), whose starring attraction might be the warped collection of funhouse mirrors.

Eat & Drink: Nathan's Famous (✉ 1310 Surf Ave. ☎ 718/333–2202 ⊕ www.nathans-famous.com) hot dogs are a Coney Island icon, and the original is still humming at the corner of Surf and Stillwell avenues. Ignore the other menu items and choose from a regular hot dog or chili cheese dog. As you eat, consider the astonishing fact that the reigning champion of the annual Nathan's Famous International Hot Dog Eating Contest (held each July 4th in Coney Island) downed 73 of these in 10 minutes.

Stay: Cross the Marine Parkway Bridge to spend the night at the **Rockaway Hotel** (✉ 108–10 Rockaway Beach Dr., Rockaway Park, NY ☎ 718/474–1216 ⊕ www.therockawayhotel.com), a stylish and modern landmark with great views back across Jamaica Bay.

Breakfast: Visit nearby **Cuisine by Claudette** (✉ 143 Beach 116th St., Rockaway Park, NY ☎ 718/945–5511 ⊕ www.cuisine-byclaudette.nyc) for superfresh juices, smoothies, and smoothie bowls, and you'll be rubbing shoulders with this spot's surfer crowd.

Chapter 9

OUTSIDE THE LOWER 48

WELCOME TO
OUTSIDE THE LOWER 48

TOP REASONS
TO GO

★ **Denali National Park:**
The most accessible of
Alaska's national parks
and one of only three
connected to the state's
highway system, the 6-mil-
lion-acre wilderness offers
spectacular mountain
views, a variety of wildlife,
striking vegetation, and
unforgettable landscapes.

★ **Haleakalā National
Park.** Some of the best
hiking in Maui can be
found in this park, along
the Road to Hāna.

★ **O'ahu's North Shore:**
As you head to the
North Shore of O'ahu,
stop along the way at
fruit stands, shrimp
trucks, beaches, world-
famous surfing spots,
and scenic overlooks.

★ **El Yunque National
Forest:** The only U.S.
tropical rain forest is laced
with hiking trails and full
of flowing waterfalls,
cool rivers, beautiful
mountain views.

1 The Best of Alaska. A
road trip from Anchorage
to Fairbanks is one of the
best ways to see all the
remarkable landscapes
that Alaska has to offer.

2 The Road to Hāna. One
of the world's most
famous drives, Maui's
precarious road has more
than 600 curves and
crosses some 50 gulch-
straddling bridges in just
52 coastline miles.

3 The Best of O'ahu.
Make a loop around the
scenic coast of Hawaii's
most popular island.

**4 The Best of Puerto
Rico.** Explore beyond the
typical tourist spots with
a road trip through the
mountains and beaches of
Puerto Rico.

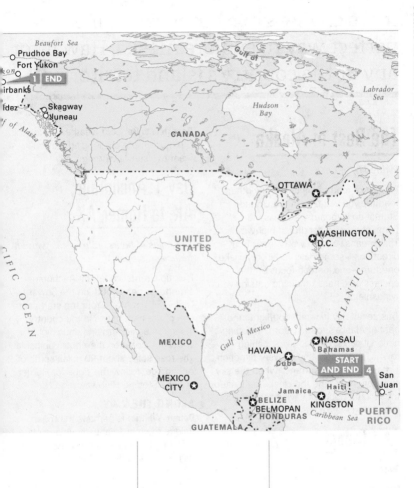

Once you leave the continental United States, taking a road trip might be a little more challenging, but it can still be the perfect way to explore Alaska, Hawaii, or any of the country's island territories.

The Best of Alaska

Written by J. Besl

An Alaska road trip is unlike any other road trip you will take in the United States: no billboards, few gas stations, and just a handful of highways. That means you can worry less about directions—some days you'll only make one turn—and instead focus on the endless epic-ness unfolding outside your windshield.

This seven-day itinerary spotlights the best of Alaska's road system, including national parks, glacier hikes, fishing towns, and mountains in every direction. Time your trip for summer when the sky stays bright around the clock. You'll need those extra hours of daylight to soak in everything Alaska has to offer.

At a Glance

Start: Anchorage, AK

End: Fairbanks, AK

Miles Traveled: 960 miles

Suggested Duration: 7 days

States Visited: Alaska

Key Sights: Alaska Native Heritage Center; Denali National Park; Kenai Fjords National Park; Museum of the North; Turnagain Arm

Best Time to Go: Cold weather makes this trip much more challenging, so you'll want to visit May through July.

Day 1: Anchorage, AK, to Homer, AK

221 miles (4 hours, 15 minutes without traffic and stops)

Pick up a rental car at the Anchorage airport and head south on the Seward Highway (aka AK-1). Your trip starts with one of the best drives in the country along Turnagain Arm and ends high above the coast on the Kenai Peninsula. The road splits about 90 miles south of Anchorage; follow the signs for Homer and the Sterling Highway.

ALONG THE WAY

Detour: Whittier is perhaps the most unique town in an already unique state. A former army base turned cruise port, its residents famously live in the same building (with a post office, market, and school attached so no one has to go outside). If you time it right, it's only an 11-mile, 25-minute drive off the Seward Highway, but this can't be a casual detour; Whittier is only accessed by a one-way tunnel through the mountains that stays open in each direction just 15 minutes of each hour. There's not much to do in town, but the views are unbeatable. Surrounding peaks cradle alpine glaciers, and when the summer weather

melts the huge winter snow load, you can catch glimpses of the brilliant blue ice underneath. You can often spot sea otters and harbor seals in the harbor.

Eat & Drink: Located right off the highway, **St. Elias Brewing Company** (✉ *434 Sharkathmi Ave., Soldotna, AK* ☎ *907/260–7837* ⊕ *www.steliasbrewingco.com*) in Soldotna serves stone-fired pizzas alongside its menu of soups and salads. Or stock up on meat and cheese at **Lucy's Market** (✉ *338 Homestead La., Soldotna, AK* ☎ *907/262–3232* ⊕ *www.lucysalaska.com*) in Soldotna for an upscale picnic on your drive.

Photo Op: Surrounded by wildflowers and overlooking the ocean, the small Russian Orthodox church in **Ninilchik** is well worth a visit. Take the marked turnoff at milepost 134.8 of the Sterling Highway.

HOMER

Do: Founded in the late 1800s as a gold-prospecting camp, today Homer is an eclectic community with an interesting mix of fishers, actors, artists, and writers. The Homer Spit is a unique landform jutting out into Kachemak Bay that houses many of the town's restaurants and hotels, along with a 360-degree view of the surrounding mountains. Step down to the docks to watch fishermen work and seagulls scavenge.

Eat & Drink: Scoop up the catch of the day at **The Little Mermaid** (✉ *162 W. Pioneer Ave., Homer, AK* ☎ *907/399–9900* ⊕ *www.littlemermaidhomer.com*), then head to the **Salty Dawg Saloon** (✉ *4380 Homer Spit Rd., Homer, AK* ☎ *907/398–5605* ⊕ *www.saltydawgsaloon.com*) for an accessible example of the textbook-Alaskan bar: dim, unfussy, dollar bills stapled all over the walls, and a bell at the bar (don't ring it unless you're buying a round for everyone).

Stay: Wake up with the waves (and possibly the whales) at **Land's End** (✉ *4786 Home Spit Rd., Homer, AK* ☎ *907/235–0400* ⊕ *www.lands-end-resort.com*), perched at the edge of Homer Spit.

Breakfast: Cozy up in the counter line at **Two Sisters Bakery** (✉ *233 E. Bunnell Ave., Homer, AK* ☎ *907/235–2280* ⊕ *www. twosistersbakery.net*). This popular spot with a wraparound porch and a kid-friendly backyard offers cakes, quiche, vegan muffins, and more.

Day 2: Homer, AK, to Seward, AK

168 miles (3 hours, 30 minutes without traffic and stops)

Take the Sterling Highway (AK-1) north to retrace yesterday's drive. Think of it as another chance to view the distant volcanoes rising over the water. Then turn right on the Seward Highway (AK-9) and head south to the seaside in Seward.

ALONG THE WAY

Eat & Drink: Odie's Deli (✉ *44315 Sterling Hwy., Soldotna, AK* ☎ *907/260–3255* ⊕ *www.odiesdeli.com*) in Soldotna offers sandwiches, soups, and a generous menu of freshly baked cookies, or you can pick up some pub food at Kenai River Brewing Co. (✉ *308 Homestead La., Soldotna, AK* ☎ *907/262–2337* ⊕ *www. kenairiverbrewing.com*).

Detour: Take the turnoff at mile 56.3 and drive 35 miles to **Hope**, where the gold rush crowds are long gone but their log cabins remain. The rust-roofed **Seaview Café & Bar** (✉ *18416 B Ave., Hope, AK* ☎ *907/782–3300* ⊕ *www.seaviewca-fealaska.com*) is a popular spot offering Reubens, brews, and bluegrass on summer weekends. Wander the few dusty

streets, clamber around the muddy tidal flats, and relish the relaxed pace in this end-of-the-road town.

SEWARD

Do: Surrounded on all sides by Kenai Fjords National Park, Chugach National Forest, and Resurrection Bay, Seward offers all the quaint realities of a small railroad town with the bonus of some jaw-dropping scenery. Stroll through Waterfront Park and swap stories with the families and camper-van crowds staying the night at the beach. Take a short drive along the coast (and past a gushing waterfall) for a quieter beach walk at Lowell Point.

Eat & Drink: Seward's restaurants cluster all along 4th Avenue. Both **Chinooks** (✉ *1404 4th Ave., Seward, AK* ☎ *907/224–2207* ⊕ *www.chinooksak. com*) and **Ray's Waterfront** (✉ *1316 4th Ave., Seward, AK* ☎ *907/224–5606* ⊕ *www.rayswaterfrontak.com*) offer seafood with harbor views. Pick up a pint at **Seward Brewing Company** (✉ *139 4th Ave., Seward, AK* ☎ *907/422–0337* ⊕ *www.sewardbrewingcompany.com*) or, for the full Alaska experience (think bright-orange ring buoys and bears in baseball hats on the wall), head to **Yukon Bar** (✉ *201 4th Ave., Seward, AK* ☎ *907/224–3063* ⊕ *www.facebook.com/ yukon.bar*).

Stay: Go big and take a 45-minute boat ride to Fox Island for a tranquil night at **Kenai Fjords Wilderness Lodge** (✉ *Fox*

Island, Resurrection Bay, AK ☎ 877/777–4053 ⊕ www.kenaifjordslodge.com). Or check in at the **Van Gilder Hotel** (✉ 308 Adams St., Seward, AK ☎ 907/224–3079 ⊕ www.vangilderseward.com) downtown, open since 1916 and listed on the National Register of Historic Places.

Breakfast: Housed in an old church and lined with local artwork, **Resurrect Art** (✉ 320 3rd Ave., Seward, AK ☎ 907/224–7161 ⊕ www.resurrectart.com) is a cozy coffee shop and gallery that's the perfect launch point for a day on the road. Lounge on the choir loft couches and watch the town wake up through the massive church window, then refill your coffee on the way out the door.

Day 3: Kenai Fjords National Park

12 miles (40 minutes)

Take a day to explore Kenai Fjords National Park, located a quick boat ride from Seward. Glacier tours dock at the small-boat harbor on 4th Avenue north of downtown. If you want to explore on foot, drive 3½ miles north on the Seward Highway (AK-9) and turn left on Herman Leirer Road (called Exit Glacier Road by locals). The road parallels Resurrection River and ends at Exit Glacier Nature Center.

This is spectacular coastal parkland incised with sheer, dark, slate cliffs rising from the sea, ribboned with white waterfalls, and tufted with deep-green spruce. Kenai Fjords offers a rare opportunity for an up close view of blue tidewater glaciers as well as some remarkable ocean wildlife.

AFTERNOON

Nature: Hankering to hike? From the **Exit Glacier Nature Center** (✉ 24620 Herman Leirer Rd., Seward, AK ☎ 907/422–0535 ⊕ www.nps.gov/kefj), it's a straightforward walk to experience views of Exit

Glacier. You can also join a ranger for a 90-minute guided walk. More adventurous types can tackle the Harding Icefield Trail, a strenuous 8.2-mile round-trip hike up the mountain that provides once-in-a-lifetime views of an endless spread of thick, ancient ice.

Photo Op: If you're on a glacier cruise, you don't need our recommendations. The entire ride will be a never-ending photo op as you cruise past calving glaciers and spot orcas, puffins, otters, harbor seals, porpoises, and sea lions.

EVENING

Do: Once you've finished exploring Kenai Fjords, head back to Seward for the night. If you can, make time for the **Alaska Sealife Center** (✉ 301 Railway Ave., Seward, AK ☎ 888/379–2525 ⊕ www.alaskasealife.org) and its charismatic crew of seals, sea lions, eiders, and octopi. The facility also offers backstage tours, allowing guests to feed puffins in the aviary or get up close with the otters.

Eat & Drink: Known for its halibut, **Thorn's Showcase Lounge** (✉ 208 4th Ave., Seward, AK ☎ 907/224–3700) is a surf-and-turf spot with a red-vinyl Rat Pack vibe. If nothing else, poke your head inside to see the wall-to-wall collection of ceramic decanters. After dinner, scoop up gelato at **Sweet Darling's** (✉ 205 4th Ave., Seward, AK ☎ 907/224–3011 ⊕ www.sweetdarlings.com).

Stay: Get a spot on the water for your second night in Seward. **Harbor 360 Hotel** (✉ 1412 4th Ave., Seward, AK ☎ 907/224–2550 ⊕ www.harbor360hotel.com) is perched on the docks near downtown, while Windsong Lodge (✉ 31772 Herman Leirer Rd., Seward, AK ☎ 907/224–7116 ⊕ www.sewardwindsong.com) is 2 miles from town along the Resurrection River.

Breakfast: Zudy's Café (✉ 501 Railway Ave., Seward, AK ☎ 907/224–4710 ⊕ www.zudyscafe.com) sits right on the waterfront, inside Seward's former

A glacier cruise is one of the best ways to see Kenai Fjords National Park.

downtown train station. Or pick up coffee on your way out of town at **13 Ravens** (✉ *411 Port Ave., Box 385, Seward, AK* ⊕ *www.facebook.com/13RavensCoffee*), a combination coffee shop and bookstore housed in an old Alaska Railroad train car.

Day 4: Seward, AK, to Hatcher Pass, AK

182 miles (3 hours, 30 minutes without traffic and stops)

Today might sound a bit confusing, but it's really just two turns. Head north on the Seward Highway (AK-1) all the way back to Anchorage, the state's only big city. Turn right on 6th Avenue near downtown and take the Glenn Highway (still AK-1) all the way past Palmer. Then turn left on Palmer Fishhook and wind your way into the mountains.

ALONG THE WAY

Town: Home to Alaska's premier ski resort, **Girdwood** offers outdoor adventures year-round. Stop at **Alyeska Resort** (✉ *1000 Arlberg Ave., Girdwood, AK* ☎ *800/880–3880* ⊕ *www.alyeskaresort. com*) and soak up some sun on the Adirondack chairs out back, or take the tram to the top of the mountain for a beer and a bite at **Bore Tide Deli & Bar** (✉ *1000 Arlberg Ave., Girdwood, AK* ☎ *907/754–2237* ⊕ *www.alyeskaresort.com*).

Eat & Drink: While in Girdwood, the **Double Musky Inn** (✉ *Mile.3, Crow Creek Rd., Girdwood, AK* ☎ *907/783–2822* ⊕ *www. doublemuskyinn.com*) offers Cajun seafood dishes and a Mardi Gras vibe. For lighter fare, grab soup and a sandwich at **The Bake Shop** (✉ *194 Olympic Mountain Loop, Girdwood, AK* ☎ *907/783–2831* ⊕ *www.thebakeshop.com*) to enjoy on the picnic tables outside.

Nature: The wide, well-maintained **Winner Creek Trail** winds through the rain forest from Alyeska Resort to a hop-aboard hand-tram over gushing Glacier Creek.

Photo Op: Just one block off your route through Anchorage, the postcard-style *Greetings from Alaska* mural offers a quick stop for a fun photo on your way out of town.

Shop: This is a great time to explore a bit more of Anchorage. Stop by the **Anchorage Museum Store** (✉ *625 C St. Anchorage, AK* ☎ *907/929–9200* ⊕ *www.anchoragemuseum.org*) to pick up art, books, and jewelry that spotlight Indigenous and Northern design. **Oomingmak** (✉ *604 H St. Anchorage, AK* ☎ *907/272–9225* ⊕ *www.qiviut.com*) is cooperatively owned by hundreds of Alaska Native women across the state who sell their wool crafts in the tiny downtown shop. Housed in an original city building from 1915, **The Kobuk** (✉ *504 W. 5th Ave., Anchorage, AK* ☎ *907/272–3626* ⊕ *www.kobukcoffee.com*) is a gift shop on Town Square Park with coffee and donuts in the back room.

Attraction: If you only have time for one sight in Anchorage, make it the **Alaska Native Heritage Center** (✉ *8800 Heritage Center Dr.* ☎ *907/330–8000* ⊕ *www.alaskanative.net*), which provides an informative introduction to Alaska's Indigenous people, with village exhibits, demonstrations, dances, storytelling, and more.

HATCHER PASS

Do: Homer's Pass is an all-season playground stocked with glacial lakes, jagged peaks, and alpine meadows to explore. Check out deep-blue Summit Lake just two miles down the gravel Hatcher Pass Road, where you can go late-summer-berry picking anywhere above the treeline and listen for whistling marmots. **Independence Mine State Historical Park** (✉ *23264 Gold Cord Rd., Palmer, AK* ⊕ *www.dnr.alaska.gov*) offers an interpretive trail through a handful of

Essential Listening

The *99 Percent Invisible* podcast episode "This is Chance: Anchor-woman of the Great Alaska Earthquake" gives listeners an unexplored look at the aftermath of the state's massive 9.2 earthquake in 1964.

well-preserved buildings from Hatcher Pass's heyday as a gold rush hub.

Eat & Drink: Hatcher Pass Lodge (✉ *Mile 175 and Fishhook Willow Rd., Gold Cord Rd., Palmer, AK* ☎ *907/745–5897* ⊕ *www.hatcherpasslodge.com*) has a small menu and a bar with incredible views in the main lodge. It's the only option up in the mountains, so consider stopping at the grocery stores along the highway in Palmer if you want something else.

Stay: The colorful A-frame cabins at **Hatcher Pass Lodge** (✉ *Mile 175 and Fishhook Willow Rd., Gold Cord Rd., Palmer, AK* ☎ *907/745–5897* ⊕ *www.hatcherpasslodge.com*) are a perfect base camp for exploring the area. The accommodations are certainly basic, but that's just more incentive to get out in the mountains.

Breakfast: Head back down the hill to **Vagabond Blues** (✉ *642 S. Alaska St., Palmer, AK* ☎ *907/745–2233*), a sunny coffee shop and community hub in downtown Palmer.

Day 5: Hatcher Pass, AK, to Talkeetna, AK

91 miles (2 hours without traffic and stops)

If you (and your car) are feeling adventurous, take the 49-mile Hatcher Pass Road for a rugged gravel trek. The road opens after the snow melts, which might not happen until July. If you prefer pavement, drive back through Palmer and hop on the Parks Highway (AK-3) to Talkeetna.

ALONG THE WAY

Town: Start your day with a stroll through **Palmer's** small downtown, popping your head into the bookstores, galleries, and coffee shops on Alaska Street. The free Palmer Museum is located alongside the visitor's center in a log cabin nearby.

Roadside Attraction: The nonprofit **Musk Ox Farm** (✉ 12850 E. Archie Rd., Palmer, AK ☎ 907/745–4151) in Palmer houses several-dozen musk oxen and collects their fur to make fine qiviut wool. Schedule a tour or pick up some wool at the gift shop.

Eat & Drink: Turkey Red (✉ 550 S. Alaska St., Palmer, AK ☎ 907/746-5544 ⊕ www.turkeyredak.com) is a bright café and bakery in Palmer where ingredients are sourced from local businesses and area farms. Or **Schwabenhof** (✉ 4115 E. Palmer-Wasilla Hwy., Wasilla, AK ☎ 9017/357–2739 ⊕ www.schwabenhof.org) is an eight-sided log cabin near Wasilla serving beer, brats, and incredible mountain views on the patio.

Detour: Want to climb a mountain but are intimidated by, well, everything you see in all directions? The (relatively) little lump known as **Bodenburg Butte,** located south of Palmer, offers 360-degree views of the Mat-Su Valley from its 874-foot summit. You just need to pay a small parking fee at the base.

TALKEETNA

Do: At this funky little mountain town, outfitters offer everything from jet boats to zipline tours, though the most celebrated adventure is a flightseeing circuit of Denali. Scoop up snacks at **Nagley's Store** (✉ 13650 E. Main St., Talkeetna, AK ☎ 907/733–3663 ⊕ www.nagleysstore.com), the former home of Talkeetna's cat mayor Stubbs, who died in 2017. Cross the railroad bridge and explore the sand bars where the Talkeetna and Susitna rivers meet.

Eat & Drink: The porch at **Mountain High Pizza Pie** (✉ 22165 C St., Talkeetna, AK ☎ 907/733–1234 ⊕ www.pizzapietalkeetna.com) is a favorite for glacier pilots, rafting guides, and mountain climbers. Denali Brewing Company's beers are available at the **Denali Brewpub** (✉ 13605 E. Main St., Talkeetna, AK ☎ 907/733–237 ⊕ www.denalibrewpub.com). End the night at the **Fairview Inn** (✉ 101 N. Main St., Talkeetna, AK ☎ 907/733–2423 ⊕ www.facebook.com/denali.inn), a historic building and bar that hosts live bands through the summer.

Stay: One of the state's last operating roadhouses, the **Talkeetna Roadhouse** (✉ 13550 E. Main St., Talkeetna, AK ☎ 907/733–1351 ⊕ www.talkeetnaroadhouse.com) is a can't-miss slice of Alaskan history. Reserve a suite, a bunk, or the "lil cabin in the back." The Roadhouse also offers coin laundry and showers, in case you've been car-camping.

Breakfast: Again, it has to be the **Talkeetna Roadhouse** (✉ 13550 E. Main St., Talkeetna, AK ☎ 907/733–1351 ⊕ www.talkeetnaroadhouse.com). With family-style tables inside and rocking chairs on the porch, prepare to swap stories with your neighbors over breakfast scrambles, cinnamon rolls, and coffee.

Day 6: Talkeetna, AK, to Denali National Park

154 miles (2 hours, 30 minutes without traffic and stops)

Drive back down the Talkeetna Spur Road and turn right onto the Parks Highway (AK-3). Get glimpses of Denali as the mighty mountain creeps closer on today's drive. Just outside the entrance to the park, in its northeast corner, you'll find a strip of hotels, restaurants, and shops; this is where you'll most likely stay for the night. You can also head 12 miles north to the town of Healy, which offers a similar collection of restaurants and hotels.

ALONG THE WAY

Nature: Kesugi K'en is a recently developed section of **Denali State Park** (✉ *Trappers Creek, AK* ☎ *907/745–3975* ⊕ *www.dnr.alaska.gov*) offering camping, cabins, and a pavilion for picnicking. There are also walking paths and the Curry Ridge trailhead, a beginner-friendly 7-mile-out-and-back climb to a subalpine lake. Turn right at mile 135.4; Alaska State Parks charges a $5 daily parking fee.

Shop: Stocked with a few things you need and most things you don't, **Wal Mike's** (✉ *Mile 114.8 West Parks Hwy., Trapper Creek, AK* ☎ *907/733–2637* ⊕ *www. wal-mikes.edan.io*), a junk emporium in Trapper Creek, is a worthy stop for Alaska knickknacks and roadside entertainment.

Roadside Attraction: Originally intended as a one-of-a-kind hotel, **Igloo City** is an abandoned four-story concrete igloo (with windows!) that never opened and now looms forever-unfinished just off the highway past mile 188.

DENALI NATIONAL PARK

Do: Alaska's most visited attraction, **Denali National Park and Preserve** (✉ *Parks Hwy., Denali National Park and Preserve, AK* ☎ *907/683–9532* ⊕ *www.nps.gov/*

dena) is a 6-million-acre wilderness that offers spectacular mountain views (including of Denali itself, the highest peak in North America), a variety of wildlife, striking vegetation, and unforgettable landscapes. You can drive your own car the first 15 miles of the Denali Park Road, or venture farther with a park bus. The National Park Service offers narrated tour buses, as well as cheaper transit buses that let you hop on and off when you want to explore. Go rafting with **New Wave Adventures** (✉ *Mile 239 Parks Hwy., Denali National Park, AK* ☎ *907/888–8385* ⊕ *www.newwaveadventures.com*); the last trips leave at 6 pm. Or check out **Cabin Nite Dinner Theatre** (✉ *Mile 231, Parks Hwy., Denali National Park, AK* ☎ *907/680–8900* ⊕ *www.denaliparkvillage.com*) just outside the park entrance for an all-you-can-eat family-style dinner bonanza where the servers are the singers.

Eat & Drink: Prospectors Pizzeria and Alehouse (✉ *238.9 George Parks Hwy., Denali National Park, AK* ☎ *907/683–7437* ⊕ *www.prospectorspizza.com*) serves only-in-Alaska toppings like elk meatballs, reindeer sausage, and king crab. With live music and dozens of beer taps, Denali Park Salmon Bake is always a classic. And for something different in this land of burgers and beer, stop by **Thai and Chinese Food To Go** (✉ *238 Parks Hwy., Denali National Park, AK* ☎ *907/306–3545*) where the creativity is on the menu and not in the name.

Stay: You'll find plenty of timber-lined lodges popping up around the park gates. Claim a cabin at **Crow's Nest** (✉ *Mile 238.5 Parks Hwy., Denali National Park, AK* ☎ *907/683–2723* ⊕ *www.denalicrowsnestcabins.com*) or a room at **Denali Bluffs Hotel** (✉ *238 Parks Hwy., Denali National Park, AK* ☎ *907/683–5800* ⊕ *www.denalialaska.com*). For a quieter experience, **Tonglen Lake Lodge** (✉ *Mile 230 Parks Hwy., Denali National Park, AK* ☎ *907/683–2570* ⊕ *www.tonglenlake.*

com) is a tucked-away B&B 10 miles south of the park.

Breakfast: Head 11 miles north to **Healy and find Rose's Café** (✉ *Aurora Denali Lodge, 249 Parks Hwy., Healy, AK* ☎ *907/683–7673*). It's not much to look at from the road, but locals love the pancakes and omelets.

Day 7: Denali National Park to Fairbanks, AK

120 miles (2 hours without traffic and stops)

Spend your morning exploring more of Denali, and then take the Parks Highway (AK-3) north all the way to Fairbanks. Return your dusty, muddy rental car in the morning at Fairbanks International Airport.

ALONG THE WAY

Eat & Drink: 49th State Brewing Company (✉ *248 Parks Hwy., Healy, AK* ☎ *907/683–2739* ⊕ *www.49statebrewing.com*) in Healy is home to a replica of the bus used in the movie *Into the Wild* (the actual bus where adventurer Christopher McCandless lived was recently airlifted from its longtime location in a remote corner of Denali after several hikers died trying to reach it; its new home is the Museum of the North in Fairbanks). Golden Eagle Saloon is a classic Alaskan dive bar just off the road in Ester, with a big front porch and burgers you grill on your own.

Town: Nenana is best known for its annual Ice Classic, a statewide split-the-pot where Alaskans try to guess the exact minute the Tanana River's melting icepack will lurch forward each spring. The whole thing is endearingly captured in the 2019 documentary *Classic*. Learn more at Nenana's log cabin visitor center.

Detour: Keep driving through Fairbanks another 14 miles to reach **North Pole**. It's

Essential Listening

Dark Winter Nights is a hilarious, heartwarming, and strange podcast that features Fairbanks residents sharing their stories at live events each winter.

nothing much, but there's a year-round Christmas store, candy-cane-striped light poles, and a city council member named Santa Claus (of course).

FAIRBANKS

Do: When you arrive in Fairbanks, the main hub of northern Alaska, tour the **Museum of the North** (✉ *1962 Yukon Dr., Fairbanks, AK* ☎ *907/474–7505* ⊕ *www.uaf.edu*) or meet the resident reindeer at the **Large Animal Research Station** (✉ *2220 Yankovich Rd., Fairbanks, AK* ⊕ *www.uaf.edu*); both are part of University of Alaska–Fairbanks. Paddle through downtown with a two-hour boat rental from **Canoe Alaska** (✉ *1101 Peger Rd., Fairbanks, AK* ☎ *907/457–2453* ⊕ *www.canoealaska.com*). Pick up a last-minute memory at the Alaska Geographic Bookstore, one of many draws at the **Morris Thompson Cultural and Visitors Center** (✉ *101 Dunkel St., Fairbanks, AK* ☎ *907/459–3700* ⊕ *www.morristhompsoncenter.org*).

Eat & Drink: Fairbanks is known for its Thai food, and **Thai House** (✉ *412 5th Ave., Fairbanks, AK* ☎ *907/452–6123* ⊕ *www.thaihousealaska.com*) downtown has been serving pads and satays since 1989. Stop by **HooDoo Brewing Co.** (✉ *1951 Fox Ave., Fairbanks, AK* ☎ *907/459–2337* ⊕ *www.hoodoobrew.com*) to see what food truck is parked at the biergarten. Aviation-inspired **East Ramp Wood-Fired Pizza** (✉ *3788 University Ave. S, Fairbanks, AK* ☎ *907/451–7492* ⊕ *www.eastramppizza.com*) has propellers on the walls and airplane seats in the lobby; pick up a pie and watch planes take off from the airport runway outside.

Stay: **Wedgewood Resort** (✉ *212 Wedgewood Dr., Fairbanks, AK* ☎ *800/528–4916* ⊕ *www.fountainheadhotels. com*) includes a wilderness sanctuary, waterfowl refuge, and an impressive antique-auto museum. Or for one last offbeat experience, hop aboard the **Aurora Express** (✉ *1550 Chena Ridge Rd., Fairbanks, AK* ☎ *907/474–0949* ⊕ *www. fairbanksalaskabedandbreakfast.com*). This B&B is built from retired Alaska Railroad train cars, with each suite designed to match a historical period.

Breakfast: The local favorite is **The Cookie Jar** (✉ *1006 Cadillac Ct., Fairbanks, AK* ☎ *907/479–8319* ⊕ *www.cookiejarfairbanks.com*), a breakfast-all-day restaurant with cinnamon rolls to-go. Or stop by **Lulu's** (✉ *364 Old Chena Pump Rd., Fairbanks, AK* ☎ *907/374–3804* ⊕ *www. lulusbagels.com*) for breads, spreads, bagels, and coffee.

The Road to Hāna

Written by Lehia Apana

California has the Pacific Coast Highway, Italy has the Amalfi Coast and Australia has the Great Ocean Road. Hawai'i's answer? The spectacular Road to Hāna on the island of Maui.

Also known as Hāna Highway (Highways 36 and 360), this famed drive is a destination in itself: 52 miles of snaking roads, single-lane bridges, and enough blind turns to give you chicken skin. The reward is arriving at one of the last unspoiled Hawaiian frontiers, whose isolation has preserved its rustic beauty and endless charm. Getting there is where the fun starts. The route from central Maui to Hāna may seem short—and those in a rush can make the drive within two to three hours—but if you do it right,

it should take all day. Along the way you'll see waterfalls, tropical forests, eclectic roadside stands, and enough Pacific Ocean panoramas to fill your camera's memory card for a lifetime.

At a Glance

Start: Kahului Airport, HI

End: Hāna, HI

Miles Traveled: 52 miles

Suggested Duration: 1 day

States Visited: Hawai'i

Key Sights: Garden of Eden; Haleakalā National Park; Twin Falls; Upper Waikani Falls; Wai'ānapanapa State Park

Best Time to Go: This route is popular year-round. The best time of day to start your drive is early morning (from 6 to 7 am). You'll get ahead of the traffic and likely enjoy many stops all to yourself.

Morning: Kahului to Hāna

33 miles (1 hour, 15 minutes without traffic and stops)

This route starts near Kahului Airport, where there are plenty of options for renting a car if you haven't already done so. In general, you'll need a vehicle to truly explore Maui, and the Road to Hāna is no exception. With so much to see in every direction—including skyward—now's the time to splurge on that convertible or pop-top Jeep.

ALONG THE WAY

Nature: Located near mile marker 2, **Twin Falls** (✉ *6300 Hana Hwy., Haiku* ☎ *808/463–1275* ⊕ *www.twinfallsmaui. net*) is what tropical dreams are made of, and if you time it right, you'll avoid the pesky crowds. Arrive when it opens at 7 am, follow an easy jungle trail to the falls, and enjoy this natural wonder to yourself.

Essential Tips

The Road to Hāna is shared by visitors and local residents, so it's understandable that while some drivers are in cruise mode, others simply need to get on with their day. It's good etiquette to pull over if there's a car on your bumper, and to stop only at designated pull-outs. As tempting as it is to get closer to [insert any number of outrageously scenic possibilities here], be sure to respect private property and keep to designated paths.

Cell reception is spotty along the Road to Hāna and some areas outside Hāna town, so it's not a bad idea to print or save maps/itineraries for offline use.

If you're prone to motion sickness, you'll want to bring a nausea remedy for the winding drive.

Bring cash, as some roadside vendors aren't set up for credit-card transactions.

It's the first of several waterfalls you'll see along your journey.

Do: After mile marker 16, Hāna Highway changes from Highway 36 to 360 and the markers start over again. Half a mile past the second 10-mile mark, you'll reach the **Garden of Eden arboretum** (✉ *10600 Hana Hwy., Haiku* ☎ *808/572–9899* ⊕ *www. mauigardenofeden.com*). It's worth a stop if you can spare at least an hour. You'll want enough time to visit the highlights of this 25-acre site, which include a vast collection of ti, one of the original "canoe plants" introduced to Hawai?i by the early Polynesians.

Photo Op: Ke'anae is a tight-knit community known for cultivating the Hawai?ian staple crop kalo, or taro, and many residents remain deeply connected to their culture. Marvel in the emerald-hued patchwork of kalo terraces and Pacific panoramas near the Ke?anae Overlook, near mile marker 17. Alternatively, take the turnoff to Ke?anae Peninsula located just before the lookout.

Roadside Attraction: Nicknamed "Three Bears," **Upper Waikani Falls** is a trio of waterfalls located past mile marker 19. It's visible from the roadside, or you can scramble down a short but steep trail to reach the water.

Eat & Drink: Hāna Harvest (✉ *800 Hana Hwy., Hana* ⊕ *www.hanaharvest.us*) serves wood-fired pizzas and smoothies, plus desserts made with Coconut Glen's ice cream near mile marker 27. Better yet, head to the original **Coconut Glen's** location (✉ *1200 Hana Hwy., Haiku* ☎ *808/248–4876* ⊕ *www.coconutglens. com*) just a few miles down the road and scoop up some of the creamy coconut-based vegan ice cream in flavors like classic coconut, spicy chili, or liliko?i (passion fruit).

Afternoon: Hāna to Kīpahulu

13 miles (45 minutes without traffic and stops)

By now the serpentine road has straightened out and you've passed the "Welcome to Hāna" sign. There's still plenty to experience on this stretch of pavement, including black-sand beaches and waterfalls.

ALONG THE WAY

Nature: Home to a black-sand beach and freshwater caves for adventurous swimmers, **Wai'ānapanapa State Park** (☎ *808/248–4843* ⊕ *www.dlnr.Hawaii.*

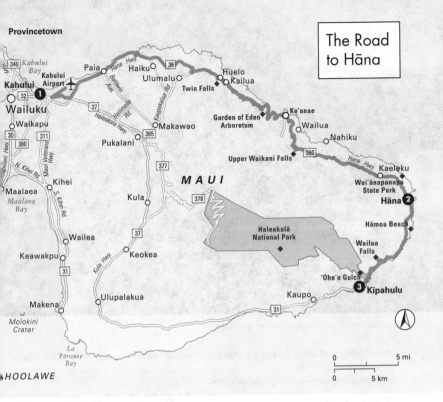

The Road to Hāna

gov) also includes a walkable 3-mile section of the ancient coastal trail known as the King's Highway, built for Maui's famed chief Piʻilani in the 1500s. The park is located near mile marker 32.

Nature: Turn off Hāna Highway near mile marker 51 to arrive at **Hāmoa Beach** (⊕ www.hamoabeach.org), which also boasts black-sand shores, but is more spacious and great for swimming. If you're staying overnight in Hāna, consider spending a few hours here tomorrow.

Nature: Venture toward Kīpahulu on Hāna Highway until you reach ʻOheʻo Gulch, a cascading series of freshwater pools that empty into the Pacific. Located within **Haleakalā National Park** (☎ 808/572–4400 ⊕ www.nps.gov/hale), the $30-per-car entrance fee is good for three days and includes entry to Haleakalā's Summit District. This is also the start of the 4-mile

round-trip Pipiwai Trail, which passes through a bamboo forest and leads to a 400-foot waterfall. You'll find this by mile marker 42 (past Hāna, mile markers count down).

Detour: Venture just a few miles past Kīpahulu and you'll encounter the drive-by waterfall known as **Wailua Falls.** It's close enough to spot while cruising by, and there's parking nearby for those who want a closer look. From here, backtrack toward Hāna.

Evening: Kīpahulu to Hāna

9.7 miles (30 minutes without traffic and stops)

Hāna is the pot of gold at the end of the rainbow. It's worth spending a night or two here so you can explore the town's

The Road to Hāna is filled with narrow, winding roads.

natural beauty at a leisurely pace. Alternatively, remain in Kīpahulu overnight and drive back toward Hāna the following day.

ALONG THE WAY

Town: Kīpahulu's drive-up camping site is located on a bluff above crashing surf, and includes tables, barbecue grills, and pit toilets. There are zero dining options nearby, so plan to cook under the stars tonight. Spots are on a first-come basis. The campground is within Haleakalā National Park, though there's no additional fee to stay overnight.

Eat & Drink: For those heading back to Hāna for the night, be warned that few eateries remain open past sunset. **Hāna Ranch Restaurant** (✉ 5031 Hana Hwy. ☎ 808/270–5280 ⊕ www.hyatt.com) is an excellent choice that does and features locally sourced ingredients.

Stay: After a long day of exploring, **Hāna-Maui Resort** (✉ 5021 Hana Hwy. ☎ 808/400–1234 ⊕ www.hyatt.com) offers a comfy place to rest your head. This landmark hotel oozes island

elegance, and its central location makes it a great base for exploring.

The Oʻahu Coast

Written by Anna Weaver

While road-tripping on an island doesn't seem like it would take too long, there's so much to see and do on Oʻahu, the busiest island in Hawaiʻi, that you can easily stretch out your travels, seeing everything "The Gathering Place" has to offer. This six-day itinerary allows you to take in Oʻahu's beauty, sample its extraordinarily diverse cuisine, and learn more about its rich history and culture while staying at a different spot on the island each night.

If you would prefer not to change hotels every night, you could set up a home base in Waikīkī and travel out to each day's destination, though you'd lose some time going back and forth.

At a Glance

Start: Waikīkī, HI

End: Honolulu, HI

Miles Traveled: 155 miles

Suggested Duration: 6 days

States Visited: Hawai'i

Key Sights: Diamond Head State Monument; 'Iolani Palace; Ka'ena Point State Park; Pearl Harbor National Memorial; Waikīkī Beach

Best Time to Go: Hawai'i can be visited year-round, though you may want to avoid the rainier season from around February through April, which also overlaps with spring break travel.

Day 1: Waikīkī

9 miles (20 minutes without traffic)

Today's route is straightforward. Whether you arrive at Honolulu International Airport in the daytime or evening, you'll head straight to Waikīkī to settle in for a night (or two) and get your bearings. Don't rent a car just yet so you can avoid pricey hotel parking fees—you can take a rideshare, cab, or TheBus from the airport to your hotel and you'll be able to explore most of Waikīkī's shops, restaurants, and its famous beach on foot or via bus/rideshare/cab/trolley.

Do: Get your souvenir shopping out of the way, take a surf lesson at Waikīkī Beach, relax with a mai tai by your hotel pool, and dive into Hawai'i cuisine. Waikīkī stays up late, so now is a good chance to try and break your jetlag while enjoying live music and drinks at the many clubs, bars, and music venues along the Waikīkī strip.

Eat & Drink: Mahina and Sun's (⊠ *412 Lewers St.* ☎ *808/924–5810* ⊕ *www. mahinaandsuns.com*) has a vintage vibe and serves farm/ocean-to-table

dishes while **Duke's Waikīkī** (⊠ *2335 Kalakaua Ave.* ☎ *808/922–2268* ⊕ *www. dukeswaikiki.com*), named after famed Hawaiian surfer Duke Kahanamoku, is a long-standing beachside favorite known for its hula pie, mai tais, and American Hawai'ian casual cuisine.

Stay: If you're okay with a larger, bustling resort, stay at the oceanfront **Sheraton Waikīkī** (⊠ *2255 Kalakaua Ave.* ☎ *808/922–4422* ⊕ *www.marriott.com*) with its infinity and family pools, cocktails, and light eats at Rumfire, along with plenty of other amenities. For a grander stay, pick the oldest hotel in Waikīkī, the **Moana Surfrider** (⊠ *2365 Kalakaua Ave.* ☎ *808/922–3111* ⊕ *www.marriott.com*), with both historic and modern rooms and an oceanfront veranda where you can enjoy the popular afternoon tea. For a midcentury modern–meets–Hawai'i vibe in a smaller space, choose the **Laylow** (⊠ *2299 Kūhiō Ave.* ☎ *808/922–6600* ⊕ *www.marriott.com*).

Breakfast: Before you head out from Waikīkī, grab pastries and 100% Kona coffee at **Kona Coffee Purveyors** (⊠ *2330 Kalakaua Ave.* ☎ *808/450–2364* ⊕ *www.konacoffeepurveyors.com*) in the International Marketplace. If you'd like a more leisurely breakfast on the way out of Waikīkī, head north a bit into Mānoa Valley for breakfast on the lanai at **Waioli Kitchen & Café** (⊠ *2950 Mānoa Rd.* ☎ *808/744–1619* ⊕ *www.waiolikitchen.com*). The eatery also serves as a vocational training site for people in recovery.

Day 2: Waikīkī, HI, to Kāhala, HI

5 miles (20 minutes with no traffic or stops)

There are several car rental options in Waikīkī. If you don't want to be spotted a mile away as a tourist, avoid renting a brightly colored convertible. It's a short

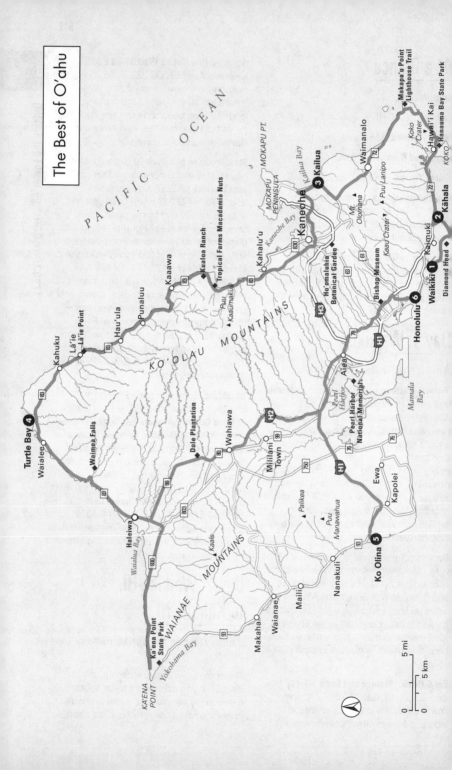

The Best of O'ahu

PACIFIC OCEAN

KAENA POINT

Ka'ena Point State Park

Yokohama Bay

WAIANAE

Makaha

Waianae

Maili

Nanakuli

Ko Olina 5

Kapolei

Ewa

H1

750

99

Mililani Town

Wahiawa

Dole Plantation

Kaala

Palikea

Puu Manawahua

WAIANAE MOUNTAINS

Waialua Bay

Haleiwa

990

803

99

80

Turtle Bay 4

Waialee

Waimea Falls

Waimea Bay

Kahuku

La'ie

La'ie Point

Hau'ula

Punaluu

Kaaawa

Kualoa Ranch

Tropical Farms Macadamia Nuts

Puu Kaaumakua

KO'OLAU MOUNTAINS

Kahalu'u

Kaneohe Bay

MOKAPU PT.

MOKAPU PENINSULA

Kailua Bay

Kailua 3

Kaneohe

830

H3

Ho'omaluhia Botanical Garden

Mt. Olomana

Kaau Crater

Puu Lanipo

Waimanalo

72

Makapu'u Point Lighthouse Trail

Koko Crater

Hawai'i Kai

Hanauma Bay State Park

KOKO

72

Kāhala 2

Kaimuki

Kaimuki

Diamond Head

Waikiki 1

Honolulu 6

H1

78

Aiea

Pearl Harbor

Pearl Harbor National Memorial

Mamala Bay

61

63

Bishop Museum

76

5 mi

5 km

0

0

route between Waikīkī and Kāhala, so there's plenty of time for stops along the way for hiking and eating; plan about five or six hours for all of today's adventures.

ALONG THE WAY

Nature: Diamond Head National Monument (☎ 808/587–0300 ⊕ www.dlnr. hawaii.gov) is where you can spend two hours hiking up to the top of the extinct volcano's rim for a panoramic view of the south shore. Although it's not an overly arduous hike, you'll want to wear good shoes and have water, a hat, and sunscreen for this mostly unshaded trek.

Eat & Drink: For lunch, head to Kaimuki, where many local foodies like to dine. Celebrity chef Lee Anne Wong runs brunch favorite **Koko Head Café** (☒ 1145 12th Ave. C ☎ 808/732–8920 ⊕ www. kokoheadcafe.com). You can also try kalua pig and barbecue at **Surfing Pig Hawai'i** (☒ 3605 Waialae Ave. ☎ 808/744– 1992 ⊕ www.thesurfingpighawaii.com).

KĀHALA

Do: Once you've arrived in upscale Kāhala, you can settle in at your hotel and choose to swim with the dolphins at your resort's lagoon, do some shopping at **Kāhala Mall** (☒ 4211 Waialae Ave. ☎ 808/732–7736 ⊕ www.kahalamall-center.com), or swim and watch the sunset at Kāhala Beach. If you're a golfer, there's a neighboring course.

Eat & Drink: Hoku's (☒ 5000 Kāhala Ave. ☎ 808/739–8760 ⊕ www.hokuskahala. com) at the Kāhala Hotel serves sophisticated island food. A good amount of the fusion menu at **Kapa Hale** (☒ 4614 Kilauea Ave. ☎ 808/888–2060 ⊕ www.kapahale. com) focuses on fresh local produce.

Stay: The midcentury-styled **Kāhala Hotel & Resort** (☒ 5000 Kāhala Ave. ☎ 808/739– 8888 ⊕ www.kahalaresort.com) has excellent service, a small but nice beach and pool, a dolphin lagoon, and several good restaurants.

Essential Listening

While you're driving in a good signal area, tune in to local radio channels 100.3 (Hawaiian contemporary), 98.5 (reggae), or 105.1 (classic Hawaiian) to get a sense of the wide range of island music.

Breakfast: Grab a quick breakfast at the hotel's Plumeria Beach House or a nearby coffee shop and get on the road to make two morning stops.

Day 3: Kāhala, HI, to Kailua, HI

22 miles (45 minutes without traffic and stops)

Today you'll have lots of options for sightseeing stops as you follow the southeastern shoreline and up the Windward Coast to the beachside community of Kailua. Be sure to pack some snacks to get you through to lunch in Kailua.

ALONG THE WAY

Nature: If you want to swim and snorkel in crystal clear waters teeming with ocean life, stop at **Hanauma Bay State Park** (☒ 7455 Kalaniana'ole Hwy. ⊕ www. honolulu.gov). Just keep in mind you'll be wasting most of your day if you don't get there a little before or right when the park opens at 6:45 am as there are no ticket reservations, only daily limited timed tickets to protect the bay's ecosystem. Arrive later and you may get a spot, but that might not be until midday or the afternoon. After 8 am, tickets are usually sold out.

Nature: A lower-pressure morning stop that's still best done first thing to avoid the sun and heat is a hike up the

paved **Makapu'u Point Lighthouse Trail**
(☎ 808/587-0300 ⊕ www.dlnr.hawaii.
gov). It's especially wonderful during
whale-watching season (December
through early May), as you'll have a great
chance of spotting whale spouts from
the lookouts along the trail. Save about
two hours for this stop.

Photo Op: You'll see several lookouts or
pull-off spots great for photos along
the coastline as you drive from Kāhala
through Hawai'i Kai and head toward
Waimānalo and Kailua.

KAILUA

Do: Once a quiet beachside town,
tourism has found Kailua and its two
stretches of beach (Kailua Beach proper
and Lanikai, which is trickier to access
parking-wise). There are many good
places to eat and shop in town, but you'll
want to spend most of your time here
on the beach. You can also take an easy
stroll or bike ride along the **Kawainui
Marsh** (☎ 808/768-3003 ⊕ www.hono-
lulu.gov) trail around sundown to take in
the beautiful wetlands and to appreciate
the way the sun hits the surrounding
hillsides at the end of the day.

Eat & Drink: For lunch, **Kalapawai Market**
(✉ 306 S. Kalaheo Ave. ☎ 808/262-4359
⊕ www.kalapawaimarket.com) is a good
grab-and-go spot near the beach. Its
sit-down spinoff in Kailua town, **Kalapawai Café and Deli** (✉ 750 Kailua Rd.
☎ 808/262-3354 ⊕ www.kalapawaimar-
ket.com), has pizzas, burgers, sandwiches, and the like at lunchtime and more
upscale fare at dinner. **Island Snow** (✉ 130
Kailua Rd. ☎ 808/263-6339 ⊕ www.
islandsnow.com) has two locations
serving the shave ice that Barack Obama
loves. For dinner, **Nico's Kailua** (✉ 970 N.
Kalaheo Ave. ☎ 808/263-3787 ⊕ www.
nicoskailua.com) along the canal has
delicious and fresh fish dishes and other
island-inspired entrées, yummy cocktails,
and live music most nights.

Shops: Kailua town is strewn with
boutiques that sell clothing, jewelry,
household items, swim attire, body products, and more. Bibliophiles will enjoy
picking up a beach read or browsing the
Hawai'iana and children's sections of the
small, independent bookstore **Bookends**
(✉ 600 Kailua Rd. ☎ 808/261-1996
⊕ www.facebook.com/BookEndsKailua).

Stay: Kailua has no hotels, so you'll want
to find a B&B or short-term lodging like
Kailua Beach Properties (☎ 808/261-1653
⊕ www.patskailua.com). In neighboring
Kaneohe, you can choose from cottages
or suites at **Paradise Bay Resort** (✉ 47-039
Lihikai Dr. ☎ 808/239-5711 ⊕ www.
paradisebayresort.com).

Breakfast: Grab some local favorite malassadas, deep-fried sweet dough rolled
in sugar, from the **Agnes' Bake Shop** (✉ 5
Ho'olai St. ☎ 808/284-4963 ⊕ www.
facebook.com/agnesbakeshop) food
truck parked in the Manuheali'i clothing
store parking lot.

Day 4: Kailua, HI, to Turtle Bay, HI

*34 miles (60 minutes without detours or
stops)*

On this day, you'll follow what locals consider a classic road trip up the Windward
Coast and ending on the North Shore.
There are usually fruit and veggie stands
and shrimp trucks along the roadsides
between Kahalu'u and up past Kahuku.

ALONG THE WAY

Detour: Take a snack to eat at **Ho'omaluhia
Botanical Garden** (✉ 45-680 Luluku Rd.
☎ 808/233-7323 ⊕ www.honolulu.gov)
in Kaneohe, which is on the way up the
coast to the North Shore. Loved by selfie
seekers for its lush and photogenic location up against the Ko'olau Mountains,
this sprawling botanical garden has easy
walking paths, campsites, and a large
man-made fish pond.

O'ahu's North Shore is one of the most famous surfing destinations in the world.

Eat & Drink: Backtrack a bit to get a Hawai'ian plate lunch at **Waiāhole Poi Factory** (✉ *48-140 Kamehameha Hwy.* ☎ *808/239–2222* ⊕ *www.Waiāholepoi-factory.com*), where you can eat freshly pounded poi and try the Sweet Lady of Waiāhole dessert. Another lunch option would be to pick from one of several delicious shrimp trucks and have a garlic shrimp with rice plate lunch. Giovanni's and Romy's are often cited as rivals for the best shrimp truck on O'ahu.

Roadside Attraction: Tropical Farms Macadamia Nuts (✉ *49-227 Kamehameha Hwy.* ☎ *808/237–1960* ⊕ *www.macnutfarm. com*) has a highly entertaining tour that includes coconut husking and fire dancing demonstrations. Browse the country store for souvenirs, coffee, and, of course, macadamia nuts.

Detour: Another potential stop on your way up to the North Shore, **Kualoa Ranch** (✉ *49-560 Kamehameha Hwy.* ☎ *808/237–7321* ⊕ *www.kualoa.com*) is a great place for movie buffs who want to take the film tour highlighting movies

and TV shows that have been shot on the ranch's 4,000 acres (*Jurassic Park* was a major one).

Photo Op: Lā'ie Point is a quick off-the-highway stop at a beautiful ocean overlook and sea arch.

TURTLE BAY

Do: After your busy day, settle in at your hotel and enjoy a relaxing dinner.

Eat & Drink: Lei Lei's Bar & Grill (✉ *Turtle Bay Resort, 57-091 Kamehameha Hwy.* ☎ *808/293–6000* ⊕ *www.turtlebayresort. com/dining/lei-leis*) at Turtle Bay Resort is a casual, seafood-centric favorite for locals and tourists.

Stay: Turtle Bay Resort (✉ *57-091 Kamehameha Hwy.* ☎ *808/293–6000* ⊕ *www. turtlebayresort.com*), a frequent backdrop for movies—perhaps most notably *Forgetting Sarah Marshall*—is a large oceanfront hotel on the tip of the North Shore offering rooms, suites, and bungalows.

Breakfast: Grab a coffee and a healthy papaya bowl at the **Sunrise**

Shack (✉ 59-158 Kamehameha Hwy. ☎ 808/638–0506 ⊕ www.sunrise-shackhawaii.com) on your way to your morning hike. Or spend a little more time with a sit-down breakfast at **Café Haleiwa** (✉ 66-460 Kamehameha Hwy. ☎ 808/637–5516 ⊕ www.cafehaleiwahawaiianislands.com).

Day 5: Turtle Bay, HI, to Ko Olina, HI

60 miles (1 hour, 40 minutes without traffic and stops)

Today you'll head west from Turtle Bay to enjoy a morning walk out to Ka☐ena Point. Stop at Haleiwa before continuing down the highway to the resort community of Ko Olina. The area you drive through from Haleiwa to Ko Olina used to be mostly sugar cane and pineapple fields.

ALONG THE WAY

Nature: It can get hot out at **Ka'ena Point State Park** (⊕ www.dlnr.hawaii.gov), so make the 40-minute drive from Turtle Bay to the north shore entrance of the gorgeous, wild, and rugged park in the morning. This nature preserve on the westernmost tip of O'ahu is home to native birds, Hawai'ian monk seals, and other endangered plants and animals.

Town: On your way back from Ka'ena Point, stop in **Haleiwa** for shopping and shave ice, and then drive along the North Shore for a look at its famous surfing beaches. If you're there in the winter, you'll likely catch sight of some big swells.

Eat & Drink: Dine on the lanai at **Haleiwa Beach House** (✉ 62-540 Kamehameha Hwy. ☎ 808/637–3435 ⊕ www.haleiwabeachhouse.com) or take your burgers, sandwiches, and shoestring fries to go from **Kua'Aina** (✉ 66-160 Kamehameha Hwy. ☎ 808/637–6067 ⊕ www.kua-aina-hawaii.com) and eat them at the beach.

Detour: After refueling in Haleiwa, you could backtrack to Waimea Valley and take the tram or walk the 30 minutes to **Waimea Falls.** There are changing facilities for those who want to swim at the lifeguard-supervised natural swimming hole. Call ahead to see if the falls are open, as excessively dry or rainy conditions will prevent swimming. On certain days you'll also be able to learn traditional Hawai☐ian games and go on history and botany walks through the lush grounds.

Roadside Attraction: If you've got a hankering for pineapple Dole Whip, head to **Dole Plantation** (✉ 64-1550 Kamehameha Hwy. ☎ 808/621–8408 ⊕ www.doleplantation.com), but skip the souvenir-stuffed store and pick-a-pearl vendors and walk around back to where the café is. Kids may like to try the pineapple maze and train ride through agriculture fields.

KO OLINA

Do: Ko Olina was transformed from agricultural land to a resort area in the early 1990s. Its four man-made lagoons and a few natural ones make this area perfect for swimming and snorkeling.

Eat & Drink: If you've been longing for a luau, **Paradise Cove** (✉ 92-1089 Ali'inui Dr. ☎ 808/842–5911 ⊕ www.paradisecove.com) has arguably the most entertaining one on the island. **Monkeypod Kitchen** (✉ 92-1048 Olani St. ☎ 808/380–4086 ⊕ www.monkeypodkitchen.com), one of Hawai☐i restauranteur Peter Merriman's eateries, has a large lanai and serves local food and cocktails. Don't skip the signature mai tai topped with whipped pineapple froth.

Stay: If you're a Disney family, splurge on **Aulani** (✉ 92-1185 Ali'inui Dr. ☎ 866/443–4763 ⊕ www.disneyaulani.com), with its nicely appointed rooms and large complex of pools, slides, and other water features for hotel guests only. **The Four Seasons Resort O'ahu at Ko Olina** (✉ 92-1001 Olani St. ☎ 808/679–0079 ⊕ www.

fourseasons.com) is your most upscale choice with great restaurants.

Breakfast: On your way out of town, grab an açaí bowl and coffee at **Island Vintage Coffee** (✉ 92-1048 Olani St. ☎ 808/678–3888 ⊕ www.islandvintagecoffee.com).

Day 6: Ko Olina, HI, to Honolulu, HI

25 miles (35 minutes without traffic and stops)

Today you'll wrap up your O'ahu road trip by driving back to Honolulu, stopping on the way to tour Pearl Harbor, and ending in Chinatown and downtown Honolulu. You'll drop off your rental car and fly out of Honolulu International Airport the next day.

ALONG THE WAY

Detour: Not too far off your path between Ko Olina and Honolulu is **Pearl Harbor National Memorial** (✉ 1 Arizona Memorial Pl. ☎ 808/422–3399 ⊕ www.nps.gov/perl), marking the spot of the attack that launched America into World War II. Reserve your tickets in advance to go out to the *USS* Arizona Memorial over the sunken battleship of the same name. WWII buffs may also want to visit the *USS* Bowfin Submarine Museum and Park, the Battleship *Missouri*Memorial, and the Pearl Harbor Aviation Museum.

Eat & Drink: Helena's Hawai'ian Food (✉ 1240 N. School St. ☎ 808/845–8044 ⊕ www.helenahawaiianfood.com) serves some of the best Hawai'ian food on the island.

Detour: Bishop Museum (✉ 1525 Bernice St. ☎ 808/847–3511 ⊕ www.bishop-museum.org) will teach you much about Hawai'ian and Pacific Islander history and culture with special attention given to the Hawai'ian monarchy.

HONOLULU

Do: Besides showing you how 19th-century Hawai'ian royals lived, a tour of **'Iolani Palace** (✉ 364 S. King St. ☎ 808/522–0822 ⊕ www.iolanipalace.org) will teach you about the monarchy's tragic history and how the United States overthrew the Hawai'ian Kingdom in 1893. Other historic buildings you can walk to are the State Capitol building, the city and county headquarters at Honolulu Hale, the King Kamehameha statue outside Ali''Iolani Hale, and the former Armed Services YMCA building that is now the Hawai'i State Art Museum.

Eat & Drink: So many of O'ahu's innovative restaurants are in Chinatown. **The Pig and the Lady** (✉ 83 N. King St. ☎ 808/585–8255 ⊕ www.thepigandthelady.com) serves modern Vietnamese cuisine while award-winning **Senia** (✉ 75 N. King St. ☎ 808/200–5412 ⊕ www.restaurant-senia.com) is a small yet upscale and inventive restaurant.

Shop: Chinatown is full of an eclectic mix of stores. You might want to walk through **Maunakea Marketplace** (✉ 1120 Maunakea St. ☎ 808/524–3409) and **Kekaulike Market** (✉ 1039 Kekaulike St.) just to marvel at the diversity of foods and goods for sale. Consider taking a guided food or culture tour through the area. You can also stop by the sprawling **Ala Moana Shopping Center** (✉ 1450 Ala Moana Blvd. ☎ 808/955–9517 ⊕ www.alamoanacenter.com) complex and **Ward Village's South Shore Market** (✉ 1170 Auahi St. ☎ 808/591–8411 ⊕ www.wardvillage.com) for last-minute gifts for others or yourself.

Stay: Check in to the **Ala Moana Hotel** (✉ 410 Atkinson Dr. ☎ 808/955–4811 ⊕ www.all.accor.com) for an affordable hotel stay on your last night before flying out. If you want to be closer to the airport, the Best Western The Plaza Hotel (✉ 3253 N. Nimitz Hwy. ☎ 808/836–3636 ⊕ www.bwtheplazahotel.com) is your best bet.

Breakfast: If you have time before heading to the airport , get the gigantic milk-and-cereal pancakes and other comfort food with a twist at **Scratch Kitchen** (✉ *1170 Auahi St.* ☎ *808/589–1669* ⊕ *www.scratch-hawaii. com*) in Ward Village.

The Best of Puerto Rico

Written by Jessica van Dop DeJesus

It's easy to have a typical Caribbean vacation in Puerto Rico, but this island offers much more than just sun and sand. By renting a car and exploring beyond the standard tourist areas of San Juan and its surrounding beaches, you'll get a deeper sense of the vibrant island, from its lush countryside and expansive mountain valleys to its booming culinary scene and fascinating history. But, of course, you'll still have time for some beach days over this seven-day adventure that takes you around the island's perimeter, with stops in legendary beach towns like Ponce and Rincon.

At a Glance

Start: San Juan, PR

End: San Juan, PR

Miles Traveled: 356 miles

Suggested Duration: 6 days

Territories Visited: Puerto Rico

Key Sights: Bosque Estatal de Guánica; Las Cavernas de Camuy; Luquillo Beach; El Yunque National Forest; Old San Juan

Best Time to Go: Puerto Rico is a great place to visit year-round. May through August is considered the low season with lower hotel rates and less crowds. Be mindful when traveling in September, October, and early November, as these are the prime months of hurricane season; sporadic rainy days are standard during this time of year.

Day 1: San Juan to Fajardo

37 miles (45 minutes without traffic and stops)

When you arrive in Puerto Rico, pick up your rental car at the San Juan International Airport (SJU). There are plenty of rental car agencies in the terminal. Take Route PR-3 and cruise through San Juan and Carolina, the bustling city surrounding San Juan. Once you leave the San Juan metro area, you will start seeing the lush green mountains that encompass the El Yunque rain forest to your right and turquoise blue beaches to your left.

ALONG THE WAY

Detour: As you head out of San Juan, take a 20-minute detour to **Piñones**, where you can enjoy *coco frío* (cold coconut water) and snacks with a beachside view.

Nature: The northeast coast of Puerto Rico is known for the must-see **El Yunque National Forest** (☎ *787/888–1880* ⊕ *www. fs.usda.gov*). The only tropical forest in the U.S. National Park System, El Yunque is home to hundreds of endemic species of birds and plants. The rain forest currently requires reservations to visit, so be sure to reserve your spot online before you go.

Photo Op: Located a few miles from the El Yunque entrance, **La Coca Falls** is a stunning spot to take a photo.

Town: After a hike in El Yunque, head to **Luquillo Beach** (⊕ *www.municiodeluquillo.com*) in the upbeat, sunny town of Luquillo to take a dip in the crystal clear, calm waters. It's one of the most popular beaches on Puerto Rico's northeast coast. If you're into surfing, check out the swells at nearby **La Pared Beach.**

Eat & Drink: Grab a bite to eat at one of Luquillo Beach's kiosks; these small restaurants offer a variety of Puerto Rican fried snacks. One of the best is **Terruño Comida Artesanal** (☎ *787/889–8989*), which offers a casual yet elevated version

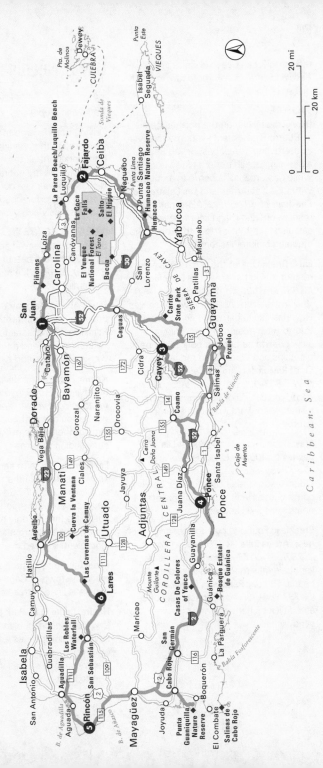

The Best of Puerto Rico

ATLANTIC OCEAN

Caribbean Sea

20 mi
20 km

San Juan ①
Fajardo ②
Cayey ③
Ponce ④
Rincón ⑤
Lares ⑥

CULEBRA
Dewey
Pta. de Molinos

Punta Este
VIEQUES
Isabel Segunda
Sonda de Vieques

La Pared Beach/Luquillo Beach
Luquillo
Ceiba
Naguabo
Punta Santiago
Punta Lima
Humacao Nature Reserve
Humacao
Yabucoa
Maunabo

Cañóvanas, La Coca Falls
Salto El Hippie
El Yunque National Forest
El Toro
Bacía
San Lorenzo

Loíza
Piñones
Carolina
Cataño
Bayamón
Dorado
Vega Baja

Caguas
Cidra
Caguas
Carite State Park de Sierra
Guayama
Jobos
Pozuelo
Patillas

Salinas
Bahía de Rincón
Coamo
Santa Isabel
Caja de Muertos

Naranjito
Corozal
Orocovia
Cerro Doña Juana
Juana Díaz
Ponce

Cueva la Ventana
Manatí
Ciales
Jayuya
Utuado
Adjuntas
CORDILLERA CENTRAL
Guayanilla
Guánica
Bosque Estatal de Guánica
La Parguera
Bahía Fosforescente

Las Cavernas de Camuy
Arecibo
Hatillo
Camuy
Lares
Maricao
Casas De Colores of Yauco

Isabela
Quebradillas
San Antonio
Aguadilla
Aguada
B. de Aguadilla
Los Robles Waterfall
San Sebastián
Rincón
Mayagüez
B. de Añasco
Joyuda
Cabo Rojo
San Germán
Boquerón
El Combate
Salinas de Cabo Rojo
Punta Guaniquilla Nature Reserve

3
37
167
172
22
149
10
111
128
155
14
155
52
15
3
53
1
149
128
116
2
115
111
109
30
52
53
Monte Guilarte

of Puerto Rican beach classics like *bacalaitos* (fried cod), *mofongo*, and rice dishes

FAJARDO

Do: A coastal city on the northeastern tip of Puerto Rico, Fajardo is home to several interesting attractions. Seven Seas is a stunning beach perfect for swimming, while Las Croabas is home to a marina with local fishermen and **Las Cabezas de San Juan** (☎ 787/691–2302), a nature reserve offering magnificent views (you can also take a kayak tour to explore the stunning bioluminescent bay).

Eat & Drink: One of the most beloved restaurants in the area is **La Estación** (✉ 987 Km 4.20 ☎ 787/863–4481 ⊕ www.laestacionpr.com), which serves Nuyorican-style barbecue and other Puerto Rican fusion dishes. Enjoy the slow-cooked barbecued pork over ripe plantains or a whole fried red snapper. Or at **Rincón del Faro** (✉ Carr. 987, Km 5.2 ☎ 787/863–0028 ⊕ www.rincondefaropr.com), you can enjoy lighthouse views and a seafood-forward menu on an ample patio.

Stay: Book a vacation rental at **Las Casitas** (✉ 1000 El Conquistador Ave. ☎ 800/455–8667); adjacent to El Conquistador Resort, these colorful little houses come with amenities such as private pools and idyllic sea views.

Breakfast: Founded by a former engineer, **Aroma Cafe** (✉ 100 Calle Unión ☎ 787/567–5173) offers pastries and various drinks made with local coffee beans. Or cozy **Panadería Monte Brisas** (☎ 787/863–3363) sells pastries, coffee, and delicious ham-egg-and-cheese sandwiches.

Day 2: Fajardo to Cayey

58 miles (1 hour, 15 minutes without traffic and stops)

Driving from Fajardo to Cayey takes you through the winding roads of the Cordillera Central, the mountain range that traverses the entire island of Puerto Rico. Keep your eye out for plenty of greenery, colorful mountainside homes, and fantastic views.

ALONG THE WAY

Detour: As you leave Fajardo, take a quick 20-minute detour to **Salto El Hippie** (☎ 941/355–7981), a stunning freshwater swimming hole.

Town: Almost halfway through today's drive, you'll encounter the city of **Humacao**. This coastal town is home to a natural reserve and a fun boardwalk area with restaurants and bars.

Nature: Stop by the **Humacao Nature Reserve** (☎ 787/397–1900 ⊕ www.facebook.com/reservanaturalhumacao), where you can rent bikes or kayaks to explore the unique mangrove vegetation surrounding the area.

Eat & Drink: The farm and restaurant known as **Bacoa** in the town of Juncos (✉ 31 Km 22 ☎ 787/244–7748 ⊕ www.bacoapr.com) is the perfect stop for lunch (just note that it's only open Thursday and Friday). The restaurant specializes in local ingredients cooked over an open flame.

Photo Op: Go for a stroll at **La Plaza de Recreo** in the town of Caguas. This cozy town square is lined with colonial architecture.

Nature: Carite State Park (☎ 787/999–2200 ⊕ www.conoceapuertorico.com) covers several municipalities leading to the town of Cayey. The dense green forest paves the way to one of the largest lakes in Puerto Rico.

The colorful streets of San Juan are filled with history.

CAYEY

Do: Nestled in the middle of the Cordillera Central, the mountain town of Cayey offers spectacular views of the island. In addition, it's home to the most *lechoneras* (restaurants specializing in roasted pork) in all of Puerto Rico.

Eat & Drink: A *lechonera* located in the mountains of Cayey, **El Cuñao** (✉ *Bo Pedro Avila Carr. 1, Km 65.5* ☎ *787/263–0511* ⊕ *www.lechoneraspr.com*) serves excellent roasted pork with classic sides like *arroz con gandules* (rice and pigeon peas) and stewed tropical root vegetables such as yuca and taro root. **El Mesón de Melquiades** (✉ *Carretera 15 Ramal* ☎ *787/738–4083* ⊕ *www.elmesonde-melquiades.com*) is an upscale restaurant serving Puerto Rican classics like cod stew and pork chops.

Stay: **El Pretexto** (✉ *Rd. 715* ⊕ *www.elpretextopr.com*) is a stunning "culinary farm lodge" located in the mountains of Cayey. The property also hosts a series of renowned communal table dinners that are open to outside guests. For something even more rustic, pack your camping gear for a night at **Cercadillo Camp Grounds** (⊕ *www.facebook.com/CercadilloCampGrounds*), which offers campsites, bathrooms, and other essential camping amenities.

Breakfast: **Montellano Bakery** (✉ *Calle Antonio R. Barceló* ☎ *787/738–6452*) is a mainstay in Cayey, selling coffee, pastries, and sandwiches.

Day 3: Cayey to Ponce

45 miles (1 hour without traffic and stops)

As you drive from Cayey to Ponce, the largest city on the southern coast of Puerto Rico, you'll travel past several southern coastal towns. The easiest and fastest way to get to Ponce is Highway 52.

ALONG THE WAY

Detour: On your way to Ponce, take a 30-minute detour to **Pozuelo**, a fishing area in Guayama, Puerto Rico. You can kayak through the mangroves or have lunch at one of the many small restaurants in the area.

Eat & Drink: Enjoy seafood on the beach at **Ladi's Place** (✉ *Calle A-86, Playa de Salinas* ☎ *787/824–1900* ⊕ *www.ladisrestaurant.com*), in the coastal town of Salinas. The restaurant's patio is pretty much right on the sandy beach; if you're there late enough, you can catch a stunning sunset.

Nature: Take a detour to the town of Coamo and relax for an hour or two in the **Coamo Hot Springs** (✉ *Río Coamo* ☎ *787/787–8787*).

Roadside Attraction: You can't miss the "Letras de Ponce" as you enter Ponce from Highway 52. These gigantic red letters spell out the town's name, giving you a warm welcome.

PONCE

Do: Known as the "Pearl of the South," Ponce is a cultural hub for the island, with several well-known museums like the **Museo de Arte de Ponce** (✉ *2325 Av. Las Américas* ☎ *787/840–1510* ⊕ *www.museoarteponce.org*) and the **Museum of Puerto Rican Music** (✉ *20, 42 Calle Reina Isabel* ☎ *787/290–6617* ⊕ *www.icp.gobierno.pr*). No trip to Ponce is complete without a photo at the Parque de Bombas, the classic red-and-black fire station erected for the 1882 World's Fair. It was a working fire station until 1990, when it became a museum.

Eat & Drink: A quaint restaurant located in Ponce city center, **Chefs Creations** (✉ *100 Calle Reina Isabel* ☎ *787/848–8384* ⊕ *www.facebook.com/chefscreations*) specializes in open-fire dishes. You will most likely catch the lively owner, chef Jorge Rivera, chatting with the guests. Or try **19 Barrios Pizza** (✉ *2638 Calle Aurora* ☎ *787/308–1988* ⊕ *www.facebook.*

com/19barrios.pr), which focuses on pizza made in a wood-fired oven, local beers, and craft cocktails. Afterward, sample craft cocktails alongside ocean views at **El Marlin**, a fun cocktail bar located within La Plaza de Mercado; don't leave without sampling a flaming tiki cocktail.

Shop: **La Plaza de Mercado de Ponce** is an indoor/outdoor market specializing in locally made artwork, local produce, and drinks.

Stay: **Hacienda la Mocha** (✉ *Cam Hoyo De San Patricio* ☎ *787/644–4469*) is a dreamy, locally owned guesthouse in the mountains of Ponce; it sits on a coffee farm that is also part of the property grounds. For something more centrally located, **Boutique Hotel Belgica** (✉ *122 Calle Villa* ☎ *787/844–3255* ⊕ *www.hotelbelgica.com*) is a quaint hotel in a beautiful colonial building in the heart of the city center.

Breakfast: Grab a toasted Mallorca bread and a cortado at **Melao Bakery** (✉ *Calle Reina, Esquina Méndez Vigo y* ☎ *787/813–5050*) located in Ponce's town square.

Day 4: Ponce to Rincón

60 miles (1 hour, 35 minutes without traffic and stops)

Take PR-2 along the southern coast of Puerto Rico and head north to the town of Rincón, which has plenty of beaches and attractions. One day might not be enough, so this is the perfect place to extend your trip for a day or two.

ALONG THE WAY

Nature: Did you know that Puerto Rico has a dry forest? The **Bosque Estatal de Guánica** (☎ 787/821–5706) is a subtropical dry forest located on the southwest coast of Puerto Rico. Plants such as cacti surround the forest, an interesting contrast from the rain forest on the northeast coast.

Roadside Attraction: The Casas de Colores of Yauco (✉ 29-37 Calle E Sanchez Lopez ☎ 787/429–7530) are a colorful spectacle located in the city center of Yauco. Although the colorful homes are popular with tourists, locals still live in them.

Town: San Germán is one of the oldest towns in Puerto Rico and home to one of the first Catholic churches in the Americas, Porta Coeli, built in 1609. Situated in a valley, the city center is surrounded by mountains and lined with colonial architecture.

Detour: Cabo Rojo is a 30-minute detour, but you will find some of the most tranquil beaches in Puerto Rico here. One highlight is Combate Beach, a stunning beach straddling a nature reserve. And don't miss the Salinas de Cabo Rojo (☎ 787/851–2999); its pink salt flats make a fantastic backdrop for a photo.

Eat & Drink: Annie's Place (✉ 101 PR-101), a fun, beachside restaurant in Cabo Rojo, makes a mean passion fruit mojito. If you come for dinner, it also has one of the most beautiful sunsets on the island.

Photo Op: Head to Punta Guaniquilla Nature Reserve to take a photo with surreal rock formations over 11 million years old.

RINCÓN

Do: The lively town of Rincón is known for its surfing community. People come from all over the globe to catch the waves here, especially during the winter months when the swells are very high. The town and its surroundings are laid-back and ideal for relaxing by the beach.

Eat & Drink: Have a delicious dinner at cozy Estela (✉ Rd. 115, Km 14 ☎ 787/823–1795), which mixes global flavors with local ingredients. Or you can treat yourself to fresh fish tacos made with the catch of the day at **La Cambija** (✉ Calle Cambija ☎ 787/823–1118 ⊕ www.facebook.com/Lacambija), a popular beach spot. For something unique, **Gylro** (✉ 24 Calle Muñoz Rivera ☎ 787/291–7410 ⊕ www.gylro.com) calls itself a "Greekrican" restaurant, specializing in gyros with a Puerto Rican twist; it's also known for its creative cocktails and live music on the weekends.

Shop: Every Thursday night, the Rincón city center hosts an art market with local artisans.

Stay: The private villas at the **Horned Dorset Primavera** (✉ Carr. 429, Km 3 ☎ 787/823–4030 ⊕ www.horneddorset.net) are the epitome of luxury. The properties have private pools, unique decor, and stunning ocean views. With picture-perfect bohemian decor, the **English Rose** (✉ 413 Carr. Bo ☎ 787/823–4032 ⊕ www.theenglishroserincon.com) in Rincón is a more affordable favorite. Perched on a hill, the property offers stunning views of the coastline.

Breakfast: A local chain originating in the neighboring town of Mayaguez, **Ricomini** (✉ PR-115, Km 12 ☎ 787/823–5707) is known for its pastries, especially its guava jelly roll.

Day 5: Rincón to Lares

31 miles (1 hour without traffic or stops)

Head deep into the Cordillera Central as you travel from Rincón to Lares, a historic small town in the center of Puerto Rico. Route PR-111 provides a dazzling scenic route through the countryside with lush vegetation, rivers, and waterfalls.

ALONG THE WAY

Detour: Head to the town of **Aguadilla** to one of the best-known beaches in Puerto Rico, Crashboat Beach. The pier has survived multiple hurricanes and is the perfect place for an adventurous dive.

Town: San Sebastián is another well-known mountain town in Puerto Rico, with several coffee-producing farms.

Eat & Drink: A local farm in San Sebastián, **Hacienda la Fe** (☎ 787/301–5707 ⊕ www. resthaciendafe.com) has an on-site restaurant with Puerto Rican favorites such as *mofongo* (mashed, fried green plantains topped with meat or seafood).

Photo Op: The area known as Gozalandia is home to **Los Robles waterfall,** and the family who owns the land also manages the parking lot and runs a small restaurant and bar. The waterfall is a short 20-minute hike from the parking lot.

LARES

Do: Lares is a small town (population 3,925), but you can use it as a base to explore the center of the island. For history buffs, Lares played an important role in Puerto Rico's independence from Spain; in 1868, it was the location of an armed uprising called El Grio de Lares. This was the first major revolt against Spanish colonial rule on the island.

Eat & Drink: Located in a scenic part of Lares, the small, locally owned **El Sartén de Fary** (✉ Carr. 135, Km 64.4 ☎ 787/645–4422) serves breakfast, lunch, and dinner. Over in the adjacent town of Adjuntas, **Restaurante Vida Ventura** (✉ PR-135, Km 13.7 ☎ 787/210–6908 ⊕ www.haciendaluzdeluna.com) is led by popular chef Ventura Vivoni, who creates an ever-changing menu of local dishes with an international twist. And when you're in Lares, you have to go to **Heladería Lares** (✉ 10 Calle Vilella ☎ 787/378–4288) to sample their famous ice cream. The shop has been around for decades, and is known for unique flavors such as rice-and-beans along with more standard flavors.

Stay: The **Hacienda El Jibarito** (✉ Carr. 445 Bo Saltos ☎ 787/280–4040 ⊕ www. haciendaeljibarito.com), located in San Sebastián, makes for a lovely farm-stay experience. The farm grows its own coffee beans and provides tours of the property. Local and family-owned, **Parador Villas Sotomayor** (✉ 7 PR-123 ☎ 787/829–1717 ⊕ www.paradorvillassotomayor. com) provides small villas perfect for families or small groups. They also have campgrounds available on their sprawling farm, with spectacular views of Adjuntas.

Breakfast: One of the best-known coffee makers in Puerto Rico, **Café Lareño** (☎ 787/897–7762 ⊕ www.cafelarenopr. com) has a small café where you can grab a coffee and pastries. The coffee farm also offers tours.

Day 6: Lares to San Juan

125 miles (2 hours, 45 minutes without traffic and stops)

This route will take you from the center of Puerto Rico to its northern coast and back to San Juan. You will go from the mountains to the Atlantic Ocean, lined with plenty of charming beaches.

ALONG THE WAY

Nature: Puerto Rico is home to the third most extensive underground cave system in the world, **Las Cavernas de Camuy** (✉ *Carr. 129, Km 18.9* ☎ *787/898–3136* ⊕ *www.islandsofpuertorico.com*). Take some time to explore its winding trails and massive sinkhole on a guided tour.

Town: Arecibo is a seaside town with several beaches, a marina, and a lighthouse. It's also home to **Cueva la Ventana** (✉ *PR-10, Km 75* ☎ *787/322–3554* ⊕ *www.cuevaventanapr.com*), a famed "window cave" that provides stunning views of the island's northwestern coast. Make sure to buy a ticket online ahead of time to secure a spot.

Eat & Drink: Get your seafood fix at lively beachside **Salitre Mesón Cosetero** (✉ *PR-681, Km 3.8* ☎ *787/816–2020* ⊕ *www.salitre.com*) in Arecibo. The menu features locally caught fish like yellowfin tuna, red snapper, and wahoo.

SAN JUAN

Do: As the capital of Puerto Rico, San Juan is one of the island's most popular tourist destinations. Take some time to explore the cobblestone streets of Old San Juan, one of the oldest cities in the Americas. Be sure to climb to the top of **El Castillo de San Felipe del Morro** (✉ *501 Calle Norzagaray* ☎ *787/729–6960* ⊕ *www.nps.gov/saju*), which was built in the 1400s to protect San Juan from pirates. Paddleboard along the Condado Lagoon, and you may spot a manatee or two.

Eat & Drink: At **Orujo** (✉ *906 Av. Juan Ponce de León*), the tasting menu is a favorite among local foodies; chef Carlos Portela focuses on local ingredients and classic techniques here, like ripe plantains topped with shredded short rib. Located in the heart of La Placita de Santurce (the city's hopping nightlife district), **Santaella** (✉ *219 Calle Canals* ☎ *787/722–7600* ⊕ *www.josesantaella.com*) is a beloved spot for locals and tourists alike, thanks to the inventive dishes like shredded green plantains topped with crab and Japanese seaweed salad. Afterward head to **Junglebird** (✉ *254 Calle Canals* ☎ *787/955–9706* ⊕ *www.junglebirdbar.com*), known for its clever cocktails and impressive bar menu from James Beard–nominated chef Paxx Caraballo.

Stay: Women-owned **La Botánica Hotel** (✉ *1808 Av. McLeary*) focuses on ayurvedic techniques in its acclaimed spa, offering facials, massages, and other healing methods. Tucked into a small side street in Old San Juan, **Villa Herencia** (✉ *23 Caleta de las Monjas* ☎ *844/468–3577* ⊕ *www.villaherencia.com*) is a quaint small hotel with antique furniture and quirky art.

Breakfast: A longtime favorite, **Kasalta** (✉ *1966 Av. McLeary* ☎ *787/727–7340* ⊕ *www.kasalta.com*) has some of the best pastries in San Juan. Order a cortado with a *quesito* (a puff pastry filled with sweetened cream cheese).

526

Index

Photo Credits

Front Cover: PauloZimmermann/iStockphoto [Description: Canyons Near Los Angeles, California During a beautiful Sunset.]. **Back cover, from left to right:** aiisha5/iStockphoto, Sean Pavone/iStockphoto, LUNAMARINA/iStockphoto. **Spine:** trekandshoot/iStockphoto. **Interior, from left to right:** S_Hoss/iStockphoto (1). Winston Tan/Shutterstock (2-3). **Chapter 1: Experience the Best Road Trips in the USA:** bluejayphoto/iStockphoto (8-9). anthony heflin/Shutterstock (10-11). Amehime/Shutterstock (11). SEASTOCK/iStockphoto (11). Linda Bair/iStockphoto (12). SNEHIT PHOTO/Shutterstock (12). Victor Maschek/Shutterstock (13). Andriy Blokhin/shutterstock (14). trekandshoot/Shutterstock (14). vermontalm/iStockphoto (14). Doug Meek/Shutterstock (15). bluejayphoto/iStockphoto (16). Stuart Monk/Shutterstock (16). felixmizioznikov/iStockphoto (16). SL_Photography/iStockphoto (16). Gimas/Shutterstock (17). R.C. Bennett/Shutterstock (17). dibrova/iStockphoto (17). Ingus Kruklitis/Shutterstock (17). Skreidzeleu/Shutterstock (18). kan_khampanya/Shutterstock (18). TRphotos/Shutterstock (18). Sara Winter/Shutterstock (18). Dan Sedran/Shutterstock (19). Don Mammoser/Shutterstock (19). Biolifepics | Dreamstime com (19). BlueBarronPhoto/Shutterstock (19). Tiago_Fernandez/iStockphoto (20). EQRoy/Shutterstock (20). northlight/Shutterstock (20). Marti Bug Catcher/Shutterstock.com (20). Susan Vineyard/iStockphoto (21). TonelsonProductions/Shutterstock (21). Jo Hunter/Shutterstock.com (21). AlizadaStudios/iStockphoto (21). **Chapter 2: Trips of a Lifetime:** funtravlr (25). Mfmegevand | Dreamstime.com (49). f11photo/Shutterstock (53). Kerrick James (71). elan7t50/iStockphoto (77). RozenskiP/Shutterstock (88). FiledIMAGE/Shutterstock (97). Jon Bilous/Shutterstock (104). Sean Pavone/Shutterstock (115). **Chapter 3: The West Coast:** Dancestrokes/Shutterstock (121). Phitha Tanpairoj/Shutterstock (129). dibrova/shutterstock (141). Pixelite/Shutterstock (150). urosr/Shutterstock (161). zschnepf/Shutterstock (172). Steven Madow/Shutterstock (180). **Chapter 4: The West and the Rockies:** Pat Tr/Shutterstock (185). chip phillips/iStockphoto (192). Dennis Frates / Alamy (202). Lukas Urwyler/Shutterstock (209). SeanXu/iStockphoto (218). Ashmephotography | Dreamstime.com (230). **Chapter 5: The Southwest and Texas:** Anton Foltin/Shutterstock (233). Sasha Buzko/Shutterstock (242). Doug Meek/Shutterstock (249). Gimas/Shutterstock (253). Evgeny Moerman/Dreamstime (268). Sean Pavone/Shutterstock (277). Fotoluminate LLC/Shutterstock (288). **Chapter 6: The Midwest and the Plains:** Checubus/Shutterstock (291). Virrage Images/Shutterstock (300). PhotoTrippingAmerica/Shutterstock (308). Niwat panket/Shutterstock (317). Nejdet Duzen/Shutterstock (326). Smontgom65 | Dreamstime.com (335). Mikesdeemer | Dreamstime com (343). Gscott54 | Dreamstime.com (353). **Chapter 7: The Southeast and Florida:** Steve Bower/iStockphoto (357). anthony heflin/Shutterstock (366). Nolichuckyjake/Shutterstock (375). Jon Bilous/Shutterstock (382). Jason Kolenda/Shutterstock (393). Michael Gordon/Shutterstock (404). Rolf_52/Shutterstock (415). NaughtyNut/Shutterstock (424). Mia2you/Shutterstock (434). **Chapter 8: The Northeast:** Tomas1111 | Dreamstime.com (439). Sean Pavone/Shutterstock (446). Roman Babakin/Shutterstock (452). Gary C. Tognoni/Shutterstock (462). JMP Traveler/iStockphoto (470). Try Media/iStockphoto (479). Jon Bilous/Shutterstock (489). **Chapter 9: Outside the Lower 48:** Tyler Westhoff (495). Tomasz Wozniak/Shutterstock (502). Linda Bair/iStockphoto (510). Gnagel | Dreamstime.com (515). mikolajn/Shutterstock (521). About Our Writers: All photos are courtesy of the writers.

*Every effort has been made to trace the copyright holders, and we apologize in advance for any accidental errors. We would be happy to apply the corrections in the following edition of this publication.

Notes

Fodor's BEST ROAD TRIPS IN THE USA

Publisher: Stephen Horowitz, *General Manager*

Editorial: Douglas Stallings, *Editorial Director*; Jill Fergus, Amanda Sadlowski, Caroline Trefler, *Senior Editors*; Kayla Becker, Alexis Kelly, *Editors*

Design: Tina Malaney, *Director of Design and Production*; Jessica Gonzalez, *Graphic Designer;* Mariana Tabares, *Design and Production Intern*

Production: Jennifer DePrima, *Editorial Production Manager*; Elyse Rozelle, *Senior Production Editor;* Monica White, *Production Editor*

Maps: Rebecca Baer, *Senior Map Editor*; Mark Stroud (Moon Street Cartography), *Cartographer*

Photography: Viviane Teles, *Senior Photo Editor*; Namrata Aggarwal, Ashok Kumar, Rebecca Rimmer, *Photo Editors*

Business and Operations: Chuck Hoover, *Chief Marketing Officer*; Robert Ames, *Group General Manager*; Devin Duckworth, *Director of Print Publishing*; Amber Zhou, *Business Analyst*

Public Relations and Marketing: Joe Ewaskiw, *Senior Director of Communications and Public Relations*

Fodors.com: Jeremy Tarr, *Editorial Director;* Rachael Levitt, *Managing Editor*

Technology: Jon Atkinson, *Director of Technology;* Rudresh Teotia, *Lead Developer*; Jacob Ashpis, *Content Operations Manager*

Writers: Kristy Alpert, Lehia Apana, J. Besl, Margot Bigg, Cassandra Brooklyn, Andrew Collins, Katherine Chou, Amber Gibson, Kristine Hansen, Aimee Heckel, Barbara Noe Kennedy, Stratton Lawrence, Chanté LaGon, Shoshi Parks, Jessica Poitevien, Elise Riley, Brandon Schultz, Jen Rose Smith, Mark Sullivan, Jessica van Dop DeJesús, Stefanie Waldek, Anna Weaver

Editor: Amanda Sadlowski

Production Editor: Jennifer DePrima

First Edition

ISBN 978-1-64097-457-9

ISSN 2769-4909

SPECIAL SALES

This book is available at special discounts for bulk purchases for sales promotions or premiums. For more information, e-mail SpecialMarkets@fodors.com.

PRINTED IN CANADA

10 9 8 7 6 5 4 3 2 1

About Our Writers

Kristy Alpert is the author of *Road Trip Activities and Travel Journal for Kids*. As a freelance travel journalist, she has unearthed ancient bread-baking secrets on Muhu Island and swam with penguins in icy Antarctic waters. See her bylines in *Cosmopolitan, Food & Wine, Men's Health, Esquire,* and Fodor's Travel, or follow along with her travels on Instagram @kristyalpert. She wrote the following trips: the Best of the Ozarks, the Best of Texas, and Texas Hill Country.

 Born and raised on Maui, **Lehia Apana** is an island girl with a wandering spirit. She has lived in Chicago, Rome, and Sydney, but she always finds her way back home. Lehia has been writing about Maui for more than a decade, and has served as an editor at *The Maui News* and *Maui Nō Ka Oi Magazine*. Find out more at ⊕ *lehiaapana. com*. She wrote the Road to Hāna trip.

 J. Besl is a university staff writer in Anchorage, sharing the stories of students and faculty and their academic adventures in the north. He's also a freelance writer, and his stories have appeared in newspapers and magazines across the state. Originally from Cincinnati, you can now find him at the bus stops and bike lanes of Alaska's big city. He wrote the Best of Alaska trip.

 Margot Bigg is a freelance travel writer and editor based in Portland, Oregon. She's lived and worked all over the world, most recently in India, where she worked at *Time Out Magazine* and contributed to the last three editions of *Fodor's Essential India*. Though now back in the States, she continues to contribute to a variety of Indian publications, including local editions of *Rolling Stone* and *National Geographic Traveler*, as well as U.S. publications ranging from *Sunset Magazine* to *VICE*. Margot wrote the following trips: the Best of the Pacific Northwest, Wine Countries of the Pacific Northwest, and Enlightenment and Wellness in the Southwest.

Cassandra Brooklyn is a freelance writer who has been published in the *New York Times, National Geographic,* and the Daily Beast, among others. She wrote the guidebook *Cuba By Bike* and runs a tour company, EscapingNY. She lives in New York City, but is usually hiking, biking, and adventuring somewhere else in the world. You can find her on Instagram @escapingny and Twitter @ escapingnewyork. She wrote the Best of the Dakotas trip.

 Former Fodor's staff editor **Andrew Collins** is based in Mexico City but spends a good bit of the year both in different parts of Oregon and Washington. A longtime contributor to more than 200 Fodor's guidebooks, including *Pacific Northwest, National Parks of the West, Utah, Santa Fe, Inside Mexico City,* and *New England,* he's also written for dozens of mainstream and LGBTQ publications—*Travel + Leisure, New Mexico Magazine, AAA Living, The Advocate,* and *Canadian Traveller* among them. Additionally, Collins teaches travel writing and food writing for New York City's Gotham Writers Workshop. You can find more of his work at AndrewsTraveling.com, and follow him on Instagram @TravelAndrew. He wrote both Ultimate Cross Country trips and the California National Parks trip.

Katherine Chou is a freelance writer and copywriter, a comedy screenwriter, and a traveler. She's journeyed extensively around the world and throughout the U.S. One of her favorite American road trips remains a pilgrimage from the northeast

About Our Writers

to Graceland, where she gained an appreciation for both Elvis and Waffle House. She wrote the Great American Music Road Trip.

Amber Gibson is a Los Angeles–based journalist specializing in travel, food, wine, and wellness. She's spearfished in Dominica, flown a private jet over the Grand Canyon, and judged international gelato competitions all in the name of work. Her work appears in *Conde Nast Traveler, National Geographic Traveler, The Telegraph,* NPR, NBC, and *Bon Appétit.* Follow her adventures on Instagram @amberyv. She wrote the Best of Southern California trip.

Based in Milwaukee, Wisconsin, **Kristine Hansen** loves to hit the road to explore what's beyond her city and doesn't hesitate to pull over for a cute café or Frank Lloyd Wright-designed home. She's the author of *Wisconsin Cheese Cookbook: Creamy, Cheesy, Sweet, and Savory Recipes from the State's Best Creameries and Wisconsin Farms* and *Farmers Markets: Tours, Trails and Attractions.* She wrote the following trips: All the Great Lakes, Underrated Cities of the Midwest, the Best of the Heartland, and A Frank Lloyd Wright Tour.

Aimee Heckel is a Colorado native who has been working at Colorado newspapers for nearly two decades. She's the head writer for TravelBoulder.com, the Colorado travel expert for Tripsavvy, and a book editor. Heckel also freelances for the *Boulder Daily Camera* and has worked as a regular travel writer for USA Today 10Best.com. She wrote the following trips: Route 66; the Best of Colorado, the Best of New Mexico, and the Ultimate Wild West Road Trip.

After many years as senior editor with NatGeo Travel Publishing, **Barbara Noe Kennedy** left in 2015 to fly solo as a freelance travel writer and editor, focusing on destinations, art, culture, food, and adventure around the world. Her website is ⊕ *barbaranoekennedy.com.* She wrote the following trips: Civil War Battlefields and History, the Blue Ridge Parkway, and the Best of the Chesapeake Bay.

Stratton Lawrence settled in Charleston in 2003 after the rambling childhood of a Navy brat and a degree in history from Davidson College. A former staff writer at *Charleston City Paper,* he's a frequent contributor to *Charleston Magazine* and managing editor of the content marketing firm, Stone Temple. He lives with his family on Folly Beach, where he drew inspiration for his first book, *Images of America: Folly Beach,* released in 2013 by Arcadia Publishing. He wrote the Best of the Carolinas and Along the Mississippi trips.

Oak Park, Illinois, native **Chanté LaGon** has nearly two decades' experience in all things word-related, from news features to poetry. She moved to Atlanta in the late '90s to join the *Atlanta Journal-Constitution,* and later served as managing editor for the weekly *Creative Loafing.* She combined her love of music and words as founding editor of a hip-hop magazine while in North Carolina, where she attended college, and has been an integral part of that scene in Atlanta, along with the electronic music, nightlife, arts and culture scenes there. She wrote the Civil Rights Trail trip.

About Our Writers

Shoshi Parks is a freelance writer, outdoor adventurer, and avid road-tripper from San Jose, CA. As a Ph.D. in anthropology, her work focuses on travel, history, food, and heritage in the U.S. and around the globe. Her writing has appeared in Atlas Obscura, *Smithsonian Magazine, Afar*, NPR, *Bon Appetit*, and elsewhere. Find her at ⊕ *shoshiparks.net*. She wrote the following trips: the Pacific Coast Highway and Route 101, the Best of Northern California, Big Sky Country, Indigenous Homelands of the Southwest, and Indigenous Homelands of the Midwest.

Jessica Poitevien is a freelance travel writer and content creator currently based in South Florida, though she spent recent years living in Spain and Colombia. Beyond Fodor's Travel, Jessica's work can be found in *Condé Nast Traveler*, *Travel+Leisure, National Geographic*, and more. When she's not working or traveling, you'll find Jessica baking, talking to strangers, and trying new foods. She wrote the Best of Southern Florida trip.

A Phoenix-based freelance writer and editor, **Elise Riley** left her native Arizona to report for newspapers across the country. She quickly learned that no place had Mexican food like the Valley, and eventually found the way back to her favorite salsas and enchiladas. Today she appreciates the striking desert sunsets more than she did in her childhood, and eagerly awaits the next out-of-state visitor she can take on a tour of her favorite local restaurants. She wrote the Best of Arizona trip.

Brandon Schultz is a travel and lifestyle writer who loves experiencing the world and telling others about it. He enjoys everything from luxury resort getaways to road trips and couchsurfing adventures, and believes that where you travel is often less important than how you travel. He's the author of six books and lives in Brooklyn, New York. He wrote the following trips: the East Coast's Best Beaches, Retracing the American Revolution, and the Great American Whiskey Road Trip.

From a home base in Vermont's Green Mountains, **Jen Rose Smith** writes about travel, adventure, and wild places. With notebook in hand, she's traveled on foot through the Borneo jungle, cycled Peru's highest passes, and gone deep into Cypriot no-man's-land. Read her work in Fodor's, *National Geographic*, the *Washington Post*, and BBC Travel—or find more at ⊕ *www.jenrosesmith.com*. She wrote the following stories: the Best of New England, New England's Great Outdoors, and Coastal New England.

Mark Sullivan has edited or contributed to more than 200 travel books. His work (appearing regularly in publications like TripAdvisor and Zagat) has been nominated for a prestigious Lowell Thomas Prize. Mark wrote the following trips: the Best of Northern and Central Florida, the Great American Baseball Road Trip, and the Best of New York State.

Jessica van Dop DeJesús is a widely published travel content creator. She's the founder of the popular foodie travel website, The Dining Traveler, and the author of the coffee-table book, *The Dining Traveler Guide to Puerto Rico*. Her writing has been featured in *Travel Channel, Modern Luxury, Washington City Paper, Southern Living,* and *Telemundo*. She was raised in Guayama, Puerto Rico. Follow her on Instagram, Facebook, Twitter, Pinterest, and YouTube @DiningTraveler. She wrote the Best of Puerto Rico trip.

About Our Writers

Stefanie Waldek is a travel, design, and space journalist for *Condé Nast Traveler*, *Travel + Leisure*, *Architectural Digest*, *Popular Science*, and Space. com, among other publications. When she's not serving as navigator on a road trip with her husband, you can find her on a plane, watching *The X-Files*, and dreaming about becoming an astronaut. She wrote the following trips: Utah's National Parks, The Loneliest Road: Nevada's Route 50, National Parks of the Southeast, and the Best of Long Island and the Jersey Shore.

Writer and multimedia journalist **Anna Weaver** is a sixth-generation *kamaaina*, born and raised in Kailua, O'ahu. She can never get enough Spam *musubi*, *malassadas*, or hiking time in her home state. Anna has written for *Slate*, *Simplemost*, and such Hawaii publications as the *Honolulu Advertiser* (now *Star-Advertiser*), *Honolulu Magazine*, and *Pacific Business News*. She wrote the Best of O'ahu trip.